Tenth Edition

# Kirszner & Mandell



# The Wadsworth Handbook

Laurie G. Kirszner
University of the Sciences, Emeritus

Stephen R. Mandell
Drexel University

WADSWORTH
CENGAGE Learning

Australia • Brazil • Japan • Korea • Mexico • Singapore • Spain • United Kingdom • United States

WADSWORTH
CENGAGE Learning™

**The Wadsworth Handbook, Tenth Edition**
**Laurie G. Kirszner and Stephen R. Mandell**

VP, Editorial Director: PJ Boardman
Editor in Chief: Lyn Uhl
Publisher: Monica Eckman
Acquisitions Editor: Kate Derrick
Development Editor: Karen Mauk
Assistant Editor: Danielle Warchol
Editorial Assistant: Marjorie Cross
Media Editor: Cara Douglass-Graff
Content Project Manager: Corinna Dibble
Executive Marketing Manager: Stacey Purviance
Senior Marketing Communications Manager: Linda Yip
Marketing Coordinator: Brittany Blais
Art Director: Marissa Falco
Manufacturing Planner: Betsy Donaghey
Rights Acquisition Specialist: Alexandra Ricciardi
Production Service: Cenveo Publisher Services
Text Designer: Cenveo Publisher Services
Cover Designer: Wing Ngan
Compositor: Cenveo Publisher Services


Library of Congress Control Number: 2012945959

Student Edition:
ISBN-13: 978-1-133-30877-5
ISBN-10: 1-133-30877-5

**Wadsworth**
20 Channel Center Street
Boston, MA 02210
USA

Cengage Learning is a leading provider of customized learning solutions with office locations around the globe, including Singapore, the United Kingdom, Australia, Mexico, Brazil and Japan. Locate your local office at **international.cengage.com/region**

Cengage Learning products are represented in Canada by Nelson Education, Ltd.

For your course and learning solutions, visit **www.cengage.com.**
Purchase any of our products at your local college store or at our preferred online store **www.cengagebrain.com.**
**Instructors:** Please visit **login.cengage.com** and log in to access instructor-specific resources.

Printed in the United States of America
1 2 3 4 5 6 7 16 15 14 13 12

# Contents

# Note to Students

We would like to introduce you to the tenth edition of *The Wadsworth Handbook*, a comprehensive writing guide for college students. Our goal in this text remains the same as it was in the first edition: to help you produce sound academic writing. To this end, we provide practical support for the writing and research projects that will be important to you in your academic career as well as in your professional life.

*The Wadsworth Handbook*, which comes out of our many years of hands-on experience as teachers of writing, offers full coverage of all the topics we see as essential for writers: the writing process, critical thinking, argumentation, common sentence errors, grammar and style, punctuation and mechanics, English for speakers of other languages, and college survival skills. In addition, the book includes the most up-to-date information on writing in a digital environment; visual rhetoric; MLA, APA, Chicago, and CSE documentation; writing in the disciplines; document design; and Web page design. Throughout the text, practice exercises are provided to reinforce writing skills.

As writers, you already know that to express your ideas clearly, you need to understand the basic principles of grammar, mechanics, and style. In addition, as writers in the digital age, you also need to know how to communicate your ideas to others more effectively, whether you are writing for an academic audience or on the job, for a business audience. In fact, in all the writing you do—regardless of your purpose or audience—technology plays an ever-increasing role in helping you to convey your ideas. For this reason, it is very important that you have a clear understanding of the relationship between technology and writing.

We revised *The Wadsworth Handbook* with these ideas in mind. The result is a book that you can depend on to give you sound, sensible advice about writing as well as about the electronic tools that define the twenty-first-century writing environment. We hope you will find *The Wadsworth Handbook* a resource that you can turn to again and again as you write in college and beyond.

Laurie Kirszner
Steve Mandell
January 2013

## Features of This Book

- **Collaborative writing icons** appear alongside features and exercises that emphasize peer review and collaborative work.
- **Frequently Asked Questions (FAQs)** appear at the beginning of each chapter. A marginal FAQ icon appears in the chapter beside each answer.
- **Grammar checker boxes** illustrating sample errors show the advantages and limitations of using a grammar checker.
- **Numerous checklists** summarize key information that you can quickly access as needed.
- **Close-up boxes** provide an in-depth look at some of the more perplexing writing-related issues you will encounter.
- **Parts 4–5** include the most up-to-date documentation and format guidelines from the Modern Language Association, the American Psychological Association, the University of Chicago Press, and the Council of Science Editors. Specially designed documentation directories make it easy for you to locate models for various kinds of sources, including those found in online databases such as *Academic Search Premier* and *LexisNexis*. In addition, color-coded and annotated diagrams of sample works-cited entries clearly illustrate the elements of proper documentation.
- **Marginal cross-references** throughout the book allow you to go directly to other sections that treat topics in more detail.
- **Marginal ESL cross-references** throughout the book direct you to sections of Part 14, "Bilingual and ESL Writers," where concepts are presented as they apply specifically to second-language writers.
- **ESL tips** are woven throughout the text to explain concepts in relation to the unique experiences of bilingual students.
- **Getting Help from the Dictionary boxes** appear throughout Chapter 64, "Grammar and Style for ESL Writers," offering bilingual students practical advice for using a dictionary effectively.
- **Numerous exercises** throughout the text allow you to practice at each stage of the writing, revising, and editing processes.
- **An extensive writing-centered treatment of grammar, punctuation, and mechanics,** including hand-edited examples, explains and illustrates specific strategies for improving your writing.

# Note to Instructors

In this tenth edition of *The Wadsworth Handbook*, our goal is to show students how they can become more effective and confident writers. To this end, the first half of the book focuses on writing and research as well as on strategies for academic success. Here we also include material on creating and interpreting visual texts as well as a chapter on writing effective and compelling literary arguments. The second half of *The Wadsworth Handbook*, which deals with grammar, punctuation, and mechanics, reflects our focus on student writing. Grammar checker boxes, which include sample screen shots, appear throughout, acknowledging the role computer technology plays in the revising and editing processes. Here we also illustrate how the rules of grammar, punctuation, and mechanics operate in real-world contexts—for example, in advertisements, emails, and text messages.

Despite our focus on the electronic tools that students have at their disposal, we have not forgotten the traditional reasons students consult a handbook: to become more effective, more confident writers. Accordingly, in addition to adding and revising Close-up boxes, we have strengthened basic discussions of the writing process, research, grammar, style, and mechanics. For example, we have updated our coverage of writing essays and research papers, and we have added more examples of electronic sources. Finally, we have revised coverage in Part 7, "Creating Documents in a Digital Age," which focuses on writing in a digital environment, designing effective documents, and designing a Web site, offering students up-to-date information about writing in the twenty-first century.

Although *The Wadsworth Handbook*, Tenth Edition, is grounded in the most current research in composition and rhetoric, it is also informed by our many years of classroom teaching. We began our careers as teachers of composition as graduate students in Temple University's basic writing program. We were colleagues before we became textbook writers, and our struggle to create useful instructional materials for the students we were teaching was our first collaboration. Today, we continue to search for what works for our students and for yours—for what they will need to succeed in college and on the job. Our goal with this new edition of *The Wadsworth Handbook* is to define the challenges that real writers will encounter in the digital writing environment of the twenty-first century and to provide students with clear choices and pragmatic advice. The result, we hope, is a book that both students and instructors will trust—and one that they will use with ease and, perhaps, even with pleasure.

## New to the Tenth Edition

- **New coverage of reading electronic texts and writing critical responses** in Chapter 2, "Reading Texts," offers students key critical reading and analysis strategies.
- **Two thoroughly revised student papers,** "*Wikipedia:* Friend or Foe?" and "The Great Debate: *Wikipedia* and College-Level Research," illustrate the writing process in Chapters 4–6 and the research process in Chapters 12 and 18. Additionally, updated and expanded coverage of **MLA, APA, Chicago, and CSE documentation styles** in Chapters 18–21 includes numerous models that help students correctly apply the latest citation guidelines when writing in various disciplines.
- **Two thoroughly revised research chapters** (Chapter 13, "Finding Information," and Chapter 14, "Evaluating Sources") reflect the way students conduct research and address the issues they are likely to encounter. Additionally, expanded coverage of **field research** in Chapter 13 and a new field research report in Chapter 25, "Writing in the Social Sciences," emphasize the importance of practical research outside the library.
- **New coverage of avoiding different kinds of plagiarism** in Chapter 17, "Avoiding Plagiarism," offers students strategies for managing their time and producing top-quality original work. Chapter 17 also features an expanded discussion of the importance of using and documenting sources correctly.
- **A streamlined new design** makes the book easier to navigate.

## Acknowledgments

We would like to take this opportunity to thank Douglas Eyman, George Mason University, for contributing his expert technology advice, and Linda Stein, University of Delaware, for sharing her research expertise.

We would also like to thank the following reviewers for their advice, which helped us develop the tenth edition:

Elizabeth Andrews, *South Florida State College*
Laura Arzola, *Houston Community College, Southeast*
Carol Copenhefer, *Central Ohio Technical College*
Ryan Cordell, *St. Norbert College*
Pamela Covert, *Valencia Community College*
Keith Huneycutt, *Florida Southern College*
Theresa James, *South Florida State College*
Stephanie Johnson, *Bowie State University*
David Kaloustian, *Bowie State University*
Michael Marsden, *St. Norbert College*
Ivan McDaniel, *South Florida State College*
Robert McWhorter, *Valencia Community College*

Michelle Moore, *College of DuPage*
Charlotte Pressler, *South Florida State College*
Karoline Szatek, *Curry College*
C. Jenise Williamson, *Bowie State University*
Nicole Wilson, *Bowie State University*

At Wadsworth, we are grateful to Lyn Uhl, Editor in Chief; Monica Eckman, Publisher; Kate Derrick, Acquisitions Editor; Leslie Taggart, Senior Development Editor; and Maggie Cross, Editorial Assistant, for keeping the project moving along, as well as to Corinna Dibble, Senior Content Project Manager, for her careful attention to detail. Our biggest thanks go to Karen Mauk, our wonderful Development Editor; as always, it has been a pleasure to work with her.

The staff of Cenveo did its usual stellar job, led by our incredibly capable Senior Project Manager and copyeditor Susan McIntyre. Carie Keller's inviting design is the icing on the cake.

We would also like to thank our families for being there when we needed them. And, finally, we each thank the person on the other side of the ampersand for making our collaboration work one more time.

Laurie Kirszner
Steve Mandell
January 2013

# Teaching and Learning Resources

### *Online College Workbook*

**ISBN:** 978-1-285-07737-6

This collection of grammar and composition exercises offers students reinforcement of basic skills.

### *Online Instructor's Resource Manual and Answer Key*

**ISBN:** 978-1-285-07738-3

Designed to give instructors maximum flexibility in planning and customizing their courses, the **Online Instructor's Resource Manual and Answer Key** is now available online. It contains an abundance of instructor materials, including sample syllabi and activities; "Questions for Teachers," which provides a variety of pedagogical questions with solutions for instructors to consider as they teach with the handbook; an ESL insert aimed at helping instructors teach writing effectively to ESL students; and an insert on disability issues as they relate to teaching first-year composition.

### *English CourseMate*

**Printed Access Card (ISBN:** 978-1-285-16674-2)
**Instant Access Code (ISBN:** 978-1-285-16675-9)

*The Wadsworth Handbook* includes English CourseMate, a complement to your textbook. English CourseMate includes:

- an interactive eBook
- interactive teaching and learning tools including:
  - Quizzes
  - Flashcards
  - Videos
  - and more
- Engagement Tracker, a first-of-its-kind tool that monitors student engagement in the course

Go to login.cengage.com to access these resources, and look for this icon which denotes a resource available within CourseMate.

### *Enhanced InSite™ for* The Wadsworth Handbook

**Printed Access Card (1 semester) (ISBN:** 978-1-285-07883-0)
**Instant Access Code (1 semester) (ISBN:** 978-1-285-07886-1)
**Printed Access Card (2 semester) (ISBN:** 978-1-285-07759-8)
**Instant Access Code (2 semester) (ISBN:** 978-1-285-07747-5)

From a single, easy-to-navigate site, instructors and students can manage the flow of papers online, check for originality, and conduct peer reviews. Students can access the multimedia eBook for a text-specific workbook, private tutoring options, and resources for writers that include anti-plagiarism tutorials and downloadable grammar podcasts. **Enhanced InSite™** provides the tools and resources instructors and students need plus the training and support they want. Learn more at **www.cengage.com/insite**. (*Access card/code is required.*)

### *Write Experience for* The Wadsworth Handbook

**Printed Access Card** (**ISBN:** 978-1-285-16678-0)
**Instant Access Code** (**ISBN:** 978-1-285-16677-3)
Assess written communication skills without adding to your workload! Instructors in all areas have told us it's important that students can write effectively in order to communicate and think critically. Through an exclusive partnership with a technology company, Cengage Learning's **Write Experience** allows you to do just that. This new product uses artificial intelligence only to not score student writing instantly and accurately, but also to provide students with detailed revision goals and feedback on their writing to help them improve.

### *InfoTrac® College Edition with InfoMarks™*

**ISBN:** 978-0-534-55853-6
**InfoTrac® College Edition,** an online research and learning center, offers over 20 million full-text articles from nearly 6,000 scholarly and popular periodicals. The articles cover a broad spectrum of disciplines and topics—ideal for every type of researcher.

### *Turnitin®*

**Printed Access Card 1-Semester User Guide 978-1-413-03018-1**
**Printed Access Card 2-Semester User Guide 978-1-413-03019-8**
**Turnitin®** is proven plagiarism-prevention software that helps students improve their writing and research skills and allows instructors to confirm originality before reading and grading student papers. Take a tour at academic.cengage.com/turnitin to see how **Turnitin** makes checking originality against billions of pages of Internet content, millions of published works, and millions of students papers fast and easy.

### *Personal Tutor*

**Printed Access Card** (**ISBN:** 978-1-285-07868-7)
**Instant Access Code** (**ISBN:** 978-1-285-07866-3)
Access to **Personal Tutor's** private tutoring resources provides students with additional assistance and review as they write their papers. With this valuable resource, students will gain access to multiple sessions to be used as either tutoring services or paper submissions—whichever they need most.

***Merriam Webster e-Dictionary***

**Printed Access Card** (**ISBN:** 978-1-285-05431-5)

**Instant Access Code** (**ISBN:** 978-1-285-05436-0)

Available only when packaged with a Wadsworth text, this high-quality, economical language reference covers the core vocabulary of everyday life with over 70,000 definitions.

PART 1

# Writing Essays

CHAPTER 1

# Understanding Purpose, Audience, and Tone

## Frequently Asked Questions



Everyone who sets out to write confronts a series of choices. In the academic, professional, public, and private writing you do in school, on the job, and in your personal life, your understanding of purpose and audience is essential, influencing the choices you make about content, emphasis, organization, style, and tone.

See Ch. 3, 28d

Note: Like written texts, visual texts—fine art, charts and graphs, photographs, maps, advertisements, and so on—are also created with specific purposes and audiences in mind.

## 1a Determining Your Purpose

Your **purpose** for writing is what you want to accomplish. Sometimes your purpose is to **reflect,** to express private feelings, as in the introspective or meditative writing that appears in personal blogs, journals, diaries, and memoirs. Or, your purpose may be to **inform,** to convey factual information as accurately and as logically as possible, as in the informational or expository writing that appears in reports, news articles, encyclopedias, and textbooks. At other times, your purpose may be to **persuade,** to convince your readers, as in advertising, proposals, editorials, and some business communications. Finally, your purpose may be to **evaluate,** to make a judgment about something, as in a book or film review, a recommendation report, or a comparative analysis.

### 1 Writing to Reflect

In diaries and journals, writers explore ideas and emotions to make sense of their experiences; in autobiographical memoirs, personal blog posts, and online course sites, they communicate their reactions and ideas to others.

At the age of five, six, well past the time when most other children no longer easily notice the difference between sounds uttered at home and words spoken in public, I had a different experience. I lived in a world magically compounded of sounds. I remained a child longer than most; I lingered too long, poised at the edge of language—often frightened by the sounds of *los gringos*, delighted by the sounds of Spanish at home. I shared with my family a language that was startlingly different from that used in the great city around us. (Richard Rodriguez, *Aria: Memoir of a Bilingual Childhood*)



## 2 Writing to Inform

In newspaper articles, writers report information, communicating factual details to readers. In reference books, instruction manuals, and textbooks, as well as in Web sites sponsored by nonprofit organizations and government agencies, writers provide definitions and explain concepts or processes, trying to help readers see relationships and understand ideas.

Most tarantulas live in the tropics, but several species occur in the temperate zone and a few are common in the southern U.S. Some varieties are large and have powerful fangs with which they can inflict a deep wound. These formidable-looking spiders do not, however, attack man; you can hold one in your hand, if you are gentle, without being bitten. Their bite is dangerous only to insects and small mammals such as mice; for man it is no worse than a hornet's sting. (Alexander Petrunkevitch, "The Spider and the Wasp")

**Note:** In your personal writing, you may write to convey information in *Facebook* updates, text messages, tweets, and instant messages.

## 3 Writing to Persuade

In proposals and editorials, as well as in advertising and on political Web sites and blogs, writers try to convince readers to accept their positions on various issues.

Market research is nothing new. The concentration of data in the hands of one company is, though, and it should raise concern. The data (and those patterns) provided by his 750 million users—us—is marketing gold that will be parlayed into enormous financial gain for Facebook and its partners (there's a Facebook IPO just around the corner).

Swept up by the feel-good effects of "friends" and "like" buttons, 750 million of us have unwittingly allowed a business model that relies on our giving away information and then celebrating the "free" access we have to it.

Shouldn't Mark Zuckerberg be paying us? (Chicagotribune.com, "Selling Our Souls to Mark Zuckerberg")

### 4 Writing to Evaluate

In reviews of books, films, or performances and in reports, critiques, and program evaluations, writers assess the validity, accuracy, and quality of information, ideas, techniques, products, procedures, or services. Sometimes they assess the relative merits of two or more things.

> Review of *A Dance with Dragons* by **George R. R. Martin.** Random House, 2011. May 16, 2012.
>
> I am a fan of the HBO series *Game of Thrones*, so I was looking forward to the release of *A Dance with Dragons*, the fifth book in the series *A Song of Ice and Fire.* Although I found the fourth book in the series slightly disappointing, *A Dance with Dragons* is a great read. Westeros, the world created by George R. R. Martin, has a complex history that stretches back thousands of years. The characters who inhabit Westeros are interesting and believable. Their various motives, flaws, and morals drive their actions in compelling ways with surprising and far-reaching consequences. It was easy to get lost in this faraway world and wrapped up in its people and history. I'm looking forward to seeing how this latest volume comes to life on the screen in *Game of Thrones.*

**Close-Up** PURPOSE AND CONTENT

Your purpose for writing determines the material you choose and the way you organize and express your ideas.

- A memoir might reflect on the negative aspects of summer camp, focusing on mosquitoes, poison ivy, homesickness, institutional food, and so on.
- A magazine article about summer camps could *inform*, presenting facts and statistics to show how camping has changed over the years.
- An advertising brochure designed to recruit potential campers could *persuade*, enumerating the benefits of the camping experience.
- A nonprofit camping association's Web site could *evaluate* various camps, assessing facilities, costs, staff-to-camper ratios, and activities in order to assist parents in choosing a camp.

Although writers write to reflect, to inform, to persuade, and to evaluate, these purposes are not mutually exclusive, and writers may have other purposes as well.

CHECKLIST

**Determining Your Purpose**

Before you begin to write, you need to determine why you are writing. Your purposes can include any of the following:

- ❑ to reflect
- ❑ to inform
- ❑ to persuade
- ❑ to evaluate
- ❑ to explain
- ❑ to amuse or entertain
- ❑ to discover
- ❑ to analyze
- ❑ to debunk
- ❑ to draw comparisons
- ❑ to make an analogy
- ❑ to define
- ❑ to criticize
- ❑ to motivate
- ❑ to satirize
- ❑ to speculate
- ❑ to warn
- ❑ to reassure
- ❑ to take a stand
- ❑ to identify problems
- ❑ to suggest solutions
- ❑ to identify causes
- ❑ to predict effects
- ❑ to interpret
- ❑ to instruct
- ❑ to inspire

## EXERCISE 1

Read the following excerpts carefully. Try to put yourself in each writer's position, considering what he or she had in mind when writing. For what purpose or purposes do you think each passage was written? What makes you think so?

1. Of course, short people have been looked down upon for years. In the matter of language, for example . . . one does not wish to be found short-tempered, short-winded or shortsighted. One does not wish to be left with the short end, caught short-handed or given short shrift. Shortages, short circuits and shortfalls are universally deplored. On the other hand, one takes pride in filling a tall order, gapes at the tall ships, admires a tall tale and—out here in the Wild West—sits tall in the saddle. Although brevity is the soul of wit and one strives to make a long story short, this quality is not equally appreciated when manifested in human form. Just as we habitually use the masculine gender to denote all people, we use tallness to measure height. Thus there are those who say they are "4 feet tall" when they are clearly 4 feet short. (Beth Luey, "Short Shrift," *Newsweek*)
2. In a hideously cruel response to an outbreak of rabies in late July, authorities in Mouding County in Southwest China ordered the killing of more than 50,000 dogs, including 4,000 who were immunized against the disease. Officials clubbed many animals to death in the street right before their guardians' eyes. Animals who were not beaten mercilessly died equally violent, gruesome deaths by poisoning or electrocution. (PETA Web site. PETA.org. Reprinted with permission.)
3. Radio began with the transatlantic "wireless" communication of Guglielmo Marconi (1874–1937) in 1901 and the development of the vacuum tube in 1904, which permitted the transmission of speech and

music. But it was only in 1920 that the first major broadcasts of special events were made in Great Britain and the United States. Lord Northcliffe, who had pioneered in journalism with the inexpensive, mass-circulation *Daily Mail*, sponsored a broadcast of "only one artist . . . the world's very best, the soprano Nellie Melba." Singing from London in English, Italian and French, Melba was heard simultaneously all over Europe on June 16, 1920. This historic event captured the public's imagination. The meteoric career of radio was launched. (McKay, Hill, Buckler, *A History of Western Society,* Vol. II)

## EXERCISE 2

The two student paragraphs that follow treat the same general subject, but their purposes are different. What do you see as the primary purpose of each paragraph? What other purposes might each writer have had?

1. Answer to an essay examination question: "Identify the Boston Massacre."

   The Boston Massacre refers to a 1770 confrontation between British soldiers and a crowd of colonists. Encouraged by Samuel Adams, the citizens had become more and more upset over issues like the British government's stationing troops and customs commissioners in Boston. When angry colonists attacked a customhouse sentry on March 5, 1770, a fight broke out. Soldiers fired into the crowd, and five civilians were killed. Although the soldiers were found guilty only of manslaughter and given only a token punishment, Samuel Adams's propaganda created the idea of a "massacre" in the minds of many Americans.

2. From "The Ohio Massacre: 1770 Revisited" (student essay):

   In two incidents that occurred exactly two hundred years apart, civilian demonstrators were shot and killed by armed troops. Although civilians were certainly inciting the British troops, starting scuffles and even brawls, these actions should not have led the Redcoats to fire blindly into the crowd. Similarly, the Ohio National Guard should not have allowed themselves to be provoked by students who were calling names, shoving, or throwing objects, and Governor Rhodes should not have authorized the troops to fire their weapons. The deaths—five civilians in Boston, Massachusetts, in 1770, and four students in Kent, Ohio, in 1970—were all unnecessary.

## EXERCISE 3

The primary purpose of the following article from the *New York Times* is to present information. Suppose you were using the information in an orientation booklet aimed at students entering your school, and your purpose was to persuade students of the importance of maintaining a good credit rating. How would you change the original article to help you achieve this purpose? Would you reorder any details? Would you add or delete anything?

**What Makes a Credit Score Rise or Fall?**

*By Jennifer Bayot*

Your financial decisions can affect your credit score in surprising ways. Two credit-scoring simulators can help consumers understand the potential impact.

The Fair Isaac Corporation, which puts out the industry-standard FICO scores, offers the myFICO simulator. A consumer with a score of 707 (considered good) and three credit cards would be likely to add or lose points from his score by making various financial moves. Following are some examples:

- By making timely payments on all his accounts over the next month or by paying off a third of the balance on his cards, he could add as many as 20 points.
- By failing to make this month's payments on his loans, he could lose 75 to 125 points.
- By using all of the credit available on his three credit cards, he could lose 20 to 70 points.
- By getting a fourth card, depending on the status of his other debts, he could add or lose up to 10 points.
- By consolidating his credit card debt into a new card, also depending on other debts, he could add or lose 15 points.

The other simulator, the What-If, comes from CreditXpert, which designs credit management tools and puts out its own, similar credit score. A consumer with a score of 727 points (also considered good) would be likely to have her score change in the following ways:

- Every time she simply applied for a loan, whether a credit card, home mortgage or auto loan, she would lose five points. (An active appetite for credit, credit experts note, is considered a bad sign. For one thing, taking on new loans may make borrowers less likely to repay their current debts.)
- By getting a mortgage, she would lose two points.
- By getting an auto loan or a new credit card (assuming that she already has several cards) she would lose three points.
- If her new credit card had a credit limit of $20,000 or more, she would lose four points, instead of three. (For every $10,000 added to the limit, the score drops a point.)
- By simultaneously getting a new mortgage, auto loan and credit card, she would lose seven or eight points.



## EXERCISE 4

Look closely at the visuals reproduced on the following page, and consider for what purpose or purposes each might have been created. (You can consult the checklist on page 5 to help you identify the purpose or purposes that best apply.)

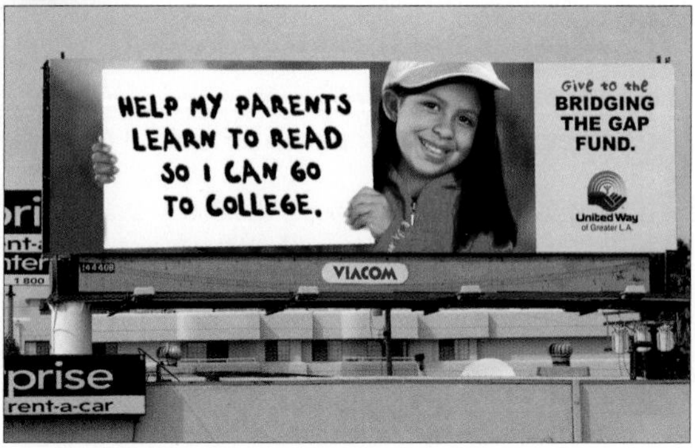


Bill Aron/PhotoEdit

FIGURE 1.1 Billboard for United Way of America.

Mario Tama/Getty Images

FIGURE 1.2 New Orleans refugees after Hurricane Katrina, 2005.

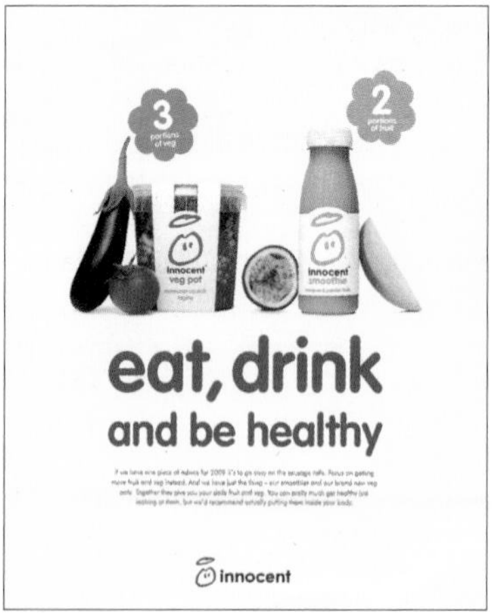


Image courtesy of the Advertising Archives

FIGURE 1.3 Health food ad.

## 1b Identifying Your Audience

When you are in the early stages of a writing project, staring at a blank screen (or a blank sheet of paper), it is easy to forget that what you write will have an audience. But except for diaries and private journals, you always write for an **audience,** a particular reader or group of readers.

### 1 Writing for an Audience

At different times, in different roles, you address a variety of audiences:

- **In your personal life,** you may send notes, emails, or text messages to friends and family members.
- **In your** public life, as a citizen, a consumer, or a member of a community, civic, political, or religious group, you may respond to pressing social, economic, or political issues by writing letters or emails to newspapers, public officials, or representatives of special interest groups. You may also be called on to write media releases, brochures, flyers, or newsletters. See Ch. 32
- **As an employee,** you may write emails, memos, proposals, and reports to your superiors, to staff members you supervise, or to coworkers; you may also be called on to address customers or critics, board members or stockholders, funding agencies or the general public.
- **As a student,** you write reflective statements and response papers as well as essays, reports, exams, and research papers for your instructors in various academic **disciplines.** You may also participate in **peer review,** writing evaluations of classmates' essays and writing responses to their comments about your own work. See Pt. 6

As you write, you shape your writing according to what you believe your audience needs and expects. Your assessment of your readers' interests, educational level, biases, and expectations determines not only the information you include but also what you emphasize and how you arrange your material.

### 2 The College Writer's Audience

***Writing for Your Instructor*** As a student, you usually write for an audience of one: the instructor who assigns the paper. Instructors want to know what you know about your subject and whether you can express your ideas clearly and accurately. They assign written work to encourage you to **think critically,** so the way you organize and express your ideas can be as important as the ideas themselves. See Ch. 8

As a group, instructors have certain expectations. Because they are trained as careful readers and critics, your instructors expect accurate information, standard grammar and correct spelling, logically presented ideas, and a reasonable degree of stylistic fluency. They also expect you to define your terms and to support your generalizations with specific examples. Finally, every

See Pts. 5–6

instructor expects you to draw your own conclusions and to provide full and accurate documentation for ideas that are not your own.

If you are writing in an instructor's academic field, you can omit long overviews and basic definitions. Remember, however, that outside their areas of expertise, most instructors are simply general readers. If you think you may know more about a subject than your instructor does, be sure to provide background and to supply the definitions, examples, and analogies that will make your ideas clear.

All academic fields of study—or **disciplines**—share certain values. All disciplines value accuracy of information, careful selection and documentation of sources, and clear, correct writing. However, instructors in different disciplines are likely to emphasize different aspects of writing and use different formats, conventions, and citation systems. Often, their requirements will be different from those you will learn in composition classes. **Part 6** of this text highlights the key features of writing in other disciplines and includes examples of assignments from disciplines in the humanities, the social sciences, and the natural and applied sciences.

**ESL TIP**

If you did not attend school in the US, you may have trouble understanding your instructor's expectations or difficulty determining how much your instructor knows about your cultural background, native language, or home country. In these situations, it is usually a good idea to ask your instructor for advice.

**CHECKLIST**

## Writing for an Academic Audience

Before you respond to an assignment in your college courses, you need to identify the audience you are writing for. The following questions can help you understand what your audience expects:

- ❑ What discipline are you writing for?
- ❑ What kinds of assignments are typical of this discipline?
- ❑ What expectations do instructors in this discipline have?
- ❑ What style considerations are important in this discipline?
- ❑ What writing conventions are used in this discipline?
- ❑ What formats are used in this discipline?
- ❑ What research sources are used in this discipline?
- ❑ What documentation style is used in this discipline?

See 6c2

***Writing for Other Students*** Before you submit a paper to an instructor, you may have an opportunity to participate in peer review, sharing your work with your fellow students and responding in writing to their work. Before you begin, you need to see your classmates as an audience whose needs you must take into account.

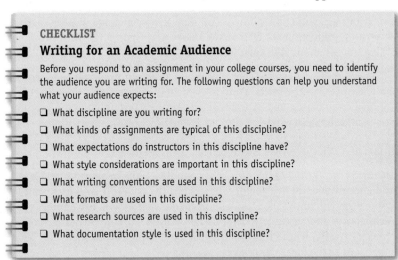

- **Writing Drafts** If you know that other students will read a draft of your paper, you need to consider how they might react to your ideas. For example, are they likely to disagree with you? To be shocked or offended by your paper's language or content? To be confused, or even mystified, by any of your references? Even if your readers are your own age, you cannot assume they share your values, political opinions, or cultural frame of reference. It is therefore very important that you maintain a neutral tone and use moderate language in your paper and that you be prepared to explain any historical, geographical, or cultural references that might be unfamiliar to your audience.
- **Writing Comments** When you respond in writing to another student's paper, you need to take into account how your reader will react to your comments. Here, too, your **tone** is important: you want to be as encouraging (and as polite) as possible. In addition, keep in mind that your purpose is not to show how clever you are but to offer constructive comments that can help your classmate write a stronger essay.

See 1c

CHECKLIST

### Audience Concerns for Peer-Review Participants

&

To get the most out of a peer-review session, keep the following guidelines in mind:

- ❑ **Know the material.** To be sure you understand what the student writer needs and expects from your comments, read the paper several times before you begin writing your response.
- ❑ **Focus on the big picture.** Try not to get bogged down in minor problems with punctuation or mechanics or become distracted by a paper's proofreading errors.
- ❑ **Look for a positive feature.** Try to zero in on what you think is the paper's greatest strength.
- ❑ **Be positive throughout.** Try to avoid words like *weak, poor,* and *bad;* instead, try using a compliment before delivering the "bad news": "Paragraph 2 is very well developed; can you add this kind of support in paragraph 4?"
- ❑ **Show respect.** It is perfectly acceptable to tell a student that something is confusing or inaccurate, but don't go on the attack.
- ❑ **Be specific.** Avoid generalizations like "needs more examples" or "could be more interesting"; instead, try to offer helpful, focused suggestions: "You could add an example after the second sentence in paragraph 2"; "Explaining how this process operates would make your discussion more interesting."
- ❑ **Don't give orders.** Ask questions, and make suggestions.
- ❑ **Include a few words of encouragement.** In your summary, try to emphasize the paper's strong points.

**EXERCISE 5**

Review the excerpts and visuals in Exercises 1 through 4. This time, try to decide what audience or audiences each seems to be aimed at. Then, consider what (if anything) might have to be changed to address the needs of each of the following audiences:

- College students
- Middle-school students
- The elderly
- People with limited English skills
- People who do not live in the United States

## 1c Setting Your Tone

Tone conveys your attitude. The attitude, or mood, that you adopt as you write may be serious or frivolous, respectful or condescending, intimate or detached. Because tone tells your readers how you feel about your material, it must remain consistent with your purpose and your audience as you write and revise.

When your general purpose is to present information, you choose words and construct sentences that make your writing objective and informative. Your choice of a factual, straightforward, reasonable—even impersonal—tone will convey your no-nonsense attitude. In such a situation, a sarcastic or playful tone would be inappropriate. However, when your primary purpose is to influence your readers—for example, to sway their opinions or appeal to their emotions, to make them angry or sympathetic—you select words and shape sentences that serve this end. Your tone can be ironic or harsh, sentimental or cold, bitter or compassionate: whatever best reflects your attitude and serves your purpose.

Your tone also reveals how you feel toward your readers—sympathetic or superior, concerned or indifferent, friendly or critical. For instance, if you identify with your readers or feel close to them, you use a personal and conversational tone. When you address readers indirectly or anonymously, you use a more distant, formal tone.

When your audience is an instructor and your purpose is to inform (as is often the case in college writing situations), you should generally use an objective tone—neither too personal and informal nor too detached and formal—as the following student paragraph does.

> One of the major characteristics of streptococci is that they are gram-positive. This means that after a series of dyes and rinses they take on a violet color. (Gram-negative organisms take on a red color.) Streptococci are also nonspore forming and nonmotile. Most strains produce a protective shield called a capsule. They use organic substances instead of oxygen for their metabolism. This process is called fermentation.

An English composition assignment asking students to write an informal essay expressing their feelings about the worst job they ever had calls for an entirely different tone. In the paragraph that follows, the student's tone effectively conveys his attitude toward his job, and his use of the first person encourages his audience to identify with him. Sarcastic comments ("good little laborer," "Now here comes the excitement!") contribute to the informal effect.

> Every day I followed the same boring, monotonous routine. After clocking in like a good little laborer, I proceeded over to a gray file cabinet, forced open the half-caved-in doors, and removed a staple gun, various packs of size cards, and a blue ballpoint pen. Now here comes the excitement! Each farmer had a specific number assigned to his name. As his cucumbers were being sorted according to their particular size, they were loaded into two-hundred-pound bins, which I had to label with a stapled size card with the farmer's number on it. I had to complete a specific size card for every bin containing that size cucumber. Doesn't it sound wonderful? Any second grader could have handled it. And all the time I worked, the machinery moaned and rattled, and the odor of cucumbers filled the air.

In a letter applying for a job, however, the same student would have a different purpose—and would, therefore, use a different tone. In this situation, his distance from his audience and his desire to impress readers with his qualifications would call for a much more objective and straightforward tone.

> My primary duty at Germaine Produce was to label cucumbers as they were sorted into bins. I was responsible for making sure each two-hundred-pound bin bore the name of the farmer who had grown those cucumbers and also for keeping track of the cucumbers' sizes. Accuracy was extremely important in this task.

**Close-Up** CONVEYING YOUR TONE

Your computer gives you options—such as different type sizes and typefaces—that can help you convey a particular tone. For example, if you are applying for a job in business or industry and want to write a résumé, you would select a conservative typeface such as Times New Roman. A plain, businesslike typeface tells readers that you are a serious applicant. If, however, you were preparing a brochure, a flyer, or another document designed to appeal to the general public, you might experiment with decorative fonts and varying type sizes.

See 33b, d

See Ch. 32

**EXERCISE 6**

1. Focus on a book that you liked or disliked very much. How would you write about the book in each of the following writing situations? Consider how each writing situation would affect your choice of content, style, organization, tone, and emphasis.
    - A post on your composition class's course site reflecting on your impressions of the book
    - An exam question that asks you to summarize the book's ideas
    - A book review for a composition class in which you evaluate the book's strengths and weaknesses
    - An email in which you try to convince your local school board that the book should (or should not) be purchased for a public high school's library
    - An editorial for your school newspaper in which you try to persuade other students that the book is worth reading
    - A text to a friend recommending (or criticizing) the book
2. Write responses for two of the writing situations listed above.

CHAPTER 2

# Reading Texts

## Frequently Asked Questions



Central to developing effective reading skills is learning the techniques of **active reading.** Being an active reader means being actively involved with the text: reading with pen in hand and physically marking the text in order to identify parallels, question ambiguities, distinguish important points from not-so-important ones, and connect causes with effects and generalizations with specific examples. The understanding you gain from active reading prepares you to think (and write) critically about a text.

## 2a Previewing a Text

Before you actually begin reading a text, you should **preview** it—that is, skim it to get a sense of the writer's subject and emphasis.

When you preview a **periodical article,** skim the introductory and concluding paragraphs for summaries of the writer's main points. (Journal articles in the sciences and social sciences often begin with summaries called **abstracts.**) Thesis statements, topic sentences, repeated key terms, transitional words and phrases, and transitional paragraphs can also help you to identify the key points a writer is making. In addition, look for the **visual cues**—such as headings and lists—that writers use to emphasize ideas.

See 28b–c

When you preview a **book,** start by looking at its table of contents; then, turn to its index. A quick glance at the index will reveal the amount of coverage the book gives to subjects that may be important to you. As you leaf through the chapters, look at pictures, graphs, or tables and the captions that appear with them.

**ESL TIP**

When you read a text for the first time, don't worry about understanding every word. Instead, just try to get a general idea of what the text is about and how it is organized. Later on, you can look up any unfamiliar words.

**CHECKLIST**

### Previewing a Text

When you preview a text, try to answer these questions:

- ❑ What is the text's general subject?
- ❑ What are the writer's main points?
- ❑ How much space does the writer devote to topics relevant to your interests or research?
- ❑ What other topics are covered?
- ❑ Who is the author of the text? What do you know about this writer?
- ❑ Is the text current?
- ❑ Does the text strike you as interesting, accessible, and useful?

**Close-Up VISUAL CUES**

When you preview a text, don't forget to note its use of color and of various typographical elements—such as typeface and type size, boldface and italics—to emphasize ideas.

## 2b Highlighting a Text

When you have finished previewing a text, photocopy relevant sections of books and articles, and print out useful material from online sources. Then, **highlight** the pages, using a system of graphic symbols and underlining to identify the writer's key points and their relationships to one another.

**CHECKLIST**

### Using Highlighting Symbols

When you read a text, use strategies like the following to help you understand the material:

- ❑ Underline to indicate information you should read again.
- ❑ Box or circle key words or important phrases.
- ❑ Put question marks next to confusing passages, unclear points, or words you need to look up.
- ❑ Draw lines or arrows to show connections between ideas.
- ❑ Number points that are discussed in sequence.
- ❑ Draw a vertical line in the margin to set off an important section.
- ❑ Star especially important ideas.

## 2c Annotating a Text

After you have read through your material once, read it again—this time, more critically. At this stage, you should **annotate** the pages, recording your responses to what you read. This process of recording notes in the margins or between the lines will help you to better understand the writer's ideas and your own reactions to those ideas.

**ESL TIP**

You may find it useful to use your native language when you annotate a text.

Some of your annotations may be relatively straightforward. For example, you may define new words, identify unfamiliar references, or jot down brief summaries. Other annotations may be more personal: you may identify a parallel between an experience of your own and one described in the text, or you may record your opinion of the writer's position.

See Ch. 8

As you start to think critically about a text, your annotations may identify points that confirm (or challenge) your own ideas, question the appropriateness or accuracy of the writer's support, uncover the writer's biases, or even question (or dispute) the writer's conclusion.

The following passage illustrates a student's highlighting and annotations of a passage from Michael Pollan's book *The Omnivore's Dilemma.*

[People drank 5x as much as they do today]

In the early years of the nineteenth century, Americans began drinking more than they ever had before or since, embarking on a collective bender that confronted the young republic with its first major public health crisis—the obesity epidemic of its day. Corn whiskey, suddenly superabundant and cheap, became the drink of choice, and in 1820 the typical American was putting away half a pint of the stuff every day. That comes to more than five gallons of spirits a year for every man, woman, and child in America. The figure today is less than one.

[!!] [?]

As the historian W. J. Rorabaugh tells the story in *The Alcoholic Republic,* we drank the hard stuff at breakfast, lunch, and dinner, before work and after and very often during. Employers were expected to supply spirits over the course of the workday; in fact, the modern coffee break began as a late-morning whiskey break called "the elevenses." (Just to pronounce it makes you sound tipsy.) Except for a brief respite Sunday morning in church, Americans simply did not gather—whether for a barn raising or quilting bee, corn husking or political rally—without passing the whiskey jug. Visitors from Europe—hardly models of sobriety themselves—marveled at the free flow of American spirits. "Come on then, if you love toping," the journalist William Cobbett wrote his fellow Englishmen in a dispatch from America. "For here you may drink yourself blind at the price of sixpence."

[*] [Did the gov't take action?]

The results of all this toping were entirely predictable: a rising tide of public drunkenness, violence, and family abandonment, and a spike in alcohol-related diseases. Several of the Founding Fathers—including George Washington, Thomas Jefferson, and John Adams—denounced the excesses of "the Alcoholic Republic," inaugurating an American quarrel over drinking that would culminate a century later in Prohibition.

[Why?] [*] [Examples from contemporary US farming?] [This is his point]

But the outcome of our national drinking binge is not nearly as relevant to our own situation as its underlying cause. Which, put simply, was this: American farmers were producing far too much corn. This was particularly true in the newly settled regions west of the Appalachians, where fertile, virgin soils yielded one bumper crop after another. A mountain of surplus corn piled up in the Ohio River Valley. Much as today, the astounding productivity of American farmers proved to be their own worst enemy, as well as a threat to public health. For when yields rise, the market is flooded with grain, and its price collapses. What happens next? The excess biomass works like a vacuum in reverse: Sooner or later, clever marketers will figure out a way to induce the human omnivore to consume the surfeit of cheap calories.

## EXERCISE 1

Preview the following passage, and then read it more carefully, highlighting and annotating it to help you understand the writer's ideas. Then, compare your highlighting and annotations with a classmate's. When you are satisfied that you have identified the most important ideas and that you both understand the passage, work together to answer the following questions:

- What is the writer's general subject?
- What is the writer's main idea—the point of the passage?
- What examples and details does the writer use to support this main idea?
- What questions do you have about the writer's ideas?

When the going gets tough, the tough take accounting. When the job market worsens, many students figure they can't indulge in an English or a history major. They have to study something that will lead directly to a job.

So it is almost inevitable that over the next few years, as labor markets struggle, the humanities will continue their long slide. There already has been a nearly 50 percent drop in the portion of liberal arts majors over the past generation, and that trend is bound to accelerate. Once the stars of university life, humanities now play bit roles when prospective students take their college tours. The labs are more glamorous than the libraries.

But allow me to pause for a moment and throw another sandbag on the levee of those trying to resist this tide. Let me stand up for the history, English and art classes, even in the face of today's economic realities.

Studying the humanities improves your ability to read and write. No matter what you do in life, you will have a huge advantage if you can read a paragraph and discern its meaning (a rarer talent than you might suppose). You will have enormous power if you are the person in the office who can write a clear and concise memo.

Studying the humanities will give you a familiarity with the language of emotion. In an information economy, many people have the ability to produce a technical innovation: a new MP3 player. Very few people have the ability to create a great brand: the iPod. Branding involves the location and arousal of affection, and you can't do it unless you are conversant in the language of romance.

Studying the humanities will give you a wealth of analogies. People think by comparison—Iraq is either like Vietnam or Bosnia; your boss is like Narcissus or Solon. People who have a wealth of analogies in their minds can think more precisely than those with few analogies. If you go through college without reading Thucydides, Herodotus and Gibbon, you'll have been cheated out of a great repertoire of comparisons.

Finally, and most importantly, studying the humanities helps you befriend The Big Shaggy.

Let me try to explain. Over the past century or so, people have built various systems to help them understand human behavior: economics, political science, game theory and evolutionary psychology. These systems are useful in many circumstances. But none completely explain behavior because deep down people have passions and drives that don't lend themselves to systemic modeling. They have yearnings and fears that reside in an inner beast you could call The Big Shaggy.

You can see The Big Shaggy at work when a governor of South Carolina suddenly chucks it all for a love voyage south of the equator, or when a smart, philosophical congressman from Indiana risks everything for an in-office affair.

You can see The Big Shaggy at work when self-destructive overconfidence overtakes oil engineers in the gulf, when go-go enthusiasm intoxicates investment bankers or when bone-chilling distrust grips politics.

Those are the destructive sides of The Big Shaggy. But this tender beast is also responsible for the mysterious but fierce determination that drives Kobe Bryant, the graceful bemusement the Detroit Tigers pitcher Armando Galarraga showed when his perfect game slipped away, the selfless courage soldiers in Afghanistan show when they risk death for buddies or a family they may never see again.

The observant person goes through life asking: Where did that come from? Why did he or she act that way? The answers are hard to come by because the behavior emanates from somewhere deep inside The Big Shaggy.

Technical knowledge stops at the outer edge. If you spend your life riding the links of the Internet, you probably won't get too far into The Big Shaggy either, because the fast, effortless prose of blogging (and journalism) lacks the heft to get you deep below.

But over the centuries, there have been rare and strange people who possessed the skill of taking the upheavals of thought that emanate from The Big Shaggy and representing them in the form of story, music, myth, painting, liturgy, architecture, sculpture, landscape and speech. These men and women developed languages that help us understand these yearnings and also educate and mold them. They left rich veins of emotional knowledge that are the subjects of the humanities.

It's probably dangerous to enter exclusively into this realm and risk being caught in a cloister, removed from the market and its accountability. But doesn't it make sense to spend some time in the company of these languages—learning to feel different emotions, rehearsing different passions, experiencing different sacred rituals and learning to see in different ways?

Few of us are hewers of wood. We navigate social environments. If you're dumb about The Big Shaggy, you'll probably get eaten by it. (David Brooks, "History for Dollars")



## 2d Reading Electronic Texts

Even when electronic documents physically resemble print documents (as they do in online newspaper articles), the way they present information can be very different. Print documents are **linear;** that is, readers move in a straight line from the beginning of a document to the end. Print documents are also self-contained, including all the background information, explanations, supporting details, and visuals necessary to make their point.

Electronic documents, however, are usually not linear. They often include advertising, marginal commentary, and graphics, and they may also include sound and video. In addition, links embedded in the text encourage readers to go to other sites for facts, statistical data, visuals, or additional articles that supplement the discussion. For example, readers of the electronic discussion of gun control pictured in Figure 2.1 could link to FBI data about the connection between "concealed carry laws" and violent crime. Once they access this material, they can choose to read it carefully, skim it, or ignore it.

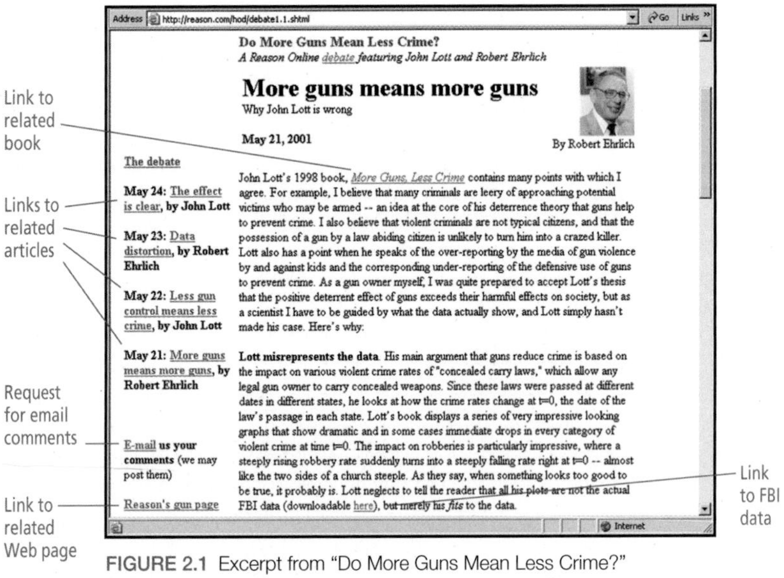


FIGURE 2.1 Excerpt from "Do More Guns Mean Less Crime?" A *Reason Online* Debate. Reprinted by permission of Reason.

The format of electronic texts presents challenges to readers. First, because links to other material interrupt the document's flow, it may be hard for readers to focus on a writer's main idea and key points or to follow an argument's logic. In addition, pages may be very busy, crowded with distracting marginalia, visuals, and advertisements. For these reasons, it makes sense to use a slightly different process when you apply active reading strategies to an electronic text.

***Previewing*** During the previewing stage, you will probably want to skim the text online, doing your best to ignore visuals, marginal commentary, advertising, and links. If the text looks like something you will want to read more closely, you should print it out (taking care to print the "printer-friendly" version, which will usually omit the distracting material and enable you to focus on the text's content).

***Highlighting and Annotating*** Once you have hard copy of an electronic text, you can proceed to highlight and annotate it just as you would a print text. Reading on hard copy will enable you to follow the writer's main idea instead of clicking on every link. However, you should be sure to circle any links that look promising so you can explore them later on.

Note: You can also highlight and annotate Web-based texts with a program like *Diigo*, which makes it possible for you to highlight and write self-stick notes on electronic documents.

### EXERCISE 2

Find an essay on the Web that focuses on the same topic discussed in the newspaper article in Exercise 1. Print the essay, and then highlight and annotate it, paying special attention to the features discussed in **2d.**

## 2e Writing a Critical Response

Once you have previewed, highlighted, and annotated a text, you should have the understanding (and the material) you need to write a **critical response** that *summarizes, analyzes,* and *interprets* the text's key ideas and perhaps *evaluates* them as well. It can also *synthesize* the ideas in the text with ideas in other texts.

> CHECKLIST
> **Elements of a Critical Response**
> When you write a critical response, you may include some or all of the following elements.
> - ❑ **Summary:** What is the writer saying?
> - ❑ **Analysis:** What elements is the text made up of?
> - ❑ **Interpretation:** What does the text mean?
> - ❑ **Synthesis:** How is the text like and unlike other texts? How are its ideas like and unlike ideas in other texts?
> - ❑ **Evaluation:** Is the text accurate and reliable? Do its ideas seem reasonable?

The following is a student's critical response to the passage from *The Omnivore's Dilemma* on page 17.

In an excerpt from his book *The Omnivore's Dilemma*, Michael Pollan discusses the drinking habits of nineteenth-century Americans and makes a connection between the cause of this "national drinking binge" and the factors behind our twenty-first-century unhealthy diets. In both cases, he blames the overproduction of grain by American farmers. He links nineteenth-century overproduction of corn with "a rising tide of public drunkenness, violence, and family abandonment, and a spike in

Author and title identified

Summary

Analysis and interpretation

alcohol-related deaths," and he also links the current overproduction of grain with a "threat to public health." Although there are certainly other causes of our current problems with obesity, particularly among young children, Pollan's analogy makes sense. As long as farmers need to sell their overabundant crops, consumers will be presented with a "surfeit of cheap calories"—with potentially disastrous results.

Evaluation

CHECKLIST

### Writing a Critical Response

As you read a text, keep the following questions in mind:

- ❑ Does the text provide any information about the writer's background? If so, how does this information affect your reading of the text?
- ❑ What is the writer's purpose? How can you tell?
- ❑ What audience is the text aimed at? How can you tell?
- ❑ What is the text's most important idea? What support does the writer provide for that idea?
- ❑ What information can you learn from the text's introduction and conclusion?
- ❑ What information can you learn from the thesis statement and topic sentences?
- ❑ What key words are repeated? What does this repetition tell you about the writer's purpose and emphasis?
- ❑ How would you characterize the writer's tone?
- ❑ Are there parallels between the writer's experiences and your own?
- ❑ Where do you agree with the writer? Where do you disagree?
- ❑ What, if anything, is not clear to you?

*Note:* For information on writing a summary, **see 15a.** For information on synthesizing sources, **see Chapter 16.** For information on evaluating electronic and print texts, **see 14a–b.**

## EXERCISE 3

Write two critical responses: one reacting to the newspaper article in Exercise 1, and one reacting to the electronic text you worked with in Exercise 2. When you have finished, write a few sentences summarizing the similarities and differences between the two articles.

CHAPTER 3

# Reading Visuals

## Frequently Asked Questions



The texts you read in college courses—books, newspapers, and periodical articles, in print or online—are often accompanied by visual images. For example, textbooks often include illustrations to make complex information more accessible, newspapers use photographs to break up columns of written text, and Web sites use graphics of all kinds to add visual appeal.

### Close-Up READING VISUALS

Visuals are used to convey information to supplement written text; they may also be used to persuade as well as to amuse.

**Fine Art**

Mary Stevenson/Bridgeman Art Library

*Profile of a Woman Wearing a Jabot* (pastel on paper) by Mary Stevenson Cassatt (1844–1926).

**Photographs**

Robert Harding Picture Library Ltd/Alamy

Photo of university student preparing backstage at Beijing Opera.


*(continued)*

## READING VISUALS *(continued)*

### Maps

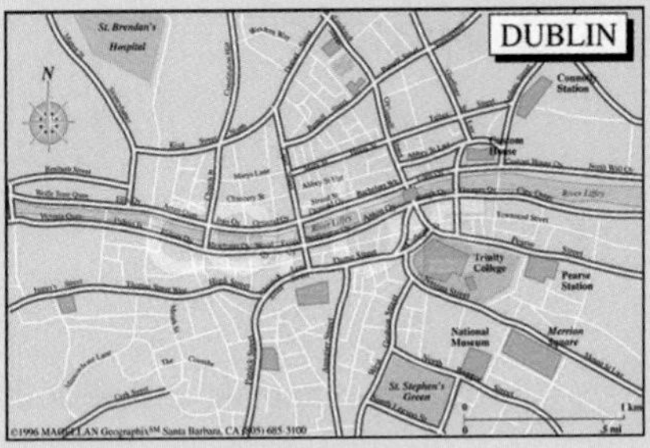


Map.com/Corbis

Map of Dublin, Ireland.

### Cartoons

© Stan Eales. Reproduction rights obtainable from www.CartoonStock.com

Cartoon by Stan Eales.

### Scientific Diagrams

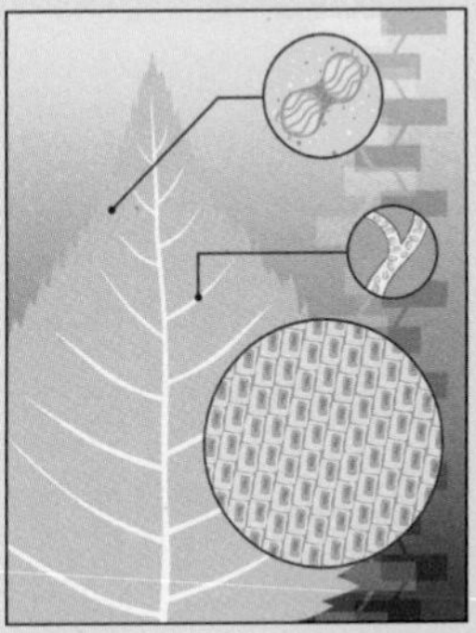

Don Bishop/Photodisc Green/Getty Images

Plant engineering diagram.

### Advertisements

Image courtesy of the Advertising Archives

Mini Cooper ad.

### Tables

Table 1

*Relationship between Sleep Deprivation and Academic Performance*

| Grade Totals | Sleep Deprived | Not Sleep Deprived | Usually Sleep Deprived | Improved | Harmed | Continue Sleep Depriva-tion? |
|---|---|---|---|---|---|---|
| A = 10 | 4 | 6 | 1 | 4 | 0 | 4 |
| B = 20 | 9 | 11 | 8 | 8 | 1 | 8 |
| C = 10 | 10 | 0 | 6 | 5 | 4 | 7 |
| D = 10 | 8 | 2 | 2 | 1 | 3 | 2 |
| Total | 31 | 19 | 17 | 18 | 8 | 21 |

© Cengage Learning

Table from student paper.

### Bar Graphs

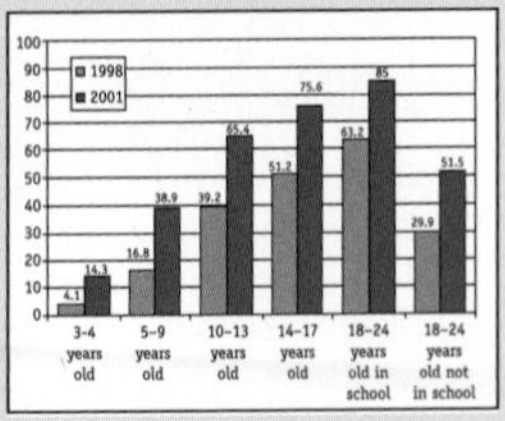


© Cengage Learning

Bar graph from student paper.

## 3a Analyzing and Interpreting Visuals

Because the world audience is becoming increasingly visual, it is important for you to acquire the skills needed to read and interpret visuals as well as to use them in your own written work. (For information on incorporating visuals into your own writing, **see 6b2.**)

The powerful photograph shown in Figure 3.1, which depicts a Marine in front of the Vietnam Veterans Memorial, uses a variety of techniques to convey its message. To **analyze and interpret** this photograph, you need to determine what strategies it uses to achieve its effect.

You might notice right away that contrasts are very important in this picture. In the background is the list of soldiers who died in the war; in the foreground, a lone Marine stands in silent vigil, seemingly as static as the names carved in granite. Still, those who view this photo know that the Marine is motionless only in the picture; when the photographer puts the camera down, the Marine lives on, in contrast to those whose names are listed behind him.

The large image of the Marine set against the smaller names in the background also suggests that the photograph's purpose is at least in part

*The whole world is watching*

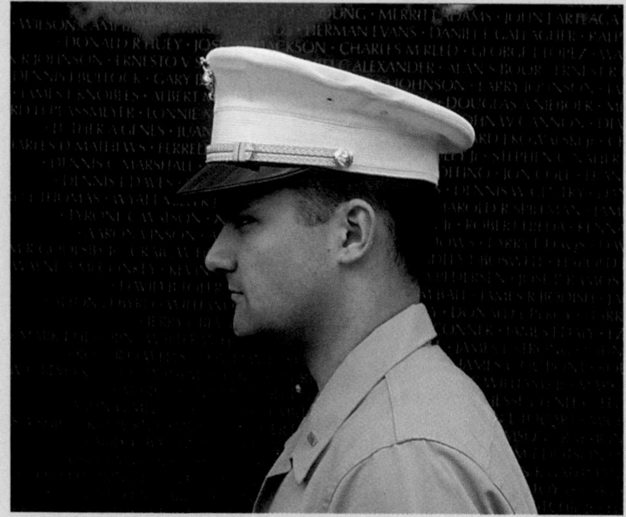

Visions of America/Superstock

A Marine passes the Vietnam memorial on which names of casualties of the war are inscribed.

**FIGURE 3.1** Photograph taken at the Vietnam Veterans Memorial.

to convey the contrast between the past and the present, the dead and the living. Thus, the photograph has a persuasive purpose: it suggests, as its title states, that "the whole world is watching" (and, in fact, *should* be watching) this scene in order to remember the past and honor the dead.

To convey their ideas, visuals often rely on contrasting light and shadow and on the size and placement of individual images (as well as on the spatial relationship of these images to one another and to the whole). In addition, visuals often use words (captions, slogans, explanatory text), and they may also include color, animation, audio narration, and even musical soundtracks. Given the complexity of most visuals and the number of individual elements each one uses to convey its message, analyzing (or "reading") visual texts can be challenging. This task will be easier, however, if you follow the same **active reading** process you use when you read a written text.

## 3b Previewing a Visual

Just as with a written text, the first step in analyzing a visual text is to **preview** it, skimming it to get a sense of its subject and emphasis. At this stage, you may notice little more than the visual's major features: its central image, its dominant colors, its use of white space, and the most prominent blocks of written text. Still, even these elements can give you a general idea of what the focus of the visual is and what purpose it might have.

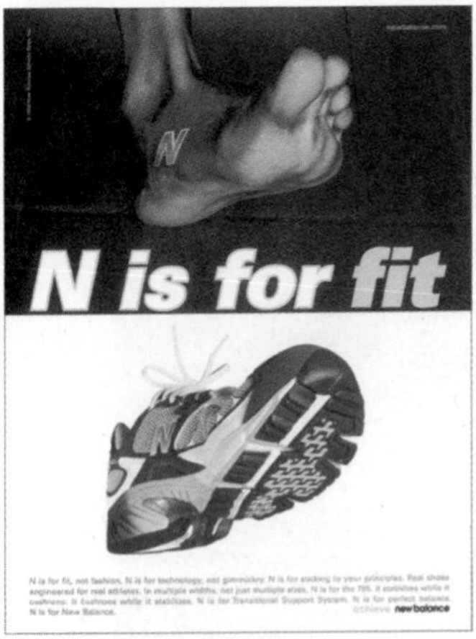


New Balance

FIGURE 3.2 Magazine ad for New Balance sneakers.

For example, the New Balance ad shown in Figure 3.2 includes two large images—a foot and a shoe—both with the distinctive New Balance "N" logo. This logo also appears in the slogan "N is for fit," which has a prominent central position. The slogan is allowed to speak for itself, with the text that explains the visual message appearing in very small type at the bottom of the page. Yellow is used to highlight the logo, the shoe's tread, and the word *fit*.

## 3c Highlighting and Annotating a Visual

When you **highlight** a visual text, you mark it to help you identify key images and their relationship to one another. You might, for example, use arrows to point to important images, or you might circle key words or details. When you **annotate** a visual text, you record your reactions to the images and words you see. (If a visual's background is dark, or if you are not permitted to write directly on it, you can do your highlighting and annotating on small self-stick notes.)

A student in a composition class was asked to analyze the advertisement for Mini Cooper automobiles shown in Figure 3.3. When she visited the company Web site, she saw that Mini Cooper was appealing to consumers who value affordability and reliability as well as the company's commitment to "minimalism" and fuel efficiency. However, the Web site was also appealing to those looking for features like high performance, sporty design, and creativity—for example, the opportunity to "build your own" car by choosing features and colors. The student's highlighting and annotating focus on how the ad's written text and visuals work together to present the company's message: that the Mini Cooper is not just a practical choice but also one that offers possibilities for excitement and adventure.

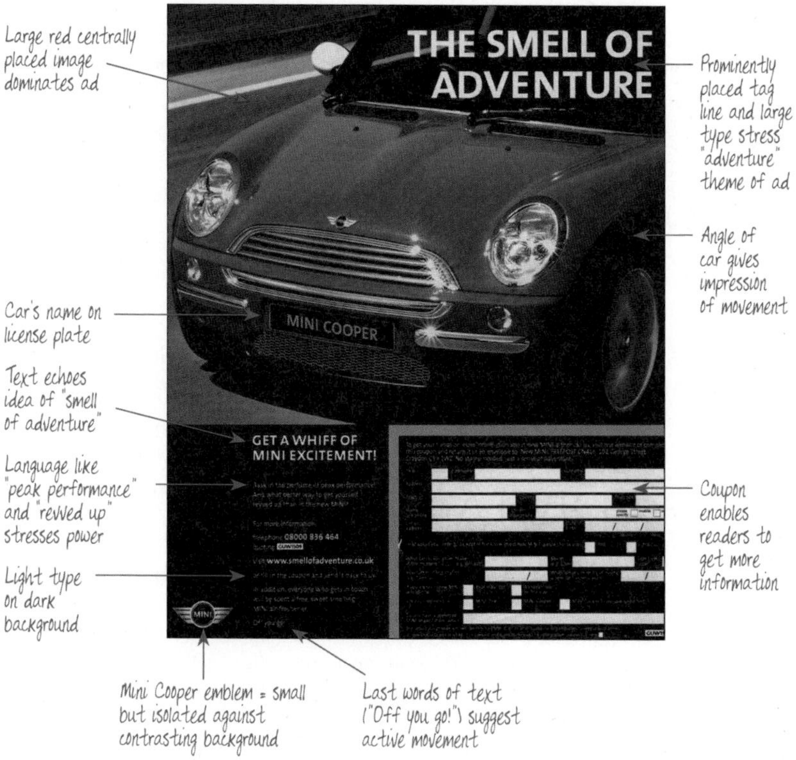


FIGURE 3.3 Mini Cooper ad. Image courtesy of The Advertising Archives.

CHECKLIST

## Analyzing Visuals

- ❑ Who has created the visual?
- ❑ For what purpose was the visual created? For example, does it seem to be designed primarily to inform? To persuade? To entertain or amuse?
- ❑ Where did the visual originally appear? What is the target audience for this publication?
- ❑ What scene does the visual depict?
- ❑ What individual images are shown in the visual? What associations do these images have for you?
- ❑ Do any people appear in the visual? What do they suggest about its target audience? What is their relationship to the scene and to one another? What are they doing?
- ❑ How would you describe the people's facial expressions? Their positions? Their body language?
- ❑ Does the visual include a lot of blank space?
- ❑ How large are the various elements (words and images)?
- ❑ Is the background light or dark? Clear or blurred? What individual elements stand out most clearly against this background?
- ❑ What general mood is suggested by the visual's use of color and shadow?
- ❑ Does the visual include any written text? What is its purpose?
- ❑ In general terms, what is the visual's message? How do its individual elements help to communicate this message?
- ❑ How would the visual's message or impact be different if something were added? If something were deleted?

*Note:* For information on writing a critical analysis of a visual, **see 22c4.** For information on using visuals (such as editorial cartoons, photos, charts, and graphs) to support an argument, **see 11a.**

### EXERCISE 1

Use the checklist above to help you write a paragraph in response to each of the following assignments.

1. On your way to campus or work, locate a billboard or a prominent sign (for example, on a train platform or bus shelter). What product or service does it promote? To what audience is it directed? How do you know? What does the image seem to assume about its intended audience (age, class, gender, and so on)?
2. Compare and contrast two magazine, television, or Internet advertisements for the same type of product (an automobile or cologne, for

instance) that are aimed at two different audiences. How are the two ads different? How does each ad aim to reach its audience? What elements contribute to the persuasive message of each ad?

3. Select a Web site related to one of your courses. What visual elements of the site—images, typeface and type size, color, and so on—contribute to its usefulness as an information resource? How might the site benefit from additional (or fewer) visual features?
4. Select a chapter from one of your textbooks, and examine the way in which content is arranged on the pages. What visual elements (headings, lists, charts, tables, photographs, and so on) can you identify? How do these elements highlight important information?

## EXERCISE 2

Write a paragraph in which you analyze the ad shown in Figure 3.4. Consider the following questions:

- What audience is being addressed?
- What is the ad's primary purpose?
- What message is being conveyed?
- How do the various visual elements work together to appeal to the ad's target audience?

FIGURE 3.4 Ad warning against texting while driving.

Editorial Image, LLC/Alamy Images

CHAPTER 4

# Planning an Essay

## Frequently Asked Questions



## 4a Understanding the Writing Process

Writing is a complex process of decision making—of selecting, deleting, and rearranging material.

**The Writing Process**

The writing process includes the following stages:

**Planning:** Consider your purpose, audience, and tone; choose your topic; discover ideas to write about.

**Shaping:** Decide how to organize your material.

**Drafting:** Write your first draft.

**Revising:** "Re-see" what you have written; write additional drafts.

**Editing:** Check grammar, spelling, punctuation, and mechanics.

**Proofreading:** Reread every word, checking for any remaining errors.

Of course, the neatly defined stages listed above do not communicate the reality of the writing process. In practice, this process is neither a linear series of steps nor an isolated activity. (In fact, in an electronic classroom, a significant part of the writing process can take place in full view of an online audience.) Writing is also often interactive: the writing process can be interrupted (and supplemented) by emailing, blogging, chat room discussions, or surfing the Internet.

Moreover, the stages of the writing process actually overlap: as you look for ideas, you begin to shape your material; as you shape your material, you begin to write; as you write a draft, you reorganize your ideas; as you revise, you continue to discover new material. These stages may be repeated again and again throughout the writing process. During your college years and in the years that follow, you will develop your own version of the writing process and use it whenever you write, adapting it to the audience, purpose, and writing situation at hand.

**Close-Up** COLLABORATIVE WRITING PROJECTS &

In school—and particularly in the workplace—you will find that writing is increasingly a collaborative effort. On a regular basis, you will work with others to plan projects, do research, draft different sections of a single document (or different components of a larger project), and offer suggestions for revision.

**EXERCISE 1**

Write a paragraph in which you describe your own writing process. (If you prefer, you may draw a diagram that represents your process.) What do you do first? What steps do you return to again and again? Which stages do you find most satisfying? Which do you find most frustrating? Compare your paragraph with the paragraph written by another student in your class. How are your processes alike and different? &

## 4b Computers and the Writing Process

Computers have changed the way we write and communicate in both academic and workplace settings. In addition to using word-processing applications for typical writing tasks, writers may rely on programs such as *PowerPoint*® for giving presentations, *Publisher*® for creating customized résumés or brochures, and Web-page authoring software such as *Dreamweaver*® or *HomeSite*® for creating Internet-accessible documents that include images, movies, and a wide range of visual effects.

See Ch. 33

See 34d2

With the prominent role of the Internet in professional, academic, and personal communication, it is increasingly likely that the feedback you receive on your writing will be electronic. For example, if your instructor uses course management software such as *WebCT*™ or *Blackboard*™, you may receive an email from your instructor about a draft that you have submitted to a digital drop box. Or, you may use discussion boards for attaching or sharing your documents with other students. Chat room and Net meeting software also allow you to discuss ideas collaboratively and to offer and receive feedback on drafts.

Although the tools you use may be course- or workplace-specific, you will still have to develop an efficient writing process. **Chapter 27** provides more comprehensive information on the options available to you as you write in a digital environment.

## 4c Understanding Your Assignment

**Planning** your essay—thinking about what you want to say and how you want to say it—begins well before you actually start recording your thoughts in any organized way. This planning is as important a part of the writing process as the writing itself. During this planning stage, you determine your **purpose** for writing and identify your **audience.** Then, you go on to focus on your assignment, choose and narrow your topic, and gather ideas.

Before you start to write, be sure you understand the exact requirements of your **assignment.** Ask questions if necessary, and be sure you understand the answers.

CHECKLIST

### Understanding Your Assignment

To help you understand your assignment, consider the following questions:

- ❑ Has your instructor assigned a specific topic, or can you choose your own?
- ❑ What is the word or page limit?
- ❑ How much time do you have to complete your assignment?
- ❑ Will you get feedback from your instructor? Will you have an opportunity to participate in peer review?
- ❑ Does your assignment require research?
- ❑ What format (for example, MLA) are you supposed to follow? Do you know what its conventions are?
- ❑ If your assignment has been given to you in writing, have you read it carefully and highlighted key words?

See 6c2

See Ch. 18

Rebecca James, a first-year composition student, was given the following assignment.

> The free online encyclopedia *Wikipedia* has become a common starting point for students seeking information on a topic. Because anyone can alter articles in this database, the reliability of *Wikipedia* as a valid source of information has been criticized by members of the academic community. In an essay of

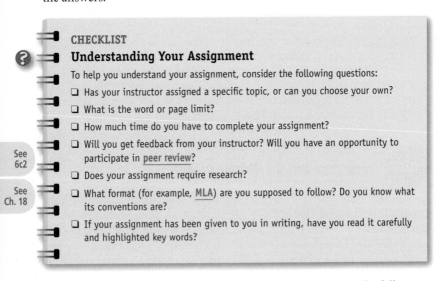

about 3–5 pages, evaluate the benefits and drawbacks of using *Wikipedia* in college research. To support your assessment, focus on a *Wikipedia* entry related to one of your courses.

The class was given three weeks to complete the assignment. Students were expected to do some research and to have the instructor and other students read and comment on at least one draft.

## 4d Choosing a Topic

Sometimes your instructor will allow you to choose your own topic; more often, however, you will be given a general assignment, which you will have to narrow to a **topic** that suits your purpose and audience.

### *From Assignment to Topic*

| **Course** | **Assignment** | **Topic** |
|---|---|---|
| American History | Analyze the effects of a social program on one segment of American society. | How did the GI Bill of Rights affect American servicewomen? |
| Sociology | Identify and evaluate the success of one resource available to the homeless population of one major American city. | The role of the Salvation Army in meeting the needs of Chicago's homeless |
| Psychology | Write a three- to five-page paper assessing one method of treating depression. | Animal-assisted therapy for severely depressed patients |

*Note:* If your instructor permits you to do so, you can work with other students to narrow your topic.

Rebecca had no trouble thinking of ways she used *Wikipedia* to find general information, but she knew that the site was controversial in the academic community because several of her instructors discouraged her from using it as a research source. As she wrote her paper, she knew she would have to find a balance between the usefulness of *Wikipedia* on the one hand and its lack of reliability on the other.

Because her assignment was so specific, Rebecca was easily able to restate it in the form of a topic.

**Topic:** *Wikipedia* and college research

## EXERCISE 2

College campuses across the US are working to achieve sustainability, making an effort to be more sensitive to environmental concerns and to become more "green."

With this exercise, you will begin the process of writing a three- to five-page essay in which you consider how your school is working toward this goal, what more it needs to do in the future, and how your suggestions for improvement will benefit your school.

Begin by looking up the word *sustainability* on the Internet. Think about this issue as it applies to your school, and (with your instructor's permission), talk to your friends and classmates about it. When you think you understand what is being done (and what is not being done) to make your campus more "green," list five specific environmental issues you could write about. Then, choose one of these areas of concern as the topic for your paper, and write a few sentences explaining why you selected this topic.

Your purpose in this essay will be to make recommendations for changes that could be adopted at your school. Your audience will be your composition instructor, members of your peer review group, and, possibly, a wider campus audience—for example, readers of your campus newspaper. (The visuals in Figures 4.1 through 4.4 can help you get started.)

Kelly-Mooney Photography

**FIGURE 4.1** Students recycling aluminum cans.

Yellow Dog Productions/Getty Images

**FIGURE 4.2** Students getting information about environmental efforts on their campus.

Chip Somodevilla/Getty Images

FIGURE 4.3 Student adjusting solar panels.

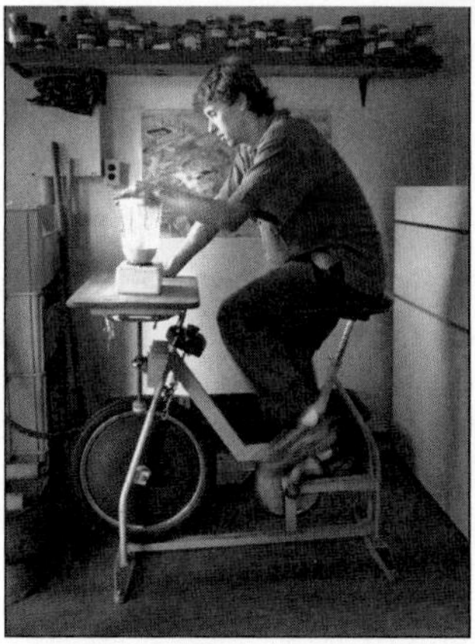

Michael Maloney/San Francisco Chronicle/Corbis

FIGURE 4.4 Student riding stationary bike to power a blender.

## 4e Finding Something to Say

Once you have a topic, you can begin to collect ideas for your essay, using one (or several) of the strategies discussed in the following pages.

### 1 Reading and Observing

As you read textbooks, magazines, and newspapers and browse the Internet, be on the lookout for ideas that relate to your topic. Films, television programs, interviews, telephone calls, letters, emails, and questionnaires can also provide material. But be sure your instructor permits such research—and remember to **document** ideas that are not your own. If you do not, you will be committing plagiarism.

**ESL TIP**

Don't use all your time making sure you are writing grammatically correct sentences. Remember, the purpose of writing is to communicate ideas. If you want to write an interesting, well-developed essay, you will need to devote plenty of time to the activities described in this section.

See Ch. 17

When students in Rebecca's composition class were assigned to read *Wikipedia*'s policy statement, "Researching with *Wikipedia*," in preparation for their essay assignment, she learned about the problems of using *Wikipedia* in college-level research. This reading assignment gave her a wider perspective on her topic and encouraged her to look beyond her own experience with *Wikipedia*.

**EXERCISE 3**

List all the potential sources you can think of for the essay you are writing: specific newspapers and magazines (including your school's publications), Web sites focusing on the environment, textbooks in related fields, newsletters and flyers, personal observations of your campus, and so on. Exchange lists with a classmate, and add two sources to his or her list.

### 2 Keeping a Journal

Many professional writers keep print or electronic **journals** (sometimes in the form of blogs), writing in them regularly whether or not they have a specific project in mind. Journals, unlike diaries, do more than simply record personal experiences and reactions. In a journal, you explore ideas, ask questions, and draw conclusions. You might, for example, analyze your position on a political issue, try to solve an ethical problem, or trace the evolution of your ideas about an academic assignment.

One of Rebecca's journal entries appears below.

#### *Journal Entry*

I use *Wikipedia* all the time, whenever something comes up that I want to know more about. Once my roommate and I were talking about graffiti art, and I started wondering how and where it began. I went to *Wikipedia* and found a long article about graffiti's origins and development as an art form. Some of my instructors say not to use *Wikipedia* as a research source, so I try to avoid going to the site for paper assignments. Still, it can be really helpful when I'm trying to find basic information. There are a lot of business and financial terms that come up in my accounting class, and I can usually find simple explanations on *Wikipedia* of things I don't understand.

### 3 Freewriting

When you **freewrite,** you write nonstop about anything that comes to mind, moving as quickly as you can. Give yourself a set period of time—say, five minutes—and don't stop to worry about punctuation, spelling, or grammar, or about where your freewriting takes you. This strategy encourages your mind to make free associations; thus, it helps you to discover ideas you probably aren't even aware you have. When your time is up, look over what you have written, and underline, circle, bracket, star, boldface, or otherwise highlight the most promising ideas. You can then use one or more of these ideas as the center of a focused freewriting exercise.

When you do **focused freewriting,** you zero in on your topic. Here, too, you write without stopping to reconsider or reread, so you have no time to be self-conscious about style or form, to worry about the relevance of your ideas, or to count how many words you have (and panic about how many more you think you need). At its best, focused freewriting can suggest new details, a new approach to your topic, or even a more interesting topic.

Excerpts from Rebecca's freewriting and focused freewriting exercises appear on the following page.

### *Freewriting (Excerpt)*

I'm just going to list a bunch of things from my accounting class notes that I've recently looked up in *Wikipedia*: shareholder, stakeholder, strategic management, core competency, certified public accountant, certified management accountant, financial accountancy, profit and loss. Not really sure which entry to focus on for this assignment. All the entries have strengths and weaknesses. I guess that's the point, but some *Wikipedia* articles are better than others. Maybe I'll choose an article that's sort of in the middle—one that provides some good basic info but could also be improved in some ways.

### *Focused Freewriting (Excerpt)*

I think I'm going to use the "Financial Accountancy" article as my focus for this paper. It explains this accounting term pretty clearly and concisely, which is good. However, it does have some problems, which are identified at the top of the article: specifically, a lack of cited sources. This article seems to represent a good balance of *Wikipedia's* benefits and drawbacks. I hope I can think of enough things to say about the article in my paper. I could start off with some background info on *Wikipedia* and then lead into the financial accountancy example. That way, I can use the financial accountancy article to support my points about *Wikipedia* in general.

## 4 Brainstorming

One of the most useful ways to collect ideas is by brainstorming (either on your own or in a group). This strategy enables you to recall bits of information and to see connections among them.

When you **brainstorm,** you list all the points you can think of that seem pertinent to your topic, recording ideas—comments, questions, single words, symbols, or diagrams—as quickly as you can, without pausing to consider their relevance or trying to understand their significance.

An excerpt from Rebecca's brainstorming notes appears below.

### *Brainstorming Notes (Excerpt)*

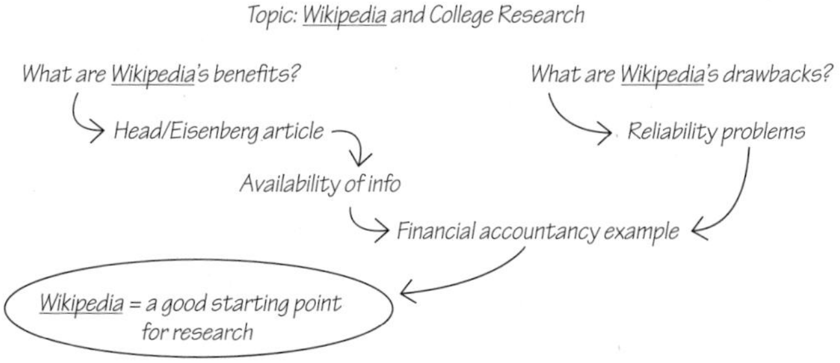
Topic: Wikipedia and College Research
What are Wikipedia's benefits?
Head/Eisenberg article
Availability of info
What are Wikipedia's drawbacks?
Reliability problems
Financial accountancy example
Wikipedia = a good starting point for research

## Close-Up COLLABORATIVE BRAINSTORMING

In addition to brainstorming on your own, you can also try **collaborative brainstorming,** working with other students to think of ideas to write about. If you and your classmates are working with similar but not identical topics—which is often the case—you will have the basic knowledge to help one another, and you can share your ideas without concern that you will all wind up focusing on the same few points.

Typically, collaborative brainstorming is an informal process. It can take place in person (in class or outside of class), on the phone, or in a chat room or class discussion board. Some instructors lead class brainstorming sessions; others arrange small-group brainstorming discussions in class.

Whatever the format, the exchange of ideas is likely to produce a lot of material that is not useful (and some that is irrelevant), but it will very likely also produce some ideas you will want to explore further. (Be sure you get your instructor's permission before you brainstorm with other students.)

### 5 Clustering

**Clustering**—sometimes called *webbing* or *mapping*—is similar to brainstorming. However, clustering encourages you to explore your topic in a more systematic (and more visual) manner.

Begin your cluster diagram by writing your topic in the center of a sheet of paper. Then, surround your topic with related ideas as they occur to you, moving outward from the general topic in the center and writing down increasingly specific ideas and details as you move toward the edges of the page. Following the path of one idea at a time, draw lines to create a diagram (often lopsided rather than symmetrical) that arranges ideas on spokes or branches radiating out from the center (your topic).

Rebecca's cluster diagram appears below.

***Cluster Diagram***

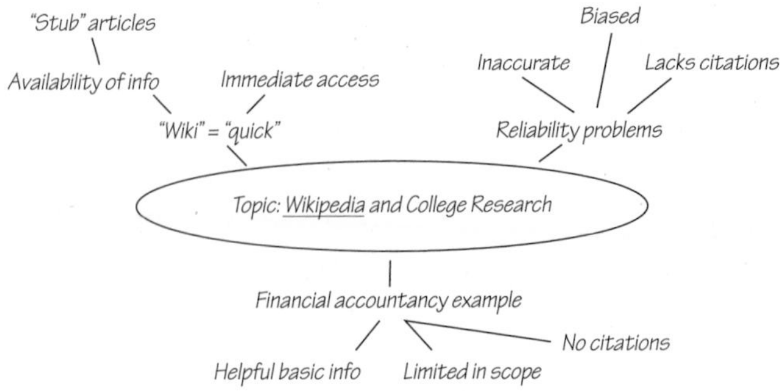

## Close-Up FINDING IDEAS

You can use the following computer strategies to help you find material to write about:

- When you **freewrite,** try turning down the brightness of the monitor, leaving the screen dark to eliminate distractions and encourage spontaneity. When you reread what you have written, you can boldface or underline important ideas (or highlight them in color).
- When you **brainstorm,** type your notes randomly. Later, after you print them out, you can add more notes and graphic elements (arrows, circles, and so on) to indicate connections between ideas.

### EXERCISE 4

Make a cluster diagram and brainstorming notes for the topic you chose in Exercise 3. If you have trouble thinking of ideas, try freewriting or collaborative brainstorming. Then, write a journal entry assessing your progress and evaluating the different strategies you used to find material for your essay. Which strategy worked best for you? Why?

### 6 Asking Journalistic Questions

**Journalistic questions** offer an orderly, systematic way of finding material to write about. Journalists ask the questions *Who? What? Why? Where? When?* and *How?* to ensure that they have explored all angles of a story, and you can use these questions to make sure you have considered all aspects of your topic.

Rebecca's list of journalistic questions appears below.

#### *Journalistic Questions*

- Who uses *Wikipedia*, and for what purposes?
- What is a wiki? What are *Wikipedia*'s benefits? What are its drawbacks?
- When was *Wikipedia* created? When did it become so popular among college students?
- Where do people go for more information after reading a *Wikipedia* article?

**ESL TIP**

Using your native language for planning activities has both advantages and disadvantages. On the one hand, if you do not have the pressure of trying to think in English, you may be able to come up with better ideas. Also, using your native language may help you record your ideas more quickly and keep you from losing your train of thought. On the other hand, using your native language while planning may make it more difficult for you to move from the planning stages of your writing to drafting. After all, you will eventually have to write your paper in English.

- Why are people drawn to *Wikipedia*? Why do some instructors discourage students from using it as a research source?
- How can *Wikipedia* be used responsibly? How can *Wikipedia* be improved?

## 7 Asking In-Depth Questions

If you have time, you can search for ideas to write about by asking a series of more focused questions about your topic. These **in-depth questions** can give you a great deal of information, and they can also suggest ways for you to eventually shape your ideas into paragraphs and essays.

**In-Depth Questions**

| | |
|---|---|
| What happened? When did it happen? Where did it happen? | Questions suggest **narration** (an account of your first day of school; a summary of Emily Dickinson's life) |
| What does it look like? What does it sound like, smell like, taste like, or feel like? | Questions suggest **description** (of the Louvre; of the electron microscope; of a Web site) |
| What are some typical cases or examples of it? | Question suggests **exemplification** (three infant day-care settings; four popular fad diets) |
| How did it happen? What makes it work? How is it made? | Questions suggest **process** (how to apply for financial aid; how a bill becomes a law) |
| Why did it happen? What caused it? What does it cause? What are its effects? | Questions suggest **cause and effect** (the events leading to the Korean War; the results of global warming; the impact of a new math curriculum on slow learners) |
| How is it like other things? How is it different from other things? | Questions suggest **comparison and contrast** (of the popular music of the 1980s and 1990s; of two paintings) |
| What are its parts or types? Can they be separated or grouped? Do they fall into a logical order? Can they be categorized? | Questions suggest **division and classification** (components of the catalytic converter; kinds of occupational therapy; kinds of dietary supplements) |

| | |
|---|---|
| What is it?<br>How does it resemble other members of its class? How does it differ from other members of its class? | Questions suggest **definition** (What is Marxism? What is photosynthesis? What is a wiki?) |

An excerpt from Rebecca's list of in-depth questions appears below.

***In-Depth Questions (Excerpt)***

What are the elements of a helpful *Wikipedia* article? Comprehensive abstracts, internal links, external links, coverage of current and obscure topics.

What are the elements of an unreliable Wikipedia article? Factual inaccuracy, bias, vandalism, lack of citations.

## EXERCISE 5

Using the two question strategies described and illustrated on pages 39–41 to supplement the work you did in Exercises 3 and 4, continue generating material for your essay-in-progress.

## EXERCISE 6

Consider what kinds of visual images might enhance your essay-in-progress. For example, would a photograph of a particular person or place be helpful? List several possibilities, and write a few sentences explaining what each visual might add to your essay.

## EXERCISE 7

Look at the visuals in Exercise 2 (pages 34–35). Which of these visuals would work best in the paper you are writing? Where would you place it? Which of your points would it support?

## EXERCISE 8

Go to *Google Images,* and find a visual to use in your essay. Using the visual as a focus, brainstorm to find additional ideas to write about.

CHAPTER 5

# Using a Thesis to Shape Your Essay

## Frequently Asked Questions



Now, it is time to start sifting through your ideas to choose those you can use. As you do this, you begin to **shape** your material into a thesis-and-support essay.

## 5a Understanding Thesis and Support

Your **thesis** is the main idea of your essay, the central point your ideas support. The concept of **thesis and support**—stating the thesis and then supplying information that explains and develops it—is central to much of the writing you will do in college.

See 7e2–3

As the following diagram illustrates, the essays you will write will consist of an introductory paragraph, which opens your essay and states your thesis; a number of **body paragraphs,** which provide the support for your thesis statement; and a concluding paragraph, which reviews your essay's major points and gives readers a sense of closure, perhaps summing up your main points or restating your thesis.

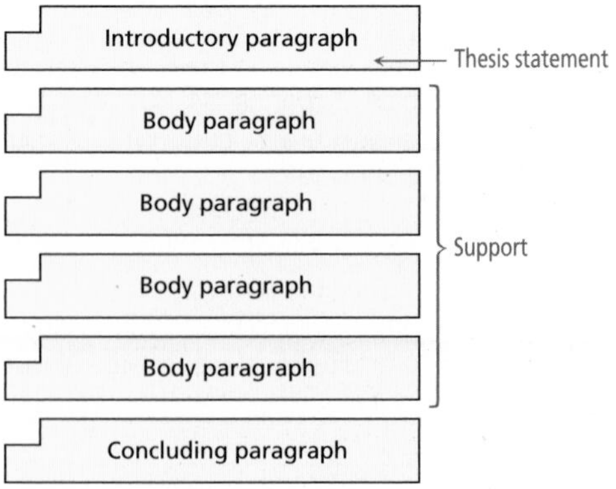

## 5b Developing an Effective Thesis Statement

An effective **thesis statement** has four characteristics:

1. **An effective thesis statement clearly communicates your essay's main idea.** It tells readers what your essay's topic is and indicates what you will say about that topic. In other words, the thesis statement is not just the topic of your essay but a specific claim you make about that topic. Thus, your thesis statement reflects your essay's purpose.

2. **An effective thesis statement is more than a general topic, a statement of fact, or an announcement of your intent.**

| Topic | Statement of Fact | Announcement |
|---|---|---|
| The environment | The environmental movement has had an impact on many college campuses. | In this essay, I will discuss the impact of the environmental movement on college campuses. |

**Effective Thesis Statement**

By encouraging sustainability, organizing conferences to raise awareness of environmental issues, and offering courses that educate students about the need to protect the planet, colleges and universities can bring the environmental movement to their campuses.

3. **An effective thesis statement is carefully worded.** Because it communicates your paper's main idea, your thesis statement should be clearly and accurately worded. Your thesis statement—usually expressed in a single concise sentence—should be direct and straightforward. It should not include abstract language, overly complex terminology, or unnecessary details that might confuse or mislead readers.

   Be particularly careful to avoid vague, wordy phrases—*centers on, deals with, involves, revolves around, has a lot to do with, is primarily concerned with,* and so on.

*is*

The real problem in our schools ~~does~~ not ~~revolve around~~ the absence of nationwide goals and standards; the problem is ~~primarily concerned with~~ the absence of resources.

Finally, an effective thesis statement should not include words or phrases such as "Personally," "I believe," "I hope to demonstrate," and "It seems to me," which weaken your credibility by suggesting that your conclusions are tentative or are based solely on opinion rather than on reading, observation, and experience.

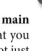

4. **An effective thesis statement suggests your essay's direction, emphasis, and scope.** Your thesis statement should not make promises that your essay will not fulfill. It should suggest where you will place your emphasis and indicate in what order your major points will be discussed, as the following thesis statement does.

**Effective Thesis Statement**

Widely ridiculed as escape reading, romance novels are important as a proving ground for many never-before-published writers and, more significantly, as a showcase for strong heroines.

This thesis statement is effective because it tells readers that the essay to follow will focus on two major roles of the romance novel: providing markets for new writers and (more important) presenting strong female characters. It also suggests that the essay will briefly treat the role of the romance novel as escapist fiction. As the following diagram shows, this effective thesis statement also indicates the order in which the various ideas will be discussed.

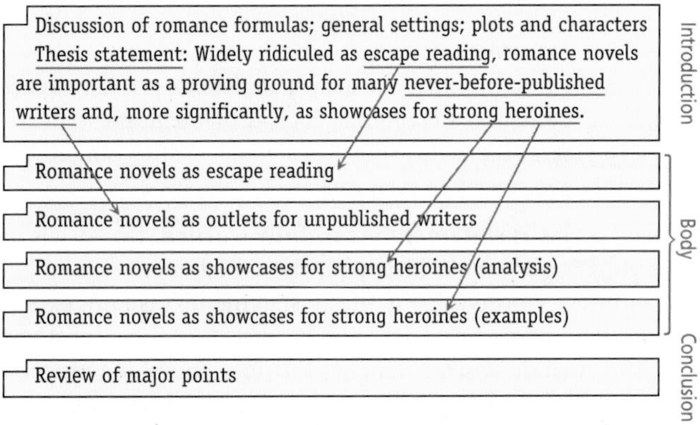

Discussion of romance formulas; general settings; plots and characters
Thesis statement: Widely ridiculed as escape reading, romance novels are important as a proving ground for many never-before-published writers and, more significantly, as showcases for strong heroines.
Introduction
Romance novels as escape reading
Romance novels as outlets for unpublished writers
Romance novels as showcases for strong heroines (analysis)
Romance novels as showcases for strong heroines (examples)
Body
Review of major points
Conclusion


**Close-Up DEVELOPING AN EFFECTIVE THESIS STATEMENT**

Here are some other problems to watch out for when you draft a thesis statement.

| Thesis Statement Too General | Effective Thesis Statement |
|---|---|
| Plagiarism is a serious problem. | Instituting an honor code can reduce plagiarism and other forms of academic cheating on our campus. |

| Thesis Statement Too Narrow | Effective Thesis Statement |
|---|---|
| Plagiarism is a form of academic cheating. | Plagiarism, a form of academic cheating, undermines the educational process. |
| **Wordy Thesis Statement** | **Effective Thesis Statement** |
| To address and curb the serious problem of the incidence of plagiarism on our college campus, I think steps must be taken by all different members of the college community, working together not only to establish but also to maintain certain mutually agreed-upon standards of academic integrity. | To solve the problem of plagiarism on our campus, all members of the college community need to work to establish and maintain standards of academic integrity. |

As she tried to decide on a thesis statement for her essay about *Wikipedia* and college research, Rebecca James reviewed her freewriting, brainstorming, and other prewriting material and also talked with friends, most of whom shared her own positive opinion of *Wikipedia*. To stress the value of *Wikipedia* in college research yet still acknowledge the drawbacks her instructors had pointed out, Rebecca drafted the following thesis statement.

> **Thesis Statement:** Despite its limitations, *Wikipedia* can be a valuable tool for locating reliable research sources.

## 5c Revising Your Thesis Statement

At this point, your thesis statement is only **tentative.** As you write and rewrite, you will think of new ideas and see new connections. As a result, you may change your essay's direction, emphasis, and scope, and if you do so, you must reword your thesis statement to reflect these modifications.

As Rebecca revised her essay, her emphasis changed, and so did her thesis statement. Because most of her research suggested that *Wikipedia* should be used with caution, she decided in her revised thesis statement to emphasize the site's usefulness not as an authoritative source but rather as a starting point for further research. Compare her tentative thesis statement above with her revised thesis statement in her paper's final draft in **6e.**

## Close-Up USING A THESIS STATEMENT TO SHAPE YOUR ESSAY

The wording of your thesis statement often suggests not only a possible order and emphasis for your essay's ideas, but also a specific pattern of development—*narration, description, exemplification, process, cause and effect, comparison and contrast, division and classification*, or *definition*. (These familiar patterns of development may also shape individual paragraphs of your essay.)

See 7d

| Thesis Statement | Pattern of Development |
|---|---|
| As the months went by and I grew more and more involved with the developmentally delayed children at the Learning Center, I came to see how important it is to treat every child as an individual. | Narration |
| Looking around the room where I spent my childhood, I realized that every object I saw told me I was now an adult. | Description |
| The risk-taking behavior that has characterized recent years can be illustrated by the increasing interest and involvement in such high-risk sports as mountain biking, ice climbing, sky diving, and bungee jumping. | Exemplification |
| Armed forces basic training programs take recruits through a series of tasks designed to build camaraderie as well as skills and confidence. | Process |
| The gap in computer literacy between rich and poor has had many significant social and economic consequences. | Cause and Effect |
| Although people who live in cities and people who live in small towns have some similarities, their views on issues like crime, waste disposal, farm subsidies, and educational vouchers tend to be very different. | Comparison and Contrast |
| The section of the proposal that recommends establishing satellite health centers is quite promising; unfortunately, however, the sections that call for the creation of alternative educational programs, job training, and low-income housing are seriously flawed. | Division and Classification |

| Thesis Statement | Pattern of Development |
|---|---|
| Many people once assumed that rape was an act perpetrated by a stranger, but today's definition is much broader. | Definition |

## EXERCISE 1

Working in a group of three or four students, analyze each of the following items, and explain why none of them qualifies as an effective thesis statement.

1. In this essay, I will examine the environmental effects of residential and commercial development on the coastal regions of the United States.
2. Residential and commercial development in the coastal regions of the United States
3. How to avoid coastal overdevelopment
4. Coastal Development: Pro and Con
5. Residential and commercial development of America's coastal regions benefits some people, but it has a number of disadvantages.
6. The environmentalists' position on coastal development
7. More and more coastal regions in the United States are being overdeveloped.
8. Residential and commercial development guidelines need to be developed for coastal regions of the United States.
9. Coastal development is causing beach erosion.
10. At one time I enjoyed walking on the beach, but commercial and residential development ruined the experience for me.

## EXERCISE 2

Draft thesis statements for three of the following topics.

1. A local or national event that changed your life
2. Cheating in college
3. US immigration laws
4. Women in combat
5. Private versus public education
6. Should college health clinics provide birth control services?
7. Is government censorship of the Internet justified?
8. What individuals can do to save the earth
9. The portrayal of an ethnic group in film or television
10. Should smoking be banned on college campuses?

## EXERCISE 3

Review all the notes you have accumulated so far, and use them to help you develop a thesis for an essay on the topic you chose in Chapter 4, Exercise 2.

## 5d Constructing an Informal Outline

Once you have a tentative thesis statement, you may want to construct an informal outline to guide you as you write. An **informal outline** arranges your essay's key points and major supporting ideas in an orderly way.

Rebecca's informal outline appears below.

### *Informal Outline*

Thesis statement: Despite its limitations, *Wikipedia* can be a valuable tool for locating reliable research sources.

Definition of wiki and explanation of *Wikipedia*

- Fast and easy
- Range of topics

*Wikipedia*'s benefits

- Internal links
- External links
- Comprehensive abstracts
- Current and popular culture topics
- "Stub" articles to be expanded

*Wikipedia*'s potential

- Current quality control
- Future enhancements

*Wikipedia*'s drawbacks

- Not accurate
- Bias
- Vandalism
- Lack of citations

Financial accountancy example: benefits

- Clear, concise
- Internal links
- External links

Financial accountancy example: drawbacks

- No citations
- Limited in scope

At this stage of the writing process, Rebecca decided that her informal outline was all she needed to guide her as she wrote a first draft. (Later on, she might decide to construct a formal outline to check her paper's organization.)

Although you may be used to constructing outlines for your written work by hand, a number of software applications and formatting features can help in this process, including the outlining feature in some desktop publishing and word-processing programs (such as *Microsoft Word*). Another useful tool for outlining (particularly for **oral presentations**) is *Microsoft PowerPoint,* presentation software that enables you to format information on individual slides with major headings, subheadings, and bulleted lists.

See 34d2

## Close-Up FORMAL OUTLINES

Sometimes—particularly when you are writing (or revising) a long or complex essay—you will need to construct a **formal outline,** which indicates both the exact order and the relative importance of all the ideas you will explore. (For information on how to construct a formal outline and for an example of a complete **sentence outline, see 6c4.** For an example of an excerpt from another sentence outline, **see 12j3.** For an example of a formal **topic outline, see 12h.**)

### EXERCISE 4

Find an editorial on your paper's topic in a newspaper or on the Internet. Then, prepare an informal outline of the editorial that includes the writer's key points and major supporting ideas.

### EXERCISE 5

Prepare an informal outline for the paper you have been developing in Chapters 4 and 5.

CHAPTER 6

# Drafting and Revising

## Frequently Asked Questions



## 6a Writing a Rough Draft

Once you are able to see a clear order for your ideas, you are ready to write a rough draft of your paper. A **rough draft** usually includes false starts, irrelevant information, and unrelated details. At this stage, though, the absence of focus and order is not a problem. You write your rough draft simply to get your ideas down so that you can react to them. You should expect to add or delete words, to reword sentences, to rethink ideas, and to reorder paragraphs. You should also be open to discovering some new ideas—and even to taking an unexpected detour.

CHECKLIST

### Drafting Strategies

The following suggestions can help you as you draft and revise:

- ❑ **Prepare your work area.** Once you begin to write, you should not have to stop because you need better lighting, important notes, or anything else.
- ❑ **Fight writer's block.** An inability to start (or continue) writing, writer's block is usually caused by fear that you will not write well or that you have nothing to say. If you really don't feel ready to write, take a short break. If you decide that you really don't have enough ideas to get you started, use one of the strategies for finding something to say.

See 4e

- ❑ **Get your ideas down on paper as quickly as you can.** Don't worry about sentence structure, spelling and punctuation, or finding exactly the right word—just write. Writing quickly helps you uncover new ideas and new connections between ideas. You may find that following an informal outline enables you to move smoothly from one point to the next, but if you find this structure too confining, go ahead and write without consulting your outline.

See 5d

- **Write notes to yourself.** As you type your drafts, get into the habit of including bracketed, boldfaced notes to yourself. These comments, suggestions, and questions can help you when you write subsequent drafts.
- **Take regular breaks as you write.** Try writing one section of your essay at a time. When you have completed a section—for example, one paragraph—take a break. Your mind will continue to focus on your assignment while you do other things. When you return to your essay, writing will be easier.
- **Leave yourself enough time to revise.** All writing benefits from revision, so be sure you have time to reconsider your work and to write as many drafts as you need.

When you write your rough draft, concentrate on the body of your essay, and don't waste time mapping out an introduction and conclusion. (These paragraphs are likely to change substantially in subsequent drafts.) For now, focus on drafting the support paragraphs of your essay.

Using her informal outline to guide her, Rebecca James wrote the following rough draft. Notice that she included boldfaced and bracketed notes to remind herself to add or check information when she revised her draft.

**ESL TIP**

Using your native language occasionally as you draft your paper may keep you from losing your train of thought. However, writing most or all of your draft in your native language and then translating it into English is generally not a good idea. This process will take a long time, and the translation into English may sound awkward.

### *Rough Draft*

*Wikipedia* and College Research

When given an assignment, students often turn first to *Wikipedia*, the popular free online encyclopedia that currently includes over 20,000,000 articles. Despite its limitations, *Wikipedia* can be a valuable tool for locating reliable research sources. **[Add more here]**

A wiki is an open-source Web site that allows users to edit or alter its content. Derived from a Hawaiian word meaning "quick," the term *wiki* conveys the swiftness and ease with which users can access information on such sites. **[Do I need to document this? Definition from *Encyclopaedia***

***Britannica Online*]** *Wikipedia* is the most popular wiki. It includes a range of topics, such as . . . . **[Include a couple of examples here]** *Wikipedia*'s editing tools make it easy for users to add new entries or edit existing ones.

The site offers numerous benefits to its users. One benefit of *Wikipedia* over traditional print encyclopedias is its "wikilinks," or internal links to other content within *Wikipedia*. **[Use info from Head and Eisenberg article on *Google* searches and wikilinks]** *Wikipedia* articles also often include external links to other sources as well as comprehensive abstracts. *Wikipedia* articles are constantly being updated and provide unmatched coverage of popular culture topics and current events. **[Make sure this is correct]** Finally, the site includes "stub" articles, which provide basic information that may be expanded by users.

*Wikipedia* claims that its articles "are never considered complete and may be continually edited and improved. Over time, this generally results in an upward trend of quality and a growing consensus over a neutral representation of information." **["About" page—need full citation]** *Wikipedia* ranks its articles according to the criteria of accuracy, neutrality, completeness, and style, letting users know which articles are among the site's best. In fact, some of *Wikipedia*'s best articles are comparable to those found in professionally edited online encyclopedias, such as *Encyclopaedia Britannica Online*. **[Check on this to make sure]** Although there's no professional editorial board to oversee the development of content within *Wikipedia*, experienced users may become editors, and this role allows them to monitor the process by which content is added and updated. Users may also use the "Talk" page to discuss an article's content and make suggestions for improvement.

*Wikipedia*'s popularity has also stimulated emergent technologies. For example, the free open-source software *MediaWiki* runs wiki Web sites worldwide. Other companies are also trying to capitalize on *Wikipedia*'s success by enhancing users' experience of the site. The online service *Pediaphon*, for instance, converts *Wikipedia* articles into MP3 audio files.

*Wikipedia* concedes that "not everything in *Wikipedia* is accurate, comprehensive, or unbiased." **["Researching with *Wikipedia*" page—need full citation]** Because anyone can create or edit *Wikipedia* articles, they can be factually inaccurate, biased, and even vandalized. Many *Wikipedia* articles also lack citations to the sources that support their claims, revealing a lack of reliability. **[Need more here]**

Personally, I have benefited from using *Wikipedia* in learning more for my accounting class. For example, the *Wikipedia* article "Financial Accountancy" defines this field in relation to basic accounting concepts. The article contains several internal links to related *Wikipedia* articles and some external links to additional resources. **[Compare this article to similar articles on sites like *Encyclopaedia Britannica Online*]**

Although the *Wikipedia* article on financial accountancy provides helpful, general information on this accounting field, it is limited in terms of reliability and scope. **[Explain more here. Add a visual?]** The limitations of the financial accountancy article suggest possible problems with *Wikipedia*.

Wikipedia articles are a good starting point for research and also link to more in-depth sources. *Wikipedia* users should understand the current shortcomings of this popular online tool. **[Add more!]**

### EXERCISE 1

Write a rough draft of the essay you began planning in Chapter 4.

## 6b Moving from Rough Draft to Final Draft

As you revise successive drafts of your essay, you should narrow your focus from larger elements, such as overall structure and content, to increasingly smaller elements, such as sentence structure and word choice.

### 1 Revising Your Drafts

After you finish your rough draft, set it aside for a day or two if you can. When you return to it, focus on only a few areas at a time. As you review this first draft, begin by evaluating your essay's thesis-and-support structure and general organization. Once you feel satisfied that your thesis statement says what you want it to say and that your essay's content supports this thesis and is logically arranged, you can turn your attention to other matters. For example, you can make sure that you have included all the transitional words and phrases that readers will need to follow your discussion. See 7b2

As you review your drafts, you may want to look at the questions in the "Revising Your Essay" checklist on pages 65–66. If you have the opportunity for peer review or a conference with your instructor, consider your readers' comments carefully.

See 6c2, 6c3

Because it can be more difficult to read text on the computer screen than on hard copy, you should print out every draft. This will enable you to make revisions by hand on printed pages and then return to the computer to type these changes into your document. (As you type your draft, you may want to leave extra space between lines. This will make any errors or inconsistencies more obvious and at the same time give you plenty of room to write questions, add new material, or edit sentences.)

If you write your revisions by hand on hard copy, you may find it helpful to develop a system of symbols. For instance, you can circle individual words or box groups of words (or even entire paragraphs) that you want to relocate, using an arrow to indicate the new location. You can also use numbers or letters to indicate the order in which you want to rearrange ideas. When you want to add words, use a caret like ^*this*.

An excerpt from Rebecca's rough draft, with her handwritten revisions, appears below.

### *Draft with Handwritten Revisions (Excerpt)*

The article contains several internal links to related *Wikipedia* articles and some external links to additional resources. ^*In comparison, the wiki Citizendium doesn't contain an article on financial accountancy, and the "Financial Accounting" article in the professionally edited Encyclopaedia Britannica Online consists only of a link to a related EB Online article.*

## Close-Up MANAGING FILES

As you revise, it is important to manage your files carefully, following these guidelines:

- First, be sure to save your drafts. Using the Save option in your word processor's file menu saves only your most recent draft. If you prefer to save every draft you write (so you can return to an earlier draft to locate a different version of a sentence or to reconsider a section you have deleted), use the Save As option instead.
- Also, be sure to label your files. To help you keep track of different versions of your paper, label every file in your folder by content and date (for example, **First Draft, Nov 5**).
- Finally, be very careful not to delete material that you may need later; instead, move this material to the end of your document so that you can assess its usefulness later on and retrieve it if necessary.

## 2 Adding Visuals

As you write and revise, you should consider whether one or more **visuals** might strengthen your paper by providing support for the points you are making. Sometimes you may want to use a visual that appears in one of your sources; at other times, you may be able to create a visual (for example, a photograph or a chart) yourself; at still other times, you may need to search *Google Images* or another image database to find an appropriate visual.

Once you have decided to add a particular visual to your paper, the next step is to determine where to insert it. (In general, you should place the visual in the part of the essay where it will have the greatest impact in terms of conveying information or persuading your audience.) Then, you need to format the visual. (Within *Microsoft Word*, you can double-click on an image to call up a picture-editing menu that allows you to alter the size, color, and position of the image within your essay and even enables you to wrap text around the image.) Next, make sure that the visual stands out in your paper: surround it with white space, add ruled lines, or enclose it in a box.

CHECKLIST

**Adding Visuals to Your Paper**

To add a visual to your paper, follow these steps:

- ❑ Find an appropriate visual.
- ❑ Place the image in a suitable location.
- ❑ Format the image, and make sure it is clearly set off from the written text.
- ❑ Introduce the visual with a sentence (or refer to it in the text).
- ❑ Label the visual.
- ❑ Document the visual (if necessary).

After you have inserted the visual where you want it, you need to integrate it into your text. You can include a sentence that introduces the visual (**The following table illustrates the similarities between the two health plans**), or you can refer to it in your text (**Figure 1 shows Kennedy as a young man**) to give it some context and explain why you are using it. You should also identify the visual by labeling it (**Fig. 1. Photo of John F. Kennedy, 1937**). In addition, if the visual is not one you have created yourself, you must **document** it. In most academic disciplines, this means including full source information directly below the image and sometimes in the list of references as well. (To see how Rebecca integrated a visual into her paper, **see 6e.**)

See Pts. 4–5

### EXERCISE 2

Look carefully at the visual you chose in Chapter 4, Exercise 8. In one sentence, state the main idea that this visual communicates to its audience. Then, list the individual elements in the visual that support this main idea. Does this visual help to support or clarify a point you are trying to make in your essay? If it does not, look for one that does. Finally, decide where to place the visual in your essay.

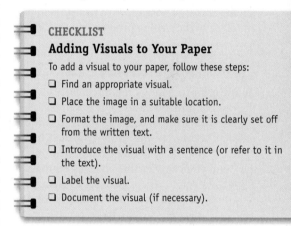

## EXERCISE 3

Start making revisions on the rough draft of your essay, following the guidelines outlined in **6b.** As you continue working on your draft, focus on the specific revision strategies explained in **6c.**

## 6c Using Specific Revision Strategies

Everyone revises differently, and every writing task calls for a slightly different process of revision. Five strategies in particular can help you revise at any stage of the writing process.

### 1 Using Word-Processing Tools

Your word-processing program includes a variety of tools designed to make the revision process easier. For example, *Microsoft Word*'s **Track Changes** feature allows you to make changes to a draft electronically and to see the original version of the draft and the changes simultaneously. Changes appear in color as underlined or crossed-out text (or as balloons in the margin), and you can view the changes on the screen or in print. This feature also allows you to accept or reject all changes or just specific changes.

Another useful tool is the **Compare Documents** feature. Whereas Track Changes allows you to keep track of changes to a single document, Compare Documents allows you to analyze the changes in two completely separate versions of a document, usually an original and its most recent update. Changes appear in color as highlighted text.

Rebecca used Track Changes as she revised her rough draft. An excerpt from her draft, along with her changes, appears below.

#### *Draft with Track Changes (Excerpt)*

A wiki is an open-source Web site that allows users to edit and add to~~or alter~~ its content. Derived from a Hawaiian word meaning "quick," the term *wiki* conveys the swiftness and ease with which users can access information on such sites as well as contribute content ("Wiki"). Since its creation in 2001 by Jimmy Wales, *Wikipedia* has grown into a huge database of articles on~~is the most popular wiki. It includes a range of~~ topics~~, such as . . . .~~ ranging from contemporary rock bands to obscure scientific and technical concepts. In accordance with the site's policies, users can edit existing articles and add new articles using *Wikipedia*'s editing tools, which do not require specialized programming knowledge or expertise.~~make it easy for users to add new entries or edit existing ones.~~

### Close-Up TRACK CHANGES VS. COMPARE DOCUMENTS

Where you are in the writing process can help you decide whether to track your changes or to compare one complete version of your document with another. **Track Changes** is especially useful in helping you follow sentence-level changes as you draft and revise; it can also be helpful later on, when you edit words and phrases. **Compare Documents** is most helpful when you are comparing global changes, such as paragraph unity and thesis-and-support structure, between one draft and another.

## 2 Participating in Peer Review

**Peer review**—a collaborative revision strategy that enables you to get feedback from your classmates—is another useful activity. With peer review, instead of trying to imagine an audience for your paper, you address a real audience, exchanging drafts with classmates and commenting on their drafts. Such collaborative work can be formal or informal, conducted in person or electronically. For example, you and a classmate may email drafts back and forth, using *Word*'s Comment tool (see page 58), or your instructor may conduct the class as a workshop, assigning students to work in groups to critique each other's essays. Students can also comment on classmates' drafts posted on a course discussion board or listserv.

### Close-Up ELECTRONIC PEER REVIEW

Some software is particularly useful for peer-review groups. For example, *Word*'s **Comment** tool allows several readers to insert comments at any point or to highlight a particular portion of the text they would like to comment on and then insert annotations. With this tool, a single paper can receive comments from multiple readers. Comments are identified by the initials of the reviewer and by a color assigned to the reviewer.

Other online programs also facilitate the peer-review process. For example, *InSite* is a Web-based application that allows students to

*(continued)*

**ELECTRONIC PEER REVIEW** *(continued)*

respond to each other's drafts with a set of peer-review questions, as shown below.

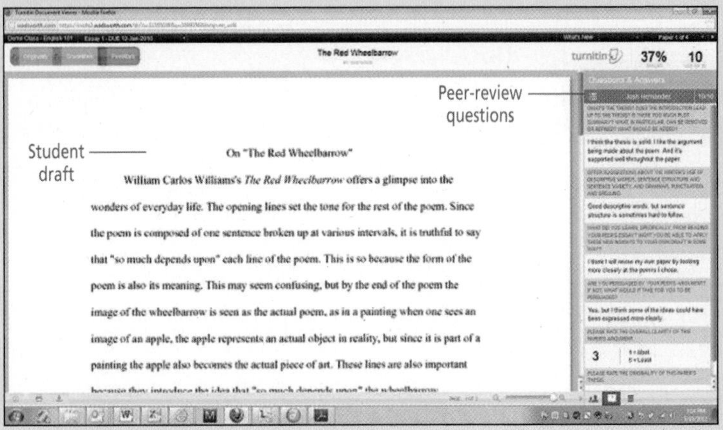

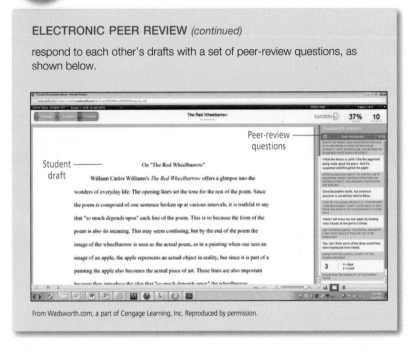

From Wadsworth.com, a part of Cengage Learning, Inc. Reproduced by permission.

An excerpt from Rebecca's rough draft with peer reviewers' comments appears below. (Note that her classmates used *Word*'s Comment tool to insert comments.)

### *Draft with Peer Reviewers' Comments (Excerpt)*

Personally, I have benefited from using *Wikipedia* in learning more for my accounting class. For example, the Wikipedia article "Financial Accountancy" defines this field in relation to basic accounting concepts. The article contains several internal links to related *Wikipedia* articles and some external links to additional resources. In comparison, the wiki *Citizendium* doesn't contain an article on financial accountancy, and the "Financial Accounting" article in the professionally edited *Encyclopaedia Britannica Online* consists only of a link to a related *EB Online* article.

Comment [KL1]: It's also helpful for other classes outside my major.

Comment [KL2]: Why is this imp.? Maybe explain more?

Comment [BR3]: Yes! This is one of my fav. features of *Wikipedia*. ☺

Comment [CB4]: But sometimes these links don't lead to the best sources either . . .

CHECKLIST

### Questions for Peer Review

The following questions can help guide you through the peer-review process:

- ❑ What is the essay about? Does the topic fulfill the requirements of the assignment?
- ❑ What is the essay's main idea? Is the thesis clearly worded? If not, how can the wording be improved?
- ❑ Is the essay arranged logically? Do the body paragraphs appear in an appropriate order?
- ❑ What ideas support the thesis? Does each body paragraph develop one of these ideas?
- ❑ Is any necessary information missing? Identify any areas that seem to need further development. Is any information irrelevant? If so, suggest possible deletions.
- ❑ Can you think of any ideas or examples from your own reading, experience, or observations that would strengthen the writer's essay?
- ❑ Can you follow the writer's ideas? If not, would clearer connections between sentences or paragraphs be helpful? Where are such connections needed?
- ❑ Is the introductory paragraph interesting to you? Would another opening strategy be more effective?
- ❑ Does the conclusion leave you with a sense of closure? Would another concluding strategy be more effective?
- ❑ Is anything unclear or confusing?
- ❑ What is the essay's greatest strength?
- ❑ What is the essay's greatest weakness?

For information on audience concerns for peer-review participants, **see 1b.**

## 3 Using Instructors' Comments

Instructors' comments—in correction symbols, in marginal comments, or in conferences—can also help you revise.

***Correction Symbols*** Your instructor may indicate concerns about style, grammar, mechanics, or punctuation by using the correction symbols listed on the inside back cover of this book. Instead of correcting a problem, the instructor will simply identify it and supply the number of the section in this handbook that deals with the error. After reading the appropriate pages, you should be able to make the necessary corrections on your own. For example, the symbol and number noted within the following sentence referred a student to **45e2,** the section in this handbook that discusses sexist language.

**Instructor's Comment:** Equal access to jobs is a desirable goal for all mankind. *Sxt—see 45e2*

After reading the appropriate section in the handbook, the student made the following change.

**Revised:** Equal access to jobs is a desirable goal for everyone.

***Marginal Comments*** Instructors frequently write marginal comments on your essays to suggest changes in content or structure. These comments may ask you to add supporting information or to arrange paragraphs differently within the essay, or they may recommend stylistic changes, such as more varied sentences. Marginal comments may also question your logic, suggest a more explicit thesis statement, ask for clearer transitions, or propose a new direction for a discussion. In some cases, you can consider these comments to be suggestions rather than corrections. You may decide to incorporate these ideas into a revised draft of your essay, or you may not. In all instances, however, you should take your instructor's comments seriously.

An excerpt from Rebecca's rough draft, along with her instructor's comments, follows. (Note that her instructor used *Microsoft Word*'s Comment tool to insert comments.)

### *Draft with Instructor's Comments (Excerpt)*

Personally, I have benefited from using *Wikipedia* in learning more for my accounting class. For example, the *Wikipedia* article "Financial Accountancy" defines this field in relation to basic accounting concepts. The article contains several internal links to related *Wikipedia* articles and some external links to additional resources. In comparison, the wiki *Citizendium* doesn't contain an article on financial accountancy, and the "Financial Accounting" article in the professionally edited *Encyclopaedia Britannica Online* consists only of a link to a related *EB Online* article.

Comment [JB1]: Revise to eliminate use of "personally" and the first person ("I") in this paper. Use this ¶ to talk about *Wikipedia*'s benefits to college students, using the accountancy article as an example.

Comment [JB2]: In your final draft, edit out all contractions. (Contractions are too informal for most college writing.) See 55b1.

***Conferences*** Many instructors require or encourage one-on-one conferences, and you should certainly schedule a conference if you can. During a conference, you can respond to your instructor's questions and ask for clarification of marginal comments. If a certain section of your paper presents a problem, use your conference time to focus on it, perhaps asking for help in sharpening your thesis or choosing more accurate words.

CHECKLIST

## Getting the Most Out of a Conference

To make your conference time as productive as possible, follow these guidelines:

- ❑ **Make an appointment.** If you are unable to keep your appointment, be sure to call or email your instructor to reschedule.
- ❑ **Review your work carefully.** Before the conference, reread your notes and drafts, and go over all your instructor's comments and suggestions. Make all the changes you can on your draft.
- ❑ **Bring a list of questions.** Preparing a list in advance will enable you to get the most out of the conference in the allotted time.
- ❑ **Bring your paper-in-progress.** If you have several drafts, you may want to bring them all, but be sure you bring any draft on which your instructor has commented.
- ❑ **Take notes.** As you discuss your paper, write down any suggestions that you think will be helpful so you won't forget them when you revise.
- ❑ **Participate actively.** A successful conference is not a monologue; it should be an open exchange of ideas.

## Close-Up WRITING CENTER CONFERENCES

If you are unable to meet with your instructor—and, in fact, even if you are—it is a good idea to make an appointment with a tutor in your school's writing center. A writing tutor (who may be either a professional or a student) is likely to know a good deal about what your instructor expects and is trained to help you produce an effective essay.

What a writing tutor can do is help you find ideas to write about and develop a thesis statement, identify parts of your essay that need more support (and help you decide what kind of support to include), and coach you as you revise your essay. What a tutor will *not* do is write your paper for you or act as a proofreader.

When you meet with a tutor, follow the guidelines in the checklist above—and always bring a copy of your assignment.

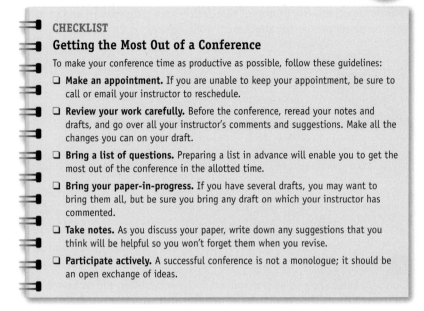

Conferences can also take place online—most commonly, through email. If you send emails to your instructor, to your writing center tutor, or to members of your peer-review group, include a specific subject line that clearly identifies the message as coming from a student writer (for example, "question about assignment" or "comments on my paper"). This is especially important if your email address does not include your name. When you attach a document to an email and send it for comments, mention the attachment in your subject line (for example, "first draft—see attachment")—and be sure your name appears on the attachment itself, not just on the email.

**Close-Up** COLLABORATION AND THE REVISION PROCESS

In a sense, the feedback you get from your instructor (or from a writing center tutor)—in conference, by email, or in written comments on a draft—opens a dialogue that is a form of collaboration. Like the comments you get from your classmates during peer review, these comments present ideas for you to react to, questions for you to answer, and answers to questions you may have. As you react to these comments, you engage in a collaboration that can help you revise your work.

## 4 Using a Formal Outline

Outlining can be helpful early in the revision process, when you are reworking the larger structural elements of your essay, or later on, when you are checking the logic of a completed draft. A formal outline reveals at once whether points are irrelevant or poorly placed—or, worse, missing. It also reveals the hierarchy of your ideas—which points are dominant and which are subordinate.

### The Conventions of Outlining

**Formal outlines** conform to specific conventions of structure, content, and style. If you follow the conventions of outlining carefully, your formal outline can help you make sure that your paper presents all relevant ideas in an effective order, with appropriate emphasis.

**Structure**

- Outline format should be followed strictly.

I. First major point of your paper
  A. First subpoint
  B. Next subpoint
    1. First supporting example
    2. Next supporting example
      a. First specific detail
      b. Next specific detail
II. Second major point

- Headings should not overlap.
- No heading should have a single subheading. (A category cannot be subdivided into one part.)
- Each entry should be preceded by an appropriate letter or number, followed by a period.
- The first word of each entry should be capitalized.

**Content**

- The outline should include the paper's thesis statement.
- The outline should cover only the body of the essay, not the introductory or concluding paragraphs.
- Headings should be concise and specific.
- Headings should be descriptive, clearly related to the topic to which they refer.

**Style**

- Headings of the same rank should be grammatically parallel.
- A **sentence outline** should use complete sentences, with all verbs in the same tense.
- In a sentence outline, each entry should end with a period.
- A **topic outline** should use words or short phrases, with all headings of the same rank using the same parts of speech.
- In a topic outline, entries should not end with periods.

As part of her revision process, Rebecca made the following sentence outline of her rough draft (shown on pages 51–53) to help her check her paper's organization.

### *Sentence Outline*

Thesis statement: Despite its limitations, *Wikipedia* can be a valuable tool for locating reliable research sources.

I. A wiki is an open-source Web site that allows users to edit or alter its content.
   A. *Wikipedia* is the most popular wiki.
   B. *Wikipedia* includes a range of topics.

II. *Wikipedia* offers numerous benefits to its users.
   A. Many *Wikipedia* articles contain internal links.
   B. Many *Wikipedia* articles contain external links.

C. Many *Wikipedia* articles contain comprehensive abstracts.

D. Many *Wikipedia* articles cover current and popular culture topics.

E. Site includes "stub" articles.

III. *Wikipedia* is making efforts to improve the quality of its content.

A. *Wikipedia* ranks its articles using the criteria of accuracy, neutrality, completeness, and style.

B. Users may serve as editors of the site's content.

C. Users may use the "Talk" page to make suggestions for improvement.

IV. *Wikipedia*'s popularity has stimulated emergent technologies.

A. The free open-source software *MediaWiki* runs wiki Web sites worldwide.

B. The online service *Pediaphon* converts *Wikipedia* articles into MP3 audio files.

V. *Wikipedia* also has several drawbacks.

A. *Wikipedia* articles may be factually inaccurate.

B. *Wikipedia* articles may be biased.

C. *Wikipedia* articles may be vandalized.

D. Many *Wikipedia* articles lack citations.

VI. The *Wikipedia* article "Financial Accountancy" offers certain benefits.

A. It defines this field in relation to basic accounting concepts.

B. It offers a visual breakdown of the key terms within the discipline.

C. It provides internal and external links to additional resources.

VII. *Wikipedia*'s "Financial Accountancy" article is limited in the information it offers.

A. It is unreliable.

B. It is limited in scope.

This outline revealed some problems in Rebecca's draft. For example, she saw that point IV was not relevant to her discussion, and she realized that she needed to develop the sections in which she discussed the benefits and drawbacks of the specific *Wikipedia* entry that she selected for this assignment. Thus, the outline helped her to revise her rough draft.

## Close-Up FORMATTING AN OUTLINE

If you use your computer's word-processing program to construct a formal outline, the Bullets and Numbering feature and the AutoFormat feature will help you to format it properly. Usually found in the Format menu, Bullets and Numbering allows you to select the format type of your outline, including styles that use roman numerals, letters, and/or numbers. Once you have selected your outline style, AutoFormat will arrange what you type in the selected format and allow you to customize the formatting further.

### EXERCISE 4

Outline the most recent draft of your paper, and use this outline to help you check the arrangement of your essay's ideas. Make any structural revisions you think are necessary. (Try not to worry at this point about stylistic issues, such as sentence variety and word choice.)

### 5 Using a Revision Checklist

The revision checklist that follows is keyed to sections of this text. Moving from global to specific concerns, it parallels the actual revision process. As your understanding of the writing process increases and you become better able to assess the strengths and weaknesses of your writing, you may want to add items to (or delete items from) this checklist. You can also use your instructors' comments to tailor the checklist to your own needs.

CHECKLIST

**Revising Your Essay**

**The Whole Essay**

- ❑ Do you understand your essay's purpose? (**See 1a.**)
- ❑ Have you taken your audience's needs into account? (**See 1b.**)
- ❑ Are your thesis and support logically related, with each body paragraph supporting your thesis statement? (**See 5a.**)
- ❑ Is your thesis statement clearly and specifically worded? (**See 5b.**)
- ❑ Have you discussed everything promised in your thesis statement? (**See 5b.**)
- ❑ Have you presented your ideas in a logical sequence? Can you think of a different arrangement that might be more appropriate for your purpose? (**See 5c.**)

*continued*

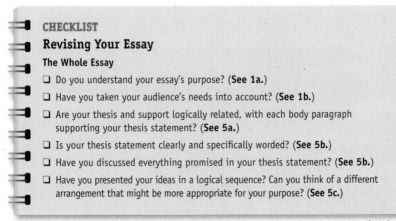

## Revising Your Essay *(continued)*

### Paragraphs

- ❑ Does each body paragraph have just one main idea? (**See 7a.**)
- ❑ Are topic sentences clearly worded and logically related to your thesis? (**See 7a1.**)
- ❑ Does each body paragraph have a clear organizing principle? (**See 7b1.**)
- ❑ Are the relationships between sentences within your paragraphs clear? (**See 7b2–4.**)
- ❑ Are your body paragraphs developed fully enough to support your points? (**See 7c.**)
- ❑ Does your introductory paragraph arouse reader interest and prepare readers for what is to come? (**See 7e2.**)
- ❑ Are your paragraphs arranged according to familiar patterns of development? (**See 7d.**)
- ❑ Have you provided transitional paragraphs where necessary? (**See 7e1.**)
- ❑ Does your concluding paragraph sum up your main points? (**See 7e3.**)

### Sentences

- ❑ Have you used correct sentence structure? (**See Chs. 40 and 41.**)
- ❑ Have you avoided potentially confusing shifts in tense, voice, mood, person, or number? (**See 44a1–4.**)
- ❑ Are your sentences constructed logically? (**See 44b–d.**)
- ❑ Have you placed modifiers clearly and logically? (**See Ch. 42.**)
- ❑ Are your sentences varied? (**See Ch. 37.**)
- ❑ Have you combined sentences where ideas are closely related? (**See 37b.**)
- ❑ Have you used emphatic word order? (**See 38a.**)
- ❑ Have you used sentence structure to signal the relative importance of clauses in a sentence and their logical relationship to one another? (**See 38b.**)
- ❑ Have you strengthened your sentences with repetition, balance, and parallelism? (**See 38c–d, 43a.**)
- ❑ Have you eliminated nonessential words and unnecessary repetition? (**See 39a–b.**)
- ❑ Have you avoided overloading your sentences with too many words, phrases, and clauses? (**See 39c.**)

### Words

- ❑ Is your level of diction appropriate for your audience and your purpose? (**See 45a.**)
- ❑ Have you selected words that accurately reflect your intentions? (**See 45b1.**)
- ❑ Have you chosen words that are specific, concrete, and unambiguous? (**See 45b3–4.**)
- ❑ Have you enriched your writing with figures of speech? (**See 45c.**)
- ❑ Have you eliminated jargon, neologisms, pretentious diction, clichés, and offensive language from your writing? (**See 44d–e.**)

### EXERCISE 5

Review the most recent draft of your paper, this time focusing on paragraphing, topic sentences, and transitions and on the way you structure your sentences and select your words. (Use the appropriate items in the checklist above as a guide.)

### EXERCISE 6

Using the revision checklist above as a model, create a ten-item customized checklist—one that reflects the specific concerns that you need to consider when you revise an essay. Then, use this checklist to help you in your revision.

### Close-Up CHOOSING A TITLE

When you are ready to decide on a title for your essay, keep these criteria in mind:

- A title should be descriptive, giving an accurate sense of your essay's focus. Whenever possible, use a key word or phrase that is central to your paper.
- A title can echo the wording of your assignment, reminding you (and your instructor) that you have not lost sight of it.
- Ideally, a title should arouse interest, perhaps by using a provocative question or a quotation or by taking a controversial position.

**Assignment:** Write about a problem on college campuses today.

**Topic:** Free speech on campus

**Possible Titles:**

Free Speech: A Problem for Today's Colleges (echoes wording of assignment and includes key words of essay)

How Free Should Free Speech on Campus Be? (provocative question)

The Right to "Shout 'Fire' in a Crowded Theater" (quotation)

Hate Speech: A Dangerous Abuse of Free Speech on Campus (controversial position)

## 6d Editing and Proofreading

Once you have revised your drafts to your satisfaction, two final tasks remain: **editing** and **proofreading.**

## 1 Editing

When you **edit,** you concentrate on grammar and spelling, punctuation and mechanics. Although you have dealt with these issues as you revised previous drafts of your paper, editing is now your primary focus. As you proceed, read each sentence carefully, consulting the items on the editing checklist below. Keep your preliminary notes and drafts and your reference books (such as this handbook and a dictionary) nearby as you work. Some reference works (such as *Dictionary.com* and *Merriam-Webster Online*) are available online.

CHECKLIST

### Editing Your Essay

**Grammar**

- ❑ Do subjects and verbs agree? (**See 50a.**)
- ❑ Do pronouns and antecedents agree? (**See 50b.**)
- ❑ Are verb forms correct? (**See 49a.**)
- ❑ Are tense, mood, and voice of verbs logical and appropriate? (**See 49b–d.**)
- ❑ Have you used the appropriate case for each pronoun? (**See 48a–b.**)
- ❑ Are pronoun references clear and unambiguous? (**See 48c.**)
- ❑ Are adjectives and adverbs used correctly? (**See Ch. 51.**)

**Punctuation**

- ❑ Is end punctuation used correctly? (**See Ch. 52.**)
- ❑ Are commas used correctly? (**See Ch. 53.**)
- ❑ Are semicolons used correctly? (**See Ch. 54.**)
- ❑ Are apostrophes used correctly? (**See Ch. 55.**)
- ❑ Are quotation marks used where they are required? (**See Ch. 56.**)
- ❑ Are quotation marks used correctly with other punctuation marks? (**See 56e.**)
- ❑ Are other punctuation marks—colons, dashes, parentheses, brackets, slashes, and ellipses—used correctly? (**See Ch. 57.**)

**Spelling**

- ❑ Are all words spelled correctly? (**See Ch. 46.**)

**Mechanics**

- ❑ Is capitalization consistent with standard English usage? (**See Ch. 58.**)
- ❑ Are italics used correctly? (**See Ch. 59.**)
- ❑ Are hyphens used where required and placed correctly within and between words? (**See Ch. 60.**)
- ❑ Are abbreviations used where convention calls for their use? (**See Ch. 61.**)
- ❑ Are numerals and spelled-out numbers used appropriately? (**See Ch. 62.**)

## 2 Proofreading

After you have completed your editing, print out a final draft and **proofread,** rereading every word carefully to make sure neither you nor your computer missed any typos or other errors.

Use the Search or Find command to look for usage errors you commonly make—for instance, confusing *it's* with *its, lay* with *lie, effect* with *affect, their* with *there*, or *too* with *to*. You can also uncover **sexist language** by searching for words like *he, his, him,* or *man*.

See 45e2

Keep in mind that neatness does not equal correctness. The clean text that your computer produces can mask flaws that might otherwise be apparent; for this reason, it is up to you to make sure no spelling errors or typos slip by.

### Close-Up PROOFREADING STRATEGIES

To help you proofread more effectively, try using these strategies:

- Read your paper aloud.
- Have a friend read your paper aloud to you.
- Read silently word by word, using your finger or a sheet of paper to help you keep your place.
- Read your paper's sentences in reverse order, beginning with the last sentence.

### Close-Up USING SPELL CHECKERS AND GRAMMAR CHECKERS

Although spell checkers and grammar checkers can make the process of editing and proofreading your papers easier, they have limitations.

- **Spell Checkers** A spell checker simply identifies strings of letters it does not recognize; it does not distinguish between homophones or spot every typographical error. For example, it does not recognize *there* in "They forgot there books" as incorrect, nor does it identify a typo that produces a correctly spelled word, such as *word* for *work* or *thing* for *think*. Moreover, a spell checker may not recognize every technical term, proper noun, or foreign word you may use.
- **Grammar Checkers** Grammar checkers scan documents for certain features (the number of words in a sentence, for example); however,

*(continued)*

**USING SPELL CHECKERS AND GRAMMAR CHECKERS** *(continued)*

they are not able to read a document to see if it makes sense. As a result, grammar checkers are not always accurate. For example, they may identify a long sentence as a run-on when it is, in fact, grammatically correct, and they generally advise against using passive voice—even in contexts where it is appropriate. Moreover, grammar checkers do not always supply answers; often, they ask questions—for example, whether *which* should be *that* or whether *which* should be preceded by a comma—that you must answer. In short, grammar checkers can guide your editing and proofreading, but you must be the one who decides when a sentence is (or is not) correct.

When you have finished proofreading, check to make sure the final typed copy of your paper conforms to your instructor's format requirements.

**EXERCISE 7**

Using the checklist on page 68 as a guide, edit your essay. Then, proofread it carefully, give it an appropriate title, and print out your final draft.

**EXERCISE 8**

Review your responses to Exercise 1 in Chapter 4. Then, write a paragraph explaining how your personal writing process has changed since you wrote those responses.

## 6e Preparing a Final Draft

The annotated essay that follows is the final draft of Rebecca James's essay, which you first saw on pages 51–53. It incorporates the suggestions that her peer reviewers and her instructor made on her rough draft.

This final draft is very different from the rough draft of the essay. As she revised, Rebecca shifted her emphasis from her own largely positive view of *Wikipedia* to a more balanced, more critical view, and she revised her thesis statement accordingly. She also provided more examples, adding specific information from sources to support her points, and she included parenthetical documentation and a works-cited list conforming to MLA documentation style. Finally, she added a visual (accompanied by a caption) to illustrate the specific shortcomings of the *Wikipedia* article she selected for the assignment.

See Ch. 18

See 6b2

## *Final Draft*

James 1

Rebecca James

Professor Burks

English 101

14 November 2011

*Wikipedia*: Friend or Foe?

When given a research assignment, students often turn first to *Wikipedia*, the popular free online encyclopedia. With over 20,000,000 articles, *Wikipedia* is a valuable source for anyone seeking general information on a topic. For college-level research, however, *Wikipedia* is most valuable when it is used not as an authoritative source but as a gateway to more reliable research sources.

Introduction

Thesis statement

A wiki is an open-source Web site that allows users to edit and add to its content. Derived from a Hawaiian word meaning "quick," the term *wiki* conveys the swiftness and ease with which users can access information on such sites as well as contribute content ("Wiki"). Since its creation in 2001 by Jimmy Wales, *Wikipedia* has grown into a huge database of articles on topics ranging from contemporary rock bands to obscure scientific and technical concepts. In accordance with the site's policies, users can edit existing articles and add new articles using *Wikipedia*'s editing tools, which do not require specialized programming knowledge or expertise.

Background on wikis and *Wikipedia*

*Wikipedia* offers several benefits to researchers seeking information on a topic. Longer *Wikipedia* articles often include comprehensive abstracts that summarize their content. Articles also often include links to other *Wikipedia* articles. In fact, *Wikipedia*'s internal links, or "wikilinks," are so prevalent that they significantly increase *Wikipedia*'s Web presence. According

Benefits of *Wikipedia*

James 2

to Alison J. Head and Michael B. Eisenberg, college students conducting a *Google* search often click first on the *Wikipedia* link, which usually appears on the first page of *Google*'s list of search results. Head and Eisenberg quote a student from their study as saying, "I don't really start with *Wikipedia*; I *Google* something and then a *Wikipedia* entry usually comes up early on, so I guess I use both in kind of a two-step process." In addition, many *Wikipedia* articles contain external links to other print and online sources, including reliable peer-reviewed sources. Finally, because its online format allows users to update its content at any time from any location, *Wikipedia* offers up-to-the-minute coverage of political and cultural events as well as information on popular culture topics that receive little or no attention in other reference sources. Even when the available information on a particular topic is limited, *Wikipedia* allows users to create "stub" articles, which provide basic information that other users can expand over time. In this way, *Wikipedia* offers an online forum for a developing bank of information on a range of topics.

Benefits of *Wikipedia*

Another benefit of *Wikipedia* is that it has the potential to become a reliable and comprehensive database of information. As *Wikipedia*'s "About" page explains, the site's articles "are never considered complete and may be continually edited and improved. Over time, this generally results in an upward trend of quality and a growing consensus over a neutral representation of information." Using the criteria of accuracy, neutrality, completeness, and style, *Wikipedia* classifies its best articles as "featured" and its second-best articles as "good." In addition, *Wikipedia*'s policy statements indicate that the information in its articles must be verifiable and must be based

James 3

on documented, preexisting research. Although no professional editorial board oversees the development of content within *Wikipedia*, experienced users may become editors, and this role allows them to monitor the process by which content is added and updated. Users may also use the "Talk" page to discuss an article's content and make suggestions for improvement. With these control measures in place, some *Wikipedia* articles are comparable to articles in professionally edited online resources.

Limitations of *Wikipedia*

Despite its numerous benefits and its enormous potential, *Wikipedia* is not an authoritative research source. As the site's "Researching with *Wikipedia*" page concedes, "not everything in *Wikipedia* is accurate, comprehensive, or unbiased." Because anyone can create or edit *Wikipedia* articles, they can be factually inaccurate or biased—and they can even be vandalized. Many *Wikipedia* articles, especially those that are underdeveloped, do not supply citations to the sources that support their claims. This absence of source information should lead users to question the articles' reliability. Of course, many underdeveloped *Wikipedia* articles include labels to identify their particular shortcomings—for example, poor grammar or missing documentation. Still, users cannot always determine the legitimacy of information contained in the *Wikipedia* articles they consult.

Strengths of "Financial Accountancy" *Wikipedia* article

For college students, *Wikipedia* can provide useful general information and links to helpful resources. For example, accounting students will find that the *Wikipedia* article "Financial Accountancy" defines this field in relation to basic accounting concepts and offers a visual breakdown of the key terms within the discipline. This article can help students in accounting classes to understand the basic

James 4

differences between this and other types of accounting. The article contains several internal links to related *Wikipedia* articles and some external links to additional resources. In comparison, the wiki *Citizendium* does not contain an article on financial accountancy, and the "Financial Accounting" article in the professionally edited *Encyclopaedia Britannica Online* consists only of a link to a related *EB Online* article.

Weaknesses of "Financial Accountancy" *Wikipedia* article

Although the *Wikipedia* article on financial accountancy provides helpful general information about this accounting field, it is limited in terms of its reliability and scope. The top of the article displays a warning label that identifies the article's shortcomings. As fig. 1 illustrates, the article's problems include a lack of cited sources. The limitations of the financial accountancy article reinforce the sense that *Wikipedia* is best used not as a source but as a path to more reliable and comprehensive research sources.

This article **needs additional** citations **for** verification. **Please help** improve this article **by** adding citations to reliable sources. **Unsourced material may be** challenged **and** removed. *(October 2007)*


Fig. 1. "Financial Accountancy"; *Wikipedia*; Wikimedia Foundation, 2011; Web; 7 Nov. 2011.

Conclusion

Like other encyclopedia articles, *Wikipedia* articles should be used only as a starting point for research and as a link to more in-depth sources. Moreover, users should keep in mind that *Wikipedia* articles can include more factual errors, bias, and inconsistencies than professionally edited encyclopedia articles. Although future enhancements to the site may make it more reliable, *Wikipedia* users should understand the current shortcomings of this popular online tool.

James 5

Works Cited

Head, Alison J., and Michael B. Eisenberg. "How College Students Use the Web to Conduct Everyday Life Research." *First Monday* 16.4 (2011): n. pag. *Google Scholar*. Web. 27 Oct. 2011.

"Wiki." *Encyclopaedia Britannica Online*. Encyclopaedia Britannica, 2011. Web. 27 Oct. 2011.

"*Wikipedia*: About." *Wikipedia*. Wikimedia Foundation, 2011. Web. 28 Oct. 2011.

"*Wikipedia*: Researching with *Wikipedia*." *Wikipedia*. Wikimedia Foundation, 2011. Web. 28 Oct. 2011.

CHAPTER 7

# Writing Paragraphs

## Frequently Asked Questions



A **paragraph** is a group of related sentences. A paragraph may be complete in itself or part of a longer piece of writing.

CHECKLIST

### When to Begin a New Paragraph

- ❑ Begin a new paragraph whenever you move from one major point to another.
- ❑ Begin a new paragraph whenever you move your readers from one time period or location to another.
- ❑ Begin a new paragraph whenever you introduce a new step in a process.
- ❑ Begin a new paragraph when you want to emphasize an important idea.
- ❑ Begin a new paragraph every time a new person speaks.
- ❑ Begin a new paragraph to signal the end of your introduction and the beginning of your conclusion.

ESL TIP

Indent the first line of each paragraph one-half inch. Set the margin at one-half inch, and press the return key on your computer every time you start a new paragraph. Do not add extra space between paragraphs.

## 7a Writing Unified Paragraphs

A paragraph is **unified** when it develops a single main idea. The **topic sentence** states the main idea of the paragraph, and the other sentences in the paragraph support that idea.

### 1 Using Topic Sentences

A topic sentence is often placed at the beginning or at the end of a paragraph. In some cases, the paragraph's main idea may be implied; if so, there is no explicitly stated topic sentence.

***Topic Sentence at the Beginning*** A topic sentence at the beginning of a paragraph tells readers what to expect and helps them to understand your paragraph's main idea immediately.

> I was a listening child, careful to hear the very different sounds of Spanish and English. Wide-eyed with hearing, I'd listen to sounds more than words. First, there were English (*gringo*) sounds. So many words were still unknown that when the butcher or the lady at the drugstore said something to me, exotic polysyllabic sounds would bloom in the midst of their sentences. Often the speech of people in public seemed to me very loud, booming with confidence. The man behind the counter would literally ask, "What can I do for you?" But by being so firm and so clear, the sound of his voice said that he was a gringo; he belonged in public society. (Richard Rodriguez, *Aria: Memoir of a Bilingual Childhood*)

***Topic Sentence at the End*** A topic sentence at the end of a paragraph is useful if you are presenting an unusual or hard-to-accept idea. By presenting a logical chain of reasoning and then stating your conclusion in the topic sentence, you are more likely to convince readers that your conclusion is reasonable.

> These sprays, dusts, and aerosols are now applied almost universally to farms, gardens, forests, and homes—nonselective chemicals that have the power to kill every insect, the "good" and the "bad," to still the song of birds and the leaping of fish in the streams, to coat the leaves with a deadly film, and to linger on in soil—all this though the intended target may be only a few weeds or insects. Can anyone believe it is possible to lay down such a barrage of poisons on the surface without making it unfit for life? They should not be called "insecticides," but "biocides." (Rachel Carson, "The Obligation to Endure," *Silent Spring*)

***Main Idea Implied*** In some narrative or descriptive paragraphs, an explicit topic sentence might seem forced. If so, it is best to imply rather than state the main idea. In the following paragraph, the writer wants readers to conclude for themselves (as she did) that because she was female, she was considered inferior.

> I am eight years old and a tomboy. I have a cowboy hat, cowboy boots, checkered shirt and pants, all red. My playmates are my brothers, two and four years older than I. Their colors are black and green, the only difference in the way we are dressed. On Saturday nights we all go to the picture show, even my mother; Westerns are her favorite kind of movie. Back home, "on the ranch," we pretend we are Tom Mix, Hopalong Cassidy, Lash LaRue (we've even named one of our dogs Lash LaRue); we chase each other for hours rustling cattle, being outlaws, delivering damsels from distress. Then my parents decide to buy my brothers guns. These are not "real" guns. They shoot "BBs," copper pellets my brothers say will kill birds. Because I am a girl, I do not get a gun. Instantly I am relegated to the position of Indian. Now there appears a great distance between us. They shoot and shoot at everything with their new guns. I try to keep up with my bow and arrows. (Alice Walker, "Beauty: When the Other Dancer Is the Self," *In Search of Our Mothers' Gardens*)

## 2 Testing for Unity

In a unified paragraph, each sentence supports the main idea in the topic sentence. The following paragraph is not unified because it includes sentences that do not support the main idea.

### *Paragraph Not Unified*

> One of the first problems I had as a college student was learning to use a computer. All students were required to buy a computer before

school started. Throughout the first semester, we took a special course to teach us to use a computer. My laptop has a lot of memory and can do word processing and spreadsheets. It has a large screen and a DVD drive. My parents were happy that I had a computer, but they were concerned about the price. Tuition was high, and when they added in the price of the computer, it was almost out of reach. To offset expenses, I got a part-time job in the school library. (student writer)

Sentences do not support main idea

When he revised, the writer deleted the sentences about his parents' financial situation and the computer's characteristics and added details related to his main idea.

### *Revised Paragraph*

One of the first problems I had as a college student was learning to use a computer. All first-year students were required to buy a computer before school started. Throughout the first semester, we took a special course to teach us to use the computer. In theory this system sounded fine, but in my case it was a disaster. In the first place, I had never owned a computer before. The closest I had ever come to my own computer was the computer I shared with my sister. In the second place, I could not type well. And to make matters worse, many of the people in my computer orientation course already knew everything there was to know about operating a computer. By the end of the first week, I was convinced that I would never be able to keep up with them.

Sentences now support main idea

## EXERCISE 1

Each of the following paragraphs is unified by one main idea, but that idea is not explicitly stated. Identify the main idea of each paragraph, write a topic sentence that expresses it, and decide where in the paragraph to place it.

A. The narrator in Ellison's novel leaves an all-black college in the South to seek his fortune—and his identity—in the North. Throughout the story, he experiences bigotry in all forms. Blacks as well as whites, friends as well as enemies, treat him according to their preconceived notions of what he should be, or how he can help to advance their causes. Clearly this is a book about racial prejudice. However, on another level, *Invisible Man* is more than the account of a young African American's initiation into the harsh realities of life in the United States before the civil rights movement. The narrator calls himself invisible because others refuse to see him. He becomes so alienated from society—black and white—that he chooses to live in isolation. But, when he has learned to see himself clearly, he will emerge demanding that others see him too.

B. "Lite" can mean that a product has fewer calories, or less fat, or less sodium, or it can simply mean that the product has a "light" color, texture, or taste. It may also mean none of these. Food can be advertised as 86 percent fat free when it is actually 50 percent fat because the term "fat free" is based on weight, and fat is extremely light. Another misleading term is "no cholesterol," which is found on some products that never had any cholesterol in the first place. Peanut butter, for example, contains no cholesterol—a fact that manufacturers have recently made an issue—but it is very high in fat and so would not be a very good food for most dieters. Sodium labeling presents still another problem. The terms "sodium free," "very low sodium," "low sodium," "reduced sodium," and "no salt added" have very specific meanings, frequently not explained on the packages on which they appear.

## 7b Writing Coherent Paragraphs

A paragraph is **coherent** when all its sentences clearly relate to one another. You can create coherence by arranging details according to an organizing principle, by using transitional words and phrases, by using parallel structure, and by repeating key words and phrases.

### 1 Arranging Details

Even if all its sentences are about the same subject, a paragraph lacks coherence if the sentences are not arranged according to a general organizing principle—that is, if they are not arranged *spatially, chronologically, or logically.*

**Spatial order** establishes the way in which readers will "see" details. For example, an object or scene can be viewed from top to bottom or from near to far. Spatial order is central to **descriptive paragraphs**.

See 7d2

**Chronological order** presents events in sequence, using transitional words and phrases to establish the time order of events—*at first, yesterday, later, in 1930,* and so on. Chronological order is central to **narrative paragraphs** and **process paragraphs**.

See 7d1, 4

**Logical order** presents details or ideas in terms of their logical relationships to one another. Transitional words and phrases such as *first, second,* and *finally* establish these relationships and lead readers through the paragraph. For example, the ideas in a paragraph may move from *general to specific,* or from *least important to most important.* Logical order is central to **exemplification paragraphs** and **comparison-and-contrast paragraphs**.

See 7d3, 6

## 2 Using Transitional Words and Phrases

**Transitional words and phrases** create coherence in paragraphs by emphasizing the spatial, chronological, and logical organizing principles discussed above. The following paragraph, which has no transitional words or phrases, illustrates just how important these words and phrases are.

### *Paragraph without Transitional Words and Phrases*

> Napoleon certainly made a change for the worse by leaving his small kingdom of Elba. He went back to Paris, and he abdicated for a second time. He fled to Rochefort in hope of escaping to America. He gave himself up to the English captain of the ship *Bellerophon*. He suggested that the Prince Regent grant him asylum, and he was refused. All he saw of England was the Devon coast and Plymouth Sound as he passed on to the remote island of St. Helena. He died on May 5, 1821, at the age of fifty-two.

In the narrative paragraph above, the topic sentence states the main idea, and the rest of the sentences support this idea. However, because of the absence of transitional words and phrases, readers cannot tell how one event in the paragraph relates to another in time. Notice how much clearer this passage is once transitional words and phrases (such as *after, finally, once again,* and *in the end*) have been added.

### *Paragraph with Transitional Words and Phrases*

> Napoleon certainly made a change for the worse by leaving his small kingdom of Elba. After Waterloo, he went back to Paris, and he abdicated for a second time. A hundred days after his return from Elba, he fled to Rochefort in hope of escaping to America. Finally, he gave himself up to the English captain of the ship *Bellerophon*. Once again, he suggested that the Prince Regent grant him asylum, and once again, he was refused. In the end, all he saw of England was the Devon coast and Plymouth Sound as he passed on to the remote island of St. Helena. After six years of exile, he died on May 5, 1821, at the age of fifty-two. (Norman Mackenzie, *The Escape from Elba*)

**Frequently Used Transitional Words and Phrases**

**To Signal Sequence or Addition**

again
also
besides
first . . . second . . . third
furthermore
in addition
moreover
one . . . another
too

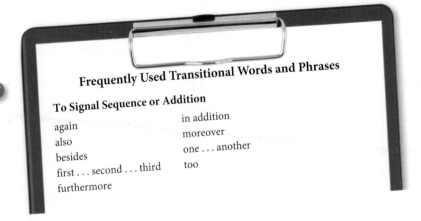

**To Signal Time**

afterward
as soon as
at first
at the same time
before
earlier
finally
in the meantime
later
meanwhile
next
now
soon
subsequently
then
until

**To Signal Comparison**

also
by the same token
in comparison
likewise
similarly

**To Signal Contrast**

although
but
despite
even though
however
in contrast
instead
meanwhile
nevertheless
nonetheless
on the contrary
on the one hand . . . on the other hand
still
whereas
yet

**To Introduce Examples**

for example
for instance
namely
specifically
thus

**To Signal Narrowing of Focus**

after all
indeed
in fact
in other words
in particular
specifically
that is

**To Introduce Conclusions or Summaries**

as a result
consequently
in conclusion
in other words
in summary
therefore
thus
to conclude

**To Signal Concession**

admittedly
certainly
granted
naturally
of course

*(continued)*

**Frequently Used Transitional Words and Phrases (*continued*)**

**To Introduce Causes or Effects**

accordingly
as a result
because
consequently
hence
since
so
then
therefore

### 3 Using Parallel Structure

See 38c, 43a

Parallelism—the use of matching words, phrases, clauses, or sentence structures to emphasize similar ideas—can create coherence in a paragraph. Note in the following paragraph how parallel constructions beginning with *He was* link Thomas Jefferson's accomplishments.

> Thomas Jefferson was born in 1743 and died at Monticello, Virginia, on July 4, 1826. During his eighty-four years, he accomplished a number of things. Although best known for his draft of the Declaration of Independence, Jefferson was a man of many talents who had a wide intellectual range. He was a patriot who was one of the revolutionary founders of the United States. He was a reformer who, when he was governor of Virginia, drafted the Statute for Religious Freedom. He was an innovator who drafted an ordinance for governing the West and devised the first decimal monetary system. He was a president who abolished internal taxes, reduced the national debt, and made the Louisiana Purchase. And, finally, he was an architect who designed Monticello and the University of Virginia. (student writer)

### 4 Repeating Key Words and Phrases

Repeating **key words and phrases** throughout a paragraph connects the sentences to one another and to the paragraph's main idea. The following paragraph repeats the key word *mercury* to keep readers focused on the subject.

> Mercury poisoning is a problem that has long been recognized. "Mad as a hatter" refers to the condition prevalent among nineteenth-century workers who were exposed to mercury during the manufacturing of felt hats. Workers in many other industries, such as mining, chemicals, and dentistry, were similarly affected. In the 1950s and 1960s, there were cases of mercury poisoning in Minamata, Japan. Research showed that there were high levels of mercury pollution in streams and lakes surrounding the village. In the

United States, this problem came to light in 1969, when a New Mexico family got sick from eating food tainted with mercury. Since then, pesticides containing mercury have been withdrawn from the market, and chemical wastes can no longer be dumped into the ocean. (student writer)

## 5 Achieving Coherence between Paragraphs

The same methods you use to establish coherence within paragraphs can also link the paragraphs in an essay. (You can also use a **transitional paragraph** as a bridge between two paragraphs.) See 7e1

The following group of related paragraphs shows how some of the strategies discussed in **7b1–4** work together to create a coherent unit.

> A language may borrow a word directly or indirectly. A direct borrowing means that the borrowed item is a native word in the language it is borrowed from. *Festa* was borrowed directly from French and can be traced back to Latin *festa*. On the other hand, the word *algebra* was borrowed from Spanish, which in turn borrowed it from Arabic. Thus *algebra* was indirectly borrowed from Arabic, with Spanish as an intermediary.
>
> Some languages are heavy borrowers. Albanian has borrowed so heavily that few native words are retained. On the other hand, most Native American languages have borrowed little from their neighbors.
>
> English has borrowed extensively. Of the 20,000 or so words in common use, about three-fifths are borrowed. Of the 500 most frequently used words, however, only two-sevenths are borrowed, and because these "common" words are used over and over again in sentences, the actual frequency of appearance of native words is about 80 percent. Morphemes such as *and, be, have, it, of, the, to, will, you, on, that,* and *is* are all native to English. (Victoria Fromkin and Robert Rodman, *An Introduction to Language*)

These paragraphs are arranged in logical order, moving from the general concept of borrowing words to a specific discussion of English. In addition, each topic sentence repeats a variation of the word group *A language may borrow*. Throughout the three paragraphs, some form of this word group (as well as *word* and the names of various languages) appears in almost every sentence.

### EXERCISE 2

A. Read the following paragraph, and determine how the author achieves coherence. Identify parallel elements, repeated words, and transitional words and phrases that link sentences.

> Some years ago the old elevated railway in Philadelphia was torn down and replaced by the subway system. This ancient El with its barnlike stations containing nut-vending machines and scattered food scraps had, for generations, been the favorite feeding ground of flocks of pigeons, generally one flock to a station along the route of the El. Hundreds of pigeons were

dependent upon the system. They flapped in and out of its stanchions and steel work or gathered in watchful little audiences about the feet of anyone who rattled the peanut-vending machines. They even watched people who jingled change in their hands, and prospected for food under the feet of the crowds who gathered between trains. Probably very few among the waiting people who tossed a crumb to an eager pigeon realized that this El was like a food-bearing river, and that the life which haunted its banks was dependent upon the running of the trains with their human freight. (Loren Eiseley, *The Night Country*)

B. Revise the following paragraph to make it more coherent.

The theory of continental drift was first put forward by Alfred Wegener in 1912. The continents fit together like a gigantic jigsaw puzzle. The opposing Atlantic coasts, especially South America and Africa, seem to have been attached. He believed that at one time, probably 225 million years ago, there was one supercontinent. This continent broke into parts that drifted into their present positions. The theory stirred controversy during the 1920s and eventually was ridiculed by the scientific community. In 1954, the theory was revived. The theory of continental drift is accepted as a reasonable geological explanation of the continental system. (student writer)

## EXERCISE 3

Read the following group of related paragraphs. Then, revise as necessary to increase coherence between paragraphs.

The period between the 1950s and the early 1990s saw dramatic changes in US families, but TV family sitcoms did not reflect these changes. *Leave It to Beaver* and *Father Knows Best* were typical of the late 1950s and early 1960s. Both were popular during a time when middle-class mothers stayed home to raise their children while fathers went to "the office." The Beaver's mother, June Cleaver, always wore a dress and high heels, even when she vacuumed. So did Margaret Anderson, the mother on *Father Knows Best*. Wally and the Beaver lived a picture-perfect, small-town life, and Betty, Bud, and Kathy never had a problem that father Jim Anderson couldn't solve.

*The Brady Bunch* featured six children and the typical Mom-at-home and Dad-at-work combination. Of course, Carol Brady did wear pants, and the Bradys were what today would be called a "blended family." Nevertheless, *The Brady Bunch* presented a hopelessly idealized picture of upper-middle-class suburban life. The Brady kids lived in a large split-level house, went on vacations, had two loving parents, and even had a live-in maid, the ever-faithful, wisecracking Alice. Everyone in town was heterosexual, employed, able-bodied, and white.

*The Cosby Show* was extremely popular. It featured two professional parents, a doctor and a lawyer. They lived in a townhouse with original art on the walls, and money never seemed to be a problem. In addition to warm relationships with their siblings, the Huxtable children also had close ties to their grandparents. *The Cosby Show* did introduce problems, such as son Theo's dyslexia, but in many ways it replicated the 1950s formula. Even in the post-1980s family, it seemed, father still knew best.

### EXERCISE 4

Consider the possible use of a visual in each of the three paragraphs in Exercise 3. What visuals would you use? How might these visuals increase the coherence of the entire passage?

## 7c Writing Well-Developed Paragraphs

A paragraph is **well developed** when it includes the support—examples, statistics, expert opinion, and so on—that readers need to understand and accept its main idea.

### Close-Up WELL-DEVELOPED PARAGRAPHS

Length does not determine whether a paragraph is well developed. To determine the amount and kind of support you need, consider your audience, your purpose, and your paragraph's main idea.

- **Consider your audience.** Will readers be familiar with your subject, or will it be new to them? Should the paragraph give readers detailed information, or should it just present a general overview of the topic? Given the needs of your audience, is your paragraph well developed?
- **Consider your purpose.** Is your purpose to inform or to persuade, or is it something else? Given your purpose, is your paragraph well developed?
- **Consider your paragraph's main idea.** Do you need to explain this idea more fully? Do you need another example, a statistic, an anecdote, or expert opinion? Given the complexity and scope of your main idea, is your paragraph well developed?

The following student paragraph is not adequately developed because it does not include enough support for its main idea—that children and parents are "bombarded by ads for violent toys and games."

### *Underdeveloped Paragraph*

From Thanksgiving until Christmas, children and their parents are bombarded by ads for violent toys and games. Toy manufacturers persist in thinking that only toys that appeal to children's aggressiveness will sell. Despite claims that they (unlike action toys) have educational value, video games have escalated the level of violence. The real question is why parents continue to buy these violent toys and games for their children.

When the student writer revised her paragraph, she added specific examples to support her topic sentence.

### Revised Paragraph (Examples Added)

From Thanksgiving until Christmas, children and their parents are bombarded by ads for violent toys and games. Toy manufacturers persist in thinking that only toys that appeal to children's aggressiveness will sell. One television commercial praises the merits of a commando team that attacks and captures a miniature enemy base. Toy soldiers wear realistic uniforms and carry automatic rifles, pistols, knives, grenades, and ammunition. Another commercial shows laughing children shooting one another with plastic rocket launchers and tanklike vehicles. Despite claims that they (unlike action toys) have educational value, video games have escalated the level of violence. The most popular video games—such as *Grand Theft Auto V* and *Resident Evil 6*—include graphic violence, criminal behavior, nudity, and other objectionable material. One game allows players to hack up and destroy zombies with a variety of weapons, such as swords, picks, and chainsaws as well as guns and grenades. Other best-selling games graphically simulate hand-to-hand combat on city streets and feature dismembered bodies and the sound of breaking bones. The real question is why parents continue to buy these violent toys and games for their children.

Examples

Examples

The student writer could also use expert opinion and statistics to develop the paragraph further.

### Revised Paragraph (Expert Opinion and Statistics Added)

From Thanksgiving to Christmas, children are bombarded by ads for violent toys and games. Toy manufacturers persist in thinking that only toys that appeal to children's aggressiveness will sell. The president of one large toy company recently observed that in spite of what people may say, they buy action toys. This is why toy companies spend so much money on commercials that promote them (Wilson 54). One such television commercial features a commando team that attacks and captures a miniature enemy base. Toy soldiers wear realistic uniforms and carry automatic rifles, pistols, knives, grenades, and ammunition. Another commercial shows laughing children shooting one another with plastic rocket launchers and tanklike vehicles. Despite claims that they (unlike action toys) have educational value, video games have escalated the level of violence. A parents' watchdog group has estimated that during the past three years, sales of violent video games have increased by almost 20 percent ("Action Toys Sell" 17). The most popular video games—such

Expert opinion

Statistics

as *Grand Theft Auto V* and *Resident Evil 6*—depict graphic violence, criminal behavior, nudity, and other objectionable material. One game allows players to hack up and destroy zombies with a variety of weapons, such as swords, picks, and chainsaws as well as guns and grenades. Other best-selling games graphically simulate hand-to-hand combat on city streets and feature dismembered bodies and chilling sound effects. The real question is why parents continue to buy these violent toys and games for their children.

Along with specific examples, this revised paragraph now includes an expert opinion—a statement by a toy manufacturer—and a statistic that shows the extent to which sales of violent video games have increased.

*Note:* The writer **documents** both the expert opinion and the statistic because they are not her own ideas.

See 18a

**EXERCISE 5**

Write a paragraph for two of the following topic sentences. Be sure to include all the examples and other support necessary to develop the paragraph adequately. Assume that you are writing your paragraph for the students in your composition class.

1. First-year students can take specific steps to make sure that they are successful in college.
2. Setting up a first apartment can be quite a challenge.
3. Whenever I get depressed, I think of __________, and I feel better.
4. The person I admire most is __________.
5. If I won the lottery, I would do three things.

## 7d Patterns of Paragraph Development

**Patterns of paragraph development**—*narration, exemplification,* and so on—reflect the way writers arrange material to express ideas most effectively.

### 1 Narration

A **narrative** paragraph tells a story by presenting events in chronological (time) order. Most narratives move in an orderly sequence from beginning to end, from first event to last. Clear transitional words and phrases (*later, after that*) and time markers (*in 1990, two years earlier, the next day*) establish the chronological sequence.

My academic career almost ended as soon as it began when, three weeks after I arrived at college, I decided to pledge a fraternity. By midterms, I was wearing a pledge cap and saying "Yes, sir" to every fraternity brother I met. When classes were over, I ran errands for the

Topic sentence identifies subject of narrative

fraternity members, and after dinner I socialized and worked on projects with the other people in my pledge class. In between these activities, I tried to study. Somehow I managed to write papers, take tests, and attend lectures. By the end of the semester, though, my grades had slipped, and I was exhausted. It was then that I began to ask myself some important questions. I realized that I wanted to be popular, but not at the expense of my grades and my future career. At the beginning of my second semester, I dropped out of the fraternity and got a job in the biology lab. Looking back, I realize that it was then that I actually began to grow up. (student writer)

Sequence of events

© Philip Gould/Corbis

**FIGURE 7.1** Student in pledge cap; one event in narrative sequence.

## 2 Description

A **descriptive** paragraph communicates how something looks, sounds, smells, tastes, or feels. The most natural arrangement of details in a description reflects the way you actually look at a person, scene, or object: near to far, top to bottom, side to side, or front to back. This arrangement of details is made clear by transitions that identify precise spatial relationships: *next to, near, beside, under, above,* and so on.

*Note:* Sometimes a descriptive paragraph does not have a topic sentence. In such cases, it is unified by a **dominant impression**—the central or unifying mood created by all the details in the description.

Details convey dominant impression

When you are inside the jungle, away from the river, the trees vault out of sight. It is hard to remember to look up the long trunks and see the fans, strips, fronds, and sprays of glossy leaves. Inside the jungle you are more likely to notice the snarl of climbers and creepers round the trees' boles, the flowering bromeliads and epiphytes in every bough's crook, and the fantastic silk-cotton tree trunks thirty or forty feet across, trunks buttressed in flanges of wood whose curves can make three high walls of a room—a shady, loamy-aired room where you would gladly live, or die. (Annie Dillard, "In the Jungle")

STILLFX/Shutterstock

**FIGURE 7.2** A jungle forest in New Zealand.

## 3 Exemplification

An **exemplification** paragraph supports a topic sentence with a series of specific examples (or, sometimes, with a single extended example). These examples can be drawn from observation, experience, or research.

Topic sentence identifies paragraph's main idea

Illiterates cannot travel freely. When they attempt to do so, they encounter risks that few of us can dream of. They cannot read traffic signs and, while they often learn to recognize and to decipher symbols, they cannot manage street names which they haven't seen before. The same is true for bus and subway stops. While ingenuity can sometimes help a man or woman to discern directions from familiar landmarks, buildings, cemeteries, churches, and the like, most illiterates are virtually immobilized. They seldom wander past the streets and neighborhoods they know. Geographical paralysis becomes a bitter metaphor for their entire existence. They are immobilized in almost every sense we can imagine. They can't move up. They can't move out. They cannot see beyond. Illiterates may take an oral test for drivers' permits in most sections of America. It is a questionable concession. Where will they go? How will they get there? How will they get home? Could it be that some of us might like it better if they stayed where they belong? (Jonathan Kozol, *Illiterate America*)

Series of examples

Art Montes De Oca/Taxi/Getty Images

FIGURE 7.3 Street signs illustrate one area of confusion for illiterates.

## 4 Process

**Process** paragraphs describe how something works, presenting a series of steps in strict chronological order. The topic sentence identifies the process, and the rest of the paragraph presents the steps. Transitional words such as *first, then, next, after this,* and *finally* link steps in the process.

Bettmann/Corbis

FIGURE 7.4 US Supreme Court justices after final step in process (handing down opinion in *Gideon v. Wainwright*, November 1962).

Topic sentence identifies process

Members of the court have disclosed, however, the general way the conference is conducted. It begins at ten A.M. and usually runs on until late afternoon. At the start each justice, when he enters the room, shakes hands with all others there (thirty-six handshakes altogether). The custom, dating back generations, is evidently designed to begin the meeting at a friendly level, no matter how heated the intellectual differences may be. The conference takes up, first, the

Steps in process

applications for review—a few appeals, many more petitions for certiorari. Those on the Appellate Docket, the regular paid cases, are considered first, then the pauper's applications on the Miscellaneous Docket. (If any of these are granted, they are then transferred to the Appellate Docket.) After this the justices consider, and vote on, all the cases argued during the preceding Monday through Thursday. These are tentative votes, which may be and quite often are changed as the opinion is written and the problem thought through more deeply. There may be further discussion at later conferences before the opinion is handed down. (Anthony Lewis, *Gideon's Trumpet*)

**Close-Up** INSTRUCTIONS

When a process paragraph presents **instructions** to enable readers to actually perform the process, it is written in the present tense and in the imperative mood—"*Remove* the cover . . . and *check* the valve."

## 5 Cause and Effect

A **cause-and-effect** paragraph explores causes or predicts or describes results; sometimes a single cause-and-effect paragraph does both. Clear, specific transitional words and phrases such as *one cause, another cause, a more important result, because,* and *as a result* convey the cause-and-effect relationship.

Paragraphs that examine **causes** explain why something happens or happened.

Topic sentence establishes major cause

Cause explored in detail

The main reason that a young baby sucks his thumb seems to be that he hasn't had enough sucking at the breast or bottle to satisfy his sucking needs. Dr. David Levy pointed out that babies who are fed every 3 hours don't suck their thumbs as much as babies fed every 4 hours, and that babies who have cut down on nursing time from 20 minutes to 10 minutes . . . are more likely to suck their thumbs than babies who still have to work for 20 minutes. Dr. Levy fed a litter of puppies with a medicine dropper so that they had no chance to suck during their feedings. They acted just the same as babies who don't get enough chance to suck at feeding time. They sucked their own and each other's paws and skin so hard that the fur came off. (Benjamin Spock, *Baby and Child Care*)

Richard Nowitz/Corbis

FIGURE 7.5 Baby sucking thumb.

Paragraphs that focus on **effects** explain how a change is or was the result of a specific set of causes or actions.

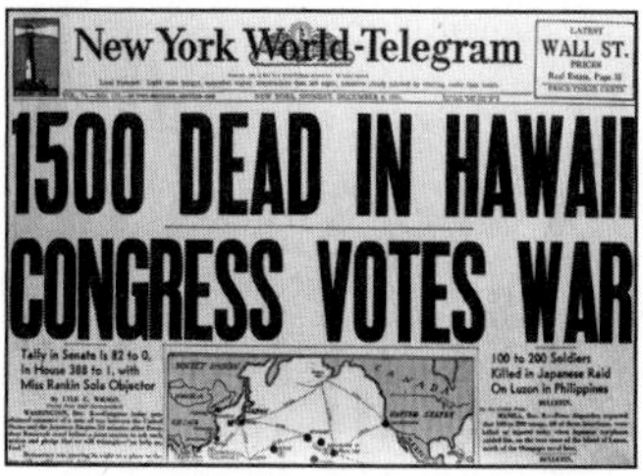
New York World-Telegram
WALL ST.
1500 DEAD IN HAWAII
CONGRESS VOTES WAR
Tally in Senate Is 82 to 0, In House 388 to 1, with Miss Rankin Sole Objector
100 to 200 Soldiers Killed in Japanese Raid On Luzon in Philippines

Bettmann/Corbis

FIGURE 7.6 Headline announcing attack on Pearl Harbor.

Topic sentence establishes major effect

On December 8, 1941, the day after the Japanese attack on Pearl Harbor in Hawaii, my grandfather barricaded himself with his family—my grandmother, my teenage mother, her two sisters and two brothers—inside of his home in La'ie, a sugar plantation village on Oahu's North Shore. This was my maternal grandfather, a man most villagers called by his last name, Kubota. It could mean either "Wayside Field" or else "Broken Dreams," depending on which ideograms he used. Kubota ran La'ie's general store, and the previous night, after a long day of bad news on the radio, some locals had come by, pounded on the front door, and made threats. One was said to have brandished a machete. They were angry and shocked, as the whole nation was in the aftermath of the surprise attack. Kubota was one of the few Japanese Americans in the village and president of the local Japanese language school. He had become a target for their rage and suspicion. A wise man, he locked all his doors and windows and did not open his store the next day, but stayed closed and waited for news from some official. (Garrett Hongo, "Kubota")

Discussion of other effects

## 6 Comparison and Contrast

**Comparison-and-contrast** paragraphs examine the similarities and differences between two subjects. **Comparison** focuses on similarities; **contrast** emphasizes differences.

A comparison-and-contrast paragraph can be organized in one of two ways: **point-by-point** or **subject-by-subject. Point-by-point** comparisons discuss the two subjects together, alternating points about one subject with comparable points about the other.

Topic sentence establishes comparison

There are two Americas. One is the America of Lincoln and Adlai Stevenson; the other is the America of Teddy Roosevelt and the modern superpatriots. One is generous and humane, the other narrowly egotistical; one is self-critical, the other self-righteous; one is sensible, the other romantic;

© Mathew B. Brady/Bettmann Corbis

© Corbis

FIGURE 7.7 Abraham Lincoln (left) and Theodore Roosevelt (right) symbolize the contrast between the two Americas.

Alternating points about the two subjects

one is good-humored, the other solemn; one is inquiring, the other pontificating; one is moderate, the other filled with passionate intensity; one is judicious and the other arrogant in the use of great power. (J. William Fulbright, *The Arrogance of Power*)

**Subject-by-subject** comparisons treat one subject completely and then move on to the other subject. In the following paragraph, notice how the writer shifts from one subject to the other with the transitional word *however*.

Topic sentence establishes comparison

First subject discussed

Second subject discussed

First, it is important to note that men and women regard conversation quite differently. For women it is a passion, a sport, an activity even more important to life than eating because it doesn't involve weight gain. The first sign of closeness among women is when they find themselves engaging in endless, secretless rounds of conversation with one another. And as soon as a woman begins to relax and feel comfortable in a relationship with a man, she tries to have that type of conversation with him as well. However, the first sign that a man is feeling close to a woman is when he admits that he'd rather she please quiet down so he can hear the TV. A man who feels truly intimate with a woman often reserves for her and her alone the precious gift of one-word answers. Everyone knows that the surest way to spot a successful long-term relationship is to look around a restaurant for the table where no one is talking. Ah . . . now that's real love. (Merrill Markoe, "Men, Women, and Conversation")

Brad Hamann/Stock Illustration Source/Getty Images

**FIGURE 7.8** Man using mute button to halt conversation (illustrates contrast between conversation styles of men and women).

An **analogy** is a special kind of comparison that explains an unfamiliar concept or object by likening it to a familiar one. In the following paragraph, the writer uses the behavior of people to explain the behavior of ants.

Topic sentence establishes analogy

Analogy explained in detail

Ants are so much like human beings as to be an embarrassment. They farm fungi, raise aphids as livestock, launch armies into wars, use chemical sprays to alarm and confuse enemies, capture slaves. The families of weaver ants engage in child labor, holding their larvae like shuttles to spin out the thread that sews the leaves together for their fungus gardens. They exchange information ceaselessly. They do everything but watch television. (Lewis Thomas, "On Societies as Organisms")

Anthony Bannister/Gallo Images/Corbis

**FIGURE 7.9** Tailor ants sewing leaves together illustrates analogy between ants and people.

## 7 Division and Classification

**Division** paragraphs take a single item and break it into its component parts.

The blood can be divided into four distinct components: plasma, red cells, white cells, and platelets. One component, plasma, is ninety percent water and holds a great number of substances in suspension. It contains proteins, sugars, fat, and inorganic salts. Plasma also contains urea and other by-products from the breaking down of proteins, hormones, enzymes, and dissolved gases. The red cells, another component of blood, give blood its distinctive color. The red cells are most numerous; they get oxygen from the lungs and release it in the tissues. The less numerous white cells are a component of blood that defends the body against invading organisms. Finally, the platelets, which occur in almost the same number as white cells, are responsible for clotting. (student writer)

Topic sentence identifies components

Components discussed

Jim Zuckerman/Corbis

FIGURE 7.10 Components of blood—blood cells and platelets—in vein.

**Classification** paragraphs take many separate items and group them into categories according to the qualities or characteristics they share.

Charles Babbage, an English mathematician, reflecting in 1830 on what he saw as the decline of science at the time, distinguished among three major kinds of scientific fraud. He called the first "forging," by which he meant complete fabrication—the recording of observations that were never made. The second category he called "trimming"; this consists of manipulating the data to make them look better, or, as Babbage wrote, "clipping off little bits here and there from those observations which differ most in excess from the mean and in sticking them on to those which are too small." His third category was data selection, which he called "cooking"—the choosing of those data that fitted the researcher's hypothesis and the discarding of those that did not. To this day, the serious discussion of scientific fraud has not improved on Babbage's typology. (Morton Hunt, *New York Times Magazine*)

Topic sentence establishes categories

Categories discussed

Presidents and Fellows Harvard University, Peabody Museum, 97-39-70/72853

FIGURE 7.11 The FeJee mermaid illustrates "forging," one of three categories of scientific fraud.

## 8 Definition

**Definition** paragraphs develop a formal definition by means of other patterns—for instance, defining *happiness* by telling a story (narration) or defining a hybrid car by explaining how it works (process).

The following definition paragraph is developed by means of exemplification: it begins with a straightforward definition of *gadget* and then cites an example.

Topic sentence gives general definition

Definition expanded with an example

A gadget is nearly always novel in design or concept and it often has no proper name. For example, the semaphore which signals the arrival of the mail in our rural mailbox certainly has no proper name. It is a contrivance consisting of a piece of shingle. Call it what you like, it saves us frequent frustrating trips to the mailbox in winter when you have to dress up and wade through snow to get there. That's a gadget! (*Smithsonian*)

Alan Schein Photography/Corbis

FIGURE 7.12 Rural mailbox with semaphore (term defined by exemplification).

## EXERCISE 6

Determine one possible pattern of development for a paragraph on each of these topics. Then, write a paragraph on one of the topics.

1. What success is (or is not)
2. How to prepare for a job interview
3. The kinds of people who appear on television reality shows
4. My worst experience
5. Two fast-food restaurants
6. The dangers of social Web sites
7. Budgeting money wisely
8. Junk food
9. Dressing for success
10. The dangers of texting while driving

## EXERCISE 7

A. Read each of the following paragraphs, and then answer these questions: In general terms, how could each paragraph be developed further? What pattern of development might be used in each case?

B. Choose one paragraph, and rewrite it to develop it further.

1. Many new words and expressions have entered the English language in the last ten years or so. Some of them come from the world of computers. Others come from popular music. Still others have politics as their source. There are even some expressions that have their origins in films or television shows.
2. Making a good spaghetti sauce is not a particularly challenging task. First, assemble the basic ingredients: garlic, onion, mushrooms, green pepper, and ground beef. Sauté these ingredients in a large saucepan. Then, add canned tomatoes, tomato paste, and water, and stir. At this point, you are ready to add the spices: oregano, parsley, basil, and salt and pepper. Don't forget a bay leaf! Simmer for about two hours, and serve over spaghetti.

3. High school and college are not at all alike. Courses are a lot easier in high school, and the course load is lighter. In college, teachers expect more from students; they expect higher quality work, and they assign more of it. Assignments tend to be more difficult and more comprehensive, and deadlines are usually shorter. Finally, college students tend to be more focused on a particular course of study—even a particular career—than high school students are.

## EXERCISE 8

Choose one of the four visuals below, and write a paragraph developed according to a pattern the visual suggests. (Note that each visual may suggest more than one pattern.)

Steve Prezant/Keepsake RM/Corbis

FIGURE 7.13 New college graduate pondering his future.

Leonard de Selva/Corbis

FIGURE 7.14 Goldilocks eating porridge.

Gideon Mendel/Corbis

FIGURE 7.15 Japanese geisha in front of soda machine.

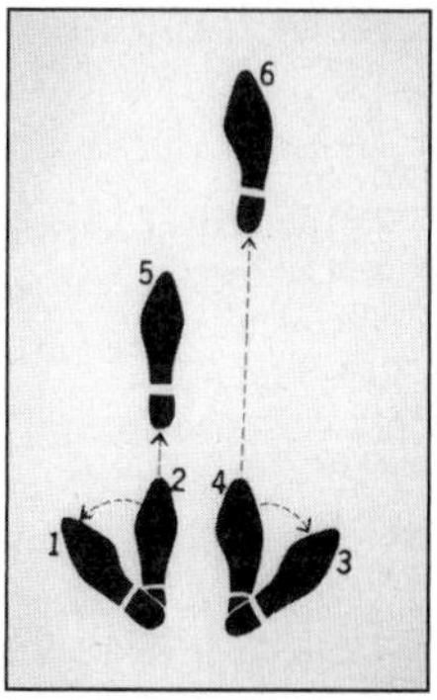


Bettmann/Corbis

FIGURE 7.16 Basic steps of the hustle.

## 7e Writing Special Kinds of Paragraphs

So far, this chapter has focused on **body paragraphs**, the paragraphs that carry the weight of your essay's discussion. Other kinds of paragraphs—*transitional paragraphs, introductory paragraphs*, and *concluding paragraphs*—have special functions in an essay.

### 1 Transitional Paragraphs

A **transitional paragraph** connects one section of an essay to another. At their simplest, transitional paragraphs can be single sentences that move readers from one point to the next.

What is true for ants is also true for people.

More often, writers use transitional paragraphs to summarize what they have already said before they move on to a new point. The following transitional paragraph uses a series of questions to sum up some of the ideas the writer has been discussing. In the next part of his essay, he goes on to answer these questions.

> Can we bleed off the mass of humanity to other worlds? Right now the number of human beings on Earth is increasing by 80 million per year, and each year that number goes up by 1 and a fraction percent. Can we really suppose that we can send 80 million people per year to the Moon, Mars, and elsewhere, and engineer those worlds to support those people? And even so, nearly remain in the same place ourselves? (Isaac Asimov, "The Case against Man")

### 2 Introductory Paragraphs

An **introductory paragraph** prepares readers for the essay to follow. It typically introduces the subject, narrows it, and then states the essay's thesis.

> Christine was just a girl in one of my classes. I never knew much about her except that she was strange. She didn't talk much. Her hair was dyed black and purple, and she wore heavy black boots and a black turtleneck sweater, even in the summer. She was attractive—in spite of the ring she wore through her left eyebrow—but she never seemed to care what the rest of us thought about her. Like the rest of my classmates, I didn't really want to get close to her. It was only when we were assigned to do our chemistry project together that I began to understand why Christine dressed the way she did. (student writer)

**ESL TIP**

A **thesis statement** is a sentence that communicates your essay's main idea. Thesis statements, which usually appear in introductory paragraphs, are an important part of US academic writing.

To arouse their audience's interest, writers may vary this direct approach by using one of the following introductory strategies.

**Strategies for Effective Introductions**

**Quotation or Series of Quotations**

When Mary Cassatt's father was told of her decision to become a painter, he said: "I would rather see you dead." When Edgar Degas saw a show of Cassatt's etchings, his response was: "I am not willing to admit that a woman can draw that well." (Mary Gordon, "Mary Cassatt")

**Question or Series of Questions**

Of all the disputes agitating the American campus, the one that seems to me especially significant is that over "the canon." What should be taught in the humanities and social sciences, especially in introductory courses? What is the place of the classics? How shall we respond to those professors who attack "Eurocentrism" and advocate "multiculturalism"? This is not the sort of tedious quarrel that now and then flutters through the academy; it involves matters of public urgency. I propose to see this dispute, at first, through a narrow, even sectarian lens, with the hope that you will come to accept my reasons for doing so. (Irving Howe, "The Value of the Canon")

**Definition**

Moles are collections of cells that can appear on any part of the body. With occasional exceptions, moles are absent at birth. They first appear in the early years of life, between ages two and six. Frequently, moles appear at puberty. New moles, however, can continue to appear throughout life. During pregnancy, new moles may appear and old ones darken. There are three major designations of moles, each with its own unique distinguishing characteristics. (student writer)

**Controversial Statement**

Many Americans would probably be surprised to learn that Head Start has not been an unqualified success. Founded in 1965, the Head Start program provides early childhood education, social services, and medical check-ups to poor children across the United States. In recent years, it has also focused on the children of migrant workers and on children who are homeless. For the most part, Americans view Head Start not just as a success but also as a model for other social programs. What many people do not know, however, is that although Head Start is a short-term success for many children, the ambitious

(*continued*)

### Strategies for Effective Introductions (*continued*)

long-term goals of the program have not been met. For example, studies have shown that children who participate in Head Start do not see long-term increases in IQ or in academic achievement. For this reason, it may be time to consider making significant changes in the way Head Start is run. (student writer)

### Close-Up INTRODUCTORY PARAGRAPHS

An introductory paragraph should make your readers want to read further.

- Avoid introductions that begin by announcing your subject ("In my paper, I will talk about Lady Macbeth").
- Avoid introductions that undercut your credibility ("I don't know much about alternative energy sources, but I would like to present my opinion about the subject").
- Avoid introductions that discuss the difficulty of the topic ("I had trouble deciding what to write about, but I finally . . .").

CHECKLIST

### Writing Effective Introductions

After you draft your introduction, check its effectiveness by asking the following questions:

- ❑ Does your introductory paragraph include a thesis statement?
- ❑ Does it lead naturally into the body of your essay?
- ❑ Does it create interest?
- ❑ Does it avoid statements that undercut your credibility?

## 3 Concluding Paragraphs

A **concluding paragraph** typically begins with specifics—reviewing the essay's main points, for example—and then moves on to more general comments. Whenever possible, it should end with a sentence that readers will remember.

As an Arab-American, I feel I have the best of two worlds. I'm proud to be part of the melting pot, proud to contribute to the tremendous diversity of cultures, customs and traditions that makes this country unique. But Arab-bashing—public acceptance of hatred and bigotry—is something no American can be proud of. (Ellen Mansoor Collier, "I Am Not a Terrorist")

Writers may use any of the following concluding strategies to sum up their essay's ideas.

### Strategies for Effective Conclusions

**Prediction**

Looking ahead, [we see that] prospects may not be quite as dismal as they seem. As a matter of fact, we are not doing so badly. It is something of a miracle that creatures who evolved as nomads in an intimate, small-band, wide-open-spaces context manage to get along at all as villagers or surrounded by strangers in cubicle apartments. Considering that our genius as a species is adaptability, we may yet learn to live closer and closer to one another, if not in utter peace, then far more peacefully than we do today. (John Pheiffer, "Seeking Peace, Making War")

**Warning**

The Internet is the twenty-first century's talking drum, the very kind of grassroots communication tool that has been such a powerful source of education and culture for our people since slavery. But this talking drum we have not yet learned to play. Unless we master the new information technology to build and deepen the forms of social connection that a tragic history has eroded, African-Americans will face a form of cyber-segregation in the next century as devastating to our aspirations as Jim Crow segregation was to those of our ancestors. But this time, the fault will be our own. (Henry Louis Gates Jr., "One Internet, Two Nations")



**Recommendation for Action**

Computers have revolutionized learning in ways that we have barely begun to appreciate. We have experienced enough, however, to recognize the need to change our thinking about our purposes, methods, and outcome of higher education. Rather than resisting or postponing change, we need to anticipate and learn from it. We must harness the technology and use it to educate our students more effectively than we have been doing. Otherwise, we will surrender our authority to those who can. (Peshe Kuriloff, "If John Dewey Were Alive Today, He'd Be a Webhead")

**Quotation**

Apart from what any critic had to say about my writing, I knew I had succeeded where it counted when my mother finished reading my book and gave me her verdict: "So easy to read." (Amy Tan, "Mother Tongue")

## Close-Up CONCLUDING PARAGRAPHS

- Don't waste time repeating sentences from your introduction in different words.
- Don't apologize or undercut your credibility ("Of course, I am not an expert" or "At least, this is my opinion").
- Don't introduce any new points or go off in new directions.

CHECKLIST

### Writing Effective Conclusions

After you draft your conclusion, check its effectiveness by asking the following questions:

- ❑ Does your concluding paragraph sum up your essay, perhaps by reinforcing the essay's main points?
- ❑ Does it do more than just repeat the introduction's wording?
- ❑ Does it avoid introducing new points?
- ❑ Does it avoid apologies?
- ❑ Does it end memorably?

PART 2

# Thinking Critically and Writing Arguments

CHAPTER 8

# Thinking Critically

## Frequently Asked Questions



See Ch. 10

As you read and write essays, you should carefully consider the ideas they present. This is especially true in argumentative essays—those that take a stand on a debatable issue.

**ESL TIP**

This chapter outlines ideas about thinking critically that are common in academic settings in the United States. In such settings, people read texts with a critical eye, testing the author's claims to see if they seem true. Reading this chapter will help you understand how your instructor expects you to read and evaluate texts.

Although some writers try their best to be fair, others are less scrupulous. They attempt to convince readers by using emotionally charged language, by emphasizing certain facts over others, and by intentionally using flawed logic. For this reason, it is particularly important that you think critically when you read and write. **Thinking critically** means learning to distinguish fact from opinion, evaluate supporting evidence, detect bias, evaluate visuals, and use the basic principles of logic to arrive at valid conclusions.

See Ch. 9

## 8a Distinguishing Fact from Opinion

**A fact** is a verifiable statement that something is true or that something occurred. An **opinion** is a personal judgment or belief that can never be substantiated beyond any doubt and is, therefore, debatable.

**Fact:** Measles is a potentially deadly disease.

**Opinion:** All children should be vaccinated against measles.

An opinion may be *supported* or *unsupported.*

**Unsupported Opinion:** I think that all children in Pennsylvania should be vaccinated against measles.

**Supported Opinion:** Despite the fact that an effective measles vaccine is widely available, several unvaccinated Pennsylvania children have died of measles each year since 1992. States that have instituted vaccination programs have had no deaths in the same time period. For this reason, all children in Pennsylvania should be vaccinated against measles.

As these examples show, supported opinion is more convincing than unsupported opinion. Remember, however, that support can only make a statement more convincing; it cannot turn an opinion into a fact.

## Close-Up SUPPORTING YOUR OPINIONS

Opinions can be supported with **examples, statistics,** or **expert opinion:**

**Examples**

The American Civil Liberties Union is an organization that has been unfairly characterized as left wing. It is true that it has opposed prayer in the public schools, defended conscientious objectors, and challenged police methods of conducting questioning and searches of suspects. However, it has also backed the antiabortion group Operation Rescue in a police brutality suit and presented a legal brief in support of a Republican politician accused of violating an ethics law.

**Statistics**

A recent National Institute of Mental Health study concludes that mentally ill people account for more than 30 percent of the homeless population (Young 27). Because so many homeless people have psychiatric disabilities, the federal government should seriously consider expanding the state mental hospital system.

**Expert Opinion**

No soldier ever really escapes the emotional consequences of war. As William Manchester, noted historian and World War II combat veteran, observes in his essay "Okinawa: The Bloodiest Battle of All," "the invisible wounds remain" (72).

### EXERCISE 1

Some of the following statements are facts; others are opinions. Identify each fact with the letter *F* and each opinion with the letter *O*. Then consider what kind of information, if any, could support each opinion.

1. The incidence of violent crime fell in the first six months of this year.
2. New gun laws and more police officers led to a decrease in crime early in the year.

3. The television rating system uses a system similar to the familiar movie rating codes to let parents know how appropriate a certain show might be for their children.
4. The television rating system would be better if it gave specifics about the violence, sexual content, and language in rated television programs.
5. Affirmative action laws and policies have helped women and minority group members advance in the workplace.
6. Affirmative action policies have outlived their usefulness.
7. Women who work are better off today than they were twenty years ago.
8. The wage gap between men and women in similar jobs is smaller now than it was twenty years ago.
9. The Charles River and Boston Harbor are less polluted now than they were ten years ago.
10. We do not need to worry about environmental legislation anymore because we have made great advances in cleaning up our environment.

## 8b Evaluating Supporting Evidence

The examples, statistics, or expert opinions that a writer uses to support a statement are called **evidence.** The more reliable the supporting evidence, the more willing readers will be to accept a statement.

See 10b1

All evidence—no matter what kind—must be *reliable, sufficient, representative,* and *relevant.*

- Evidence is likely to be **reliable** if it comes from a trustworthy source—one whose author is generally recognized as an expert in a particular field. Such a source quotes accurately and does not present remarks out of context. It does not contain factual, grammatical, or typographical errors. It also presents examples, statistics, and expert testimony fairly, drawing them from other reliable sources. Finally, it includes documentation to help readers evaluate both the writer and the evidence. (See **Parts 4 and 5** for more information on documentation.)
- Evidence is **sufficient** if a writer presents an adequate amount of information. It is not enough, for instance, for a writer to cite just one example in an attempt to demonstrate that most poor women do not receive adequate prenatal care. Similarly, the opinions of a single expert, no matter how reputable, would not be enough to support this position.
- Evidence is **representative** if it reflects a fair range of sources and viewpoints. Writers should not just choose evidence that supports their position and ignore evidence that does not. In other words, they should not permit their biases to govern their choice of evidence. For example, a writer who is making the point that the United States Congress should pass a bill that grants amnesty to undocumented immigrants should not just include evidence from people who agree with this position. The

writer should also address the arguments against this position and point out their weaknesses or inaccuracies.

- Evidence is **relevant** if it specifically applies to the case being discussed. For example, a writer cannot support the position that increased airport security in the United States has discouraged terrorist attacks by citing only examples from European airports. To be relevant, evidence must also be current. Statistics on terriorism that are several years old are not likely to be relevant for an essay about present-day security practices at airports.

### EXERCISE 2

Evaluate the supporting evidence in the following student paragraph.

> The United States is becoming more and more violent every day. I was talking to my friend Gayle, and she mentioned that a guy her roommate knows was attacked at dusk and had his skull crushed by the barrel of a gun. Later she heard that he was in the hospital with a blood clot in his brain. Two friends of mine were walking home from a party when they were attacked by armed men right outside the A-Plus Mini Market. These two examples make it very clear to me how violent our nation is becoming. My English professor, who is in his fifties, remembers a few similar violent incidents occurring when he was growing up, and he was even mugged in London last year. He believes that if more London police carried guns, the city would be safer. Two of the twenty-five people in our class have been the victims of violent crime, and I feel lucky that I am not one of them.

## 8c Detecting Bias

Bias is the tendency to base conclusions on emotions or preconceived ideas rather than on evidence. As a critical reader, you should be aware that bias may sometimes lead writers to see what they want to see and to ignore evidence that is inconsistent with their own points of view.

### Close-Up DETECTING BIAS

When you read, look for the following kinds of bias:

- **The Writer's Stated Beliefs** If a writer says that he or she is skeptical about global warming, you should be alert to the possibility that the writer may not present an accurate (or balanced) view of the subject.

*(continued)*

**DETECTING BIAS** *(continued)*

- **Sexist or Racist Statements** A writer who assumes that all engineers are male or all nurses are female reflects a clear bias. A researcher who assumes that certain racial or ethnic groups are intellectually superior to others is also likely to present a biased view.
- **Slanted Language** Some writers use **slanted language**—language that contains value judgments—to influence readers' reactions. For example, a newspaper article that states "The politician gave an impassioned speech" gives one impression; the statement "The politician delivered a diatribe" gives another.
- **Biased Tone** The tone of a piece of writing indicates a writer's attitude toward readers or toward his or her subject. An angry or sarcastic tone might suggest that the writer is not presenting his or her case fairly; a dismissive tone might suggest that a writer is ignoring opposing points of view.

See 1c

- **Biased Choice of Evidence** Frequently, the examples or statistics cited in a piece of writing reveal the writer's bias. For instance, a writer may include only examples that support a point and leave out examples that contradict it. Or, the writer may cite a single study that supports his or her point but ignore several others that undercut it.
- **Biased Choice of Experts** A writer should cite experts who represent a fair range of opinion. If, for instance, a writer assessing a state government's policy on same-sex marriage includes only statements by experts who vehemently oppose the policy, he or she is presenting a biased case.

*Note:* Your own biases can also affect your response to a text. When you read, it is important to remain aware of your own values and beliefs and to be alert to how they affect your reactions.

CHECKLIST

**Thinking Critically**

- ❑ Are the writer's points supported primarily by fact or by opinion?
- ❑ Does the writer offer supporting evidence for his or her opinions?
- ❑ What kind of evidence is provided? How convincing is it?
- ❑ Is the evidence accurate? sufficient? representative? relevant? authoritative? documented?
- ❑ Does the writer display any bias? If so, is the bias revealed through language, tone, or choice of evidence?
- ❑ Does the writer present a balanced picture of the issue?
- ❑ Are any alternative viewpoints overlooked?
- ❑ Does the writer omit pertinent examples?`

## EXERCISE 3

Read the following essay about home schooling, a movement supported by parents who have abandoned traditional schools in favor of teaching their children at home. After evaluating the quality of the writer's supporting evidence, identify her biases, and decide if these biases undercut her argument in any way. Use the questions in the "Thinking Critically" checklist on page 106 as a guide.

### Questioning the Motives of Home-Schooling Parents

America's most famous home-schooling parents at the moment are Andrea Yates and JoAnn McGuckin. Yates allegedly drowned her five children in a Houston suburb. McGuckin was arrested and charged with child neglect in Idaho. Her six kids barricaded themselves in the family's hovel when child-care workers came to remove them.

The intention here is not to smear the parents who instruct 1.5 million mostly normal children at home. But a social phenomenon that isolates children from the outside world deserves closer inspection.

The home-schooling movement runs an active propaganda machine. It portrays its followers in the most flattering terms—as bulwarks against the moral decay found in public, and presumably private, schools. Although now associated with conservative groups, modern home-schooling got its start among left-wing dropouts in the '60s.

Home-schooled students do tend to score above average on standardized tests. The most likely reason, however, is that most of the parents are themselves upper income and well educated. Students from those backgrounds also do well in traditional schools.

Advocates of home-schooling have become a vocal lobbying force in Washington, D.C. Children taught at home may be socially isolated, but the parents have loads of interaction. Membership in the anti-public-education brigade provides much comradeship.

The mouthpiece for the movement, the Home School Legal Defense Association (*www.hslda.org*), posts articles on its Web site with headlines like, "The Clinging Tentacles of Public Education." Trashing the motivations of professional teachers provides much sport.

Perhaps the time has come to question the motives of some home-schooling parents. Are the parents protecting their children from a cesspool of bad values in the outside world? Or are the parents just people who can't get along with others? Are they "taking charge" of their children's education? Or are they taking their children captive?

Yates and McGuckin are, of course, extreme cases and probably demented. But a movement that insists on parents' rights to do as they wish with their children gives cover for the unstable, for narcissists and for child-abusers.

In West Akron, Ohio, reporters would interview Thomas Lavery on how he successfully schooled his five children in their home. The kids all had top grades and fine manners. They recalled how their father loved to strut before the media.

Eventually, however, the police came for Lavery and charged him with nine counts of child endangerment. According to his children, Lavery smashed a daughter over the head with a soda can after she did poorly in a basketball game. Any child who wet a bed would spend the night alone, locked in the garage.

A child who spilled milk had to drop on his or her knees and lick it up from the floor. And in an especially creepy attempt to establish himself as master, Lavery would order his children to damn the name of God.

The best way to maintain the sanctity of a family madhouse is to keep the inmates inside. Allowing children to move about in the world could jeopardize the deal.

In some cases, it might also prevent tragedy. Suppose one of Andrea Yates' children had gone to a school and told a teacher of the mother's spiraling mental state. The teacher could have called a child-welfare officer and five little lives might have been saved.

Putting the horror stories aside, there's something sad about home-schooled children. During the New Hampshire presidential primary race, I attended an event directed at high-school and college students. The students were a lively bunch, circulating around the giant room, debating and arguing. Except for my table.

About four young people and a middle-aged woman were just sitting there. The teenagers were clearly intelligent and well behaved. I tried to chat, but they seemed wary of talking with strangers. The woman proudly informed me that they were her children and home-schooled.

The Home School Legal Defense Association condemns government interference in any parent's vision of how a child might be educated. The group's chairman, Michael Farris, says things like, "We just want to say to the government: We are doing a good job, so leave us alone."

Could that be where JoAnn McGuckin found her twisted sense of grievance? "Those are my kids," she said as Idaho removed her children from their filthy home. "The state needs to mind its own business." (Froma Harrop, *Seattle Times*)

"Questioning the Motives of Home-Schooling Parents" by Froma Harrop as appeared in the *Seattle Times*, June 28, 2001. Reprinted by permission of The Providence Journal Company.

CHAPTER 9

# Using Logic

## Frequently Asked Questions



Argumentative essays rely primarily on **logic**—the study of the principles of correct reasoning. Logical reasoning enables you to construct arguments that reach valid conclusions in a persuasive and systematic way. Before you can read and evaluate argumentative writing (and write an argumentative essay of your own), you need to understand the basic principles of *inductive* and *deductive reasoning*.

See Ch. 10

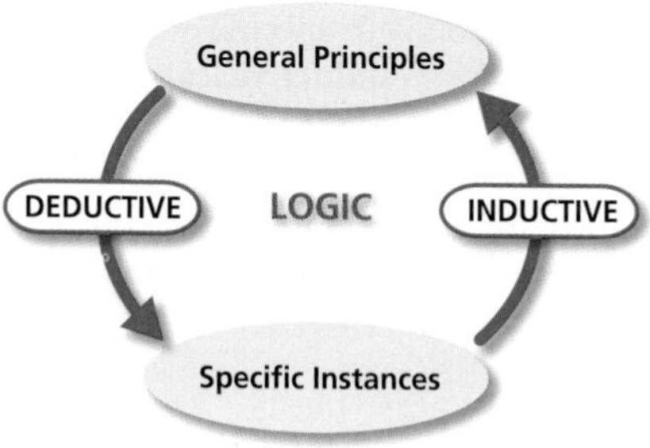


## 9a Understanding Inductive Reasoning

### 1 Moving from Specific to General

**Inductive reasoning** moves from specific facts, observations, or experiences to a general conclusion. Writers use inductive reasoning when they address a skeptical audience that requires a great deal of evidence before it will accept a conclusion. You can see how inductive reasoning operates by studying the following list of specific statements about the relationship between SAT scores and admissions at one particular college:

- The SAT is an admission requirement for all applicants.
- High school grades and rank in class are also examined.
- Nonacademic factors, such as sports, activities, and interests, are taken into account as well.
- Special attention is given to the applications of athletes, minorities, and children of alumni.

- Fewer than 52 percent of applicants for a recent class with SAT verbal scores between 600 and 700 were accepted.
- Fewer than 39 percent of applicants with similar math scores were accepted.
- Approximately 18 percent of applications with SAT verbal scores between 450 and 520 and about 19 percent of applicants with similar SAT math scores were admitted.

After reading the statements above you can use inductive reasoning to draw the general conclusion that although they are important, SAT scores are not the single factor that determines whether or not a student is admitted to this college.

### 2 Making Inferences

No matter how much evidence you provide, an inductive conclusion is never certain, only probable. The best you can do is present a convincing case to readers. You arrive at an inductive conclusion by making an **inference,** a statement about the unknown based on the known.

In order to bridge the gap that exists between your specific observations and your general conclusion, you have to make an **inductive leap,** a mental process that enables you to draw a reasonable inference from the available information. If you have presented enough specific evidence, this gap will be relatively small and your readers will readily accept your conclusion. If the gap is too big, your readers will accuse you of making a **hasty generalization** and will not accept your conclusion.

See 9d

### EXERCISE 1

Read the paragraph below, and then determine which of the statements that follow it can be inferred from the paragraph.

Americans are becoming more ecologically aware with each passing year, but their awareness may be limited. Most people know about the destruction of rain forests in South America, for example, or the vanishing African elephant, but few realize what is going on in their own backyards in the name of progress. Even people who are knowledgeable about such topics as the plight of the wild mustang, the dangers of toxic waste disposal, and acid rain frequently fail to realize either the existence or the importance of "smaller" ecological issues. The wetlands are a good case in point. In recent decades, more than 500,000 acres of wetlands a year have been filled, and it seems unlikely that the future will see any great change. What has happened in recent times is that United States wetlands are filled in one area and "restored" in another area, a practice that is legal according to Section 404 of the Clean Water Act and one that does in fact result in "no net loss" of wetlands. Few see the problems with this. To most, wetlands are mere swamps, and getting rid of swamps is viewed as something positive. In addition, the wetlands typically contain few spectacular species—the sort of glamour animals, such as condors and grizzlies, that easily attract publicity and sympathy. Instead, they contain boring specimens of flora and fauna unlikely to generate great concern among the masses. Yet the delicate balance of the ecosystem is upset by the elimination or "rearrangement" of such marshy areas. True, cosmically speaking, it matters little if one organism (or many) is wiped out. But even obscure subspecies might provide some much-needed product or information in the future. We should not forget that penicillin was made from a lowly mold.

1. The loss of even a single species may be disastrous to the ecosystem of the wetlands.
2. Even though the wetlands are considered swamps, most people are very concerned about their fate.
3. Section 404 of the Clean Water Act is not sufficient to protect the wetlands.
4. Few Americans are concerned about environmental issues.
5. Most people would agree that the destruction of rain forests is worse than the destruction of the wetlands.

## 9b Understanding Deductive Reasoning

### 1 Moving from General to Specific

**Deductive reasoning** moves from a generalization believed to be true or self-evident to a more specific conclusion. Writers use deductive reasoning when they address an audience that is more likely to be influenced by logic than by evidence. The process of deduction has traditionally been illustrated with a **syllogism,** a three-part set of statements or propositions that includes a **major premise,** a **minor premise,** and a **conclusion.**

**Major Premise:** All high-fat food is unhealthy.

**Minor Premise:** French fries are a high-fat food.

**Conclusion:** Therefore, french fries are unhealthy.

The **major premise** of a syllogism makes a general statement that the writer believes to be true. The **minor premise** presents a specific example of the belief that is stated in the major premise. If the reasoning is sound, the conclusion should follow from the two premises. (Note that the conclusion introduces no terms that have not already appeared in the major and minor premises.) The strength of a deductive argument is that if readers accept the premises, they have to grant the conclusion.

Note: When you write an **argument,** you can use a syllogism during the planning stage (to test the validity of your points), or you can use it as a revision strategy (to test your logic). In either case, the syllogism enables you to express your deductive argument in its most basic form and to see whether it makes sense.

See Ch. 10

## 2 Constructing Sound Syllogisms

A syllogism is **valid** (or logical) when its conclusion follows from its premises. A syllogism is **true** when it makes accurate claims—that is, when the information it contains is consistent with the facts. To be **sound,** a syllogism must be both valid and true. However, a syllogism may be valid without being true or true without being valid. The following syllogism, for example, is valid but not true.

**Major Premise:** All politicians are male.

**Minor Premise:** Nancy Pelosi is a politician.

**Conclusion:** Therefore, Nancy Pelosi is male.

As odd as it may seem, this syllogism is valid. In the major premise, the phrase *all politicians* establishes that the entire class *politicians* is male. After Nancy Pelosi is identified as a politician, the conclusion that she is male automatically follows—but, of course, she is not. Because the major premise of this syllogism is not true, no conclusion based on it can be true. Even though the logic of the syllogism is correct, its conclusion is not. Therefore, the syllogism is not sound.

## 3 Recognizing Enthymemes

An **enthymeme** is a syllogism in which one of the premises—often the major premise—is unstated. Enthymemes often occur as sentences containing words that signal conclusions—*therefore, consequently, for this reason, for, so, since,* or *because.*

Melissa is on the Dean's List; therefore, she is a good student.

The preceding sentence contains the minor premise and the conclusion of a syllogism. The reader must fill in the missing major premise in order to complete the syllogism and see whether or not the reasoning is logical.

**Major Premise:** All those on the Dean's List are good students.

**Minor Premise:** Melissa is on the Dean's List.

**Conclusion:** Therefore, Melissa is a good student.

Bumper stickers often take the form of enthymemes, stating just a conclusion ("Eating meat is murder") and leaving readers to supply both the major and minor premises. Careful readers, however, are not so easily fooled. They supply the missing premise (or premises), and then determine if the resulting syllogism is sound.

### EXERCISE 2

Read the following two enthymemes:

- Tax cuts help the economy, so we should support the new tax proposals.

- Eating meat is murder.

Now, supply the missing premises, and determine whether the resulting syllogisms are sound—in other words, whether they are both valid and true.

## 9c Using Toulmin Logic

Stephen Toulmin, a contemporary philosopher and logician, has formulated another way of analyzing arguments. According to Toulmin, the traditional syllogistic approach, while useful for identifying flaws in logic, is not useful for analyzing arguments that occur in the real world because these arguments tend to be far more complex than a three-part syllogism suggests. To address this shortcoming, Toulmin created a system that enables writers and readers of argument to compose or analyze arguments at a deeper level than the traditional syllogism permits.

According to Toulmin, most arguments contain the following elements: the *claim,* the *qualifiers,* the *support,* the *warrant,* the *backing,* and the *rebuttal.* The Toulmin model of argument is illustrated in the box below.

### The Toulmin Model of Argument

**Claim (the point a writer is trying to prove):** College athletes should receive salaries for the time they spend competing in sports.

**Qualifiers (words or phrases that limit the claim):** College athletes *who participate in programs that bring money into the school* should receive salaries for the time they spend competing in sports.

**Support (facts, examples, and expert opinion that support the claim):** Examples showing that colleges and universities make a great deal of money from their sports programs.

**Warrant (underlying assumption that connects the support with the claim):** Athletic scholarships do not adequately compensate student athletes in successful sports programs.

**Backing (facts and examples that support the warrant):** Studies show that the compensation given to student athletes in major football and basketball programs is small in comparison to the millions of dollars the teams raise for their schools.

**Rebuttal (acknowledgment of an exception to the claim):** Some say that if student athletes were paid, they would be professionals, not students.

See 10b1

In an argumentative essay, the **claim** is the thesis, an opinion that must be supported with evidence. For example, in the Toulmin argument in the box above, the claim is "College athletes should receive salaries for the time they spend competing in sports."

The **qualifiers** are words (*probably, sometimes, many,* and *few,* for example) or phrases that limit the claim. Qualifiers demonstrate to readers that you are reasonable and that you have not overstated your claim. In the argument above, for example, the qualifier limits the claim by saying that only student athletes who participate in programs that make money for the school (not all student athletes) should receive a salary.

The **support** convinces readers that the claim is worth considering. For example, in the argument on page 113, the claim would be supported with facts, examples, and expert opinion establishing that colleges can make a great deal of money from their sports programs.

The **warrant** (or **warrants**) is the assumption that readers must accept in order for the argument to succeed. Sometimes a writer will think that a warrant is so obvious (or self-evident) that it need not be stated. In this case, readers would have to infer the unstated warrant in order to evaluate the argument. At other times, a writer will explicitly state the warrant.

Whether the warrant is implied or explicit, readers have to determine whether the writer has supplied the **backing,** the facts and examples needed to support it. For example, in the argument on page 113, the underlying assumption is that athletic scholarships do not adequately compensate student athletes. To establish the validity of this assumption, you would have to provide data to show that sports scholarships do not equitably compensate student athletes.

The **rebuttal** introduces arguments that disagree with the claim. A persuasive argument often presents opposing arguments and *refutes* them by demonstrating their weakness. In the argument on page 113, the writer introduces the argument that student athletes who are paid should be considered professional athletes and not students. To refute this argument, the writer should provide evidence that undercuts the counterargument—for example, pointing out that other students who are paid for work they do for the school are not considered professionals.

## EXERCISE 3

Read this newspaper editorial carefully.

> A nation succeeds only if the vast majority of its citizens succeed. It therefore stands to reason that with immigrants accounting for about 40 percent of our population growth, the future economic and social success of the United States is bound up with the success of these new Americans. Demography, in a word, is destiny.

This is an important principle to keep in mind as we try to come to grips with the problems and opportunities presented by the flood of legal and illegal immigrants from Mexico and other parts of South and Central America, who now constitute by far our largest immigrant group.

How are we doing in our efforts to assimilate these largely Hispanic newcomers and provide them with a bright future? Some signs are disturbing.

John Garcia, associate professor of political science at the University of Arizona, writing in *International Migration Review,* finds that the average rate of naturalization of Mexican immigrants is one-tenth that of other immigrant naturalization rates. The Select Commission on Immigration and Refugee Policy made a similar finding. Increasingly, immigrants are separated from everyone else by language, geography, ethnicity and class.

The future success of this country is closely linked to the ability of our immigrants to succeed. Yet 50 percent of our children of Hispanic background do not graduate from high school. Hispanic students score 100 points under the average student on Scholastic Aptitude Test scores. Hispanics have much higher rates of poverty, illiteracy and need for welfare than the national average. This engenders social crisis.

Not all the indicators of assimilation are pessimistic: the success of many Indochinese immigrants has been gratifying. But the warning signs of nonassimilation are increasing and ominous.

America must make sure the melting pot continues to melt: immigrants must become Americans. Seymour Martin Lipset, professor of political science and sociology at the Hoover Institution, Stanford University, observes: "The history of bilingual and bicultural societies that do not assimilate are histories of turmoil, tension and tragedy. Canada, Belgium, Malaysia, Lebanon—all face crises of national existence in which minorities press for autonomy, if not independence. Pakistan and Cyprus have divided. Nigeria suppressed an ethnic rebellion. France faces difficulties with its Basques, Bretons and Corsicans."

The United States is at a crossroads. If it does not consciously move toward greater integration, it will inevitably drift toward more fragmentation. It will either have to do better in assimilating all of the other peoples in its boundaries or it will witness increasing alienation and fragmentation. Cultural divisiveness is not a bedrock upon which a nation can be built. It is inherently unstable.

The nation faces a staggering social agenda. We have not adequately integrated blacks into our economy and society. Our education system is rightly described as "a rising tide of mediocrity." We have the most violent society in the industrial world; we have startlingly high rates of illiteracy, illegitimacy and welfare recipients.

It bespeaks a hubris to madly rush, with these unfinished social agendas, into accepting more immigrants and refugees than all of the rest of the world and then to still hope to keep a common agenda.

America can accept additional immigrants, but we must be sure that they become American. We can be a Joseph's coat of many nations, but we must be unified. One of the common glues that hold us together is language—the English language.

We should be color-blind but linguistically cohesive. We should be a rainbow but not a cacophony. We should welcome different peoples but not adopt different languages. We can teach English through bilingual education, but we should take great care not to become a bilingual society. (Richard D. Lamm, "English Comes First")



A. Answer the following questions about the essay.

1. Former Colorado governor Richard D. Lamm relies on a number of unstated premises about his subject that he expects his audience to accept. What are some of these premises?
2. What kinds of information does Lamm use to support his position?
3. Where does Lamm state his conclusion? Restate the conclusion in your own words.
4. In paragraph 1, Lamm uses deductive reasoning. Express this reasoning as a syllogism.
5. Express the syllogism in paragraph 1 in terms of Toulmin logic.

B. Evaluate the reasoning in each of the following statements. (If the statement is in the form of an enthymeme, supply the missing term before evaluating it.)

1. All immigrants should speak English. If they do not, they are not real Americans.
2. Richard D. Lamm was born in the United States and grew up in an English-speaking household. Therefore, he has no credibility on the subject of bilingualism.
3. Spanish-speaking immigrants should be required by law to learn English. After all, most Eastern European immigrants who came to this country early in the twentieth century learned English.
4. If immigrants do not care enough about our country to learn English, we should not allow them to become citizens.
5. Some immigrants have become financially successful even though they did not learn English. Obviously, then, learning English does not increase an immigrant's chances for success.
6. All Cuban immigrants speak Spanish. Former Secretary of Housing and Urban Development Henry Cisneros speaks Spanish, so he must be a Cuban immigrant.
7. As sociologist Seymour Martin Lipset points out, bilingual societies can be threatened by tension and political unrest. Therefore, it is important that immigrants not be bilingual.

## 9d Recognizing Logical Fallacies

**Logical fallacies** are flawed arguments. A writer who inadvertently uses fallacies is not thinking clearly or logically; a writer who intentionally uses them is trying to deceive readers. It is important that you learn to recognize fallacies—to challenge them when you read and to avoid them when you write.

**ESL TIP**

In many cultures, people present arguments in order to persuade others to believe something. However, the rules for constructing such arguments are different in different cultures. In US academic settings, writers are discouraged from using the types of arguments listed in the box below because they are not considered fair.

### Logical Fallacies

- **Hasty Generalization** Drawing a conclusion based on too little evidence

  The person I voted for is not doing a good job in Congress. Therefore, voting is a waste of time. (One disappointing experience does not warrant the statement that you will never vote again.)

- **Sweeping Generalization** Making a generalization that cannot be supported no matter how much evidence is supplied

  Everyone should exercise. (Some people, for example those with severe heart conditions, might not benefit from exercise.)

- **Equivocation** Shifting the meaning of a key word or phrase during an argument

  It is not in the public interest for the public to lose interest in politics. (Although clever, the shift in the meaning of the term *public interest* clouds the issue.)

- **Non Sequitur (Does Not Follow)** Arriving at a conclusion that does not logically follow from what comes before it

  Kim Williams is a good lawyer, so she will make a good senator. (Kim Williams may be a good lawyer, but it does not necessarily follow that she will make a good senator.)

- **Either/Or Fallacy** Treating a complex issue as if it has only two sides

  Either we institute universal health care, or the health of all Americans will be at risk. (Good health does not necessarily depend on universal health care.)

(*continued*)

### Logical Fallacies (*continued*)

- **Post Hoc** Establishing an unjustified link between cause and effect
  The United States sells wheat to China. This must be why the price of wheat is so high. (Other factors, unrelated to the sale, could have caused the price of wheat to rise.)
- **Begging the Question (Circular Reasoning)** Stating a debatable premise as if it were true
  Stem-cell research should be banned because nothing good can come from something so inherently evil. (Where is the evidence that stem-cell research is "inherently evil"?)
- **False Analogy** Assuming that because things are similar in some ways, they are similar in other ways
  When forced to live in crowded conditions, people act like rats. They turn on each other and act violently. (Both people and rats might dislike living in crowded conditions, but unlike rats, people do not necessarily resort to violence in this situation.)
- **Red Herring** Changing the subject to distract readers from the issue
  Our company may charge high prices, but we give a lot to charity each year. (What does charging high prices have to do with giving to charity?)
- **Argument to Ignorance** Saying that something is true because it cannot be proved false, or vice versa
  How can you tell me to send my child to a school where there is a child who has AIDS? After all, doctors can't say for sure that my child won't catch AIDS, can they? (Just because a doctor cannot prove the writer's claim to be false, it does not follow that the claim is true.)
- **Bandwagon** Trying to establish that something is true because everyone believes it is true
  Everyone knows that eating candy makes children hyperactive. (Where is the evidence to support this claim?)
- **Argument to the Person (*Ad Hominem*)** Attacking the person and not the issue
  Of course the former Vice President supports drilling for oil in the Arctic. He once worked for an oil company. (By attacking his opponent, the writer attempts to sidestep the issue.)

## EXERCISE 4

Form groups of three students. Then, identify the logical fallacies in the following statements. In each case, name the fallacy, and then rewrite the statement to correct the problem. Finally, select one student in each group to present one rewritten statement to the class.

1. Membership in the Coalition Against Pornography has more than quadrupled since the 1990s. Convenience stores in many parts of

the country have limited their selection of pornography and, in many cases, taken pornography off the shelves. In 1995, the defense appropriations bill included a ban on the sale of pornography on military installations. The American public clearly believes that pornography has a harmful effect on its audience.

2. With people like Larry Flynt and Hugh Hefner arguing that pornography is harmless, you know that pornography is causing its readers to live immoral lifestyles.
3. The Republican Party and conservative thinkers are all for the free market when the issue is environmental degradation, but they will be the first ones to call for a limit to what can be shown on movies, television, and the Internet.
4. Television is out of control. There is more foul language, sex, and sexual innuendo on television than there has ever been before. The effects of this obscene and pornographic material have been clearly documented in studies that proved that serial killers and other criminals were much more likely to be regular consumers of pornographic materials.
5. We know that television causes children to be more violent. So what can we use to control television? More governmental control of television content will help us reduce violence.
6. Study after study has been completed, and none of the researchers has presented incontrovertible evidence that rap music causes an increase in violent behavior among its listeners.
7. A boy in Idaho set fire to his family's home after watching a television stunt show. From this incident, we can see that television has a negative influence on children's behavior.
8. We want our children to grow up in safe neighborhoods. We would like to see less violence in the schools and on the playgrounds. We would like to be less fearful when we have to go out at night. If we stop polluting our culture with violent images from television and popular music, we can reclaim our communities and our children.
9. Ted Bundy and Richard Ramirez, two of the most violent serial killers ever caught, both viewed pornography regularly. Pornography caused them to kill women.
10. Some people believe that violent content on the Internet affects children and want the government to limit it. Others believe that children are unaffected by violent Internet content. I do not think that violence on the Internet causes children to become violent.

## EXERCISE 5

Read the following excerpt and identify as many logical fallacies as you can. Then, write a letter to the author pointing out the fallacies and explaining how they weaken his argument.

Hunting and eating a free-roaming wild deer is one thing; slaughtering and eating a [wounded] deer is another.

The point . . . is that—despite what our enemies are saying—hunters are just as compassionate as the next fellow. It hurts us to see an animal suffer, and when we can help an animal in need, we go out of our way to do whatever we can.

A case in point is the story . . . about SCI Alaska vice president Dave Campbell's efforts to help a cow moose. That animal had carried a poorly shot arrow in its body for weeks until Campbell saw it and made certain it got help.

Despite how some media handled that story, there is no irony in hunters coming to the rescue of the same species we hunt.

We do it all the time.

A story of hunters showing compassion for an animal is something you'll never see in *The Bunny Huggers' Gazette* (yes, there is such a publication. It's a bimonthly magazine produced on newsprint. According to the publisher's statement, it provides information about vegetarianism, and "organizations, protests, boycotts or legislation on behalf of animal liberation . . .").

Among the protests announced in the June issue of *BHG* are boycotts against the countries of Ireland and Spain, the states and provinces of the Yukon Territory, Alberta, British Columbia, Pennsylvania and Alaska, the companies of American Express, Anheuser-Busch, Bausch & Lomb, Bloomingdale's, Coca-Cola Products, Coors, Gillette, Hartz, L'Oreal, McDonald's, Mellon Bank, Northwest Airlines, Pocono Mountain resorts and a host of others.

Interestingly, *BHG* tells how a subscribing group, Life Net of Montezuma, New Mexico, has petitioned the US Forest Service to close portions of the San Juan and Rio Grande National Forests between April and November to all entry "to provide as much protection as possible" for grizzly bears that may still exist there. Another subscriber, Predator Project of Bozeman, Montana, is asking that the entire North Cascades region be closed to coyote hunting because gray wolves might be killed by "sportsmen (who) may not be able to tell the difference between a coyote and a wolf."

Although it's not a new idea, another subscriber, Prairie Dog Rescue, is urging persons who are opposed to hunting to apply for limited quota hunting permits because "one permit in peaceful hands means one less opportunity for a hunter to kill."

And if you ever doubted that the vegetarian/animal rights herd is a wacko bunch, then consider the magazine's review of *Human Tissue, A Neglected Experimental Resource*. According to the review, the 24-page essay encourages using human tissues to test "medicines and other substances, any of which would save animals' lives." (Bill Quimby, "The World of Hunting")

CHAPTER 10

# Writing an Argumentative Essay

## Frequently Asked Questions



For most people, the true test of their critical thinking skills comes when they write an **argumentative essay,** one that takes a stand on an issue and uses logic and evidence to convince readers. When you write an argument, you follow the same process you use when you write any essay. However, because the purpose of an argument is to change the way readers think, you need to use some additional strategies to present your ideas to your audience.

See Chs. 4–6

## 10a Planning an Argumentative Essay

### 1 Choosing a Topic

As with any type of essay, choosing the right topic for your argumentative essay is important. First, you should choose a topic that you already know something about. The more you know about your topic, the easier it will be to gather the information you need to write your argumentative essay. You should also choose a topic that interests and challenges you, one in which you have an emotional and intellectual stake.

It stands to reason that the more you care about a topic, the more enthusiastically you will pursue it. Still, you should be willing to consider other people's viewpoints—even those that contradict your own beliefs. If the situation warrants—for example, if the evidence goes against your position—you should be willing to change your position. If you find that you cannot be open-minded, you should consider choosing another topic. Remember, in order to be persuasive, you will have to demonstrate to readers that your position is fair and that you have considered both the strengths and the weaknesses of opposing arguments.

Your topic should also be narrow enough so that you can write about it within the assigned page limit. If your topic is too broad, you will not be able to treat it in enough detail. Finally, your topic should be interesting to your readers. Keep in mind that some topics—such as "The Need for Gun Control" or "The Fairness of the Death Penalty"—have been discussed and written about so often that you may not be able to say anything new or interesting about them. Instead of relying on an overused topic, choose one that enables you to contribute something to the debate.

Finally, make sure you have access to the information that you will need to develop your topic. Do some preliminary research about your topic. Many times, this survey will enable you to get a sense of your topic and the conflicting opinions that people have about it. If you are unable to find the information you will need, choose another topic—one that you can reasonably discuss.

## 2 Developing a Thesis

See 5b

After you have chosen a topic, your next step is to take a stand—to summarize your position in a thesis statement. Properly worded, this thesis statement lays the foundation for the rest of your argument. A thesis statement for an argumentative essay challenges readers, calling on them to consider your points and to think in ways that they may not have anticipated. It almost always raises questions that have no easy or pat answers.

When you develop your thesis statement, make sure that it is *clearly stated* and that it is *debatable.*

Your argumentative thesis should be **clearly stated.** A good thesis statement leaves no doubts in readers' minds what you intend to discuss or what direction your argument will take. It is a good idea to write a preliminary draft of your thesis statement. If you write down this tentative thesis, you will be able to think critically about it and make sure that it says exactly what you want to say.

Your argumentative thesis should also be **debatable**—that is, it should take a side on an issue. Because your thesis statement determines the direction your argumentative essay will take, you should make sure that it accurately presents your side of the argument.

A **factual statement**—a verifiable assertion about which reasonable people do *not* disagree—is not suitable as a thesis statement for an argumentative essay.

> **Fact:** First-year students are not required to purchase a meal plan from the university.
>
> **Thesis Statement:** First-year students should not be required to purchase a meal plan from the university.

One way to make sure that your thesis statement is actually debatable is to formulate an **antithesis,** a statement that takes the opposite position. If you can state an antithesis, you can be certain that your thesis statement is one that is debatable.

**Thesis Statement:** Term limits would be beneficial because they would bring in people with fresh ideas every few years.

**Antithesis:** Term limits would not be beneficial because elected officials would always be inexperienced.

**Effective Thesis Statements for Argumentative Essays**

The following thesis statements are both clearly stated and debatable. Each one takes a stand that the writer will support with evidence in the rest of the essay.

Even though some people say that green technology will eliminate the need for foreign oil, this is not the case.

The use of Ethanol should be discontinued because it has caused worldwide shortages of food.

Developing alternate energy sources is the most important challenge facing scientists today.

Instead of continuing its reliance on fossil fuels, the United States should increase its use of renewable energy.

**Close-Up DEVELOPING AN ARGUMENTATIVE THESIS**

To make sure your argumentative thesis is effective, ask the following questions:

- Is your thesis one with which reasonable people might disagree?
- Can you formulate an antithesis?
- Can your thesis be supported by evidence?
- Does your thesis make your position clear to readers?

### EXERCISE 1

Working on your own or in a group, determine which of the following thesis statements are effective and which are not. Then, rewrite the ineffective thesis statements so that they are clear and debatable.

1. There are many different reasons for cheating.
2. Gun violence in the United States is on the rise.
3. The advantages of a flat tax clearly outweigh those of the current tax system.
4. In this paper, I'm going to discuss *The Hunger Games*.
5. Although many people think buying counterfeit goods is all right, this activity harms the legitimate businesses whose merchandise is being copied.

## 3 Defining Your Terms

You should always define the key terms you use in your argument—especially those you use in your thesis statement. After all, the soundness of an entire argument may hinge on the definition of a word that may mean one thing to one person and another thing to someone else. For example, in the United States, democratic elections involve the selection of government officials by popular vote; in other countries, the word *democratic* may be used to describe elections in which only one candidate is running or in which all candidates represent the same party. For this reason, if your argument hinges on a key term like *democratic,* you should make sure that your readers know exactly what you mean.

### Close-Up USING PRECISE LANGUAGE

Be careful to use precise language in your thesis statement. Avoid vague and judgmental words, such as *wrong, bad, good, right,* and *immoral*.

**Vague:** Censorship of the Internet would be wrong.

**Clearer:** Censorship of the Internet would unfairly limit free speech.

## 4 Considering Your Audience

See 1b

As you plan your essay, keep a specific audience in mind. Are your readers unbiased observers or people deeply concerned about the issue you plan to discuss? Can they be cast in a specific role—concerned parents, victims of discrimination, irate consumers—or are they so diverse that they cannot be categorized?

Always assume a **skeptical audience**—one that is likely to question or even challenge your assumptions. Even sympathetic readers will need to be convinced that your argument is logical and that your evidence is solid. Skeptical readers will need reassurance that you understand their concerns and that you are willing to concede some of their points. However, no matter what you do, you may never be able to convince hostile readers that your conclusion is valid or even worth considering. The best you can hope for is that these readers will acknowledge the strengths of your argument even if they reject your conclusion.

**ESL TIP**

If you have not lived in the United States very long, it may be difficult for you to assess what your readers know and believe. Since your instructor is one of your primary readers, consult him or her about this issue.

### 5 Refuting Opposing Arguments

As you develop your argument, you should briefly summarize and then **refute**—that is, argue against—opposing arguments.

**Refuting Opposing Arguments**

In order to effectively refute opposing arguments, follow these steps:

- Accurately summarize the argument that you intend to refute. Do not slant your summary or misrepresent the opposition.
- Identify areas where the opposition is incorrect, misguided, weak, or irrelevant. For example, are there problems with reasoning? Does the opponent's argument contain logical fallacies? Is the evidence weak? Are there factual errors?
- If an opponent's argument is particularly strong, concede this fact and then identify its limitations.
- Make sure that you explain the importance of your refutation. Readers should have a clear sense of why your criticism is relevant to your own argument.

In the following paragraph, a student refutes the argument that Sea World is justified in keeping whales in captivity.

> Of course, some will say that Sea World wants to capture only a few whales, as George Will points out in his commentary in *Newsweek*. Unfortunately, Will downplays the fact that Sea World wants to capture a hundred whales, not just "a few." And, after releasing ninety of these whales, Sea World intends to keep ten for "further work." At hearings in Seattle last week, several noted marine biologists went on record as condemning Sea World's research program.

*Note:* When you acknowledge an opposing view, be careful not to distort or oversimplify it. This tactic, known as creating a **straw man,** can seriously undermine your credibility.

### Close-Up CHOOSING ARGUMENTS TO REFUTE

As you plan your argumentative essay, try creating a two-column table or chart that organizes all the arguments against your position. Label the first column "Opposing Arguments" and the second column "Refutations." List the arguments against your position in the first column and your refutations of these arguments in the second column. When you are finished, delete the weakest opposing arguments. When you write your essay, discuss and refute only those opposing arguments that remain.

### EXERCISE 2

Choose one of the following five statements, and list the arguments in favor of it. Then, list the arguments against it. Finally, choose one position (pro or con), and write a paragraph or two supporting it. Be sure to refute the arguments against your position.

1. Public school students who participate in extracurricular activities should have to submit to random drug tests.
2. The federal government should limit the amount of violence shown on television.
3. A couple applying for a marriage license should be required to take AIDS tests.
4. Retirees making more than $50,000 a year should not be eligible for Social Security benefits.
5. Colleges and universities should provide free day care for students' children.

## 10b Using Evidence Effectively

### 1 Supporting Your Argument

Most arguments are built on **assertions**—statements that you make about your topic—backed by evidence—supporting information, in the form of examples, statistics, or expert opinion. Some of the most common sources of evidence are scholarly journals, magazines, newspapers, Web sites, and books. You may also get evidence from observations, interviews, surveys, and your own personal experience. See 8b

Keep in mind that all information—words and ideas—that you get from a source requires documentation. Only assertions that are **self-evident** ("All human beings are mortal"), **true by definition** ("2 + 2 = 4"), or **factual** ("The Atlantic Ocean separates England and the United States") need no documentation. See Pts. 4–5

Even though you support your points with evidence from your sources, your argument should not be a patchwork of other people's ideas. In other words, *your* voice—not those of your sources—should dominate the discussion. You should present your points, introduce and interpret your evidence, and make sure that readers know how your ideas relate to one another and to your thesis. In this way, you let readers know that you are in control of the argument and that you have something to add to the discussion.

Note: Remember that you can never prove a thesis conclusively; if you could, there would be no argument. The best you can do is to provide enough evidence to establish a high probability that your thesis is reasonable or valid.

### 2 Establishing Credibility

Clear reasoning, compelling evidence, and strong refutations go a long way toward making an argument solid. But these elements in themselves are not sufficient to create a convincing argument. In order to convince readers, you have to satisfy them that you are someone they should listen to—in other words, that you have **credibility.**

Some people, of course, bring credibility with them every time they speak. When a Nobel Prize winner in physics makes a speech about the need to control the proliferation of nuclear weapons, we assume that he or she speaks with authority. But most people do not have this kind of inherent credibility. When you write an argument, you must work to establish your credibility by *establishing common ground, demonstrating knowledge, maintaining a reasonable tone,* and *presenting yourself as someone worth listening to.*

***Establishing Common Ground*** When you engage in argument, it is tempting to go on the attack, emphasizing the differences between your position and those of your opponents. Writers of effective arguments, however, know they can gain a greater advantage by establishing common ground between their opponents and themselves.

> **Close-Up** USING ROGERIAN ARGUMENT
>
> One way to establish common ground is to use the techniques of **Rogerian argument.** According to the psychologist Carl Rogers, you should think of the members of your audience as colleagues with whom you must collaborate to find solutions to problems. Instead of verbally assaulting them, you emphasize points of agreement. In this way, rather than taking a confrontational stance, you establish common ground and work toward a resolution of the problem you are discussing.

***Demonstrating Knowledge*** Including relevant personal experiences in your argumentative essay can show readers that you know a lot about your subject; demonstrating this kind of knowledge gives you authority. For example, describing what you observed at a National Rifle Association convention can give you authority in an essay arguing for (or against) gun control.

See Pts. 4–5

You can also establish credibility by showing you have done research into a subject. By referring to important sources of information and by providing accurate **documentation** for your information, you show readers that you have done the necessary background reading. Including references to a range of sources—not just one—suggests that you have a balanced knowledge of your subject. However, questionable sources, inaccurate (or missing) documentation, and factual errors can undermine your credibility. For many readers, an undocumented quotation or even an incorrect date can put an entire argument into question.

See 1c

***Maintaining a Reasonable Tone*** Your **tone** is almost as important as the information you convey. Talk to your readers, not at them. If you lecture your readers or appear to talk down to them, you will alienate them. Remember that readers are more likely to respond to a writer who is conciliatory than to one who is strident or insulting.

In addition, never engage in name-calling or personal attacks against your opponent. This type of behavior undercuts your credibility and makes it easy for readers to dismiss you as unreasonable or mean-spirited.

As you write your essay, use moderate language, and qualify your statements so that they seem reasonable. Try to avoid words and phrases such as *never, all,* and *in every case,* which can make your claims seem exaggerated and unrealistic. The statement "Euthanasia is never acceptable," for example, leaves you no room for compromise. A more conciliatory statement might be "In cases of extreme suffering, a patient's desire for death is certainly understandable, but in most cases, the moral, social, and legal implications of euthanasia make it unacceptable."

***Presenting Yourself as Someone Worth Listening To*** When you write an argument, you should make sure you present yourself as someone your readers will want to listen to. Present your argument in positive and forceful terms, and don't apologize for your views. For example, do not rely on phrases—such as "In my opinion" and "It seems to me"—that undercut your credibility. Be consistent, and be careful not to contradict yourself. Finally, limit your use of the first person ("I"), and avoid slang and colloquialisms.

### 3 Being Fair

Because argument advances one point of view over another, it is seldom objective. However, college writing requires that you stay within the bounds of fairness and avoid bias. To be sure that the support for your argument is not misleading or distorted, you should take the following steps.

See 8c

***Avoid Distorting Evidence*** You **distort** evidence when you misrepresent it. Writers sometimes intentionally misrepresent their opponents' views by exaggerating them and then attacking this extreme position. For example, a senator of a northeastern state proposed requiring unmarried mothers receiving welfare to identify their children's fathers and to supply information about them. Instead of challenging this proposal directly, a critic distorted the senator's position and attacked it unfairly.

> What is the senator's next idea in his headlong rush to embrace this extreme position? A program of tattoos for welfare mothers? Badges sewn on to their clothing identifying them as welfare recipients? Creation of colonies in which welfare recipients would be forced to live like lepers? How about an involuntary relocation program that settles welfare recipients in concentration camps?

***Avoid Quoting Out of Context*** You **quote out of context** when you take someone's words from their original setting and use them in another. When you select certain statements and ignore others, you can change the meaning of what someone has said or suggested.

> **Mr. N, Township Resident:** I don't know why you are opposing the new highway. According to your own statements, the highway will increase land values and bring more business into the area.
>
> **Ms. L, Township Supervisor:** I think you should look at my statements more carefully. I have a copy of the paper that printed my interview,

and what I said was [*reading*]: "The highway will increase land values a bit and bring some business to the area. But at what cost? One hundred and fifty families will be displaced, and the highway will divide our township in half." My comments were not meant to support the new highway but to underscore the problems that its construction will cause.

***Avoid Slanting*** You **slant** an argument when you select only information that supports your case and ignore information that does not. Slanting also occurs when you use judgmental or inflammatory language to create bias. For example, a national magazine slanted information when it described a person accused of a crime as "a hulk of a man who looks as if he could burn out somebody's eyes with a propane torch." Although one-sided presentations frequently appear in tabloids and some popular magazines, you should avoid such distortions in your argumentative essays.

***Avoid Using Unfair Appeals*** Traditionally, writers of arguments use three kinds of appeals to influence readers: **logical appeals** address a reader's sense of reason; **emotional appeals** play on the emotions of a reader; and **ethical appeals** call the reader's attention to the credibility of the writer.

See 9d

Problems arise when these appeals are used unfairly. For example, writers can use fallacies to fool readers into thinking that a conclusion is logical when it is not. Writers can also employ inappropriate emotional appeals—to prejudice or fear, for example—to influence readers. And finally, writers can unfairly use their credentials in one area of expertise to bolster their stature in another area that they are not qualified to discuss.

## 10c Organizing an Argumentative Essay

See 9a–b

In its simplest form, an argument consists of a thesis statement and supporting evidence. However, argumentative essays frequently use **inductive and deductive reasoning** and other specialized strategies to win audience approval and overcome potential opposition.

### Close-Up ELEMENTS OF AN ARGUMENTATIVE ESSAY

**Introduction**

See 7e2

The introduction of your argumentative essay acquaints your readers with your subject. Here you can show how your subject concerns your audience, establish common ground with your readers, and perhaps explain how your subject has been misunderstood.

**Thesis Statement**

Your thesis statement can appear anywhere in your argumentative essay. Most often, you state your thesis in your introduction. However, if you are presenting a highly controversial argument—one to which you believe your readers might react negatively—you may postpone stating your thesis until later in your essay.

See 5b, 10a2

**Background**

In this section, you can briefly present a narrative of past events, an overview of others' opinions on the issue, definitions of key terms, or a review of basic facts.

**Arguments in Support of Your Thesis**

Here you present your arguments and the evidence that supports them. Begin with your weakest argument, and work up to your strongest. If all your arguments are equally strong, you might begin with those with which your readers are already familiar and therefore perhaps more likely to accept.

**Refutation of Opposing Arguments**

If the opposing arguments are relatively weak, summarize and refute them after you have made your case. However, if the opposing arguments are strong, concede their strengths and then discuss their limitations.

**Conclusion**

Your conclusion should reinforce the main point you are making in your argument. Here you can summarize key points, restate your thesis, remind readers of the weaknesses of opposing arguments, or underscore the logic of your position. Many writers like to end their arguments with a strong last line, such as a quotation or a statement that sums up the argument.

See 7e3

## 10d Writing and Revising an Argumentative Essay

The following student essay includes many of the elements discussed in this chapter. The writer, Samantha Masterton, was asked to write an argumentative essay on a topic of her choice, drawing her supporting evidence from her own knowledge and experience as well as from other sources.

Masterton 1

Samantha Masterton

Professor Egler

English 102

14 April 2012

The Returning Student: Older Is Definitely Better

Introduction

After graduating from high school, young people must decide what they want to do with the rest of their lives. Many graduates (often without much thought) decide to continue their education uninterrupted, and they go on to college. This group of teenagers makes up what many see as typical first-year college students. Recently, however, this stereotype has been challenged by an influx of older students, including myself, into American colleges and universities (Palmer). Not only do these students make a valuable contribution to the schools they attend, but they also offer an alternative to young people who go to college simply because they do not know what else to do. A few years off between high school and college can give many students the life experience they need to appreciate the value of higher education and to gain more from it.

Thesis statement

Background

The college experience of an eighteen-year-old is quite different from that of an older "nontraditional" student. The typical high school graduate is often concerned with things other than studying—for example, going to parties, dating, and testing personal limits. However, older students—those who are twenty-five years of age or older—are serious about the idea of returning to college. Although many high school students do not think twice about whether or not to attend college, older students have much more to consider when they think about returning to college. For example, they must decide how much time they can spend getting their degree

Masterton 2

and consider the impact that attending college will have on their family and their finances.

In the United States, the makeup of college students is changing. According to the US Department of Education report *Nontraditional Undergraduates,* the percentage of students who could be classified as "nontraditional" has increased over the last decade (7). So, despite the challenges that older students face when they return to school, more and more are choosing to make the effort.

Background (continued)

Most older students return to school with clear goals. The *Nontraditional Undergraduates* report shows that more than one-third of nontraditional students decided to attend college because it was required by their job, and 87 percent enrolled in order to gain skills (10). Getting a college degree is often a requirement for professional advancement, and older students are therefore more likely to take college seriously. In general, older students enroll in college with a definite course of study in mind. For older students, college is an extension of work rather than a place to discover what they want to be when they graduate. A study by psychologists R. Eric Landrum, Je T'aime Hood, and Jerry M. McAdams concluded, "Nontraditional students seemed to be more appreciative of their opportunities, as indicated by their higher enjoyment of school and appreciation of professors' efforts in the classroom" (744).

Argument in support of thesis

Older students also understand the actual benefits of doing well in school; as a result, they take school seriously. The older students I know rarely cut classes or put off studying. This is because older students are often balancing the demands of home and work and because they know how

Argument in support of thesis

Masterton 3

important it is to do well. The difficulties of juggling school, family, and work force older students to be disciplined and focused—especially concerning their schoolwork. This pays off: older students tend to spend more hours per week studying and tend to have a higher GPA than younger students do (Landrum, Hood, and McAdams 742-43).

Argument in support of thesis

My observations of older students have convinced me that many students would benefit from delaying entry into college. Eighteen-year-olds are often immature and inexperienced. They cannot be expected to have formulated definite goals or developed firm ideas about themselves or about the world in which they live. In contrast, older students have generally had a variety of real-life experiences. Most have worked for several years, many have started families. Their years in the "real world" have helped them become more focused and more responsible than they were when they graduated from high school. As a result, they are better prepared for college than they would have been when they were younger.

Refutation of opposing argument

Of course, postponing college for a few years is not for everyone. Certainly some teenagers have a definite sense of purpose and these individuals would benefit from an early college experience. Charles Woodward, a law librarian, went to college directly after high school, and for him the experience was positive. "I was serious about learning, and I loved my subject," he said. "I felt fortunate that I knew what I wanted from college and from life." Many younger students, however, are not like Woodward; they graduate from high school without any clear sense of purpose. For this reason, it makes sense for them to postpone college until they are mature enough to benefit from the experience.

Masterton 4

Granted, some older students have difficulties when they return to college. Because they have been out of school so long, these students may have problems studying and adapting to academic life. As I have seen, though, most of these problems disappear after a period of adjustment. Of course, it is true that many older students find it difficult to balance the needs of their family with college and to deal with the financial burden of tuition. However, this challenge is becoming easier with the growing number of online courses, the availability of distance education, and the introduction of governmental programs, such as educational tax credits (Agbo 164-65).

Refutation of opposing argument

All things considered, higher education is often wasted on the young, who are either too immature or too unfocused to take advantage of it. Taking a few years off between high school and college would give these students the time they need to make the most of a college education. The increasing number of older students returning to college seems to indicate that many students are taking this path. According to a US Department of Education report, *Digest of Education Statistics, 2007,* 31.3 percent of students enrolled in American colleges in 2005 were twenty-five years of age or older (273). Older students such as these have taken time off to serve in the military, to gain valuable work experience, or to raise a family. In short, they have taken the time to mature. By the time they get to college, these students have defined their goals and made a firm commitment to achieve them.

Conclusion

Concluding statement

Masterton 5

Works-cited list begins new page

Works Cited

Agbo, S. "The United States: Heterogeneity of the Student Body and the Meaning of 'Nontraditional' in U.S. Higher Education." *Higher Education and Lifelong Learners: International Perspectives on Change*. Ed. Hans G. Schuetze and Maria Slowey. London: Routledge, 2000. 149-69. Print.

Landrum, R. Eric, Je T'aime Hood, and Jerry M. McAdams. "Satisfaction with College by Traditional and Nontraditional College Students." *Psychological Reports* 89.3 (2001): 740-46. Print.

Palmer, Corburn. "Older Workers Head Back to College." *USA Today College*. USA Today, 27 Jan. 2012. Web. 6 Apr. 2012.

United States. Dept. of Educ. Office of Educ. Research and Improvement. Natl. Center for Educ. Statistics. *Digest of Education Statistics, 2007*. By Thomas D. Snyder, Sally A. Dillow, and Charlene M. Hoffman. 2008. *National Center for Education Statistics*. Web. 5 Apr. 2012.

---. ---. ---. ---. *Nontraditional Undergraduates*. By Susan Choy. 2002. *National Center for Education Statistics*. Web. 7 Apr. 2012.

Woodward, Charles B. Personal interview. 21 Mar. 2012.

Four sets of three unspaced hyphens indicate that *United States, Dept. of Educ., Office of Educ. Research and Improvement,* and *Natl. Center for Educ. Statistics* are repeated from the previous entry

CHECKLIST

## Writing Argumentative Essays

- ❑ Does your essay have a debatable thesis?
- ❑ Have you adequately defined the terms you use in your argument?
- ❑ Have you considered the opinions, attitudes, and values of your audience?
- ❑ Have you supported your points with evidence?
- ❑ Have you summarized and refuted opposing arguments?
- ❑ Have you established your credibility?
- ❑ Have you been fair?
- ❑ Have you constructed your arguments logically?
- ❑ Have you avoided logical fallacies?
- ❑ Have you provided your readers with enough background information?
- ❑ Have you presented your points clearly and organized them logically?
- ❑ Have you written an interesting introduction and a strong conclusion?
- ❑ Have you documented all information that is not your own?

Close-Up

## USING TRANSITIONS IN ARGUMENTATIVE ESSAYS

Argumentative essays should include transitional words and phrases to indicate which paragraphs are arguments in support of the thesis, which are refutations of arguments that oppose the thesis, and which are conclusions.

**Arguments in Support of Thesis**

accordingly
because
for example
for instance
generally
given
in general
since

**Refutations**

admittedly
although
certainly
despite
granted
in all fairness
naturally
nonetheless
of course

**Conclusions**

all things considered
as a result
in conclusion
in summary
therefore
thus

**EXERCISE 3**

Samantha Masterton deleted the following paragraph from her essay "The Returning Student: Older Is Definitely Better." Do you think Samantha was right to delete it? If it belongs in the essay, where would it go? Would it need any revision?

> The dedication of adult students is evident in the varied roles they must play. Many of the adults who return to school are seeking to increase their earning power. They have established themselves in the working world, only to find they cannot advance without more education or a graduate degree. The dual-income family structure enables many of these adults to return to school, but it is unrealistic for them to put their well-established lives on hold while they pursue their education. In addition to the rigors of college, older students are often juggling homes, families, and jobs. However, adult students make up in determination what they lack in time. In contrast, younger students often lack the essential motivation to succeed in school. Teenagers in college often have no clear idea of why they are there and, lacking this sense of purpose, may do poorly even though they have comparatively few outside distractions.

CHAPTER 11

# Using Visuals as Evidence

## Frequently Asked Questions



## 11a Using Visuals

See 6b2, 28d

**Visuals** can add a persuasive dimension to your argumentative essays. Because visual images can have such an immediate impact, they can make a good argumentative essay even more persuasive.

In this sense, visuals are another type of **evidence** that can support your thesis statement. For example, the addition of a photograph of a roadway work zone choked with traffic (Figure 11.1) could help support your assertion that your township should provide more effective work-zone strategies to reduce congestion. In addition, a graph or chart could reinforce the point that traffic congestion has gotten considerably worse over the past twenty years (Figure 11.2).

US Department of Transportation

FIGURE 11.1 Traffic jam in a roadway work zone.

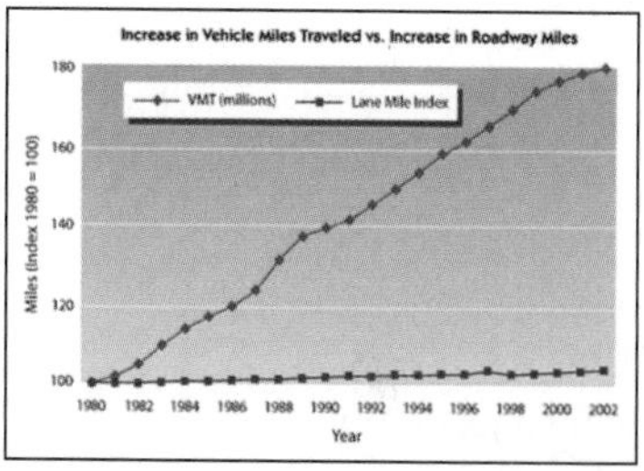


© Cengage Learning

FIGURE 11.2 Chart showing the increase in vehicle miles traveled versus the increase in roadway miles.

To persuade readers, visuals rely on elements such as images, written text, and color. Consider, for example, the editorial cartoon in Figure 11.3, which comments on the high cost of a college education and on students' difficulties in meeting these costs. The structure of the cartoon is simple and direct: graduating students are shown walking up a steep staircase that represents the challenges that they must meet in order to graduate. Once they receive their diplomas, however, they encounter two very large steps that represent the daunting challenges they face upon graduation.

© 2009 Jeff Parker, *Florida Today*/Cagle Cartoons, Inc.

FIGURE 11.3 Cartoon by Jeff Parker from *Florida Today*.

The use of written text is simple and direct. The person handing out diplomas congratulates the students and advises them to watch their step; the two large steps are labeled "cost of college" and "sour job market." (In addition, muted blue and grey colors reinforce the somber message of the cartoon.) Thus, with very few words, the visual forcefully makes the cartoonist's point: that in spite of the challenges graduating students have already overcome, they face ever greater—and perhaps insurmountable—challenges in the future. If you were writing an argument that took the same position, this cartoon could certainly help you make your point.

Remember, visuals should not be used simply for decoration or to break up the text of your essay. To be effective, they must contribute something useful to your discussion. Irrelevant or inappropriate visuals will not only distract readers, but also confuse them. Moreover, misleading or unfair visuals will damage your credibility, thereby undercutting your argument. For this reason, when you select visuals, keep in mind your purpose and audience and the tone you wish to establish. Just as you would with any other evidence in an argumentative essay, you should evaluate the visuals you use to make sure that they are not taken out of context and that they do not make their points unfairly.

CHECKLIST

**Selecting Visuals**

- ❑ What point does the visual make?
- ❑ Does the visual clearly support your argument?
- ❑ How do the various elements of the visual reinforce your argument?
- ❑ Is the visual aimed at a particular type of audience?
- ❑ Could the visual confuse or distract your readers in any way?
- ❑ Could the visual seem unfair to readers?

## EXERCISE 1

Look carefully at the political cartoon in Figure 11.4.

King Features Syndicate

FIGURE 11.4 Cartoon from Arizona *Tribune*.

Using the questions in the checklist above to guide you, determine whether the cartoon would provide useful evidence to support the following argumentative thesis statements:

- Because public opinion seems to be turning against the death penalty, it should be abolished as soon as possible.
- If the death penalty is abolished, violent criminals will be more likely to commit violent crimes.
- Because the death penalty seems to be carried out in such an arbitrary way, it should be abolished as soon as possible.
- Until an exhaustive study of the death penalty can be carried out, state governors should declare a moratorium on capital punishment.
- Although many consider the death penalty to be "cruel and unusual punishment," it is still appropriate for particularly heinous crimes.

### EXERCISE 2

Visit two Web sites that take opposing positions on a controversial topic. What visuals are used on each site, and how are they used to support each site's position?

## 11b Evaluating Visuals

Just as you have to think critically about the ideas you read, you also have to think critically about the visuals that accompany these texts.

Almost all photographs that appear in print have been altered in some way. The most common changes involve **cropping** (cutting or trimming) a picture to eliminate distracting background objects, **recoloring** a background to emphasize subjects in the foreground, and **altering the brightness and contrast** of an image to enhance its overall quality.

Problems arise, however, when an overly zealous editor, reporter, or photographer deliberately alters a photograph in order to further a particular point of view. Problems also occur when a researcher or reporter misrepresents experimental data in a graph or chart. Occasionally, this kind of error is caused by carelessness, but sometimes it is an intentional attempt to mislead or deceive.

### Close-Up ALTERING IMAGES

With the advent of desktop digital imaging programs, altering images is no longer something only professionals can do. Programs such as *Adobe Photoshop®* give users access to a wide range of digital image editing techniques.

*(continued)*

**ALTERING IMAGES** *(continued)*

Keep in mind, however, that you are only allowed to alter a person's **copyrighted work** under very specific circumstances that fall under the **fair use doctrine.** The fair use doctrine permits you to use copyrighted visual material (with proper acknowledgment) in a research paper, but it generally does not permit you to distort, misrepresent, or otherwise alter this material. If you use a copyrighted work in a publicly accessible document and you are unsure if it is an acceptable "fair use," you should obtain written permission from the copyright holder to use that work.

## EXERCISE 3

Look at the following photograph in its original and altered form (Figures 11.5 and 11.6). Compare the two representations of the scenery. How does the cropped image differ from the original image? Do you think the cropping misrepresents the photographer's original intention in any significant way?

**FIGURE 11.5** Waikiki Beach, OaHu, Hawaii.

**FIGURE 11.6** Cropped image.

## 1 Recognizing Doctored Photographs

A photograph is **doctored** when it has been intentionally falsified in some significant way. Consider the doctored photograph shown in Figure 11.7. The government of Iran posted this photograph on the Internet to announce the test of a new long-range missile. Within days, this photograph appeared in many major newspapers all around the world—including the *New York Times*, the *Chicago Tribune*, and the *Los Angeles Times*.

FIGURE 11.7 Doctored photograph of Iranian missiles.

Soon after its publication, however, people began to suspect that this image had been digitally manipulated. Eventually, the Iranian government took down the doctored picture and released the original photograph shown in Figure 11.8. Apparently, the original photo had been altered to cover up the fact that one of the rockets in the test had failed to launch.

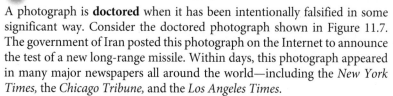

FIGURE 11.8 Undoctored photograph of Iranian missiles.

Unfortunately, incidents such as this one are becoming quite common. For example, after the 9/11 attacks, a picture circulated on the Internet that purportedly showed a Hungarian tourist on top of the World Trade towers just before a plane highjacked by terrorists hit. The background of the photo shows the plane flying toward the unsuspecting tourist. In fact, this picture was a fake, a composite of several pictures put together with *Photoshop*.

Another example of doctored photographs appeared after the Israeli air force bombed Beirut in 2006. Newspapers published a picture of the city covered by dense, billowing clouds of black smoke. The repeated patterns of smoke, however, caused some people to suspect that the picture had been altered to make the smoke (and the damage) seem heavier than it actually was. After some investigation, it was discovered that a Lebanese photographer had used *Photoshop*'s "clone" tool to alter the original photograph, adding both smoke and buildings to the picture, to make a political point.

With digital cameras and personal computers, as well as software such as *Photoshop*, it is easy to manipulate the images in photographs. As a result, you have to be very careful when using photographs as support for your arguments. If you suspect that a picture has been altered in some way, research it on the Internet and try to determine its validity, just as you would for a print source.

### EXERCISE 4

& Go to a Web site such as *Photo Tampering throughout History,* and look at several doctored images. Then, working with two or three other students, determine what the person who doctored the picture was trying to accomplish.

## 2 Recognizing Staged Photographs

Another questionable tactic is the use of **staged photographs,** visual images that purport to be spontaneous when they are actually posed. Even the hint of staging can discredit a visual image.

One of the most famous debates about staged photographs concerns the flag-raising photograph at the battle of Iwo Jima during World War II (see Figure 11.9). Photographer Joe Rosenthal's Pulitzer Prize–winning image is perhaps the most famous war photograph ever taken. When it appeared in newspapers on February 25, 1945, it immediately captured the attention of the American public, so much so that it became the model for the Marine Corps monument in Washington, DC. Almost immediately, however, people began to question whether the photograph was staged. Rosenthal did not help matters when he seemed to admit to a correspondent that it was. Later, however, he said that he had been referring to a posed shot he took the same day (see Figure 11.10), not the famous flag-raising picture. Historians now agree that the flag-raising picture was not staged, but the charge that it was haunted Rosenthal his entire life and is still repeated by some as if it were fact.

FIGURE 11.9 Soldiers raise a flag at the battle of Iwo Jima, February 1945.

FIGURE 11.10 Soldiers pose before the camera at Iwo Jima, February 1945.

## 3 Recognizing Misleading Charts and Graphs

Charts and graphs are effective tools for showing relationships among statistical data in science, business, and other disciplines, where they are often used as supporting evidence. However, charts can skew results and mislead readers when their components (titles, labels, and so on) are manipulated—for example, to show just partial or mislabeled data. Whenever you encounter a chart or graph in a document, examine it carefully to be certain that visual information is labeled clearly and accurately and that data increments are large enough to be significant.

Consider, for example, the potentially misleading nature of the two salary charts below. At first glance, it appears as if the salaries in the "Salaries Up!" chart (Figure 11.11) rose dramatically while those in the "Salaries Stable!" chart (Figure 11.12) remained almost the same. A closer analysis of the two charts, however, reveals that the salaries in the two charts are nearly identical across the six-year period. The data in the two charts seem to differ dramatically because of the way each chart displays salary increases: in the first chart, salary increases are given in $500 increments; in the second chart, salary increases are given in $5,000 increments. For this reason, a $1,000 increase in the first chart registers quite visibly, whereas in the second chart it hardly shows at all.

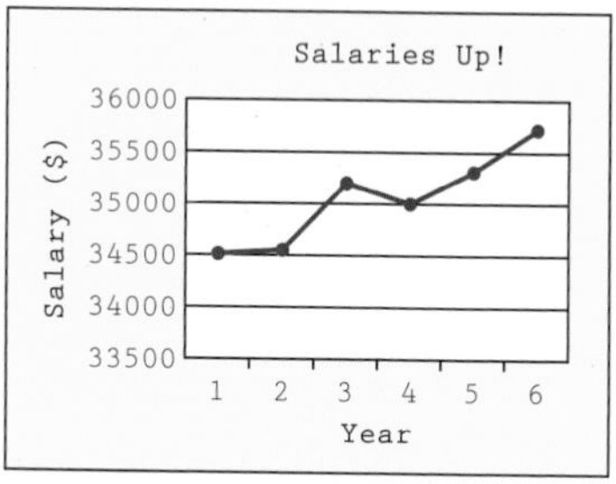


FIGURE 11.11 Salary chart 1 from the *CPIT Maths2Go* online tutorial, New Zealand, www.cpit.ac.nz/maths2go. Reprinted with permission.

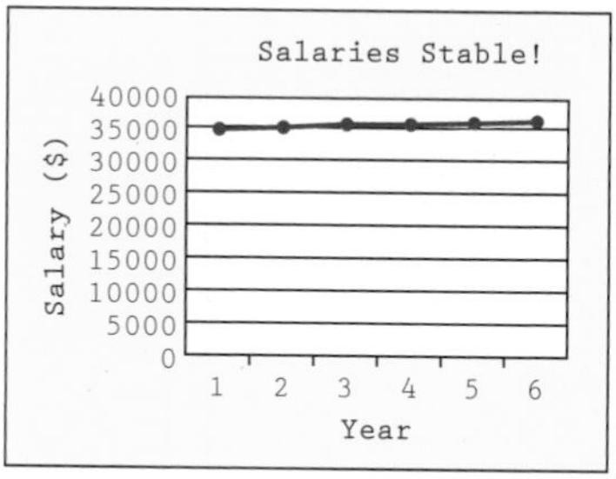


FIGURE 11.12 Salary chart 2 from the *CPIT Maths2Go* online tutorial. New Zealand, www.cpit.ac.nz/maths2go. Reprinted with permission.

## Close-Up INTEGRATING VISUALS INTO YOUR ESSAYS

To make sure that your visuals are smoothly integrated into your argumentative essays, follow these guidelines:

- Place your visual as close as possible to the point in the essay where you discuss it.
- Include a specific reference to the visual—for example, *See Figure 3* or *See the figure below*.
- Explain the visual in the text of your paper so readers will understand what they are supposed to learn from it.
- Make sure the visual is large enough so readers can see its individual elements and read any words or numbers.
- If you take a visual from a source, be sure to document it.

### EXERCISE 5

Find a chart or a graph (in a report or an advertisement, for instance) that you think is misleading. Identify the elements that seem to distort the data being portrayed.

PART 3

# Doing Research

CHAPTER 12

# Writing a Research Paper

## Frequently Asked Questions

**Research** is the systematic investigation of a topic outside your own knowledge and experience. However, doing research means more than just reading other people's ideas. When you undertake a research project, you become involved in a process that requires you to **think critically**: to evaluate and interpret the ideas explored in your sources and to develop ideas of your own.

See Ch. 8

Although the research process is much richer and more complex than the list of activities in the following box suggests, your research will be most efficient if you follow a systematic process.

**The Research Process**

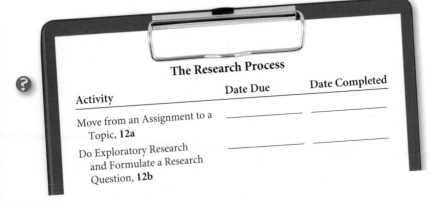

| Activity | Date Due | Date Completed |
|---|---|---|
| Move from an Assignment to a Topic, **12a** | ______ | ______ |
| Do Exploratory Research and Formulate a Research Question, **12b** | ______ | ______ |

| Activity | Date Due | Date Completed |
|---|---|---|
| Assemble a Working Bibliography, **12c** | ______ | ______ |
| Develop a Tentative Thesis, **12d** | ______ | ______ |
| Do Focused Research, **12e** | ______ | ______ |
| Take Notes, **12f** | ______ | ______ |
| Fine-Tune Your Thesis, **12g** | ______ | ______ |
| Outline Your Paper, **12h** | ______ | ______ |
| Draft Your Paper, **12i** | ______ | ______ |
| Revise Your Paper, **12j** | ______ | ______ |
| Prepare Your Final Draft, **12k** | ______ | ______ |

## 12a Moving from Assignment to Topic

### 1 Understanding Your Assignment

Every research paper begins with an assignment. Before you can find a direction for your research, you must be sure you understand the exact requirements of the specific assignment.

CHECKLIST

**Understanding Your Assignment**

Asking yourself the following questions will help you focus on your research project:

- ❑ Has your instructor provided a list of possible topics, or are you expected to select a topic on your own?
- ❑ Is your purpose to explain, to persuade, or to do something else?
- ❑ Is your audience your instructor? Your fellow students? Both? Someone else?
- ❑ Can you assume that your audience knows a lot (or just a little) about your topic?
- ❑ When is the completed research paper due?
- ❑ About how long should it be?
- ❑ Will you be given a specific research schedule to follow, or are you expected to set your own schedule?

*continued*

**Understanding Your Assignment *(continued)***

- ❑ Is peer review permitted? Is it encouraged? If so, at what stages of the writing process?
- ❑ Does your instructor expect you to prepare a formal outline?
- ❑ Are instructor–student conferences required? Are they encouraged?
- ❑ Will your instructor review notes, outlines, or drafts with you at regular intervals?
- ❑ Does your instructor require you to keep a research notebook?
- ❑ What manuscript guidelines and documentation style are you to follow?
- ❑ What help is available to you—from your instructor, from other students, from experts on your topic, from community resources, from your library staff?

In **Chapters 4–6** of this text, you followed the writing process of Rebecca James as she planned, drafted, and revised a short essay for her first-semester composition course. In her second-semester composition class, Rebecca was given the following assignment:

> Write a ten- to fifteen-page research paper that takes a position on any issue related to the Internet. Keep a research notebook that traces your progress.

Throughout this chapter, you will see examples of the work Rebecca did in response to this assignment.

## 2 Finding a Topic

Once you understand the requirements and scope of your assignment, you need to decide on a topic. In many cases, your instructor will help you choose a topic, either by providing a list of suitable topics or by suggesting a general subject area—for example, a famous trial, an event that happened on the day you were born, a problem on college campuses. Keep in mind, though, that you will still need to narrow your topic to one you can write about: one trial, one event, one problem.

If your instructor requires you to select a topic on your own, you should consider several possible topics and weigh both their suitability for research and your interest in them. You decide on a topic for your research paper in much the same way you decide on a topic for a short essay: you read, brainstorm, talk to people, and ask questions. Specifically, you talk to friends and family, coworkers, and perhaps your instructor; read magazines and newspapers; take stock of your interests; consider possible topics suggested by your other courses (historical events, scientific developments, and so on); talk to a reference librarian; and, of course, browse the Internet. (The

**subject guides** in your search engine and in your library's catalog can be particularly helpful as you look for a promising topic for your research or try to narrow a broad subject area.) See 13b2

CHECKLIST

### Choosing a Research Topic

As you look for a suitable research topic, keep the following guidelines in mind:

- ❑ **Are you genuinely interested in your research topic?** Remember that you will be deeply involved with the topic you select for weeks—perhaps even for an entire semester. If you lose interest in your topic, you are likely to see your research as a tedious chore rather than as an opportunity to discover new information, new associations, and new insights.
- ❑ **Is your topic suitable for research?** Topics limited to your personal experience and those based on value judgments are not suitable for research. For example, "Why Freud's work is superior to Jung's" might sound promising, but no amount of research can establish that one person's work is "better" than another's.
- ❑ **Are the boundaries of your research topic appropriate?** A research topic should be neither too broad nor too narrow. For example, "O.J. Simpson: Murderer or Scapegoat?" is far too broad a topic for a ten-page—or even a hundred-page—treatment, and "One piece of evidence that played a decisive role in the O.J. Simpson murder trial" would probably be too narrow for a ten-page research paper. But how one newspaper reported the trial or how a particular group of people (law-enforcement professionals or college students, for example) reacted to the verdict at the time would work well.

## 3 Starting a Research Notebook

Keeping a **research notebook,** a combination journal of your reactions and log of your progress, is an important part of the research process. A research notebook maps out your direction and keeps you on track; throughout the research process, it helps you define and redefine the boundaries of your assignment.

In your research notebook (which can be an actual notebook or a computer file), you can record lists of things to do, sources to check, leads to follow up on, appointments, possible community contacts, questions to which you would like to find answers, stray ideas, possible thesis statements or titles, and so on. (Be sure to date your entries and to check off and date work completed.)

As she began her research, Rebecca James set up a computer file in which she planned to keep all the electronic documents for her paper. In a *Word* document that she labeled "Research Notebook," she outlined her schedule and explored some preliminary ideas.

Following is an entry from Rebecca's research notebook in which she discusses how she chose a topic for her research paper.

### *Excerpt from Research Notebook*

Last semester, I wrote an essay for Professor Burks about using *Wikipedia* for college-level research. In class, we'd read *Wikipedia*'s policy statement, "Researching with *Wikipedia*," which helped me to understand *Wikipedia*'s specific limitations for college research. In that paper, I used a sample *Wikipedia* entry related to my accounting class to support my points about the site's strengths and weaknesses. For this research paper, which has to be about the Internet, I want to expand the paper I wrote for my first-semester composition course. This time, I want to talk more about the academic debate surrounding *Wikipedia*. (I asked Professor Burks if I could use this topic for her class this semester, and she said I could. In fact, she really liked the idea.)

### EXERCISE 1

Enter information about your assignment and your schedule in your research notebook. Next, using your instructor's guidelines for selecting a research topic, begin thinking of possible topics for your paper. Then, explore some preliminary ideas about these topics in your research notebook, and decide which one you want to write about.

## 12b Doing Exploratory Research and Formulating a Research Question

During **exploratory research,** you develop an overview of your topic, searching the Internet and perhaps also looking through general reference works such as encyclopedias, bibliographies, and specialized dictionaries (either in print or online). Your goal at this stage is to formulate a **research question** that you want your research paper to answer. A research question helps you to decide which sources to seek out, which to examine first, which to examine in depth, and which to skip entirely. (The answer to your research question will be your paper's **thesis statement**.)

See 12d

When developing a list of keywords to help you focus your online database searches, it is often helpful to see how others have framed questions about the same topic. To gather a list of words and phrases (paying particular attention to specific words that appear together), you can look at social-networking and collaboratively produced sites such as *Wikipedia* and *Twitter* and at social-bookmarking sites such as *Delicious* and *Diigo*. Searching for a broad term like *censorship* on these sites will help you see how it is used in a wide range of contexts.

Rebecca began her exploratory research with a preliminary search on *Google* (see Figure 12.1). When she entered the keywords *Wikipedia and academia,* they generated millions of hits, but she wasn't overwhelmed. She had learned in her library orientation that the first ten to twenty items would be most useful to her because the results of a *Google* search are listed in order of relevance to the topic, with the most relevant sites listed first. After a quick review of these items, she did a keyword search on *InfoTrac College Edition*, a database to which her library subscribed (see Figure 12.2).

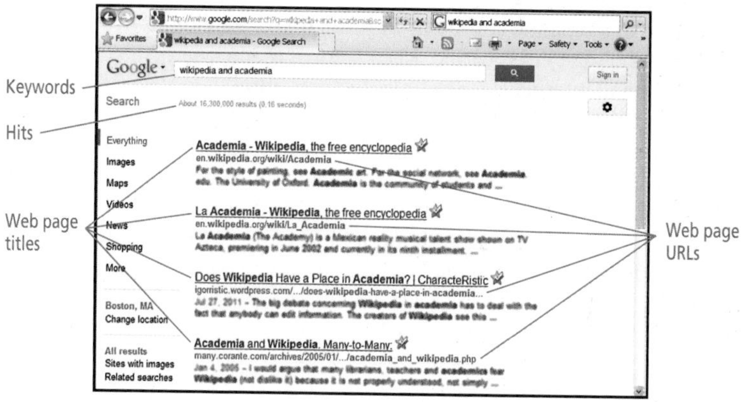


FIGURE 12.1 *Google* search engine. © Google, Inc.

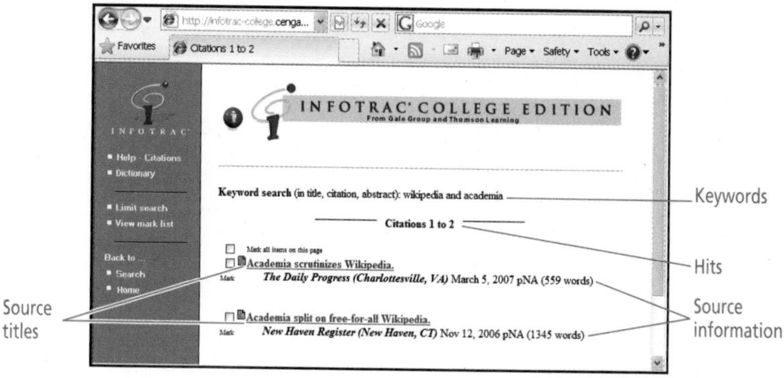


FIGURE 12.2 *InfoTrac College Edition*. © Cengage Learning.

When she finished her exploratory research, Rebecca was able to decide on a research question for her paper.

> **Research Question:** What effect has *Wikipedia* had on academic research?

## 12c Assembling a Working Bibliography

During your exploratory research, you begin to assemble a **working bibliography** of the sources you consult. This working bibliography will be the basis for your works-cited list, which will include all the sources you cite in your paper.

See 18a2

### 1 Recording Bibliographic Information

As you consider each potential source, record full and accurate bibliographic information in a separate computer file designated "Bibliography" (or, if you prefer, on individual index cards). Keep records of interviews (including telephone and email interviews), meetings, lectures, films, and electronic sources as well as articles and books. For each source, include basic identifying details—such as the date of an interview, the call number of a library book, the URL of an Internet source and the date you downloaded it (and perhaps the search engine you used to find it as well), or the author of an article accessed from a database. Also write up a brief evaluation that includes your comments about the kind of information the source contains, the amount of information offered, its relevance to your topic, and its limitations.

**Close-Up** ASSEMBLING A WORKING BIBLIOGRAPHY

As you record bibliographic information for your sources, include the following information:

- **Article** Author(s); title of article (in quotation marks); title of journal (italicized in computer file, underlined on index card); volume and issue numbers; date; inclusive page numbers; medium; date downloaded (if applicable); URL (if applicable); brief evaluation
- **Book** Author(s); title (italicized in computer file, underlined on index card); call number (for future reference); city of publication; publisher; date of publication; medium; brief evaluation

Figure 12.3 shows two of the sources Rebecca found as she put together her working bibliography.

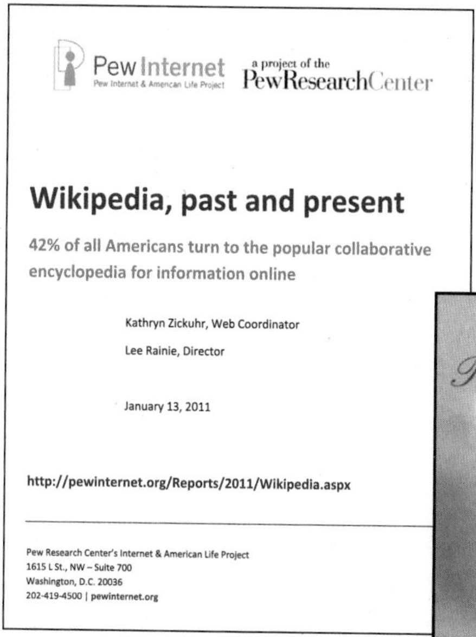

Pew Internet
Pew Internet & American Life Project
a project of the PewResearchCenter

**Wikipedia, past and present**

42% of all Americans turn to the popular collaborative encyclopedia for information online

Kathryn Zickuhr, Web Coordinator

Lee Rainie, Director

January 13, 2011

http://pewinternet.org/Reports/2011/Wikipedia.aspx

Pew Research Center's Internet & American Life Project
1615 L St., NW – Suite 700
Washington, D.C. 20036
202-419-4500 | pewinternet.org

*Putting the* LIBRARY *in* WIKIPEDIA

by Lauren Pressley
and Carolyn J. McCallum

Few online resources provoke so much controversy in the library community as Wikipedia. Some librarians hate it, arguing that since anyone can edit it, it can't be trusted. Others love it, because it is fast, easy to use, and a good starting point for research. With such a conflicted relationship, there's no clear answer as to where (or whether) Wikipedia belongs in libraries. We librarians are not sure what we should do with it.

In the March/April 2008 issue of *ONLINE*, William Badke wondered about, in his InfoLit Land column, "What to Do With Wikipedia" (www.infotoday.com/online/mar08/Badke.shtml). The column describes how this online encyclopedia is snubbed by academia but widely accepted by many others as a valid place to find information. He proposes that academia should participate in Wikipedia and makes several suggestions as to how professors and their students could improve Wikipedia by contributing new scholarly content, evaluating existing articles, and editing those that are less than scholarly. Badke's article fails to mention one academic group that could positively impact the content and scholarship in Wikipedia—librarians.

Based on work done at the University of Washington by Ann M. Lally and Carolyn E. Dunford, described in their May/June 2007 *D-Lib Magazine* article "Using Wikipedia to Extend Digital Collections" (www.dlib.org/dlib/may07/lally/05lally.html), librarians at Wake Forest University began experimenting with Wikipedia as a platform for sharing and expanding our web presence in relation to our digital collections. Although we agreed that there were many reasons to begin this project, we encountered a few roadblocks.

SEP | OCT 2008 ONLINE 39

FIGURE 12.3 Sources for working bibliography. Left: From "Wikipedia, Past and Present" by Kathryn Zickuhr and Lee Rainie, Pew Internet and American Life Project, copyright © 2011 by Pew Research Center. Reprinted with permission. Right: "Putting the Library in Wikipedia," by Lauren Pressley and Carolyn J. McCallum, *Online*, September/October 2008. Reprinted by permission.

Following are examples of records Rebecca kept for her working bibliography.

### *Information for Working Bibliography (in Computer File)*

| | |
|---|---|
| Author | Badke, William |
| Title | "What to Do with *Wikipedia*" |
| Publication information and medium | *Online* Mar.-Apr. 2008: 48-50. *Academic Search Elite*. Web. Accessed April 7, 2012. |
| URL | <http://www.infotoday.com/online/mar08/Badke.shtml> |
| Evaluation | Argues that it's important for the academic community to be involved in *Wikipedia*'s development. |

### *Information for Working Bibliography (on Index Card)*

Author — Bauerlein, Mark

Title — <u>The Dumbest Generation: How the Digital Age Stupefies Young Americans and Jeopardizes Our Future (or, Don't Trust Anyone Under 30)</u>

Publication information — NY: Penguin, 2008.

Medium — Print

Evaluation — Book is several years old, so information may be dated. Chapter 4, "Online Learning and Non-Learning," includes useful discussion of poor writing in <u>Wikipedia</u> articles.

As you go about collecting sources and building your working bibliography, be careful to evaluate the quality and relevance of all the materials you examine. Making informed choices early in the research process will save you a lot of time in the long run. (For guidelines on evaluating sources, **see Chapter 14.**)

## 2 Preparing an Annotated Bibliography

Some instructors require an **annotated bibliography,** a list of all your sources accompanied by a brief summary and evaluation of each source. The following is an excerpt from Rebecca's annotated bibliography.

### *Annotated Bibliography (Excerpt)*

Zickuhr, Kathryn, and Lee Rainie. "*Wikipedia,* Past and Present." *Pew Internet & American Life Project*. Pew Research Center, 13 Jan. 2011. Web. 7 Apr. 2012. <pewinternet.org/Reports/2011/Wikipedia.aspx>. This report discusses the kinds of people who most commonly consult *Wikipedia*, considering factors such as age, race and ethnicity, income level, and education level. It includes a table that gives percentages of *Wikipedia* users within various categories.

This report provides important data on *Wikipedia* users. It shows that the majority of American *Wikipedia* users are educated adults.

### EXERCISE 2

Do some exploratory research to find a research question for your paper, carefully evaluating the relevance and usefulness of each source. Then, compile a working bibliography. When you have finished, list five sources you decided *not* to use, and be prepared to explain why.

Then, reevaluate the usefulness of your sources and plan additional research if necessary. If your instructor requires you to do so, prepare an annotated bibliography.

## 12d Developing a Tentative Thesis

See 12g

Your **tentative thesis** is a preliminary statement of the main point you think your research will support. This statement, which you will eventually refine into your paper's **thesis statement,** should answer your research question.

As Rebecca James did exploratory research, she learned that some academics see *Wikipedia* as a challenge to their traditional notion of how to conduct research. She thought this would be a good angle to explore further, and she worded her tentative thesis to reflect this idea.

Rebecca's progress from assignment to tentative thesis appears below.

### *Tentative Thesis*

| Assignment | Topic | Research Question |
|---|---|---|
| Issue related to the Internet | Using *Wikipedia* for college-level research | What effect has *Wikipedia* had on academic research? |

**Tentative Thesis:** The debate surrounding *Wikipedia* has challenged those in the academic community, forcing them to confront the fact that college-level research has changed in recent years.

Because your tentative thesis suggests the specific direction your research will take as well as the scope and emphasis of your argument, it can help you generate a list of the main points you plan to develop in your paper. This list can help you to zero in on the specific areas to explore as you read and take notes.

Rebecca used her tentative thesis to help her generate the following list of points to explore further.

### *Points to Explore*

Tentative thesis: The debate surrounding *Wikipedia* has challenged those in the academic community, forcing them to confront the fact that college-level research has changed in recent years.

- Give background about *Wikipedia;* explain its benefits and drawbacks.
- Talk about who uses *Wikipedia* and for what purposes.
- Explain possible future enhancements to the site.
- Explain college professors' resistance to *Wikipedia*.
- Talk about efforts made by librarians and others to incorporate *Wikipedia* into academic research.

### EXERCISE 3

Following your instructor's guidelines, develop a tentative thesis for your research paper, and compile a list of the points you plan to develop.

## 12e Doing Focused Research

During exploratory research, you consult general reference works to get an overview of your topic. During **focused research,** you dig deeper into your topic: you consult periodical articles, books, and other sources (in print and online) to find the specific information—facts, examples, statistics, definitions, quotations—you need to support your points. Once you have decided on a tentative thesis and made a list of the points you plan to explore, you are ready to begin your focused research.

### 1 Reading Sources

As you look for information, try to explore as many sources as possible. It makes sense to examine more sources than you actually intend to use so that you can proceed even if some of your sources turn out to be biased, outdated, unreliable, superficial, or irrelevant—in other words, not suitable.

As you explore various sources, quickly evaluate each source's potential usefulness. For example, if your source is a journal article, read the abstract; if your source is a book, skim the table of contents and the index. Then, if an article or a section of a book seems useful, photocopy it for future reference. As you explore sources online, you may find that you have multiple windows open at once. If this is the case, be especially careful not to paste material you see onscreen directly into your paper. (This practice can lead to plagiarism.) Instead, send yourself links to any promising sources—or print the material out—so you can evaluate it further later on. (For information on evaluating electronic and print sources, **see Chapter 14.**)

See Ch. 17

### 2 Balancing Primary and Secondary Sources

See 13a

During your focused research, you will encounter both primary sources (original documents and observations) and secondary sources (interpretations of original documents and observations).

> **Primary Source:** United States Constitution, Amendment XIV (Ratified July 9, 1868). Section I.
>
> All persons born or naturalized in the United States, and subject to the jurisdiction thereof, are citizens of the United States and the state wherein they reside. No state shall make or enforce any law which shall abridge the privileges or immunities of citizens of the United States; nor shall any state deprive any person of life, liberty, or property, without the process of law; nor deny to any person within its jurisdiction the equal protection of the laws.

**Secondary Source:** Paula S. Rothenberg, *Racism and Sexism: An Integrated Study.*

Congress passed the Fourteenth Amendment . . . in July 1868. This amendment, which continues to play a major role in contemporary legal battles over discrimination, includes a number of important provisions. It explicitly extends citizenship to all those born or naturalized in the United States and guarantees all citizens due process and "equal protection" of the law.

For some research projects, primary sources are essential; however, most research projects in the humanities rely heavily on secondary sources, which provide scholars' insights and interpretations. Remember, though, that the further you get from the primary source, the more chances exist for inaccuracies caused by misinterpretations or distortions.

**Primary and Secondary Sources**

| Primary Source | Secondary Source |
|---|---|
| Novel, poem, play, film | Criticism |
| Diary, autobiography | Biography |
| Letter, historical document, speech, oral history | Historical analysis |
| Newspaper article | Editorial |
| Raw data from questionnaires or interviews | Social science article; case study |
| Observation/experiment | Scientific article |

## 12f Taking Notes

As you locate information, take notes to create a record of what you found and where you found it. These notes will help you to fine-tune your tentative thesis and decide how to develop your paper.

### 1 Recording Source Information

Each piece of information you record in your notes (whether **summarized**, **paraphrased**, or **quoted** from your sources) should be accompanied by a short descriptive heading that indicates its relevance to one of the points you will develop in your paper. Because you will use these headings to guide you as you organize your notes, you should make them as specific as possible. For example, labeling every note for a paper on *Wikipedia* ***Wikipedia*** or **Internet** will not be very helpful later on. More focused headings—for example, ***Wikipedia*'s popularity** or **college professors' objections**—will be much more useful.

See Ch. 15

Also include brief comments that make clear your reasons for recording the information. These comments (enclosed in brackets so you will know they are your own ideas, not those of your source) should establish the purpose of your note—what you think it can explain, support, clarify, describe, or contradict—and perhaps suggest its relationship to other notes or other sources. Any questions you have about the information or its source can also be included in your comment.

Finally, each note should fully and accurately identify the source of the information you are recording. You do not have to write out the complete citation, but you do have to include enough information to identify your source. For example, **Rainie and Tancer** would be enough to send you back to your working bibliography, where you would be able to find the complete documentation for the authors' article.

Following are examples of notes that Rebecca took.

### *Notes (in Computer File)*

Short heading — Source

*Growth potential* Spinellis and Louridas 71

Note (quotation) — "the apparently chaotic *Wikipedia* development process delivers growth at a sustainable rate."

Comment — **[Does this mean *Wikipedia* will eventually become a reliable research source?]**

---

*Unreliability—vandalism* Spinellis and Louridas 68

Note (paraphrase) — In 2006, 11% of *Wikipedia*'s articles were vandalized at least once, but only 0.13% of at-risk articles were locked.

Comment — **[Are *Wikipedia*'s current control measures sufficient to prevent vandalism?]**

---

*Benefit—stubs* Spinellis and Louridas 71

Note (summary) — "Stub" articles have the potential to become complete articles. Data show that, over time, the coverage of various topics in *Wikipedia* tends to even out.

Comment — **[Do the benefits of stubs outweigh their drawbacks?]**

### *Notes (on Index Card)*

Short heading — Source

Drawback— poor writing — Bauerlein 153-54

Note — Bauerlein notes that Wikipedia articles are written in a "flat, featureless, factual style." He goes on to say that "Wikipedia prose sets the standard for intellectual style. Students relying on Wikipedia alone, year in and year out, absorb the prose as proper knowledge discourse, and knowledge itself seems blank and uninspiring."

Comment — [Does Wikipedia's poor writing actually influence students' writing?]

Note: Various note-taking programs, such as *Evernote* or *Notely*, can help you to keep track of your notes.

## Close-Up TAKING NOTES

When you take notes, your goal is flexibility: you want to be able to arrange and rearrange information easily and efficiently as your paper takes shape.

**If you take notes at your computer,** type each individual note (accompanied by source information) under a specific heading rather than listing all information from a single source under the same heading, and be sure to divide notes from one another with extra space or horizontal lines, as illustrated on page 160. (As you revise, you can move notes around so notes on the same topic are grouped together.)

**If you take notes by hand,** use the time-tested index-card system, taking care to write on only one side of the card and to use a separate index card for each individual note rather than running several notes together on a single card. (Later, you can enter the information from these notes into your computer file.)

CHECKLIST

### Taking Notes

- ❑ **Identify the source of each piece of information,** including the page numbers for quotations from paginated sources.

*continued*

**Taking Notes *(continued)***

- ❑ **Include everything now that you will need later** to understand your note—names, dates, places, connections with other notes—and to remember why you recorded it.
- ❑ **Distinguish quotations from paraphrases and summaries and your own ideas from those of your sources.** If you copy a source's words, place them in quotation marks. (If you take notes by hand, circle the quotation marks; if you type your notes, put the quotation marks in boldface.) If you write down your own ideas, enclose them in brackets—and, if you are typing, boldface them as well. These techniques will help you avoid accidental plagiarism in your paper.
- ❑ **Put an author's ideas into your own words whenever possible,** summarizing and paraphrasing material as well as adding your own observations and analyses.
- ❑ **Copy quoted material accurately,** using the exact words, spelling, punctuation marks, and capitalization of the original.
- ❑ **Never paste information from a source directly into your paper.** This practice can lead to **plagiarism.**

See Ch. 17

## 2 Managing Photocopies and Downloaded Material

Much of the information you gather will be in the form of photocopies (of articles, book pages, and so on) and material downloaded (and perhaps printed out) from the Internet or from a library database. Learning to manage this source information efficiently will save you a lot of time.

First, do not use the ease of copying and downloading as an excuse to postpone decisions about the usefulness of your sources. After all, you can easily accumulate so many pages that it will be almost impossible for you to keep track of all your information.

Also keep in mind that photocopies and downloaded articles are just raw material, not information that you have already interpreted and evaluated. Making copies of sources is only the first step in the process of taking thorough, careful notes. You still have to evaluate, paraphrase, and summarize your sources' ideas and make connections among them.

Moreover, photocopies and downloaded material do not give you much flexibility. For example, a single page of text may include information that should be earmarked for several different sections of your paper. This lack of flexibility makes it almost impossible for you to arrange

**ESL TIP**

Taking notes in English (rather than in your native language) will make it easier for you to transfer the notes into a draft of your paper. However, you may find it faster and more effective to use your native language when writing your own comments about each note.

source material into any meaningful order. Just as you would with any source, you will have to take notes on the information you read. These notes will give you the flexibility you need to write your paper.

See Ch. 17

## Close-Up AVOIDING PLAGIARISM

To avoid the possibility of accidental plagiarism, be sure to keep all downloaded material in a separate file—not in your Notes file. After you read this material and decide how to use it, you can move the information you use into your Notes file (along with full source information).

### CHECKLIST
### Working with Photocopies and Downloaded Material

To get the most out of photocopies and material downloaded from the Internet, follow these guidelines:

- ❑ Record full and accurate source information, including the inclusive page numbers, electronic address (URL), and any other relevant information, on the first page of each copy.
- ❑ For printed material, clip or staple together consecutive pages of a single source.
- ❑ Do not photocopy or print out a source without reminding yourself—*in writing*—why you are doing so. In pencil or on removable self-stick notes, record your initial responses to the source's ideas, jot down cross-references to other works or notes, and highlight important sections.
- ❑ Photocopying can be time-consuming and expensive, so try to avoid copying material that is only marginally relevant to your paper.
- ❑ Keep photocopies and printouts in a separate file so you will be able to find them when you need them. Keep all electronic copies of source material together in one clearly labeled folder.

Note: Many **electronic tools** give you other options for saving and organizing your source material. For example, *Zotero* can help you manage citations and build your bibliography, and a wiki can help you work with others to upload material, organize it into folders, and record your evaluations of various sources. **See 17b** for information on how using such resources can help you to avoid unintentional plagiarism.

### EXERCISE 4

Begin focused research for your paper, reading sources carefully and taking notes as you read. Your notes should include paraphrase, summary, and your own observations and analysis as well as quotations.

## 12g Fine-Tuning Your Thesis

After you have finished your focused research and note-taking, you should be ready to refine your tentative thesis into a carefully worded statement that expresses a conclusion your research can support. This **thesis statement** should accurately convey the direction, emphasis, and scope of your paper. Also keep in mind that the revised thesis statement isn't just a reworded or more polished version of your tentative thesis. In many cases, it has a different focus or emphasis. Remember: if you revise the scope or emphasis of your essay, you will need to revise your thesis statement so that it is consistent with the rest of your paper.

See 5b–c

As Rebecca did her focused research and took notes, she began to see *Wikipedia* as an important influence on college research—not just an unwelcome upheaval but a challenge with a potentially positive outcome.

Compare Rebecca's tentative thesis with her final thesis statement.

### *Thesis Statement*

| Tentative Thesis | Thesis Statement |
|---|---|
| The debate surrounding *Wikipedia* has challenged those in the academic community, forcing them to confront the fact that college-level research has changed in recent years. | All in all, the debate over *Wikipedia* has been a positive development because it has led the academic community to confront the challenges of open, collaborative software on the Web. |

### EXERCISE 5

Read the following passages. Assume that you are writing a research paper on the influences that shaped young writers in the 1920s. What possible thesis statements could be supported by the information in these passages?

1. Yet in spite of their opportunities and their achievements the generation deserved for a long time the adjective ["lost"] that Gertrude Stein had applied to it. The reasons aren't hard to find. It was lost, first of all, because it was uprooted, schooled away and almost wrenched away

from its attachment to any region or tradition. It was lost because its training had prepared it for another world than existed after the war (and because the war prepared it only for travel and excitement). It was lost because it tried to live in exile. It was lost because it accepted no older guides to conduct and because it formed a false picture of society and the writer's place in it. The generation belonged to a period of transition from values already fixed to values that had to be created. (Malcolm Cowley, *Exile's Return*)

2. The 1920s were a time least likely to produce substantial support among intellectuals for any sound, rational, and logical program. Prewar stability and convention were condemned because all evidences of stability seemed illusory and artificial. The very lively and active interest in science was perhaps the decade's most substantial contribution to modern civilization. Yet in this case as well, achievement became a symbol of disorder and a source of disenchantment. (Frederick J. Hoffman, *The 20's*)
3. Societies do not give up old ideals and attitudes easily; the conflicts between the representatives of the older elements of traditional American culture and the prophets of the new day were at times as bitter as they were extensive. Such matters as religion, marriage, and moral standards as well as the issues over race, prohibition, and immigration were at the heart of the conflict. (Introduction to *The Twenties,* ed. George E. Mowry)

### EXERCISE 6

Review the tentative thesis you developed for Exercise 3. Carefully read all the notes you have collected during your focused research, and develop a thesis statement for your paper.

## 12h Constructing an Outline

Once you have a thesis statement, you are ready to make an outline to guide you as you draft your essay.

A formal outline is different from a list of the main points you tentatively plan to develop in your paper. A **formal outline**—which may be either a **topic outline** or a **sentence outline**—includes all the ideas you will develop in your paper, indicating both the exact order in which you will present these ideas and the relationship between main points and supporting details.

See 6c4

*Note:* The outline you construct at this stage is only a guide for you to follow as you draft your paper. During the revision process, you may want to construct another outline to check the logic of your paper's organization.

Rebecca James made the following topic outline to guide her as she wrote the first draft of her research paper.

### Formal (Topic) Outline

Thesis statement: All in all, the debate over *Wikipedia* has been a positive development because it has led the academic community to confront the challenges of open, collaborative software on the Web.

I. Definition of wiki and explanation of *Wikipedia*
  A. Fast and easy
  B. Range of topics
II. Introduction to *Wikipedia*'s drawbacks
  A. Warnings on "Researching with *Wikipedia*" page
  B. Criticisms in "Reliability of *Wikipedia*" article
  C. Criticisms by academics
    1. Villanova University
    2. Washington College
    3. Middlebury College history department
III. *Wikipedia*'s unreliability
  A. Lack of citations
  B. Factual inaccuracy and bias
  C. Vandalism
IV. *Wikipedia*'s poor writing
  A. *Wikipedia*'s coding system
  B. *Wikipedia*'s influence on students' writing (Bauerlein)
V. *Wikipedia*'s popularity and benefits
  A. Pew report statistic and table
  B. Comprehensive abstracts, links to other sources, and current and comprehensive bibliographies
VI. *Wikipedia*'s advantages over other online encyclopedias
  A. Very current information
  B. More coverage of popular culture topics
  C. "Stub" articles
VII. *Wikipedia*'s ongoing improvements
  A. Control measures
  B. Users as editors
  C. "Talk" page

VIII. *Wikipedia*'s content
    A. Spinellis and Louridas's view
    B. Graph showing *Wikipedia*'s topic coverage
IX. Academic community's reservations about *Wikipedia*
    A. Academics' failure to keep up with technology
    B. Academics' qualifications to improve *Wikipedia*
X. Librarians' efforts to use and improve *Wikipedia*
    A. Badke, Bennington, and Morrill's support of *Wikipedia*
    B. Pressley, McCallum, and other librarians' successes
XI. *Wikipedia* in the classroom
    A. *Wikipedia*'s "classroom coordination project" and "School and University Projects" page
    B. Collaborative and critical thinking assignments
XII. Academics' changing view of *Wikipedia*
    A. Academics' increasing acceptance
    B. Academics' increasing involvement
    C. Recent *Wikipedia* initiatives
        1. "Rate This Page"
        2. PPI

## EXERCISE 7

Carefully review your notes. Then, sort and group them into categories and construct a topic outline for your paper.

### Close-Up OUTLINING

Before you begin writing, create a separate file for each major section of your outline. Then, copy your notes into these files in the order in which you intend to use them.

Make sure that you label the files clearly for later reference. Each file name should include a reference to the class and assignment for which it was written. For instance, Rebecca's file for the section of her English 102 essay on *Wikipedia*'s growth potential is called "102 Wikipedia Growth Potential." The individual files relating to this paper are all collected in a folder titled "Eng 102 Wikipedia." By organizing your files in this way, you can print out each file as you need it and use it as a guide as you write.

## 12i Writing a Rough Draft

See 6a

When you are ready to write your **rough draft**, check to be sure you have arranged your notes in the order in which you intend to use them. Follow your outline as you write, using your notes as needed. As you draft, write notes to yourself in brackets, jotting down questions and identifying points that need further clarification and areas that need more development. You can also use your word processor's Comment tool to add notes.

As you move along, leave space for material you plan to add, and identify phrases or whole sections that you think you may later decide to move or delete. In other words, lay the groundwork for revision.

As your draft takes shape, be sure to supply transitions between sentences and paragraphs to indicate how your points are related. To make it easy for you to revise later on, you might want to triple-space your draft. Also be careful to copy source information fully and accurately in this and every subsequent draft, placing documentation as close as possible to the material it identifies.

### 1 Shaping the Parts of the Paper

Like any other essay, a research paper has an introduction, a body, and a conclusion. In your rough draft, as in your outline, you focus on the body of your paper. Don't spend too much time planning your introduction or conclusion at this stage; your ideas will change as you write, and you will need to revise and expand your opening and closing paragraphs later to reflect those changes.

***Introduction*** In your **introduction,** you identify your topic and establish how you will approach it, perhaps presenting an overview of the problem you will discuss or summarizing research already done on your topic. Your **introduction** also includes your thesis statement, which presents the position you will support in the rest of the paper.

See 7e2

***Body*** As you draft the **body** of your paper, you lead readers through your discussion with clearly worded **topic sentences** that correspond to the divisions of your outline.

See 7a1

> Without a professional editorial board to oversee its development, *Wikipedia* has several shortcomings that ultimately limit its trustworthiness as a research source.

See 28b

You can also use **headings** if they are a convention of the discipline in which you are writing.

> *Wikipedia*'s Advantages
>
> *Wikipedia* has advantages over other, professionally edited online encyclopedias.

See 7d

Use different **patterns of development** to shape the individual sections of your paper, and be sure to connect your sentences and paragraphs with clear transitions. If necessary, connect two sections of your paper with a transitional paragraph that shows their relationship.

See 7e1

***Conclusion*** In the **conclusion** of your research paper, you may want to restate your thesis. This is especially important in a long paper because by the time your readers get to the end, they may have lost sight of your paper's main idea. Your conclusion can also include a summary of your key points, a call for action, or perhaps an apt quotation. (Remember, however, that in your rough draft, your concluding paragraph is usually very brief.)

See 7e3

## 2 Working Source Material into Your Paper

In the body of your paper, you evaluate and interpret your sources, comparing different ideas and assessing various points of view. As a writer, your job is to draw your own conclusions, synthesizing information from various sources into a paper that coherently and forcefully presents your own original viewpoint.

See Ch. 16

To turn your notes into well-developed paragraphs, begin with a topic sentence that states the point you want the source to support. Next, introduce the source with an **identifying tag,** followed by the information in the form of summary, paraphrase, or quotation. Then, in a sentence or two, interpret the source material for your readers, explaining its significance to the point you want to make. (Don't forget to include parenthetical documentation.)

See Ch. 15

See 18a1

Be sure to integrate source material smoothly into your paper, clearly and accurately identifying the relationships among various sources (and between those sources' ideas and your own). Your goal here is to interpret your source's ideas for readers and to give these ideas the emphasis you need to support your own points. If two sources present conflicting interpretations, you should be especially careful to use precise language and accurate transitions to make the contrast apparent (for instance, **Although some academics believe that *Wikipedia* should not be a part of college-level research, Pressley and McCallum argue . . .**). When two sources agree, you should make this clear (for example, **Like Badke, Bennington claims . . .** or **Spinellis and Louridas's findings support Pressley and McCallum's point**). Such phrasing will provide a context for your own comments and conclusions. If different sources present complementary information about a subject, blend details from the sources carefully, keeping track of which details come from which source.

See 15d

## 3 Integrating Visuals

Photographs, diagrams, graphs, and other visuals can be very useful in your research paper because they can provide additional support for the points you make. You can create a visual on your own (for example, by taking a photograph or creating a bar graph). You can also scan an appropriate visual from a book or magazine or access an image database. When you add

See Ch. 3, 28d

a visual to a paper, be sure to provide a caption that identifies the name of the person who created it. This will enable readers to find full source information in your works-cited list.

When Rebecca searched *Google*'s image database, she found a visual to include in her paper (see Figure 12.4).

FIGURE 12.4 Image database search results. © Google, Inc.

## EXERCISE 8

Write a rough draft of your paper, being careful to incorporate source material and visuals smoothly and to record source information accurately. Begin by drafting the section for which you have the most material.

## 12j Revising Your Drafts

As you review your drafts, you follow the revision procedures that apply to any paper (**see 6b–c**). In addition, you should review the questions in the checklist on page 173, which apply specifically to research papers.

### 1 Instructor's Comments

Your instructor's suggestions for revisions can come in a conference or in handwritten comments on your paper. Your instructor can also use a word processor's Comment tool to make comments electronically on a draft that you send by email. When you revise, you can incorporate these suggestions into your paper, as Rebecca did.

### Draft with Instructor's Comments (Excerpt)

Emory University English professor Mark Bauerlein asserts that *Wikipedia* articles are written in a "flat, featureless, factual style" (153). Even though *Wikipedia* has instituted a coding system in which it labels the shortcomings of its less-developed articles, a warning about an article's poor writing style is likely to go unnoticed by the typical user.

Comment [JB1]: You need a transition sentence before this one to show that this ¶ is about a new idea. See 7b2.

Comment [JB2]: Wordy. See 39a.

### Revision (Incorporating Instructor's Suggestions)

Because they can be edited by anyone, *Wikipedia* articles are often poorly written. Emory University English professor Mark Bauerlein asserts that *Wikipedia* articles are written in a "flat, featureless, factual style" (153). Even though *Wikipedia* has instituted a coding system to label the shortcomings of its less-developed articles, a warning about an article's poor writing style is likely to go unnoticed by the typical user.

## 2 Peer Review

Feedback you get from **peer review**—other students' comments, handwritten or electronic—can also help you revise. As you incorporate your classmates' suggestions, as well as your own changes and any suggested by your instructor, you can use *Microsoft Word*'s Track Changes tool to help you keep track of the revisions you make on your draft.

& See 6c2

Following are two versions of an excerpt from Rebecca's paper. The first version includes comments (inserted with *Microsoft Word*'s Comment tool) from three peer reviewers. The second uses the Track Changes tool to show the revisions Rebecca made in response to these comments.

### Draft with Peer Reviewers' Comments (Excerpt)

Because users can update articles in real time from any location, *Wikipedia* offers up-to-the-minute coverage of political and cultural events as well as timely information on popular culture topics that receive little or no attention in other reference sources. In addition, because *Wikipedia* has such a broad user

Comment [RS1]: I think you need a better transition here.

base, more topics are covered in *Wikipedia* than in other online resources. Even when there is little information on a particular topic, *Wikipedia* allows users to create "stub" articles, which provide minimal information that users can expand over time. Thus, *Wikipedia* can be a valuable first step in finding reliable research sources.

Comment [TG2]: I think some examples here would really help.

Comment [DL3]: I agree. Maybe talk about a useful *Wikipedia* article you found recently.

Comment [RS4]: Why?

### *Revision with Track Changes*

*Wikipedia* has advantages over other online encyclopedias. Because users can update articles in real time from any location, *Wikipedia* offers up-to-the-minute coverage of political and cultural events as well as timely information on popular culture topics that receive little or no attention in other reference sources. In addition, because *Wikipedia* has such a broad user base, more topics are covered in *Wikipedia* than in other online resources. For example, a student researching the history of video gaming would find *Wikipedia*'s "Wii" article, with its numerous pages of information and nearly two hundred references, to be a valuable resource. In contrast, the "Nintendo Wii" article in the professionally edited *Encyclopaedia Britannica Online* consists of a few paragraphs and a handful of external resources. Even when there is little information on a particular topic, *Wikipedia* allows users to create "stub" articles, which provide minimal information that users can expand over time. Thus, by offering immediate access to information on relatively obscure topics, *Wikipedia* can be a valuable first step in finding reliable research sources on such topics.

## 3 Outlining

See 6c4, 12h

As you move closer to a final draft, you can make a formal outline of your paper-in-progress to check the logic of its organization and the relationships among sections. An excerpt from the **sentence outline** Rebecca constructed to check the structure of her paper is shown below.

### *Sentence Outline (Excerpt)*

Thesis statement: All in all, the debate over *Wikipedia* has been a positive development because it has led the academic community to confront the challenges of open, collaborative software on the Web.

I. *Wikipedia* is the most popular wiki.
  A. Users can edit existing articles and add new articles using *Wikipedia*'s editing tools.
  B. *Wikipedia* has grown into a huge database.
II. *Wikipedia* has several shortcomings that limit its trustworthiness.
  A. *Wikipedia*'s "Researching with *Wikipedia*" page acknowledges existing problems.
  B. *Wikipedia*'s "Reliability of *Wikipedia*" page presents criticisms.
  C. Academics have objections.
III. *Wikipedia* is not always reliable or accurate.
  A. Many *Wikipedia* articles do not include citations.
  B. *Wikipedia* articles can be inaccurate or biased.
  C. *Wikipedia* articles can be targets for vandalism.

CHECKLIST

### Revising a Research Paper

As you revise your research paper, consider the following questions:

- ❑ Should you do more research to find support for certain points?
- ❑ Do you need to reorder the major sections of your paper?
- ❑ Should you rearrange the order in which you present your points within sections?
- ❑ Do you need to add section headings? transitional paragraphs?
- ❑ Have you integrated source material smoothly into your paper? See 15d
- ❑ Have you chosen visuals carefully and integrated them smoothly into your paper?
- ❑ Are quotations blended with paraphrase, summary, and your own observations and reactions?
- ❑ Have you avoided plagiarism by carefully documenting all borrowed ideas? See Ch. 17
- ❑ Have you analyzed and interpreted the ideas of others rather than simply stringing those ideas together?
- ❑ Do your own ideas—not those of your sources—define the focus of your discussion?

*Note:* You will probably take your paper through several drafts, changing different parts of it each time or working on one part over and over again. After revising each draft thoroughly, print out a corrected version, and label it *First Draft, Second Draft*, and so on. Then, make additional corrections by hand on that draft before typing in your changes to create the next draft. Be sure to save and clearly label every electronic draft of your paper so you can go back to a previous draft if necessary.

**Close-Up PREPARING YOUR WORKS-CITED LIST**

When you finish revising your paper, copy the file that contains your working bibliography and insert it at the end of your paper. Keep the original file for your working bibliography as a backup in case any data is lost in the process. Delete any irrelevant entries, and then create your works-cited list. (Make sure the format of the entries in your works-cited list conforms to the documentation style you are using.)

If you save multiple drafts of your works-cited list, be sure to name each file with the date or some other label so that it is readily identifiable. Keep all files pertaining to a single project in a folder dedicated to that paper or assignment.

*Note:* You can use a citation software program, such as *Zotero, CiteMe, RefWorks, EndNote*, or *EasyBib*, to create your bibliography and to make sure that all the sources you used—and only those sources—appear in your works-cited list.

**EXERCISE 9**

Following the guidelines in **12j** and **6c**, revise your research paper until you are ready to prepare your final draft.

## 12k Preparing a Final Draft

See 6d

Before you print out the final version of your paper, edit and proofread hard copy of both your paper and your works-cited list. Next, consider (or reconsider) your paper's **title.** It should be descriptive enough to tell your readers what your paper is about, and it should create interest in your subject. Your title should also be consistent with the purpose and tone of your paper. (You would hardly want a humorous title for a paper about famine in sub-Saharan Africa or inequities in the American education system.) Finally, your title should be engaging and to the point—perhaps even provocative. Often, a quotation from one of your sources will suggest a likely title.

See 1a, 1c

When you are satisfied with your title, read your paper one last time, proofreading for grammar, spelling, or typing errors you may have missed. Pay particular attention to parenthetical documentation and works-cited entries. (Remember that every error undermines your credibility.) Once you are satisfied that your paper is as accurate as you can make it, print out your final draft. Then, fasten the pages with a paper clip (do not staple the pages or fold the corners together), and hand it in. Some instructors will allow you to email your final draft. (For the final draft of Rebecca's research paper, along with her works-cited list, **see 18c.**)

**EXERCISE 10**

Prepare a works-cited list for your research paper. Then, edit your paper and your works-cited list, decide on a title, and check to make sure your paper follows the format your instructor requires. Proofread your final draft carefully before you hand it in.

CHAPTER 13

# Finding Information

## Frequently Asked Questions



## 13a Finding Information in the Library

If you are like most students, you go to the Internet when you begin a research project. Certainly, the Internet enables you to quickly access a tremendous amount of information. When it comes to finding trustworthy, high-quality, and authoritative sources, however, nothing beats your college library. A modern college library offers resources that you cannot find anywhere else—even on the Internet. In the long run, you will save a good deal of time and effort as well as gain a deeper understanding of your topic if you begin your research by consulting your library's print and electronic resources.

**Close-Up** WHY USE THE LIBRARY?

Although the Internet can help you get an overview of your subject—and can be a useful resource as you brainstorm and look for a topic—once you start looking for sources for your paper, your college library is the best place to go:

- Many important publications are available only in print or through the library's databases.
- The information in your college library is cataloged and classified.
- Because the library's databases list only published sources, the information you access will always be available, unlike the information on the Internet.
- Because librarians screen the resources in your college library, these resources are likely to meet academic standards of reliability. (Even so, you still have to evaluate any information before you use it in a paper.)
- Bibliographic information for the documents in your college library is easy to determine, unlike that of documents on the Internet.
- The library staff is available to answer your questions and to help you find material.

See 14a

*Note:* When looking for information, be sure you understand the difference between primary and secondary sources. **Primary sources** are original documents: letters, diaries, speeches, government records, contemporary newspaper accounts, photographs, statistics, research results, original literary works, and interviews. **Secondary sources** are interpretations of primary sources: textbooks, literary criticism, encyclopedia and journal articles, and so on.

See 12e2

## 1 Searching the Library's Online Catalog

The best way to get started with your research is to visit your college library's **Web site.** The Web site's home page is a gateway to a vast amount of information—for example, the library's catalog, the databases the library makes available, special library services, and general information about the library. Many libraries also offer online help to students—for example, study guides on a wide variety of topics and email answers to questions. Figure 13.1 shows the home page of a library's Web site.

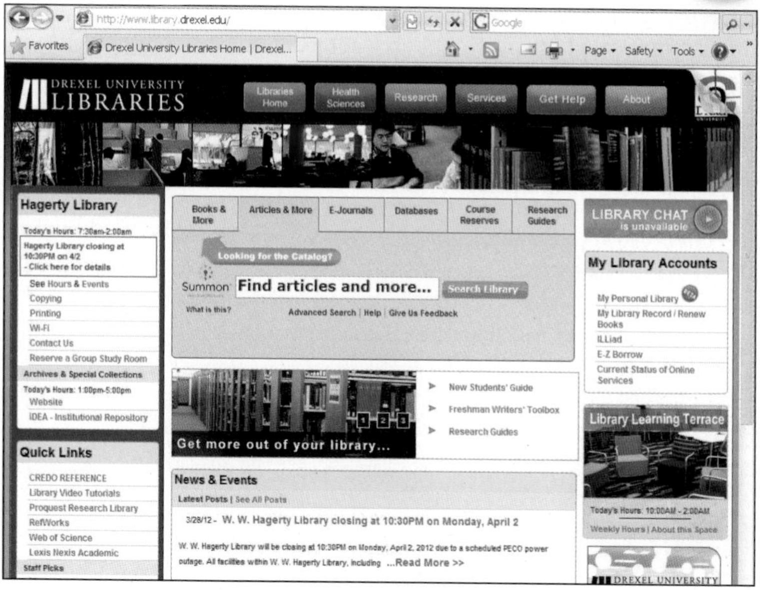


FIGURE 13.1 Home page of an academic library's Web site. © Drexel University.

Your next step is to search the library's **online catalog,** a comprehensive database that lists all the material held in the library's collections. When you search the online catalog for information, you may do either a *keyword search* or a *subject search.*

***Doing a Keyword Search*** When you do a **keyword search,** you enter into the online catalog's Search box a word (or words) associated with your topic. The computer then displays a list of entries (called **hits**) that contain these words. The more precise your keywords, the more specific and useful the information you retrieve will be. For example, *Civil War* will yield many thousands of hits; *The Wilderness Campaign* will yield far fewer.

Because vague or inaccurate keyword searching can yield thousands of irrelevant hits, you need to focus your search by using **search operators,** words or symbols that narrow (or broaden) your query. One way to focus your search is to put quotation marks around your keywords. By doing this, you limit your search to entries containing this exact phrase (for example, "*climate change*"). An asterisk at the end of the root word enables you to retrieve the singular, plural, and other forms of the word (for example, *parent** will retrieve *parent*, *parents*, and *parenting*). Finally, a question mark tells the search engine to look for words with one varying character (for example, *?at* will retrieve *hat*, *cat*, *bat*, *mat*, *fat*, and so on).

Another way to limit (or broaden) your search is to carry out a **Boolean search,** a procedure named after George Boole, a nineteenth-century British logician and mathematician. Boolean searches combine keywords with the search operators *and*, *or*, or *not*. Some library catalogs enable you to use a plus or minus sign to focus your search and to eliminate irrelevant entries.

CHECKLIST

### Using Search Operators

When you do a keyword search, follow these guidelines:

- ❑ Use **quotation marks** to search for a specific phrase: *"Baltimore Economy."*
- ❑ Use an **asterisk** after a word to retrieve a root word with any ending: *photo** will yield *photograph*, *photographer*, *photojournalist*, *photoactive*, and so on.
- ❑ Use a **question mark** to replace a single character inside or at the end of a word: *wom?n* will yield *woman* and *women*.
- ❑ Use **and** to search for sites that contain both terms: *Baltimore* and *Economy*.
- ❑ Use **or** to search for sites that contain either term: *Baltimore* or *Philadelphia*.
- ❑ Use **not** to exclude the term that comes after the *not: Baltimore* and *Economy* not *Agriculture*.

***Doing a Subject Search*** When you do a **subject search,** you enter a subject heading into the online catalog's search box. The resources in an academic library are classified under specific subject headings. Many online catalogs list subject headings to help you identify the exact words that you need for your search. One good strategy is to start your research with a keyword search, identify some appropriate titles, and then use the subject headings assigned to these titles to find more material. (The subject headings in your library's catalog can also help you to narrow your search and to find a topic.) Figure 13.2 shows the results of a subject search in a university library's online catalog.

Close-Up **KEYWORD SEARCHING VERSUS SUBJECT SEARCHING**

When deciding whether to do a keyword search or a subject search, consider the strengths and weaknesses of each method.

| Keyword Searching | Subject Searching |
|---|---|
| • Searches many subject areas | • Searches only a specific subject area |
| • Can use any significant word or phrase | • Can use only specific subject headings |
| • Retrieves a large number of items | • Retrieves a smaller number of items |
| • May retrieve many irrelevant items | • Retrieves few irrelevant items |

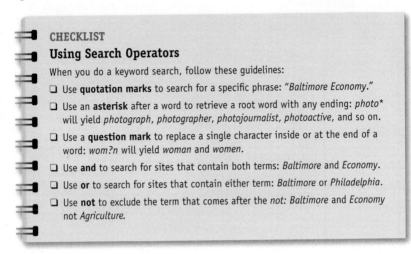

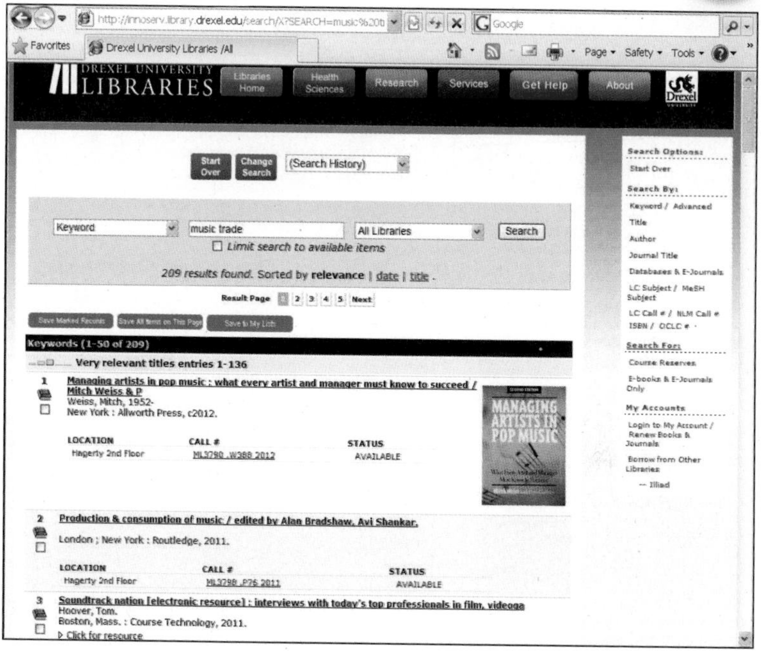


FIGURE 13.2 Online catalog search results for the subject heading *Music Trade*. © Drexel University.

**Note:** *WorldCat* and *WorldCat Local* are "super" catalogs of millions of items. If your college library provides access to these resources, you can locate books, DVDs, music, photographs, and specialized databases from thousands of participating libraries around the world and in your community. Check with your reference librarian for information about *WorldCat* and *WorldCat Local*.

## 2 Searching the Library's Databases

Through your college library's Web site, you can access a variety of online databases to which the library subscribes. **Online databases** are collections of digital information—such as newspaper, magazine, and journal articles—arranged for easy access and retrieval. (You search these databases the same way you search the library's online catalog—by doing a **keyword search** or a **subject search**.) See 13a1

One of the first things you should do is find out which databases your library subscribes to. You can usually access a list of these databases through the library's Web site, and if necessary, you can ask a reference librarian for more information. Figure 13.3 shows a partial list of databases to which one library subscribes.

College libraries subscribe to information service companies, such as Gale Cengage Learning, which provide access to hundreds of databases

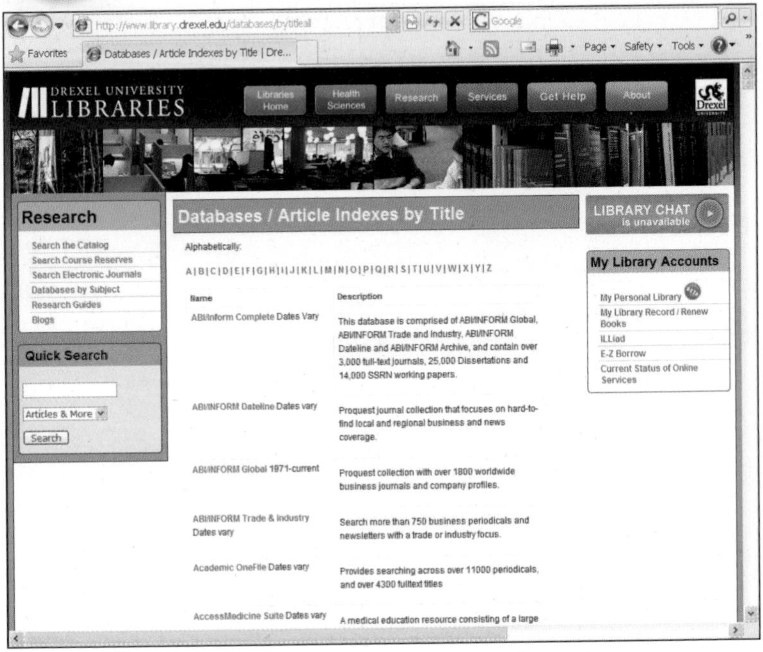


FIGURE 13.3 Excerpt from list of databases to which one academic library subscribes. © Drexel University.

not available for free on the Internet. These databases enable you to access current information from scholarly journals, abstracts, books, reports, case studies, government documents, magazines, and newspapers. Some library databases cover many subject areas (*Expanded Academic ASAP Plus* or *LexisNexis Academic*, for example); others cover a single subject area in great detail (*PsycINFO* or *Sociological Abstracts*, for example).

Assuming that your library offers a variety of databases, how do you know which ones will be best for your research? First, you should determine the level of the periodical articles listed in the database. A **periodical** is a scholarly journal, magazine, newspaper, or other publication that appears at regular intervals (weekly, monthly, or quarterly, for example). **Scholarly journals** are often the most reliable sources you can find on a subject. They contain articles written by experts in a field, and because journals focus on a particular subject area, they usually provide in-depth analysis. However, because journal articles are aimed at experts, they can be difficult for general readers to understand. **Popular periodicals** are magazines and newspapers that publish articles aimed at general readers. These periodicals are more accessible, but they are less reliable than those in scholarly journals because they can vary greatly in quality. Some articles might conform to academic standards of reliability, but others may be totally unsuitable as sources. (**See 14a** for a discussion of scholarly versus popular publications.)

Next, you should look for a database that is suitable for your topic. Most libraries list databases alphabetically by title or arrange them by subject area. Some offer online study guides that list databases (as well as other resources) that are appropriate for research in a given subject area. If you know what database you are looking for, you can find it in the alphabetical listing. If you don't, go to the subject list and locate your general subject area—*History*, *Nursing*, or *Linguistics*, for example. Then, look at the databases that are listed under this heading.

You can begin with a multisubject **general database** that includes full-text articles. Then, you can move on to more **specialized databases** that examine your specific subject in detail. The specialized databases are more likely to include scholarly and professional sources as well as **abstracts** (short summaries) that can help you determine the usefulness of a source. Figure 13.4 shows a printout from a library's database.

Date | Volume number | Issue number | First page of article | Total number of pages

**Title:** The Supply Side of the Digital Divide: Is There Equal Availability in the Broadband Internet Access Market?

**Periodical:** *Economic Inquiry,* April 2003 v41 i2 p346(18).

**Author:** James E. Prieger

**Author's Abstract:** The newest dimension of the digital divide is access to broadband (high-speed) Internet service. Using comprehensive US data covering all forms of access technology (chiefly DSL and cable modem), I look for evidence of unequal broadband availability in areas with high concentrations of poor, minority, or rural households. . . .

**Subjects:** Digital Divide (Technology) = Demographic Aspects

Internet = Usage

**Features:** tables; figures

FIGURE 13.4 Library subscription database printout. "The Supply Side of the Digital Divide: Is There Equal Availability in the Broadband Internet Access Market?" by James E. Prieger from *Economic Inquiry*, April 2003, Vol. 41, No. 2, p. 346.

Note: Remember that an abstract, such as the one shown in Figure 13.4, is not an acceptable source. However, reading an abstract can help you decide if you want to read the full article it summarizes.

## Close-Up FREQUENTLY USED GENERAL DATABASES

| Database | Description |
|---|---|
| *Academic OneFile* | Articles from journals and reference sources in a number of disciplines |
| *Credo Reference* | A database of over two hundred reference books |
| *Expanded Academic Plus* | Articles from journals in the humanities, social sciences, and the natural and applied sciences |
| *FirstSearch* | Full-text articles from many popular and scholarly periodicals |
| *LexisNexis Academic* | Full-text articles from national news publications as well as legal and business publications |
| *Opposing Viewpoints Resource Center* | A library of debates on current topics |
| *ProQuest Research Library* | An index of journal articles in various disciplines, many full text |
| *Readers' Guide Full-Text Mega Edition* | Full-text articles from over two hundred journals from as far back as 1994 and popular periodicals from as far back as 1983 |

Before using a database, you should survey it to get a general sense of how useful it will be for your research and what it will add to your view of your topic. Check to make sure that any database you select includes the resources you need. A database usually includes a description of its scope, resources, and range of dates. Some enable you to limit your search to articles in scholarly journals or to articles in magazines and newspapers aimed at general readers. Finally, keep in mind that in order to get a fuller understanding of your topic, it is often best to look at it from more than one perspective—for example, by searching more than one database.

### 3 Surveying Specialized Databases

Academic libraries usually subscribe to specialized databases, such as those listed on pages 183–185. These databases give you access to journal articles as well as other resources that you can use in your research. Be sure to consult your library's Web site or a reference librarian to see which specialized databases are available to you.

### Specialized Databases

HUMANITIES

| Database | Description |
|---|---|
| **Art** | |
| *Art Full Text* | A bibliographic database that includes abstracts |
| **Communication** | |
| *Communication & Mass Media Complete* | Index and abstracts for more than four hundred journals and coverage of two hundred more |
| **History** | |
| *History Reference Center* | Full-text articles and other resources for the study of history |
| **Literature** | |
| *MLA International Bibliography* | An index for books, articles, and Web sites focusing on literature |
| *Gale Literature Criticism Online* | Full-text articles on literary criticism and analysis |
| **Music** | |
| *International Index to Music Periodicals Full Text* | Full-text journals covering a wide body of research |
| **Performing Arts** | |
| *International Bibliography of Theater and Dance Full Text* | An annotated collection of over sixty thousand resources on all aspects of theater and performance |
| **Philosophy** | |
| *Philosopher's Index* | Index and abstracts from over five hundred fifty journals from forty countries |

SOCIAL SCIENCES

| Database | Description |
|---|---|
| **Anthropology** | |
| *Anthropology Plus* | The most comprehensive database of anthropological resources |
| **Business** | |
| *ABI/INFORM Global* | A ProQuest collection of over eighteen hundred journals and company profiles |

*(continued)*

**Specialized Databases** ***(continued)***

| Database | Description |
| --- | --- |
| *Business Source Premier* | Indexes more than seventy-eight hundred publications |
| **Economics** | |
| *EconLit* | Offers a wide range of economics-related resources |
| **Education** | |
| *Education Research Complete* | The world's largest collection of full-text education journals |
| *ERIC* | A database of citations for education research |
| **Political Science** | |
| *Worldwide Political Science Abstracts* | Bibliographic information from one thousand journals |
| **Psychology** | |
| *PsycINFO* | Indexes books and journal articles in the psychological and behavioral sciences |
| **Sociology and Social Work** | |
| *Sociological Abstracts* | An index of literature in sociology |
| *Social Work Abstracts* | An index of current research in social work |

NATURAL AND APPLIED SCIENCES

| Database | Description |
| --- | --- |
| **Biology** | |
| *Biological Sciences* | Abstracts and citations from a wide range of biological research |
| **Chemistry** | |
| *American Chemical Society Publications* | Articles from over thirty peer-reviewed journals |
| **Computer Science** | |
| *ACM Guide to Computing Literature* | Over 750,000 citations and abstracts of literature about computing |
| **Engineering** | |
| *AccessScience* | Research updates in all areas of science and technology |
| *IEEE Xplore* | Full-text access to all IEEE journals, magazines, and conference proceedings |
| **Environmental Science** | |
| *Environmental Science Database* | Information on environmental subjects |

| Database | Description |
| --- | --- |
| **Health and Medicine** | |
| *PubMed (Medline)* | Full text of articles in medical journals |
| **Nursing** | |
| *ProQuest Nursing & Allied Health Source* | Resources for nursing and the allied health fields |
| **Physical Sciences** | |
| *INSPEC* | Bibliographic database for resources in engineering, physics, information technology, and manufacturing |

Figure 13.5 shows the search page from *LexisNexis Academic,* a general library subscription database.

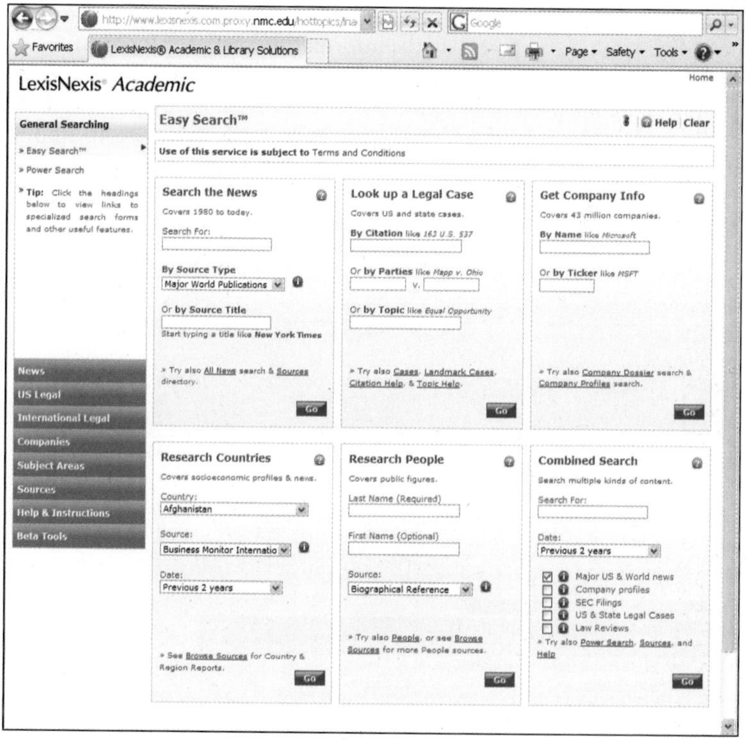


FIGURE 13.5 Search page from *LexisNexis Academic*, a general library subscription database. Courtesy of LexisNexis.

## Close-Up CHOOSING THE RIGHT DATABASE

Before you decide which database to use, ask the following questions:

- Is the database suited to your subject? Is it too general or too specialized?
- What types of sources are included in the database? Are they scholarly journals, popular publications, or both?
- Does the database contain the full text of articles or just citations?
- What search features does the database offer? Are you able to limit your search—for example, to just scholarly publications or to just peer-reviewed publications?
- How easy (or difficult) is the database to use?
- Does the database allow you to download and/or email documents?
- What years does the database cover?

### 4 Finding Books

The online catalog also gives you the information you need for locating specific books. Catalog entries for books include the author's name, the title, the subject, publication information, and a call number. A **call number** is like a book's address in the library: it tells you exactly where to find the book you are looking for. (Figure 13.6 shows the results of an author search in a university library's online catalog.) Once you become familiar with the physical layout of the library, you should have no trouble locating the books you need.

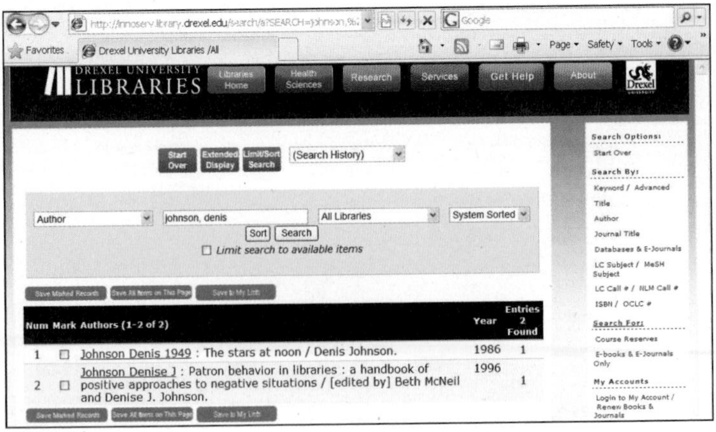


**FIGURE 13.6** Online catalog search results for the author *Denis Johnson*.
© Drexel University.

CHECKLIST

### Tracking Down a Missing Source

| Problem | Possible solution |
| --- | --- |
| 1. Book is checked out of library. | ❑ Consult the person at the circulation desk. |
| 2. Book is not in the library's collection. | ❑ Ask your instructor if he or she owns a copy.<br>❑ Arrange for an interlibrary loan (if time permits). |
| 3. Periodical is not in the library's collection. | ❑ See if the article is available in a full-text database.<br>❑ Check *WorldCat* to see if other local libraries have what you need.<br>❑ Arrange for an interlibrary loan (if time permits).<br>❑ Ask a librarian if the article has been reprinted as part of a collection. |

## 5 Consulting General Reference Sources

**General reference sources**—dictionaries, encyclopedias, almanacs, atlases, bibliographies, and so on—can provide an overview of your topic as well as essential background and factual information (see Figure 13.7). Even though they do not discuss your topic in enough depth to be used as research sources, the following general reference works can be useful for gathering information and for focusing your research on the specific issues you want to explore in depth.

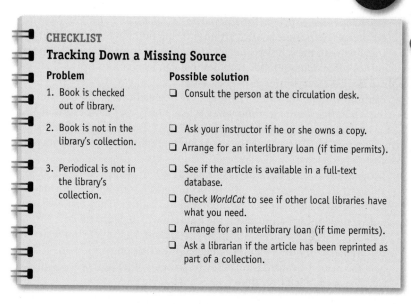

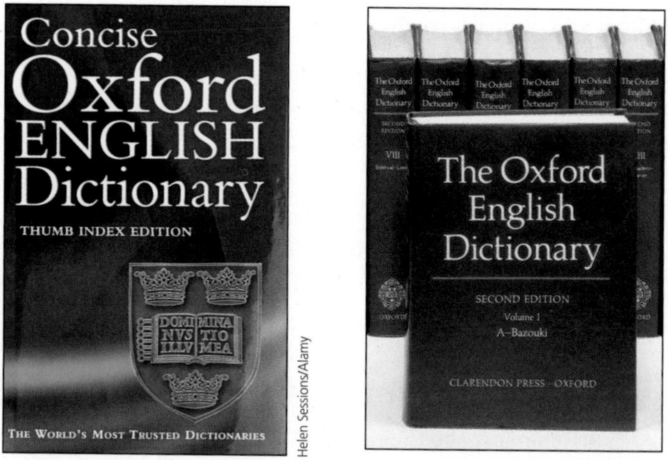


Helen Sessions/Alamy

Jon Stipe/Alamy

FIGURE 13.7 General reference sources.

- **Encyclopedias**—such as the *Encyclopedia Americana* and *The New Encyclopaedia Britannica*—provide an introduction to your topic and give you a sense of the scholarly debates related to it. Individual encyclopedia entries often contain bibliographies that can lead you to works that you can use as research sources.
- **Bibliographies** are lists of sources on a specific topic. For example, the *MLA International Bibliography* lists books and articles published in literature, and the *Bibliographic Guide to Education* lists published sources on all aspects of education. Bibliographic entries often include abstracts.
- **Biographical reference books**—such as *Who's Who in America, Who's Who,* and *Dictionary of American Biography*—provide information about people's lives as well as bibliographic listings. They can also provide general information about the times in which people lived.
- **Unabridged dictionaries**—such as the *Oxford English Dictionary*—are comprehensive works that give detailed information about words. They give the history of words and show how their connotations and denotations have changed over time.
- Some **special dictionaries** focus on topics such as synonyms, slang and idioms, rhyming, symbols, proverbs, sign language, and foreign phrases. Other special dictionaries concentrate on specific academic disciplines, such as law, medicine, and computing.
- A **yearbook or almanac** is an annual publication that updates factual and statistical information—for example, *Facts on File, Information Please Almanac,* and *World Almanac.* An **atlas** contains maps and charts as well as historical, cultural, and economic information—for example, *National Geographic Atlas of the World* and *We the People: An Atlas of America's Ethnic Diversity.*

### 6 Using Special Library Services

In addition to their standard services, libraries provide a number of special services. As you do your research, consult a librarian if you would like to take advantage of any of the following special services.

#### Close-Up SPECIAL LIBRARY SERVICES

- **Interlibrary Loans** Your library may be part of a system that allows you to borrow books from other libraries.
- **Document Delivery** Some libraries are able to request the electronic delivery of journal articles and book chapters.
- **Online Communication** Some libraries answer student questions by email.

- **Services for the Visually Impaired** Many libraries offer special services—for example, large print books, braille texts, or audio-described video—to students with reading impairments or other disabilities.
- **Special Collections** Your college library may house special collections of books, manuscripts, or documents. These items are usually listed on the library's Web site.
- **Government Documents** A large university library may have a separate area, with its own listing or index, for government documents.
- **Vertical File** The vertical file includes pamphlets from a variety of organizations and interest groups, reprints, newspaper clippings, and other miscellaneous material collected by librarians. These can be idiosyncratic but useful in certain cases.

### EXERCISE 1

Which library research sources would you consult to find the following information?

1. A review of the movie *Brick Lane* (2008), based on Monica Ali's 2003 novel
2. A government publication about how to heat your home with solar energy
3. Biographical information about the American anthropologist Margaret Mead
4. Books about Margaret Mead and her work
5. Information about what is being done to prevent the killing of wolves in North America
6. Information about the theories of Albert Einstein
7. Current information about the tobacco lobby
8. The address at which to contact Edward P. Jones, an American writer
9. Whether your college library has *The Human Use of Human Beings* by Norbert Wiener
10. Current information about AmeriCorps

## 13b Finding Information on the Internet

The Internet (more specifically, the Web) gives users access to vast amounts of information, but this strong point is also one of the Internet's primary drawbacks. Because Internet searches can yield thousands of hits, students can be overwhelmed by material and have a difficult time distinguishing valuable research sources from questionable material. Internet documents can vary significantly, so it is important to evaluate them carefully before you use them as sources. See 14b

Even with its drawbacks, the Internet is an extremely valuable research tool. For example, *Google Scholar* provides links to many scholarly sources that are as reliable as those found in your college library's databases. In addition, *The*

*Directory of Open Access Journals* <doaj.org> provides access to almost six thousand open-access scholarly journals—many of which are highly respected.

To do a Web search, you need a **Web browser**—such as *Microsoft Internet Explorer, Mozilla Firefox, Safari, Opera,* or *Google Chrome*—that enables you to access the Web.

**Close-Up** USING A BROWSER TO MANAGE YOUR RESEARCH

In addition to connecting you to the Web, a browser can help you keep track of your research.

- You can use your browser's Bookmark function to save useful URLs.
- You can use your browser's History function to see a list of the sites you have accessed during a research session.

Once you are connected to the Web, you use a **search engine** such as *Google* or *Yahoo!* to search for and retrieve documents. There are two ways to use search engines to find information: by *doing a keyword search* and by *using subject directories.*

## 1 Doing a Keyword Search

See 13a1

The most common method of locating information is through a keyword search, entering a keyword (or words) into your search engine's search box. (Figure 13.8 shows a search engine's keyword search page.) The search engine will identify any site in its database on which the keywords appear.

You can create a list of useful keywords by looking online at the subject catalog of your college library and using its headings. You can also find keywords by accessing an online encyclopedia, such as *Wikipedia*, and looking at the category list that follows each article.

Pixelbully/Alamy

FIGURE 13.8 *Google* keyword search page in *Google Chrome*.

Many search engines have advanced options that enable you to limit the number of irrelevant results. For example, you can tailor your search so that it retrieves only documents with a particular reading level, domain (*.gov* or *.org*, for example), or file type (*.pdf* or *.ppt*, for example). (Figure 13.9 shows a search engine's Advanced Search page.)

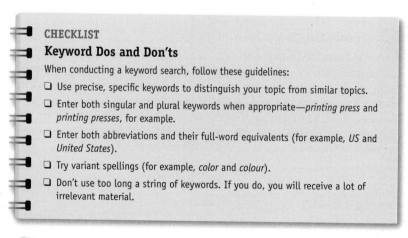

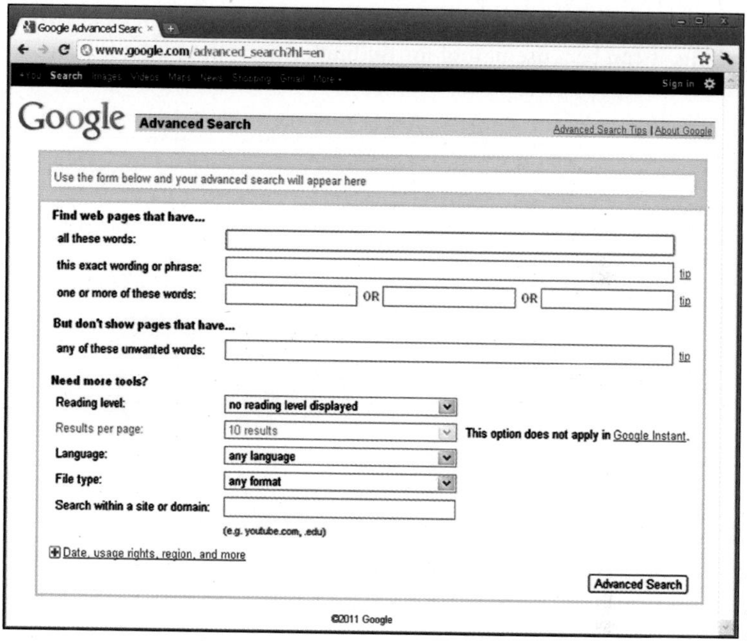


Studiomode/Alamy

FIGURE 13.9 *Google* Advanced Search page in *Google Chrome*.

**CHECKLIST**

### Keyword Dos and Don'ts

When conducting a keyword search, follow these guidelines:

- ❑ Use precise, specific keywords to distinguish your topic from similar topics.
- ❑ Enter both singular and plural keywords when appropriate—*printing press* and *printing presses*, for example.
- ❑ Enter both abbreviations and their full-word equivalents (for example, *US* and *United States*).
- ❑ Try variant spellings (for example, *color* and *colour*).
- ❑ Don't use too long a string of keywords. If you do, you will receive a lot of irrelevant material.

## 2 Using Subject Directories

Some search engines, such as *Yahoo!* and *About.com,* contain subject directories—lists of general categories from which you can choose. Other sites, such as *Academic Info* <academicinfo.net/subject-guides>, the *Open Directory Project* <dmoz.com>, and *INFOMINE* <infomine.ucr.edu> provide directories of Web sites by topic. Each general category will lead you to a more specific list of categories and subcategories until you get to the topic you want. For example, clicking on *Society and Culture* could lead you to *Activism* and then to *Animal Rights* and eventually to an article about factory farming. Although using subject guides is not as efficient as keyword searching, it can be a useful tool for finding or narrowing a topic. (Figure 13.10 shows the *About.com* subject directory.)

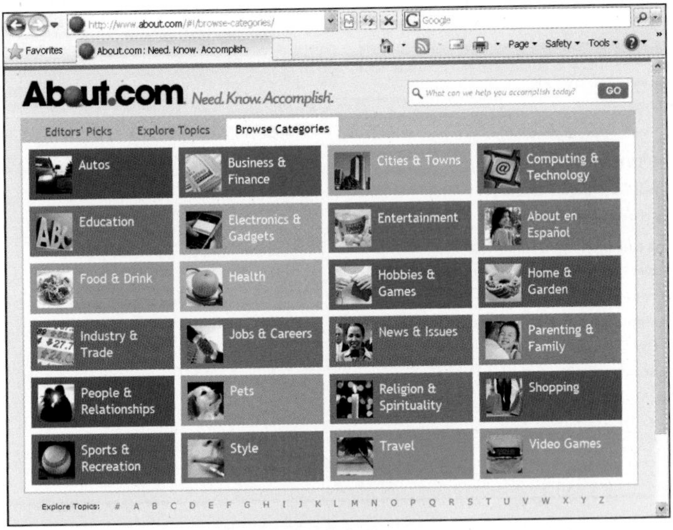


M4OS Photos/Alamy

FIGURE 13.10 *About.com* subject directory page.

## 3 Choosing the Right Search Engine

***General-Purpose Search Engines*** The most widely used search engines are **general-purpose search engines** that focus on a wide variety of topics. Some of these search engines are more user-friendly than others; some allow for more sophisticated searching functions; some are updated more frequently; and some are more comprehensive than others. As you try out various search engines, you will probably settle on a favorite that you will turn to first whenever you need to find information.

### Close-Up POPULAR SEARCH ENGINES

*AltaVista* <altavista.com>: Good, precise engine for focused searches. Fast and easy to use. Large database.

*Ask.com* <ask.com>: Allows you to narrow your search by asking questions, such as *Are dogs smarter than pigs?*

*Bing* <bing.com>: Currently the second most widely used search engine on the Web, *Bing* has a variety of specialized functions that sort responses into categories. By clicking on progressively narrower categories, you get more specific results. In some searches, a single "Best Match" response may appear. Excellent image and video functions.

*Excite* <excite.com>: Good for general topics. Because it searches a vast number of Web sites, you often receive more information than you need.

*Google* <google.com>: Arguably the best search engine available, it accesses a large database that includes both text and graphics. It is easy to navigate, and searches usually yield a high percentage of useful hits. (See pages 194–195 for more information about *Google* resources.)

*HotBot* <hotbot.com>: Excellent, fast search engine for locating specific information. Good search options allow you to fine-tune your searches.

*Lycos* <lycos.com>: One of the oldest search engines on the Web, *Lycos* lets you see results on one side of the page and the actual Web pages on another. At the bottom of the page, it offers additional search terms as well as a "second opinion" feature that links to another search engine.

*Yahoo!* <yahoo.com>: Good for exploratory research. Enables you to search using either subject headings or keywords. Searches its own indexes as well as the Web.

Because even the best search engines search only a fraction of the material available on the Web, if you use only one search engine, you will most likely miss much valuable information. It is therefore a good idea to repeat each search with several different search engines or to use a **metasearch** or **metacrawler** engine that uses several search engines simultaneously.

### Close-Up METASEARCH ENGINES

*Dogpile* <dogpile.com>

*Kartoo* <kartoo.com>

*Mamma* <mamma.com>

*MetaCrawler* <metacrawler.com>

*SurfWax* <surfwax.com>

*Vivisimo* <vivisimo.com>

***Specialized Search Engines*** In addition to the popular general-purpose search engines and metasearch engines, there are also numerous **specialized search engines** devoted entirely to specific subject areas, such as literature, business, sports, and women's issues. Hundreds of specialized search engines are indexed at <listofsearchengines.info>. These search engines are especially useful when you are looking for in-depth information about your topic.

### Close-Up *GOOGLE* RESOURCES

*Google* is the most-used search engine on the Internet. In fact, many people now say that they are going to "Google" a subject rather than search it. Few people who use *Google,* however, actually know its full potential. Following are just a few of the resources that *Google* offers:

- ***Blog Search*** Enables users to find blogs on specific subjects
- ***Blogger*** A tool for creating and posting blogs online
- ***Book Search*** A database that allows users to access millions of books that they can either preview or read for free
- ***Google Earth*** A downloadable, dynamic global map that enables users to see satellite views of almost any place on the planet
- ***Finance*** Business information, news, and interactive charts
- ***News*** Enables users to search thousands of news stories
- ***Patent Search*** Enables users to search the full text of US patents
- ***Google Scholar*** Searches scholarly literature, including peer-reviewed papers, books, and abstracts
- ***Google Translate*** A free online language translation service that instantly translates text and Web pages

You can access these tools by going to the *Google* home page, clicking on MORE in the upper left of your screen, and then clicking on EVEN MORE on the pull-down menu.

Even though all search engines rank results according to relevance, they have different ways of "deciding" what is relevant. For this reason, search engines have strengths and weakness. *NoodleTools* <noodletools.com> is a useful Web site that lists a large number of search engines (some general and some specialized) and helps you choose the one that is best suited for finding the information you need.

### Close-Up *GOOGLE SCHOLAR*

*Google Scholar* gives you access to some high-quality resources—such as full-text peer-reviewed articles, books, and abstracts—and ranks results according to relevance. It also has a "cited by" feature that links to articles in the *Google Scholar* database that have been cited in the article being viewed. Even so, it does have some drawbacks that users should be aware of:

- Because it does not clearly define *scholar,* you have to make sure that the material conforms to academic standards of reliability.
- Some articles are only abstracts, and others are pay-per-view. (Often, you can get the pay-per-view articles for free through your library's databases.)
- *Google Scholar* is uneven across disciplines and does not index many pre-1990 sources.
- The sources you find may not be current or comprehensive.
- Many important scholarly journals are not indexed in *Google Scholar*.

## 4 Surveying Specialized Web Resources

The Web offers access to a number of specialized sites that you can use in your research. These Web sites can give you access to more focused and more authoritative resources than you get when you do a general keyword or subject search.

### *Web Resources: General Research*

- *ipl2* (Internet Public Library)—A public library for the Internet; thousands of students are involved in answering questions and maintaining the *ipl2*'s collections <ipl.org>
- *INFOMINE*—A search engine with links to many librarian-selected scholarly and educational Internet resources <infomine.ucr.edu>
- *The Library of Congress Online Catalog*—A searchable catalog that contains over 130 million items <catalog.loc.gov>
- *The Library of Congress Digital Collections*—A searchable database of the Library of Congress's digitized material <loc.gov/library/libarch-digital.html>
- *The National Archives*—A list of all the National Archives' research tools and databases <archives.gov/research/start/online-tools.html>
- *Smithsonian Institution Libraries*—A collection of resources in twenty libraries from the world's largest museum complex <sil.si.edu>

### *Web Resources: Humanities*

**Art**

- *Guggenheim Museum*—A collection of works by over 160 artists, searchable by artist name, title, date, movement, medium, concept, and museum <guggenheimcollection.org/index.html>
- *Humanities Web*—A Web site that shows the interconnections between history, arts, and culture <humanitiesweb.org>

- *The National Gallery of Art*—A searchable catalog of the museum's 110,000 objects, with more than 6,000 images <nga.gov/collection/index.shtm>

**Literature**

- *Project Gutenberg*—A searchable catalog of full-text books <gutenberg.org/wiki/Main_Page>
- *Voice of the Shuttle*—A comprehensive humanities search engine (still a valuable resource, but not as well maintained as it once was) <vos.ucsb.edu>

**History**

- *American FactFinder*—A collection of Census Bureau data searchable by city, county, or ZIP code <factfinder2.census.gov/main.html>
- *FedStats*—A gateway to statistics from over one hundred US federal agencies <fedstats.gov>
- *Historical Census Browser*—A repository of historical US census data dating back to 1790, compiled by the University of Virginia <mapserver.lib.virginia.edu>
- *United States Government Printing Office* (GPO)—A search engine for multiple government databases <gpo.gov/fdsys>

### *Web Resources: Social Sciences*

**Business**

- *BEOnline*—A searchable database of Internet resources on the study of entrepreneurship and small business, compiled by the Library of Congress <loc.gov/rr/business/beonline/beohome.html>
- *Biznar*—A Web site that gives access to numerous business collections <biznar.com>

**Psychology**

- *CyberPsych*—A site that provides information about psychoanalysis and psychotherapy <cyberpsych.com>
- *Psych Web*—This site contains information for students and teachers of psychology <psychwww.com>

**Social Science**

- *Social Science Research Network*—A site that provides access to research in the social sciences and humanities <ssrn.com>
- *SocioWeb*—A guide to sociological resources on the Internet <socioweb.com>

### *Web Resources: Natural and Applied Sciences*

**General Science**

- *Science.gov*—A searchable portal that provides access to scientific information provided by the US government <science.gov>

**Biology**

- *BioOne*—Abstracts of over fifty peer-reviewed scientific journals in biology, ecology, and the environment <bioone.org>

**Chemistry**

- *ChemXSeer*—An integrated digital library allowing the search of documents and data obtained from chemical kinetics <chemxseer.ist.psu.edu>
- *PubChem*—A free database of small organic molecules <pubchem.ncbi.nlm.nih.gov>

**Engineering**

- *Engineering Web Site*—A gateway site for engineering resources on the Internet <mastep.sjsu.edu/resources/engineer.htm>

**Physics**

- *Physics.org*—A site maintained by the Institute of Physics <physics.org/index.asp>

CHECKLIST

### Tips for Effective Web Searches

- ❑ **Choose the right search engine.** No single all-purpose search engine exists. Review the list of search engines in the boxes on pages 192–194.
- ❑ **Choose your keywords carefully.** A search engine is only as good as the keywords you use.
- ❑ **Include enough terms.** If you are looking for information on housing, for example, search for several variations of your keyword: *housing, houses, home buyer, buying houses, residential real estate,* and so on.
- ❑ **Use more than one search engine.** Because different search engines index different sites, try several. If one does not yield results after a few tries, try another. Also, don't forget to try a metasearch engine like *MetaCrawler.*
- ❑ **Add useful sites to your Bookmark or Favorites list.** Whenever you find a particularly useful Web site, **bookmark** it by selecting this option on the menu bar of your browser (with some browsers, such as *Microsoft Internet Explorer,* this option is called Favorites).

## 5 Using *Wikipedia* as a Research Source

Although no encyclopedia—electronic or print—should be used as a research source, *Wikipedia* requires an extra level of scrutiny.

*Wikipedia* is an open-source, online general encyclopedia created through the collaborative efforts of its users. Anyone (not necessarily experts) registered with the site can write an article, and in most cases, anyone who views the site can edit an article. The theory is that if enough people contribute, over time, entries will become more and more accurate. Needless to say, *Wikipedia* has its critics—especially in academia. Many instructors point out that the coverage in *Wikipedia* is uneven; some articles follow acceptable standards of academic research, but many others do not. Because some articles have little or no documentation, it is difficult to judge their merit. In addition, because *Wikipedia* does not have an editorial staff responsible for checking entries for accuracy, it is not a reliable source of information. Finally, critics point out that there is no foolproof way that *Wikipedia* can guard against **vandalism**—the purposeful addition of factual inaccuracies, obscenities, or libelous charges into an entry.

Still, *Wikipedia* does have its strengths. Currently, it contains almost four million entries and many of its articles focus on subjects not treated by other encyclopedias. Because it is constantly being revised, it can be more up to date than other reference sources. In addition, many articles contain bibliographic citations that enable users to link to reliable sources of information. Keep in mind, however, that even though you can use *Wikipedia* to get a general overview of your topic, most instructors do not consider it trustworthy, let alone authoritative.

### EXERCISE 2

Choose a topic that interests you—for example, artificial intelligence or student loans. Then, choose two popular search engines listed in the box on pages 192–193 and do a search of your topic on each. When you finish, compare the results, and answer the following questions:

1. How many results did you get from each search engine?
2. How useful were the results?
3. How easy is it to access visuals about your topic? video? blogs? news?
4. Which search engine seemed the most helpful? Why?
5. Which search features were similar, and which were different?

## 13c Doing Field Research

In addition to using the library's resources, you can find valuable information by doing **field research** (sometimes called **primary research**). Field research involves gathering your own information by making observations (of people, places, objects, and events); by conducting an interview; or by conducting a survey.

### 1 Making Observations

Your own observations can be a useful source of information. For example, an art or music paper can be enriched by information gathered during a visit to a museum or attending a concert. An education paper may include an account of a classroom visit, and a psychology or sociology paper may include observations (as well as photographs) of an individual's or a group's behavior.

**CHECKLIST**

**Making Observations**

- ❑ Decide what you want to observe and where you want to observe it.
- ❑ Determine in advance what information you hope to gain from your observations.
- ❑ Bring a laptop, notepad, or audio recorder so you can keep a record of your observations.
- ❑ Bring any additional items you may need—a camera or timer, for example.
- ❑ Make sure you record the date, place, and time of your observations.

## 2 Conducting an Interview

**Interviews** (conducted in person or by email) often give you material that you cannot find in a library—for instance, biographical information, a firsthand account of an event, or the opinions of an expert.

The kinds of questions you ask in an interview depend on the information you want. **Open-ended questions**—questions designed to elicit general information—allow a respondent great flexibility in answering: *"Do you think students today are motivated? Why or why not?"* **Closed-ended questions**—questions intended to elicit specific information—zero in on a particular detail about a subject: *"How much money did the government's cost-cutting programs actually save?"* (Figure 13.11 shows sample interview questions from a student oral history project.)

- What is the most important lesson you have learned in life?
- What accomplishment are you most proud of?
- What was the happiest moment of your life? the saddest?
- Who has been the biggest influence on your life? What lessons did this person teach you?
- How would you like to be remembered?

FIGURE 13.11 Excerpt from list of interview questions.

**CHECKLIST**

**Conducting an Interview**

- ❑ Always make an appointment.
- ❑ Prepare a list of specific questions tailored to the subject matter and the time limit of your interview.

*continued*

**Conducting an Interview *(continued)***

- ❑ Do background reading about your topic. (Do not ask for information that you can easily find elsewhere.)
- ❑ Have a pen and paper with you. If you want to record the interview electronically, get your subject's permission in advance.
- ❑ Allow the person you are interviewing to complete an answer before you ask another question.
- ❑ Take notes, but continue to pay attention as you do so.
- ❑ Pay attention to the reactions of your interview subject.
- ❑ Be willing to depart from your prepared list of questions to ask follow-up questions.
- ❑ At the end of the interview, thank your subject for his or her time and cooperation.
- ❑ Send a brief note of thanks.

**Close-Up** CONDUCTING AN EMAIL INTERVIEW

Using email to conduct an interview can save you a great deal of time. Before you email your questions, make sure the person is willing to cooperate. If the person agrees to be interviewed, send a short list of specific questions. After you have received the answers, send an email thanking the person for his or her cooperation. When you conduct an email interview, make sure you follow the guidelines for writing emails.

See 33g

### 3 Conducting a Survey

If your research project is examining a contemporary social, political, or economic issue, a **survey** of attitudes or opinions could be very useful. You begin conducting a survey by identifying the group of individuals that you will poll. This group can be a **convenient sample**—for example, people in your composition class—or a **random sample**—names chosen from the campus directory or a class roster. When you identify a sample, your goal is to select a population that is both *representative*—that accurately reflects the group you are studying—and *significant*—that includes enough respondents to convince people that your results are valid. If you poll ten people in your French class about a university policy and your university has thousands of students, you cannot expect your conclusion to be valid.

You should also make sure that your questions are clearly worded and designed to elicit the information you want. For example, multiple-choice questions or closed-ended questions that require a simple "yes" or "no" will yield more usable data than questions that call for paragraph-length answers. Also, be sure that you do not ask so many questions that respondents lose interest and stop answering. Finally, be careful not to ask biased or **leading questions**—questions asked in a way that suggests an answer.

CHECKLIST

**Conducting a Survey**

- ❑ Determine what you want to know.
- ❑ Select your sample.
- ❑ Design your questions.
- ❑ Distribute questionnaires.
- ❑ Collect the responses.
- ❑ Analyze the responses.
- ❑ Decide how you will use the results in your paper.

Figure 13.12 shows sample survey questions from a community service project. For an example of a student paper that uses information from a survey, **see 19c.**

| **Section 2:** Please indicate how strongly you agree or disagree with the following statement at this point in time. | Strongly Disagree 1 | Disagree 2 | Undecided 3 | Agree 4 | Strongly Agree 5 |
|---|---|---|---|---|---|
| Being involved in a program to improve my community is important. | ☐ | ☐ | ☐ | ☐ | ☐ |
| It is important to work toward equal opportunity (e.g. social political, vocational) for all people. | ☐ | ☐ | ☐ | ☐ | ☐ |
| It is not necessary to volunteer my time to help people in need. | ☐ | ☐ | ☐ | ☐ | ☐ |
| I think that people should find time to contribute to their community. | ☐ | ☐ | ☐ | ☐ | ☐ |
| I feel I can have a poitive impact on local social problems. | ☐ | ☐ | ☐ | ☐ | ☐ |

FIGURE 13.12 Excerpt from list of survey questions <servicelearning.org>.

CHAPTER 14

# Evaluating Sources

## Frequently Asked Questions



The sources that you use in your research papers help to establish the level of trustworthiness and authority that readers believe you have. If you use high-quality, reliable sources, your readers are likely to assume that you have more than a superficial knowledge of your subject. If, however, you use questionable sources, readers will begin to doubt your authority, and they may dismiss your ideas. For these reasons, it is very important to make sure that the research sources you use to support your ideas are trustworthy and reliable.

Whenever you find a source (either print or electronic), you should take the time to **evaluate** it—to assess its usefulness. Of course, some sources have to be evaluated more carefully than others. For example, a scholarly book or journal article that you find in your college library presents fewer problems than an anonymous source you find on the Internet. The library source has most likely gone through some sort of **peer-review** or **referee** process (that is, it has been screened by experts in a field) and was probably published by a reputable publisher. In addition, a librarian may have prescreened this item. On the other hand, the anonymous Internet source could have been posted by anyone, and for this reason, it is highly suspect. In the final analysis, however, it is your responsibility—not a librarian's or an editor's—to determine if the sources you use in your papers are reliable as well as relevant to your topic and suitable for your purpose.

## 14a Evaluating Library Sources

The fact that something is in the library does not necessarily mean that it meets academic standards or that it is an appropriate source for your paper. For example, an article in a popular magazine in the library's browsing room may not include documentation, and an article in a scholarly journal may present only one side of a debatable issue.

Before you decide to use a library source (print or electronic), you should assess its suitability according to the following criteria:

- **Reliability:** *Is the source trustworthy?* Does the writer support his or her conclusions with facts and expert opinion, or does the source rely on unsupported opinion? Is the information accurate and free of factual errors? Does the writer include documentation and a bibliography?
- **Credibility:** *Is the source respected?* A contemporary review of a source can help you make this assessment. *Book Review Digest,* available in print and online, lists popular books that have been reviewed in at least three newspapers or magazines and includes excerpts from representative reviews as well as abstracts. Is the writer well known in his or her field? Can you check the writer's credentials? Is the article **refereed** (that is, chosen by experts in the field)?
- **Objectivity:** *Does the writer strive to present a balanced discussion?* Sometimes a writer has a particular agenda to advance. Compare a few statements from the source with a neutral source—a textbook or an encyclopedia, for example—to see whether the writer seems to be exhibiting bias or slanting facts.
- **Currency:** *Is the source up to date?* The date of publication tells you whether the information in a book or article is current. A source's currency is particularly important for scientific and technological subjects, but even in the humanities, new discoveries and new ways of thinking lead scholars to reevaluate and modify their ideas.
- **Scope of coverage:** *Does the source treat your topic in enough detail?* To be useful, a source should treat your topic comprehensively. For example, a book should include a section or chapter on your topic, not simply a brief reference or a note. To evaluate an article, either read the abstract or skim the entire article for key facts, looking closely at section headings, information set in boldface type, and topic sentences. An article should have your topic as its central subject (or at least one of its main concerns).

In general, **scholarly publications**—books and journals aimed at an audience of expert readers—are more reliable than **popular publications**—books, magazines, and newspapers aimed at an audience of general readers. However, assuming they are current, written by reputable authors, and documented, articles from substantive popular publications (such as the *Atlantic* and *Scientific American*) may be appropriate for your research. Other popular publications—especially sensational tabloids such as the *Globe* and the *National Enquirer*—are almost never appropriate for your research. Check with your instructor to be sure.

## Scholarly versus Popular Publications

Courtesy of AIP

The Atlantic Publication

FIGURE 14.1 Scholarly (left) and popular (right) publications.

| Scholarly Publications | Popular Publications |
|---|---|
| Report the results of research | Entertain and inform |
| Are often published by a university press or have some connection with a university or other academic organization | Are published by commercial presses |
| Are usually peer reviewed—that is, reviewed by other experts in the author's field before they are published | Are usually not peer reviewed |
| Are usually written by someone who is a recognized authority in the field | May be written by experts in a particular field but more often are written by freelance or staff writers |
| Are written for a scholarly audience so often use technical vocabulary and include challenging content | Are written for general readers so tend to use an accessible vocabulary and do not include challenging content |
| Nearly always contain extensive documentation as well as a bibliography of works consulted | Rarely cite sources or use documentation |
| Are published primarily because they make a contribution to a particular field of study | Are published primarily to make a profit |

## Close-Up EVALUATING POPULAR PERIODICALS

To find out how reliable a popular periodical is, go to the reference desk of your college library and find out if the library owns (or has access to) the following book:

LaGuardia, Cheryl, ed. *Magazines for Libraries.* 19th ed. Created by Bill Katz. New York: Bowker, 2010.

This book lists over six thousand periodicals by subject. Each entry includes an abstract that identifies the political orientation and scope of the publication. To locate a periodical, use the index at the end of the book.

### EXERCISE 1

Read the following paragraphs carefully, paying close attention to the information provided about their sources and authors as well as to their content. Decide which sources would be most useful and reliable in supporting the thesis "Winning the right to vote has (or has not) significantly changed the role of women in national politics." Which sources, if any, should be disregarded? Which would you examine first? Why?

1. Woman has been the great unpaid laborer of the world, and although within the last two decades a vast number of new employments have been opened to her, statistics prove that in the great majority of these, she is not paid according to the value of the work done, but according to sex. The opening of all industries to women, and the wage question as connected with her, are the most subtle and profound questions of political economy, closely interwoven with the rights of self-government. (Susan B. Anthony; first appeared in Vol. I of *The History of Woman Suffrage;* reprinted in *Voices from Women's Liberation,* ed. Leslie B. Tanner, NAL, 1970. *An important figure in the battle for women's suffrage, Susan B. Anthony* [1820–1906] *also lectured and wrote on abolition and temperance*.)
2. Women have had an impact in the voting booth since Lydia Taft cast a ballot in Uxbridge, Mass., on whether the town should spend money on troops in the French and Indian War. The year was 1756. Taft was allowed to vote on her dead husband's behalf because of the considerable wealth and land she inherited from him. Women certainly have made strides since then, says Lara Brown, a political scientist at Villanova University. "But I think it is important to remember that we've had 55 presidential elections and we've only ever had men as the major-party presidential nominees." Only two women have been major-party vice-presidential picks: the late Geraldine Ferraro, a New York Democrat and congresswoman, and Sarah Palin, Alaska's Republican

governor. (Salena Zito, "Women's Impact Grows," *Pittsburgh Tribune-Review,* 2011. *The author examines American women's voting habits since they gained the right to vote.*)



3. Nineteen eighty-two was the year that time ran out for the proposed equal rights amendment. Eleanor Smeal, president of the National Organization for Women, the group that headed the intense 10-year struggle for the ERA, conceded defeat on June 24. Only 24 words in all, the ERA read simply: "Equality of rights under the law shall not be denied or abridged by the United States or by any state on account of sex." Two major opinion polls had reported just weeks before the ERA's defeat that a majority of Americans continued to favor the amendment. (June Foley, "Women 1982: The Year That Time Ran Out," *The World Almanac & Book of Facts*, 1983.)
4. It won't happen this year. But the next chance at the White House is only four years away, and more women than you might think are already laying the groundwork for their own presidential bids. Bolstered by changing public attitudes, women in politics no longer assume that the Oval Office will always be a male bastion. In 1936, when George Gallup first asked people whether they would "vote for a woman for president if she qualified in every other respect," 65 percent said they would not. Back then, women were only slightly more open to the idea than men. Things are far different today. A recent poll shows that 90 percent of Americans, men included, say they could support a woman for president. (Eleanor Clift and Tom Brazaitis, *Madam President*, © 2000 by Eleanor Clift and Tom Brazaitis. *The authors profile the women who they say are positioning themselves to be president.*)

## 14b Evaluating Internet Sources

Because anyone can post anything on the Internet, you can easily be overwhelmed by unreliable material. As you sort through and attempt to evaluate this information, there are some general guidelines you can follow.

If you use the library's databases to find digital versions of print journal articles, you can assume that they conform to academic standards (even so, you still have to evaluate them). To a lesser degree, the same is true for digital versions of print newspaper or magazine articles. You still have to check the credentials of the authors, the reputation of the periodicals, and possibly the accuracy of the information, but these publications usually give you the information you need to do this checking. Many Internet sources—for example, anonymous blog posts, e-zines that post no standards for publication, and personal and commercial Web sites—often do not provide the specific information you need to fully evaluate them. For this reason, you should not use them as research sources unless you are able to assess the quality of the information they contain.

**Close-Up ACCEPTABLE VERSUS UNACCEPTABLE INTERNET SOURCES**

**Acceptable**

- Web sites sponsored and maintained by reliable organizations
- Articles in established online encyclopedias, such as <britannica.com>
- Web sites sponsored by reputable newspapers and magazines
- Blogs by reputable authors

**Unacceptable**

- Information from anonymous sources (blogs, Web sites, and so on)
- Information found in chat rooms and on discussion boards
- Articles in questionable e-zines and other online publications

Before you use an Internet source, you should evaluate it for *reliability, credibility, objectivity, currency,* and *scope of coverage.*

***Reliability*** **Reliability** refers to the accuracy of the material itself and to its use of proper documentation.

Factual errors—especially errors in facts that are central to the main idea of the source—should cause you to question the reliability of the material you are reading. To evaluate a site's reliability, ask these questions:

- Is the text free of basic grammatical and mechanical errors?
- Does the site contain factual errors?
- Does the site provide a list of references?
- Are working links available to other sources?
- Can information be verified by print or other sources?

***Credibility*** **Credibility** refers to the credentials of the person or organization responsible for the site.

Web sites operated by well-known institutions (the Smithsonian or the Library of Congress, for example) have a high degree of credibility. Those operated by individuals (personal Web pages or blogs, for example) are often less reliable. To evaluate a site's credibility, ask these questions:

- Does the site list an author (or authors)? Are credentials (for example, professional or academic affiliations) provided for the author?
- Is the author a recognized authority in his or her field?
- Is the site **refereed?** That is, does an editorial board or a group of experts determine what material appears on the Web site?
- Can you determine how long the Web site has existed?

***Objectivity*** **Objectivity** refers to the degree of bias that a Web site exhibits.

Some Web sites strive for objectivity, but others make no secret of their biases. They openly advocate a particular point of view or action, or they clearly try to sell something. Some Web sites may try to hide their biases. For example, a Web site may present itself as a source of factual information when it is actually advocating a political point of view. To evaluate a site's objectivity, ask these questions:

- Does advertising appear in the text?
- Does a business, a political organization, or a special interest group sponsor the site?
- Does the site express a particular viewpoint?
- Does the site contain links to other sites that express a particular viewpoint?

***Currency*** **Currency** refers to how up to date the Web site is.

The easiest way to assess a site's currency is to see when it was last updated. Keep in mind, however, that even if the date on the site is current, the information that the site contains may not be. To evaluate a site's currency, ask these questions:

- Does the site include the date when it was last updated?
- Are all the links to other sites still functioning?
- Is the actual information on the page up to date?
- Does the site clearly identify the date it was created?

CHECKLIST

### Determining the Legitimacy of an Anonymous or Questionable Web Source

When a Web source is anonymous (or has an author whose name is not familiar to you), you have to take special measures to determine its legitimacy:

- ❑ **Follow the links.** Follow the hypertext links in a document to other documents. If the links take you to legitimate sources, you know that the author is aware of these sources of information.
- ❑ **Find out what Web pages link to the site.** You can go to <alexa.com> to find information about a Web site. Type the Web site's URL into *Alexa*'s search box, and you will be given the volume of traffic to the site, the ownership information for the site, and the other sites visited by people who visited the URL. In addition, you will also be given a link to the "Wayback Machine" <archive.org/web/web.php>, an archive that shows what the page looked like in the past.
- ❑ **Do a keyword search.** Do a search using the name of the sponsoring organization or the author as keywords. Other documents (or citations in other works) may identify the author.

- ❑ **Verify the information.** Check the information you find against a reliable source—a textbook or a reputable Web site, for example. Also, see if you can find information that contradicts what you have found.
- ❑ **Check the quality of the writing.** Review the writing on the Web site to see if there are typos, misspellings, and errors in grammar or word choice. If the writer is careless about these things, he or she has probably not spent much time checking facts.
- ❑ **Look at the URL.** Although a Web site's URL is not a foolproof guide to the site's purpose, it does give you some useful information. The last part of a Web site's URL (immediately following the **domain name**) can often tell you whether the site is sponsored by a commercial entity (*.com*), a nonprofit organization (*.org*), an educational institution (*.edu*), the military (*.mil*), or a government agency (*.gov*). Knowing this information can help you assess its legitimacy.

***Scope of Coverage*** **Scope of coverage** refers to the comprehensiveness of the information on a Web site.

More coverage is not necessarily better, but some sites may be incomplete. Others may provide information that is no more than common knowledge. Still others may present discussions that are not suitable for college-level research. To evaluate the scope of a site's coverage, ask these questions:

- Does the site provide in-depth coverage?
- Does the site provide information that is not available elsewhere?
- Does the site identify a target audience? Does this target audience suggest the site is appropriate for your research needs?

### Close-Up EVALUATING MATERIAL FROM ONLINE FORUMS

Be especially careful with material posted on discussion boards, blogs, newsgroups, and other online forums. Unless you can adequately evaluate this material—for example, determine its accuracy and the credibility of the author or authors—you should not use it in your paper. In most cases, online forums are not good sources of high-quality information.

### EXERCISE 2

Working in a group of three or four students, study the two Web pages shown in Figures 14.2 and 14.3 on page 210. Use the criteria outlined in **14b** to help you evaluate their content. &

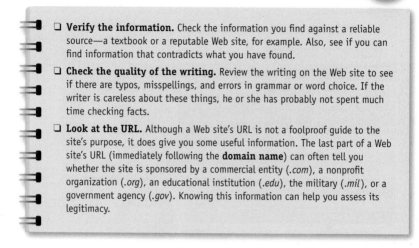

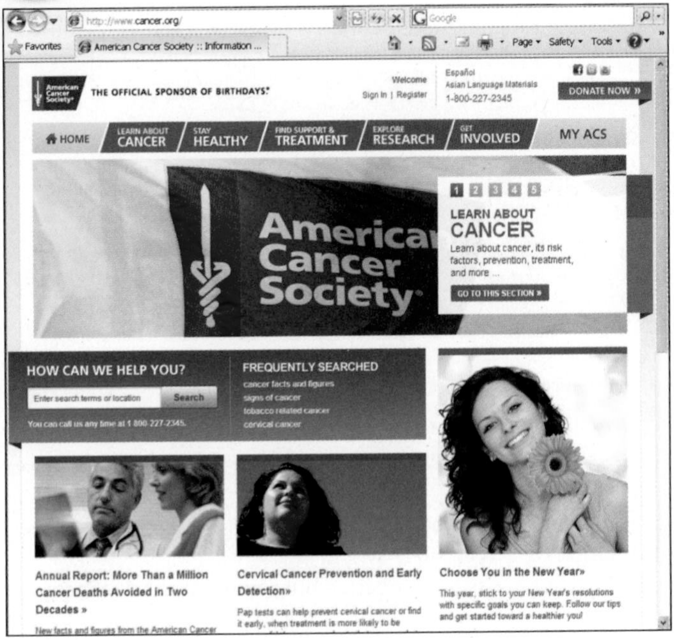


FIGURE 14.2 American Cancer Society home page <cancer.org>.

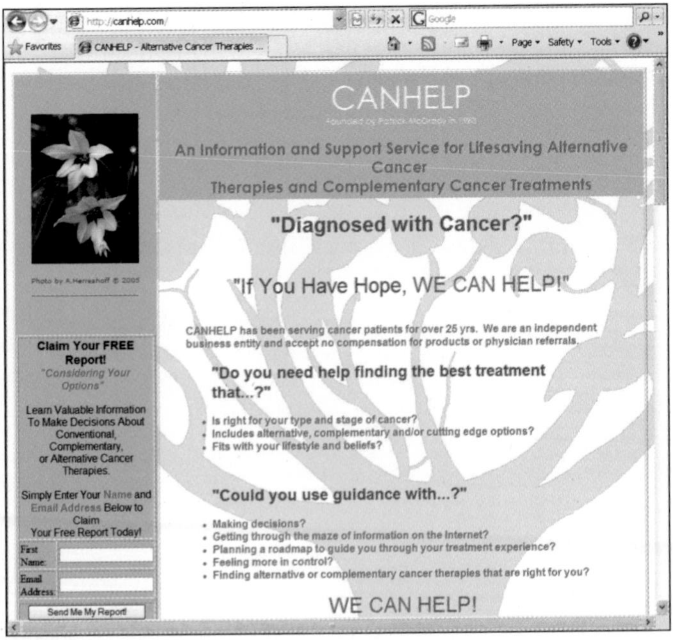


FIGURE 14.3 CANHELP home page <canhelp.com>.

## EXERCISE 3

Examine the home page for the *National Geographic* Web site (Figure 14.4). Using the criteria discussed in **14b,** write a paragraph in which you evaluate the site's content in terms of accuracy, credibility, objectivity, currency, and scope of coverage.

Netphotos/Alamy

FIGURE 14.4 The *National Geographic* home page.

CHAPTER 15

# Summarizing, Paraphrasing, and Quoting Sources

## Frequently Asked Questions



See 12f

Although it may seem like a good strategy, copying down the exact words of a source is the least efficient way of **taking notes**. Experienced researchers know that a better strategy is to take notes that combine summary and paraphrase with direct quotation. By doing so, they make sure they understand the material and see its relevance to their research.

## 15a Writing a Summary

A **summary** is a brief restatement of the main idea of a passage or an article. A summary is always much shorter than the original because it omits the examples, asides, analogies, and rhetorical strategies that writers use to add emphasis and interest.

When you summarize, *use your own words,* not the exact language or phrasing of your source. Remember that your summary should include only the main idea of your source, not your own interpretations or opinions. Finally, be sure to include **parenthetical documentation**.

See 18a1

**Summaries**

- **Summaries are original.** They should use your own language and phrasing, not the language and phrasing of your source.
- **Summaries are concise.** They should always be much shorter than the original.

- **Summaries are accurate.** They should express the main idea of your source.
- **Summaries are objective.** They should not include your opinions.
- **Summaries are complete.** They should convey a sense of the entire passage, not just a part of it.

Compare the following three passages. The first is an original source; the second, an acceptable summary; and the third, an unacceptable summary.

**Original Source**

Today, the First Amendment faces challenges from groups who seek to limit expressions of racism and bigotry. A growing number of legislatures have passed rules against "hate speech"—[speech] that is offensive on the basis of race, ethnicity, gender, or sexual orientation. The rules are intended to promote respect for all people and protect the targets of hurtful words, gestures, or actions.

Legal experts fear these rules may wind up diminishing the rights of all citizens. "The bedrock principle [of our society] is that government may never suppress free speech simply because it goes against what the community would like to hear," says Nadine Strossen, president of the American Civil Liberties Union and professor of constitutional law at New York University Law School. In recent years, for example, the courts have upheld the right of neo-Nazis to march in Jewish neighborhoods; protected cross-burning as a form of free expression; and allowed protesters to burn the American flag. The offensive, ugly, distasteful, or repugnant nature of expression is not reason enough to ban it, courts have said.

But advocates of limits on hate speech note that certain kinds of expression fall outside of First Amendment protection. Courts have ruled that "fighting words"—words intended to provoke immediate violence—or speech that creates a clear and present danger are not protected forms of expression. As the classic argument goes, freedom of speech does not give you the right to yell "Fire!" in a crowded theater. (Sudo, Phil. "Freedom of Hate Speech?")



The following acceptable summary gives an accurate, objective overview of the original without using its exact language or phrasing.

**Acceptable Summary:** Some people think that stronger laws against the use of hate speech weaken the First Amendment, but others argue that some kinds of speech remain exempt from this protection (Sudo 17).

The following unacceptable summary uses words and phrases from the original. In addition, the unacceptable summary expresses the student writer's opinion (**Other people have the sense to realize . . .**).

> **Unacceptable Summary:** Today, the First Amendment faces challenges from lots of people. Some of these people are legal experts who want to let Nazis march in Jewish neighborhoods. Other people have the sense to realize that some kinds of speech fall outside of First Amendment protection because they create a clear and present danger (Sudo 17).

**CHECKLIST**

**Writing a Summary**

- ❑ Reread your source until you understand it.
- ❑ Write a one-sentence restatement of the main idea.
- ❑ Use your own words and phrasing, not those of your source.
- ❑ Add appropriate documentation.

## 15b Writing a Paraphrase

A summary conveys just the main idea of a source; a **paraphrase** gives a *detailed* overview of a source's important ideas. It not only presents the source's main points, but it also reflects its tone and emphasis.

When you paraphrase, make certain that you use your own words, except when you want to quote to give readers a sense of the original. Try not to look at the source as you write, use language and syntax that come naturally to you, and avoid duplicating the phrasing or sentence structure of the original. Whenever possible, use synonyms that accurately convey the meaning of the original word or phrase. If you cannot think of a synonym for an important term, quote it. Remember that your paraphrase should reflect the ideas of your source—not your analysis or interpretation of those ideas. Finally, be sure to include parenthetical documentation.

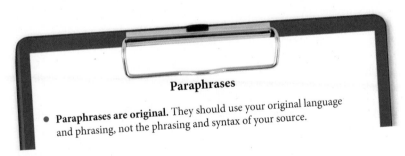

**Paraphrases**

- **Paraphrases are original.** They should use your original language and phrasing, not the phrasing and syntax of your source.

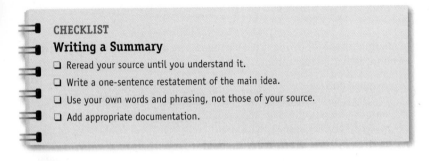

- **Paraphrases are accurate.** They should precisely convey both the key ideas and the emphasis of your source.
- **Paraphrases are objective.** They should not include your opinions or interpretations.
- **Paraphrases are complete.** They should include all the important ideas in your source.

Compare the following three passages. The first is an original source, the second is an acceptable paraphrase, and the third is an unacceptable paraphrase.

**Original Source**

When you play a video game, you enter into the world of the programmers who made it. You have to do more than identify with a character on a screen. You must act for it. Identification through action has a special kind of hold. Like playing a sport, it puts people into a highly focused and highly charged state of mind. For many people, what is being pursued in the video game is not just a score, but an altered state.

The pilot of a race car does not dare to take . . . attention off the road. The imperative of total concentration is part of the high. Video games demand the same level of attention. They can give people the feeling of being close to the edge because, as in a dangerous situation, there is no time for rest and the consequences of wandering attention [are] dire. With pinball, a false move can be recuperated. The machine can be shaken, the ball repositioned. In a video game, the program has no tolerance for error, no margin for safety. Players experience their every movement as instantly translated into game action. The game is relentless in its demand that all other time stop and in its demand that the player take full responsibility for every act, a point that players often sum up [with] the phrase "One false move and you're dead." (Turkle, Sherry. *The Second Self: Computers and the Human Spirit.*)

The following acceptable paraphrase conveys the key ideas and emphasis of the source and maintains an objective tone. It quotes a key phrase, but its wording and sentence structure are very different from those of the source.

**Acceptable Paraphrase:** The programmer defines the reality of the video game. The game forces a player to merge with the character who is part of the game. The character becomes an extension of the player, who determines how he or she will think and act. According to Turkle, like sports, video games put a player into a very intense "altered state" of mind that is the most important part of the activity (83).

The total involvement they demand is what attracts many people to video games. These games can simulate the thrill of participating in a dangerous activity without any of the risks. Players cannot stop to rest, and there is no opportunity to correct errors of judgment. Unlike video games, pinball games are forgiving. A player can—within certain limits—manipulate a pinball game to correct minor mistakes. With video games, however, every move has immediate consequences. The game forces a player to adapt to its rules and to act carefully. One mistake can cause the death of the character on the screen and the end of the game (Turkle 83-84).

The following unacceptable paraphrase simply echoes the phrasing and syntax of the original, borrowing words and expressions without enclosing them in quotation marks. This constitutes **plagiarism**. In addition, the paraphrase digresses into a discussion of the student writer's own opinions about the relative merits of pinball and video games (**That is why I like . . .**).

See Ch. 17

**Unacceptable Paraphrase:** Playing a video game, you enter into a new world—one the programmer of the game made. You can't just play a video game; you have to identify with it. Your mind goes to a new level, and you are put into a highly focused state of mind.

Just as you would if you were driving a race car or piloting a plane, you must not let your mind wander. Video games demand complete attention. But the sense that at any time you could make one false move and lose is their attraction—at least for me. That is why I like video games more than pinball. Pinball is just too easy. You can always recover. By shaking the machine or quickly operating the flippers, you can save the ball. Video games, however, are not so easy to control. Usually, one slip and you're dead (Turkle 83-84).

CHECKLIST

**Writing a Paraphrase**

- ❑ Reread your source until you understand it.
- ❑ Write your paraphrase, following the tone and emphasis of the original.
- ❑ Avoid using the words or phrasing of the original. (Enclose any borrowed material within quotation marks.)
- ❑ Add appropriate documentation.

## 15c Quoting Sources

When you **quote,** you copy a writer's statements exactly as they appear in a source, word for word and punctuation mark for punctuation mark, enclosing the borrowed material in quotation marks. As a rule, you should not quote extensively in a research paper. Numerous quotations interrupt the flow of your discussion and give readers the impression that your paper is just a collection of other people's ideas.

CHECKLIST

**When to Quote**

Quote a source only in the following situations:

- ❑ Quote when a source's wording or phrasing is so distinctive that a summary or paraphrase would diminish its impact.
- ❑ Quote when a source's words will lend authority to your discussion.
- ❑ Quote when a writer's words are so concise that paraphrasing would change the meaning of the original.
- ❑ Quote when you go on to disagree with a source. Using a source's exact words helps convince readers you are being fair.

Note: Remember to document all quotations that you use in your paper.

## EXERCISE 1

Choose a debatable issue from the following list:

- Illegal immigrants' rights to medical care
- Helmet requirements for motorcycle riders
- Community service requirements for college students
- Making English the official language of the United States
- Requiring every citizen to carry a national identification card
- A constitutional amendment prohibiting the defacing of the American flag

Write a one-sentence summary of your own position on the issue; then, interview a classmate and write a one-sentence summary of his or her position on the same issue. Be sure each sentence includes the reasons that support the position. Next, write a single sentence that compares and contrasts the two positions.

## EXERCISE 2

Assume that in preparation for a paper on the effects of the growth of the suburbs, you read the following paragraph from the book *Great Expectations: America and the Baby Boom Generation* by Landon Y. Jones. Reread the paragraph, and write a brief summary. Then, write a paraphrase of the paragraph, quoting only those words and phrases you consider especially distinctive.

> As an internal migration, the settling of the suburbs was phenomenal. In the twenty years from 1950 to 1970, the population of the suburbs doubled from 36 million to 72 million. No less than 83 percent of the total population growth in the United States during the 1950s was in the suburbs, which were growing fifteen times faster than any other segment of the country. As

people packed and moved, the national mobility rate leaped by 50 percent. The only other comparable influx was the wave of European immigrants to the United States around the turn of the century. But as *Fortune* pointed out, more people moved to the suburbs every year than had ever arrived on Ellis Island.



## 15d Integrating Source Material into Your Writing

Weave quotations, paraphrases, and summaries smoothly into your discussion, adding your own analysis or explanation to increase coherence and to show the relevance of your source material to the points you are making.

### Integrating Source Material into Your Writing

To make sure your sentences do not all sound the same, experiment with different methods of integrating source material into your paper:

- Vary the verbs you use to introduce a source's words or ideas (instead of repeating *says*).

| | | | |
|---|---|---|---|
| acknowledges | concludes | implies | proposes |
| admits | concurs | indicates | reports |
| affirms | discloses | insists | speculates |
| believes | explains | notes | suggests |
| claims | finds | observes | summarizes |
| comments | illustrates | predicts | warns |

- Vary the placement of the **identifying tag** (the phrase that identifies the source), putting it in the middle or at the end of the quoted material instead of always at the beginning.

**Quotation with Identifying Tag in Middle:** "A serious problem confronting Amish society from the viewpoint of the Amish themselves," observes Hostetler, "is the threat of absorption into mass society through the values promoted in the public school system" (193).

**Paraphrase with Identifying Tag at End:** The Amish are also concerned about their children's exposure to the public school system's values, notes Hostetler (193).

## 1 Integrating Quotations

Be sure to work quotations smoothly into your sentences. Quotations should never be awkwardly dropped into your paper, leaving the relationship between the quoted words and your point unclear. Use brief introductory remarks to provide a context for the quotation, and quote only those words you need to make your point.

**Acceptable:** For the Amish, the public school system is a problem because it represents "the threat of absorption into mass society" (Hostetler 193).

**Unacceptable:** For the Amish, the public school system represents a problem. "A serious problem confronting Amish society from the viewpoint of the Amish themselves is the threat of absorption into mass society through the values promoted in the public school system" (Hostetler 193).

Whenever possible, use an identifying tag to introduce the source of the quotation.

**Identifying Tag:** As John Hostetler points out, the Amish see the public school system as a problem because it represents "the threat of absorption into mass society" (193).

### Close-Up PUNCTUATING IDENTIFYING TAGS

Whether or not to use a comma with an identifying tag depends on where you place the tag in the sentence. If the identifying tag immediately precedes a quotation, use a comma.

As Hostetler points out, "The Amish are successful in maintaining group identity" (56).

If the identifying tag does not immediately precede a quotation, do not use a comma.

Hostetler points out that the Amish frequently "use severe sanctions to preserve their values" (56).

**Note:** Never use a comma after *that:* Hostetler says that/ Amish society is "defined by religion" (76).

***Substitutions or Additions within Quotations*** Indicate changes or additions that you make to a quotation by enclosing your changes in brackets.

**Original Quotation:** "Immediately after her wedding, she and her husband followed tradition and went to visit almost everyone who attended the wedding" (Hostetler 122).

**Quotation Edited to Make Verb Tenses Consistent:** Nowhere is the Amish dedication to tradition more obvious than in the events surrounding marriage. Right after the wedding celebration, the Amish bride and groom "visit almost everyone who [has] attended the wedding" (Hostetler 122).

**Quotation Edited to Supply an Antecedent for a Pronoun:** "Immediately after her wedding, [Sarah] and her husband followed tradition and went to visit almost everyone who attended the wedding" (Hostetler 122).

**Quotation Edited to Change an Uppercase to a Lowercase Letter:** The strength of the Amish community is illustrated by the fact that "[i]mmediately after her wedding, she and her husband followed tradition and went to visit almost everyone who attended the wedding" (Hostetler 122).

See 57f1

***Omissions within Quotations*** When you delete unnecessary or irrelevant words, substitute an **ellipsis** (three spaced periods) for the deleted words.

**Original Quotation:** "Not only have the Amish built and staffed their own elementary and vocational schools, but they have gradually organized on local, state, and national levels to cope with the task of educating their children" (Hostetler 206).

**Quotation Edited to Eliminate Unnecessary Words:** "Not only have the Amish built and staffed their own elementary and vocational schools, but they have gradually organized . . . to cope with the task of educating their children" (Hostetler 206).

**Close-Up** OMISSIONS WITHIN QUOTATIONS

Be sure you do not misrepresent or distort the meaning of quoted material when you shorten it. For example, do not say, "the Amish have managed to maintain . . . their culture" when the original quotation is "the Amish have managed to maintain *parts of* their culture."

See Ch. 18

*Note:* If the passage you are quoting already contains ellipses, **MLA style** requires that you place brackets around any ellipses you add.

***Long Quotations*** Set off a quotation of more than four typed lines of prose (or more than three lines of poetry) by indenting it one inch from the margin. Double-space, and do not use quotation marks. See 56b

If you are quoting a single paragraph, do not indent the first line. If you are quoting more than one paragraph, indent the first line of each complete paragraph an additional one-quarter inch. Integrate the quotation into your paper by introducing it with a complete sentence followed by a colon. Place parenthetical documentation one space after the end punctuation.

> According to Hostetler, the Amish were not always hostile to public education:
>
> > The one-room rural elementary school served the Amish community well in a number of ways. As long as it was a public school, it stood midway between the Amish community and the world. Its influence was tolerable, depending upon the degree of influence the Amish were able to bring to the situation. (196)

## 2 Integrating Paraphrases and Summaries

Introduce your paraphrases and summaries with identifying tags, and end them with appropriate documentation. By doing so, you make certain that your readers are able to see the boundaries of the source material so they can differentiate your ideas from those of your sources.

**Correct (Identifying Tag Differentiates Ideas of Source from Ideas of Writer):** Art can be used to uncover many problems that children have at home, in school, or with their friends. For this reason, many therapists use art therapy extensively. According to William Alschuler in *Art and Self-Image,* children's views of themselves in society are often reflected by their art style. For example, a cramped, crowded art style using only a portion of the paper shows a child's limited role (260).

**Misleading (Ideas of Source Blend with Ideas of Writer):** Art can be used to uncover many problems that children have at home, in school, or with their friends. For this reason, many therapists use art therapy extensively. Children's views of themselves in society are often reflected by their art style. For example, a cramped, crowded art style using only a portion of the paper shows their limited role (Alschuler 260).

### EXERCISE 3

Look back at the summary and paraphrase that you wrote for Exercise 2. Write three possible identifying tags for each, varying the verbs you use for attribution and the placement of the identifying tag. Be sure to include appropriate documentation at the end of each passage.

CHAPTER 16

# Synthesizing Sources

## Frequently Asked Questions



To *synthesize* means to combine two or more things to form something new. In academic settings, writers must often synthesize source information, combining borrowed material with their own ideas in order to express an original viewpoint. Synthesis allows writers to explore relationships among ideas and to arrange those ideas in a logical way.

## 16a Understanding Synthesis

While summaries and paraphrases rephrase a source's key ideas, and quotations reproduce a source's exact language, a **synthesis** combines these strategies to create an essay or a paragraph that develops the writer's own viewpoint. An effective synthesis shows the relevance of each source to the writer's points.

To synthesize source material, you need to discover connections among sources that may seem unrelated. For this reason, you need to think critically about your topic and your sources, trying to understand both your topic and your own point of view.

The first step in synthesizing material is to determine how your sources are alike and how they are different, where they agree and disagree, and whether they reach the same conclusions. As you identify connections between one source and another or between a source and your own ideas, you will develop your own perspective on your subject. It is this viewpoint, summarized in a thesis statement (in the case of an entire paper) or in a topic sentence (in the case of a paragraph), that becomes the focus of your synthesis.

**Close-Up** QUESTIONS FOR MAKING CONNECTIONS AMONG SOURCES

As you plan your synthesis, ask yourself these questions:

- What positions do the sources take on the issue?
- What key terms do the sources identify and define?
- What background information do the sources provide?
- How do the sources address their audiences?
- How do the sources agree?
- How do the sources disagree?
- What evidence do the sources use to support their assertions?
- How do the sources address opposing points of view?
- How do the sources organize their main ideas?

CHECKLIST

**Writing a Synthesis**

As you write your synthesis, follow these guidelines:

- ❑ Begin with a statement that sums up the main point of your synthesis.
- ❑ Develop your points one at a time, using your sources as support.
- ❑ Identify each source, naming its author(s) and title.
- ❑ Be sure to identify the similarities and differences among your sources.
- ❑ Carefully analyze and interpret source material.
- ❑ Use identifying tags as well as transitional words and phrases to help your readers follow your discussion.
- ❑ Be sure to differentiate your ideas from those of your sources.
- ❑ Document all summaries, paraphrases, and quotations that you use in your synthesis.

## 16b Writing an Explanatory Synthesis

An **explanatory synthesis** (whether essay or paragraph length) combines material from two or more sources to help readers understand a topic. The purpose of an explanatory synthesis is not to argue a point but simply to present information in a reasonably straightforward (and logical) way.

In a first-semester composition class, Jay Gilman, a computer science major, was given the following assignment:

> Choose an area that you think others would benefit from learning more about. Then, using three sources as support, write a paragraph that explains

this topic to an audience unfamiliar with the field. Summarize, paraphrase, and quote source material as appropriate, using MLA documentation style.

After carefully reading his sources and thinking critically about them, Jay wrote the following explanatory synthesis.

Topic sentence states student's main point

Computers carry out many of the tasks that make our way of life possible. For example, computer billing, with all its faults, makes modern business possible, and without computers we would not have access to the cellular services and cable or satellite television that we take for granted. But computers are more than fast calculators; they are also equipped with artificial intelligence (AI), which has transformed fields such as medicine, agriculture, and manufacturing. One technology writer defines artificial intelligence (AI) as "a field that attempts to provide machines with humanlike reasoning and language-processing capabilities" (Havenstein). Farming is an industry that is now using AI technology: with new, high-tech agricultural sprayers that treat crops precisely and accurately, farmers are able to improve the output and quality of their yield ("More Machine Intelligence").

Quotation from Havenstein article

Source

There's no precise definition of AI, but broadly, it's a field that attempts to provide machines with humanlike reasoning and language-processing capabilities.

Paraphrase of unsigned article's text and visual content

Source

Researchers at Oklahoma State University, meanwhile, have demonstrated the potential for adding machine intelligence to agricultural sprayers (photo). Enhanced with sensors and computers, the field sprayers dramatically increased the application efficiency by applying fertilizers and herbicides only where needed, reports John B. Solie, professor, power and machinery at Oklahoma State.

F. Schussler/PhotoLink/Getty Images

Summary of Howell article

AI has also made possible numerous medical advances—for example, helping scientists to generate human tissue, bone, and organs for patients in need (Howell). Given the importance of AI technology, it is certain that computers will change our lives even more in the future.

Conclusion summarizes student writer's position

Source

**Human 2.0**
News that an artificial pancreas has been developed, which could help millions of diabetes patients, is only the tip of the iceberg as far as augmentation of the human body goes. We can already grow skin, cartilage, bone, ears and bladders.

This synthesis effectively defines the term *artificial intelligence (AI)* and uses information from three short articles to explain AI and briefly describe its use in various fields. The writer introduces his paragraph with a summary of computer applications familiar to his readers and then moves into a discussion of AI.

**EXERCISE 1**

Examine a group of advertisements (on television, in print, or in electronic media) that either target the same group of consumers (children, for example) or focus on a similar product (teeth whiteners, for example). Then, integrate information from at least three ads in a paragraph-length explanatory synthesis that discusses the message the ads are trying to convey.

## 16c Writing an Argumentative Synthesis

Like an explanatory synthesis, an **argumentative synthesis** (whether essay or paragraph length) also combines information from two or more sources. However, its primary purpose is to convey the writer's own point of view—supported by material from the sources. The thesis of an argumentative synthesis should be debatable, expressing a position about which reasonable people can disagree. In an argumentative synthesis, a writer synthesizes sources to develop a chain of logic that supports a thesis.

In a second-semester composition class, Angela Gray, a psychology major, was given the following assignment:

> Choose a controversy related to your major. Then, locate source material on this topic. Integrate four print sources and one visual source in an essay that takes a stand on the issue. Summarize, paraphrase, and quote source material as support, using MLA documentation style.

In response to this assignment, Angela wrote the argumentative synthesis shown on pages 226–232.

Gray 1

Angela Gray

Professor Morgan

English 102

2 April 2012

Spirituality in Therapy:
Should Secular Psychologists Accommodate
Religious Patients?

Introduction

Thesis statement

Religious people have motives for their actions that are different from those who are secular, and psychologists can benefit from understanding these motives. In fact, it is possible that the use of spirituality in a therapy setting could be beneficial not only to religious patients, but also to the psychologists who treat them.

Summary of Young, Wiggins-Frame, and Cashwell article

A great many Americans are religious and are looking for help from professionals who share their convictions (Young, Wiggins-Frame, and Cashwell 47). Still, many people go to a member of the clergy for counseling because they think that a psychologist may ridicule their beliefs. As a result, these patients may receive inadequate support from clergy who are not equipped to deal with complicated psychological problems. In such cases, the use of spirituality in psychotherapy sessions may enable religious individuals to receive more effective treatment.

Paraphrase of and quotation from Blanton article

The need to believe in a higher power can sometimes cause great emotional distress in clients. Psychotherapist and scholar P. Gregg Blanton suggests that the postmodern era has caused people to feel disconnected from God (69), resulting in feelings of isolation and abandonment. Lacking support or a sense of direction, religious people may become convinced that they are "seeking something besides God" (Blanton 69).

Source: Young, Wiggins-Frame, and Cashwell

that religion and spirituality are important to them (University of Pennsylvania, 2003). Indeed, a majority of families adhere to some religious system for the expression of their spirituality (Campbell & Moyers, 1988). Because there is such widespread commitment of the general population to some form of spirituality, it is not surprising that when faced with a major difficulty, two thirds of Gallup respondents indicated that they would prefer to see a counselor who held similar spiritual values and beliefs (Lehman, 1993). Furthermore, counselors themselves report spiritual and religious beliefs and practices at rates comparable with those of the general population (Kelly, 1995). Not to address issues of spirituality and religion in counseling is to ignore a vital aspect of clients' lives (Burke et al., 1999; Ellison, 1991; Frame, 2003; Hadaway, Marler, & Chaves, 1993; Miller, 1999; Wuthnow, 1994).

Source: Blanton

***The Problem***

***Spiritual Direction.*** Operating from a Christian worldview, instead of a postmodern one, spiritual direction has a very different view of the problem. Because of the Fall of humankind, people have fallen away from their awareness of and responsiveness to God's Spirit in their souls. The image of God is hidden, because they have fallen into an overly separated sense of themselves (Edwards, 2001).

We are not actually separate from God. According to spiritual direction, the problem is that we do not realize that we are united with God. Our usual experience is that we are "here" and God is "there" (May, 2004). As we lose sensitivity to the spiritual level, "we can cease to feel the touch of the Mystery that bends so near us in order to communicate with us" (Gratton, 1992, p. 2).

May (2004) suggests that we feel separate from God for two fundamental reasons. First, he quotes St Teresa from The Interior Castles: "We just don't understand ourselves or who we are" (p. 51). The second reason is that we have become attached to things other than God. The root of our problem is that we are seeking something besides God.

Gray 2

Summary of Phillips and Henderson article and table data

Patients who experience spiritually directed therapy may be better able to cope with stress and stress-induced illness. A recent study shows that rates of depression are lower in religious college students than in their nonreligious counterparts (Phillips and Henderson 169). For this reason, psychotherapists should consider integrating spirituality into their treatment.

Paraphrase of and single-word quotation from Young, Wiggins-Frame, and Cashwell article

Of course, the incorporation of spirituality into counseling is not without problems. Most psychologists do not have formal training in religion and, for this reason, have traditionally "neglected" spiritual matters in counseling (Young, Wiggins-Frame, and Cashwell 47). As noted by Young, Wiggins-Frame, and Cashwell, many religious people distrust the field of psychology because of the divide between science and religion (47). They may even resist counseling, a situation that can lead to inadequate treatment or to no treatment at all.

Quotation from Langberg article and paraphrase of two sections from article

Paraphrase of and quotation from Langberg article

However, despite the divide between the social sciences and religion, psychologist Diane Langberg sees benefits in including spirituality in psychological treatment. Langberg points out that all people are "image bearers" and incorporate into themselves the emotions and knowledge they perceive in others (259). The difficult work of therapists involves experiencing, along with their patients, the impact of their patients' stories and the distressing images evoked by those stories. Langberg suggests that offsetting such images with "the image of God" can offer new hope to both psychologists and patients (262).

Paraphrase of Blanton article

Perhaps one reason for hope lies in the growing interest among psychologists in including spirituality in therapy (Blanton 68). Therapists are, after all, human beings with

Source: Phillips and Henderson

***Symptom Differences and Subjective Religiousness***

Earlier we hypothesized that students who describe themselves as more religious will exhibit fewer symptoms of depression than those who are less religious or not at all religious. To test this hypothesis, the authors of this study examined respondents' mean symptom scores for each response category of the question measuring religiousness. The results of an ANOVA comparing these means appear in Table 2. The statistically significant value of F (F=41.93 p<.05) denotes that there is more variability in symptoms of depression between the categories of the religiousness variable than within them. The analysis also shows that respondents who rate themselves as "very," "some," or "a little" religious have significantly fewer symptoms of depression than those who declare that they are "not at all" religious (p<.05). This is consistent with the hypothesis outlined above. Those who report that they are "very" religious rank the lowest on the depression scale (mean=28.2), followed by those who say "some" (mean=29.0), and those who say that they are "a little" religious (mean=29.1). The differences between these three groups, however, are not statistically significant. This suggests that the presence or absence of religious devotion in the population under investigation matters more than the intensity of that devotion.

**Table 2: Means and Standard Deviations for Depression by Level of Religiousness**

| | N | Mean | $S$ |
|---|---|---|---|
| Very | 2826 | 28.2 * | 4.01 |
| Some | 4609 | 29.0 * | 3.94 |
| A Little | 3089 | 29.1 * | 3.89 |
| Not at all | 2731 | 29.4 | 4.19 |

F statistic = 41.93, $p<.05$

* Mean difference from non-religious significant at $p<.05$

Source: Young, Wiggins-Frame, and Cashwell

Until recently, many mental health professionals neglected issues related to religion and spirituality in their work with clients (Bergin, 1980, 1983; Frame, 2003; Henning & Tirrell, 1982; Hodge, 2001; Richards & Bergin, 1997; Schulte, Skinner, & Claiborn, 2002; Slife, Hope, & Nebeker, 1999; Zinnbauer & Pargament, 2000). Part of the explanation for excluding religion and spirituality from clinical work came from the conflict between the scientific, objective perspective of psychology and the transcendent, subjective aspects of religion (Burke et al., 1999; Lovinger, 1984; Pattison, 1978; Prest & Keller, 1993; Rayburn, 1985; Reisner & Lawson, 1992; Wallwork & Wallwork, 1990).

Source: Langberg

All of us are image bearers, mirrors. When we talk with one another we see reflected in each our histories, our country or locality of origin, the physical characteristics of our parents. If you listen carefully to me for a long enough time you may see the reflection of my political preference, what I have read lately, or the areas with which I struggle. We read such reflections all the time in the lives of our patients. We often see there the reflection of things they have never explicitly stated. Our ability to do so makes them nervous. They think we can read minds.

Now I believe this principle runs even deeper. I believe that because we as humans are soft, malleable, and permeable, that we not only reflect but we also assimilate.[1] To assimilate means to take something up and make it part of yourself. We carry within that which we reflect. We are image *bearers*, not simply image reflectors. If you stand in front of a mirror you see yourself reflected there. But if you walk away the image is gone. Nothing within the substance of the mirror is any different than before you were reflected in it. Mirrors do not assimilate your image. I believe that human beings, over time, take into their very substance the things that they reflect. They hold such reflections preserved within themselves.

Source: Langberg

was lost (for the image of God in us was shattered). He came to set free the captives and to make all things new. I believe that you and I as believers first, and as therapists, second, are to live in such a way that we too explain the Father to others. While bearing the image of suffering in ourselves we are to habitually reflect the Father so as to serve as a redemptive force in this world. I believe that is true because Scripture calls us to walk as Jesus walked. That means that if we want the work that we do to restore and make new, if we want who we are to reflect the image of Christ to others, then we ourselves must incarnate who God is. We must learn to bear God's image in our persons. We must learn to be under God's influence more than any other influence, for to live with God is to become like God.

Source: Blanton

During the past decade, mental health professionals have become increasingly interested in integrating religion and spirituality into psychotherapy (Griffith & Griffith, 2002). A more specific focus that has received greater attention recently is the integration of spiritual direction and psychotherapy (Tan, 2004).

Gray 3

emotional, psychological, and spiritual complexities. Many of them, as Table 1 shows, also hold religious beliefs of their own.

Incorporation of Walker, Gorsuch, and Tan table summarizing relevant data

Table 1

Differences in Religious Denomination by Professional Background

| | **Psychologists**[a] | | **Marriage and Family Therapists**[b] | | **Social Workers**[c] | |
|---|---|---|---|---|---|---|
| Affiliation | *N* | % | *N* | % | *N* | % |
| Protestant | 593 | 35.85 | 433 | 50.0 | 109 | 40.1 |
| Jewish | 339 | 20.49 | 110 | 12.7 | 56 | 20.6 |
| Catholic | 250 | 15.11 | 126 | 14.6 | 32 | 11.8 |
| Atheist | 31 | 1.87 | 3 | 0.03 | 3 | 1.1 |
| Agnostic | 74 | 4.47 | 6 | 0.07 | 6 | 2.2 |
| No religion | 270 | 16.32 | 71 | 8.2 | 27 | 9.9 |
| Other | 297 | 17.96 | 117 | 13.5 | 33 | 14.3 |

Note: Percentages do not total 100 due to rounding.

[a]Ten studies. [b]Six studies. [c]Three studies.

Source: Donald F. Walker, Richard L. Gorsuch, and Siang-Yang Tan; "Therapists' Integration of Religion and Spirituality in Counseling: A Meta-Analysis"; *Counseling and Values* 49 (2004): 74; *Academic Search Elite*; Web; 19 Mar. 2012.

Summary of Young, Wiggins-Frame, and Cashwell table data

Summary of Blanton article

Religious therapists may be better able to identify with religious patients because they understand the ways in which religious beliefs make a person unique. In fact, according to a recent survey of American Counseling Association members, many therapists actually regard spirituality as important to their work (Young, Wiggins-Frame, and Cashwell 49). Blanton also argues that spiritually directed therapy closely mirrors the proven method of family narrative therapy.

Conclusion and recommendations

Despite possible objections, the incorporation of spirituality in a psychotherapeutic setting could have significant benefits for both patient and psychologist. First, religious individuals with emotional and psychological problems could seek treatment without worrying about their

Source: Young, Wiggins-Frame, and Cashwell

TABLE 2

**Mean Importance and Percentage of Agreement Scores for All Competencies**

| Competency[a] | *M* | *SD* | % Agree | 95% CI |
|---|---|---|---|---|
| Sensitivity to communication . . . (5) | 4.7 | 1.43 | 92 | 4.64–4.76 |
| Limits to own understanding . . . (6) | 4.7 | 0.70 | 92 | 4.64–4.76 |
| Respectful of spiritual themes . . . (8) | 4.6 | 0.68 | 92 | 4.54–4.66 |
| Engage in self-exploration . . . (3) | 4.3 | 1.02 | 80 | 4.21–4.39 |
| Assess relevance of spiritual domains . . . (7) | 4.1 | 0.95 | 77 | 4.02–4.18 |
| Use client's beliefs in treatment . . . (9) | 4.0 | 0.95 | 70 | 3.92–4.08 |
| Describe practices in a cultural context . . . (2) | 3.8 | 1.02 | 66 | 3.71–3.89 |
| Explain the relationship . . . (1) | 3.8 | 1.03 | 65 | 3.71–3.89 |
| Explain self/models of development . . . (4) | 3.5 | 1.15 | 51 | 3.40–3.60 |

*Note.* $N = 505$. CI = confidence interval.

[a]A complete list of competencies is available in the Appendix.

Gray 4

religious beliefs being challenged. Second, psychologists could receive more trust from the religious community. Thus, by incorporating spirituality, psychologists could have another tool with which to explore mind, body, and spirit.

Gray 5

Works Cited

Blanton, P. Gregg. "Narrative Family Therapy and Spiritual Direction: Do They Fit?" *Journal of Psychology and Christianity* 24.1 (2005): 68-79. *Academic Search Elite*. Web. 21 Mar. 2012.

Langberg, Diane. "The Spiritual Life of the Therapist: We Become What We Habitually Reflect." *Journal of Psychology and Christianity* 25.3 (2006): 258-66. *Academic Search Elite*. Web. 20 Mar. 2012.

Phillips, Rick, and Andrea Henderson. "Religion and Depression among US College Students." *International Social Science Review* 82.3-4 (2006): 166-72. *Academic Search Elite*. Web. 21 Mar. 2012.

Young, J. Scott, Marsha Wiggins-Frame, and Craig S. Cashwell. "Spirituality and Counselor Competence: A National Survey of American Counseling Association Members." *Journal of Counseling & Development* 85.1 (2007): 47-52. *Academic Search Elite*. Web. 19 Mar. 2012.

This synthesis effectively argues for the benefits of incorporating spirituality into therapy. The student writer weaves information from four academic articles and a table from a fifth article into her discussion. She clearly states and develops an argumentative thesis on a debatable topic, synthesizing source material to develop her points. In addition, she considers and refutes opposing arguments. Finally, she concludes the essay with recommendations that take the multiple perspectives of her sources into account.

### EXERCISE 2

Read the following four sources. Then, write an essay-length argumentative synthesis that integrates at least three of the sources. Develop your own perspective on the topic of women and advertising and summarize it in a clear thesis statement. Summarize, paraphrase, and quote from sources, using MLA parenthetical reference style.

**Source A**

The following passage is excerpted from a book exploring the relationship between advertising and consumer behavior.

> The gap between boys and girls is closing, but this is not always for the best. According to a 1998 status report by a consortium of universities and research centers, girls have closed the gap with boys in math performance and are coming close in science. But they are also now smoking, drinking, and using drugs as often as boys their own age. And, although girls are not nearly as violent as boys, they are committing more crimes than ever before and are far more often physically attacking each other.
>
> It is important to understand that these problems go way beyond individual psychological development and pathology. Even girls who are raised in loving homes by supportive parents grow up in a toxic cultural environment, at risk for self-mutilation, eating disorders, and addictions. The culture, both reflected and reinforced by advertising, urges girls to adopt a false self, to bury alive their real selves, to become "feminine," which means to be nice and kind and sweet, to compete with other girls for the attention of boys, and to value romantic relationships with boys above all else. Girls are put into a terrible double bind. They are supposed to repress their power, their anger, their exuberance and be simply "nice," although they also eventually must compete with men in the business world and be successful. They must be overtly sexy and attractive but essentially passive and virginal. It is not surprising that most girls experience this time as painful and confusing, especially if they are unconscious of these conflicting demands. (Kilbourne, Jean. *Can't Buy My Love: How Advertising Changes the Way We Think and Feel*. New York: Simon, 1999. 129–30. Print.)

**Source B**

The following is a magazine advertisement for women's fashion.

Image courtesy of the Advertising Archives

(Wal-Mart. Advertisement. *The Advertising Archives*. Advertising Archives, 2009. Web. 28 Mar. 2012.)

**Source C**

The following is excerpted from a study analyzing the depiction of women in magazine advertisements since 1955.

This study was designed to examine the portrayal of women in advertisements in a general interest magazine (i.e., *Time*) and a women's fashion magazine (i.e., *Vogue*) over the last 50 years. The coding scheme used for this analysis was based on the one developed by sociologist Erving Goffman in the 1970s, which focuses primarily on the subtle and underlying clues in the picture content of advertisements that contain messages in terms of (stereotypical) gender roles. The results of this study show that, overall, advertisements in *Vogue*, a magazine geared toward a female audience, depict women more stereotypically than do those in *Time*, a magazine with the general public as a target audience. In addition, only a slight decrease in the stereotypical depiction of women was found over time, despite the influence of the Women's Movement. . . .

In this study, a longitudinal approach was taken to analyze the portrayal of women in a general interest magazine and a women's fashion magazine from 1955 to 2002. The sample consisted of the issues of *Time* in the first 4 weeks of January and June in the years 1955, 1965, 1975, 1985, 1995, and 2002 as well as the January and June issues of *Vogue* in the same years. The months of January and June were selected to avoid a bias in the sample based on the time of the year the advertisements were published. (It could be expected, for example, that advertisements in magazine issues of the summer months include more instances of "body display.") By including summer as well as winter issues, the sample was expected to reveal greater insight regarding the overall picture of the way women are portrayed. (Lindner, Katharina. "Images of Women in General Interest and Fashion Magazine Advertisements from 1955 to 2002." *Sex Roles* 51.7–8 [2004]: 409–21. Print.)

**Source D**

The following is excerpted from a book about the impact of popular notions of feminine beauty.

When this book first came out [in 1991], general public opinion considered anorexia and bulimia to be anomalous marginal behavior, and the cause was not assumed to be society's responsibility, insofar as it created ideals and exerted pressure to conform to them—but rather personal crises, perfectionism, poor parenting, and other forms of individual psychological maladjustment. In reality, however, these diseases were widely suffered by many ordinary young women from unremarkable backgrounds, women and girls who were simply trying to maintain an unnatural "ideal" body shape and weight. I knew from looking around me in high school and at college that eating disorders were widespread among otherwise perfectly well balanced young women, and that the simple, basic social pressure to be thin was a major factor in the development of these diseases. . . . Disordered eating, which was understood to fit a disordered ideal, was one of the causes of the disease, and not necessarily, as popular opinion of the day held, a manifestation of an underlying neurosis.

Now, of course, education about the dangers of obsessive dieting or exercise is widespread, and information about eating disorders, their addictive nature, and how to treat them is available in every bookstore, as well as in middle schools, doctors' offices, gyms, high schools, and sororities. *This*, now, is progress.

Yet, on the down side, those very disorders are now so widespread, in fact, almost destigmatized by such intense publicity that they have become virtually normal. Not only do whole sororities take for granted that bulimia is mainstream behavior, but models now openly talk to *Glamour* magazine about their starvation regimes. A newspaper feature about a group of thin, ambitious young women talking about weight quotes one of them as saying,

"Now what's wrong with throwing up?" And "pro-an" Web sites have appeared on the Internet, indicating a subculture of girls who are "pro-anorexia," who find the anorexic look appealing and validate it. This is definitely *not* progress. (Wolf, Naomi. *The Beauty Myth: How Images of Beauty Are Used against Women.* New York: Harper, 2002. 5–6. Print.)

CHAPTER 17

# Avoiding Plagiarism

## Frequently Asked Questions



## 17a Defining Plagiarism

Throughout high school, students are taught that they should not plagiarize. They hear this so often that they never stop to consider why teachers are so insistent about this issue. The answer to this question is not as simple as it may seem.

Most likely, you already understand the basic concept of plagiarism. If, for example, a friend reposted something you said on *Twitter* or *Facebook* without acknowledging the comments as yours, you would instinctively know that your friend did something wrong. You would be upset that your friend took your posts and passed them off as his or her own. The same would be true if you heard that a reporter made up a story that he or she said was factual or that the author of a book took information from another book and submitted it as his or her own. No one would have to explain to you that these actions were wrong.

In an academic setting, however, the issue is a bit more complicated. **Plagiarism** occurs when a writer (intentionally or unintentionally) uses the words, ideas, or distinctive style of others without acknowledging their source. In other words, you plagiarize when you submit someone else's work as your own or fail to document appropriately. The harm plagiarism does, however, extends beyond the act itself. Instructors assign research for a reason; they want students to become part of a community of scholars and to take part in the conversations that define this community. When you misappropriate the work of others, you deprive yourself of a unique opportunity to learn. Moreover, by plagiarizing, you devalue the work of other students who have acted ethically and responsibly. Finally, plagiarism (as well as other forms of academic dishonesty) compromises the academic mission of your school, weakens the intellectual foundation on which all colleges and universities rest, and undermines the climate of mutual trust and respect that must exist for learning to take place.

Most plagiarism is **unintentional plagiarism**—for example, inadvertently pasting a quoted passage into a paper and forgetting to include the quotation marks and documentation.

There is a difference, however, between an honest mistake and **intentional plagiarism**—for example, copying a passage word for word from a journal article or submitting a paper that someone else has written. The penalties for unintentional plagiarism may sometimes be severe, but intentional plagiarism is almost always dealt with harshly: students who intentionally plagiarize can receive a failing grade for the paper (or the course) and can even be expelled from school.

**Understanding Plagiarism**

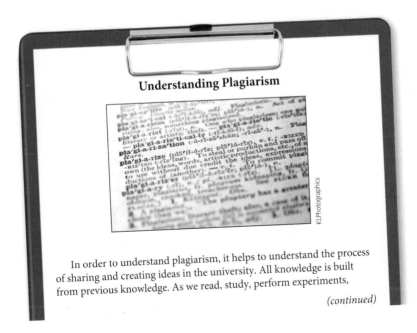

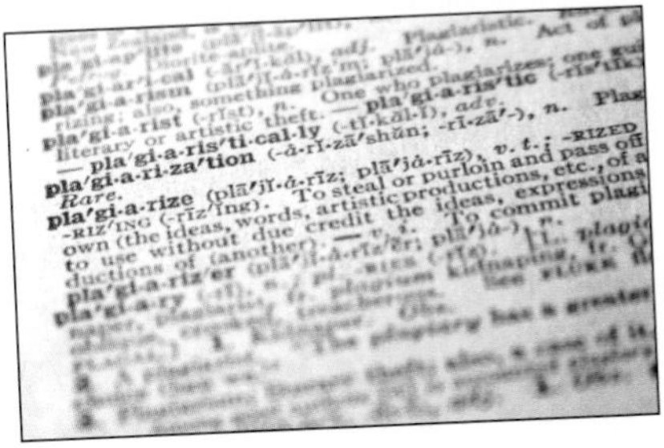

KLPhotographics

In order to understand plagiarism, it helps to understand the process of sharing and creating ideas in the university. All knowledge is built from previous knowledge. As we read, study, perform experiments,

*(continued)*

### Understanding Plagiarism (*continued*)

and gather perspectives, we are drawing on other people's ideas. Building on their ideas and experiences, we create our own. When you put your ideas on paper, your instructors want to distinguish between the building block ideas borrowed from other people and your own newly reasoned perspectives or conclusions. You make these distinctions in a written paper by citing the sources for your building block ideas. Providing appropriate citations will also help readers who are interested in your topic find additional, related material to read—in this way, they will be able to build on the work you have done to find sources.

—"Plagiarism" from The Writing Center at UNC Chapel Hill. © 2010–2012 by The Writing Center at UNC Chapel Hill.

[W]eb surfing encourages the free flow and exchange of ideas. Sharing and borrowing are integral parts of the online experience. Shareware is a positive example of this philosophy in use. Plagiarism, whether it is unintentional or not, is a negative example.

—From "Encourage Academic Integrity and Prevent Plagiarism" from the City College of San Francisco, Library and Learning Resources.

In my experience, people usually don't consciously decide to plagiarize, but they may end up plagiarizing "by accident" because they run out of time, or they get confused about the assignment, or maybe they copy-and-paste, intending to go back and edit later but forgetting to do so. Every time that I have seen plagiarism in an assignment, the person swore that the plagiarism happened "by accident." That does not change the fact of the matter: plagiarism, even when it happens by accident, is still plagiarism, and the consequences are serious. It's like when you are caught speeding or running a red light: it doesn't matter if you ran the red light because you were not paying attention or because you did not know you were speeding—you are still going to get a speeding ticket.

—From "Orientation Week: Original Writing and Plagiarism" by Laura Gibbs, University of Oklahoma, http://onlinecourselady.pbworks.com/w/page/12763870/plagiarism.

Drawing on the ideas of others as you develop your own is an essential and exciting component of intellectual work. Whenever you use other writers' ideas, however, you must acknowledge your sources. Doing so allows you to distinguish between your ideas and those of others; it directs your readers to relevant sources; and it allows you to give credit where credit is due.

—From "Using Sources" from Nesbitt-Johnston Writing Center, Hamilton College, Clinton, NY 13323. https://my.hamilton.edu/documents/writing-center/Using_Sources.PDF.

The values that underpin the concept of academic integrity go beyond simply not cheating or plagiarizing. Embracing these values mean[s] that you are responsible for your own learning; you have an obligation to be honest—with yourself and others; and you have the responsibility to treat other students and your professors with respect and fairness.

—From "Academic Integrity for Students" from *Guide to Plagiarism and Cyber-Plagiarism*, University of Alberta Libraries, August 8, 2011, http://guides.library.ualberta.ca/content.php?pid=62200&sid=460084.

At its core, academic integrity requires honesty. This involves giving credit where it is due and acknowledging the contributions of others to one's own intellectual efforts. It also includes assuring that one's own work has been completed in accordance with the standards of one's course or discipline. Without academic integrity, neither the genuine innovations of the individual nor the progress of a given field of study can adequately be assessed, and the very foundation of scholarship itself is undermined. Academic integrity, for all these reasons, is an essential link in the process of intellectual advancement.

—Student Judicial Services at the University of Texas

## Close-Up DETECTING PLAGIARISM

The same technology that has made unintentional plagiarism more common has also made plagiarism easier to detect. By doing a *Google* search, an instructor can quickly find the source of a phrase that has been plagiarized from an Internet source. In addition, plagiarism detection services, such as Turnitin.com, can search scholarly databases and identify plagiarized passages in student papers.

*(continued)*

## DETECTING PLAGIARISM *(continued)*

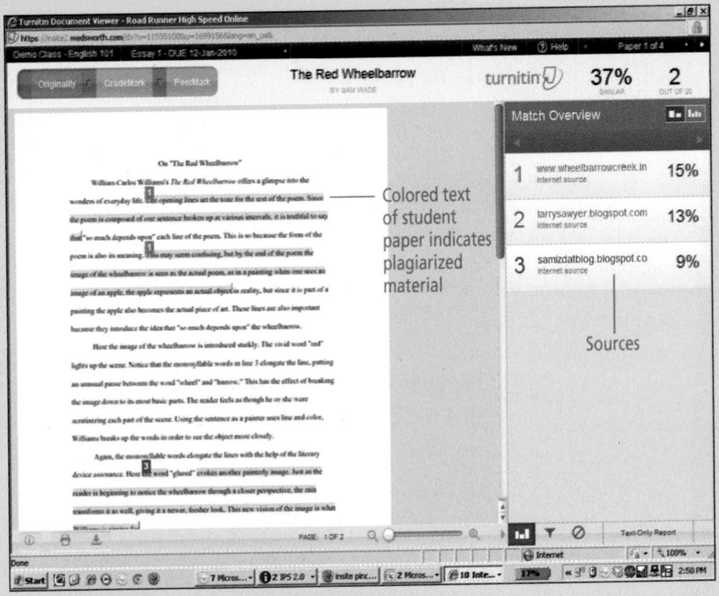


Courtesy of Turnitin.com

## 17b Avoiding Unintentional Plagiarism

The most common cause of unintentional plagiarism is sloppy research habits. To avoid this problem, start your research paper early. Do not cut and paste text from a Web site or full-text database directly into your paper. If you paraphrase, do so correctly by following the advice in **15b**.

In addition, take care to manage your sources—especially those you download—so that they do not overwhelm you. Unintentional plagiarism often occurs when students use source material thinking that it is their own. If you are writing a short paper, keep source material in a file. For longer papers, create separate files for each section of your paper.

### ESL TIP

Plagiarism is a difficult concept for many ESL students to grasp because it is not a concern in all countries. In cultures that value the group over the individual, including some Asian, African, and Latin American cultures, plagiarism is less of a concern because the group is thought to own the original work.

In places such as the United States, however, where the individual is valued over the group, plagiarism is considered stealing because the individual who originally developed the idea or work is considered to be its owner. Although you may be tempted to closely follow the syntax and word choice of your sources, be aware that this practice constitutes plagiarism.

A number of Web-based tools can help you manage your sources. For example, *Delicious* <delicious.com> enables you to tag and keep track of your research sources. *Zotero* <zotero.org> helps you to collect, organize, store, and share your research sources. Other programs can also be helpful. For example, *Evernote* <evernote.com> enables you to take notes and synchronize them with a calendar, and *Backpack* <backpackit.com> is a wiki page that lets you keep files, images, and notes in a single place.

Another cause of unintentional plagiarism is failure to use proper **documentation.** In general, you must document the following information:

- Direct quotations, summaries, and paraphrases of material in sources (including Web sources)
- Images that you borrow from a source (print or electronic)
- Facts and opinions that are another writer's original contributions
- Information that is the product of an author's original research
- Statistics, charts, graphs, or other compilations of data that are not yours

See Chs. 18–21

Material that is considered **common knowledge** (information most readers probably know) need not be documented. This includes facts available from a variety of reference sources, familiar sayings, and well-known quotations. Your own original research (interviews and surveys, for example) also does not require documentation.

So, although you do not have to document the fact that John F. Kennedy graduated from Harvard in 1940 or that he was elected president in 1960, you do have to document information from a historian's evaluation of his presidency. The best rule to follow is if you have doubts, document.

## Close-Up WHY DOCUMENT SOURCES?

There are a number of reasons to document sources:

- **To give credit** By documenting your sources, you acknowledge the original work of others.
- **To become part of a conversation** When you discuss the work of other scholars, you join an ongoing intellectual discussion.
- **To establish your credibility** By indicating what sources you have consulted, you show readers that your conclusions should be taken seriously.
- **To differentiate your ideas from the ideas of your sources** Documentation enables readers to identify the original ideas you have contributed to the discussion.

## 17c Avoiding Intentional Plagiarism

When students **intentionally plagiarize,** they make a decision to misappropriate the ideas or words of others—and this is no small matter. Not only does intentional plagiarism deprive the student of a valuable educational experience (instructors assign research for a reason), it also subverts the educational goals of other students as well as of the institution as a whole. Because academic honesty is absolutely central to any college or university, intentional plagiarism is taken very seriously.

So why do some students engage in this unethical (and risky) behavior? Research has shown that many students who intentionally plagiarize do so out of procrastination and fear. They put off working on their writing projects until they have no time to complete them. Or, they have trouble finding source materials. Some students find that as they do their research, their ideas change. As a result, they discover at the last minute that they have to shift the focus of their papers, and they panic. Finally, other students think that they are not up to the job of writing a research paper. The easiest way to deal with all these types of problems is to ask for help.

Of course, some students plagiarize out of laziness or because they mistakenly believe that buying a paper from a paper mill or paying someone to write a paper is "no big deal." Fortunately, these students are in the minority. Most, if not all, students realize that plagiarism is simply wrong.

## 17d Avoiding Other Kinds of Plagiarism

When instructors assign a research paper, they expect it to be your original work. They also expect your paper to be written in response to specific assignments they give. For this reason, you should not submit a paper that you have written for another course. (This is considered **self-plagiarism.**) If you intend to substantially rework or expand the paper, however, you may be able to use it. Check with your instructor before doing so.

A paper prepared in collaboration with other students can also present challenges. It is not uncommon in some courses to do work as part of a team. This collaborative work is acceptable in the course for which it was assigned. Even so, each member of the group should clearly identify the sections on which he or she worked.

Finally, although your instructors may encourage you to go the writing center for help, they do not expect your paper to include passages written by a tutor. Passages written (or revised and edited) by a friend or a family member are also unacceptable. If you present material contributed by others as if it were your own, you are committing plagiarism.

## 17e Revising to Eliminate Plagiarism

You can avoid plagiarism by using documentation wherever it is required and by following these guidelines.

### 1 Enclose Borrowed Words in Quotation Marks

**Original:** Historically, only a handful of families have dominated the fireworks industry in the West. Details such as chemical recipes and mixing procedures were cloaked in secrecy and passed down from one generation to the next. . . . One effect of familial secretiveness is that, until recent decades, basic pyrotechnic research was rarely performed, and even when it was, the results were not generally reported in scientific journals. (Conkling, John A. "Pyrotechnics.")

**Plagiarism:** John A. Conkling points out that until recently, little scientific research was done on the chemical properties of fireworks, and when it was, the results were not generally reported in scientific journals (96).

Even though the preceding example includes documentation, the student writer uses the source's exact words without placing them in quotation marks.

The writer can correct this problem either by putting the borrowed words in quotation marks or by paraphrasing them.

**Correct (Borrowed Words in Quotation Marks):** John A. Conkling points out that until recently, little scientific research was done on the chemical properties of fireworks, and when it was, "the results were not generally reported in scientific journals" (96).

**Correct (Paraphrase):** John A. Conkling points out that the little research conducted on the chemical composition of fireworks was seldom reported in the scientific literature (96).

**Close-Up** PLAGIARISM AND INTERNET SOURCES

Any time you download text from the Internet, you run the risk of committing unintentional plagiarism. To avoid the possibility of plagiarism, follow these guidelines:

- Download information into individual files so that you can keep track of your sources.
- Do not cut and paste blocks of downloaded text directly into your paper; first summarize or paraphrase this material.

*(continued)*

**PLAGIARISM AND INTERNET SOURCES** *(continued)*

- If you record the exact words of your source, enclose them in quotation marks.
- Even if your information is from emails, online discussion groups, blogs, or Web sites, provide appropriate documentation.
- Always document figures, tables, charts, and graphs obtained from the Internet or from any other electronic source.

## 2 Do Not Imitate a Source's Syntax and Phrasing

**Original:** In the early years of the nineteenth century, Americans began drinking more than they ever had before or since, embarking on a collective bender that confronted the young republic with its first major public health crisis—the obesity epidemic of its day. Corn whiskey, suddenly superabundant and cheap, became the drink of choice, and in 1820 the typical American was putting away half a pint of the stuff every day. That comes to more than five gallons of spirits a year for every man, woman, and child in America. The figure today is less than one. (Pollan, Michael. *The Omnivore's Dilemma.*)



**Plagiarism:** Early in the nineteenth century, Americans started to drink more than ever before or since, beginning a collective bender that was the first major public health crisis for the new nation—a crisis similar to our present-day obesity epidemic. The most popular drink was corn whiskey, which was plentiful and cheap. In 1920, the average American was drinking a half pint each day—more than five gallons a year for each American man, woman, and child. Today's figure is not even one gallon per year (Pollan 100).

The student example above not only closely follows the original's syntax and phrasing but also uses some of Pollan's distinctive phrasing without placing these phrases in quotation marks.

In the revised passage below, the writer uses her own syntax and phrasing and puts a borrowed phrase in quotation marks.

**Correct (Paraphrase; One Distinctive Phrase Placed in Quotation Marks):** As Michael Pollan points out in his book *The Omnivore's Dilemma*, the availability of cheap corn whiskey in the early nineteenth century led Americans to go on a "collective bender," drinking more than ever before. This presented a serious public health problem—a problem Pollan compares to today's obesity crisis. In 1820, the average American drank more than five gallons of whiskey per year (half a pint per day), compared to today's yearly consumption of less than one gallon per person (100).

*Note:* When it is clear that all information in a passage is from the same source, only one parenthetical reference is needed. For this reason, the brief quotation in the passage above does not require separate documentation.

### 3 Document Statistics Obtained from a Source

Although many people assume that statistics are common knowledge, they are usually the result of original research and must, therefore, be documented. Moreover, providing the source of the statistics helps readers to assess their validity.

> **Correct:** According to one study, male drivers between the ages of sixteen and twenty-four accounted for the majority of accidents. Of 303 accidents recorded almost one half took place before the drivers were legally allowed to drive at eighteen (Schuman et al. 1027).

### 4 Differentiate Your Words and Ideas from Those of Your Source

> **Original:** At some colleges and universities traditional survey courses of world and English literature . . . have been scrapped or diluted. At others they are in peril. At still others they will be. What replaces them is sometimes a mere option of electives, sometimes "multicultural" courses introducing material from Third World cultures and thinning out an already thin sampling of Western writings, and sometimes courses geared especially to issues of class, race, and gender. Given the notorious lethargy of academic decision-making, there has probably been more clamor than change; but if there's enough clamor, there will be change. (Howe, Irving. "The Value of the Canon.")

> **Plagiarism:** Debates about expanding the literary canon take place at many colleges and universities across the United States. At many universities, the Western literature survey courses have been edged out by courses that emphasize minority concerns. These courses are "thinning out an already thin sampling of Western writings" in favor of courses geared especially to issues of "class, race, and gender" (Howe 40).

Because the student example above does not differentiate the writer's ideas from those of his source, it appears that only the quotations in the last sentence are borrowed when, in fact, the second sentence also owes a debt to the original.

In the revised passage below, the writer clearly identifies the boundaries of the borrowed material by introducing it with an identifying tag and ending with documentation.

> **Correct:** Debates about expanding the literary canon take place at many colleges and universities across the United States. According to critic Irving Howe, at many universities the Western literature survey courses have been edged out by courses that emphasize minority concerns. These courses, says

Howe, are "thinning out an already thin sampling of Western writings" in favor of "courses geared especially to issues of class, race, and gender" (40).

CHECKLIST

## Avoiding Plagiarism

The following strategies can help you avoid plagiarism:

- ❑ **Take careful notes.** Be sure you have recorded information from your sources carefully and accurately.
- ❑ **Keep track of your sources.** Place all source material, along with pertinent bibliographic information, in the appropriate files.
- ❑ **In your notes, clearly identify summaries, paraphrases, and quotations.** In handwritten notes, put all words borrowed from your sources inside circled quotation marks. In typed notes, boldface all quotation marks. Always enclose your own comments within brackets.
- ❑ **In your paper, differentiate your ideas from those of your sources** by clearly introducing borrowed material with an identifying tag and by following it with parenthetical documentation.
- ❑ **Enclose all direct quotations** used in your paper within quotation marks.
- ❑ **Review all paraphrases and summaries** in your paper to make certain that they use your own phrasing and syntax and that any distinctive words and phrases from a source are quoted.
- ❑ **Document all quoted material and all paraphrases and summaries** of your sources.
- ❑ **Document all information** that is not common knowledge.
- ❑ **Document all opinions, conclusions, figures, tables, statistics, graphs, and charts** taken from a source.
- ❑ **Never use sources that you have not actually read (or invent sources that do not exist).**

## EXERCISE 1

The following paragraph uses material from three sources, but its student author has neglected to cite them. After reading the paragraph and the three sources that follow it, identify the material that has been quoted directly from a source. Compare the wording to the original for accuracy, and insert quotation marks where necessary, making sure the quoted passages fit smoothly into the paragraph. Differentiate the ideas of the student from those of each of the three sources by using identifying tags to introduce any quotations. (If you think the student did not need to quote a passage, paraphrase it instead.) Finally, add parenthetical documentation for each piece of information that requires it.

**Student Paragraph**

Oral history is an important way of capturing certain aspects of the past that might otherwise be lost. While history books relate the stories of great men and great events, rarely do they include the experiences of ordinary people—slaves, concentration camp survivors, and the illiterate, for example. By providing information about the people and emotions of the past, oral history makes sense of the present and gives a glimpse of the likely future. But because any particular rendition of a life history relies heavily on personal memory, great care must be taken to evaluate and explain the context of an oral history. Like any other historical account, oral history is just one of many possible versions of an individual's past.

**Source 1**

Oral history relies heavily on memory, a notoriously malleable entity; people remake the past in light of present concerns and knowledge. Yet not all memories are false, and oral history gives us testimony that might otherwise be lost—stories of slaves, of concentration camp survivors, of the illiterate and the obscure, of the legion "ordinary people" who rarely find their way into the history books. Oral history gives us the human element, the thoughts and emotions and confusions that lie beneath the calm surface of written documents. Even when people remake the past because memories are faulty or unbearable, we can learn much about the ways in which the past affects the present. (Freedman, Jean R. "Never Underestimate the Power of a Bus: My Journey to Oral History." *Oral History Review* 29.2 [2002]: 30. Print.)

**Source 2**

[There is a] widely held view that history belongs to great men and great events, not ordinary people or ordinary life. Yet we know that "ordinary" people in our local districts have important stories to tell. . . . Local histories tell us, on the one hand, that things were done differently in the past, but on the other hand, that in essence people and emotions were much the same. We need to learn from the past to make sense of the present, and get a glimpse of the likely future. (Gregg, Alison. "Planning and Managing an Oral History Collection." *Aplis* 13.4 [2000]: 174. Print.)

**Source 3**

One aspect of oral history . . . concerns the way in which any particular rendition of a life history is a product of the personal present. It is well-recognized that chronicles of the past are invariably a product of the present, so that different "presents" inspire different versions of the past. Just as all historical accounts—the very questions posed or the interpretive framework imposed—are informed by the historian's present, so, too, is a life history structured by both the interviewer's and the narrator's present. . . . [O]ral history cannot be treated as a source of some narrative truth, but rather as one of many possible versions of an individual's past. . . . [and] the stories told in an oral history are not simply the source of explanation, but rather require explanation. (Honig, Emily. "Getting to the Source: Striking Lives: Oral History and the Politics of Memory." *Journal of Women's History* 9.1 [1997]: 139. Print.)

PART 4

MLA

# Documenting Sources: MLA Style

## Directory of MLA Parenthetical References



## Directory of MLA Works-Cited List Entries

### PRINT SOURCES: *Entries for Articles*

#### Articles in Scholarly Journals



#### Articles in Magazines and Newspapers



### PRINT SOURCES: *Entries for Books*

#### Authors

### Paintings, Photographs, Cartoons, and Maps on the Internet



## OTHER ELECTRONIC SOURCES

### DVD-ROMs, CD-ROMs, and Computer Software



### Digital Files

CHAPTER 18

# MLA Documentation Style

## Frequently Asked Questions



**Documentation** is the formal acknowledgment of the sources you use in your paper. This chapter explains and illustrates the documentation style recommended by the Modern Language Association (MLA). Chapter 19 discusses the documentation style of the American Psychological Association (APA), Chapter 20 gives an overview of the format recommended by *The Chicago Manual of Style,* and Chapter 21 presents the format recommended by the Council of Science Editors (CSE) and the formats used by organizations in other disciplines.

### Close-Up CITATION GENERATORS

A number of Web sites can help you generate properly formatted citations for the most commonly used documentation styles. The most popular are *CiteMe* <citeme.com>, *EasyBib* <easybib.com>, *Zotero* <zotero.org>, and *Son of Citation Machine* <citationmachine.net>.

Although these sites can save you time and effort, most have limitations. For example, most citation generators occasionally make basic formatting errors. For this reason, you still have to proofread bibliographic entries carefully before you submit your paper.

## 18a Using MLA Style

**MLA style*** is required by instructors of English and other languages as well as by many instructors in other humanities disciplines. MLA documentation has three parts: *parenthetical references in the body of the paper (also known as in-text citations), a works-cited list,* and *content notes.*

*MLA documentation style follows the guidelines set in the *MLA Handbook for Writers of Research Papers,* 7th ed. (New York: MLA, 2009).

## 1 Parenthetical References

MLA documentation uses parenthetical references in the body of the paper keyed to a works-cited list at the end of the paper. A typical parenthetical reference consists of the author's last name and a page number.

The colony appealed to many idealists in Europe (Kelley 132).

If you state the author's name or the title of the work in your discussion, do not also include it in the parenthetical reference.

Penn's political motivation is discussed by Joseph J. Kelley in *Pennsylvania, The Colonial Years, 1681-1776* (44).

To distinguish two or more sources by the same author, include a shortened title after the author's name. When you shorten a title, begin with the word by which the work is alphabetized in the list of works cited.

Penn emphasized his religious motivation (Kelley, *Pennsylvania* 116).

### Close-Up PUNCTUATING WITH MLA PARENTHETICAL REFERENCES

**Paraphrases and Summaries** Parenthetical references are placed *before* the sentence's end punctuation.

Penn's writings epitomize seventeenth-century religious thought (Dengler and Curtis 72).

**Quotations Run In with the Text** Parenthetical references are placed *after* the quotation but *before* the end punctuation.

As Ross says, "Penn followed his conscience in all matters" (127).

According to Williams, "Penn's utopian vision was informed by his Quaker beliefs . . ." (72).

**Quotations Set Off from the Text** When you quote more than four lines of prose or more than three lines of poetry, parenthetical references are placed one space after the end punctuation.

See 56b

According to Arthur Smith, William Penn envisioned a state based on his religious principles:

> Pennsylvania would be a commonwealth in which all individuals would follow God's truth and develop according to God's law. For Penn, this concept of government was self-evident. It would be a mistake to see Pennsylvania as anything but an expression of Penn's religious beliefs. (314)

## Sample MLA Parenthetical References

### 1. A Work by a Single Author

Fairy tales reflect the emotions and fears of children (Bettelheim 23).

### 2. A Work by Two or Three Authors

The historian's main job is to search for clues and solve mysteries (Davidson and Lytle 6).

With the advent of behaviorism, psychology began a new phase of inquiry (Cowen, Barbo, and Crum 31-34).

### 3. A Work by More Than Three Authors

List only the first author, followed by **et al.** ("and others").

Helping each family reach its goals for healthy child development and overall family well-being was the primary approach of Project EAGLE (Bartle et al. 35).

Or, list the last names of all authors in the order in which they appear on the work's title page.

Helping each family reach its goals for healthy child development and overall family well-being was the primary approach of Project EAGLE (Bartle, Couchonnal, Canda, and Staker 35).

### 4. A Work in Multiple Volumes

If you list more than one volume of a multivolume work in your works-cited list, include the appropriate volume and page number (separated by a colon followed by a space) in the parenthetical citation.

Gurney is incorrect when he says that a twelve-hour limit is negotiable (6: 128).

### 5. A Work without a Listed Author

Use the full title (if brief) or a shortened version of the title (if long), beginning with the word by which it is alphabetized in the works-cited list.

The group later issued an apology ("Satire Lost" 22).

### 6. A Work That Is One Page Long

Do not include a page reference for a one-page article.

Sixty percent of Arab Americans work in white-collar jobs (El-Badru).

### 7. An Indirect Source

If you use a statement by one author that is quoted in the work of another author, indicate that the material is from an indirect source with the abbreviation **qtd. in** ("quoted in").

> According to Valli and Lucas, "the form of the symbol is an icon or picture of some aspect of the thing or activity being symbolized" (qtd. in Wilcox 120).

### 8. More Than One Work

Cite each work as you normally would, separating one citation from another with a semicolon.

> The Brooklyn Bridge has been used as a subject by many American artists (McCullough 144; Tashjian 58).

*Note:* Long parenthetical references distract readers. Whenever possible, present them as **content notes**.

See 18a3

### 9. A Literary Work

When citing a work of **fiction,** it is often helpful to include more than the author's name and the page number in the parenthetical citation. Follow the page number with a semicolon, and then include any additional information that might be helpful.

> In *Moby-Dick*, Melville refers to a whaling expedition funded by Louis XIV of France (151; ch. 24).

Parenthetical references to **poetry** do not include page numbers. In parenthetical references to *long poems,* cite division and line numbers, separating them with a period.

> In the *Aeneid*, Virgil describes the ships as cleaving the "green woods reflected in the calm water" (8.124).

(In this citation, the reference is to book 8, line 124 of the *Aeneid.*)

When citing *short poems,* identify the poet and the poem in the text of the paper, and use line numbers in the citation.

> In "My mistress' eyes are nothing like the sun," Shakespeare's speaker says, "I have seen roses damasked red and white, / But no such roses see I in her cheeks," (lines 5-6).

*Note:* When citing lines of a poem, include the word **line** (or **lines**) in the first parenthetical reference; use just the line numbers in subsequent references.

When citing a **play,** include the act, scene, and line numbers (in arabic numerals), separated by periods. Titles of classic literary works (such as Shakespeare's plays) are often abbreviated (**Mac. 2.2.14-16**).

### 10. Sacred Texts

When citing sacred texts, such as the Bible or the Qur'an, include the version (italicized) and the book (abbreviated if longer than four letters, but not italicized or enclosed in quotation marks), followed by the chapter and verse numbers (separated by a period).

> The cynicism of the speaker is apparent when he says, "All things are wearisome; no man can speak of them all" (*New English Bible*, Eccles. 1.8).

Note: The first time you cite a sacred text, include the version in your parenthetical reference; after that, include only the book. If you are using more than one version of a sacred text, however, include the version in each in-text citation.

### 11. An Entire Work

When citing an entire work, include the author's name and the work's title in the text of your paper rather than in a parenthetical reference.

> Lois Lowry's *Gathering Blue* is set in a technologically backward village.

### 12. Two or More Authors with the Same Last Name

To distinguish authors with the same last name, include their initials in your parenthetical references.

> Increases in crime have caused thousands of urban homeowners to install alarms (L. Cooper 115). Some of these alarms use sophisticated sensors that were developed by the army (D. Cooper 76).

### 13. A Government Document or a Corporate Author

Cite such works using the organization's name (usually abbreviated) followed by the page number (**Amer. Automobile Assn. 34**). You can avoid long parenthetical references by working the organization's name (not abbreviated) into your discussion.

> According to the President's Commission for the Study of Ethical Problems in Medicine and Biomedical and Behavioral Research, the issues relating to euthanasia are complicated (76).

### 14. A Legal Source

Titles of acts or laws that appear in the text of your paper or in the works-cited list should not be italicized or enclosed in quotation marks. In the parenthetical reference, titles are usually abbreviated, and the act or law is referred to by sections. Include the USC (United States Code) and the year the act or law was passed (if relevant).

Such research should include investigations into the cause, diagnosis, early detection, prevention, control, and treatment of autism (42 USC 284q, 2000).

Names of legal cases are usually abbreviated (**Roe v. Wade**). They are italicized in the text of your paper but not in the works-cited list.

In *Goodridge v. Department of Public Health*, the court ruled that the Commonwealth of Massachusetts had not adequately provided a reasonable constitutional cause for barring homosexual couples from civil marriages (2003).

### 15. An Electronic Source

If a reference to an electronic source includes paragraph numbers rather than page numbers, use the abbreviation **par.** or **pars.** followed by the paragraph number or numbers.

The earliest type of movie censorship came in the form of licensing fees, and in Deer River, Minnesota, "a licensing fee of $200 was deemed not excessive for a town of 1000" (Ernst, par. 20).

If the electronic source has no page or paragraph numbers, cite the work in your discussion rather than in a parenthetical reference. By consulting your works-cited list, readers will be able to determine that the source is electronic and may therefore not have page numbers.

In her article "Limited Horizons," Lynne Cheney observes that schools do best when students read literature not for practical information but for its insights into the human condition.

## 2 Works-Cited List

The **works-cited list,** which appears at the end of your paper, is an alphabetical listing of all the research materials you cite. Double-space within and between entries on the list, and indent the second and subsequent lines of each entry one-half inch. (**See 18b** for full manuscript guidelines.)

### MLA PRINT SOURCES Entries for Articles

Article citations include the author's name; the title of the article (in quotation marks); the title of the periodical (italicized); the volume and issue numbers (when applicable; see page 260); the year or date of publication; the pages on which the full article appears, without the abbreviation *p.* or *pp.*; and the publication medium (**Print**). Figure 18.1 shows where you can find this information.

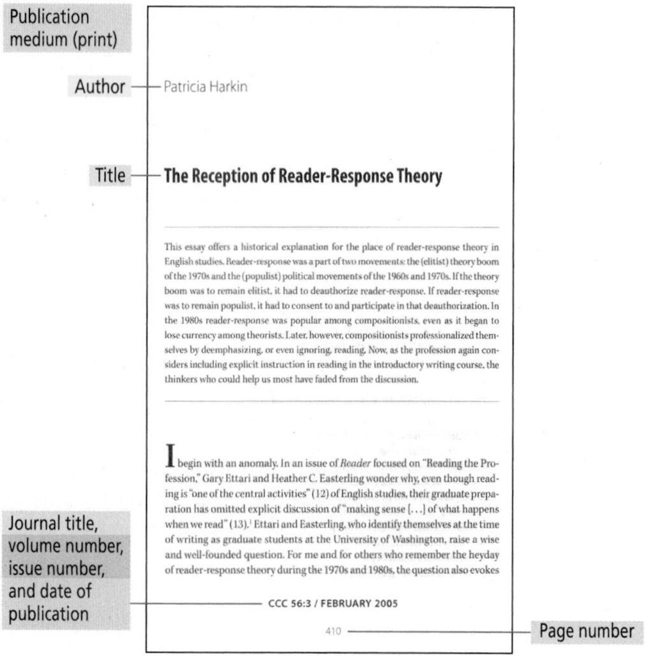


Patricia Harkin

**The Reception of Reader-Response Theory**

This essay offers a historical explanation for the place of reader-response theory in English studies. Reader-response was a part of two movements: the (elitist) theory boom of the 1970s and the (populist) political movements of the 1960s and 1970s. If the theory boom was to remain elitist, it had to deauthorize reader-response. If reader-response was to remain populist, it had to consent to and participate in that deauthorization. In the 1980s reader-response was popular among compositionists, even as it began to lose currency among theorists. Later, however, compositionists professionalized themselves by deemphasizing, or even ignoring, reading. Now, as the profession again considers including explicit instruction in reading in the introductory writing course, the thinkers who could help us most have faded from the discussion.

I begin with an anomaly. In an issue of *Reader* focused on "Reading the Profession," Gary Ettari and Heather C. Easterling wonder why, even though reading is "one of the central activities" (12) of English studies, their graduate preparation has omitted explicit discussion of "making sense [. . .] of what happens when we read" (13).[1] Ettari and Easterling, who identify themselves at the time of writing as graduate students at the University of Washington, raise a wise and well-founded question. For me and for others who remember the heyday of reader-response theory during the 1970s and 1980s, the question also evokes

CCC 56:3 / FEBRUARY 2005

410

**FIGURE 18.1** First page of a journal article showing the location of the information needed for documentation. © College Composition and Communication/National Council of Teachers of English.

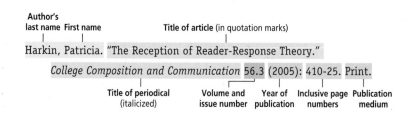

**Author's last name** | **First name** | **Title of article** (in quotation marks)

Harkin, Patricia. "The Reception of Reader-Response Theory."
*College Composition and Communication* 56.3 (2005): 410-25. Print.

**Title of periodical** (italicized) | **Volume and issue number** | **Year of publication** | **Inclusive page numbers** | **Publication medium**

## *Articles in Scholarly Journals*

### 1. An Article in a Scholarly Journal

MLA guidelines recommend that you include both the volume number and the issue number (separated by a period) for all scholarly journal articles that you cite, regardless of whether they are paginated continuously through an annual volume or separately in each issue. Follow the volume and issue numbers with the year of publication (in parentheses), the inclusive page numbers, and the publication medium.

Siderits, Mark. "Perceiving Particulars: A Buddhist Defense." *Philosophy East and West* 54.3 (2004): 367-83. Print.

*Articles in Magazines and Newspapers*

**2. An Article in a Weekly Magazine (Signed)**

For signed articles, start with the author, last name first. In dates, the day precedes the month (abbreviated except for May, June, and July).

Corliss, Richard. "His Days in Hollywood." *Time* 14 June 2004: 56-62. Print.

**3. An Article in a Weekly Magazine (Unsigned)**

For unsigned articles, start with the title of the article.

"Ronald Reagan." *National Review* 28 June 2004: 14-17. Print.

**4. An Article in a Monthly Magazine**

Thomas, Evan. "John Paul Jones." *American History* Aug. 2003: 22-25. Print.

**5. An Article That Does Not Appear on Consecutive Pages**

When, for example, an article begins on page 120 and then skips to page 186, include only the first page number, followed by a plus sign.

Di Giovanni, Janine. "The Shiites of Iraq." *National Geographic* June 2004: 62+. Print.

**6. An Article in a Newspaper (Signed)**

Krantz, Matt. "Stock Success Not Exactly Unparalleled." *Wall Street Journal* 11 June 2004: B1+. Print.

**7. An Article in a Newspaper (Unsigned)**

"A Steadfast Friend on 9/11 Is Buried." *New York Times* 6 Aug. 2002, late ed.: B8. Print.

*Note:* Omit the article *the* from the title of a newspaper even if the newspaper's actual title includes the article.

**8. An Editorial in a Newspaper**

"The Government and the Web." Editorial. *New York Times* 25 Aug. 2009, late ed.: A20. Print.

**9. A Letter to the Editor of a Newspaper**

Chang, Paula. Letter. *Philadelphia Inquirer* 10 Dec. 2012, suburban ed.: A17. Print.

**10. A Book Review in a Newspaper**

Straw, Deborah. "Thinking about Tomorrow." Rev. of *Planning for the 21st Century: A Guide for Community Colleges*, by William A.

Wojciechowski and Dedra Manes. *Community College Week* 7 June 2004: 15. Print.

**11. An Article with a Title within Its Title**

If the article you are citing contains a title that is normally enclosed in quotation marks, use single quotation marks for the interior title.

Zimmerman, Brett. "Frantic Forensic Oratory: Poe's 'The Tell-Tale Heart.'" *Style* 35 (2001): 34-50. Print.

If the article you are citing contains a title that is normally italicized, use italics for the title in your works-cited entry.

Lingo, Marci. "Forbidden Fruit: The Banning of *The Grapes of Wrath* in the Kern County Free Library." *Libraries and Culture* 38 (2003): 351-78. Print.

## MLA PRINT SOURCES Entries for Books

Book citations include the author's name; book title (italicized); and publication information (place, publisher, date, publication medium). Figures 18.2 and 18.3 show where you can find this information.

### Close-Up PUBLISHERS' NAMES

MLA requires that you use abbreviated forms of publishers' names in the works-cited list. In general, omit articles; abbreviations, such as *Inc.* and *Corp.*; and words such as *Publishers, Books,* and *Press*. If the publisher's name includes a person's name, use the last name only. Finally, use standard abbreviations whenever you can—*UP* for University Press and *P* for Press, for example.

| Name | Abbreviation |
|---|---|
| Basic Books | Basic |
| Government Printing Office | GPO |
| The Modern Language Association of America | MLA |
| Oxford University Press | Oxford UP |
| Alfred A. Knopf, Inc. | Knopf |
| Random House, Inc. | Random |
| University of Chicago Press | U of Chicago P |

In each works-cited entry, capitalize all major words of the book's title except articles, coordinating conjunctions, prepositions, and the *to* of an infinitive (unless such a word is the first or last word of the title or subtitle). Do not italicize the period that follows a book's title.

**Author's last name** | **First name and middle initial** | **Italicized title** (all major words and first word of subtitle capitalized)

Kleiner, Fred S. *Gardner's Art through the Ages: A Global History.*
    Enhanced 13th ed. Boston: Wadsworth, 2011. Print.

**Edition** | **City** | **Publisher's name** (abbreviated) | **Year of publication** | **Publication medium**

FIGURE 18.2 Title page from a book showing the location of the information needed for documentation. © Cengage Learning, 2011.

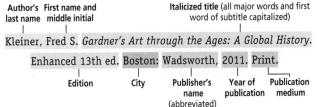

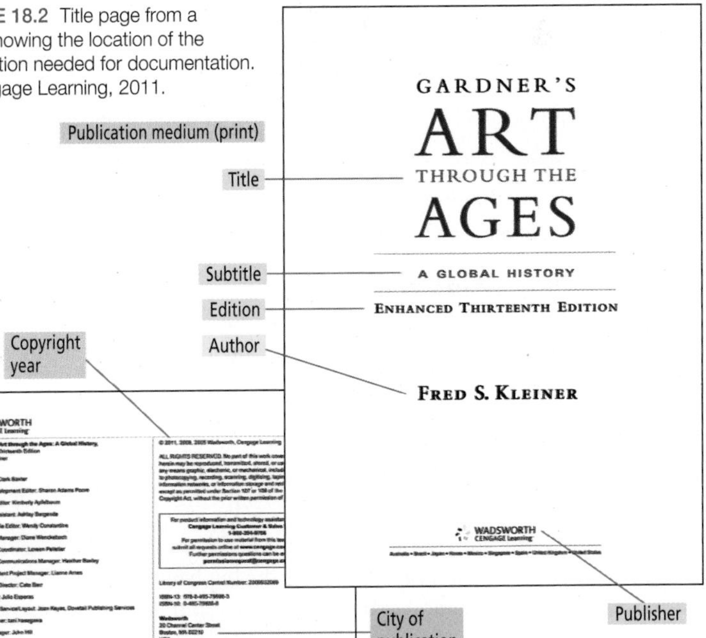


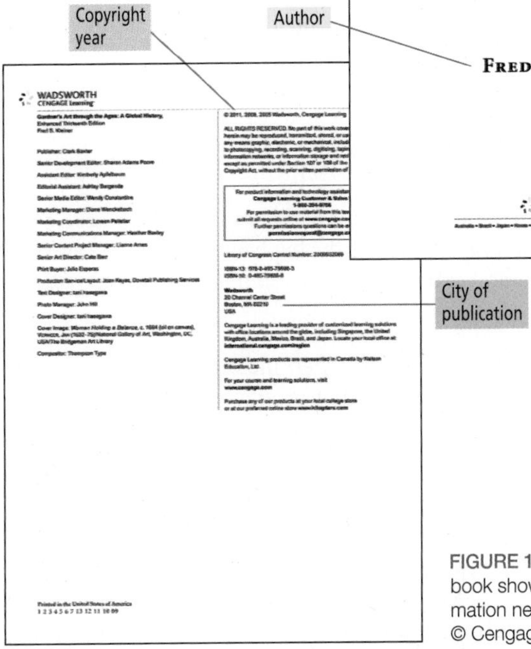


FIGURE 18.3 Copyright page from a book showing the location of the information needed for documentation. © Cengage Learning, 2011.

*Authors*

### 12. A Book by One Author

Bettelheim, Bruno. *The Uses of Enchantment: The Meaning and Importance of Fairy Tales*. New York: Knopf, 1976. Print.

### 13. A Book by Two or Three Authors

List the first author with last name first. List subsequent authors with first name first in the order in which they appear on the book's title page.

Peters, Michael A., and Nicholas C. Burbules. *Poststructuralism and Educational Research*. Lanham: Rowman, 2004. Print.

### 14. A Book by More Than Three Authors

List the first author only, followed by **et al.** ("and others").

Badawi, El Said, et al. *Modern Written Arabic*. London: Routledge, 2004. Print.

Or, include all the authors in the order in which they appear on the book's title page.

Badawi, El Said, Daud A. Abdu, Mike Carfter, and Adrian Gully. *Modern Written Arabic*. London: Routledge, 2004. Print.

### 15. Two or More Books by the Same Author

List books by the same author in alphabetical order by title. After the first entry, use three unspaced hyphens followed by a period in place of the author's name.

Ede, Lisa. *Situating Composition: Composition Studies and the Politics of Location*. Carbondale: Southern Illinois UP, 2004. Print.

---. *Work in Progress*. 6th ed. Boston: Bedford, 2004. Print.

*Note:* If the author is the editor or translator of the second entry, place a comma and the appropriate abbreviation after the hyphens (**---, ed.**). See entry 17 for more on edited books and entry 25 for more on translated books.

### 16. A Book by a Corporate Author

A book is cited by its corporate author when individual members of the association, commission, or committee that produced it are not identified on the title page.

American Automobile Association. *Western Canada and Alaska*. Heathrow: AAA, 2010. Print.

### 17. An Edited Book

An edited book is a work prepared for publication by a person other than the author. If your focus is on the *author's* work, begin your citation with the author's name. After the title, include the abbreviation **Ed.** ("Edited by"), followed by the editor or editors.

Twain, Mark. *Adventures of Huckleberry Finn*. Ed. Michael Patrick Hearn. New York: Norton, 2001. Print.

If your focus is on the *editor's* work, begin your citation with the editor's name followed by the abbreviation **ed.** ("editor") if there is one editor or **eds.** ("editors") if there is more than one. After the title, give the author's name, preceded by the word **By**.

Hearn, Michael Patrick, ed. *Adventures of Huckleberry Finn*. By Mark Twain. New York: Norton, 2001. Print.

### Editions, Multivolume Works, Graphic Narratives, Forewords, Translations, and Sacred Works

#### 18. A Subsequent Edition of a Book

When citing an edition other than the first, include the edition number that appears on the work's title page.

Wilson, Charles Banks. *Search for the Native American Purebloods*. 3rd ed. Norman: U of Oklahoma P, 2000. Print.

#### 19. A Republished Book

Include the original publication date after the title of a republished book—for example, a paperback version of a hardcover book.

Wharton, Edith. *The House of Mirth*. 1905. New York: Scribner's, 1975. Print.

#### 20. A Book in a Series

If the title page indicates that the book is a part of a series, include the series name, neither italicized nor enclosed in quotation marks, and the series number, followed by a period, after the publication information. Use the abbreviation **Ser.** if *Series* is part of the series name.

Davis, Bertram H. *Thomas Percy*. Boston: Twayne, 1981. Print. Twayne's English Authors Ser. 313.

#### 21. A Multivolume Work

When all volumes of a multivolume work have the same title, include the number of the volume you are using.

Fisch, Max H., ed. *Writings of Charles S. Peirce: A Chronological Edition*. Vol. 4. Bloomington: Indiana UP, 2000. Print.

If you use two or more volumes that have the same title, cite the entire work.

Fisch, Max H., ed. *Writings of Charles S. Peirce: A Chronological Edition.* 6 vols. Bloomington: Indiana UP, 2000. Print.

When the volume you are using has an individual title, you may cite the title without mentioning any other volumes.

Mareš, Milan. *Fuzzy Cooperative Games: Cooperation with Vague Expectations.* New York: Physica-Verlag, 2001. Print.

If you wish, however, you may include supplemental information, such as the number of the volume, the title of the entire work, the total number of volumes, or the inclusive publication dates.

### 22. An Illustrated Book or a Graphic Narrative

An **illustrated book** is a work in which illustrations accompany the text. If your focus is on the *author's* work, begin your citation with the author's name. After the title, include the abbreviation **Illus.** ("Illustrated by") followed by the illustrator's name and then the publication information.

Frost, Robert. *Stopping by Woods on a Snowy Evening.* Illus. Susan Jeffers. New York: Dutton-Penguin, 2001. Print.

If your focus is on the *illustrator's* work, begin your citation with the illustrator's name followed by the abbreviation **illus.** ("illustrator"). After the title, give the author's name, preceded by the word **By**.

Jeffers, Susan, illus. *Stopping by Woods on a Snowy Evening.* By Robert Frost. New York: Dutton-Penguin, 2001. Print.

A **graphic narrative** is a work in which text and illustrations work together to tell a story. Cite a graphic narrative as you would cite a book.

Bechdel, Alison. *Fun Home: A Family Tragicomic.* Boston: Houghton, 2006. Print.

### 23. The Foreword, Preface, or Afterword of a Book

Campbell, Richard. Preface. *Media and Culture: An Introduction to Mass Communication.* By Bettina Fabos. Boston: Bedford, 2005. vi-xi. Print.

### 24. A Book with a Title within Its Title

If the book you are citing contains a title that is normally italicized (a novel, play, or long poem, for example), do not italicize the interior title.

Fulton, Joe B. *Mark Twain in the Margins: The Quarry Farm Marginalia and* A Connecticut Yankee in King Arthur's Court. Tuscaloosa: U of Alabama P, 2000. Print.

If the book you are citing contains a title that is normally enclosed in quotation marks, keep the quotation marks.

Hawkins, Hunt, and Brian W. Shaffer, eds. *Approaches to Teaching Conrad's "Heart of Darkness" and "The Secret Sharer."* New York: MLA, 2002. Print.

**25. A Translation**

García Márquez, Gabriel. *One Hundred Years of Solitude*. Trans. Gregory Rabassa. New York: Avon, 1991. Print.

**26. The Bible**

*The New English Bible with the Apocrypha.* Oxford Study ed. New York: Oxford UP, 1976. Print.

**27. The Qur'an**

*Holy Qur'an*. Trans. M. H. Shakir. Elmhurst: Tahrike Tarsile Qur'an, 1999. Print.

### *Parts of Books*

**28. A Short Story, Play, Poem, or Essay in a Collection of an Author's Work**

Bukowski, Charles. "lonely hearts." *The Flash of Lightning behind the Mountain: New Poems*. New York: Ecco, 2004. 115-16. Print.

*Note:* The title of the poem in the entry above is not capitalized because it appears in lowercase letters in the original.

**29. A Short Story, Play, or Poem in an Anthology**

Chopin, Kate. "The Storm." *Literature: Reading, Reacting, Writing*. Ed. Laurie G. Kirszner and Stephen R. Mandell. 8th ed. Boston: Wadsworth, 2013. 306-09. Print.

Shakespeare, William. *Othello, the Moor of Venice. Shakespeare: Six Plays and the Sonnets*. Ed. Thomas Marc Parrott and Edward Hubler. New York: Scribner's, 1956. 145-91. Print.

**30. An Essay in an Anthology or Edited Collection**

Crevel, René. "From *Babylon*." *Surrealist Painters and Poets: An Anthology*. Ed. Mary Ann Caws. Cambridge: MIT P, 2001. 175-77. Print.

*Note:* Supply inclusive page numbers for the entire essay, not just for the page or pages you cite in your paper.

### 31. More Than One Essay from the Same Anthology

List each essay from the same anthology separately, followed by a cross-reference to the entire anthology. Also list complete publication information for the anthology itself.

Agar, Eileen. "Am I a Surrealist?" Caws 3-7.

Caws, Mary Ann, ed. *Surrealist Painters and Poets: An Anthology*. Cambridge: MIT P, 2001. Print.

Crevel, René. "From *Babylon*." Caws 175-77.

### 32. A Scholarly Article Reprinted in a Collection

Booth, Wayne C. "Why Ethical Criticism Can Never Be Simple." *Style* 32.2 (1998): 351-64. Rpt. in *Mapping the Ethical Turn: A Reader in Ethics, Culture, and Literary Theory*. Ed. Todd F. Davis and Kenneth Womack. Charlottesville: UP of Virginia, 2001. 16-29. Print.

### 33. An Article in a Reference Book (Signed/Unsigned)

For a **signed** article, begin with the author's name. For unfamiliar reference books, include full publication information.

Drabble, Margaret. "Expressionism." *The Oxford Companion to English Literature*. 6th ed. New York: Oxford UP, 2000. Print.

If the article is **unsigned,** begin with the title. For familiar reference books, do not include full publication information.

"Cubism." *The Encyclopedia Americana*. 2006 ed. Print.

Note: Omit page numbers when the reference book lists entries alphabetically. If you are listing one definition among several from a dictionary, include the abbreviation **Def.** ("Definition") along with the letter and/or number that corresponds to the definition.

"Justice." Def. 2b. *The Concise Oxford Dictionary*. 11th ed. 2008. Print.

## *Dissertations, Pamphlets, Government Publications, and Legal Sources*

### 34. A Dissertation (Published)

Cite a published dissertation the same way you would cite a book, but add relevant dissertation information before the publication information.

Rodriguez, Jason Anthony. *Bureaucracy and Altruism: Managing the Contradictions of Teaching*. Diss. U of Texas at Arlington, 2003. Ann Arbor: UMI, 2004. Print.

Note: University Microfilms, which publishes most of the dissertations in the United States, is also available online by subscription. For the proper format for citing online databases, see entries 53–58.

**35. A Dissertation (Unpublished)**

Use quotation marks for the title of an unpublished dissertation.

Bon Tempo, Carl Joseph. "Americans at the Gate: The Politics of American Refugee Policy." Diss. U of Virginia, 2004. Print.

**36. A Pamphlet**

Cite a pamphlet as you would a book. If no author is listed, begin with the title (italicized).

*The Darker Side of Tanning*. Schaumburg: The American Academy of Dermatology, 2010. Print.

**37. A Government Publication**

If the publication has no listed author, begin with the name of the government, followed by the name of the agency. You may use an abbreviation if its meaning is clear: **United States. Cong. Senate.**

United States. Office of Consumer Affairs. *2003 Consumer's Resource Handbook*. Washington: GPO, 2003. Print.

When citing two or more publications by the same government, use three unspaced hyphens (followed by a period) in place of the name for the second and subsequent entries. When you cite more than one work from the same agency of that government, use an additional set of unspaced hyphens in place of the agency name.

United States. FAA. *Passenger Airline Safety in the Twenty-First Century*. Washington: GPO, 2003. Print.

---. ---. *Recycled Air in Passenger Airline Cabins*. Washington: GPO, 2002. Print.

**38. A Historical or Legal Document**

In general, you do not need a works-cited entry for familiar historical documents. Parenthetical references in the text are sufficient—for example, **(US Const., art. 3, sec. 2)**.

If you cite an act in the works-cited list, include the name of the act, its Public Law (Pub. L.) number, its Statutes at Large (Stat.) cataloging number, its enactment date, and its publication medium.

Children's Health Act. Pub. L. 106-310. 114 Stat. 1101. 17 Oct. 2000. Print.

In works-cited entries for **legal cases,** abbreviate names of cases, but spell out the first important word of each party's name. Include the volume number, abbreviated name (not italicized), and inclusive page numbers of the law report; the name of the deciding court; the decision year; and publication information for the source. Do not italicize the case name in the works-cited list.

Abbott v. Blades. 544 US 929. Supreme Court of the US. 2005. *United States Reports*. Washington: GPO, 2007. Print.

## MLA ENTRIES FOR MISCELLANEOUS PRINT AND NONPRINT SOURCES

### *Lectures and Interviews*

#### 39. A Lecture

Grimm, Mary. "An Afternoon with Mary Grimm." Visiting Writers Program. Dept. of English, Wright State U, Dayton. 16 Apr. 2004. Lecture.

#### 40. A Personal Interview

Tannen, Deborah. Telephone interview. 8 June 2012.

West, Cornel. Personal interview. 28 Dec. 2011.

#### 41. A Published Interview

Huston, John. "The Outlook for Raising Money: An Investment Banker's Viewpoint." *NJBIZ* 30 Sept. 2002: 2-3. Print.

### *Letters*

#### 42. A Personal Letter

Include the abbreviation **TS** (for "typescript") after the date of a typed letter.

Tan, Amy. Letter to the author. 7 Apr. 2010. TS.

#### 43. A Published Letter

Joyce, James. "Letter to Louis Gillet." 20 Aug. 1931. *James Joyce*. By Richard Ellmann. New York: Oxford UP, 1965. 631. Print.

#### 44. A Letter in a Library's Archives

Include the abbreviation **MS** (for "manuscript") after the date of a handwritten letter.

Stieglitz, Alfred. Letter to Paul Rosenberg. 5 Sept. 1923. MS. Stieglitz Archive. Yale U Arts Lib., New Haven.

### *Films, Videotapes, Radio and Television Programs, and Recordings*

#### 45. A Film

Include the title of the film (italicized), the distributor, and the date, along with other information that may be useful to readers, such as the names of the performers, the director, and the screenwriter. Conclude with the publication medium.

*Citizen Kane*. Dir. Orson Welles. Perf. Welles, Joseph Cotten, Dorothy Comingore, and Agnes Moorehead. RKO, 1941. Film.

If you are focusing on the contribution of a particular person, begin with that person's name.

Welles, Orson, dir. *Citizen Kane*. Perf. Welles, Joseph Cotten, Dorothy Comingore, and Agnes Moorehead. RKO, 1941. Film.

### 46. A Videotape, DVD, or Laser Disc

Cite a videotape, DVD, or laser disc as you would cite a film, but include the original release date (when available).

*Bowling for Columbine*. Dir. Michael Moore. 2002. United Artists and Alliance Atlantis, 2003. DVD.

### 47. A Radio or Television Program

"War Feels Like War." *P.O.V.* Dir. Esteban Uyarra. PBS. WPTD, Dayton, 6 July 2004. Television.

### 48. A Recording

List the composer, conductor, or performer (whomever you are focusing on), followed by the title, publisher, year of issue, and publication medium (**CD-ROM**, **MP3 file**, and so on).

Boubill, Alain, and Claude-Michel Schönberg. *Miss Saigon*. Perf. Lea Salonga, Claire Moore, and Jonathan Pryce. Cond. Martin Koch. Geffen, 1989. CD-ROM.

Marley, Bob. "Crisis." *Kaya*. Kava Island, 1978. LP.

## *Paintings, Photographs, Cartoons, and Advertisements*

### 49. A Painting

Hopper, Edward. *Railroad Sunset*. 1929. Oil on canvas. Whitney Museum of American Art, New York.

### 50. A Photograph

Cite a photograph in a museum's collection in the same way you cite a painting.

Stieglitz, Alfred. *The Steerage*. 1907. Photograph. Los Angeles County Museum of Art, Los Angeles.

For a personal photograph, include a descriptive title (without quotation marks or italics), the name of the photographer, and the date.

Rittenhouse Square in winter. Personal photograph by the author. 8 Feb. 2012.

### 51. A Cartoon or Comic Strip

Trudeau, Garry. "Doonesbury." Comic strip. *Philadelphia Inquirer* 15 Sept. 2003, late ed.: E13. Print.

### 52. An Advertisement

Microsoft. Advertisement. *National Review* 8 June 2010: 17. Print.

## MLA ELECTRONIC SOURCES Entries for Sources from Online Databases

To cite information from an online database, supply the publication information (including page numbers, if available; if unavailable, use **n. pag.**) followed by the name of the database (italicized), the publication medium (**Web**), and the date of access. Figure 18.4 shows where you can find this information.

Author's last name | First name | Title of short story (in quotation marks) | Title of periodical (italicized) | Date of publication | Inclusive page numbers

Keillor, Garrison. "Love Me: A Short Story." *Atlantic* July-Aug. 2003: 115-22. *Academic Search Elite.* Web. 2 May 2011.

Name of database (italicized) | Publication medium | Date of access

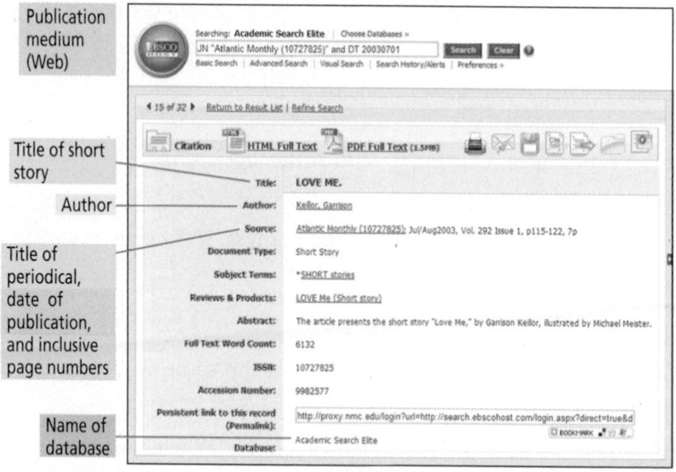


FIGURE 18.4 Opening screen from an online database showing the location of the information needed for documentation. © EBSCO.

### *Journal Articles, Magazine Articles, News Services, and Dissertations from Online Databases*

**53. A Scholarly Journal Article with a Print Version**

Schaefer, Richard J. "Editing Strategies in Television News Documentaries." *Journal of Communication* 47.4 (1997): 69-89. *InfoTrac OneFile Plus*. Web. 2 Oct. 2011.

**54. A Scholarly Journal Article with No Print Version**

Maeseele, Thomas. "From Charity to Welfare Rights? A Study of Social Care Practices." *Social Work and Society: The International Online-Only Journal* 8.1 (2010): n. pag. *Academic Search Elite*. Web. 20 May 2011.

**55. A Monthly Magazine Article**

Livermore, Beth. "Meteorites on Ice." *Astronomy* July 1993: 54-58. *Expanded Academic ASAP Plus*. Web. 12 Nov. 2010.

Wright, Karen. "The Clot Thickens." *Discover* Dec. 1999: n. pag. *MasterFILE Premier*. Web. 10 Oct. 2010.

**56. A News Service**

Ryan, Desmond. "Some Background on the Battle of Gettysburg." *Knight Ridder/Tribune News Service* 7 Oct. 1993: n. pag. *InfoTrac OneFile Plus*. Web. 16 Nov. 2011.

**57. A Newspaper Article**

Meyer, Greg. "Answering Questions about the West Nile Virus." *Dayton Daily News* 11 July 2002: Z3-7. *LexisNexis*. Web. 17 Feb. 2006.

**58. A Published Dissertation**

Rodriguez, Jason Anthony. *Bureaucracy and Altruism: Managing the Contradictions of Teaching*. Diss. U of Texas at Arlington, 2003. *ProQuest*. Web. 4 Mar. 2009.

## MLA ELECTRONIC SOURCES Entries for Sources from Internet Sites

MLA style* recognizes that full source information for Internet sources is not always available. Include in your citation whatever information you can reasonably obtain: the author or editor of the site (if available); the name of

*The documentation style for Internet sources presented here conforms to the most recent guidelines published in the *MLA Handbook for Writers of Research Papers* (7th ed.) and found online at <http://www.mlahandbook.org>.

the site (italicized); the version number of the source (if applicable); the name of any institution or sponsor (if unavailable, include the abbreviation **N.p.** for "no publisher"); the date of electronic publication or update (if unavailable, include the abbreviation **n.d.** for "no date of publication"); the publication medium (**Web**); and the date you accessed the source. MLA recommends omitting the URL from the citation unless it is necessary to find the source (as in entry 62). Figure 18.5 shows where you can find this information.

Author's last name | First name | Title of article (in quotation marks) | Name of site (italicized) | Sponsor of site

Keim, Brandon. "What's in a Hurricane Name?" *Wired Science*. Condé Nast Digital, 26 Aug. 2009. Web. 27 Aug. 2011.

Date of publication | Publication medium | Date of access

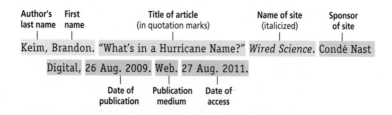

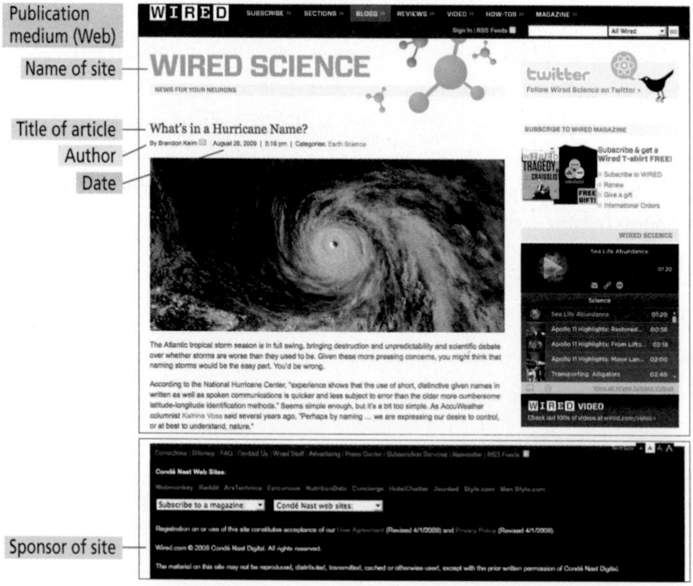


FIGURE 18.5 Part of an online article showing the location of the information needed for documentation. Wired.com © 2009 Condé Nast Digital. All rights reserved. Image from NOAA.

## *Internet-Specific Sources*

### 59. An Entire Web Site

Nelson, Cary, ed. *Modern American Poetry*. Dept. of English, U of Illinois, Urbana-Champaign, 2002. Web. 26 May 2011.

### 60. A Document within a Web Site

"June 6, 1944: D-Day." *History.com*. History Channel, 1999. Web. 7 June 2011.

### 61. A Home Page for a Course

Walker, Janice R. "ENGL 1101-Composition I, Fall 2010." Course home page. *Georgia Southern University*. Dept. of Writing and Linguistics, Georgia Southern U, 6 Aug. 2010. Web. 8 Sept. 2012.

### 62. A Personal Home Page

Gainor, Charles. Home page. U of Toronto, 22 July 2010. Web. 10 Nov. 2011. <http://www.chass.utoronto.ca:9094/~char>.

*Note:* If an electronic address (URL) is necessary, MLA requires that you enclose the URL within angle brackets to distinguish the address from the punctuation in the rest of the citation. If a URL will not fit on a line, the entire URL will be automatically carried over to the next line. If you prefer to divide the URL, divide it only after a slash. (Do not insert a hyphen.)

### 63. A Radio Program Accessed from an Internet Archive

"Teenage Skeptic Takes on Climate Scientists." Narr. David Kestenbaum. *Morning Edition*. Natl. Public Radio. WNYC, New York, 15 Apr. 2008. Transcript. *NPR*. Web. 30 Mar. 2010.

### 64. An E-mail

Mauk, Karen R. Message to the author. 28 June 2012. E-mail.

### 65. A Posting on an Online Forum or Blog

Schiller, Stephen. "Paper Cost and Publishing Costs." *New York Times*. New York Times, 24 Apr. 2002. Web. 17 May 2002.

Merry. "The Way We Roll. . . ." *EnviroMom*. EnviroMom, 27 June 2008. Web. 3 July 2010.

## *Articles, Books, Reviews, Letters, and Reference Works on the Internet*

### 66. An Article in a Scholarly Journal

When you cite an article you accessed from an electronic source that also has a print version, include the publication information for the print source, the inclusive page numbers (if available), the publication medium (**Web**), and the date you accessed it.

DeKoven, Marianne. "Utopias Limited: Post-Sixties and Postmodern American Fiction." *Modern Fiction Studies* 41.1 (1995): 75-97. Web. 20 Jan. 2005.

### 67. An Article in a Magazine

Weiser, Jay. "The Tyranny of Informality." *Time*. Time, 26 Feb. 1996. Web. 1 Mar. 2009.

### 68. An Article in a Newspaper

Bilton, Nick. "Three Reasons Why the iPad Will Kill Amazon's Kindle." *New York Times*. New York Times, 27 Jan. 2010. Web. 16 Feb. 2011.

### 69. An Article in a Newsletter

Sullivan, Jennifer S., comp. "Documentation Preserved, New Collections." *AIP Center for History of Physics* 39.2 (2007): 2-3. Web. 26 Feb. 2011.

### 70. A Book

Douglass, Frederick. *My Bondage and My Freedom*. Boston, 1855. *Google Book Search*. Web. 8 June 2012.

### 71. A Review

Ebert, Roger. Rev. of *Star Wars: Episode I—The Phantom Menace,* dir. George Lucas. *Chicago Sun-Times*. Digital Chicago, 8 June 2000. Web. 22 June 2007.

### 72. A Letter to the Editor

Chen-Cheng, Henry H. Letter. *New York Times*. New York Times, 19 July 1999. Web. 1 Jan. 2011.

### 73. An Article in an Encyclopedia

Include the article's title, the title of the database (italicized), the version number (if available), the sponsor, the date of electronic publication, the publication medium (**Web**), and the date of access.

"Hawthorne, Nathaniel." *Encyclopaedia Britannica Online*. Encyclopaedia Britannica, 2010. Web. 16 May 2011.

### 74. A Government Publication

Cite an online government publication as you would cite a print version; end with the information required for an electronic source.

United States. Dept. of Justice. Office of Justice Programs. *Violence against Women: Estimates from the Redesigned National Crime Victimization Survey*. By Ronet Bachman and Linda E. Saltzman. Aug. 1995. *Bureau of Justice Statistics*. Web. 10 July 2009.

### *Paintings, Photographs, Cartoons, and Maps on the Internet*

#### 75. A Painting

Seurat, Georges-Pierre. *Evening, Honfleur*. 1886. Museum of Mod. Art, New York. *MoMA.org*. Web. 8 Jan. 2012.

#### 76. A Photograph

Brady, Mathew. *Ulysses S. Grant 1822-1885*. 1864. *Mathew Brady's National Portrait Gallery*. Web. 2 Oct. 2011.

#### 77. A Cartoon

Stossel, Sage. "Star Wars: The Next Generation." Cartoon. *Atlantic Unbound*. Atlantic Monthly Group, 2 Oct. 2002. Web. 14 Nov. 2009.

#### 78. A Map

"Philadelphia, Pennsylvania." Map. *U.S. Gazetteer*. US Census Bureau, n.d. Web. 17 July 2012.

## MLA OTHER ELECTRONIC SOURCES

### *DVD-ROMs, CD-ROMs, and Computer Software*

#### 79. A Nonperiodical Publication on DVD-ROM or CD-ROM

Cite a nonperiodical publication on DVD-ROM or CD-ROM the same way you would cite a book, but include the appropriate medium of publication.

"Windhover." *The Oxford English Dictionary*. 2nd ed. Oxford: Oxford UP, 2001. DVD-ROM.

"Whitman, Walt." *DiskLit: American Authors*. Boston: Hall, 2000. CD-ROM.

#### 80. A Periodical Publication on DVD-ROM or CD-ROM

Zurbach, Kate. "The Linguistic Roots of Three Terms." *Linguistic Quarterly* 37 (1994): 12-47. CD-ROM. *InfoTrac: Magazine Index Plus*. Information Access. Jan. 2009.

#### 81. Computer Software or a Video Game

*The Sims 3 Deluxe*. Redwood City: Electronic Arts. 2010. DVD.

### *Digital Files*

#### 82. A Word-Processing Document

Russell, Brad. "Work Trip Notes." File last modified on 22 Mar. 2009. *Microsoft Word* file.

#### 83. An MP3 File

U2. "Beautiful Day." *All That You Can't Leave Behind*. Universal-Island, 2000. MP3 file.

## Close-Up HOW TO CITE SOURCES NOT LISTED IN THIS CHAPTER

The examples listed in this chapter represent the sources you will most likely encounter in your research. If you encounter a source that is not listed here, find the model that most closely matches it, and adapt the guidelines for your use.

For example, suppose you wanted to include **an obituary** from a print newspaper in your list of works cited. The models that most closely resemble this type of entry are *an editorial in a newspaper* (entry 8) and *a letter to the editor* (entry 9). If you used these models as your guide, your entry would look like this:

Boucher, Geoff, and Elaine Woo. "Michael Jackson's Life Was Infused with Fantasy and Tragedy." Obituary. *Los Angeles Times* 2 July 2009: 4. Print.

Follow the same procedure for an electronic source. Suppose you wanted to include a posting from a **social networking site,** such as *Facebook*. The models that most closely resemble this type of entry are a *personal home page* (entry 62) and a *blog posting* (entry 65). If you used these models as your guide, your entry would look like this:

Branagh, Kenneth. Wall post. *Facebook.com*. 15 Mar. 2012. Web. 16 Mar. 2012.

## EXERCISE 1

The following notes identify sources used in a paper on censorship and the Internet. Following the proper format for MLA parenthetical documentation, create a parenthetical reference for each source, and then create a works-cited list, arranging the sources in the proper order.

1. Page 72 in a book called Banned in the USA by Herbert N. Foerstel. The book has 231 pages and was published in a third edition in 2006 by Greenwood Press, located in Westport, Connecticut. The author's name appears in the text of your paper.
2. A statement made by Esther Dyson in her keynote address at the Newspapers 1996 Conference. Her statement is quoted in an article by Jodi B. Cohen called Fighting Online Censorship. The speech has not been printed in any other source. The article is in the April 13, 1996, edition of the weekly business journal Editor & Publisher. Dyson's quotation appears on page 44. The article begins on page 44 and continues on page 60. Dyson's name is mentioned in the text of your paper.

3. If You Don't Love It, Leave It, an essay by Esther Dyson in the New York Times Magazine, July 15, 1995, on pages 26 and 27. Your quotation comes from the second page of the essay. No author's name is mentioned in the text of your paper.
4. An essay by Nat Hentoff titled Speech Should Not Be Limited on pages 22–26 of the book Censorship: Opposing Viewpoints, edited by Terry O'Neill. The book is published by Greenhaven Press in St. Paul, Minnesota. The publication year is 2005. The quotation you have used is from page 24, and the author is mentioned in the text of your paper.
5. An essay by Robert Cannon on the Internet called A Parent's Guide to Supervising a Child Online. The essay appeared on the Web site Internet Issues, which was updated May 10, 2002. Although the essay prints out on four pages, the pages are not numbered. In your paper, you summarize information from the second and third pages of the document. You accessed the information on January 20, 2012, from the online database *Expanded Academic Plus*.

## 3 Content Notes

**Content notes**—multiple bibliographic citations or other material that does not fit smoothly into your paper—are indicated by a **superscript** (raised numeral) in the text. Notes can appear either as footnotes at the bottom of the page or as endnotes on a separate sheet entitled **Notes**, placed after the last page of the paper and before the works-cited list. Content notes are double-spaced within and between entries. The first line is indented one-half inch, and subsequent lines are typed flush left.

### *For Multiple Citations*

***In the Paper***

Many researchers emphasize the necessity of having dying patients share their experiences.[1]

***In the Note***

1. Kübler-Ross 27; Stinnette 43; Poston 70; Cohen and Cohen 31-34; Burke 1: 91-95.

### *For Other Material*

***In the Paper***

The massacre during World War I is an event the survivors could not easily forget.[2]

***In the Note***

2. For a firsthand account of these events, see Bedoukian 178-81.

## 18b MLA-Style Manuscript Guidelines

Although MLA papers do not usually include abstracts or internal headings, this situation is changing. Be sure you know what your instructor expects.

The guidelines in the three checklists that follow are based on the latest version of the *MLA Handbook for Writers of Research Papers.*

**CHECKLIST**

### Typing Your Paper

When typing your paper, use the student paper in **18c** as your model.

- ❑ Leave a one-inch margin at the top and bottom and on both sides of the page. Double-space your paper throughout.
- ❑ Capitalize all important words in your title, but not prepositions, articles, coordinating conjunctions, or the *to* in infinitives (unless they begin or end the title or subtitle). Do not italicize your title or enclose it in quotation marks. Never put a period after the title, even if it is a sentence.
- ❑ Number all pages of your paper consecutively—including the first—in the upper right-hand corner, one-half inch from the top, flush right. Type your last name followed by a space before the page number on every page.
- ❑ Set off quotations of more than four lines of prose or more than three lines of poetry by indenting the whole quotation one inch. If you quote two or more paragraphs, indent the first line of each paragraph an additional quarter inch. (If the first sentence does not begin a paragraph, do not indent it. Indent the first line only in successive paragraphs.)
- ❑ Citations should follow MLA documentation style.

See 18a

**CHECKLIST**

### Using Visuals

See 28d

- ❑ Insert visuals into the text as close as possible to where they are discussed.
- ❑ For **tables**, follow these guidelines: *Above the table*, label each table with the word **Table** followed by an arabic numeral (for instance, **Table 1**). Double-space, and type a descriptive caption, with the first line flush with the left-hand margin; indent subsequent lines one-quarter inch. Capitalize the caption as if it were a title.

  *Below the table*, type the word **Source,** followed by a colon and all source information. Type the first line of the source information flush with the left-hand margin; indent subsequent lines one-quarter inch.
- ❑ Label other types of visual material—graphs, charts, photographs, drawings, and so on—**Fig.** (Figure) followed by an arabic numeral (for example, **Fig. 2**). Directly below the visual, type the label and a title or caption on the same

line, followed by source information. Type all lines flush with the left-hand margin.

- ❑ Do not include the source of the visual in the works-cited list unless you use other material from that source elsewhere in the paper.

CHECKLIST

**Preparing the MLA Works-Cited List**

When typing your works-cited list, follow these guidelines:

- ❑ Begin the works-cited list on a new page after the last page of text or content notes, numbered as the next page of the paper.
- ❑ Center the title **Works Cited** one inch from the top of the page. Double-space between the title and the first entry.
- ❑ Each entry on the works-cited list has three divisions: author, title, and publication information. Separate divisions with a period and one space.
- ❑ List entries alphabetically, with last name first. Use the author's full name as it appears on the title page. If a source has no listed author, alphabetize it by the first word of the title (not counting the article).
- ❑ Type the first line of each entry flush with the left-hand margin; indent subsequent lines one-half inch.
- ❑ Double-space within and between entries.

See 18a3

## 18c Model MLA-Style Research Paper

The following student paper, "The Great Debate: *Wikipedia* and College-Level Research," by Rebecca James, uses MLA documentation style. It includes MLA-style in-text citations, a line graph, a notes page, and a works-cited list. Marginal annotations explain format conventions and reproduce corresponding sections of the outline Rebecca used to guide her writing (**see 12h**).

## Title Pages

Although MLA does not require a separate title page, some instructors prefer that you include one. If so, follow this format:

About ⅓ page down

Title — The Great Debate:
*Wikipedia* and College-Level Research

2"

by

Name — Rebecca James

2"

Instructor — Professor Burks

Course — English 102

Date submitted — 24 April 2012

Double-space

1″ ½″

James 1 Student's last name and page number on every page (including the first)

Rebecca James

Professor Burks

English 102

24 April 2012

Center title → The Great Debate: *Wikipedia* and College-Level Research

Indent ½″ → When confronted with a research assignment, students and professionals alike often turn first to *Wikipedia,* the popular free online encyclopedia. With over 20,000,000 articles, *Wikipedia* is a valuable resource for anyone seeking general information on a topic. Recently, however, *Wikipedia* has become a source of controversy. Many college instructors say that students should not rely on *Wikipedia* as an authoritative research source or cite it in their bibliographies; they say that *Wikipedia* (like other encyclopedias) should be used only as a starting point for in-depth research. Some academics, troubled by the site's lack of reliability, even discourage the use of *Wikipedia* as a source of factual information. On the other hand, some instructors (along with some college librarians) believe that the issue is not so clear-cut. They say that *Wikipedia* is here to stay and that if the site has problems, it is their responsibility to help improve it. All in all, the debate over *Wikipedia* has been a positive development because it has led the academic community to confront the challenges of open, collaborative software on the Web.

Double-space

1″ 1″

Thesis statement

**Outline point I: Definition of wiki and explanation of *Wikipedia***

*Wikipedia* is the most popular wiki, an open-source Web site that allows users to edit as well as contribute content. Derived from a Hawaiian word meaning "quick," the term *wiki* suggests the swiftness and ease with which users can access information on and contribute content to a site ("Wiki"). In accordance with the site's policies, users can edit existing

Parenthetical documentation refers to material accessed from a Web site

1″

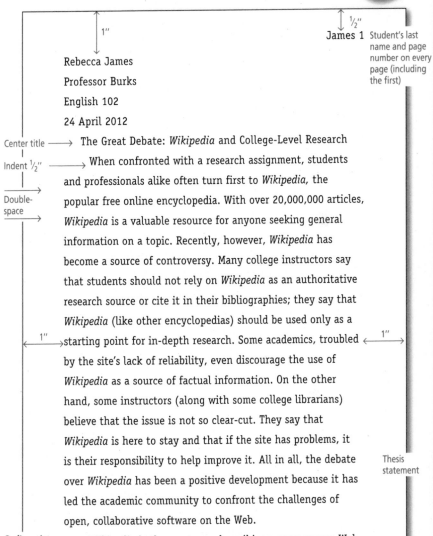

James 2

Student's original conclusions; no documentation necessary

articles and add new articles using *Wikipedia*'s editing tools, which do not require specialized programming knowledge or expertise. Since its creation in 2001 by Jimmy Wales, *Wikipedia* has grown into a huge database of articles on topics ranging from contemporary rock bands to obscure scientific and technical concepts. Because anyone can edit or add content to the site, however, many members of the academic community consider *Wikipedia* unreliable.

Outline point II: Introduction to *Wikipedia*'s drawbacks

Quotations from Internet source, introduced by author's name, are not followed by a paragraph or page number because this information was not provided in the electronic text

Without a professional editorial board to oversee its development, *Wikipedia* has several shortcomings that limit its trustworthiness. As *Wikipedia*'s own "Researching with *Wikipedia*" page concedes, "not everything in *Wikipedia* is accurate, comprehensive, or unbiased." "Reliability of *Wikipedia*," an article on *Wikipedia*, discusses the many problems that have been identified, presenting criticisms under categories such as "areas of reliability," "susceptibility to bias," and "false biographical information." Academics have similar objections. Villanova University communication department chair Maurice L. Hall has reservations about *Wikipedia*:

Quotation of more than four lines is typed as a block, indented 1", and double-spaced, with no quotation marks

> As an open source that is not subjected to traditional forms of peer review, *Wikipedia* must be considered only as reliable as the credibility of the footnotes it uses. But I also tell students that the information can be skewed in directions of ideology or other forms of bias, and so that is why it cannot be taken as a final authority. (qtd. in Burnsed)

*Qtd. in* indicates that Hall's and Kehm's comments were quoted in Burnsed's article

Similarly, Karl Kehm, an associate professor of physics at Washington College, does not allow his students to cite *Wikipedia*. However, he does "encourage them to use it as one of many launch points for pursuing original source material.

James 3

The best *Wikipedia* entries are well researched with extensive citations" (qtd. in Burnsed). In fact, in 2007, *Wikipedia*'s unreliability led Middlebury College's history department to prohibit students from citing *Wikipedia* as a research source—although it does not prohibit them from using the site for reference. Since then, however, many academics have qualified their criticisms of *Wikipedia*, arguing that although the site is not a reliable research source, it is a valuable stepping stone to more in-depth research. As retired reference librarian Joe Schallan explains, "*Wikipedia* can be useful, especially as a starting point for information on offbeat topics or niche interests that traditional encyclopedias omit." However, he believes that information from *Wikipedia* should be taken "with a very large grain of salt."

Outline point III: *Wikipedia*'s unreliability

Because it is an open-source site, *Wikipedia* is not always reliable or accurate. Although many *Wikipedia* articles include citations, many others—especially those that are underdeveloped—do not. In addition, because anyone can create or edit them, *Wikipedia* articles can be inaccurate, biased, and even targets for vandalism. For example, some *Wikipedia* users tamper with the biographies of especially high-profile political or cultural figures.[1] According to the 2011 article "*Wikipedia* Vandalism Detection," 7% of *Wikipedia*'s articles are vandalized in some way (Adler et al. 277). Although *Wikipedia* has an extensive protection policy that restricts the kinds of edits that can be made to its articles ("*Wikipedia*: Protection Policy"), there are limitations to *Wikipedia*'s control measures. As William Badke, an associate librarian at Trinity Western University, notes, *Wikipedia* can be "an environment for shallow thinking, debates over interpretation, and the settling of scores" (50).

Superscript number identifies content note

James 4

Because they can be edited by anyone, *Wikipedia* articles are often poorly written. Emory University English professor Mark Bauerlein asserts that *Wikipedia* articles are written in a "flat, featureless, factual style" (153). Even though *Wikipedia* has instituted a coding system to label the shortcomings of its less-developed articles, a warning about an article's poor writing style is likely to go unnoticed by the typical user. Bauerlein argues that the poor writing of many *Wikipedia* articles reaffirms to students that sloppy writing and grammatical errors are acceptable in their own writing as well: "Students relying on *Wikipedia* alone, year in and year out, absorb the prose as proper knowledge discourse, and knowledge itself seems blank and uninspiring" (153-54). Thus, according to Bauerlein, *Wikipedia* articles have actually lowered the standards for what constitutes acceptable college-level writing.

Outline point IV: *Wikipedia*'s poor writing

Despite *Wikipedia*'s drawbacks, there is no denying the popularity of the site among both college students and professionals, who turn to it first for general factual information on a variety of topics. According to a 2011 report by the Pew Internet & American Life Project, 53% of American adults use *Wikipedia,* with the majority of users having or pursuing higher-education degrees (Zickuhr and Rainie 2). Table 1 shows a breakdown of the people who most commonly consult *Wikipedia*.

Outline point V. A: *Wikipedia*'s popularity and benefits: Pew report statistic and table

There are good reasons why so many educated adults use *Wikipedia*. Longer *Wikipedia* articles often include comprehensive abstracts that summarize their content. *Wikipedia* articles also often include links to other *Wikipedia* articles, allowing users to navigate quickly through related content. In addition, many *Wikipedia* articles link to other print and online sources, including reliable peer-reviewed

Outline point V. B: *Wikipedia*'s popularity and benefits: comprehensive abstracts, links to other sources, and current and comprehensive bibliographies

James 5

Table 1

*Wikipedia* User Profile

| Total | 53% |
|---|---|
| Men | 56 |
| Women | 50 |
| **Age** | |
| 18-29 | 62 |
| 30-49 | 52 |
| 50-64 | 49 |
| 65+ | 33 |
| **Race/Ethnicity** | |
| White, non-Hispanic | 55 |
| Black, non-Hispanic (n=85) | 43 |
| Hispanic (n=61) | 40 |
| **Household Income** | |
| Less than $30,000 | 44 |
| $30,000-$49,999 | 49 |
| $50,000-$74,999 | 63 |
| $75,000+ | 61 |
| **Education level** | |
| Less than High School (n=46) | 30 |
| High School Diploma | 41 |
| Some College | 52 |
| College+ | 69 |
| **Home internet connection type** | |
| Dial-up (n=76) | 26 |
| Broadband | 59 |

**Source:** Pew Research Center's Internet & American Life Project, April 29-May 30, 2010 Spring Change Assessment Survey. N=852 internet users age 18 and older.



Source: Kathryn Zickuhr and Lee Rainie; "*Wikipedia,* Past and Present"; *Pew Internet & American Life Project*; Pew Research Center, 13 Jan. 2011; Web; 7 Apr. 2012; 2.

Table summarizes relevant data. Source information is typed directly below the table.

sources. Another benefit, noted earlier by Villanova University's Maurice L. Hall and Washington College's Karl Kehm, is the inclusion of current and comprehensive bibliographies in some *Wikipedia* articles. According to Alison J. Head and Michael B. Eisenberg, "*Wikipedia* plays an important role when students are formulating and defining a topic."[2] Assuming that *Wikipedia* users make the effort to connect an

Superscript number identifies content note

James 6

article's content with more reliable, traditional research sources, *Wikipedia* can be a valuable first step for serious researchers.

*Wikipedia* has advantages over other online encyclopedias. Because users can update articles in real time from any location, *Wikipedia* offers up-to-the-minute coverage of political and cultural events as well as timely information on popular culture topics that receive little or no attention in other reference sources. In addition, because *Wikipedia* has such a broad user base, more topics are covered in *Wikipedia* than in other online resources. For example, a student researching the history of video gaming would find *Wikipedia*'s "Wii" article, with its numerous pages of information and nearly two hundred references, to be a valuable resource. In contrast, the "Nintendo Wii" article in the professionally edited *Encyclopaedia Britannica Online* consists of a few paragraphs and a handful of external resources. Even when there is little information on a particular topic, *Wikipedia* allows users to create "stub" articles, which provide minimal information that users can expand over time. Thus, by offering immediate access to information on relatively obscure topics, *Wikipedia* can be a valuable first step in finding reliable research sources on such topics.

Outline point VI: *Wikipedia*'s advantages over other online encyclopedias

In their 2008 landmark study, Diomidis Spinellis and Panagiotis Louridas accurately predict that *Wikipedia* would become an even more comprehensive database of information that could eventually gain acceptance in the academic community. *Wikipedia*'s "About" page claims that the site's articles "are never considered complete and may be continually edited and improved. Over time, this generally results in an upward trend of quality and a growing consensus over a neutral

Outline point VII: *Wikipedia*'s ongoing improvements

James 7

representation of information." In fact, *Wikipedia* has instituted control measures to help weed out inaccurate or biased information and to make its content more reliable. For example, evaluating articles on the basis of accuracy, neutrality, completeness, and style, *Wikipedia* ranks its best articles as "featured" and its second-best articles as "good."[3] Although no professional editorial board oversees the development of content within *Wikipedia,* experienced users may become editors, and this role allows them to monitor the process by which content is added and updated. Users may also use the "Talk" page to discuss an article's content and make suggestions for improvement. With such controls in place, some *Wikipedia* articles are comparable in scope and accuracy to articles in professionally edited online resources.

Superscript number identifies content note

Outline point VIII: *Wikipedia*'s content

Although critics argue that the collaborative nature of the wiki format does not necessarily help improve content, Spinellis and Louridas's study seems to suggest the opposite. In examining trends of content development in *Wikipedia,* Spinellis and Louridas affirm that the coverage of various topics in *Wikipedia* tends to become more balanced over time:

> *Wikipedia*'s topic coverage has been criticized as too reflective of and limited to the interests of its young, tech-savvy contributors, covering technology and current affairs disproportionably more than, say, world history or the arts. We hypothesize that the addition of new *Wikipedia* articles is not a purely random process following the whims of its contributors but that references to nonexistent articles trigger the eventual creation of a corresponding article. Although it is difficult to claim

James 9

Parenthetical documentation is placed one space after end punctuation

> that this process guarantees even and unbiased coverage of topics (adding links is also a subjective process), such a mechanism could eventually force some kind of balance in *Wikipedia* coverage. (71)

Spinellis and Louridas summarize their findings with a positive conclusion: "the apparently chaotic *Wikipedia* development process delivers growth at a sustainable rate" (71). Fig. 1 supports this conclusion, illustrating how, in recent years, *Wikipedia* has achieved a relative balance between complete and incomplete (or stub) articles. In offering increasingly more consistent (as well as broader) coverage, *Wikipedia* is becoming a more reliable source of information than some of its critics might like to admit.

Graph summarizes relevant data. Source information is typed directly below the figure.

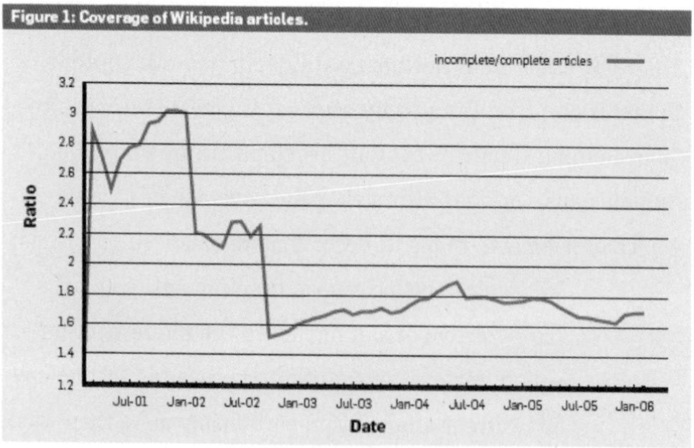




Fig. 1. Diomidis Spinellis and Panagiotis Louridas, "The Collaborative Organization of Knowledge"; *Communications of the ACM* 51.8 (2008): 71; *Academic Search Elite*; Web; 3 Apr. 2012.

Some argue that the academic community's reservations about *Wikipedia* have less to do with *Wikipedia*'s shortcomings

**Outline point IX: Academic community's reservations about *Wikipedia***

James 9

and more to do with resistance to emergent digital research technologies. Harvard Law professor Jonathan L. Zittrain suggests that academia has, in effect, fallen behind, observing that although "many projects by universities and libraries are about knowledge and information online, . . . they just couldn't get *Wikipedia* going, or anything like it" (qtd. in Foster). William Badke, the Trinity Western University librarian, agrees, stating, "*Wikipedia* is an affront to academia, because it undercuts what makes academics the elite in society. . . . *Wikipedia* doesn't depend on elite scholars" (49). Although he acknowledges that *Wikipedia* should serve only as a starting point for more in-depth research, Jimmy Wales, cofounder of *Wikipedia,* calls for the academic community to recognize *Wikipedia* as one of several new, important digital platforms that change the way people learn and disseminate knowledge: "Instead of fearing the power, complexity, and extraordinary potential of these new platforms, we should be asking how we can gain from their success" (qtd. in Goldstein). As Badke and others argue, members of the academic community are uniquely qualified to improve *Wikipedia* by expanding stub articles and by writing new articles about their areas of expertise. As Badke suggests, "The most daring solution would be for academia to enter the world of *Wikipedia* directly" (50). According to Badke, professors should not be asking whether college students should use *Wikipedia* in their research but rather how the academic community can improve this bank of information that students consult before any other research source.

Ellipsis indicates that the student has omitted words from the quotation

In recent years, librarians across the country have committed their time and resources to enhancing *Wikipedia*

James 10

Outline point X: Librarians' efforts to use and improve *Wikipedia*

Paragraph synthesizes several sources cited in paper

articles that pertain to their own special collections and areas of expertise. Like William Badke, librarian Adam Bennington argues that the *Wikipedia* phenomenon presents a "teachable moment" that enables librarians and other members of the academic community to develop students' information literacy skills (47). Similarly, Richard Morrill, a reference/instruction librarian at Lake-Sumter Community College, proposes, "Surely the thing that librarians and English instructors should be doing is giving students assignments to find and evaluate critically information in . . . *Wikipedia*." In their article "Putting the Library in *Wikipedia*," Wake Forest University librarians Lauren Pressley and Carolyn J. McCallum argue that librarians can play a pivotal role in making *Wikipedia* a more reliable source of information, as demonstrated by their own contributions as well as those made by librarians at the University of Washington Digital Initiatives, the University of North Texas, and Villanova University. "Through this type of collaboration," Pressley and McCallum suggest, "perhaps we will reach a whole new group of users that wouldn't have come through our doors another way" (42). Badke, Bennington, Morrill, Pressley, McCallum, and other librarians believe that it is the responsibility of the academic community to bridge the divide between traditional research sources and the digital tools and technologies students are increasingly using to conduct college-level research.

Outline point XI: *Wikipedia* in the classroom

Already, college instructors have found new uses and benefits of *Wikipedia* by incorporating it into their classrooms. In fact, *Wikipedia* has implemented a "classroom coordination project" to help instructors around the world build writing assignments based on *Wikipedia*. *Wikipedia*'s

James 11

"School and University Projects" page offers guidelines and other resources as well as a list of more than fifty schools that incorporate *Wikipedia* into the classroom, noting that "An advantage of this over regular homework is that the student is dealing with a real world situation, which is not only more educational but also makes it more interesting." Jeff Byers, a professor of chemistry and biochemistry at Middlebury College (where one of the more famous *Wikipedia* "bans" was instituted not long ago), has developed an assignment for his advanced organic chemistry course that has students write and edit *Wikipedia* entries. Similarly, in her article "Writing for the World: *Wikipedia* as an Introduction to Academic Writing," Christine M. Tardy, an associate professor of writing, rhetoric, and discourse at DePaul University, encourages instructors to use *Wikipedia* in the classroom and outlines some sample writing assignments. Tardy explains, "In producing a text for *Wikipedia*, students gain a real sense of audience and enjoy the satisfaction of seeing their work published on a high-traffic global website" (18). Instructors like Byers and Tardy emphasize the collaborative nature of *Wikipedia* writing assignments, which offer students a unique opportunity to experience the kinds of writing they are likely to do after college. Additionally, *Wikipedia* writing assignments encourage students to use critical thinking skills, since they require students to evaluate the articles they find on the site and to use *Wikipedia* bibliographies as a starting place to find more suitable research sources.

Outline point XII: Academics' changing view of *Wikipedia*

With emerging research on *Wikipedia* use and with new efforts by colleges and universities around the country to incorporate *Wikipedia* into the classroom, the debate

James 12

surrounding *Wikipedia* seems to be shifting. Although instructors used to seek ways to prevent students from using *Wikipedia* as a research source, some in the academic community are acknowledging the importance and usefulness of this online resource—at least for general reference. Many former critics are acknowledging that *Wikipedia* offers academics an opportunity to participate in emergent digital technologies that have changed the ways students conduct research. In other words, instructors acknowledge, they need to come to terms with *Wikipedia* and develop guidelines for its use. More and more academics are realizing that improving *Wikipedia* actually benefits students, since the site is often the first place students go when starting a research project. To its credit, *Wikipedia* has taken steps to improve the site's reliability and accuracy. In her article "Boosting *Wikipedia* Quality," Robin Peek, an associate professor at Simmons College, describes two major initiatives *Wikipedia* has recently undertaken. The first is the "Rate This Page" feature, which allows users to evaluate articles on the basis of trustworthiness, objectivity, completeness, and writing quality. The second is the Public Policy Initiative, or PPI, which encourages instructors in public policy programs to develop *Wikipedia* writing assignments. *Wikipedia* plans to expand the PPI over time by involving other disciplines as well.

Conclusion restates the thesis and summarizes key points

Like any encyclopedia, *Wikipedia* is not a suitable source for college-level research. Beyond this fact, however, it may also not yet be as reliable as some other reference sources. Still, it is a valuable starting point for research. As academics and others continue to examine *Wikipedia*'s strengths and weaknesses, they may become more open to its use and more

James 13

willing to work to improve it. In this sense, the debate over *Wikipedia* is likely to have a positive outcome. Meanwhile, however, students should exercise caution when evaluating general information they find on *Wikipedia* and refrain from citing it as a source.

1"

James 14

Center title → Notes

Indent ½" → 1. In one well-known example, the reputation of journalist John Seigenthaler was tarnished when a *Wikipedia* user edited his biography to claim inaccurately that Seigenthaler was involved in the Kennedy assassination, a lie that spread to other online sources.

Double-space

2. Head and Eisenberg also note, however, that "when students are in a deep research mode, . . . it is library databases, such as *JSTOR* and *PsycINFO*, for instance, that students use more frequently than *Wikipedia*."

1" ↔ 1"

3. In addition, *Wikipedia*'s policies state that the information in its articles must be verifiable and must be based on documented, preexisting research.

1/2"

James 15

1"

Works Cited

Center title

Double-space

1"

1"

Adler, B. Thomas, et al. "*Wikipedia* Vandalism Detection: Combining Natural Language, Metadata, and Reputation Features." *Lecture Notes in Computer Science* 6609 (2011): 277-88. *Google Scholar*. Web. 3 Apr. 2012.

Badke, William. "What to Do with *Wikipedia*." *Online* Mar.-Apr. 2008: 48-50. *Academic Search Elite*. Web. 7 Apr. 2012.

Bauerlein, Mark. *The Dumbest Generation: How the Digital Age Stupefies Young Americans and Jeopardizes Our Future (or, Don't Trust Anyone Under 30)*. New York: Penguin, 2008. Print.

Bennington, Adam. "Dissecting the Web through *Wikipedia*." *American Libraries* Aug. 2008: 46-48. Print.

Burnsed, Brian. "*Wikipedia* Gradually Accepted in College Classrooms." *USNews.com*. US News & World Rept., 20 June 2011. Web. 25 Mar. 2012.

Foster, Andrea L. "Professor Predicts Bleak Future for the Internet." *Chronicle of Higher Education* 18 Apr. 2008: A29. *Academic Search Elite*. Web. 3 Apr. 2012.

Newspaper article accessed from an online database

Goldstein, Evan R. "The Dumbing of America?" *Chronicle of Higher Education* 21 Mar. 2008: B4. *Academic Search Elite*. Web. 3 Apr. 2012.

Head, Alison J., and Michael B. Eisenberg. "How Today's College Students Use *Wikipedia* for Course-Related Research." *First Monday* 15.3 (2010): n. pag. *Google Scholar*. Web. 3 Apr. 2012.

Journal article without pagination accessed from *Google Scholar*

Morrill, Richard. "Who Says *Wikipedia* Isn't Trustworthy?" Letter. *Chronicle of Higher Education* 2 Oct. 2011: n. pag. *Academic Search Elite*. Web. 3 Apr. 2012.

1"

Peek, Robin. "Boosting *Wikipedia* Quality." *Information Today* Oct. 2011: 25. *Academic Search Elite*. Web. 3 Apr. 2012.

Pressley, Lauren, and Carolyn J. McCallum. "Putting the Library in *Wikipedia*." *Online* Sept.-Oct. 2008: 39-42. *Academic Search Elite*. Web. 3 Apr. 2012.

"Reliability of *Wikipedia*." *Wikipedia*. Wikimedia Foundation, 2012. Web. 25 Mar. 2012.

Signed letter to the editor in a montly magazine

Schallan, Joe. "*Wikipedia* Woes." Letter. *American Libraries* Apr. 2010: 9. Print.

Spinellis, Diomidis, and Panagiotis Louridas. "The Collaborative Organization of Knowledge." *Communications of the ACM* 51.8 (2008): 68-73. *Academic Search Elite*. Web. 3 Apr. 2012.

Tardy, Christine M. "Writing for the World: *Wikipedia* as an Introduction to Academic Writing." *English Teaching Forum* 48.1 (2010): 12+. *ERIC*. Web. 3 Apr. 2012.

Article in an online encyclopedia

"Wiki." *Encyclopaedia Britannica Online*. Encyclopaedia Britannica, 2012. Web. 25 Mar. 2012.

"*Wikipedia*: About." *Wikipedia*. Wikimedia Foundation, 2012. Web. 25 Mar. 2012.

Unsigned document within a Web site

"*Wikipedia:* Protection Policy." *Wikipedia*. Wikimedia Foundation, 2012. Web. 25 Mar. 2012.

"*Wikipedia*: Researching with *Wikipedia*." *Wikipedia*. Wikimedia Foundation, 2012. Web. 25 Mar. 2012.

"*Wikipedia:* School and University Projects." *Wikipedia*. Wikimedia Foundation, 2012. Web. 25 Mar. 2012.

Zickuhr, Kathryn, and Lee Rainie. "*Wikipedia*, Past and Present." *Pew Internet & American Life Project*. Pew Research Center, 13 Jan. 2011. Web. 7 Apr. 2012.

PART 5

# Documenting Sources: APA and Other Styles

## Directory of APA In-Text References



## Directory of APA Reference List Entries

### PRINT SOURCES: *Entries for Articles*

#### Articles in Scholarly Journals



#### Articles in Magazines and Newspapers



### PRINT SOURCES: *Entries for Books*

#### Authors



#### Editions, Multivolume Works, and Forewords

### Parts of Books



### Government and Technical Reports



## ENTRIES FOR MISCELLANEOUS PRINT SOURCES

### Letters



## ENTRIES FOR OTHER SOURCES

### Television Broadcasts, Films, CDs, Audiocassette Recordings, Interviews, and Computer Software



## ELECTRONIC SOURCES: *Entries for Sources from Internet Sites*

### Internet-Specific Sources



### Abstracts and Newspaper Articles

CHAPTER 19

# APA Documentation Style

## Frequently Asked Questions



## 19a Using APA Style

**APA style*** is used extensively in the social sciences. APA documentation has three parts: *parenthetical references in the body of the paper*, a *reference list*, and optional *content footnotes.*

### 1 Parenthetical References

APA documentation uses short parenthetical references in the body of the paper keyed to an alphabetical list of references at the end of the paper. A typical parenthetical reference consists of the author's last name (followed by a comma) and the year of publication.

> Many people exhibit symptoms of depression after the death of a pet (Russo, 2009).

If the author's name appears in an introductory phrase, include the year of publication there as well.

> According to Russo (2009), many people exhibit symptoms of depression after the death of a pet.

When quoting directly, include the page number, preceded by **p.** in parentheses after the quotation.

> According to Weston (2006), children from one-parent homes read at "a significantly lower level than those from two-parent homes" (p. 58).

Note: A long quotation (forty words or more) is not set in quotation marks. It is set as a block, and the entire quotation is double-spaced and indented one-half inch from the left margin. Parenthetical documentation is placed one space after the final punctuation.

*APA documentation format follows the guidelines set in the *Publication Manual of the American Psychological Association,* 6th ed. Washington, DC: APA, 2010.

## Sample APA In-Text Citations

### 1. A Work by a Single Author

Many college students suffer from sleep deprivation (Anton, 2009).

### 2. A Work by Two Authors

There is growing concern over the use of psychological testing in elementary schools (Albright & Glennon, 2010).

### 3. A Work by Three to Five Authors

If a work has more than two but fewer than six authors, mention all names in the first reference; in subsequent references in the same paragraph, cite only the first author followed by **et al.** ("and others"). When the reference appears in later paragraphs, include the year.

*First Reference*

(Sparks, Wilson, & Hewitt, 2009)

*Subsequent References in the Same Paragraph*

(Sparks et al.)

*References in Later Paragraphs*

(Sparks et al., 2009)

### 4. A Work by Six or More Authors

When a work has six or more authors, cite the name of the first author followed by **et al.** and the year in all references.

(Miller et al., 2008)

#### Close-Up CITING WORKS BY MULTIPLE AUTHORS

When referring to multiple authors in the text of your paper, join the last two names with **and.**

According to Rosen, Wolfe, and Ziff (2009). . . .

Parenthetical references (as well as reference list entries) require an **ampersand (&)**.

(Rosen, Wolfe, & Ziff, 2009)

### 5. Works by Authors with the Same Last Name

If your reference list includes works by two or more authors with the same last name, use each author's initials in all in-text citations.

Both F. Bor (2010) and S. D. Bor (2009) concluded that no further study was needed.

### 6. A Work by a Corporate Author

If the name of a corporate author is long, abbreviate it after the first citation.

*First Reference*

(National Institute of Mental Health [NIMH], 2010)

*Subsequent Reference*

(NIMH, 2010)

### 7. A Work with No Listed Author

If a work has no listed author, cite the first two or three words of the title (followed by a comma) and the year. Use quotation marks around titles of periodical articles and chapters of books; use italics for titles of books, periodicals, brochures, reports, and the like.

("New Immigration," 2009)

### 8. A Personal Communication

Cite letters, memos, telephone conversations, personal interviews, emails, messages from electronic bulletin boards, and so on only in the text of your paper—*not* in the reference list.

(R. Takaki, personal communication, October 17, 2009)

### 9. An Indirect Source

Cogan and Howe offer very different interpretations of the problem (cited in Swenson, 2009).

### 10. A Specific Part of a Source

Use abbreviations for the words *page* (**p.**), and *pages* (**pp.**), but spell out *chapter* and *section*.

These theories have an interesting history (Lee, 2010, chapter 2).

### 11. An Electronic Source

For an electronic source that does not show page numbers, use the paragraph number preceded by the abbreviation **para.**

Conversation at the dinner table is an example of a family ritual (Kulp, 2010, para. 3).

In the case of an electronic source that has neither page nor paragraph numbers, cite both the heading in the source and the number of the paragraph following the heading in which the material is located.

> Healthy eating is a never-ending series of free choices (Shapiro, 2008, Introduction section, para. 2).

If the source has no headings, you may not be able to specify an exact location.

#### 12. Two or More Works within the Same Parenthetical Reference

List works by different authors in alphabetical order, separated by semicolons.

> This theory is supported by several studies (Barson & Roth, 1995; Rose, 2001; Tedesco, 2010).

List two or more works by the same author or authors in order of date of publication (separated by commas), with the earliest date first.

> This theory is supported by several studies (Rhodes & Dollek, 2008, 2009, 2010).

For two or more works by the same author published in the same year, designate the work whose title comes first alphabetically *a*, the one whose title comes next *b*, and so on; repeat the year in each citation.

> This theory is supported by several studies (Shapiro, 2009a, 2009b).

#### 13. A Table

If you use a table from a source, give credit to the author in a note at the bottom of the table. Do not include this information in the reference list.

> *Note*. From "Predictors of Employment and Earnings Among JOBS Participants," by P. A. Neenan and D. K. Orthner, 1996, *Social Work Research, 20*(4), p. 233.

### 2 Reference List

The **reference list** gives the publication information for all the sources you cite. It should appear at the end of your paper on a new numbered page titled **References.** Entries in the reference list should be arranged alphabetically. Double-space within and between reference list entries. The first line of each entry should start at the left margin, with the second and subsequent lines indented one-half inch. (**See 19b** for full manuscript guidelines.)

## APA PRINT SOURCES Entries for Articles

Article citations include the author's name (last name first); the date of publication (in parentheses); the title of the article; the title of the periodical (italicized); the volume number (italicized); the issue number, if any (in parentheses); and the inclusive page numbers (including all digits). Figure 19.1 shows where you can find this information.

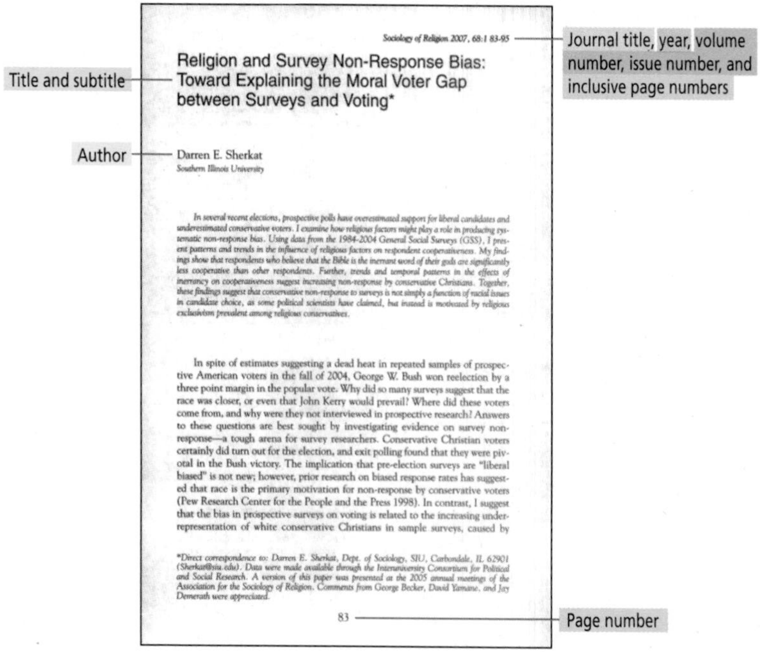


*Sociology of Religion 2007, 68:1 83-95*

Religion and Survey Non-Response Bias: Toward Explaining the Moral Voter Gap between Surveys and Voting*

Darren E. Sherkat
*Southern Illinois University*

*In several recent elections, prospective polls have overestimated support for liberal candidates and underestimated conservative voters. I examine how religious factors might play a role in producing systematic non-response bias. Using data from the 1984-2004 General Social Surveys (GSS), I present patterns and trends in the influence of religious factors on respondent cooperativeness. My findings show that respondents who believe that the Bible is the inerrant word of their gods are significantly less cooperative than other respondents. Further, trends and temporal patterns in the effects of inerrancy on cooperativeness suggest increasing non-response by conservative Christians. Together, these findings suggest that conservative non-response to surveys is not simply a function of racial issues in candidate choice, as some political scientists have claimed, but instead is motivated by religious exclusivism prevalent among religious conservatives.*

In spite of estimates suggesting a dead heat in repeated samples of prospective American voters in the fall of 2004, George W. Bush won reelection by a three point margin in the popular vote. Why did so many surveys suggest that the race was closer, or even that John Kerry would prevail? Where did these voters come from, and why were they not interviewed in prospective research? Answers to these questions are best sought by investigating evidence on survey non-response—a tough arena for survey researchers. Conservative Christian voters certainly did turn out for the election, and exit polling found that they were pivotal in the Bush victory. The implication that pre-election surveys are "liberal biased" is not new; however, prior research on biased response rates has suggested that race is the primary motivation for non-response by conservative voters (Pew Research Center for the People and the Press 1998). In contrast, I suggest that the bias in prospective surveys on voting is related to the increasing under-representation of white conservative Christians in sample surveys, caused by

**Direct correspondence to: Darren E. Sherkat, Dept. of Sociology, SIU, Carbondale, IL 62901 (Sherkat@siu.edu). Data were made available through the Interuniversity Consortium for Political and Social Research. A version of this paper was presented at the 2005 annual meetings of the Association for the Sociology of Religion. Comments from George Becker, David Yamane, and Jay Demerath were appreciated.*

83

**FIGURE 19.1** First page of an article showing the location of the information needed for documentation. © Association for the Sociology of Religion. Used by permission of Association for the Sociology of Religion, Inc.

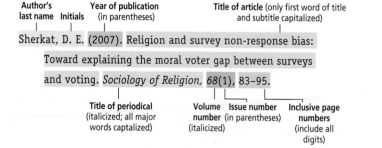

**Author's last name** | **Initials** | **Year of publication** (in parentheses) | **Title of article** (only first word of title and subtitle capitalized)

Sherkat, D. E. (2007). Religion and survey non-response bias: Toward explaining the moral voter gap between surveys and voting. *Sociology of Religion, 68*(1), 83–95.

**Title of periodical** (italicized; all major words captalized) | **Volume number** (italicized) | **Issue number** (in parentheses) | **Inclusive page numbers** (include all digits)

Capitalize the first word of the article's title and subtitle as well as any proper nouns. Do not underline or italicize the title of the article or enclose it in quotation marks. Give the periodical title in full, and capitalize all words except articles, prepositions, and conjunctions of fewer than four letters. Use **p.** or **pp.** when referring to page numbers in newspapers, but omit this abbreviation when referring to page numbers in journals and popular magazines.

### *Articles in Scholarly Journals*

#### 1. An Article in a Scholarly Journal with Continuous Pagination throughout an Annual Volume

Miller, W. (1969). Violent crimes in city gangs. *Journal of Social Issues, 27,* 581–593.

#### 2. An Article in a Scholarly Journal with Separate Pagination in Each Issue

Williams, S., & Cohen, L. R. (2004). Child stress in early learning situations. *American Psychologist, 21*(10), 1–28.

Note: Do not leave a space between the volume and issue numbers.

#### 3. A Book Review in a Scholarly Journal (Unsigned)

A review with no author should be listed by title, followed by a description of the reviewed work in brackets.

Coming of age and joining the cult of thinness [Review of the book *The cult of thinness,* by Sharlene Nagy Hesse-Biber]. (2008, June). *Psychology of Women Quarterly, 32*(2), 221–222.

### *Articles in Magazines and Newspapers*

#### 4. A Magazine Article

McCurdy, H. G. (2003, June). Brain mechanisms and intelligence. *Psychology Today, 46,* 61–63.

#### 5. A Newspaper Article

If an article appears on nonconsecutive pages, give all page numbers, separated by commas (for example, **A1, A14**). If the article appears on consecutive pages, indicate the full range of pages (for example, **A7–A9**).

James, W. R. (1993, November 16). The uninsured and health care. *Wall Street Journal,* pp. A1, A14.

#### 6. A Newspaper Editorial (Unsigned)

An editorial with no author should be listed by title, followed by the label **Editorial** in brackets.

The plight of the underinsured [Editorial]. (2008, June 12). *The New York Times,* p. A30.

### 7. A Letter to the Editor of a Newspaper

Williams, P. (2006, July 19). Self-fulfilling stereotypes [Letter to the editor]. *Los Angeles Times,* p. A22.

## APA PRINT SOURCES Entries for Books

Book citations include the author's name (last name first); the year of publication (in parentheses); the book title (italicized); and publication information. Figures 19.2 and 19.3 show where you can find this information.

Capitalize only the first word of the title and subtitle and any proper nouns. Include any additional necessary information—edition, report number, or volume number, for example—in parentheses after the title. In the publication information, write out in full the names of associations, corporations, and university presses. Include the words **Book** and **Press**, but do not include terms such as **Publishers, Co.**, or **Inc.**

**Author's last name** | **Initial** | **Year of publication** (in parentheses) | **Title** (italicized, with only first word of title and subtitle capitalized)

Straubhaar, J., LaRose, R., & Davenport, L. (2012). *Media now: Understanding media, culture, and technology* (7th ed.). Boston, MA: Wadsworth Cengage Learning.

**Edition** (in parentheses) | **City and state** | **Publisher** (not including terms Publishers, Co., or Inc.)

### *Authors*

### 8. A Book with One Author

Maslow, A. H. (1974). *Toward a psychology of being.* Princeton, NJ: Van Nostrand.

### 9. A Book with More Than One Author

List up to seven authors by last name and initials, using an ampersand (&) to connect the last two names. For more than seven authors, insert an ellipsis (three spaced periods) and add the last author's name.

Wolfinger, D., Knable, P., Richards, H. L., & Silberger, R. (2007). *The chronically unemployed.* New York, NY: Berman Press.

### 10. A Book with No Listed Author or Editor

*Teaching in a wired classroom.* (2012). Philadelphia, PA: Drexel Press.

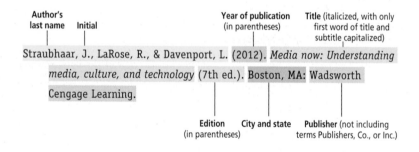

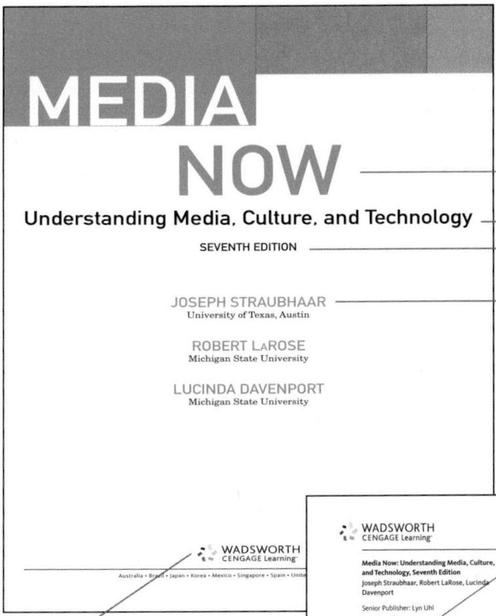
MEDIA NOW
**Understanding Media, Culture, and Technology**
SEVENTH EDITION
JOSEPH STRAUBHAAR
University of Texas, Austin
ROBERT LaROSE
Michigan State University
LUCINDA DAVENPORT
Michigan State University
WADSWORTH
CENGAGE Learning
Australia • Brazil • Japan • Korea • Mexico • Singapore • Spain • Unite


FIGURE 19.2 Title page from a book showing the location of the information needed for documentation. © Cengage Learning, 2012; reprinted with permission.

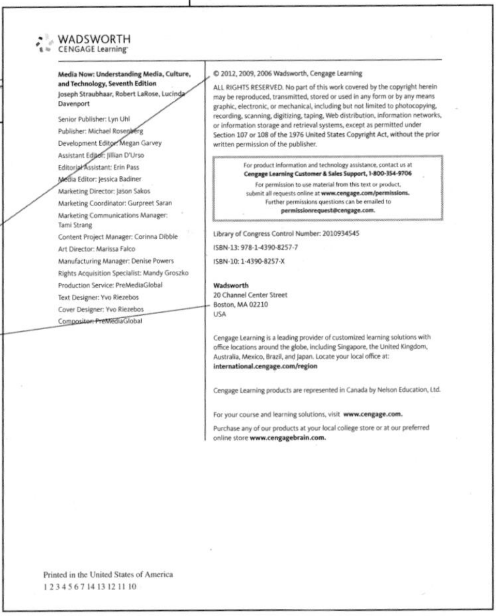
WADSWORTH
CENGAGE Learning

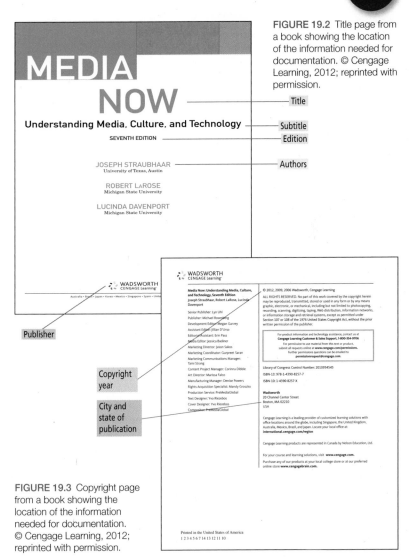

**Media Now: Understanding Media, Culture, and Technology, Seventh Edition**
Joseph Straubhaar, Robert LaRose, Lucinda Davenport

Senior Publisher: Lyn Uhl
Publisher: Michael Rosenberg
Development Editor: Megan Garvey
Assistant Editor: Jillian D'Urso
Editorial Assistant: Erin Pass
Media Editor: Jessica Badiner
Marketing Director: Jason Sakos
Marketing Coordinator: Gurpreet Saran
Marketing Communications Manager: Tami Strang
Content Project Manager: Corinna Dibble
Art Director: Marissa Falco
Manufacturing Manager: Denise Powers
Rights Acquisition Specialist: Mandy Groszko
Production Service: PreMediaGlobal
Text Designer: Yvo Riezebos
Cover Designer: Yvo Riezebos
Compositor: PreMediaGlobal

© 2012, 2009, 2006 Wadsworth, Cengage Learning

ALL RIGHTS RESERVED. No part of this work covered by the copyright herein may be reproduced, transmitted, stored or used in any form or by any means graphic, electronic, or mechanical, including but not limited to photocopying, recording, scanning, digitizing, taping, Web distribution, information networks, or information storage and retrieval systems, except as permitted under Section 107 or 108 of the 1976 United States Copyright Act, without the prior written permission of the publisher.

For product information and technology assistance, contact us at
**Cengage Learning Customer & Sales Support, 1-800-354-9706**
For permission to use material from this text or product, submit all requests online at **www.cengage.com/permissions.**
Further permissions questions can be emailed to
**permissionrequest@cengage.com.**

Library of Congress Control Number: 2010934545
ISBN-13: 978-1-4390-8257-7
ISBN-10: 1-4390-8257-X

**Wadsworth**
20 Channel Center Street
Boston, MA 02210
USA

Cengage Learning is a leading provider of customized learning solutions with office locations around the globe, including Singapore, the United Kingdom, Australia, Mexico, Brazil, and Japan. Locate your local office at: **international.cengage.com/region**

Cengage Learning products are represented in Canada by Nelson Education, Ltd.

For your course and learning solutions, visit **www.cengage.com.**

Purchase any of our products at your local college store or at our preferred online store **www.cengagebrain.com.**

Printed in the United States of America
1 2 3 4 5 6 7 14 13 12 11 10


FIGURE 19.3 Copyright page from a book showing the location of the information needed for documentation. © Cengage Learning, 2012; reprinted with permission.

### 11. A Book with a Corporate Author

When the author and the publisher are the same, include the word **Author** at the end of the citation instead of repeating the publisher's name.

League of Women Voters of the United States. (2008). *Local league handbook*. Washington, DC: Author.

### 12. An Edited Book

Lewin, K., Lippitt, R., & White, R. K. (Eds.). (1985). *Social learning and imitation*. New York, NY: Basic Books.

## *Editions, Multivolume Works, and Forewords*

### 13. A Work in Several Volumes

Jones, P. R., & Williams, T. C. (Eds.). (1990–1993). *Handbook of therapy* (Vols. 1–2). Princeton, NJ: Princeton University Press.

### 14. The Foreword, Preface, or Afterword of a Book

Taylor, T. (1979). Preface. In B. B. Ferencz, *Less than slaves* (pp. ii–ix). Cambridge, MA: Harvard University Press.

## *Parts of Books*

### 15. A Selection from an Anthology

Give inclusive page numbers preceded by **pp.** (in parentheses) after the title of the anthology. The title of the selection is not enclosed in quotation marks.

Lorde, A. (1984). Age, race, and class. In P. S. Rothenberg (Ed.), *Racism and sexism: An integrated study* (pp. 352–360). New York, NY: St. Martin's Press.

**Note:** If you cite two or more selections from the same anthology, give the full citation for the anthology in each entry.

### 16. An Article in a Reference Book

Edwards, P. (Ed.). (2006). Determinism. In *The encyclopedia of philosophy* (Vol. 2, pp. 359–373). New York, NY: Macmillan.

## *Government and Technical Reports*

### 17. A Government Report

U.S. Department of Health and Human Services, National Institutes of Health, National Institute of Mental Health. (2007). *Motion pictures and violence: A summary report of research* (DHHS Publication No. ADM 91-22187). Washington, DC: Government Printing Office.

### 18. A Technical Report

Attali, Y., & Powers, D. (2008). *Effect of immediate feedback and revision on psychometric properties of open-ended GRE® subject test items* (ETS GRE

Board Research Report No. 04-05). Princeton, NJ: Educational Testing Service.

## APA ENTRIES FOR MISCELLANEOUS PRINT SOURCES

### *Letters*

#### 19. A Personal Letter

References to unpublished personal letters, like references to all other personal communications, should be included only in the text of the paper, not in the reference list.

#### 20. A Published Letter

Joyce, J. (1931). Letter to Louis Gillet. In Richard Ellmann, *James Joyce* (p. 631). New York, NY: Oxford University Press.

## APA ENTRIES FOR OTHER SOURCES

### *Television Broadcasts, Films, CDs, Audiocassette Recordings, Interviews, and Computer Software*

#### 21. A Television Broadcast

Murphy, J. (Executive Producer). (2006, March 4). *The CBS evening news* [Television broadcast]. New York, NY: Columbia Broadcasting Service.

#### 22. A Television Series

Sorkin, A., Schlamme, T., & Wells, J. (Executive Producers). (2002). *The west wing* [Television series]. Los Angeles, CA: Warner Bros. Television.

#### 23. A Film

Spielberg, S. (Director). (1994). *Schindler's list* [Motion picture]. United States: Universal.

#### 24. A CD Recording

Marley, B. (1977). Waiting in vain. On *Exodus* [CD]. New York, NY: Island Records.

#### 25. An Audiocassette Recording

Skinner, B. F. (Speaker). (1972). *Skinner on Skinnerism* [Cassette recording]. Hollywood, CA: Center for Cassette Studies.

#### 26. A Recorded Interview

Bartel, S. S. (1978, November 5). Interview by L. Clark [Tape recording]. Billy Graham Center, Wheaton College. BGC Archives, Wheaton, IL.

**27. A Transcription of a Recorded Interview**

Berry, D. W. (1986, February 14). *Interview with Donald Wesley Berry—Collection 325*. Billy Graham Center, Wheaton College. BGC Archives, Wheaton, IL.

**28. Computer Software**

Sharp, S. (2009). Career Selection Tests (Version 7.0) [Software]. Chico, CA: Avocation Software.

## APA ELECTRONIC SOURCES Entries for Sources from Internet Sites

APA guidelines for documenting electronic sources focus on Web sources, which often do not include all the bibliographic information that print sources do. For example, Web sources may not include page numbers or a place of publication. At a minimum, a Web citation should have a title, a date (the date of publication, update, or retrieval), and a Digital Object Identifier (DOI) (when available) or an electronic address (URL). If possible, also include the author(s) of a source. Figure 19.4 shows where you can find this information.

When you need to divide a URL at the end of a line, break it after a double slash or before most other punctuation (do not add a hyphen). Do not add a period at the end of the URL.

**Author's last name** — **Initials** — **Year of publication** (in parentheses) — **Title of article** (only first word of title and subtitle as well as proper nouns capitalized)

Yip, T., Gee, G. C., & Takeuchi, D. T. (2008). Racial discrimination and psychological distress: The impact of ethnic identity and age among immigrant and United States-born Asian adults. *Developmental Psychology, 44*(3), 787–800. doi:10.1037/0012-1649.44.3.787

**Volume number** (italicized) — **Issue number** (in parentheses) — **Inclusive page numbers** (include all digits) — **DOI** (without period at end) — **Title of periodical** (italicized)

### *Internet-Specific Sources*

**29. An Internet Article Based on a Print Source**

If the article has a DOI, you do not need to include the retrieval date or the URL. Always include the volume number (italicized) and the issue number (in parentheses, if available).

Rutledge, P. C., Park, A., & Sher, K. J. (2008). 21st birthday drinking: Extremely extreme. *Journal of Consulting and Clinical Psychology, 76*(3), 511–516. doi:10.1037/0022-006X.76.3.511

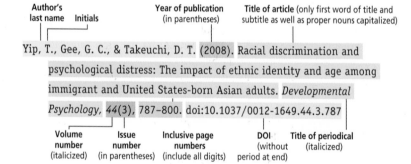

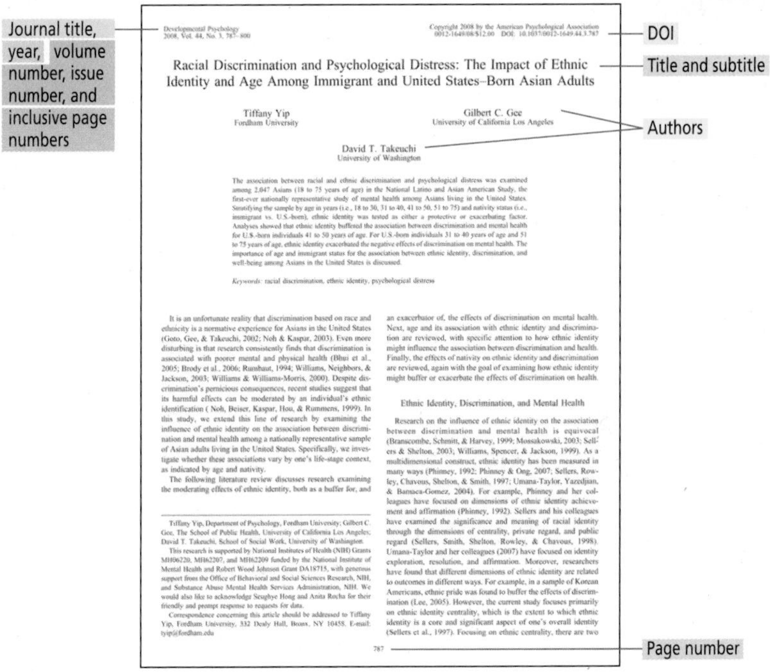


Developmental Psychology
2008, Vol. 44, No. 3, 787–800

Copyright 2008 by the American Psychological Association
0012-1649/08/$12.00 DOI: 10.1037/0012-1649.44.3.787

Racial Discrimination and Psychological Distress: The Impact of Ethnic Identity and Age Among Immigrant and United States–Born Asian Adults

Tiffany Yip
Fordham University

Gilbert C. Gee
University of California Los Angeles

David T. Takeuchi
University of Washington

The association between racial and ethnic discrimination and psychological distress was examined among 2,047 Asians (18 to 75 years of age) in the National Latino and Asian American Study, the first-ever nationally representative study of mental health among Asians living in the United States. Stratifying the sample by age in years (i.e., 18 to 30, 31 to 40, 41 to 50, 51 to 75) and nativity status (i.e., immigrant vs. U.S.-born), ethnic identity was tested as either a protective or exacerbating factor. Analyses showed that ethnic identity buffered the association between discrimination and mental health for U.S.-born individuals 41 to 50 years of age. For U.S.-born individuals 31 to 40 years of age and 51 to 75 years of age, ethnic identity exacerbated the negative effects of discrimination on mental health. The importance of age and immigrant status for the association between ethnic identity, discrimination, and well-being among Asians in the United States is discussed.

*Keywords:* racial discrimination, ethnic identity, psychological distress

It is an unfortunate reality that discrimination based on race and ethnicity is a normative experience for Asians in the United States (Goto, Gee, & Takeuchi, 2002; Noh & Kaspar, 2003). Even more disturbing is that research consistently finds that discrimination is associated with poorer mental and physical health (Bhui et al., 2005; Brody et al., 2006; Rumbaut, 1994; Williams, Neighbors, & Jackson, 2003; Williams & Williams-Morris, 2000). Despite discrimination's pernicious consequences, recent studies suggest that its harmful effects can be moderated by an individual's ethnic identification ( Noh, Beiser, Kaspar, Hou, & Rummens, 1999). In this study, we extend this line of research by examining the influence of ethnic identity on the association between discrimination and mental health among a nationally representative sample of Asian adults living in the United States. Specifically, we investigate whether these associations vary by one's life-stage context, as indicated by age and nativity.

The following literature review discusses research examining the moderating effects of ethnic identity, both as a buffer for, and an exacerbator of, the effects of discrimination on mental health. Next, age and its association with ethnic identity and discrimination are reviewed, with specific attention to how ethnic identity might influence the association between discrimination and health. Finally, the effects of nativity on ethnic identity and discrimination are reviewed, again with the goal of examining how ethnic identity might buffer or exacerbate the effects of discrimination on health.

Ethnic Identity, Discrimination, and Mental Health

Research on the influence of ethnic identity on the association between discrimination and mental health is equivocal (Branscombe, Schmitt, & Harvey, 1999; Mossakowski, 2003; Sellers & Shelton, 2003; Williams, Spencer, & Jackson, 1999). As a multidimensional construct, ethnic identity has been measured in many ways (Phinney, 1992; Phinney & Ong, 2007; Sellers, Rowley, Chavous, Shelton, & Smith, 1997; Umana-Taylor, Yazedjian, & Bamaca-Gomez, 2004). For example, Phinney and her colleagues have focused on dimensions of ethnic identity achievement and affirmation (Phinney, 1992). Sellers and his colleagues have examined the significance and meaning of racial identity through the dimensions of centrality, private regard, and public regard (Sellers, Smith, Shelton, Rowley, & Chavous, 1998). Umana-Taylor and her colleagues (2007) have focused on identity exploration, resolution, and affirmation. Moreover, researchers have found that different dimensions of ethnic identity are related to outcomes in different ways. For example, in a sample of Korean Americans, ethnic pride was found to buffer the effects of discrimination (Lee, 2005). However, the current study focuses primarily on ethnic identity centrality, which is the extent to which ethnic identity is a core and significant aspect of one's overall identity (Sellers et al., 1997). Focusing on ethnic centrality, there are two

Tiffany Yip, Department of Psychology, Fordham University; Gilbert C. Gee, The School of Public Health, University of California Los Angeles; David T. Takeuchi, School of Social Work, University of Washington.

This research is supported by National Institutes of Health (NIH) Grants MH06220, MH62207, and MH62209 funded by the National Institute of Mental Health and Robert Wood Johnson Grant DA18715, with generous support from the Office of Behavioral and Social Sciences Research, NIH, and Substance Abuse Mental Health Services Administration, NIH. We would also like to acknowledge Seughye Hong and Anita Rocha for their friendly and prompt response to requests for data.

Correspondence concerning this article should be addressed to Tiffany Yip, Fordham University, 332 Dealy Hall, Bronx, NY 10458. E-mail: tyip@fordham.edu

787

FIGURE 19.4 Part of an online article showing the location of the information needed for documentation. © 2008 by the American Psychological Association. Reproduced by permission. The use of this information does not imply endorsement by the publisher.

### 30. An Article in an Internet-Only Journal

If the article does not have a DOI, include the URL. Always include the URL (when available) for the archived version of the article. If you accessed the article through an online database, include the URL for the home page of the journal. (If a single URL links to multiple articles, include the URL for the journal's home page.) No retrieval date is needed for content that is not likely to be changed or updated—for example, a journal article or a book.

Hill, S. A., & Laugharne, R. (2006). Patient choice survey in general adult psychiatry. *Psychiatry On-Line*. Retrieved from http://www.priory.co.uk/psych.htm

### 31. A Document from a University Web Site

Beck, S. E. (2008, April 3). *The good, the bad & the ugly: Or,why it's a good idea to evaluate web sources.* Retrieved July 7, 2008, from New Mexico State University Library website: http://lib.nmsu.edu/instruction/evalcrit.html

#### 32. A Web Document (No Author Identified, No Date)

A document with no author or date should be listed by title, followed by the abbreviation **n.d.** (for "no date"), the retrieval date, and the URL.

*The stratocaster appreciation page.* (n.d.). Retrieved July 27, 2008, from http://members.tripod.com/~AFH

#### 33. An Email

As with all other personal communications, citations for email should be included only in the text of your paper, not in the reference list.

#### 34. A Posting to a Newsgroup

List the author's full name—or, if that is not available, the author's screen name. In brackets after the title, provide information that will help readers access the posting.

Silva, T. (2007, March 9). Severe stress can damage a child's brain [Online forum comment]. Retrieved from http://groups.google.com/group/sci.psychology.psychotherapy.moderated

#### 35. A Posting to a Blog

Jamie. (2010, June 26). Re: Trying to lose 50 million pounds [Web log comment]. Retrieved from http://blogs.wsj.com/numbersguy

#### 36. A Searchable Database

Include the database name only if the material you are citing is obscure, out of print, or otherwise difficult to locate. No retrieval date is needed.

Murphy, M. E. (1940, December 15). When war comes. *Vital Speeches of the Day, 7*(5), 139–144. Retrieved from http://www.vsotd.com

### *Abstracts and Newspaper Articles*

#### 37. An Abstract

Qiong, L. (2008, July). After the quake: Psychological treatment following the disaster. *China Today, 57*(7), 18–21. Abstract retrieved from http://www.chinatoday.com.cn/ctenglish/index.htm

#### 38. An Article in a Daily Newspaper

Fountain, H. (2008, July 1). In sleep, we are birds of a feather. *The New York Times.* Retrieved from http://www.nytimes.com

## 3 Content Footnotes

APA format permits content notes, indicated by **superscripts** in the text. The notes are listed on a separate numbered page, titled **Footnotes,** after the reference list and before any appendices. Double-space all notes, indenting the first line of each note one-half inch and beginning subsequent lines flush left. Number the notes with superscripts that correspond to the numbers in your text.

## 19b APA-Style Manuscript Guidelines

Social science papers label sections with headings. Sections may include an introduction (untitled), followed by headings like **Background, Method, Results,** and **Conclusion.** Each section of a social science paper is a complete unit with a beginning and an end so that it can be read separately and still make sense out of context. The body of the paper may include charts, graphs, maps, photographs, flowcharts, or tables.

CHECKLIST

### Typing Your Paper

When you type your paper, use the student paper in **19c** as your model.

- ❑ Leave one-inch margins at the top and bottom and on both sides. Double-space your paper throughout.
- ❑ Indent the first line of every paragraph and the first line of every content footnote one-half inch from the left-hand margin.
- ❑ Set off a **long quotation** (more than forty words) in a block format by indenting the entire quotation one-half inch from the left-hand margin. Do not indent the first line further.
- ❑ Number all pages consecutively. Each page should include a **page header** (an abbreviated title and a page number) typed one-half inch from the top of the page. Type the page header flush left and the page number flush right.
- ❑ Center major **headings**, and type them with uppercase and lowercase letters. Place minor headings flush left, typed with uppercase and lowercase letters. Use boldface for both major and minor headings. See 28b
- ❑ Format items in a series as a numbered **list.** See 28c
- ❑ Arrange the pages of the paper in the following order:
    - ❑ **Title page** (page 1) with a running head (in all uppercase letters), page number, title, your name, and the name of your school. (Your instructor may require additional information.)
    - ❑ **Abstract and keywords** (page 2)
    - ❑ **Text of paper** (beginning on page 3)
    - ❑ **Reference list** (new page)
    - ❑ **Content footnotes** (new page)
    - ❑ **Appendices** (start each appendix on a new page)
- ❑ Citations should follow **APA documentation style.** See 19a

CHECKLIST

## Using Visuals

APA style distinguishes between two types of visuals: **tables** and **figures** (charts, graphs, photographs, and diagrams). In manuscripts not intended for publication, tables and figures are included in the text. A short table or figure should appear on the page where it is discussed; a long table or figure should be placed on a separate page just after the page where it is discussed.

### Tables

Number all **tables** consecutively. Each table should have a *label* and a *title*.

- ❑ The **label** consists of the word **Table** (not in italics), along with an arabic numeral, typed flush left above the table.
- ❑ Double-space and type a brief explanatory **title** for each table (in italics) flush left below the label. Capitalize the first letters of principal words of the title.

  Table 7

  *Frequency of Negative Responses of Dorm Students to Questions Concerning*

  *Alcohol Consumption*

### Figures

Number all **figures** consecutively. Each figure should have a *label* and a *caption*.

- ❑ The **label** consists of the word **Figure** (typed flush left below the figure) followed by the figure number (both in italics).
- ❑ The **caption** explains the figure and serves as a title. Double-space the caption, but do not italicize it. Capitalize only the first word and any proper nouns, and end the caption with a period. The caption follows the label (on the same line).

  *Figure 1.* Duration of responses measured in seconds.

Note: If you use a table or figure from an outside source, include full source information in a note at the bottom of the table or figure. This information does not appear in your reference list.

CHECKLIST

## Preparing the APA Reference List

When typing your reference list, follow these guidelines:

- ❑ Begin the reference list on a new page after the last page of text, numbered as the next page of the paper.
- ❑ Center the title **References** at the top of the page.
- ❑ List the items in the reference list alphabetically (with author's last name first).
- ❑ Type the first line of each entry at the left margin. Indent subsequent lines one-half inch.
- ❑ Separate the major divisions of each entry with a period and one space.
- ❑ Double-space the reference list within and between entries.

### Close-Up ARRANGING ENTRIES IN THE APA REFERENCE LIST

- Single-author entries precede multiple-author entries that begin with the same name.

  Field, S. (1987).

  Field, S., & Levitt, M. P. (1984).

- Entries by the same author or authors are arranged according to date of publication, starting with the earliest date.

  Ruthenberg, H., & Rubin, R. (1985).

  Ruthenberg, H., & Rubin, R. (1987).

- Entries with the same author or authors and date of publication are arranged alphabetically according to title. Lowercase letters (*a*, *b*, *c*, and so on) that indicate the order of publication are placed within parentheses.

  Wolk, E. M. (1996a). Analysis . . .

  Wolk, E. M. (1996b). Hormonal . . .

## 19c Model APA-Style Research Paper

The following student paper, "Sleep Deprivation in College Students," uses APA documentation style. It includes a title page, an abstract, a reference list, a table, and a bar graph. The Web citations in this student paper do not have DOIs, so URLs have been provided instead.

| | |
|---|---|
| Page header | Running head: SLEEP DEPRIVATION 1 |
| Title | Sleep Deprivation in College Students |
| Your name | Andrew J. Neale |
| School | University of Texas |
| Course title | Psychology 215, Section 4 |
| Instructor's name | Dr. Reiss |
| Date | April 12, 2012 |

½"

insert

Page header on every page

SLEEP DEPRIVATION 2

(Running Head)

1″

Abstract

Center heading

A survey was conducted of 50 first-year college students in an introductory biology class. The survey consisted of five questions regarding the causes and results of sleep deprivation and specifically addressed the students' study methods and the grades they received on the fall midterm. The study's hypothesis was that although students believe that forgoing sleep to study will yield better grades, sleep deprivation may actually cause a decrease in performance. The study concluded that while only 43% of the students who received either an A or a B on the fall midterm deprived themselves of sleep in order to cram for the test, 90% of those who received a C or a D were sleep deprived.

Abstract typed as a single paragraph in block format (not indented)

*Keywords:* sleep disorders, sleep deprivation, grade performance, grades and sleep, forgoing sleep

An optional list of keywords helps readers find your work in databases. Check with your instructor to see if this list is required.

Full title (centered)

Indent ½"

Double-space

Thesis statement

Heading (centered and boldfaced)

1"

Literature review (paras. 2–7)

Quotation requires its own documentation and a page number (or a paragraph number for Internet sources)

Introduction

1"

1"

SLEEP DEPRIVATION 3

Sleep Deprivation in College Students

For many college students, sleep is a luxury they feel they cannot afford. Bombarded with tests and assignments and limited by a 24-hour day, students often attempt to make up time by doing without sleep. Unfortunately, students may actually hurt their academic performance by failing to get enough sleep. According to several psychological and medical studies, sleep deprivation can lead to memory loss and health problems, both of which are likely to harm a student's academic performance.

**Background**

Sleep is often overlooked as an essential part of a healthy lifestyle. Each day, millions of Americans wake up without having gotten enough sleep. This fact indicates that for many people, sleep is viewed as a luxury rather than a necessity. As National Sleep Foundation Executive Director Richard L. Gelula observes, "Some of the problems we face as a society—from road rage to obesity—may be linked to lack of sleep or poor sleep" (National Sleep Foundation, 2002, para. 3). In fact, according to the National Sleep Foundation, sleep deprivation causes "impairment in mood, attention and memory, behavior control and quality of life; lower academic performance and a decreased motivation to learn; and health-related effects including increased risk of weight-gain, lack of exercise and use of stimulants" (2010, para. 5).

Sleep deprivation is particularly common among college students, many of whom have busy lives and are required to absorb a great deal of material before their exams. It is common for college students to take a quick nap between classes or fall asleep while studying in the library because they are sleep deprived.

1"

Approximately 44% of young adults experience daytime sleepiness at least a few days a month (National Sleep Foundation, 2002, para. 6). In particular, many students are sleep deprived on the day of an exam because they stayed up all night studying. These students believe that if they read and review immediately before taking a test—even though this usually means losing sleep—they will remember more information and thus get better grades. However, this is not the case.

A study conducted by professors Mary Carskadon at Brown University in Providence, Rhode Island, and Amy Wolfson at the College of the Holy Cross in Worcester, Massachusetts, showed that high school students who got adequate sleep were more likely to do well in their classes (Carpenter, 2001). According to this study, students who went to bed early on both weeknights and weekends earned mainly A's and B's. The students who received D's and F's averaged about 35 minutes less sleep per day than the high achievers (cited in Carpenter). The results of this study suggest that sleep is associated with high academic achievement.

Student uses past tense when discussing other researchers' studies

*Cited in* indicates an indirect source

Once students reach college, however, many believe that sleep is a luxury they can do without. For example, students believe that if they use the time they would normally sleep to study, they will do better on exams. A survey of 144 undergraduate students in introductory psychology classes disproved this assumption. According to this study, "long sleepers," those individuals who slept 9 or more hours out of a 24-hour day, had significantly higher grade point averages (GPAs) than "short sleepers," individuals who slept less than 7 hours out of a 24-hour day. Therefore, contrary to the belief of many college students, more sleep is often associated with a high GPA (Kelly, Kelly, & Clanton, 2001).

Many students believe that sleep deprivation is not the cause of their poor performance, but rather that a host of other factors are to blame. A study in the *Journal of American College Health* tested the effect that several factors have on a student's performance in school, as measured by students' GPAs. Some of the factors considered were exercise, sleep, nutritional habits, social support, time management techniques, stress management techniques, and spiritual health (Trockel, Barnes, & Egget, 2000). The most significant correlation discovered in the study was between GPA and the sleep habits of students. Sleep deprivation had a more negative impact on GPAs than any other factor (Trockel et al.).

First reference includes all three authors; *et al.* replaces second and third authors in subsequent reference in same paragraph

Despite these findings, many students continue to believe that they will be able to remember more material if they do not sleep before an exam. They fear that sleeping will interfere with their ability to retain information. Pilcher and Walters (1997), however, showed that sleep deprivation actually impaired learning skills. In this study, one group of students was sleep deprived, while the other got 8 hours of sleep before the exam. The students in each group estimated how well they had performed on the exam. The students who were sleep deprived believed their performance on the test was better than did those who were not sleep deprived, but actually the performance of the sleep-deprived students was significantly worse than that of those who got 8 hours of sleep prior to the test (Pilcher & Walters, 1997, cited in Bubolz, Brown, & Soper, 2001). This study supports the hypothesis that sleep deprivation harms cognitive performance.

A survey of students in an introductory biology class at the University of Texas, which demonstrated the effects of sleep deprivation on academic performance, also supported the hypothesis that despite students' beliefs, forgoing sleep does not lead to better test scores.

Student uses past tense when discussing his own research study

**Method**

To determine the causes and results of sleep deprivation, a study of the relationship between sleep and test performance was conducted. Fifty first-year college students in an introductory biology class were surveyed, and their performance on the fall midterm was analyzed.

Each student was asked to complete a survey consisting of the following five questions about their sleep patterns and their performance on the fall midterm:

1. Do you regularly deprive yourself of sleep when studying for an exam?
2. Did you deprive yourself of sleep when studying for the fall midterm?
3. What was your grade on the exam?
4. Do you feel your performance was helped or harmed by the amount of sleep you had?
5. Will you deprive yourself of sleep when you study for the final exam?

Numbered list is indented ½" and set in block format

To maintain confidentiality, the students were asked not to put their names on the survey. Also, to determine whether the students answered question 3 truthfully, the group grade distribution from the surveys was compared to the number of A's, B's, C's, and D's shown in the instructor's record of the test results. The two frequency distributions were identical.

## Results

Table 1 introduced

Analysis of the survey data indicated a significant difference between the grades of students who were sleep deprived and the grades of those who were not. The results of the survey are presented in Table 1.

The grades in the class were curved so that out of 50 students, 10 received A's, 20 received B's, 10 received C's, and 10 received D's. For the purposes of this survey, an A or B on the exam indicates that the student performed well. A grade of C or D on the exam is considered a poor grade.

Table placed on page where it is discussed

Table 1

*Results of Survey of Students in University of Texas Introduction to Biology Class Examining the Relationship between Sleep Deprivation and Academic Performance*

Table created by student; no documentation necessary

| Grade totals | Sleep deprived | Not sleep deprived | Usually sleep deprived | Improved | Harmed | Continue sleep deprivation? |
|---|---|---|---|---|---|---|
| A = 10 | 4 | 6 | 1 | 4 | 0 | 4 |
| B = 20 | 9 | 11 | 8 | 8 | 1 | 8 |
| C = 10 | 10 | 0 | 6 | 5 | 4 | 7 |
| D = 10 | 8 | 2 | 2 | 1 | 3 | 2 |
| Total | 31 | 19 | 17 | 18 | 8 | 21 |

Statistical findings in table discussed

Of the 50 students in the class, 31 (or 62%) said they deprived themselves of sleep when studying for the fall midterm. Of these students, 17 (or 34% of the class) reported that they regularly deprive themselves of sleep before an exam.

Of the 31 students who said they deprived themselves of sleep when studying for the fall midterm, only 4 earned A's, and the majority of the A's in the class were received by those students who were not sleep deprived. Even more significant was the fact that of the 4 students who were sleep deprived and got A's, only one student claimed to usually be sleep deprived on the day of an exam. Thus, assuming the students who earn A's in a class do well in general, it is possible that sleep deprivation did not help or harm these students' grades. Not surprisingly, of the 4 students who received A's and were sleep deprived, all said they would continue this behavior pattern.

The majority of those who deprived themselves of sleep received B's and C's on the exam. A total of 20 students earned a grade of B on the exam. Of those students, only 9, or 18% of the class, said they were deprived of sleep when they took the test.

Students who said they were sleep deprived when they took the exam received the majority of the poor grades. Ten students got C's on the midterm, and of these 10 students, 100% said they were sleep deprived when they took the test. Of the 10 students (20% of the class) who got D's, 8 said they were sleep deprived. Figure 1 shows the significant relationship that was found between poor grades on the exam and sleep deprivation.

Figure 1 introduced

**Conclusion**

For many students, sleep is viewed as a luxury rather than as a necessity. Particularly during exam periods, students use the hours in which they would normally sleep to study. However, this behavior does not seem to be effective. The survey discussed here reveals a definite correlation between sleep deprivation and lower exam scores. In fact,

SLEEP DEPRIVATION 9

Figure placed as close as possible to discussion in paper

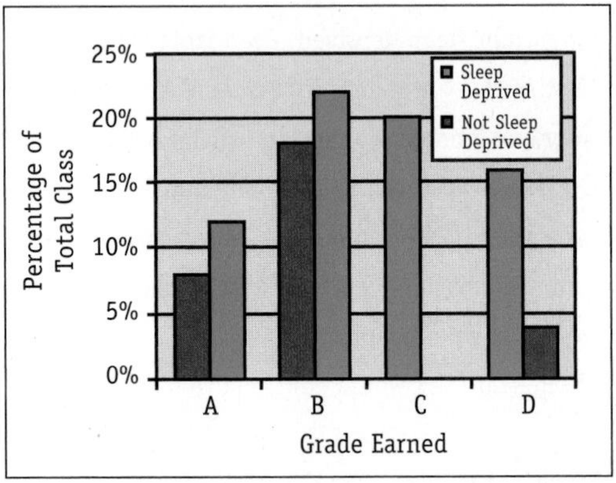




Label and caption

(No source information needed for graph based on student's original data)

*Figure 1.* Results of a survey of students in a University of Texas Introduction to Biology class, examining the relationship between sleep deprivation and academic performance.

the majority of students who performed well on the exam, earning either A's or B's, were not deprived of sleep. Therefore, students who choose studying over sleep should consider that sleep deprivation may actually lead to impaired academic performance.

SLEEP DEPRIVATION 10

1″

**References**

Center heading

Indent ½″

Double-space

Entries listed in alphabetical order

URL is provided for Web citation that does not have a DOI

Bubolz, W., Brown, F., & Soper, B. (2001). Sleep habits and patterns of college students: A preliminary study. *Journal of American College Health, 50,* 131–135.

Carpenter, S. (2001). Sleep deprivation may be undermining teen health. *Monitor on Psychology, 32*(9). Retrieved from http://www.apa.org/monitor/oct01/sleepteen.html

Kelly, W. E., Kelly, K. E., & Clanton, R. C. (2001). The relationship between sleep length and grade-point average among college students. *College Student Journal, 35*(1), 84–90.

National Sleep Foundation. (2002, April 2). *Epidemic of daytime sleepiness linked to increased feelings of anger, stress and pessimism*. Retrieved from http://www.sleepfoundation.org

National Sleep Foundation. (2010, July 6). *Later school start times improved adolescent alertness*. Retrieved from http://www.sleepfoundation.org

Trockel, M., Barnes, M., & Egget, D. (2000). Health-related variables and academic performance among first-year college students: Implications for sleep and other behaviors. *Journal of American College Health, 49,* 125–131.

# Directory of Chicago-Style Endnotes and Bibliography Entries

## PRINT SOURCES: *Entries for Articles*

### Articles in Scholarly Journals



### Articles in Magazines and Newspapers



## PRINT SOURCES: *Entries for Books*

### Authors and Editors



### Editions and Multivolume Works



### Parts of Books



### Religious Works

## ENTRIES FOR MISCELLANEOUS PRINT AND NONPRINT SOURCES



## ELECTRONIC SOURCES: *Entries for Sources from Online Publications*



## ELECTRONIC SOURCES: *Entries for Sources from an Online Database*



## ELECTRONIC SOURCES: *Entries for Sources from Internet Sites*

CHAPTER 20

# Chicago Documentation Style

## Frequently Asked Questions


- When should I use Chicago-style documentation? 330
- What should a Chicago-style paper look like? 344


## 20a Using Chicago Humanities Style

*The Chicago Manual of Style* includes two citation methods, a notes-bibliography style used in history, in the humanities, and in some social science disciplines and an author-date style used in the sciences and social sciences. **Chicago humanities style*** has two parts: *notes at the end of the paper* (**endnotes**) and usually a *list of bibliographic citations* (**bibliography**). (Chicago style encourages the use of endnotes, but allows the use of footnotes at the bottom of the page.)

### 1 Endnotes and Footnotes

The notes format calls for a **superscript** (raised numeral) in the text after source material you have either quoted or referred to. This numeral, placed after all punctuation marks except dashes, corresponds to the numeral that precedes the endnote or footnote.

#### *Endnote and Footnote Format: Chicago Style*

***In the Text***

By November of 1942, the Allies had proof that the Nazis were engaged in the systematic killing of Jews.[1]

***In the Note***

1. David S. Wyman, *The Abandonment of the Jews: America and the Holocaust 1941–1945* (New York: Pantheon Books, 1984), 65.

---

*Chicago humanities style follows the guidelines set in *The Chicago Manual of Style*, 16th ed. Chicago: University of Chicago Press, 2010. The manuscript guidelines and sample research paper at the end of this chapter follow guidelines set in Kate L. Turabian's *A Manual for Writers of Research Papers, Theses, and Dissertations*, 7th ed. Chicago: University of Chicago Press, 2007. Turabian style, which is based on Chicago style, addresses formatting concerns specific to college writers.

Close-Up SUBSEQUENT REFERENCES TO THE SAME WORK

In a paper with no bibliography, use the full citation in the first note for a work; in subsequent references to the same work, list only the author's last name, a comma, an abbreviated title, another comma, and a page number. In a paper with a bibliography, you may use the short form for all notes.

**First Note on Espinoza**

1. J. M. Espinoza. *The First Expedition of Vargas in New Mexico, 1692* (Albuquerque: University of New Mexico Press, 1949), 10–12.

**Subsequent Note**

5. Espinoza, *First Expedition,* 29.

Note: You may use the abbreviation *ibid.* ("in the same place") for subsequent references to the same work as long as there are no intervening references. *Ibid.* takes the place of the author's name, the work's title, and the page number if they are the same as those in the previous note. If the page number is different, cite *Ibid.* and the page number.

**First Note on Espinoza**

1. J. M. Espinoza. *The First Expedition of Vargas in New Mexico, 1692* (Albuquerque: University of New Mexico Press, 1949), 10–12.

**Next Note**

2. Ibid., 23.

## 2 Bibliography

The **bibliography** provides complete publication information for the works consulted. Bibliography entries are arranged alphabetically by the author's last name or the first major word of the title (if there is no author). Single-space within an entry; double-space between entries.

## Sample Chicago-Style Endnotes and Bibliography Entries

### CHICAGO PRINT SOURCES Entries for Articles

Article citations generally include the name of the author (last name first); the title of the article (in quotation marks); the title of the periodical (in italics); the volume number, issue number, and date; and the page reference. Months are spelled out in full, not abbreviated.

**Author's last name** | **First name and middle initial** | **Title of article** (in quotation marks)

Strauss, David A. "Common Law, Common Ground, and Jefferson's Principle." *Yale Law Journal* 112, no. 7 (2003): 1717–55.

**Periodical title** (italicized) | **Volume number** | **Issue number** | **Year of publication** (in parentheses) | **Inclusive page numbers**

### *Articles in Scholarly Journals*

#### 1. An Article in a Scholarly Journal with Continuous Pagination throughout an Annual Volume

***Endnote***

1. John Huntington, "Science Fiction and the Future," *College English* 37 (Fall 1975): 341.

***Bibliography***

Huntington, John. "Science Fiction and the Future." *College English* 37 (Fall 1975): 340–58.

#### 2. An Article in a Scholarly Journal with Separate Pagination in Each Issue

***Endnote***

2. R. G. Sipes, "War, Sports, and Aggression: An Empirical Test of Two Rival Theories," *American Anthropologist* 4, no. 2 (1973): 80.

***Bibliography***

Sipes, R. G. "War, Sports, and Aggression: An Empirical Test of Two Rival Theories." *American Anthropologist* 4, no. 2 (1973): 65–84.

### *Articles in Magazines and Newspapers*

#### 3. An Article in a Weekly Magazine (Signed/Unsigned)

***Endnote***

*Signed*

3. Pico Iyer, "A Mum for All Seasons," *Time,* April 8, 2002, 51.

*Unsigned*

3. "Burst Bubble," *New Scientist,* July 27, 2002, 24.

Although both endnotes above specify page numbers, the corresponding bibliography entries include page numbers only when the pages are consecutive (as in the second example that follows).

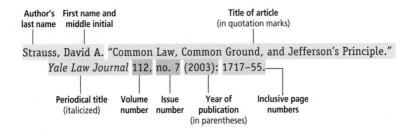

***Bibliography***

*Signed*

Iyer, Pico. "A Mum for All Seasons." *Time,* April 8, 2002.

*Unsigned*

"Burst Bubble." *New Scientist,* July 27, 2002, 24–25.

### 4. An Article in a Monthly Magazine (Signed)

***Endnote***

4. Tad Suzuki, "Reflecting Light on Photo Realism," *American Artist,* March 2002, 47.

***Bibliography***

Suzuki, Tad. "Reflecting Light on Photo Realism." *American Artist,* March 2002, 46–51.

### 5. An Article in a Monthly Magazine (Unsigned)

***Endnote***

5. "Repowering the U.S. with Clean Energy Development," *BioCycle,* July 2002, 14.

***Bibliography***

"Repowering the U.S. with Clean Energy Development." *BioCycle,* July 2002, 14.

### 6. An Article in a Newspaper (Signed)

***Endnote***

Because the pagination of newspapers can change from edition to edition, Chicago style recommends not giving page numbers for newspaper articles.

6. Francis X. Clines, "Civil War Relics Draw Visitors, and Con Artists," *New York Times,* August 4, 2002, national edition.

***Bibliography***

Clines, Francis X. "Civil War Relics Draw Visitors, and Con Artists." *New York Times,* August 4, 2002, national edition.

### 7. An Article in a Newspaper (Unsigned)

***Endnote***

7. "Feds Lead Way in Long-Term Care," *Atlanta Journal-Constitution,* July 21, 2002, sec. E.

Note: Omit the initial article the from the newspaper's title, but include a city name in the title, even if it is not part of the actual title.

If you provide a note or mention the name of the newspaper and publication date in your text, you do not need to list unsigned articles or other newspaper items in your bibliography.

### 8. A Letter to the Editor of a Newspaper

***Endnote***

8. Arnold Stieber, letter to the editor, *Seattle Times,* July 4, 2009.

***Bibliography***

Stieber, Arnold. Letter to the editor. *Seattle Times,* July 4, 2009.

### 9. A Book Review in a Newspaper

***Endnote***

9. Janet Maslin, "The Real Lincoln Bedroom: Love in a Time of Strife," review of *The Lincolns: Portrait of a Marriage,* by Daniel Mark Epstein, *New York Times*, July 3, 2008.

***Bibliography***

Maslin, Janet. "The Real Lincoln Bedroom: Love in a Time of Strife." Review of *The Lincolns: Portrait of a Marriage,* by Daniel Mark Epstein. *New York Times*, July 3, 2008.

## **CHICAGO** PRINT SOURCES Entries for Books

Capitalize the first, last, and all major words of titles and subtitles. Chicago style italicizes book titles.

**Author's last name** | **First name and middle Initial** | **Title** (italicized, all major words capitalized) | **City and state** (to clarify unfamiliar or ambiguous city)

Wartenberg, Thomas E. *The Nature of Art.* Belmont, CA: Wadsworth, 2002.

**Publisher's name** | **Year of publication**

### *Authors and Editors*

### 10. A Book by One Author or Editor

***Endnote***

10. Robert Dallek, *An Unfinished Life: John F. Kennedy, 1917–1963* (New York: Little, Brown, 2003), 213.

***Bibliography***

Dallek, Robert. *An Unfinished Life: John F. Kennedy, 1917–1963*. New York: Little, Brown, 2003.

If the book has an editor rather than an author, add a comma and **ed.** after the name: **John Fields, ed.** Follow with a comma in a note.

### 11. A Book by Two or Three Authors or Editors

***Endnote***

*Two Authors*

11. Jack Watson and Grant McKerney, *A Cultural History of the Theater* (New York: Longman, 1993), 137.

*Three Authors*

11. Nathan Caplan, John K. Whitmore, and Marcella H. Choy, *The Boat People and Achievement in America: A Study of Economic and Educational Success* (Ann Arbor: University of Michigan Press, 1990), 51.

***Bibliography***

*Two Authors*

Watson, Jack, and Grant McKerney. *A Cultural History of the Theater*. New York: Longman, 1993.

*Three Authors*

Caplan, Nathan, John K. Whitmore, and Marcella H. Choy. *The Boat People and Achievement in America: A Study of Economic and Educational Success*. Ann Arbor: University of Michigan Press, 1990.

### 12. A Book by More Than Three Authors or Editors

***Endnote***

Chicago style favors **et al.** rather than **and others** after the first name in endnotes. Add a comma and **eds.** after the names of the editors in both the endnotes and the bibliography.

12. Robert E. Spiller et al., eds., *Literary History of the United States* (New York: Macmillan, 1953), 24.

***Bibliography***

List all authors' or editors' names in the bibliography.

Spiller, Robert E., Willard Thorp, Thomas H. Johnson, and Henry Seidel Canby, eds. *Literary History of the United States*. New York: Macmillan, 1953.

### 13. A Book with No Listed Author or Editor

***Endnote***

13. *Merriam-Webster's Guide to Punctuation and Style*, 4th ed. (Springfield, MA: Merriam-Webster, 2008), 22.

***Bibliography***

*Merriam-Webster's Guide to Punctuation and Style*. 4th ed. Springfield, MA: Merriam-Webster, 2008.

### 14. A Book by a Corporate Author

If a publication issued by an organization does not identify a person as the author, the organization is listed as the author even if its name is repeated in the title, in the series title, or as the publisher.

***Endnote***

14. National Geographic Society, *National Parks of the United States,* 6th ed. (Washington, DC: National Geographic Society, 2009), 77.

***Bibliography***

National Geographic Society. *National Parks of the United States.* 6th ed. Washington, DC: National Geographic Society, 2009.

### 15. A Book with an Author and an Editor

***Endnote***

15. William Bartram, *The Travels of William Bartram,* ed. Mark Van Doren (New York: Dover Press, 1955), 85.

***Bibliography***

Bartram, William. *The Travels of William Bartram*. Edited by Mark Van Doren. New York: Dover Press, 1955.

### 16. A Book Quoted in a Secondary Source

***Endnote***

16. Henry Adams, *Mont Saint-Michel and Chartres* (New York: Penguin Books, 1986), 296, quoted in Karen Armstrong, *A History of God: The 4000-Year Quest of Judaism, Christianity and Islam* (New York: Ballantine Books, 1993), 203–4.

***Bibliography***

Adams, Henry. *Mont Saint-Michel and Chartres,* 296. New York: Penguin Books, 1986. Quoted in Armstrong, *A History of God,* 203–4.

Armstrong, Karen. *A History of God: The 4000-Year Quest of Judaism, Christianity, and Islam.* New York: Ballantine Books, 1993.

## *Editions and Multivolume Works*

### 17. A Subsequent Edition of a Book

***Endnote***

17. Laurie G. Kirszner and Stephen R. Mandell, *The Wadsworth Handbook,* 10th ed. (Boston: Wadsworth, 2014), 52.

***Bibliography***

Kirszner, Laurie G., and Stephen R. Mandell. *The Wadsworth Handbook.* 10th ed. Boston: Wadsworth, 2014.

### 18. A Multivolume Work

***Endnote***

18. Kathleen Raine, *Blake and Tradition* (Princeton, NJ: Princeton University Press, 1968), 1:143.

***Bibliography***

Raine, Kathleen. *Blake and Tradition.* Vol. 1. Princeton, NJ: Princeton University Press, 1968.

## *Parts of Books*

### 19. A Chapter in a Book

***Endnote***

19. Roy Porter, "Health, Disease, and Cure," in *Quacks: Fakers and Charlatans in Medicine* (Stroud, UK: Tempus Publishing, 2003), 188.

***Bibliography***

Porter, Roy. "Health, Disease, and Cure." In *Quacks: Fakers and Charlatans in Medicine,* 182–205. Stroud, UK: Tempus Publishing, 2003.

### 20. An Essay in an Anthology

***Endnote***

20. G. E. R. Lloyd, "Science and Mathematics," in *The Legacy of Greece,* ed. Moses Finley (New York: Oxford University Press, 1981), 270.

***Bibliography***

Lloyd, G. E. R. "Science and Mathematics." In *The Legacy of Greece,* edited by Moses Finley, 256–300. New York: Oxford University Press, 1981.

## *Religious Works*

### 21. Sacred Texts

References to religious works (such as the Bible or Qur'an) are usually limited to the text or notes and not listed in the bibliography. In citing the Bible, include the book (abbreviated), the chapter (followed by a colon), and the verse numbers. Identify the version, but do not include a page number.

***Endnote***

21. Phil. 1:9–11 (King James Version).

## CHICAGO ENTRIES FOR MISCELLANEOUS PRINT AND NONPRINT SOURCES

### *Interviews*

**22. A Personal Interview**

***Endnote***

22. Cornel West, interview by author, tape recording, June 8, 2011.

Personal interviews are cited in the notes or text but are usually not listed in the bibliography.

**23. A Published Interview**

***Endnote***

23. Gwendolyn Brooks, interview by George Stavros, *Contemporary Literature* 11, no. 1 (Winter 1970): 12.

***Bibliography***

Brooks, Gwendolyn. Interview by George Stavros. *Contemporary Literature* 11, no. 1 (Winter 1970): 1–20.

### *Letters and Government Documents*

**24. A Personal Letter**

***Endnote***

24. Julia Alvarez, letter to the author, April 10, 2009.

Personal letters are mentioned in the text or a note but are not listed in the bibliography.

**25. A Government Document**

***Endnote***

25. US Department of Transportation, *The Future of High-Speed Trains in the United States: Special Study, 2007* (Washington, DC: Government Printing Office, 2008), 203.

***Bibliography***

US Department of Transportation. *The Future of High-Speed Trains in the United States: Special Study, 2007*. Washington, DC: Government Printing Office, 2008.

### *Videotapes, DVDs, and Recordings*

**26. A Videotape or DVD**

***Endnote***

26. *Interview with Arthur Miller,* directed by William Schiff (Mequon, WI: Mosaic Group, 1987), videocassette (VHS), 17 min.

***Bibliography***

*Interview with Arthur Miller*. Directed by William Schiff. Mequon, WI: Mosaic Group, 1987. Videocassette (VHS), 17 min.

### 27. A Recording

***Endnote***

27. Bob Marley and the Wailers, "Crisis," *Kaya,* Kava Island Records 423 095-3, 1978, compact disc.

***Bibliography***

Marley, Bob, and the Wailers. "Crisis." *Kaya*. Kava Island Records 423 095-3, 1978, compact disc.

## **CHICAGO** ELECTRONIC SOURCES Entries for Sources from Online Publications

Author's last name | First name | Title of article (in quotation marks)

Dekoven, Marianne. "Utopias Limited: Post-Sixties and Postmodern American Fiction." *Modern Fiction Studies* 41, no. 1 (1995). doi:10.1353/mfs.1995.0002.

DOI | Title of periodical (italicized) | Volume number | Issue number | Year of publication (in parentheses)

Citations of sources from online publications usually include the author's name; the title of the article; the title of the publication; the publication information and date; the page numbers (if applicable); and the DOI (digital object identifier), a permanent identifying number, or URL (followed by a period). If no publication date is available or if your instructor or discipline requires one, include an access date before the DOI or URL.

You may break a DOI or URL that continues to a second line after a colon or double slash; before a comma, a period, a hyphen, a question mark, a percent symbol, a number sign, a tilde, or an underscore; or before or after an ampersand or equals sign.

## *Articles, Books, and Reference Works on the Internet*

### 28. An Article in an Online Scholarly Journal

***Endnote***

28. Richard J. Schaefer, "Editing Strategies in Television Documentaries," *Journal of Communication* 47, no. 4 (1997): 80, doi:10.1111/j1460-2446.1997.tb02726.x.

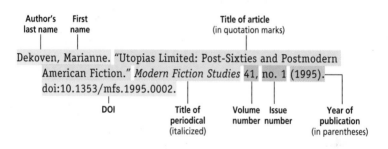

*Bibliography*

Schaefer, Richard J. "Editing Strategies in Television Documentaries." *Journal of Communication* 47, no. 4 (1997): 69–89. doi:10.1111/j1460-2446.1997.tb02726.x.

### 29. An Article in an Online Magazine

*Endnote*

29. Steven Levy, "I Was a Wi-Fi Freeloader," *Newsweek,* October 9, 2002, http://www.msnbc.com/news/816606.asp.

If there is no DOI for a source, cite the URL.

*Bibliography*

Levy, Steven. "I Was a Wi-Fi Freeloader." *Newsweek,* October 9, 2002. http://www.msnbc.com/news/816606.asp.

### 30. An Article in an Online Newspaper

*Endnote*

30. William J. Broad, "Piece by Piece, the Civil War *Monitor* Is Pulled from the Atlantic's Depths," *New York Times on the Web,* July 18, 2002, http://query.nytimes.com.

*Bibliography*

Broad, William J. "Piece by Piece, the Civil War *Monitor* Is Pulled from the Atlantic's Depths." *New York Times on the Web,* July 18, 2002. http://query.nytimes.com.

### 31. An Article in an Encyclopedia

If the reference book lists entries alphabetically, put the abbreviation **s.v.** (Latin for *sub verbo,* "under the word") before the entry name. If there is no publication or revision date for the entry, give the date of access before the DOI or URL.

*Endnote*

31. *Encyclopaedia Britannica Online*, s.v. "Adams, John," accessed July 5, 2010, http://www.britannica.com/EBchecked/topic/5132/John-Adams.

Dictionary and encyclopedia entries are not listed in the bibliography.

### 32. A Book

*Endnote*

32. Frederick Douglass, *My Bondage and My Freedom* (Boston, 1855), http://etext.virginia.edu/toc/modeng/public/DouMybo.html.

*Bibliography*

Douglass, Frederick. *My Bondage and My Freedom*. Boston, 1855. http://etext.virginia.edu/toc/modeng/public/DouMybo.html.

Older works available online may not include all publication information. Give the DOI or URL as the last part of the citation.

### 33. A Government Publication

***Endnote***

33. US Department of Transportation, Federal Motor Carrier Safety Administration, *Safety Belt Usage by Commercial Motor Vehicle Drivers (SBUCMVD) 2007 Survey, Final Report* (Washington, DC: Government Printing Office, 2008), http://www.fmcsa.dot.gov/safety-security/safety-belt/exec-summary-2007.htm.

***Bibliography***

US Department of Transportation. Federal Motor Carrier Safety Administration. *Safety Belt Usage by Commercial Motor Vehicle Drivers (SBUCMVD) 2007 Survey, Final Report*. Washington, DC: Government Printing Office, 2008. http://www.fmcsa.dot.gov/safety-security/safety-belt/exec-summary-2007.htm.

## **CHICAGO** ELECTRONIC SOURCES Entries for Sources from an Online Database

### *Sources from an Online Database*

Many articles and other materials published in print and electronically are also archived and available online through free or subscription databases.

### 34. A Scholarly Journal Article

***Endnote***

34. Monroe Billington, "Freedom to Serve: The President's Committee on Equality of Treatment and Opportunity in the Armed Forces, 1949–1950," *Journal of Negro History* 51, no. 4 (1966): 264, http://www.jstor.org/stable/2716101.

Use a DOI, a number that applies to an article in all of the media in which it may be published, rather than a URL if one is available. If you use a URL, cite the shorter, more stable form that will take you to the article's location in a database.

***Bibliography***

Billington, Monroe. "Freedom to Serve: The President's Committee on Equality of Treatment and Opportunity in the Armed Forces, 1949–1950," *Journal of Negro History* 51, no. 4 (1966): 262–74. http://www.jstor.org/stable/2716101.

If there is no stable URL, include the name of the database and put any identifying database number in parentheses: (**ERIC**). If the article or document does not have a date of publication or revision, include an access date.

**CHICAGO ELECTRONIC SOURCES** Entries for Sources from Internet Sites

### *Internet-Specific Sources*

**35. A Web Site or Home Page**

***Endnote***

35. David Perdue, "Dickens's Journalistic Career," David Perdue's Charles Dickens Page, accessed October 25, 2010, http://www.fidnet.com/~dap1955/dickens.

Titles of Web sites are in regular type (roman). Titles of pages or sections on a site are in quotation marks. If there is no date of publication, give an access date. Web site content is not usually listed in a bibliography.

**36. An Email**

***Endnote***

36. Meg Halverson, "Scuba Report," email message to author, April 2, 2010.

Email messages can also be mentioned in the text; they are not listed in the bibliography.

**37. A Listserv Posting**

Include the name of the list, the date of the individual posting, and the URL for the archive.

***Endnote***

37. Dave Shirlaw to Underwater Archeology discussion list, September 6, 2010, http://lists.asu.edu/archives/sub-arch.html.

Listserv postings are not listed in the bibliography.

## 20b Chicago Humanities Manuscript Guidelines

**CHECKLIST**

**Typing Your Paper**

When you type your paper, use the student paper in **20c** as your model.

- ❑ On the title page, type the full title of your paper in capitals. Also include your name, the course title, and the date.
- ❑ Double-space all text in your paper. Single-space block quotations, table titles, figure captions, footnotes, endnotes, and bibliography entries. Double-space between footnotes, endnotes, and bibliography entries.

- ❑ Leave a one-inch margin at the top, at the bottom, and on both sides of the page.
- ❑ Indent the first line of each paragraph one-half inch. Set off a long prose block quotation (five or more lines) from the text by indenting the quotation one-half inch from the left-hand margin. Do not use quotation marks. Double-space before and after the block quotation.
- ❑ Number all pages consecutively at the top of the page (centered or flush right) or centered at the bottom. Page numbers should appear at a consistent distance (at least three-fourths of an inch) from the top margin. Do not number the title page; the first full page of the paper is page 1.
- ❑ Use superscript numbers to indicate in-text citations. Type superscript numbers at the end of cited material (quotations, paraphrases, or summaries). Place the note number at the end of a sentence or clause (with no intervening space). The number follows any punctuation mark except a dash, which it precedes.
- ❑ Citations should follow **Chicago humanities documentation style**.

See 20a

CHECKLIST

## Using Visuals

According to *The Chicago Manual of Style,* there are two types of visuals: **tables** and **figures** (or **illustrations**), including charts, graphs, photographs, maps, and diagrams.

### Tables

- ❑ Give each **table** a label and a consecutive arabic number (**Table 1, Table 2**) followed by a period.
- ❑ Give each table a concise descriptive title in noun form without a period. Place the title after the table number.
- ❑ Place both the label and the title flush left above the table.
- ❑ Place source information flush left below the table, introduced by the word **Source** or **Sources**. Otherwise style the source as a complete footnote.

  *Source:* David E. Fisher and Marshall Jon Fisher, *Tube: The Invention of Television* (Washington, DC: Counterpoint Press, 1996), 185.

  If you do not cite this source elsewhere in your paper, do not list it in your bibliography.

### Figures

- ❑ Give each **figure** a label, a consecutive arabic number, and a caption.
- ❑ Place the label, the number, and a period flush left below the figure. Then, leave a space and add the caption.
- ❑ Place source information (credit line) at the end of the caption after a period.

  Figure 1. Television and its influence on young children. Photograph from ABC Photos.

CHECKLIST

### Preparing the Chicago-Style Endnotes Page

When typing your endnotes page, follow these guidelines:

- ❑ Begin the endnotes on a new page after the last page of the text of the paper and preceding the bibliography.
- ❑ Type the title **NOTES** entirely in capitals and center it one inch from the top of the page. Then double-space and type the first note.
- ❑ Number the page on which the endnotes appear as the next page of the paper.
- ❑ Type and number notes in the order in which they appear in the paper, beginning with number 1. Type the note number on (not above) the line, followed by a period and one space.
- ❑ Indent the first line of each note one-half inch; type subsequent lines flush with the left-hand margin.
- ❑ Single-space lines within a note. Double-space between notes.
- ❑ Break DOIs and URLs after a colon or double slashes, before punctuation marks (period, single slash, comma, hyphen, and so on), or before or after the symbols = and &.

CHECKLIST

### Preparing the Chicago-Style Bibliography

When typing your bibliography, follow these guidelines:

- ❑ Begin entries on a separate page after the endnotes.
- ❑ Type the title **BIBLIOGRAPHY** entirely in capitals, and center it one inch from the top of the page. Then double-space and type the first entry.
- ❑ List entries alphabetically according to the author's last name.
- ❑ Type the first line of each entry flush with the left-hand margin. Indent subsequent lines one-half inch.
- ❑ Single-space within an entry; double-space between entries.

## 20c Model Chicago Humanities Research Paper (Excerpts)

The following pages are from a student paper, "The Flu of 1918 and the Potential for Future Pandemics," written for a history course. It uses Chicago humanities documentation and has a title page, notes page, and bibliography. The Web citations in this student paper do not have DOIs, so URLs have been provided instead.

Title page is not numbered

THE FLU OF 1918 AND THE POTENTIAL FOR FUTURE PANDEMICS

Title (all capitals) centered

Rita Lin
American History 301
May 3, 2012

Name
Course title
Date

1″ ¾″ 1

Title if required by instructor (centered)

The Flu of 1918 and the Potential for
Future Pandemics

Indent ½″

Double-space the text of the paper

Introduction

Superscript numbers refer to endnotes

In November 2002, a mysterious new illness surfaced in China. By May 2003, what became known as SARS (Severe Acute Respiratory Syndrome) had been transported by air travelers to Europe, South America, South Africa, Australia, and North America, and the worldwide death toll had grown to 250.[1] By June 2003, there were more than 8,200 suspected cases of SARS in 30 countries and 750 deaths related to the outbreak, including 30 in Toronto. Just when SARS appeared to be waning in Asia, a second outbreak in Toronto, the hardest hit of all cities outside of Asia, reminded everyone that SARS remained a deadly threat.[2] As SARS continued to claim more victims and expand its reach, fears of a new pandemic spread throughout the world.

1″ 1″

The belief that a pandemic could occur in the future is not a far-fetched idea. During the twentieth century, there were three, and the most deadly one, in 1918, had several significant similarities to the SARS outbreak. As David Brown points out, the 1918 influenza pandemic is in many ways a mirror reflecting the causes and symptoms, as well as the future potential, of SARS. Both are caused by a virus, lead to respiratory illness, and spread through casual contact and coughing. Outbreaks of both are often traced to one individual, quarantine is the major weapon against the spread of both, and both probably arose from mutated animal viruses. Moreover, as Brown observes, the greatest fear regarding SARS was that it would become so widespread that transmission chains would be undetectable, and health officials would be helpless to restrain outbreaks. Such was the case with the 1918 influenza, which also began mysteriously in China and was transported around the globe (at that time by World War I

1″

2

military ships). By the time the flu lost its power in the spring of 1919, just one year later, it had killed more than 50 million people worldwide,[3] more than twice as many as those who died during the four and a half years of World War I. Thus, if SARS is a reflection of the potential for a future flu pandemic—and experts believe it is—the international community needs to acknowledge the danger, accelerate its research, and develop an extensive virus surveillance system.

Thesis statement

Clearly, the 1918 flu was different from anything previously known to Americans. Among the peculiarities of the pandemic were its origin and cause. In the spring of 1918, the virus, in relatively mild form, mysteriously appeared on a Kansas military base. After apparently dying out, the flu returned to the United States in late August. At that point, the influenza was no ordinary flu; it "struck with incredible speed, often killing a victim within hours of contact[,] . . . so fast that such infections rarely had time to set in."[4] Unlike previous strains, the 1918 flu struck healthy young people.

History of 1918 pandemic

Brackets indicate that comma was added by student writer

The initial spring outbreak in the United States, confined primarily to military bases, was largely ignored by public officials and the press because the nation's attention was focused on the war overseas. As a result, little was done to prepare for the deadly fall and winter to come. During the

1″

10

Center title and double-space before first note →

NOTES

1. Nancy Shute, "SARS Hits Home," *U.S. News & World Report*, May 5, 2003, 42.

Indent ½″ →

2. "Canada Waits for SARS News as Asia Under Control," *Sydney Morning Herald on the Web*, June 2, 2003, http://www.smh.com.au.

Single-space within a note; double-space between notes

3. David Brown, "A Grim Reminder in SARS Fight: In 1918, Spanish Flu Swept the Globe, Killing Millions," MSNBC News Online, June 4, 2003, http://www.msnbc.com/news/921901.asp.

A long URL for an online newspaper article can be shortened after the first single slash

4. Doug Rekenthaler, "The Flu Pandemic of 1918: Is a Repeat Performance Likely?—Part 1 of 2," Disaster Relief: New Stories, February 22, 1999, http://www.disasterrelief.org/Disasters/990219Flu.

5. Lynette Iezzoni, *Influenza 1918: The Worst Epidemic in American History* (New York: TV Books, 1999), 40.

Endnotes listed in order in which they appear in the paper

6. "1918 Influenza Timeline," *Influenza 1918,* 1999, http://www.pbs.org/wgbh/amex/influenza/timeline/index.html.

7. Iezonni, *Influenza 1918,* 131–32.

8. Brown, "Grim Reminder."

9. Iezonni, *Influenza 1918,* 88–89.

10. Ibid., 204.

*Ibid.* is used for a subsequent reference to the same source when there are no intervening references

Subsequent references to the same source include author's last name, shortened title, and page number(s)

1″

13

BIBLIOGRAPHY

"1918 Influenza Timeline." *Influenza 1918,* 1999. http://www.pbs.org/wgbh/amex/influenza/timeline/index.html.

Billings, Molly. "The Influenza Pandemic of 1918." Human Virology at Stanford: Interesting Viral Web Pages, June 1997. http://www.stanford.edu/group/virus/uda/index.html.

Brown, David. "A Grim Reminder in SARS Fight: In 1918, Spanish Flu Swept the Globe, Killing Millions." MSNBC News Online, June 4, 2003. http://www.msnbc.com/news/921901.asp.

"Canada Waits for SARS News as Asia Under Control." *Sydney Morning Herald on the Web,* June 2, 2003. http://www.smh.com.au/text.

Cooke, Robert. "Drugs vs. the Bug of 1918: Virus' Deadly Code Is Unlocked to Test Strategies to Fight It." *Newsday,* October 1, 2002.

Crosby, Alfred W., Jr. *America's Forgotten Pandemic: The Influenza of 1918.* New York: Cambridge University Press, 1989.

Dandurant, Daren. "Virus Changes Can Make Flu a Slippery Foe to Combat." MSNBC News Online, January 17, 2003. http://www.msnbc.com/local/sco/m8052.asp.

Center title and double-space before first entry

First line of each entry is flush with the left-hand margin; subsequent lines are indented ½″

Single-space within entries; double-space between them

URLs are provided for Web citations that do not have DOIs

Entries are listed alphabetically according to the author's last name

## Directory of CSE Reference List Entries

CHAPTER 21

# CSE and Other Documentation Styles

## Frequently Asked Questions



## 21a Using CSE Style

**CSE style,*** recommended by the Council of Science Editors (CSE), is used in biology, zoology, physiology, anatomy, and genetics. CSE style has two parts—*documentation in the text* and a *reference list.*

### 1 Documentation in the Text

**CSE style** permits either of two documentation formats: *citation-sequence format* and *name-year format.*

*Citation-Sequence Format* The **citation-sequence format** calls for either **superscripts** (raised numbers) in the text of the paper (the preferred form) or numbers inserted parenthetically in the text of the paper.

One study[1] has demonstrated the effect of low dissolved oxygen.

These numbers refer to a list of references at the end of the paper. Entries are numbered in the order in which they appear in the text of the paper. For example, if **James** is mentioned first in the text, **James** will be number 1 in the reference list. When you refer to more than one source in a single note, the numbers are separated by a hyphen if they are in sequence and by a comma if they are not.

Some studies[2-3] dispute this claim.

Other studies[3,6] support these findings.

---

*CSE style follows the guidelines set in the style manual of the Council of Science Editors: *Scientific Style and Format: The CSE Manual for Authors, Editors, and Publishers,* 7th ed. New York: Rockefeller UP, 2006.

*Note:* The **citation-name** format is a variation of the citation-sequence format. In the citation-name format, the names in the reference list are listed in alphabetical order. The numbers assigned to the references are used as in-text references, regardless of the order in which they appear in the paper.

***Name-Year Format*** The **name-year format** calls for the author's name and the year of publication to be inserted parenthetically in the text. If the author's name is used to introduce the source material, only the date of publication is needed in the parenthetical citation.

> A great deal of heat is often generated during this process (McGinness 2010).

> According to McGinness (2010), a great deal of heat is often generated during this process.

When two or more works are cited in the same parentheses, the sources are arranged chronologically (from earliest to latest) and separated by semicolons.

> Epidemics can be avoided by taking tissue cultures (Domb 2010) and by intervention with antibiotics (Baldwin and Rigby 2005; Martin and others 2006; Cording 2010).

*Note:* The citation **Baldwin and Rigby 2005** refers to a work by two authors; the citation **Martin and others 2006** refers to a work by three or more authors.

## 2 Reference List

The format of the reference list depends on the documentation format you use. If you use the **name-year** documentation format, your reference list will resemble the reference list for an **APA** paper (**see Chapter 19**). If you use the **citation-sequence** documentation style (as in the paper in **21c**), your sources will be listed by number, in the order in which they appear in your paper, on a **References** page. In either case, double-space within and between entries; type each number flush left, followed by a period and one space; and align the second and subsequent lines with the first letter of the author's last name. (The following examples illustrate citation-sequence documentation style.)

### **CSE** PRINT SOURCES Entries for Articles

List the author or authors by last name; after one space, list the initial or initials (unspaced) of the first and middle names (followed by a period); the title of the article (not in quotation marks, and with only the first word capitalized); the abbreviated name of the journal (with all major words capitalized, but not italicized or underlined); the year (followed by a semicolon); the volume number, the issue number (in parentheses), followed by a colon; and inclusive page numbers. No spaces separate the year, the volume number, and the page numbers.

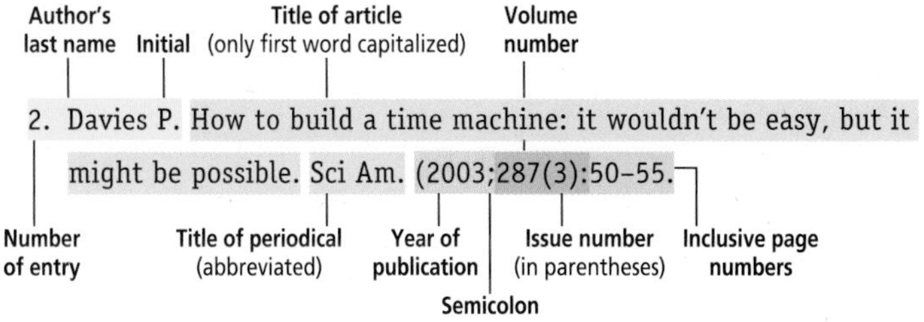


### *Articles in Scholarly Journals*

#### 1. An Article in a Journal Paginated by Issue

1. Sarmiento JL, Gruber N. Sinks for anthropogenic carbon. Phy Today. 2002;55(8):30-36.

#### 2. An Article in a Journal with Continuous Pagination

2. Brazil K, Krueger P. Patterns of family adaptation to childhood asthma. J Pediatr Nurs. 2002;17:167-173.

*Note:* Omit the month (and the day for weeklies) and issue number for journals with continuous pagination through an annual volume.

### *Articles in Magazines and Newspapers*

#### 3. A Magazine Article (Signed)

3. Nadis S. Using lasers to detect E.T. Astronomy. 2002 Sep:44-49.

*Note:* Month names longer than three letters are abbreviated by their first three letters.

#### 4. A Magazine Article (Unsigned)

4. Brown dwarf glows with radio waves. Astronomy. 2001 Jun:28.

#### 5. A Newspaper Article (Signed)

5. Husted B. Don't wiggle out of untangling computer wires. Atlanta Journal-Constitution. 2002 Jul 21;Sect Q:1 (col 1).

#### 6. Newspaper Article (Unsigned)

6. Scientists find gene tied to cancer risk. New York Times (Late Ed.). 2002 Apr 22;Sect A:18 (col 6).

## CSE PRINT SOURCES Entries for Books

List the author or authors (last name first); the title (not underlined, and with only the first word capitalized); the place of publication; the full name of the publisher (followed by a semicolon); the year (followed by a period); and the total number of pages (including back matter, such as the index).

**Author's last name** | **Initials** (unspaced) | **Title** (only first word capitalized) | **City and state**

1. Abbott EA. Flatland: a romance of many dimensions. Boston (MA): Shambhala; 1999. 238 p.

**Number of entry** | **Publisher** | **Semicolon** | **Year of publication** | **Total number of pages**

### *Authors*

#### 7. A Book with One Author

7. Hawking SW. A brief history of time: from the big bang to black holes. New York (NY): Bantam; 1995. 198 p.

*Note:* No comma follows the author's last name, and no period separates the unspaced initials of the first and middle names.

#### 8. A Book with More Than One Author

8. Horner JR, Gorman J. Digging dinosaurs. New York (NY): Workman; 1988. 210 p.

#### 9. An Edited Book

9. Goldfarb TD, editor. Taking sides: clashing views on controversial environmental issues. 2nd ed. Guilford (CT): Dushkin; 1987. 323 p.

*Note:* The publisher's state, province, or country can be added within parentheses to clarify the location. The two-letter postal service abbreviation can be used for the state or province.

#### 10. An Organization as Author

10. National Institutes of Health (US). Human embryonic stem-cell derived neurons treat stroke in rats. Bethesda (MD): US Dept. of Health and Human Services; 2008. 92 p.

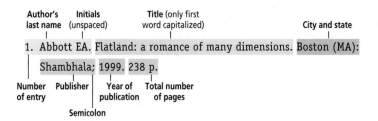

### *Parts of Books*

#### 11. A Chapter or Other Part of a Book with a Separate Title but with the Same Author

11. Asimov I. Exploring the earth and cosmos: the growth and future of human knowledge. New York (NY): Crown; 1984. Part III, The horizons of matter; p. 245-294.

#### 12. A Chapter or Other Part of a Book with a Different Author

12. Gingerich O. Hints for beginning observers. In: Mallas JH, Kreimer E, editors. The Messier album: an observer's handbook. Cambridge (GB): Cambridge Univ Pr; 1978. p. 194-195.

### *Professional and Technical Publications*

#### 13. Published Proceedings of a Conference

13. Al-Sherbini A. New applications of lasers in photobiology and photochemistry. Modern Trends of Physics Research, 1st International Conference; 2004 May 12-14; Cairo, Egypt. Melville (NY): American Institute of Physics; 2005. 14 p.

#### 14. A Technical Report

14. Forman, GL. Feature selection for text classification. 2007 Feb 12. Hewlett-Packard technical reports HPL-2007-16R1. 24 p. Available from www.hpl.hp.com/techreports/2007/HPL-2007-16R1.html

## **CSE** ENTRIES FOR MISCELLANEOUS PRINT AND NONPRINT SOURCES

### *Films, Videotapes, Recordings, and Maps*

#### 15. An Audiocassette

15. Bronowski J. The ascent of man [audiocassette]. New York: Jeffrey Norton Pub; 1974. 1 audiocassette: 2-track, 55 min.

#### 16. A Film, Videotape, or DVD

16. Stoneberger B, Clark R, editors. Women in science [videocassette]. American Society for Microbiology, producer. Madison (WI): Hawkhill; 1998. 1 videocassette: 42 min., sound, color, 1/2 in. Accompanied by: 1 guide.

### 17. A Map

#### *A Sheet Map*

17. Amazonia: a world resource at risk [ecological map]. Washington (DC): National Geographic Society; 2008. 1 sheet.

#### *A Map in an Atlas*

17. Central Africa [political map]. In: Hammond citation world atlas. Maplewood (NJ): Hammond; 2008. p. 114-115. Color, scale 1:13,800,000.

## **CSE** ELECTRONIC SOURCES Entries for Sources from Internet Sites

With Internet sources, include a description of the medium, the date of access, and the URL.

Author's last name | Initials (unspaced) | Title of article (only first word capitalized) | Title of periodical (abbreviated)

3. Sarra SA. The method of characteristics with applications to conservation laws. J Online Math and Its Apps [Internet]. 2003 [cited 2003 Aug 26];3. Available from: http://www.joma.org/vol3/articles/sarra/sarra.html

Number of entry | Year of publication | Date of access (abbreviated: in brackets) | Semicolon | Volume number | URL | Description of medium (in brackets)

### *Internet-Specific Sources*

### 18. An Online Journal

18. Lasko P. The *Drosophila melanogaster* genome: translation factors and RNA binding proteins. J Cell Biol [Internet]. 2000 [cited 2008 Aug 15]; 150(2):F51-56. Available from: http://www.jcb.org/search.dtl

### 19. An Online Book

19. Bohm D. Causality and chance in modern physics [Internet]. Philadelphia: Univ of Pennsylvania Pr; c1999 [cited 2008 Aug 17]. Available from: http://www.netlibrary.com/ebook_info.asp?product_id517169

## 21b CSE-Style Manuscript Guidelines

**CHECKLIST**

### Typing Your Paper

When you type your paper, use the student paper in **21c** as your model.

- ❑ Do not include a title page. Type your name, the course, and the date flush left one inch from the top of the first page.
- ❑ If required, include an **abstract** (a 250-word summary of the paper) on a separate numbered page.
- ❑ Double-space throughout.
- ❑ Insert tables and figures in the body of the paper. Number tables and figures in separate sequences (**Table 1, Table 2; Fig. 1, Fig. 2;** and so on).
- ❑ Number pages consecutively in the upper right-hand corner; include a shortened title before the number.
- ❑ When you cite source material in your paper, follow CSE documentation style.

See 21a

**CHECKLIST**

### Preparing the CSE Reference List

When typing your reference list, follow these guidelines:

- ❑ Begin the reference list on a new page after the last page of the paper, numbered as the next page.
- ❑ Center the title **References, Literature Cited,** or **References Cited** one inch from the top of the page.
- ❑ For citation-sequence format, list entries in the order in which they first appear in the paper—not alphabetically. For name-year format, list entries alphabetically.
- ❑ Number the entries consecutively; type the note numbers flush left on (not above) the line, followed by a period.
- ❑ Leave one space between the period and the first letter of the entry; align subsequent lines directly beneath the first letter of the author's last name.
- ❑ Double-space within and between entries.

## 21c Model CSE-Style Research Paper (Excerpts)

The following pages are from a student paper that explores the dangers of global warming for humans and wildlife. The paper, which cites seven sources and includes a line graph, illustrates CSE citation-sequence format.

1"
½"
Abbreviated title and page number
Center title
Indent ½"
Double-space
Introduction
Thesis statement
1"
1"
Superscript numbers correspond to sources in the reference list
Figure 1 Introduced
1"

Polar Ice Caps 1

Sara Castillo

Ecology 4223.01

April 10, 2012

Polar Ice Caps Could Melt by the End of This Century

The Arctic and Antarctica are homes to the earth's polar ice caps, and global warming appears to be melting them. When polar temperatures increase, parts of floating ice sheets and glaciers break off and melt. This process could eventually cause the ocean levels to rise and have disastrous effects on plants, animals, and human beings. There are ways to minimize this disaster, but they will only be effective if governments act immediately.

The polar ice caps are melting at a rapid rate, and much of the scientific community agrees that global warming is one of the causes. The greenhouse effect, the mechanism that causes global warming, occurs when molecules of greenhouse gases in the atmosphere reflect the rays of the sun back to the earth. This mechanism enables our planet to maintain a temperature adequate for life. However, as the concentration of greenhouse gases in the atmosphere increases, more heat from the sun is retained, and the temperature of the earth rises.[1]

Greenhouse gases include carbon dioxide ($CO_2$), methane, and nitrous oxide.[2] Since the beginning of the industrial revolution in the late 1800s, people have been burning fossil fuels that create $CO_2$.[3] This $CO_2$ has led to an increase in the greenhouse effect and has contributed to the global warming that is melting the polar ice caps. As Figure 1 shows, the surface temperature of the earth has

Polar Ice Caps 2

increased by about 1 degree Celsius (1.8 degrees Fahrenheit) since the 1850s. Some scientists have predicted that temperatures will increase even further.

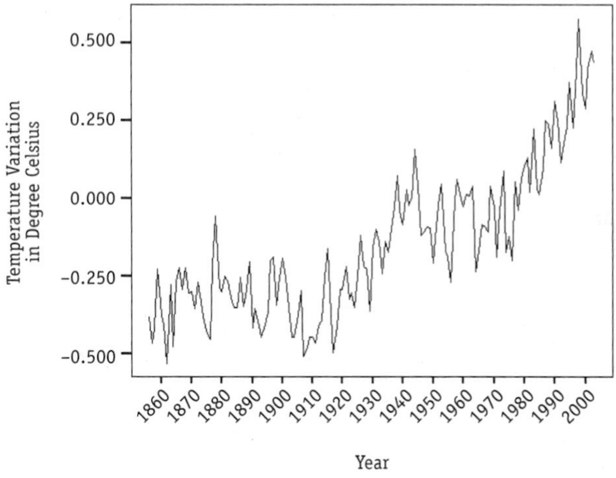


Reprinted by permission of Climatic Research Unit, School of Environmental Sciences, University of East Anglia.

Figure placed close to where it is discussed

Fig. 1. Global temperature variation from the average during the base period 1860-2000 (adapted from Climatic research unit: data: temperature 2003) [Internet]. [cited 2012 Mar 11]. Available from: http://www.cru.uea.ac.uk/cru/data/temperature.

Label, caption, and full source information

It is easy to see the effects of global warming. For example, the Pine Island Glacier in Antarctica was depleted at a rate of 1.6 meters per year between 1992 and 1999. This type of melting is very likely to increase the fresh water that

1″

Polar Ice Caps 8

References

Book with one author — 1. Edmonds A. A closer look at the greenhouse effect. Brookfield (CT): Copper Beach Books; 1997. 32 p.

Book with more than one author — 2. Smith RL, Smith TM. Elements of ecology. 5th ed. San Francisco (CA): Benjamin Cummings; 2003. 534 p.

Double-space

Entries listed in order in which they first appear in the paper

3. Pringle L. Global warming: the threat of earth's changing climate. New York (NY): Sea and Star Books; 2001. 48 p.

4. Perkins S. Antarctic glacier thins and speeds up. Sci News. 2001;159(5):70.

1″ — 1″

Online journal — 5. Pearce F. Arctic to lose all summer ice by 2100. NewScientist [Internet]. 2002 [cited 2012 Mar 11]; 70(2):99-133. Available from: http://www.newscientist .com

Print journal — 6. The pacific decadal oscillation. BioSci. 2000 Aug:32-39.

7. Woods M. Science on ice. Brookfield (CT): Millbrook Press; 1995. 96 p.

## 21d Using Other Documentation Styles

The following style manuals describe documentation formats and manuscript guidelines used in various fields.

**CHEMISTRY**

Coghill, Anne M., and Lorrin R. Garson, eds. *The ACS Style Guide: Effective Communication of Scientific Information*. 3rd ed. Washington: American Chemical Society, 2006. Print.

**GEOLOGY**

Hansen, Wallace R., ed. *Suggestions to Authors of the Reports of the United States Geological Survey*. 7th ed. Washington: GPO, 1991. Print.

**GOVERNMENT DOCUMENTS**

Cheney, Debora. *The Complete Guide to Citing Government Information Resources: A Manual for Social Science & Business Research*. 3rd ed. Bethesda: Congressional Information Service, 2002. Print.

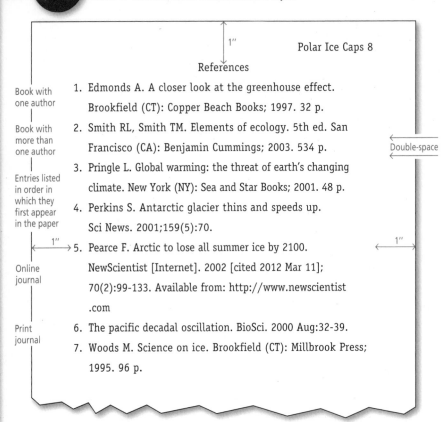

United States Government Printing Office. *Style Manual.* Washington: GPO, 2009. Print.

#### JOURNALISM

Christian, Darrell, Sally Jacobsen, and David Minthorn, eds. *The Associated Press Stylebook and Briefing on Media Law 2011.* 46th ed. New York: Basic, 2011. Print.

#### LAW

*The Bluebook: A Uniform System of Citation.* Comp. Editors of Columbia Law Review et al. 18th ed. Cambridge: Harvard Law Review Association, 2008. Print.

#### MATHEMATICS

American Mathematical Society. *AMS Author Handbook.* Providence: American Mathematical Society, 2010. Web.

#### MEDICINE

Iverson, Cheryl. *AMA Manual of Style: A Guide for Authors and Editors.* 10th ed. Oxford: Oxford UP, 2007. Print.

#### MUSIC

Holoman, D. Kern. *Writing about Music: A Style Sheet.* 2nd ed. Berkeley: U of California P, 2008. Print.

#### PHYSICS

American Institute of Physics. *AIP Style Manual.* 5th ed. Melville: American Institute of Physics, 2000. Print.

#### SCIENTIFIC AND TECHNICAL WRITING

Rubens, Philip, ed. *Science and Technical Writing: A Manual of Style.* 2nd ed. New York: Routledge, 2001. Print.

PART 6

# Writing in the Disciplines

CHAPTER 22

# Writing in the Humanities

## Frequently Asked Questions



**Humanities** disciplines include art history, drama, film, history, languages, literature, music, philosophy, and religion. In these disciplines, research often involves analyzing or interpreting a **primary source**—a literary work, a historical document, a musical composition, or a painting or piece of sculpture—or making connections between one work and another. Scholars in humanities disciplines may also cite **secondary sources**—commentaries on primary sources—to support their points or develop new interpretations.

## 22a Understanding Purpose, Audience, and Tone

See Ch. 18

Writing assignments in the humanities may be formal or informal. While formal writing may require you to use academic discourse and MLA documentation style and format, informal writing assignments may call for no more than your personal responses to your reading and observations. Each of these two types of writing has a distinct purpose and tone.

**Informal** writing assignments—for example, journals, reflections, or response papers—may use a relatively conversational, even colloquial, style and use the first person (*I*). Often, your instructor will specify an audience: your classmates, the instructor, or someone else. Sometimes you may be asked to share these writings, perhaps by posting regular responses to a class discussion board. At other times, you may keep these writings entirely private—for example, in a journal that reflects on your learning throughout a semester.

See Ch. 16

More **formal** writing assignments—literary analyses, research papers, literature reviews, and so on—often require that you summarize, analyze, or evaluate print and electronic sources and synthesize information from a variety of sources. Because the purpose of a formal writing assignment is often to persuade an audience to accept a particular point of view or position, these assignments require a more objective tone and a more formal level of diction than informal assignments do.

See 45b

## 22b Collaborative Work

Most assignments in the humanities are designed to be completed by students working on their own. Sometimes, however, humanities courses give students opportunities to work collaboratively. The most common kind of collaborative work in the humanities is peer review, a process by which students evaluate the written work of their classmates and make suggestions for revisions. Students can also do collaborative research projects, perhaps setting up group presentations or panel discussions to report the results of their research. In various humanities disciplines, students can conduct interviews and then work together to compile information for a report or an oral history. They can also work in groups to stage a debate or collaborate online to write and edit a wiki Web site article.

See 6c2

## 22c Writing Assignments

### 1 Response Paper

In some humanities disciplines (particularly literature, music, and art), you may be asked to write a **response paper,** an informal first-person account of your reactions to a literary work, a painting, a dance performance, or a concert.

*Assignment (World Music)*

Attend one of the performances offered by the Music and Drama Department during the upcoming month. Then, write an informal paper that communicates your response to the performance. What was memorable or remarkable? How did the audience react at particular moments? How did you feel as you were watching and listening, and how did you feel when the performance was over?

*Sample Response Paper (Excerpt)*

When I first arrived, I saw that the people in the audience were pretty much who I expected to see at a classical music recital, including quite a few faculty. (I'm sure they were shocked to see me there.) The audience was quiet as they waited for Chu's entrance; everyone just kind of sat looking at the darkened stage, which contained a very large grand piano and a cello. When Chu came on stage, the applause was almost deafening. I hadn't realized he was so famous. The audience quieted down when he sat down and picked up his bow. The first item on the program was a solo titled

*Allegretto Minimoso*. I have to admit that once Chu started to play his cello, I didn't even notice what was going on in the audience anymore. His music made me think of tall cliffs towering over the ocean under a bright sky during a storm. I was hooked from the first moment.

## 2 Book or Film Review

Instructors in the humanities may require students to write **reviews** of books, films, or art exhibits. The purpose of a review is to evaluate a work, exhibit, or performance and perhaps make recommendations to readers.

### *Assignment (Journalism)*

Write an informal review of a film you liked when you were a child, contrasting your reactions to the film then with your reactions to it now. In choosing a film, remember that your review will be submitted to our school newspaper, where your primary audience will be students about your age.

### *Sample Film Review*

I have always been a fan of musicals, handsome boys, and history lessons. Kenny Ortega's 1992 film *Newsies* finds a way to incorporate all these elements into one entertaining (although flawed) package.

The film begins with a narrator describing New York City in 1899 through the eyes of the poor newspaper boys who sell papers on the street. The "newsies" walk the dirty streets of New York shoeless and homeless while the rich and powerful newspaper publishers squeeze as much money as they can from the public. *Newsies* focuses on two young boys who sell newspapers for some of the most famous publishers of the time, including Joseph Pulitzer.

When Pulitzer (Robert Duvall) decides to raise the cost of the boys' newspaper purchase by a tenth of a percent, they are outraged. Jack Kelly (Christian Bale) and David Jacobs (David Moscow) set out to rally the rest of their gang, as well as the "street rats" of the other boroughs, to help fight "old man Pulitzer." At the same time, Warden Snyder (Kevin Tighe), the operator of The Refuge, a poorly run and corrupt orphanage, is trying to find Jack to bring him back to the orphanage. While trying to start a strike and evade Warden Snyder, the boys attract the attention of Bryan Denton (Bill Pullman), a reporter for the New York *Sun* who finds their troubles newsworthy.

Musicals like *Newsies* are a guilty pleasure of mine because they are films I loved when I was growing up. The first time I saw this movie, I was swept up by the singing and dancing as well as by the glimpse into a time and place I knew nothing about. And, of course, I loved watching my former heartthrob, Christian Bale; with a handful of strappingly handsome young boys thrown into the mix, *Newsies* is basically the early 1990s version of the present-day *Twilight* films, where young girls' love is directed at Jacob and Edward.

Recently, I watched *Newsies* again, and it was not the pleasurable experience I remembered. Although the film is historically accurate and has a catchy soundtrack, I found it disappointing. The young actors are not always all that talented, and some of the singers and dancers are just not polished enough. And, with all the new advances in film and cinematography that have taken place since *Newsies* was made in 1992, it is startling to see backgrounds that are all too noticeably digitally imaged.

As much as I liked this movie when it first came out, I see now that it is not as good as I thought it was. Still, there are not enough drawbacks to make me completely write it off. It may be too cute for adults, but it helps me remember what it was like to be young.

## 3 Literature Review

When you are writing a research paper, your instructor may ask you to prepare an **annotated bibliography**—a list of sources (accompanied by full source information) followed by summary and evaluation. In some cases, you may also be asked to write a literature review that discusses these sources and their relevance to your research.

See 12c2

### *Assignment (Nineteenth-Century American History)*

Write a literature review that discusses three of the sources you use in your research paper. Do not simply describe or summarize your sources; synthesize, compare, and contrast them, developing your own point of view. Be sure to include paraphrases and quotations from your sources as well as a works-cited list.

### *Sample Literature Review (Excerpt)*

The women mill operatives of Lowell, Massachusetts, produced a variety of writings in different genres that portray the ways in which they negotiated their everyday urban experiences in their boardinghouses and on the factory production line. While their descriptions of daily life in the mill town can be read as a story of their journey to financial independence, these writings also reveal the women's collective coming of political age.

The *Lowell Offering*, first published in 1840, was a "monthly magazine, thirty pages long, priced at six and one-quarter cents an issue" (Eisler 33) that began as a corporately owned concern but later was bought, run, and edited by two women who were both former mill operatives. While the publishers of the *Offering* focused on presenting the working women's own creations, the *Factory Girl's Garland*, also begun in 1840 (only to fold less than a year later), was more of a "liberal reformist paper [that] spoke paternalistically in favor of the mill women, and at times even preached at them" (Vogel 791).

Jean Marie Lutes explains that some labor reformists among the operatives found the "sentimental tales, romantic stories, and poetic rhyme" of the *Offering* too "neutral," accusing it of having "neglected the operative as a working being" (8). Therefore, they chose to represent their concerns through the *Voice of Industry*, a newspaper whose "case for reform," Lutes argues, was only made possible through the preliminary cultural work performed by the less critical *Offering*: while the *Voice* explicitly called for recognition of working class women's rights, it was the *Offering* that "initiate[d] the discourse of female working-class culture" (9). These periodicals demonstrate various ways in which the operatives initiated change for white working-class women through both their physical and their literary labors.

Works Cited

Eisler, Benita. *The Lowell Offering: Writings by New England Mill Women (1840-1845)*. New York: Norton, 1998. Print.

Lutes, Jean Marie. "Cultivating Domesticity: Labor Reform and the Literary Culture of the Lowell Mill Girls." *Works and Days* 22.11 (1993): 7-27. Print.

Vogel, Lise. "Their Own Work: Two Documents from the Nineteenth-Century Labor Movement." *Signs: Journal of Women in Culture and Society* 1.3 (1976): 787-802. Print.

## 4 Critical Analysis

Instructors in various humanities disciplines often ask students to analyze texts. (For an example of a literary analysis, **see 23c.**) A critical analysis takes apart a print or visual text, considering its various components in order to make sense of the whole.

### *Assignment (Mass Communications)*

Research an ad campaign for a specific product, service, or cause. Select a poster, billboard, or other visual from the campaign, and write an essay analyzing the ad's purpose, target audience, and overall message. Describe how the ad's words and images work together to reach the intended audience, and explain who benefits from the ad's message, and how.

### *Sample Critical Analysis (Excerpt)*

The National Teen Dating Abuse Helpline, along with Texas Attorney General Greg Abbott, recently launched a multimedia campaign aimed at helping to prevent teen dating abuse. The "LOVE" campaign has produced posters as well as public service announcements, songs, Web site images, and other materials to alert teens to the prevalence and danger of dating abuse. One poster (see fig. 1) shows the word *Love* written in a graffiti style, superimposed over a photograph of a teen couple. This ad illustrates the techniques the campaign uses to promote respectful and supportive romantic relationships to its teen audience.

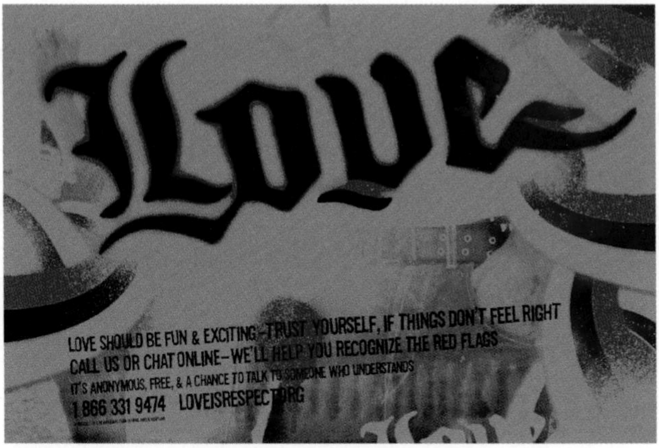


Courtesy of loveisrespect.org

Fig. 1. "LOVE" campaign poster; *loveisrespect.org*; Natl. Teen Dating Abuse Helpline, 2009; Web; 15 Oct. 2012.

The "LOVE" poster uses words and images to convey the campaign's overall message: that teens can prevent and stop dating abuse when they are given the resources they need to identify warning signs and to get help. The central image of a neon pink stylized "Love" logo, framed with splattered paint and a smaller, repeated version of the logo, emphasizes the ad's positive focus on what love should be: fun, exciting, and—above all—respectful. In addition, the text beneath the logo uses an informal, conversational style (rather than formal, grammatically correct language) to appeal to its young audience. The whitewashed image behind the logo, showing the close-up embrace of a teen couple, subtly supports the ad's message that teens should trust their own instincts and ask for help when "things don't feel right."

Together, the poster's words and images work to empower teens to build healthy, loving relationships and to recognize the signs of dating abuse in time to stop it. By focusing on *love* rather than *abuse,* the ad maintains an upbeat message that supports teen dating as long as it is loving and respectful. The concluding advice to "call us or chat online," along with the Helpline's contact information, gives teens a place to go when abuse happens, enabling them not just to recognize the problem but also to do something about it.

## 22d Conventions of Style, Format, and Documentation

### 1 Style and Format

Each humanities discipline has its own specialized vocabulary. You should use the technical terms used in the field, but be careful not to overuse such terminology. You can use the first person (*I*) when you are expressing your own reactions and convictions—for example, in a response paper or **reflective statement**. In other situations, however, avoid the first person.

See 30c

Although papers in the humanities do not usually include abstracts, internal headings, tables, or graphs, this situation is changing. Be sure you know what your instructor expects.

See Ch. 23; Ch. 24

*Note:* When you write papers about **literature**, follow the special conventions that apply to literary analysis.

### 2 Documentation

See Ch. 18; Ch. 20

Literature and modern and classical language scholars, as well as scholars in music and sometimes in art history, use **MLA documentation style**; history scholars generally use **Chicago style**.

## 22e Avoiding Plagiarism

When plagiarism occurs in the humanities, it is often the result of inaccurate summarizing and paraphrasing, failure to use quotation marks where they are required, and confusion between your ideas and those of your sources. See Ch. 17

Whenever you use sources, you must be careful to document them. In this way, you acknowledge the work of others who influenced your ideas or contributed to your conclusions. Take accurate notes, avoid cutting and pasting chunks of information from online sources directly into your paper, and whenever you quote, summarize, or paraphrase, do so honestly. Document ideas as well as words, no matter where they come from. "Borrowing" without acknowledgment is plagiarism, and the penalties for plagiarism can be severe. (You do not have to document **common knowledge.** If you have any questions about what constitutes common knowledge in a particular humanities discipline, be sure to check with your instructor.) See 17b

## 22f Research Sources

Each discipline within the humanities has its own methodology, so it is important to know not only the sources or tools that are used by scholars in a particular field but also the way students and scholars conduct research.

In literature, for example, scholars may analyze, explain, interpret, or evaluate the text of a poem, short story, novel, or play or the work of a particular author. They study the text itself, but often they also consult other sources for evidence that will support their conclusions. They use the tools of their discipline: library resources (online catalogs, specialized databases, periodical indexes, bibliographies, and so on) and Internet resources to locate that evidence.

In other humanities disciplines—such as history—specialized databases, periodical indexes, reference works, and Web sites also exist. But **primary sources,** such as narratives, letters, diaries, or other original documents, also provide important evidence.

In some cases, you may be asked to provide your own analysis, interpretation, or evaluation of an original text, work of art, or musical composition, without reading what has already been written about it. More often, however, you will be asked to use **secondary sources** to reinforce your conclusions, especially when you are an undergraduate student, and you must be sure to evaluate those sources carefully before you use them. See Ch. 14

Doing library research in the humanities does not usually require that you know what the latest thinking is about a particular work, author, idea, or theory. Older books and journal articles may be as valuable as recent ones. When you begin your research, you can consult the *Humanities Index*, a general resource that lists articles from more than two hundred scholarly journals in areas such as history, language, literary criticism, philosophy, and religion. (*Humanities Abstracts* and *Humanities Full Text* are available as databases.)

Many specialized sources are also available for each humanities discipline. They include databases that cover the literature of that discipline and other sources that provide background information about people, creative works, literary or artistic movements, or historical time periods. Some of these specialized sources will be found in your library's reference collection; many will be available online, either on the Web or through your library's databases.

**Close-Up** FINDING ADDITIONAL SOURCES

Some online indexes offer citation searching, allowing you to search for any articles that cite articles you have found useful. Reading the lists of works cited at the ends of books, chapters, or journal articles may help you to identify other relevant sources. Reference works also frequently include lists of sources for further reading. Finally, annotated bibliographies can help you distinguish the useful sources from the irrelevant ones, saving you a good deal of time in the long run.

## 1 Reference Works

Library research is an important part of study in many humanities disciplines. When you do research in any subject area, the *Humanities Index* is one general source you can use. Another excellent index available in print and as a computer-searchable database is the *Arts and Humanities Citation Index. The New Grove Dictionary of Music and Musicians*, available in print and online, offers full-text bibliographies, biographies, and articles on music and musicians. For information on reference works in specific humanities disciplines, consult a reference librarian. For information on general reference works, see **13a5.**

## 2 Databases for Computer Searches

Some of the most helpful databases for humanities disciplines include *Arts and Humanities Citation Index; Art Abstracts/Art Full Text; MLA International Bibliography; JSTOR: Scholarly Journal Archive; ARTstor* Digital Image Collection; *Religion Index; Philosopher's Index; Essay and General Literature Index; Art Bibliographies Modern; America: History and Life; Historical Abstracts; Linguistics and Language Behavior Abstracts (LLBA);* and *RILM Abstracts of Music Literature.* Ask a reference librarian about the availability of these and other databases in your library. (Additional databases for specific humanities disciplines are listed in **13a3.**)

### 3 Web Sites

For links to Web sites for specific humanities disciplines, see **13b4.**

### 4 Other Sources of Information

Research in the humanities is not limited to print and electronic resources. For example, historians may do interviews and archival work or consult records collected in town halls, houses of worship, or courthouses; art historians visit museums and galleries; and music scholars attend concerts and recitals.

In addition, nonprint sources, such as surveys and interviews, can be important resources for a paper in any humanities discipline. See 13c

# CHAPTER 23

# Writing a Literary Analysis

## Frequently Asked Questions



## 23a Reading Literature

When you read a literary work you plan to write about, you use the same critical thinking skills and active reading strategies you apply to other works you read: **preview** the work and **highlight** it to identify key ideas and cues to meaning; then, **annotate** it carefully. See Ch. 2

As you read and take notes, focus on the special concerns of literary analysis, considering elements such as a short story's plot, a poem's rhyme or meter, or a play's staging. Look for *patterns*, related groups of words, images, or ideas that run through a work. Look for *anomalies*, unusual forms, unique uses of language, unexpected actions by characters, or original treatments of topics. Finally, look for *connections*, links with other literary works, with historical events, or with biographical information.

When you read a work of literature, keep in mind that you do not read to discover the one correct meaning the writer has hidden between the lines—there *is* no "one correct meaning." The meaning of a literary work is created by the interaction between a text and its readers. Do not assume, however, that a work can mean whatever you want it to mean; ultimately, your interpretation must be consistent with the stylistic signals, thematic suggestions, and patterns of imagery in the text.

Note: Before you begin planning a literary analysis, review **Chapter 17** to be sure you understand exactly what **plagiarism** is and how to avoid it.

## 23b Writing about Literature

When you have finished your reading and annotating, you decide on a topic; then, you follow the writing process outlined in **Chapters 4–6.** First, you **brainstorm** to find ideas to write about; next, you decide on a thesis and use it to help you organize your material. As you arrange related material into categories, you will begin to see a structure for your paper. At this point, you are ready to start drafting your essay.

When you write about literature, your goal is to make a point and support it with appropriate references to the work under discussion or to related works or secondary sources. In this sense, an essay on a literary topic is often a kind of argumentative essay in which you use sources and your own insights to support a thesis statement.

See Ch. 10; Ch. 24

As you write, you observe the conventions of literary criticism, which has its own specialized vocabulary and formats. You also respond to certain discipline-specific assignments. For instance, you may be asked to **analyze** a work, to take it apart and consider one or more of its elements—perhaps the plot or characters in a story or the use of language in a poem. Or, you may be asked to **interpret** a work, to explore its possible meanings. Finally, you may be called on to **evaluate** a work, to judge its strengths and weaknesses.

More specifically, you may be asked to trace the critical or popular reactions to a work, to compare two works by a single writer (or by two different writers), or to consider the relationship between a work of literature and a literary movement or historical period. You may also be asked to analyze a character's motives or the relationship between two characters or to comment on a story's setting or tone.

When you write a literary analysis, you will often be asked to use sources to support the points you are making about a particular work of fiction, poetry, or drama. Sometimes, however, you may be asked to analyze, interpret, or evaluate a literary work solely on the basis of your own reactions. Whatever the case, understanding exactly what you are expected to do will make your writing task easier.

## Conventions of Writing about Literature

When you write about a literary work, keep the following conventions in mind:

- Use present-tense verbs when discussing works of literature (**The character of Mrs. Mallard's husband is not developed**).
- Use past-tense verbs only when discussing historical events (**Owen's poem conveys the destructiveness of World War I, which at the time the poem was written was considered to be. . . .**); when presenting historical or biographical data (**Her first novel, published in 1811 when Austen was thirty-six, . . .**); or when identifying events that occurred prior to the time of the story's main action (**Miss Emily is a recluse; since her father died she has lived alone except for a servant**).
- Support your points with specific, concrete examples from the work you are discussing, *briefly* summarizing key events, quoting dialogue or description, describing characters or setting, or paraphrasing ideas.
- Combine paraphrase, summary, and quotation with your own interpretations, weaving quotations smoothly into your paper (**see Ch. 15**).
- Be careful to acknowledge all the sources you use, including the literary work or works under discussion. Introduce the words or ideas of others with a reference to the source, and follow borrowed material with appropriate parenthetical documentation (**see 18a1**). Be sure you have quoted accurately and enclosed the words of others in quotation marks.
- Include a works-cited list in accordance with MLA documentation style.
- When citing a part of a short story or novel, supply the page number (**168**). For a poem, give the line numbers (**2-4**) if they are included in the text; in your first reference, include the word *line* or *lines* (**lines 2-4**). For a classic verse play, include act, scene, and line numbers (**1.4.29-31**). For other plays, supply act and/or scene numbers. (When quoting more than four lines of prose or more than three lines of poetry, follow the guidelines outlined in **56b.**)
- Avoid subjective expressions like *I feel, I believe, it seems to me,* and *in my opinion.* These weaken your paper by suggesting that its ideas are "only" your opinion and have no validity in themselves.
- Avoid unnecessary plot summary. Your goal is to draw a conclusion about one or more works and to support that conclusion with pertinent details. If a plot development supports a point you wish to make, a *brief* summary is acceptable, but plot summary is no substitute for analysis.
- Use literary terms accurately. For example, be careful not to confuse *narrator* or *speaker* with *writer*. Feelings or opinions expressed by a narrator or character do not necessarily represent those of the writer. You should not say, **In the poem's last stanza, Frost expresses his indecision,** when you mean the poem's *speaker* is indecisive.

(*continued*)

See 18a2

**Conventions of Writing about Literature** (*continued*)

- Italicize titles of books and plays (**see 59a**); enclose titles of short stories and poems in quotation marks (**see 56c**). Book-length poems are treated as long works, and their titles should be italicized.

## 23c Writing about Fiction

See Chs. 4–6

When you write a literary analysis of a work of fiction, you follow the same writing process you use when you write any paper about literature. However, you concentrate on elements—such as plot, character, setting, and point of view—central to works of fiction.

CHECKLIST

**Writing about Fiction**

- ❑ **Plot** What happens in the story? What conflicts can you identify? Are they resolved? In what order are the events arranged? Does the story include flashbacks or foreshadowing?
- ❑ **Character** Who is the protagonist? the antagonist? What role do minor characters play? What are each character's most striking traits? Does the protagonist grow and change during the story? Are the characters portrayed sympathetically? How do characters interact with one another? What motivates the characters?
- ❑ **Setting** Where and when is the story set? How does the setting influence the plot? How does it affect the characters' lives and relationships?
- ❑ **Point of View** Is the story told by an anonymous third-person narrator or by a character who uses first-person (*I* or *we*) point of view? Is the first-person narrator trustworthy? Is the narrator a participant in the action or just a witness to the story's events? How would a different point of view change the story?
- ❑ **Style, Tone, and Language** Is the style simple or complex? Is the tone intimate or distant? What kind of imagery is used? Is the level of diction formal or informal?
- ❑ **Theme** What central theme or themes does the story explore?

See Ch. 18

Tim Westmoreland, a student in an introductory literature class, was asked to write a source-based analysis of John Updike's short story "A&P." The paper, which follows, uses MLA documentation style and a variety of print and nonprint sources.

### *Model Literary Analysis: Fiction*

Westmoreland 1

Tim Westmoreland

Professor Adkins

Literature 2101

25 February 2012

"A&P": A Class Act

John Updike's "A&P," like many of his other works, is a "profoundly American" story about social inequality and an attempt to bridge the gap between social classes (Steiner). The story is told by an eighteen-year-old boy who is working as a checkout clerk in an A&P in a small New England town five miles from the beach. The narrative is delivered in a slangy, colloquial voice that tells of a brief but powerful encounter with a "beautiful but inaccessible girl" from another social and economic level (Wells 128). Sammy, the narrator, is working his cash register on a slow Thursday afternoon when, as he says, "In walks these three girls in nothing but bathing suits" (Updike, "A&P" 259). Lengel, the store's manager—a Sunday school teacher and "self-appointed moral policeman"—confronts the girls, telling them that they should be decently dressed (Wells 131). It is a moment of embarrassment and insight for all parties concerned, and in an apparently impulsive act, Sammy quits his job. Although the plot is simple, what is at the heart of the story is complex: a noble gesture that serves as a futile attempt to cross social and economic boundaries.

Introduction (combines paraphrase, summary, and quotation)

Title included because paper cites two sources by Updike

Thesis statement

Through Sammy's eyes, we see the class conflict that defines the story. The privileged young girls in bathing suits are very different from the few customers who are shopping in the store. Sammy refers to the customers as "sheep" (Updike,

Westmoreland 2

"A&P" 260) and describes one of them as "a witch about fifty with rouge on her cheekbones and no eyebrows" (259). Other customers are characterized in equally negative terms—for example, "houseslaves in pin curlers" (260) and "an old party in baggy gray pants" (261). Unlike the other customers, the leader of the three girls is described as a "queen":

Long prose quotation (more than four lines) is set off from text and introduced by a colon. Quotation is indented 1" from left margin; no quotation marks are used.

> She came down a little hard on her heels, as if she didn't walk in her bare feet that much, putting down her heels and then letting the weight move along to her toes as if she was testing the floor with every step, putting a little deliberate extra action into it. (259-60)

It seems clear that Sammy realizes that Queenie and her friends come from farther away than just the beach. They have come to test the floors of a store patronized by the less well-off and do it openly, in defiance of social rules. In a sense, they are "slumming."

Queenie, whose name suggests her superior status, understands her position in social as well as sexual terms. Sammy has to spend the summer working, but she has come to the A&P just to purchase "Kingfish Fancy Herring Snacks in Pure Sour Cream" for her parents. (The exotic and expensive herring snacks hints at their different backgrounds.) Regardless, the two act in ways that are not all that different. Both are self-consciously trying out new roles, with Sammy trying to rise above his station in life and Queenie trying to move below hers. As Queenie arrives at the register, Sammy observes, "Now her hands are empty, not a ring or a bracelet, . . . and I wonder where the money's coming from. Still with that prim look she lifts a folded dollar bill out of the hollow at the center of her nubbled pink top" (Updike, "A&P" 261).

Westmoreland 3

With this gesture, she not only tests her own sexual powers but also sinks to the level of the supermarket. Despite her act, though, Sammy knows how different Queenie's world is from his:

> I slid right down her voice into her living room. Her father and the other men were standing around in ice-cream coats and bow ties and the women were in sandals picking up herring snacks on toothpicks off a big plate and they were all holding drinks the color of water with olives and sprigs of mint in them. When my parents have somebody over they get lemonade and if it's a real racy affair Schlitz in tall glasses with "They'll Do It Every Time" cartoons stencilled on. (262)

As Updike says in an interview with writer Donald Murray, "[Sammy] is a blue-collar kid longing for a white-collar girl."

At this point in the story, as Sammy says, "everybody's luck begins to run out" (Updike, "A&P" 261). Lengel, the store manager, who represents "the cruel and unethical" rules that govern matters of social etiquette (Updike, Interview), confronts the girls, telling them that they are indecently dressed. "'We *are* decent,' Queenie says suddenly, her lower lip pushing, getting sore now that she remembers her place, a place from which the crowd that runs the A&P must look pretty crummy" (262). Suddenly, Sammy can no longer be a detached observer and, in a gesture of defiance, he quits. The real question here is *why* he quits. In fact, Updike himself wonders "to what extent his gesture of quitting has to do with the fact that she is rich and he is poor" (Interview).

Parenthetical reference cites filmed interview

By quitting, Sammy challenges social inequality, but is his response really just heroic posturing—or simply an expression of his long-standing frustration? In other words, does Sammy quit because of what Updike calls a

Westmoreland 4

"misunderstanding of how the world is put together" (Updike, Interview) or because he is "a boy who's tried to reach out of his immediate environment towards something bigger and better" (Updike,"Still Afraid")? Although Sammy's action may be simply impulsive—Sammy even states it would be "fatal" (Updike, "A&P" 263) not to go through with his initial gesture—it seems likely that he is taking a deliberate stand against what he sees as social injustice. Unlike Queenie's act of defiance, Sammy's gesture will have long-term consequences (Oates). As Updike points out, in Sammy's small town everyone will find out what he has done, and he may be "known . . . as a quitter" (Interview). Sammy's understanding and acceptance of these consequences ("'You'll feel this for the rest of your life.' Lengel says, and I know that's true, . . . "), and of the limitations his social class imposes on him, constitute his initiation into adulthood ("A&P" 263). Whether quitting is Sammy's first step toward overcoming these limitations or a romantic gesture he will live to regret remains to be seen. As Updike says, "How blind we are, as we awkwardly push outward into the world!" ("Still Afraid").

Citation for Internet source does not include page or paragraph numbers

Conclusion

Although it is true that both Queenie and Sammy attempt to cross social boundaries, the reasons for their actions are different. Queenie's provocative gesture is well thought out: she deliberately relinquishes her trappings, her clothes and jewelry. If only for a few minutes, she sheds her dignity and her wealth in order to flaunt her sexuality and her power. In contrast, Sammy chooses impulsively, in what Updike calls a "hot flash," a "moment of manly decisiveness," to take action and, ultimately, gives up both his dignity and his power (Updike, Interview). He gains only a brief moment of glory before he finds himself alone in the parking lot. In this instant, he confronts the social inequality and the

Westmoreland 5

unspeakable frustration it represents. According to Updike, Sammy cannot win—even though in a "noble surrender of his position," he gains an understanding of the weight he must bear (Interview).

Westmoreland 6

Works Cited

Oates, Joyce Carol. "John Updike's American Comedies." *Joyce Carol Oates on John Updike*. U of San Francisco, 5 Apr. 1998. Web. 15 Jan. 2012.

Steiner, George. "Supreme Fiction: America Is in the Details." *The New Yorker*. Condé Nast, 11 Mar. 1996. Web. 20 Feb. 2012.

Updike, John. "A&P." *Literature: Reading, Reacting, Writing*. Ed. Laurie G. Kirszner and Stephen R. Mandell. 8th ed. Boston: Wadsworth, 2013. 259-63. Print.

---. Interview by Donald Murray. *The Heinle Original Film Series in Literature*. Dir. Bruce Schwartz. Thomson, 2004. DVD.

---. "Still Afraid of Being Caught." *New York Times*. New York Times, 8 Oct. 1995. Web. 16 Feb. 2012.

Wells, Walter. "John Updike's 'A&P': A Return Visit to Araby." *Studies in Short Fiction* 30.2 (1993): 127-33. *Magazine Index Plus*. Web. 15 Feb. 2012.

## 23d Writing about Poetry

When you write a paper about poetry, you concentrate on the elements poets use to create and enrich their work—for example, voice, form, sound, meter, language, and tone.

CHECKLIST

### Writing about Poetry

- ❑ **Voice** Who is the poem's speaker? What is the speaker's attitude toward the poem's subject? How would you characterize the poem's tone?
- ❑ **Word Choice and Word Order** What words seem important? Why? What does each word say? What does it suggest? Are any words repeated? Why? Is the poem's diction formal or informal? Is word choice unusual—or even surprising? Is the arrangement of words conventional or unconventional?
- ❑ **Imagery** What images are used in the poem? To what senses (sight, sound, smell, taste, or touch) do they appeal? Is one central image important? Why? Does the poem develop a pattern of related images?
- ❑ **Figures of Speech** Does the poet use simile? metaphor? personification? What do figures of speech add to the poem?
- ❑ **Sound** Does the poem include rhyme? Where? Does it have regular meter (that is, a regular pattern of stressed and unstressed syllables)? Does the poem include repeated consonant or vowel sounds? What do these elements contribute to the poem?
- ❑ **Form** Is the poem written in **open form** (with no pattern of line length, rhyme, or meter) or in **closed form** (conforming to a pattern)? Why do you think this kind of form is used?
- ❑ **Theme** What central theme or themes does the poem explore?

ESL TIP

You may find English-language poetry difficult to understand, but you should know that even native English speakers may have trouble understanding poetry because of the special ways in which poets use words. Do your best, and remember that as a person who speaks more than one language, you may have a greater sensitivity to language than people who speak only one language.

Daniel Johanssen, a student in an introductory literature class, was assigned to write an essay analyzing a poem from a list his instructor provided. (He was asked not to consult outside sources.) Daniel chose to write about Delmore Schwartz's 1959 poem, "The True-Blue American," which appears on the facing page. Daniel's essay appears on pages 384–86.

THE TRUE-BLUE AMERICAN

Jeremiah Dickson was a true-blue American,
For he was a little boy who understood America, for he felt that he must
Think about *everything;* because that's all there is to think about,
Knowing immediately the intimacy of truth and comedy,
Knowing intuitively how a sense of humor was a necessity
For one and for all who live in America. Thus, natively, and
Naturally when on an April Sunday in an ice cream parlor Jeremiah
Was requested to choose between a chocolate sundae and a banana split
He answered unhesitatingly, having no need to think of it
Being a true-blue American, determined to continue as he began:
Rejecting the either-or of Kierkegaard,[1] and many another European;
Refusing to accept alternatives, refusing to believe the choice of between;
Rejecting selection; denying dilemma; electing absolute affirmation: knowing
    in his breast
        The infinite and the gold
        Of the endless frontier, the deathless West.
"Both: I will have them both!" declared this true-blue American
In Cambridge, Massachusetts, on an April Sunday, instructed
    By the great department stores, by the Five-and-Ten,
Taught by Christmas, by the circus, by the vulgarity and grandeur of Niagara Falls and the Grand Canyon,
Tutored by the grandeur, vulgarity, and infinite appetite gratified and
    Shining in the darkness, of the light
On Saturdays at the double bills of the moon pictures,
The consummation of the advertisements of the imagination of the light
Which is as it was—the infinite belief in infinite hope—of Columbus, Barnum, Edison, and Jeremiah Dickson.

[1]Søren Kierkegaard (1813–1855)—Danish philosopher who greatly influenced twentieth-century existentialism. *Either-Or* (1841) is one of his best-known works.

### *Model Literary Analysis: Poetry*

Johanssen 1

Daniel Johanssen

Professor Stang

English 1001

8 April 2012

Title of poem is in quotation marks

Irony in "The True-Blue American"

The poem "The True-Blue American," by Delmore Schwartz, is not as simple and direct as its title suggests. In fact, the title is extremely ironic. At first, the poem seems patriotic, but actually the flag-waving strengthens the speaker's criticism. The poem may seem to support and celebrate America, but it is in fact a bitter critique of the negative aspects of American culture.

Thesis statement

According to the speaker, the primary problem with America is that its citizens falsely believe themselves to be authorities on everything. The following lines introduce the theme of the "know-it-all" American: "For he was a little boy who understood America, for he felt that he must / Think about *everything*; because that's all there is to think about" (lines 2-3). This theme is developed later in a series of parallel phrases that seem to celebrate the value of immediate intuitive knowledge and a refusal to accept or to believe anything other than what is American (4-6).

Slash separates lines of poetry (space before and after slash)

Parenthetical documentation indicates line numbers (the word *line* or *lines* is included only in the first reference)

Americans are ambitious and determined, but these qualities are not seen in the poem as virtues. According to the speaker, Americans reject sophisticated "European" concepts like doubt and choices and alternatives and instead insist on "absolute affirmation" (13)—simple solutions to complex problems. This unwillingness to compromise translates into stubbornness and materialistic greed. This tendency is illustrated by the boy's

Johanssen 2

asking for *both* a chocolate sundae *and* a banana split at the ice cream parlor—not "either-or" (11). Americans are characterized as pioneers who want it all, who will stop at nothing to achieve "The infinite and the gold / Of the endless frontier, the deathless West" (15-16). For the speaker, the pioneers who seek this "endless frontier" are not noble or self-sacrificing; they are like greedy little boys at an ice cream parlor.

According to the speaker, the greed and materialism of America began as grandeur but ultimately became mere vulgarity. Similarly, the "true-blue American" is not born a vulgar parody of grandeur; he learns from his true-blue fellow Americans, who in turn were taught by experts:

> By the great department stores, by the
> Five-and-Ten,
> Taught by Christmas, by the circus, by the
> vulgarity and grandeur of Niagara Falls
> and the Grand Canyon,
> Tutored by the grandeur, vulgarity, and
> infinite appetite gratified. . . . (19-21)

Among the "tutors" the speaker lists are such American institutions as department stores and national monuments. Within these institutions, grandeur and vulgarity coexist; in a sense, they are one and the same.

The speaker's negativity climaxes in the phrase "Shining in the darkness, of the light" (22). This paradoxical statement suggests that negative truths are hidden beneath America's glamorous surface. All the grand and illustrious things of which Americans are so proud are personified by Jeremiah Dickson, the spoiled brat in the ice cream parlor.

More than 3 lines of poetry are set off from text and introduced by a colon. Quotation is indented 1" from left margin; no quotation marks are used.

Documentation is placed one space after final punctuation.

Johanssen 3

Conclusion

Like America, Jeremiah has unlimited potential. He has native intuition, curiosity, courage, and a pioneer spirit. Unfortunately, however, both America and Jeremiah Dickson are limited by their willingness to be led by others, by their greed and impatience, and by their preference for quick, easy, unambiguous answers rather than careful philosophical analysis. Regardless of his—and America's—potential, Jeremiah Dickson is doomed to be hypnotized and seduced by glittering superficialities, light without substance, and to settle for the "double bills of the moon pictures" (23) rather than the enduring truths of a philosopher such as Kierkegaard.

Johanssen 4

Work Cited

Schwartz, Delmore. "The True-Blue American." *Selected Poems: Summer Knowledge*. New York: New Directions, 1967. 163. Print.

## 23e Writing about Drama

When you write a paper about a play, you focus on the special conventions of drama. For example, you might consider not just the play's plot and characters but also its staging.

CHECKLIST

### Writing about Drama

- ❑ **Plot** What happens in the play? What conflicts are developed? How are they resolved? Are there any subplots? What events, if any, occur offstage?
- ❑ **Character** Who are the major characters? The minor characters? What relationships exist among them? What are their most distinctive traits? What do we learn about characters from their words and actions? from what other characters tell us? Does the main character change or grow during the course of the play? What motivates the characters?
- ❑ **Staging** When and where is the play set? How do the scenery, props, costumes, lighting, and music work together to establish this setting? What else do these elements contribute to the play?
- ❑ **Theme** What central theme or themes does the play explore?

Kimberly Allison, a student in an introductory literature class, was assigned to write a short paper focusing on one element—plot, character, staging, or theme—in a one-act play. Kimberly's analysis was to be based on her own understanding of the play, not on the interpretations of literary critics. She chose to write about the characters in Susan Glaspell's 1916 play *Trifles.* Her completed paper, with annotations that highlight some conventions of writing about drama, appears on pages 388–92.

## Model Literary Analysis: Drama

Allison 1

Kimberly Allison

Professor Johnson

English 1013

3 March 2012

Desperate Measures: Acts of Defiance in *Trifles*

Opening sentence identifies author and work

Introduction places play in historical context

Susan Glaspell wrote her best-known play, *Trifles,* in 1916, at a time when married women were beginning to challenge their socially defined roles, realizing that their identities as wives kept them in a subordinate position in society. Because women were demanding more autonomy, traditional institutions such as marriage, which confined women to the home and made them mere extensions of their husbands, were beginning to be reexamined.

Thesis statement

Evidently touched by these concerns, Glaspell chose as her play's protagonist a married woman, Minnie Wright, who challenged society's expectations in an extreme way: by murdering her husband. Minnie's defiant act has occurred before the action begins; during the play, two women, Mrs. Peters and Mrs. Hale, who accompany their husbands on an investigation of the murder scene, piece together the details of the situation surrounding the murder. As the events unfold, however, it becomes clear that the focus of *Trifles* is not on who killed John Wright but on the themes of the subordinate role of women, the confinement of the wife in the home, and the experiences all women share. With these themes, Glaspell shows her audience the desperate measures women had to take to achieve autonomy.

Topic sentence identifies first point paper will discuss: women's subordinate role

The subordinate role of women, particularly Minnie's role in her marriage, becomes evident in the first few minutes of the play, when Mr. Hale observes that the victim, John Wright, had little concern for his wife's opinions: "I didn't know as what his

Allison 2

wife wanted made much difference to John—" (1244). Here Mr. Hale suggests that Mrs. Wright was powerless against the wishes of her husband. Indeed, as these characters imply, Mrs. Wright's every act and thought was controlled by her husband, who tried to break her spirit by forcing her to stay alone in the house, performing repetitive domestic chores. Mrs. Wright's only source of power in the household was her kitchen work, a situation that Mrs. Peters and Mrs. Hale understand because their own behavior is also determined by their husbands. Therefore, when Sheriff Peters makes fun of Minnie's concern about her preserves, saying, "Well, can you beat the women! Held for murder and worryin' about her preserves" (1245), he is, in a sense, criticizing all three of the women for worrying about domestic matters rather than about the murder that has been committed. Indeed, the sheriff's comment suggests that he assumes women's lives are trivial, an attitude that influences the thoughts and speech of all three men.

Mrs. Peters and Mrs. Hale are similar to Minnie Wright in another way as well: throughout the play, they are confined to the kitchen of the Wrights' house. As a result, the kitchen becomes the focal point of the play—and, ironically, the women find that the kitchen holds the clues to Mrs. Wright's loneliness and to the details of the murder. Mrs. Peters and Mrs. Hale remain confined to the kitchen while their husbands enter and exit the house at will. This situation mirrors Minnie Wright's daily life, as she remained in the home while her husband went to work and into town. As they move about the kitchen, the two women discuss Minnie Wright's isolation: "Not having children makes less work—but it makes a quiet house, and Wright out to work all day, and no company when he did come in" (1250). Beginning to identify with Mrs. Wright's

Topic sentence introduces second point paper will discuss: women's confinement in the home

Allison 3

loneliness, Mrs. Peters and Mrs. Hale recognize that, busy in their own homes, they have participated in isolating and confining Minnie Wright. Mrs. Hale declares, "Oh, I *wish* I'd come over here once in a while! That was a crime! That was a crime! Who's going to punish that? . . . I might have known she needed help!" (1252).

Transitional paragraph discusses women's observations and conclusions

Soon the two women discover that Mrs. Wright's only connection to the outside world was her bird, the symbol of her confinement; she herself was a caged bird who was kept from singing and communicating with others because of her husband. And piecing together the evidence—the disorderly kitchen, the misstitched quilt pieces, and the dead canary—the women come to believe that John Wright broke the bird's neck, just as he had broken his wife's spirit. At this point, Mrs. Peters and Mrs. Hale understand the connection between the dead canary and Minnie Wright's motivation. The stage directions describe the moment when the women become aware of the truth behind the murder: *"Their eyes meet,"* and the women share *"A look of growing comprehension, of horror"* (1251).

Topic sentence introduces third point paper will discuss: experiences women share

Through their observations and discussions in Mrs. Wright's kitchen, Mrs. Hale and Mrs. Peters come to understand the commonality of women's experiences. Mrs. Hale speaks for both of them when she says, "I know how things can be—for women. . . . We all go through the same things—it's all just a different kind of the same thing" (1252). And once the two women realize the experiences they share, they begin to recognize that they must join together in order to challenge their male-oriented society; although their experiences may seem trivial to the men, the "trifles" of their lives are significant to them. They realize that Minnie's independence and identity were crushed by her husband and that their own husbands also believe that women's lives are

Allison 4

trivial and unimportant. This realization leads them to commit an act as defiant as the one that got Minnie into trouble: they conceal their discovery from their husbands and from the law.

Significantly, Mrs. Peters does acknowledge that "the law is the law" (1248), yet she still seems to believe that because Mr. Wright treated his wife badly, she is justified in killing him. They also realize, however, that for men the law is black and white and that an all-male jury will not take into account the extenuating circumstances that prompted Minnie Wright to kill her husband. And even if Mrs. Wright were allowed to communicate to the all-male court the psychological abuse she has suffered, the law would undoubtedly view her experience as trivial because a woman who complained about how her husband treated her would be seen as ungrateful.

Nevertheless, because Mrs. Hale and Mrs. Peters empathize with Mrs. Wright's situation, they suppress the evidence they find, enduring their husbands' condescension rather than standing up to them. And through this desperate action, the women break through the boundaries of their social role, just as Minnie Wright has done. Although Mrs. Wright is imprisoned for her crime, she has freed herself; and although Mrs. Peters and Mrs. Hale conceal their knowledge, fearing the men will laugh at them, these women are really challenging society and, in this way, freeing themselves as well.

Conclusion places play in historical context

In *Trifles*, Susan Glaspell addresses many of the problems shared by early-twentieth-century women, including their subordinate status and their confinement in the home. In order to emphasize the pervasiveness of these problems and the desperate measures women had to take to break out of restrictive social roles, Glaspell does more than focus on the plight of a woman who has ended her isolation and loneliness

Allison 5

by committing a heinous crime against society. By presenting characters who demonstrate the vast differences between male and female experience, she illustrates how men define the roles of women and how women must challenge these roles in search of their own significance in society and their eventual independence.

Allison 6

Work Cited

Glaspell, Susan. *Trifles. Literature: Reading, Reacting, Writing.* Ed. Laurie G. Kirszner and Stephen R. Mandell. 8th ed. Boston: Wadsworth, 2013. 1242-53. Print.

CHAPTER 24

# Writing a Literary Argument

## Frequently Asked Questions



See Ch. 23

When you write a literary argument, you follow the same process you do when you write a **literary analysis**. However, because the purpose of an argument is to convince readers, you need to use some additional strategies to present your ideas.

# 24a Planning a Literary Argument

## 1 Choosing a Topic

Your first step in writing a literary argument is to decide on a specific topic to write about. Just as you would for any argumentative essay, you should choose a topic that engages you. If you are interested in fantasy or horror, you might decide to write about one of Edgar Allan Poe's short stories—for example, "The Cask of Amontillado" or "The Fall of the House of Usher." If you are interested in women's issues, you could write about some poems that focus on this subject—for example, "Woman Work" and "Phenomenal Women," by Maya Angelou. It stands to reason that the more you like your topic, the more enthusiasm you will bring to your writing.

You should also make sure that your topic is suitable for the paper you are going to write. If you are assigned to write a three-page paper, you will probably write about just one character in a play or novel or just one poem. In a longer paper, you could cover more ground and go into more depth. In addition, if your paper requires research, you should make sure that you are able to find the information you need. Do you have access to the journal articles and books that you will need? Can you find high-quality material in the library's online databases or on the Internet? If not, you should choose another topic.

## 2 Formulating a Thesis

After you have chosen your topic, your next step is to take a stand—to state your position in an **argumentative thesis.** Properly worded, this thesis statement will lay the foundation for the rest of your argument.

Because an argumentative essay attempts to change the way readers think, it must have a thesis that is **debatable,** a statement about which reasonable people may disagree. **Factual statements**—statements about which reasonable people do *not* disagree—are therefore inappropriate as thesis statements for argument.

> **Factual Statement:** Linda Loman is Willy Loman's long-suffering wife in Arthur Miller's play *Death of a Salesman*.
>
> **Thesis Statement:** More than a stereotype of the long-suffering wife, Linda Loman in Arthur Miller's play *Death of a Salesman* is a multidimensional character.

One way to make sure that your thesis takes a stand is to formulate an **antithesis**—a statement that takes an arguable position opposite from yours. If you can construct an antithesis, you can be certain that your thesis statement takes a stand. If you cannot, your thesis statement needs further revision to give it an argumentative edge.

**Thesis Statement:** The last line of Richard Wright's short story "Big Black Good Man" indicates that Jim was fully aware all along of Olaf's deep-seated racial prejudice.

**Antithesis:** The last line of Richard Wright's short story "Big Black Good Man" indicates that Jim remained unaware of Olaf's feelings toward him.

## 3 Defining Your Terms

You should always define the key terms you use in your literary argument. For example, if you are using the term *narrator*, make sure that your readers know whether you are referring to a first-person or a third-person narrator. In addition, you may need to clarify the distinction between an **unreliable narrator**—someone who misrepresents or misinterprets events—and a **reliable narrator**—someone who accurately describes events. Without clear definitions of the terms you are using, readers will have a difficult time understanding the points you are making.

### Close-Up DEFINING YOUR TERMS

Be especially careful to use precise terms in your thesis statement. Avoid vague and judgmental words, such as *wrong*, *bad*, *good*, *right*, and *immoral*.

**Vague:** The poem "Birmingham Sunday (September 15, 1963)" by Langston Hughes shows how bad racism can be.

**Clear:** The poem "Birmingham Sunday (September 15, 1963)" by Langston Hughes makes a moving statement about how destructive racism can be.

## 4 Considering Your Audience

As you plan your essay, keep your audience in mind. For example, if you are writing about a work that has been discussed in class, you can assume that your readers are familiar with it; include plot summary only when it is needed to explain or support a point you are making. Keep in mind that you will be addressing an academic audience—your instructor and possibly other students. For this reason, you should be sure to follow the conventions of writing about literature as well as the conventions of standard written English.

See 23b

When you write an argumentative essay, always assume that you are addressing a skeptical audience. Remember, your thesis is debatable, so not everyone will agree with you—and even if your readers are sympathetic to your position, you cannot assume that they will accept your ideas without question.

### 5 Refuting Opposing Arguments

As you develop your literary argument, you may need to **refute**—that is, to argue against—opposing arguments by demonstrating that they are false, misguided, or illogical. By summarizing and refuting opposing views, you make opposing arguments seem less credible to readers; thus, you strengthen your case. See 10a5

In the following paragraph, a student refutes the argument that Homer Barron, a character in William Faulkner's short story "A Rose for Emily," is gay.

> Several critics have suggested that Homer Barron, Miss Emily's suitor, is gay. Certainly, there is some evidence in the story to support this interpretation. For example, the narrator points out that Homer enjoys "the company of men" (Faulkner 220) and that he is not "a marrying man" (220). In addition, the narrator describes Homer as wearing yellow gloves when he takes Emily for drives. According to the critic William Greenslade, in the 1890s yellow was associated with homosexuality (24). This evidence, however, does not establish that Homer is gay. During the nineteenth century, many men preferred the company of other men (as many do today). This, in itself, did not mean they were gay. Neither does the fact that Homer wears yellow gloves. According to the narrator, Homer is a man who likes to dress well. It is certainly possible that he wears these gloves to impress Miss Emily, a woman he is trying to attract.

Summary of opposing argument concedes point

Refutation

## 24b Supporting Your Literary Argument

### 1 Using Evidence Effectively

Many literary arguments are built on **assertions**—statements made about a topic—that are backed by **evidence**—supporting examples in the form of references to the text, quotations, and the opinions of literary critics. For example, if you stated that Torvald Helmer, Nora's husband in Henrik Ibsen's play *A Doll House,* is as much a victim of society as his wife is, you could support this assertion with relevant quotations and examples from the play. You could also paraphrase, summarize, or quote the ideas of literary critics who also hold this opinion. Remember, only assertions that are **self-evident** (**All plays include characters and dialogue**) or **factual** (***A Doll House* was published in 1879**) need no supporting evidence. All other kinds of assertions require support.

## 2 Establishing Credibility

Some people bring **credibility** to whatever they write. When a well-known literary critic evaluates the contributions of a particular writer, you can assume that he or she speaks with authority. (Although you might question the critic's opinions, you do not question his or her expertise.) But most people do not have this kind of credibility. When you write a literary argument, you must constantly work to establish credibility. You do this by *demonstrating knowledge, maintaining a reasonable tone,* and *presenting yourself as someone worth listening to.*

***Demonstrating Knowledge*** One way to establish credibility is by presenting your own carefully considered ideas about a subject. A clear argument and compelling support can demonstrate to readers that you know what you are talking about.

You can also establish credibility by showing readers that you have thoroughly researched your subject. By referring to important sources, by including the ideas of experts, and by providing accurate documentation for your information, you indicate that you have done the necessary background reading.

***Maintaining a Reasonable Tone*** Your **tone**—your attitude toward your readers or subject—is almost as important as the information you convey. Talk *to* your readers not *at* them. If you lecture your readers or appear to talk down to them, you will alienate them. Generally speaking, readers are more likely to respond to a writer who seems balanced and respectful than one who seems strident or condescending.

As you write your essay, use moderate language, and qualify your statements so that they seem reasonable. Try to avoid words and phrases such as *all, never, always,* and *in every case,* which can make your points seem simplistic, exaggerated, or unrealistic. Also, avoid absolute statements. For example, the statement **In "Doe Season," the ocean symbolizes Andy's attachment to her mother** leaves no room for other interpretations. A more measured and accurate statement might be **In "Doe Season," the ocean suggests Andy's identification with her mother and her realization that she is becoming a woman.**

***Presenting Yourself as Someone Worth Listening To*** When you write a literary argument, you should try to present yourself as someone your readers will want to listen to. Make your argument confidently, and don't apologize for your views. For example, do not use phrases such as *in my opinion* and *it seems to me,* which undercut your credibility. Finally, avoid the use of *I* (unless you are asked to give your opinion or to write a reaction statement) as well as slang and colloquialisms.

## 3 Being Fair

College writing requires that you stay within the bounds of fairness and that you avoid conclusions based on **bias** (preconceived ideas) rather than on evidence. To make sure that the support for your argument is not misleading, follow these guidelines:

- ***Avoid distorting the evidence.*** Distortion is misrepresentation. Writers sometimes misrepresent the extent to which critical opinion supports their thesis. For example, by saying that "many critics" think that something is so when only one or two do, they try to make a weak case stronger than it actually is.
- ***Avoid quoting out of context.*** You quote out of context when you take words out of their original setting and use them in another in order to change their meaning. For example, you are quoting out of context if you say **"Emily Dickinson's poems are so idiosyncratic that they do not appeal to readers"** when your source says "Emily Dickinson's poems are so idiosyncratic that they do not appeal to readers *who are accustomed to safe, conventional subjects.*" By eliminating a key portion of the original source's sentence, you alter its meaning.
- ***Avoid slanting.*** When you select only information that supports your position and ignore information that does not, you are guilty of slanting. You can eliminate this problem by including (and discussing) a full range of opinions, not just opinions that support your thesis.
- ***Avoid using unfair appeals.*** Writers of literary arguments rely on logic to convince readers that their ideas are worth considering. Problems arise, however, when writers use logical fallacies—flawed arguments—to fool readers into thinking that a conclusion is valid when it is not. Writers can also undercut their credibility if they use questionable support—books and articles by writers who have little or no expertise on the topic. This is especially true when information is obtained from the Internet, where the credentials of a writer may be difficult or impossible to assess. See 9d

## 4 Using Visuals as Evidence

**Visuals**—photographs, drawings, diagrams, and the like—can add a persuasive dimension to your essay. Because visual images have an immediate impact, they can sometimes make a good literary argument even better. For example, a discussion of a play's staging can be enhanced by photos that show its scenery, props, lighting, and so on. In a sense, visuals are another type of evidence that can support your thesis.

Of course, not all visuals will be appropriate or effective for a literary argument. Before using a visual, make certain it supports the point you are making. If it does not, it will distract readers and thereby undercut your argument. To ensure that readers understand your reason for including a visual, introduce it with a sentence that establishes its context; then, discuss its significance, paying particular attention to how it helps you make your point. Finally, be sure to document any visual that is not your original creation.

## 24c Organizing a Literary Argument

In its simplest form, a literary argument—like any argumentative essay—consists of a thesis statement and supporting evidence. Like other argumentative essays, however, literary arguments frequently include additional elements to win audience approval and to overcome potential opposition.

**Elements of Literary Arguments**

- **Introduction:** The introduction should orient readers to the subject of your essay, presenting the issue you will discuss and explaining its significance.
- **Thesis statement:** In most literary arguments, you will present your thesis statement in your introduction. However, if you think your readers may not be familiar with the issue you are discussing (or if it is controversial), you may want to postpone stating your thesis until later in the essay—perhaps until after the background section.
- **Background:** In this section, you can survey critical opinion about your topic, perhaps pointing out the shortcomings of these opinions. You can also define key terms, review basic facts, or briefly summarize the plot of the work or works you will discuss.
- **Arguments in support of your thesis:** Here you present your assertions and the evidence to support them. It makes sense to move from the least controversial to the most controversial point or from the most familiar to the least familiar idea.
- **Refutation of opposing arguments:** In a literary argument, you may want to summarize and refute the most obvious arguments against your thesis. If you do not address these opposing arguments, doubts about your position will remain in your readers' minds.
- **Conclusion:** Your conclusion will often restate your main point as well as the major arguments in support of it. Your conclusion can also summarize key points, remind readers of the weaknesses of opposing arguments, or underscore the logic of your position.

## 24d Model Literary Argument

The following student paper presents a literary argument about Dee, a character in Alice Walker's short story "Everyday Use." The student author supports her thesis with ideas she developed as she read the story as well as with information she found when she did research. She also includes two visuals from a film version of the story on DVD.

Chase 1

Margaret Chase

Professor Sierra

English 1001

16 April 2012

The Politics of "Everyday Use"

Introduction

Alice Walker's "Everyday Use" focuses on a mother, Mrs. Johnson, and her two daughters, Maggie and Dee, and how they view their heritage. The story's climax comes when Mrs. Johnson rejects Dee's request for a hand-stitched quilt that she wants to hang on her wall. Knowing that Maggie will put the quilt to "everyday use," Dee is horrified, and she tells her mother and Maggie that they do not understand their heritage. Although many literary critics see Dee's desire for the quilt as materialistic and shallow, a closer examination of the social and historical circumstances in which Walker wrote this 1973 story suggests a different interpretation of Dee's behavior.

Thesis statement

Background

On the surface, "Everyday Use" is a story about two sisters, Dee and Maggie, and Mrs. Johnson, their mother. Mrs. Johnson tells the reader that "Dee, . . . would always look anyone in the eye. Hesitation was no part of her nature" (465). Unlike her sister Dee, Maggie is shy and introverted. She is described as looking like a lame animal that has been run over by a car. According to the narrator, "She has been like this, chin on chest, eyes on ground, feet in shuffle" (465) ever since she was burned in a fire.

Unlike Dee, Mrs. Johnson never got an education. After second grade, she explains, the school closed down. She says, "Don't ask me why: in 1927 colored asked fewer questions than they do now" (466). Mrs. Johnson admits that she accepts the status quo even though she knows that it is unjust.

Chase 2

This admission further illustrates the difference between Mrs. Johnson and Dee: Mrs. Johnson has accepted her circumstances, while Dee has worked to change hers. Their differences are illustrated in a film version of the story by their contrasting dress. As shown in fig. 1, Dee and her boyfriend Hakim dress in a style that celebrates their African heritage. However, Mrs. Johnson and Maggie dress in plain, conservative clothing.

Bruce R. Schwartz

Fig. 1. Dee and Hakim arrive at the family home; *The Wadsworth Original Film Series in Literature: "Everyday Use,"* dir. Bruce R. Schwartz; Wadsworth, 2005; DVD.

Background continued

When Dee arrives home with her new boyfriend, it soon becomes obvious that her character is, for the most part, unchanged. As she eyes her mother's belongings and asks Mrs. Johnson if she can take the top of the butter churn home with her, it is clear that she is still very materialistic. However, her years away from home have also politicized her.

Chase 3

Dee now wants to be called "Wangero" because she believes (although mistakenly) that her given name comes from whites who owned her ancestors. She talks about how a new day is dawning for African Americans.

The meaning and political implications of Dee's decision to adopt an African name and to wear African clothing cannot be understood without knowledge of the social and political context in which Walker wrote this story. Walker's own comments about this time period explain Dee's behavior and add meaning to it.

Social and historical context used as evidence to support thesis

In an interview with her biographer, Evelyn C. White, Walker explains that the late 1960s was a time of cultural and intellectual awakening for African Americans. Many turned ideologically and culturally to Africa, adopting the dress, hairstyles, and even the names of their African ancestors. Walker admits that as a young woman she too became interested in discovering her African roots. (In fact, she herself was given the name "Wangero" during a visit to Kenya in the late 1960s.) Walker tells White that she considered keeping this new name but eventually realized that to do so would be to "dismiss" her family and her American heritage. When she researched her American family, she found that her great-great-grandmother had walked from Virginia to Georgia carrying two children. "If that's not a Walker," she says, "I don't know what is." Thus, Walker realized that, over time, African Americans had actually transformed the names they had originally taken from their enslavers. To respect the ancestors she knew, Walker says, she decided it was important to retain her name.

Along with adopting symbols of their African heritage, many African Americans also worked to elevate these symbols, such as the quilt shown in fig. 2, to the status of art. According

Chase 4

to Kalamu Ya Salaam, one way of doing this was to put these objects in museums; another was to hang them on the walls of their homes. Such acts were aimed at convincing whites that African Americans had an old and rich culture, and that consequently, they deserved not only basic civil rights, but also respect. These gestures were also meant to improve self-esteem and pride within black communities (42-43).

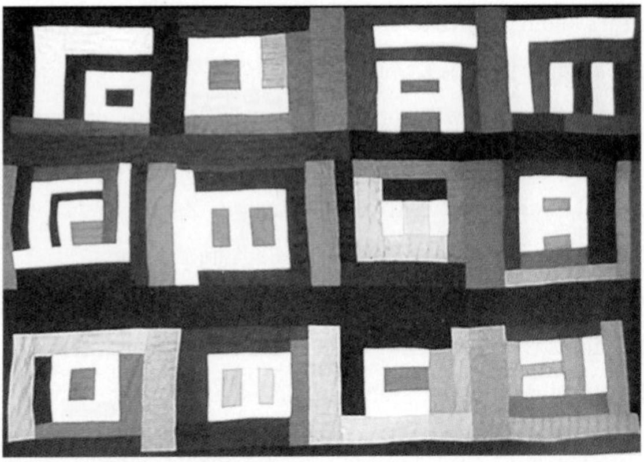


Fig. 2. Traditional hand-stitched quilt; Evelyn C. White, "Alice Walker: Stitches in Time," interview, *The Wadsworth Original Film Series in Literature: "Everyday Use,"* dir. Bruce R. Schwartz; Wadsworth, 2005; DVD.

Summary of opposing argument

Admittedly, as some critics have pointed out, Dee is more materialistic than political. For example, although Mrs. Johnson makes several statements throughout the story that suggest her admiration of Dee's defiant character, she also identifies incidents that highlight Dee's materialism and selfishness. When their first house burned down, Dee watched it burn while she stood under a tree with "a look of concentration" (465) rather than remorse. Mrs. Johnson knows that Dee hated their small,

Chase 5

dingy house, and she knows too that Dee was glad to see it destroyed. Furthermore, Walker acknowledges in the interview with Evelyn C. White that as she was writing the story, she imagined that Dee might even have set the fire that destroyed the house and scarred her sister. Even now, Dee is ashamed of the tin-roofed house her family lives in, and she has said that she would never bring her friends there. Although these examples indicate that Dee is materialistic and self-serving, they also show positive traits: pride and a strong will. Knowing that she will encounter strong opposition wherever she goes, she works to use her appearance to establish power. Thus, her desire for the quilt can be seen as an attempt to establish herself and her African-American culture in a society dominated by whites.

Refutation of opposing argument

Mrs. Johnson knows Dee wants the quilt, but she decides to give it to Maggie. According to literary critics Houston Baker and Charlotte Pierce-Baker, when Mrs. Johnson decides to give the quilt to Maggie, she is challenging Dee's understanding of her heritage. Unlike Dee, Mrs. Johnson recognizes that quilts signify "sacred generations of women who have made their own special kind of beauty separate from the traditional artistic world" (qtd. in Piedmont-Marton 45). According to Baker and Pierce-Baker, Mrs. Johnson realizes that her daughter Maggie, whom she has long dismissed because of her quiet nature and shyness, understands the true meaning of the quilt in a way that Dee never will (Piedmont-Marton 45). Unlike Dee, Maggie has paid close attention to the traditions and skills of her mother and grandmother: she has actually learned to quilt. More important, by staying with her mother instead of going to school, she has gotten to know her family. She poignantly underscores this fact when she tells her mother that Dee can have the quilt because she does not need it to remember her grandmother.

Analysis of Mrs. Johnson's final act

Chase 6

Conclusion

Even though Maggie's and Mrs. Johnson's understanding of heritage may be more emotionally profound than Dee's, it is important not to dismiss Dee's interest in elevating the quilt to the status of art. The political stakes of defining an object as art in the late 1960s and early 1970s were high, and the fight for equality went beyond basic civil rights. At the time the story was written, displaying the quilt would have been a political act—an act with important, positive results. The final message of "Everyday Use" may just be that an accurate understanding of the quilt (and, by extension, of African-American culture) requires both views—Maggie's and Mrs. Johnson's "everyday use" and Dee's elevation of the quilt to art.

Chase 7

Works Cited

Piedmont-Marton, Elisabeth. "An Overview of 'Everyday Use.'" *Short Stories for Students* 2 (1997): 42-45. *Literature Resource Center*. Web. 2 Apr. 2012.

Salaam, Kalamu Ya. "A Primer of the Black Arts Movement: Excerpts from *The Magic of Juju: An Appreciation of the Black Arts Movement*." *Black Renaissance/Renaissance Noire* (2002): 40-59. *Expanded Academic ASAP*. Web. 10 Apr. 2012.

Walker, Alice. "Alice Walker: Stitches in Time." Interview by Evelyn C. White. *The Wadsworth Original Film Series in Literature: "Everyday Use."* Dir. Bruce R. Schwartz. Wadsworth, 2005. DVD.

---. "Everyday Use." *Literature: Reading, Reacting, Writing*. Ed. Laurie G. Kirszner and Stephen R. Mandell. 8th ed. Boston: Wadsworth, 2013. 464-70. Print.

CHAPTER 25

# Writing in the Social Sciences

## Frequently Asked Questions



The **social sciences** include anthropology, business, criminal justice, economics, education, political science, psychology, social work, and sociology. When you approach an assignment in the social sciences, your purpose is often to study the behavior of individuals or groups. You may be seeking to understand causes; predict results; define a policy, habit, or trend; or analyze a problem.

Before you can consider a problem in the social sciences, you must develop a **hypothesis,** an educated guess about what you believe your research will suggest. Then, you can gather the data that will test that hypothesis. Data may be quantitative or qualitative. **Quantitative data** are numerical—the "countable" results of surveys and polls. **Qualitative data** are less exact and more descriptive—the results of interviews or observations, for example.

Many assignments in the social sciences call for responses to a problem. For this reason, a clear **problem statement** at the beginning of a piece of writing, such as a proposal or a case study, is necessary to define and guide the discussion. Not only does this statement keep the reader on track, but it also helps the writer stay focused. In this sense, a problem statement establishes the structure for the piece of writing and presents the rationale for the rest of the discussion.

## 25a Understanding Purpose, Audience, and Tone

Like writing assignments in the humanities, writing assignments in the social sciences can be *informal* or *formal.*

**Informal** writing assignments require you to examine ideas, phenomena, and data in the world around you. One example of an informal writing assignment is a personal experience essay, in which you are asked to relate your own observations of an event or an experience. Because you are being asked for your personal reactions, it is acceptable to use the first person (*I*) as well as a conversational tone.

**Formal** writing assignments—such as case studies, research essays, and proposals—use an objective tone and a technical vocabulary. These assignments often require you to examine similarities and differences between what you have observed and what you have read or to evaluate terms and concepts from your course readings and lectures. While the purpose of writing in the social sciences is often to **inform,** it may also be to **persuade**—for example, to propose changes in an after-school tutoring center or to convince readers that binge drinking is a problem on college campuses.

Sometimes your instructor will define an audience for your assignment—your classmates, a supervisor of a social agency, or a public official, for example—but at other times you have to come up with your own or assume that you are addressing a general audience of readers in your field.

**Close-Up USING THE PASSIVE VOICE**

Unlike writers in the humanities, writers in the social sciences often use the passive voice, particularly in the parts of the paper that describe the research methods. Passive voice allows writers to avoid the first person and to present their research in objective terms.

See 49d

## & 25b Collaborative Work

Collaborative writing is common in the social sciences. As a result, there are numerous possibilities for collaborative writing in social science courses. Students are routinely asked to collaborate on the writing of case studies, proposals, and research papers. Sometimes they meet as a group to brainstorm, developing ideas for study and sharing ideas about topics to explore. A collaborative writing group can also divide up writing tasks for a single project. For example, one person can write the abstract of a report, another the introduction, and another the description of the research. Finally, the group can meet to decide if a project is ready for submission or if it needs more work.

Collaborative groups can meet in person—in a classroom, in the library, or at the student union—or they can meet online in a chat room. Increasingly, social science instructors encourage groups to use Internet technology to facilitate collaboration. For example, a document can be posted on a wiki site where all members of the group can work on it together. Not only does this technology help students communicate, but it also prepares them for the workplace, where online collaboration is becoming the norm.

## 25c Writing Assignments

### 1 Personal Reaction Report

In some social science disciplines (particularly psychology, education, and sociology), you may be asked to write an informal **personal reaction report,** an account of a site visit or a visit with a professional who works in your area of study. In this kind of assignment, you record specific details about your experience. For example, students in a sociology class might report on a visit to a state correctional facility or to a homeless shelter.

#### *Assignment (Anthropology: Service Learning)*

Write a personal reaction report in which you describe your first visit to your service-learning field site. What expectations did you have? Record your initial impressions of the site: How did you feel as you were walking in? What were the first things you noticed? What surprises did you find?

#### *Sample Personal Reaction Report (Excerpt)*

Working with animals was my first choice for the service-learning part of this course. I have loved animals ever since I was a child. However, normally I interact with the pets in people's homes, so I was not accustomed to the behaviors of the affection-starved animals that I encountered at the Humane Society. Each animal has its own sad story. Each has its own personality traits as well. On my first day at the Humane Society, I met Barney, a dog with an interesting personality. He had a bright blue collar around his neck and was full of energy. During our 30-minute walk, he purposely walked around me and tangled me up in his leash. He repeated this "game" as often as I would allow him to, and he reacted well to affection. Because he wasn't hand-shy, I concluded that his owner probably had not abused him. Barney and I have already formed a close bond.

### 2 Book Review

Instructors in the social sciences may ask you to write a book review. A **book review** should include a summary to familiarize your audience with the book's content. It should also include your evaluation of the book and your analysis of its contribution to the discipline. Be sure to include the author, date, and title of the book in your first paragraph.

#### *Assignment (Political Science)*

Write a book review summarizing the content and commenting on the usefulness to the field of Steven Kelman's *Making Public Policy: A Hopeful*

*View of American Government*. (This book will be one of your sources for your group research project.) Reviews will be evaluated according to how well they demonstrate your understanding of the book, what insights they provide into your research topic, and how well they are written.

### *Sample Book Review (Excerpt)*

In the next section of his book, Kelman effectively explores the relationship between the Presidency and the bureaucracy. Rather than dividing the Executive and the bureaucracy into the Senior Executive Service and the Civil Service, Kelman limits his discussion to the Executive Office of the President (EOP) and direct political appointments.

Kelman's observations concerning the importance of organizational structure, ground rules, and operating tradition are key. Particularly significant is how organizational characteristics affect the flow of debate, information, and decision making. For example, when a congressional committee debates legislation, the consequences of different organizational structures become visible and are subject to change. When a committee chair excludes an issue from debate, however, the different organizational structures never become visible. According to Kelman, political decision makers may not even be conscious of the exclusion.

## 3 Case Study

Social science courses, especially psychology, sociology, and anthropology, frequently require **case studies** that focus on individuals or small groups. Case studies often describe a problem and suggest solutions or treatments. In psychology, social work, and education, case studies typically focus on individuals and their interaction with peers or with agency professionals.

### *Assignment (Psychology of the Family)*

Write a formal case study of the family you have been observing.

### *Sample Case Study*

**Family Profile**

The Newberg family consists of Tom and Tina and their children David (8), Angela (6), and Cristina (4).

**Problem**

Tom has been laid off from his automobile production-line job. Tina is not employed outside the home. They have a mortgage on their home as well as $10,000 in credit card debt.

The loss of income when Tom was laid off from his job caused a change in the economic status of the Newberg family. Initially, Tom tried to maintain his traditional family role, wanting to be the sole provider, while Tina continued to stay at home with their children. Both Tom and Tina saw no way to alleviate their financial difficulties. Both were heavy smokers, and this habit increased their expenses.

**Observations**

Tom spent so much time looking for a job that he had little time with his family—especially the children. Eventually, Tina borrowed money from her parents to start a door-to-door beauty products business. When this failed, she found a job driving a school bus, but it was only part time. Tom and Tina's financial situation severely strained the family. Even so, the couple made no plans for the future; they just kept hoping things would improve.

**Discussion**

Even when the Newbergs both managed to get full-time jobs, they could not maintain the lifestyle they were used to. Image is very important to Tom and Tina: they thought they had to look like a traditional family in order to have self-esteem. This is especially important to Tom. The prognosis for the Newberg family is not promising unless they make some changes. They have to learn to cooperate, set goals as a family, and share responsibilities. Both debt counseling and family counseling are strongly recommended.

## 4 Field Research Report

Social science instructors may ask you to write a **field research report.** Field research involves gathering information by observing people, places, or things. (It can also involve conducting an interview or carrying out a survey.) Field research reports often conform to guidelines established by your instructor, typically including how information was gathered, the information itself, and conclusions based on the information.

See 13c

### *Assignment (Anthropology)*

Groups of two or three students will engage in a firsthand observational exercise of present-day Philadelphia or its suburbs. Each group will walk along a major suburban or urban thoroughfare such as Lancaster Avenue or Market Street. While walking, group members should observe the shifting patterns of buildings as well as the landscape configurations. Beforehand, you will be given detailed maps and survey documents that will enable you to see the buildings and the property lines as they existed over a century ago. Then, in a two- to three-page paper, you will describe what you observe and discuss the changes that have taken place over the years—and, if possible, account for these changes.

### *Sample Field Research Report (Excerpt)*

Our group walked southwest on Buck Lane, a small street that runs perpendicular to Lancaster Avenue. As we walked away from Lancaster Avenue, The Haverford School was on our left. The school was built in 1901 on a 25-acre tract that was purchased from Howell Evans. As the years went by, the school's prestige increased, and the campus grew (see Figure 1).

On our right, the houses were small and well kept, not particularly fancy or on large lots. In 1881, almost all of the land on the right side of the road was owned by Michael Gallagher, who sold the land between 1900 and 1913 to the Kerrigan family. The Kerrigan family held the land until 1948, when it was divided into smaller subplots (in Figure 1, this tract is called the "Kerrigan Heir Plan").

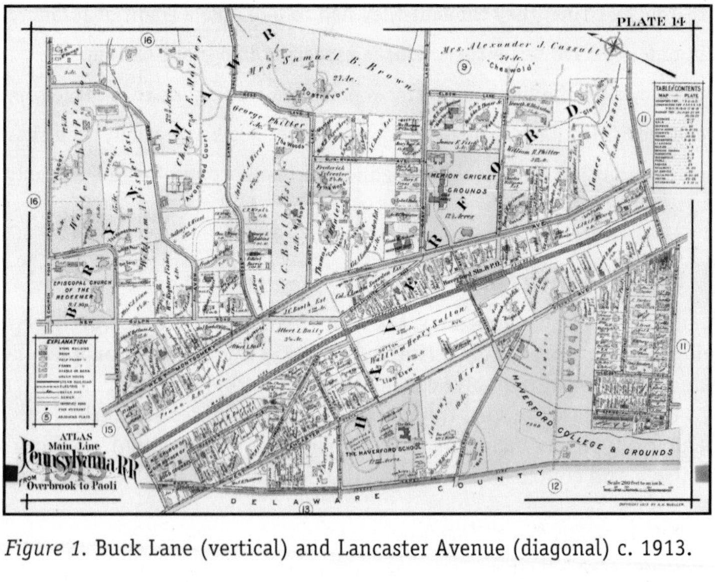




*Figure 1.* Buck Lane (vertical) and Lancaster Avenue (diagonal) c. 1913.

At the turn of the century, many wealthy people, like the Kerrigan family, moved to the western suburbs to escape the noise and congestion of Philadelphia, which was experiencing an industrial boom. The development of the Philadelphia and Western Railroad (currently the Norristown High-Speed Line) in 1907 gave these individuals easy and inexpensive transportation into the city. They built houses on large plots of land. Eventually, these tracts were divided and developed for the middle-class families who were moving into the area. However, a few wealthy families chose not to subdivide, and even today, their houses occupy large plots of land. The major trends that affected the development of the suburbs northwest of Philadelphia were the expansion of train lines and the growth of the middle class after World War II. As the area changed, many of the older wealthy families sold their estates and moved farther from the city.

## 5 Annotated Bibliography and Literature Review

Social science instructors may ask you to write an **annotated bibliography** in which you summarize and evaluate each of your research sources. You may also be asked to write a **literature review,** an essay in which you discuss the entries in your annotated bibliography and perhaps compare them. (The literature review is often part of a social science research paper.)

### *Assignment (Sociology)*

Research an issue that interests you and that has a significant impact on particular populations in your state. Then, compile an annotated bibliography of at least six sources. Finally, write a literature review that discusses these sources.

### *Sample Annotated Bibliography (Excerpt)*

Adams, J. R. (2010). Farm bill funding boosts FMNP. *National Association of Farmers' Market Nutrition Programs*. Retrieved from http://www.nafmnp.org. This article provides current information on the Farmers' Market Nutrition Program (FMNP), with particular emphasis on its legislative appropriation status. The author stresses the need for lobbying to keep the FMNP program alive.

### *Sample Literature Review (Excerpt)*

J. R. Adams (2010) discusses the successful efforts farmers and lobbyists have made in securing funding for the Farmers' Market Nutrition Program. For example, even though funding had originally been cut by half in the projected budget for 2010, this shortfall was corrected (Rosen, 2010). Farmers stand to benefit from this program and from the similar Seniors Farmers' Market Nutrition Program (SFMNP). Similarly, as S. Z. Greenberg et al. (2009) point out, these programs not only create a potential new market for farmers' products, but also may benefit from private grants to supplement government funding.

### 6 Proposal

A **proposal** is often the first stage of a research project. In a proposal, you define the scope and nature of the problem to be addressed, outline your research project, and suggest possible solutions. The proposal is where you make a convincing case for your research project.

### *Assignment (Psychology of Substance Abuse)*

Write a proposal to solve a problem associated with alcohol abuse. Each source you use—including Web sites, journal articles, monographs, and interviews—should be documented in APA style.

See 19a

### *Sample Proposal (Excerpt)*

**Statement of the Problem**

It is a fact that alcohol can impair coordination. The severity of this effect depends on an individual's Blood Alcohol Concentration (BAC), which is determined by the individual's weight, speed of alcohol consumption, and amount of alcohol consumed. If an individual's BAC is greater than .08, he or she can be charged with Driving Under the Influence (DUI).

As Figure 1 illustrates, the number of DUIs in Frewsdale is high, with 1067 DUI charges in the past 5 years. Of course, this number reflects only the individuals who were actually caught; the number of people driving with a BAC higher than .08 is probably much greater, as shown by

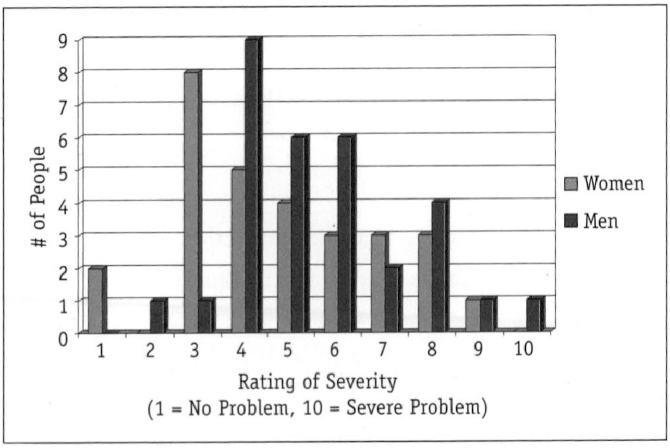




*Figure 1.* Drunk driving in Frewsdale.

our survey of Frewsdale University students, in which more than 80% of respondents—none of whom had ever received a DUI charge—indicated that they or someone they knew had driven drunk.

An alternative transportation method for people who have been drinking would greatly reduce the number of DUIs in Frewsdale. Furthermore, such a program would reduce the number of people who walk home alone late at night and potentially put themselves at risk.

To address this problem, we propose a safe-ride program aimed primarily at providing a free ride home on weekends (when people most frequently go out, as Figure 2 shows) for residents of Frewsdale who have been drinking.

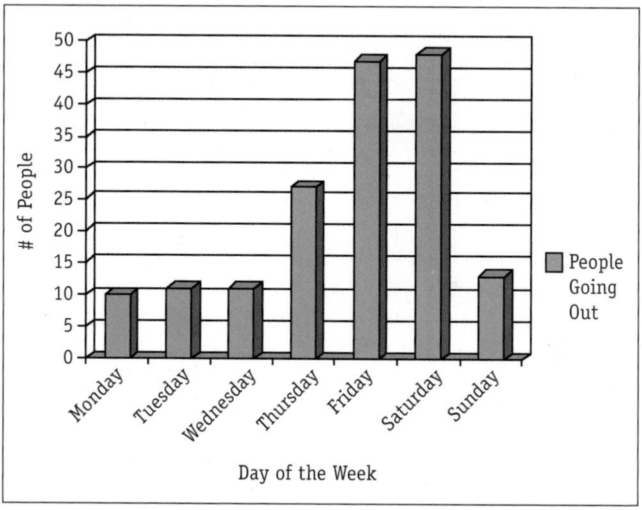




*Figure 2.* Nights people go out in Frewsdale.

## 25d Conventions of Style, Format, and Documentation

### 1 Style and Format

Because you are addressing specialists, you should use the specialized vocabulary of the discipline and, when you discuss charts and tables, you should use statistical terms, such as *mean, percentage,* and *chi square.* Keep in mind, however, that you should use plain language to explain what *percentages, means,* and *standard deviations* signify in terms of your analysis.

A social science research paper follows a specific format. For example, APA manuscript guidelines require a title page that includes a **running head** (if the paper is being submitted for publication), a **title,** and a **byline**

See 19b

(your name, school, and so on). Every page of the paper, including the title page, should have a **page header,** an abbreviated title and page number printed at the top. Social science papers also include **internal headings.** The body of the paper may present and discuss graphs, maps, photographs, flowcharts, or tables.

### 2 Documentation

See Ch. 19

Many of the journals in the various social science disciplines use APA documentation style.

## 25e Avoiding Plagiarism

See Ch. 17

When writing in the social sciences, it is important to avoid plagiarism by correctly documenting paraphrases, summaries, and quotations as well as the statistics and visuals of others that you use in your paper.

In addition, social scientists are bound by ethical considerations regarding the treatment of research subjects, the protection of privacy, and the granting of credit to those who have made substantial contributions to a research project.

## 25f Research Sources

Social scientists engage in both library and field research.

See 13c

In **library research,** social scientists consult print and electronic compilations of statistics, government documents, and newspaper articles, in addition to scholarly books and articles. In **field research,** social scientists conduct interviews and surveys and observe individuals and groups. Because so much of their data are quantitative, social scientists must know how to analyze statistics and how to read and interpret tables.

Social scientists may also review the literature on a topic to discover what research has already been done, or they may analyze research reports. Social scientists are particularly interested in case studies and published reports of surveys, opinion polls, interviews, experiments, and observations that may be useful in proving or disproving a theory.

Social scientists are expected to base their studies on the most current thinking surrounding a topic. For this reason, statistics must be up to date, and so researchers rely on electronic databases to locate the most recent scholarly journal articles and government publications.

See 13b

Some excellent databases and print indexes cover the literature of the social sciences. *Social Sciences Citation Index* is available online as part of the database *Web of Science*. Other databases and indexes cover specific disciplines within the social sciences. In addition to databases, the Internet may be very helpful to social scientists who are looking for government information, including census data, statistics, congressional reports, laws, and reports issued by government agencies.

### 1 Newspaper Articles

Newspaper articles are particularly good resources for research topics in political science, economics, and business. Useful sources of information from newspapers are *NewsBank, National Newspaper Index,* and *LexisNexis Academic.*

### 2 Reference Works

For information on reference works for specific social science disciplines, consult a reference librarian. For information on general reference works, **see 13a5.**

### 3 Government Documents

Government documents are important resources for social scientists because they contain complete and up-to-date facts and figures on a wide variety of subjects. Government documents can be located through the *Monthly Catalog,* which contains the list of documents (in print and electronic form) published each month. Other useful indexes include *The Congressional Information Service Index, The American Statistics Index,* and *The Index to U.S. Government Periodicals.*

The Web site <gpo.gov/fdsys> provides direct access to the documents published by the Government Printing Office for all three branches of government without the intermediate step of searching through the print *Monthly Catalog.* In addition, <thomas.loc.gov>, via the Library of Congress, is a good resource for federal legislative information and government documents.

### 4 Databases for Computer Searches

Some of the more widely used databases for social science disciplines are *Cendata; General BusinessFile ASAP; Social Sciences Citation Index; Social Sciences Index; PsycINFO; ERIC; Sociological Abstracts; Social Sciences Full Text; Science and Technology Abstracts; PAIS International; Population Bibliography; EconLit; ABI/INFORM; Management Contents; LexisNexis Academic;* and *Facts on File.* Additional databases for specific social science disciplines are listed in **13a3.**

### 5 Web Sites

For links to Web sites for specific social science disciplines, **see 13b4.**

### 6 Other Sources of Information

Interviews, surveys, and observations of the behavior of various groups and individuals are important nonlibrary sources for social science research.

CHAPTER 26

# Writing in the Natural and Applied Sciences

## Frequently Asked Questions



## 26a Understanding Purpose, Audience, and Tone

See Ch. 21

Writing assignments in the natural and applied sciences—for example, in courses in biology, chemistry, geology, astronomy, physics, engineering, nursing, and computer science—use a formal, objective tone and follow documentation guidelines such as those published by the Council of Science Editors (CSE).

Most scientific writing is aimed at readers who are familiar with the technical language and writing conventions of a particular scientific discipline, but occasionally it may be aimed at general readers. Its purpose is to report **empirical data** (data that are obtained through observations and experiments).

### Close-Up THE SCIENTIFIC METHOD

The scientific method relies on empirical data to explain and solve problems. After using secondary sources to research a problem, you gather and interpret information by following these steps:

1. Propose a **hypothesis** that makes a claim about the cause and effect of the problem.
2. Plan a research design and methodology.
3. Carry out the experiment, recording observations and data.
4. Analyze the results of the experiment, carefully comparing the initial hypothesis with the actual results.
5. Make recommendations for further experiments.

## 26b Collaborative Work

Much of the writing produced in the natural sciences is done collaboratively. Papers that appear in scientific journals frequently have multiple authors who have participated to varying degrees in the research and writing. Students in the natural sciences frequently collaborate on lab reports, abstracts, literature surveys, and research reports. In advanced courses, students may also work collaboratively on grant proposals and articles for possible publication in journals or in newspapers, magazines, and Web sites aimed at general readers. Writing is sometimes done in computer labs in an integrated computer environment that facilitates collaboration. Increasingly, however, students in the natural sciences are using wikis in order to collaborate on planning, structuring, writing, and revising and editing texts.

## 26c Writing Assignments

### 1 Observation

Some science instructors may ask you to write about and analyze your own observations of the natural world. This is one of the few assignments in the natural and applied sciences in which you will be encouraged to use the first person (*I*). In this type of assignment, you first record your observations (using scientific terminology where necessary) and then analyze the phenomena you describe.

#### *Assignment (Ecology)*

Write a report in which you describe a natural setting and then discuss the environmental impact of human beings on that setting.

#### *Sample Observation (Excerpt)*

Lake Wenatchee, part of the Alpine Lakes, is in the Wenatchee National Forest, where over 700 small freshwater lakes are scattered throughout the central Cascade region. The average annual precipitation is 40 inches; this heavy rainfall accounts for the mixed conifers—Douglas firs, grand firs, and cedars—that thrive there. The rain-shadow effect also causes the soils in the region to be rich in organic materials as well as in basalt, pumice, and volcanic ash. However, human activity—clear-cutting of old-growth forest, damming of rivers, and fire suppression—is altering the area's natural ecology. These activities lead to a build-up of debris, a higher number of forest fires, severe soil erosion, and the endangerment of local species of animals and fish.

While climbing one part of a barely distinguishable trail, I noticed a very large area on the side of the mountain that had no trees. This was an alarming sign. Because the terrain is sloped, clear-cutting the trees causes extreme soil erosion, including mudslides. Clear-cutting also destroys animal habitats, so many species of owl, woodpecker, and squirrel will very likely be threatened.

## 2 Biographical Report

In a science or math course, an instructor may ask you to write a report about a historical figure. When writing your essay, try to relate the information you find about your subject to the work you have been doing in the course—for example, you might consider how Mendel's experiments with genetics relate to your class's work on heredity.

### *Assignment (Geometry)*

Select a figure whose life and work we have discussed in class. Then, write a biographical essay in which you summarize his or her contributions to geometry.

### *Sample Biographical Report (Excerpt)*

Jean-Victor Poncelet was born in Metz, northeastern France, in July 1788. He studied calculus with Gaspard Monge at the École Polytechnique and then joined the army as a lieutenant of engineers, following Napoleon to Russia. While he was a prisoner of war in Saratoff on the River Volga, he began researching projective geometry, investigating the projective properties of figures later in his great work *Traité des Propriétés Projectives des Figures*.

Projective geometry is a branch of geometry concerned with properties of geometric figures that retain their character. The basic elements of projective geometry are points, lines, and planes. The concept of parallel does not exist in projective geometry because any pair of distinct lines intersects in a point, and if these lines are parallel in the sense of Euclidean geometry, then their point of intersection is at infinity.

## 3 Abstract

An **abstract**—a concise technical summary of a journal article—is a standard part of many assignments in the natural sciences. Abstracts are usually about two hundred words long. In the natural sciences, the purpose of an abstract is to summarize the goals, methods, and results of the research.

You begin writing an abstract after you have finished writing your paper. When writing an abstract, follow the organization of your paper, devoting a sentence or two to each of its major sections. State the purpose, the method of research, results, and conclusions in the order in which they appear in the paper, but include only essential information. Keep in mind that abstracts do not include quotations or paraphrases.

The following abstract was written as part of the assignment on page 420.

### *Sample Abstract*

This project used Wisconsin Fast Plants to determine the effect of gibberellic acid on plants. Gibberellic acid is a growth hormone that stimulates a plant to grow taller by elongation of internode length. The research tested the hypothesis that plants that are treated with gibberellic acid will grow taller than plants that are untreated, and the internode length on treated plants will be longer than that on untreated plants. Results supported this hypothesis: the internode length on treated plants was longer than that on untreated plants. Furthermore, even the dwarf plants that were treated with gibberellic acid grew longer, reaching almost the same height as the control standard plants by the last day of measurement. Therefore, the results of this experiment indicate that gibberellic acid can stimulate the growth of plants by elongation of internode length, though not by internode number.

## 4 Literature Survey

Literature surveys are common in the sciences, often appearing as a section of a proposal or as part of a report or a research paper. A **literature survey** summarizes a number of studies and sometimes compares and contrasts them. By doing so, the literature survey provides a theoretical context for the paper's discussion.

Sometimes, however, a literature survey can be a paper on its own, and in this case it makes an argument about how to view the literature. In other words, a literature review paper doesn't simply survey the literature but also evaluates it.

Keep in mind that in the natural sciences *literature* means peer-reviewed primary sources. A literature review most often comments on **primary research literature**—articles reporting the results of original research. Typically, literature reviews do not discuss **secondary sources,** articles that comment on the work of others. See 14a

A literature survey should have a formal tone and be aimed at readers who know the field. The purpose of a literature survey is to give these readers an overview of a range of scholarly publications about a subject. Your primary focus should be on the most current research available.

### *Assignment (Biology)*

Research an aspect of plant biology, and present your findings in a report that contains the following sections: Abstract, Introduction, Literature Survey, Materials, Methods, Results, Discussion, Conclusions, Reference List, and Appendix (if necessary).

### *Sample Literature Survey (Excerpt)*

The cell *Myxococcus xanthus* responds to starvation by initiating a cycle that culminates with the cell forming spore-filled fruiting bodies. This developmental cycle, which is dependent upon changes in gene expression, ensures cell sporulation at the appropriate time and place. Thousands of cells are affected by this process. Recent studies strongly suggest that NtrC-like activators are a crucial component of the complex regulatory controls of *M. xanthus'* developmental program. Twelve NtrC activators were found to be most important in the process.[1] These findings led to further research that examined the specific developmental moments at which NtrC proteins activate specific sets of genes throughout the process.[2] In addition, Garza and others[3] identified two inductive components of the early part of the developmental process.

References

1. Gorski L, Kaiser D. Targeted mutagenesis of $\sigma^{54}$ activator proteins in *Myxococcus xanthus*. J Bacteriol. 2010;180:5896-5905.
2. Keseler IM, Kaiser D. An early A-signal-dependent gene in *Myxococcus xanthus* has a $\sigma^{54}$-like promoter. J Bacteriol. 2007;177:4638-4644.
3. Garza AG, Pollack JS, Harris BZ, Lee A, Keseler IM, Licking EF, Singer M. SdeK is required for early fruiting body development in *Myxococcus xanthus*. J Bacteriol. 2010;180:4628-4637.

## 5 Lab Report

The **lab report** is one of the most frequently assigned writing tasks in the sciences. Lab reports typically contain the following sections: *Purpose, Apparatus, Method, Procedure, Data, Results,* and *Conclusion*. However, not every section will be necessary for every experiment, and some experiments may require additional components, such as an abstract or a reference list. In addition, lab reports may include tables, charts, graphs, and diagrams. The format for a lab report is usually defined by a course's lab manual.

## 26d Conventions of Style, Format, and Documentation

### 1 Style and Format

Because writing in the sciences focuses on experiments, not on those conducting the experiments, writers often use the passive voice.

Another stylistic convention concerns verb tense: a conclusion or a statement of generally accepted fact should be in the present tense ("Objects in motion *tend* to stay in motion"); a summary of a study, however, should be in the past tense ("Watson and Crick *discovered* the structure of DNA"). Finally, note that direct quotations are seldom used in scientific papers.

Keep in mind that each scientific discipline prescribes its own formats for **tables** and other visuals and the way they are to be presented. See 28d1

Remember that different scientific journals may use different paper formats. For example, the *Journal of Immunology* might have a format different from that of the *Journal of Parasitology*. Your instructor may ask you to prepare your paper according to the style sheet of a particular journal to which you could submit your work. Although publication may seem a remote possibility to you, following a style sheet reminds you that writing in the sciences involves writing for a specific audience.

### 2 Documentation

Citation systems (documentation styles) within the sciences vary from one scientific discipline to another; even within a given discipline, the citation system may vary from one journal to another. For this reason, ask your instructor which system is required.

## 26e Avoiding Plagiarism

In the sciences, it is especially important to acknowledge the work of others who contributed to your research results. If many people contribute to a research project, the work of each one must be properly cited. Falsifying data or using the experimental results, computer codes, chemical formulas, graphs, images, ideas, or words of others without proper acknowledgment is particularly serious because it undermines the integrity of your work.

If you need more information about what constitutes **plagiarism** in the sciences or how to cite the work of individual collaborators in a research project, be sure to check with your instructor. See Ch. 17

## 26f Research Sources

Although much scientific research takes place in the laboratory or in the natural world, it is also important that scientists know how to do library research. Literature surveys allow scientists to discover what research has already been done. Building on this research, they can conduct meaningful experiments that prove or disprove a theory or solve a problem. Much of this research is collaborative. It is not uncommon for several people to work on different aspects of a research problem in the laboratory or in the library and then jointly report on the results.

Scientists must always use the most current information available. Although books may provide background material, scholarly journal articles, conference proceedings, technical reports, and research reports provide the most up-to-date information.

Numerous comprehensive databases cover the sciences. *Science Citation Index* covers all the natural and applied sciences. Others cover specific disciplines: *PubMed* (medicine), *Biological Abstracts* (biology), and *Chemical Abstracts* (chemistry) are examples of specialized databases.

### 1 Reference Works

For information on reference works for specific natural and applied science disciplines, consult a reference librarian. For information on general reference works, **see 13a5.**

### 2 Databases for Computer Searches

Helpful databases for research in the sciences include: *Agricola; Aquatic Sciences and Fisheries Abstracts; Aquatic Sciences Set; Columbia Earthscape; CAB Abstracts; CINAHL; Compendex; NTIS; Inspec; PubMed; MathSciNet; Life Sciences Collection; GEOREF; Environmental Sciences and Pollution Management; Science Citation Index Expanded; Wildlife and Ecology Studies Worldwide; GEOBASE;* and *Zoological Record Plus.* Check with a reference librarian about the availability of these and other databases in your library. Additional databases for specific natural and applied science disciplines are listed in **13a3.**

### 3 Web Sites

For links to Web sites for specific natural and applied science disciplines, **see 13b4.**

### 4 Other Sources of Information

Opportunities for research outside the library vary widely because of the many ways in which scientists can gather information. In agronomy, for example, researchers collect soil samples; in toxicology, they test air or water quality; and in chemistry, they conduct experiments to identify unknown substances. Scientists also conduct surveys. And, of course, the Internet is an important source of up-to-date scientific information.

PART 7

# Creating Documents in a Digital Age

CHAPTER 27

# Writing in a Digital Environment

## Frequently Asked Questions



In email, social networking sites, computerized classroom environments, blogs, wikis, and chat rooms, electronic communication occurs daily on a wide variety of topics. Because of the nature of the Internet, online communication is somewhat different from print communication. In order to write effectively for an online audience, you should be aware of the demands of writing in an electronic environment.

## 27a Considering Audience and Purpose

The most obvious difference between electronic communication and print communication is the nature of the **audience.** Audiences for print documents are relatively passive: they read a discussion from beginning to end, form their own ideas about it, and then stop. Depending on the writing situation, however, audiences for electronic documents often respond differently. Although in some cases readers may be passive, in other cases they can be quite active, posting and emailing responses and directly communicating with the writer (sometimes in real time) as well as with one another.

The **purpose** of electronic communication may sometimes be different from that of print communication. Unlike print documents, which appear as carefully crafted finished products, electronic documents may be written in immediate response to other people's arguments or ideas. In fact, by including links to a writer's email address or to a blog, some online documents are works in progress, encouraging readers to respond—or, in the case of wikis, to add or edit content. For this reason, in addition to trying to inform or persuade, the purpose of electronic documents may also be to support, refute, react, clarify, expand, or to elicit a response.

Increasingly, the line between print and electronic documents is blurring. for one thing, all different types of writing are now being published online. For example, scholarly articles are often published in online-only journals, and news stories appear both in print and online. When a print article is published online, it usually includes some Web-specific features, such as links to other articles or streaming video. In addition, some distinctly online formats, such as blogs, are increasingly becoming conduits for a wide range of writing—some of it quite formal. In any case, as online writing becomes the norm, writers need to understand the advantages that this medium offers.

## 27b Writing in a Wired Classroom

Much of the writing you do in a wired classroom involves collaboration, a process in which more than one person contributes to the creation of a document. In some cases, students write a draft of a paper and then post it or distribute it electronically to members of a peer-editing group, who then make revision suggestions. Comments can be sent via email or they can be inserted into the document with *Microsoft Word*'s Comment tool or with Track Changes. In other cases, students meet in groups and jointly contribute to the prewriting, drafting, and revision and editing of an entire document. See 27c

Central to this type of instruction is communication between students and between instructors and students. With **synchronous communication,** all parties involved in the communication process are online at the same time and can be involved in a real-time conversation. Chatrooms, instant messaging, and texting are examples of synchronous communication. With **asynchronous communication,** there is a delay between the time a message is sent and the time it is received. Asynchronous exchanges occur with email, blogs, wikis, Web forums, and discussion groups.

Increasingly—both in distance-learning situations and in traditional classrooms—instructors are using the Internet as well as specific Web-based technology to teach writing. Some of the most popular tools that students use to create Web-based content in an electronic writing environment are discussed in the pages that follow.

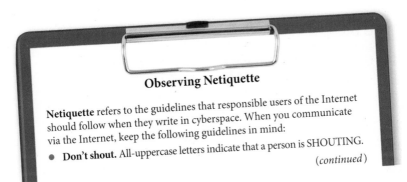

### Observing Netiquette

**Netiquette** refers to the guidelines that responsible users of the Internet should follow when they write in cyberspace. When you communicate via the Internet, keep the following guidelines in mind:

- **Don't shout.** All-uppercase letters indicate that a person is SHOUTING.

*(continued)*

**Observing Netiquette** *(continued)*

- **Watch your tone.** Make sure you send the message you actually intend to send. What might seem humorous to you may seem disrespectful to someone else.
- **Be careful what you write.** Remember, once you hit *Send*, it is often too late to call the message back. Be sure to consider carefully what you have written.
- **Don't flame.** When you flame, you send an insulting electronic message. This tactic is not only immature, but also rude and annoying.
- **Make sure you use the correct electronic address.** Be certain that your message goes to the right person. Nothing is more embarrassing than sending an email to the wrong address.
- **Use your computer ethically and responsibly.** Don't use computer labs for personal communications or for entertainment. Not only is this a misuse of the facility but it also ties up equipment that others may be waiting to use.

## 1 Using Email

Email enables you to exchange ideas with classmates, ask questions of your instructors, and communicate with the writing center or other campus services. You can insert email links in Web documents, and you can transfer files as email attachments from one computer to another. In many classes, writing assignments are submitted as email attachments.

CHECKLIST

**Writing Emails**

Although personal email tends to be extremely informal, email to classmates and instructors should be more formal. For academic and public writing, follow these guidelines:

- ❑ **Include your actual name with your email.** Campus email addresses don't always contain easily identifiable names.
- ❑ **Write in complete sentences.** Avoid the slang, imprecise diction, abbreviations, and emoticons that are commonplace in personal emails.
- ❑ **Include a subject line that clearly identifies your content.** If your subject line is vague, your email may be deleted without being read.
- ❑ **Make your email as short as possible.** Because most emails are read on the screen, long discussions are difficult to follow.
- ❑ **Use short paragraphs.** If your email message is more than five or six lines long, divide it into paragraphs, and leave extra space between paragraphs.

- ❑ **Do not use text slang or abbreviations.** These terms may be appropriate for your friends, but they are absolutely out of place in an email to an instructor. When you write to your instructors, you should maintain a certain level of formality. For example, begin your emails with "Dear Professor ____________," not "Hey Prof" or "Doc."
- ❑ **Edit and proofread before you send your email.** Look carefully for typos and other errors that will undermine your credibility.
- ❑ **Check your routing list.** Be careful not to send your email to unintended recipients.
- ❑ **Respect other people's privacy.** Don't forward an email unless you have the permission of the sender.

**Close-Up EMAIL ADDRESSES**

Avoid using an email address that is cute or witty or that contains puns or double entendres. Although it may be fine for your friends, this kind of address is not appropriate for the classroom or for a résumé or job application letter.

## 2 Using Blogs

A **blog** (short for Web log) is like an online personal journal. Most blogs offer commentary, news, or personal reactions—usually presented in reverse chronological order, with the most recent entry first. Blogs can also function as online diaries, communicating the personal views of the author.

Blogs are not limited to text; they can contain photographs, videos, music, audio, and personal artwork as well as links to Web sites. Most course management systems (such as *Blackboard, Moodle,* and *Angel*) make it easy for instructors or students to create a blog and post comments. Although many blogs are open to everyone, some are password protected.

On a class blog, students can post informal responses to readings and class discussions, and they can also brainstorm or try out ideas there before they write. Blogs also give students a chance to get comments from other students who read and react to their posts.

The following excerpt shows a post and two comments on a class blog for a first-year writing course. The student posted her draft on the course Web site and received comments from several students. These comments, along with advice in an email from her instructor, helped her to revise her paper.

**Wednesday, September 26, 2012**

***The Omnivore's Dilemma*** **by Michael Pollan**

In an excerpt from his book *The Omnivore's Dilemma,* Michael Pollan discusses the drinking habits of nineteenth-century Americans and makes a connection between the cause of this "national drinking binge" and the factors behind our twenty-first-century unhealthy diets. In both cases, he blames the overproduction of grain by American farmers. He links nineteenth-century overproduction of corn and the current overproduction of grain with various social crises. Although there are certainly other causes of our current problems with obesity, particularly among young children, Pollan's analogy makes sense.

Posted by Julie at 7:14 PM

**2 COMMENTS:**

**Alison said . . .**
You did a good job of summarizing Pollan's main points in that part of the book. But I think you could give more details about the "various social crises" Pollan is writing about. I feel like I need to know what they are to understand why he's writing about them in the first place. Maybe use a quote here?

**Jeremy said . . .**
My response to Pollan was like yours, but at the end I gave more of an evaluation of Pollan's book, I think. Yours just ends with "Pollan's analogy makes sense," and I guess I want to know why you think it makes sense, and why it's important. I'm thinking you could just add another sentence that kind of sums things up—and explains your opinion of the book.

CHECKLIST

## Writing a Blog

When writing a blog, keep the following guidelines in mind:

- ❑ **Write about what matters to you.** Don't write just to fill up space; write about ideas that are important to you.
- ❑ **Don't use clichés.** Try to use original, effective language. Don't litter your blog with tired, overused expressions.
- ❑ **Get to the point.** The point of a blog is to communicate ideas quickly and efficiently. Focus each blog post on one subject, and use short paragraphs.
- ❑ **Use multimedia and links.** Using multimedia (pictures, video, audio, or any other medium) is a good way to break up text. Links enable you to give your readers more information. However don't include too many links because they will distract readers from your main point.

### 3 Using Wikis

Unlike a blog, which is created by an individual and does not allow visitors to edit the posted content, a **wiki** (Hawaiian for *fast*) is a Web site that allows users to add, remove, or change content. The best-known wiki is *Wikipedia*, the online encyclopedia.

In the writing classroom, wikis are used for collaborative writing. They allow students to engage in peer review and to add (or delete) content. Groups of students use wikis to plan projects and to compile class notes. Wiki sites also enable students to view the history of a revision and to compare the relative merits of various drafts of a paper. In research projects, wikis allow students to collaborate on developing research questions, to exchange hyperlinks, to share bibliographical information, to collaborate on drafts of their papers, and to get help with documentation.

CHECKLIST

**Using a Wiki**

When working on a wiki, keep the following guidelines in mind:

- ❑ **Be constructive.** Be sure your suggestions are useful. Your purpose is to help other students, not to show off how much you know.
- ❑ **Avoid slang and abbreviations.** Make sure you write in a way that is easy to understand.
- ❑ **Do not delete the work of others.** Don't delete other students' writing unless it is absolutely necessary.
- ❑ **Don't overedit.** Be sure your edits actually improve the text's content and style.
- ❑ **Keep the assignment in mind.** Be sure your edits reflect the assignment's purpose.
- ❑ **Proofread before you hit Enter.** Make sure your work is accurate, grammatical, and spelled and punctuated correctly before you post it.

### 4 Using Discussion Lists

**Discussion lists,** electronic mailing lists to which users must subscribe, enable individuals to communicate with groups of people interested in particular topics. (Many schools, and even individual courses, have discussion lists.) Subscribers to a discussion list send emails to a main email address, and these messages are routed to all members of the group. Discussion lists can be especially useful in composition classes, permitting students to post comments on reading assignments as well as to discuss other subjects with the entire class.

### 5 Using Newsgroups

Like discussion lists, **newsgroups** are sites where users exchange ideas. Unlike discussion list messages, which are sent as email, newsgroup messages are collected on the Usenet system, a global collection of news servers, where anyone who subscribes can access them. In a sense, newsgroups function as gigantic bulletin boards where users post messages that others read and respond to. Thus, newsgroups can provide specific information as well as suggestions about where to look for specific information.

Some composition instructors establish newsgroups for their classes. Students access the newsgroup to get messages from their classmates or to download papers and assignments. An advantage of newsgroups is that messages are posted and downloaded only when the need arises, so they don't take up space in students' email files.

## 6 Using Podcasts

Originally, the term **podcast** referred to material that could be downloaded to Apple's iPod. Now, however, it refers to any audio broadcast that has been converted to an MP3 or similar format for playback on the Internet. You can access a podcast with a computer, with an iPad or iPhone, or with an MP3 playback device.

Podcasting is becoming increasingly common in college classrooms. On the most basic level, instructors podcast class lectures that students can access at their leisure. Instructors also use podcasts to present commentary on students' writing, to distribute supplementary material such as audio recordings or speeches, to record student presentations, or to communicate class information or news. Students may also be asked to analyze podcasts of political speeches, radio programs, or short stories from radio programs such as National Public Radio's *Selected Shorts*. Some instructors even ask students to make their own podcasts. For example, students can read their own essays and add sound clips or visual files.

CHECKLIST

### Producing a Podcast

When producing a podcast, keep the following guidelines in mind:

- ❑ **Consider your purpose and audience.** Just as you would for any other oral presentation, consider your purpose and your audience, and decide on the main point you want to make.
- ❑ **Consider the form of your podcast.** Decide in advance what form your podcast will take. For example, will it be a monologue, an interview, or a series of interviews connected by commentary?
- ❑ **Write a script.** Make presentation notes, and then revise and edit them into a script that will guide you through your podcast. Be sure to rehearse.
- ❑ **Get access to the equipment you need.** A good podcast requires the right equipment—a video camera, a microphone, and something to record onto (most likely, a computer). Find out if there is a campus facility that has the equipment you'll need to produce a high-quality podcast.
- ❑ **Publish your podcast.** Find out how to publish your podcast. Most likely, your instructor will want you to use *Blackboard* or some other course management software package to make your podcast available to others.

### 7 Using *Twitter* and *Facebook*

Some instructors use *Twitter* as a tool to teach writing. Because tweets have a one-hundred-and-forty character limit, they force students to be concise. As a result, in some writing classes, instructors ask students to tweet their thesis statements to the class. This exercise encourages students to state the thesis in clear, concise language. In addition, instructors can use *Twitter* as an easy way to get in touch with students (*Don't forget. Class cancelled tomorrow.*) and to reinforce important course concepts (*Your arguments must be supported by evidence. Look out for logical fallacies.*).

Some instructors form *Facebook* groups and post links to Web sites, documents, and other links on the group pages. Students can ask questions about class assignments and discuss topics that interest them. Joining these groups is usually optional because some students have concerns about *Facebook*'s privacy policies.

## 27c Writing Collaboratively Online

As you already know, **writing collaboratively** means creating a piece of writing that has more than one author. Every time you post a written passage and get feedback from a member of a class, you are engaging in collaborative writing. (In fact, when your instructor writes comments on a rough draft of an essay or discusses your work with you in conference, he or she is collaborating with you.) Digital writing environments present special opportunities for collaboration. For example, if your writing class has an online component, your instructor has most likely set up a virtual space where writing can be posted and commented on. In addition, electronic tools such as email, text messages, and blogs allow for collaboration at every stage of the writing process. &

### 1 Peer Review

Participating in peer review online has a number of advantages. You can easily exchange papers with members of a group or even with the entire class, and you can get feedback on your work from a number of people. If you are working on a group project, you do not have to arrange meetings or travel to campus. In fact, most of your collaborative activities can take place in front of your computer. In many cases, you can get information from classmates at any time simply by posting a message on an electronic bulletin board or by sending an email. Finally, because most of your communications are archived, you will usually have a record of your drafts and your correspondence. See 6c2

Although online writing environments present unique opportunities for collaboration, they also present challenges. Because feedback can come from so many different sources—for example, from blogs, chat rooms, and wikis as well as from editorial suggestions made with *Word*'s Comment tool—it is easy to become overwhelmed by your classmates' comments and suggestions. For this reason, it is extremely important to keep track of the various drafts of your essay and to keep your own ideas separate from the comments you get in response to your essay.

One way to avoid confusion is to think carefully before you set up files for any writing project that will be peer reviewed. When you save a draft of your essay (or any other document related to your writing—brainstorming notes, for example), make sure you clearly label and date it—and possibly even number it. In addition, save all emails you receive from members of your peer-review group in files that contain the name of the assignment and the date. Even if your course management program archives and categorizes all discussion board communication into threads, it is a good idea to download and file important messages.

If for some reason you need to compare two drafts of a paper, use the Track Changes "Compare Versions" tool. Everything that was deleted will be shaded, and everything that has been changed will be highlighted. Some document management systems—*Writeboard,* for example—allow you to access every version of a piece of writing that you have saved. This feature enables you to revise and edit a document without losing an earlier version that might be better.

### 2 Group Projects

See 32c–d

Sometimes you may be assigned to a group or team to work together on a writing project—for example, a proposal, a **brochure**, a **flyer**, or even a Web page. When you work online as part of a group, you follow many of the same procedures that you do in any online collaboration. In addition, you follow procedures that are specifically tailored to working as a group. As you set up and organize your group, keep the following advice in mind:

- **Decide how your group will meet.** Will you exchange comments in a chat room or post comments on a discussion board? (Often, your instructor will make this decision for you, but sometimes you will have to decide for yourself.) Some instant message and chat room technologies allow multiuser discussions and enable you to record and save transcripts of discussions for use later.
- **Divide tasks.** Make sure each member of the group knows exactly what his or her role is. For example, one person might be responsible for coordinating the project, another for finding information, another for finding visuals, another for writing, and still another for revising and editing.
- **Determine how you will collaborate.** Will you send drafts to each other as email attachments? Will you work on a wiki site? Or, will you use some other method?
- **Keep a list of email and phone numbers.** Set up an email group so that you can easily communicate with everyone at the same time.

- **Set up files to store communications.** Make sure you keep a file (or files) of all communications sent and received from members of the group.
- **Agree on technology.** Make sure everyone is using compatible technology. For example, make sure everyone is using the same version of *Word*. In addition, if you are using a tool such as a wiki, make sure that all members of the group understand how it works.
- **Decide on editing guidelines in advance.** To avoid confusion, agree on a consistent way to respond to writing—for example, offering suggestions with *Word*'s Comment tool.
- **Set up a realistic schedule.** Be sure to set up a schedule that includes deadlines and due dates, and be sure each person understands his or her responsibilities and is willing (and able) to meet deadlines.
- **Agree on specific dates for checking progress.** Check in with one another periodically to make sure you are all on schedule. Don't let a missed deadline take the group by surprise.
- **Get your instructor's approval.** Before you begin working on your group project, make sure your instructor approves of your plans.

CHAPTER 28

# Designing Effective Documents

## Frequently Asked Questions



**Document design** is a set of guidelines that help you determine how to design a piece of written work so that it communicates your ideas clearly and effectively. Although formatting conventions—for example, how tables and charts are constructed and how information is arranged on a title page—may differ from discipline to discipline, all well-designed documents share the same general characteristics: *an effective format, clear headings, useful lists,* and *helpful visuals.*

## 28a Creating an Effective Visual Format

An effective document contains visual cues that help readers find, read, and interpret information on a page. For example, wide margins can give a page a balanced, uncluttered appearance; white space can break up a long discussion; and a distinctive type size and typeface can make a word or phrase stand out on a page.

### 1 Margins

**Margins** frame a page and keep it from looking overcrowded. Because long lines of text can overwhelm readers and make a document difficult to read, every page should have margins. Different disciplines have somewhat different specifications concerning margins. For example, MLA style requires a one-inch margin at the top, bottom, and sides of a paper. APA style calls for *at least* a one-inch margin on all sides of a paper. CSE style, however, does not specify a style for an undergraduate paper. Because conventions vary from discipline to discipline, before you type a paper for a course, you should be familiar with your instructor's formatting guidelines.

Except for documents such as flyers and brochures, where you might want to isolate blocks of text for emphasis, you should **justify** (uniformly align, except for paragraph indentations) the left-hand margin. You should leave a ragged edge on the right because fully justified documents (those whose words are aligned evenly on both the right and left margins) are more difficult to read.

### 2 White Space

**White space** is the area of a page that is intentionally left blank. Used effectively, white space can isolate material and focus a reader's attention on it. You can use white space around a block of text—a paragraph or a section, for example—or around visuals such as charts, graphs, and photographs. White space can eliminate clutter, break a discussion into manageable chunks, and help readers process information more easily.

#### Close-Up BORDERS, HORIZONTAL RULES, AND SHADING

Your word-processing program enables you to create borders, horizontal rules, and shaded areas of text. Border and shading options are usually found under the Format menu (or in the Formatting Palette). With these features, you can select line style, thickness, and color and adjust white space, boxed text, and the degree of shading. Keep in mind that these features should be used only when appropriate, so check with your instructor.

## 3 Color

**Color** (when used in moderation) can help to emphasize and clarify information while making it visually appealing. For example, color can draw attention to certain items in a document and show their connections to other items. In addition to using color to emphasize information, you can use a color scheme to distinguish certain types of information. For example, titles can be one color and subheadings can be another, complementary color. (You can also use color to differentiate the segments of a chart or the bars of a graph.) Software applications, including *Microsoft Word* and *PowerPoint*, contain templates (such as the one shown in Figure 28.1) that make it easy for you to choose a color scheme of your own.

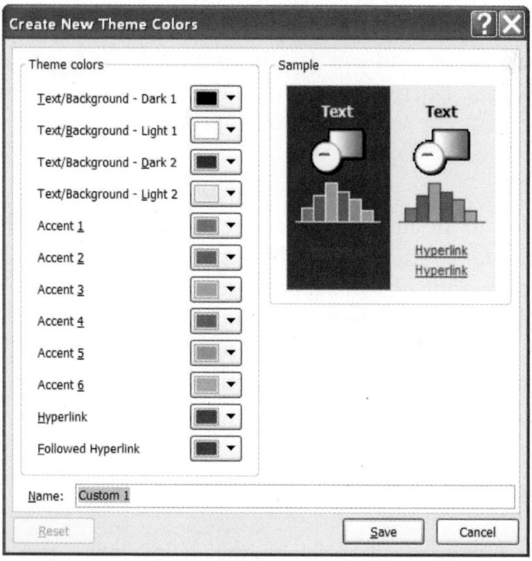


FIGURE 28.1 *Microsoft PowerPoint* color scheme menu.


Remember that color, when used carefully, can greatly enhance the effectiveness of your documents. For example, studies have shown that judicious use of color in a document increases readers' attention spans as well as their recall of information. Conversely, using color haphazardly or using too many colors will confuse readers and detract from the visual emphasis.

## 4 Typeface and Type Size

Your computer gives you a wide variety of typefaces and type sizes (measured in **points**) from which to choose.

**Typefaces** are distinctively designed sets of letters, numbers, and punctuation marks. The typeface you choose should be suitable for your purpose and audience. In your academic writing, avoid fancy or elaborate typefaces—script or old English, for example—that call attention to themselves and distract readers. Instead, select a typeface that is simple and direct—Cambria, Times New Roman, or Arial, for example. In nonacademic documents—such as Web pages and flyers—decorative typefaces may be used to emphasize information or attract a reader's attention.

The use of some type styles (*italics,* **boldface,** and so on) is a matter of convention. For example, most style guides (MLA, APA, and so on) require italics for the title of a book. Italics are also used when a word is referred to as a word (for example, "the word *juxtapose*"). Boldface is commonly used to set off an important term or the major headings of a report. When you use type styles for headings it is important to be consistent—for example, to use boldface for all corresponding headings, not just for some.

See Ch. 59

You also have a wide variety of **type sizes** available to you. For most of your academic papers, you will use 10- or 12-point type (headings will sometimes be larger). Documents such as advertisements, brochures, and Web pages, however, may require a variety of type sizes.

### 5 Line Spacing

**Line spacing** refers to the amount of space between the lines of a document. If the lines are too far apart, the text will seem to lack cohesion; if the lines are too close together, the text will appear crowded and be difficult to read. The type of writing you do determines the line spacing. For example, the paragraphs of business letters, memos, and some reports are usually single-spaced and separated by a double space, but the paragraphs of academic papers are usually double-spaced.

## 28b Using Headings

Used effectively, **headings** act as signals that help readers process information, and they also break up a text, making it inviting and easy to read. In addition, headings add a sense of structure and organization to a document. Because different academic disciplines have different requirements concerning headings, you should consult the appropriate style manual (or your instructor) before inserting headings in a paper.

### 1 Number of Headings

The number of headings you use depends on the document. A long, complicated document will need more headings than a shorter, less complicated one. Keep in mind that too few headings may not be of much use, but too many headings will make your document look like an outline.

### 2 Phrasing

Headings should be brief, informative, and to the point. They can be single words—**Summary** or **Introduction**, for example—or they can be phrases (always stated in parallel terms): **Traditional Family Patterns, Alternative Family Patterns, Modern Family Patterns**. Finally, headings can be questions (**How Do You Choose a Major?**) or statements (**Choose Your Major Carefully**).

See 43a

## 3 Indentation

**Indenting** is one way of distinguishing one level of heading from another. Keep in mind, however, that style guides for different disciplines provide different guidelines concerning the placement of headings. For example, the APA style guide makes the following recommendations: first-level headings should be centered, second-level headings should be justified left, and third-level headings should be indented one-half inch. Consult the appropriate style manual for guidelines on this issue.

## 4 Typographical Emphasis

You can emphasize important words in headings (and further distinguish different levels) by using **boldface,** *italics,* or ALL CAPITAL LETTERS. Used in moderation, these distinctive type styles make a text easier to read. Used excessively, however, they slow readers down.

### Close-Up HEADING STYLES

Most word-processing programs offer style options that keep headings distinctive and consistent. For example, *Word* has various options that enable you to automatically format headings throughout a document.

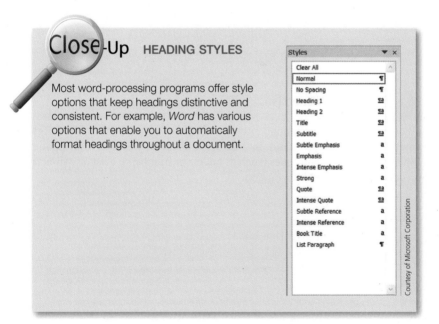

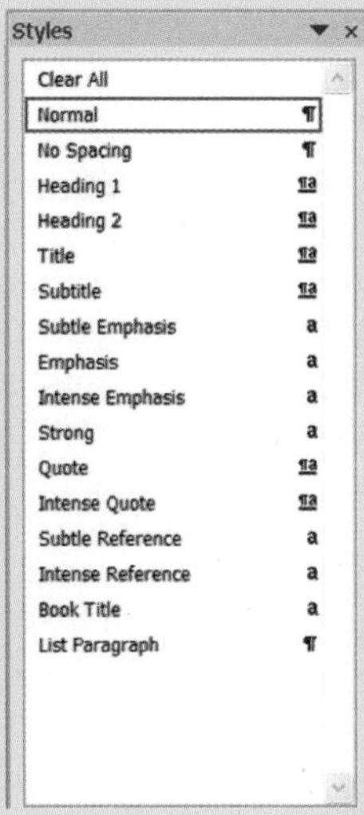


Courtesy of Microsoft Corporation

## 5 Consistency

Headings at the same level should have the same type style, type size, spacing, and color. In addition, if one first-level heading is boldfaced and centered, all other first-level headings must be boldfaced and centered. Using consistent patterns reinforces the connection between content and ideas and makes a document easier to understand.

Note: Never separate a heading from the text that goes with it: if a heading is at the bottom of one page and the text that goes with it is on the next page, move the heading onto the next page along with the text.

**Close-Up** SAMPLE HEADING FORMATS

**Flush Left, Boldfaced, Uppercase and Lowercase**

**Indented, Boldfaced, Uppercase and Lowercase**

*Indented, italicized, lowercase; run into the text at the beginning of a paragraph; ends with a period.*

*Or*

**Centered, Boldfaced, Uppercase and Lowercase**

Flush Left, Underlined, Uppercase and Lowercase

Indented, underlined, lowercase; run into the text at the beginning of a paragraph; ends with a period.

*Or*

ALL CAPITAL LETTERS, CENTERED

## 28c Constructing Lists

By breaking long discussions into a series of key ideas, a list makes information easier to understand. By isolating individual pieces of information and by providing visual cues (such as bullets or numbers), a list also directs readers to important information.

CHECKLIST

### Constructing Effective Lists

When constructing a list, follow these guidelines:

- ❑ **Indent each item.** Each item in a list should be indented so that it stands out from the text around it.
- ❑ **Set off items with bullets or numbers.** Use **bullets** when items are not organized according to any particular sequence (the members of a club, for example). Use **numbers** when you want to indicate that items are organized according to a sequence (the steps in a process, for example).
- ❑ **Introduce a list with a complete sentence.** Do not simply drop a list into a document; introduce it with a complete sentence (followed by a colon) that tells readers what to look for in the list.

- ❑ **Use parallel structure.** Lists are easiest to read when all items are parallel and about the same length.

  A decrease in several factors can cause high unemployment:
  - consumer spending
  - factory orders
  - factory output

- ❑ **Capitalize and punctuate correctly.** If the items in a list are fragments (as in the example above), begin each item with a lowercase letter, and do not end with a period. However, if the items in a list are complete sentences (as in the example below), begin each item with a capital letter and end with a period.

  Here are the three steps we must take to reduce our spending:
  1. We must cut our workforce by 10 percent.
  2. We must use less expensive vendors.
  3. We must decrease overtime payments.

- ❑ **Don't overuse lists.** Too many lists will give readers the impression that you are simply enumerating points instead of discussing them.

Figure 28.2 shows a page from a student's report for an introduction to cultural anthropology course that incorporates some of the effective design elements discussed in **28a–c.** Notice that the use of different typefaces and type sizes contributes to the document's overall readability.

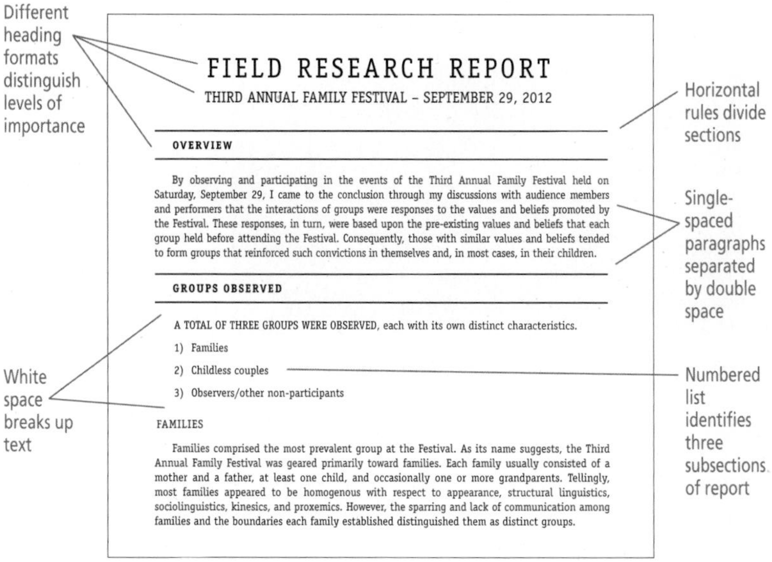
FIELD RESEARCH REPORT

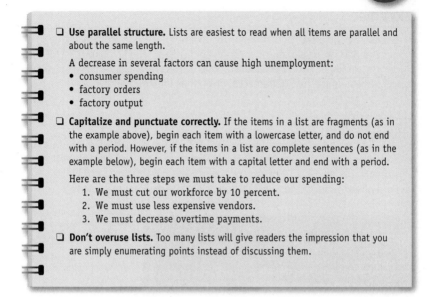

THIRD ANNUAL FAMILY FESTIVAL - SEPTEMBER 29, 2012

OVERVIEW

By observing and participating in the events of the Third Annual Family Festival held on Saturday, September 29, I came to the conclusion through my discussions with audience members and performers that the interactions of groups were responses to the values and beliefs promoted by the Festival. These responses, in turn, were based upon the pre-existing values and beliefs that each group held before attending the Festival. Consequently, those with similar values and beliefs tended to form groups that reinforced such convictions in themselves and, in most cases, in their children.

GROUPS OBSERVED

A TOTAL OF THREE GROUPS WERE OBSERVED, each with its own distinct characteristics.

1) Families
2) Childless couples
3) Observers/other non-participants

FAMILIES

Families comprised the most prevalent group at the Festival. As its name suggests, the Third Annual Family Festival was geared primarily toward families. Each family usually consisted of a mother and a father, at least one child, and occasionally one or more grandparents. Tellingly, most families appeared to be homogenous with respect to appearance, structural linguistics, sociolinguistics, kinesics, and proxemics. However, the sparring and lack of communication among families and the boundaries each family established distinguished them as distinct groups.



FIGURE 28.2 A well-designed page from a student's report. © Cengage Learning.

### EXERCISE 1

Select two different documents—for example, a page from a procedure manual and an invitation, or a report and a flyer. Then, make a list of the design elements each document contains. Finally, evaluate the relative effectiveness of the two documents, given their intended audiences.

### EXERCISE 2

Look at the advertisement in Figure 28.3, noting its organization, format, and design. How does the ad make use of margins, typefaces and type sizes, line spacing, and other document design features to emphasize important elements of the text? Can any design elements be improved?

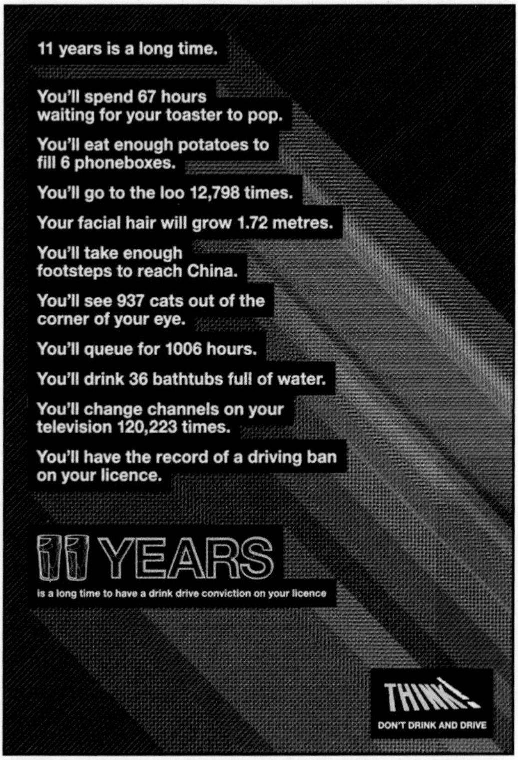


Image courtesy of The Advertising Archives

FIGURE 28.3 Advertisement warning against drunk driving.

## 28d Using Visuals

**Visuals,** such as tables, graphs, diagrams, and photographs, can help you convey complex ideas that are difficult to communicate with words. They can also help you attract readers' attention.

**Note:** Use a visual in the text only if you plan to discuss it in your paper (otherwise, place the visual in an appendix).

## 1 Tables

**Tables** present data in a condensed, visual format—arranged in rows and columns. Tables may contain numerical data, text, or a combination of the two. When you plan a table, make sure you include only the data that you will need; discard information that is too detailed or difficult to understand. Keep in mind that tables interrupt the flow of a discussion, so include only those that are necessary to support your point. (The table in Figure 28.4 reports the student writer's original research and therefore needs no documentation.)

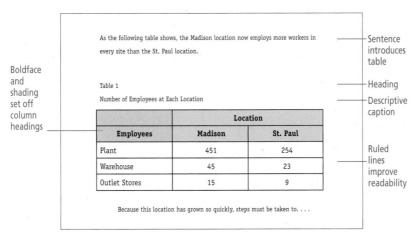

As the following table shows, the Madison location now employs more workers in every site than the St. Paul location.

Sentence introduces table

Table 1

Heading

Number of Employees at Each Location

Descriptive caption

Boldface and shading set off column headings

| | Location | |
|---|---|---|
| **Employees** | **Madison** | **St. Paul** |
| Plant | 451 | 254 |
| Warehouse | 45 | 23 |
| Outlet Stores | 15 | 9 |

Ruled lines improve readability

Because this location has grown so quickly, steps must be taken to. . . .

FIGURE 28.4 Sample table from a student paper. © Cengage Learning.

## 2 Graphs

Like tables, **graphs** present data in visual form. Whereas tables may present specific numerical data, graphs convey the general pattern or trend that the data suggest. Because graphs tend to be more general (and therefore less accurate) than tables, they are frequently accompanied by tables. Figure 28.5 on page 442 is an example of a bar graph showing data from a source.

## 3 Diagrams

A **diagram** calls readers' attention to specific details of a mechanism or object. Diagrams are often used in scientific and technical writing to clarify concepts that are difficult to explain in words. Figure 28.6 on page 442, which illustrates the sections of an orchestra, serves a similar purpose in a music education paper.

the demographics of college students is changing. According to a 2002 US Department of Education report entitled *Nontraditional Undergraduates*, the percentage of students who could be classified as "nontraditional" has increased over the last decade (see fig. 1).

Data

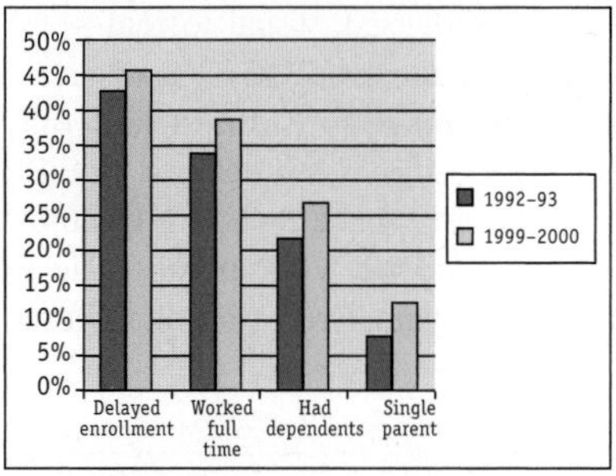


Label and citation

Fig. 1. United States, Dept. of Educ., Office of Educ. Research and Improvement, Natl. Center for Educ. Statistics; *Nontraditional Undergraduates*, by Susan Choy; 2002; *National Center for Education Statistics*; Web; 27 Feb. 2012.

**FIGURE 28.5** Sample graph from a student paper. Data © US Department of Education. © Cengage Learning.

The sections of an orchestra are arranged precisely to allow for a powerful and cohesive performance. Fig. 1 illustrates the placement of individual sections of an orchestra.

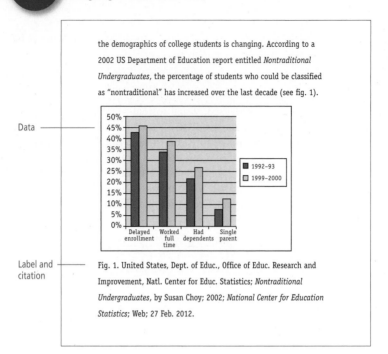

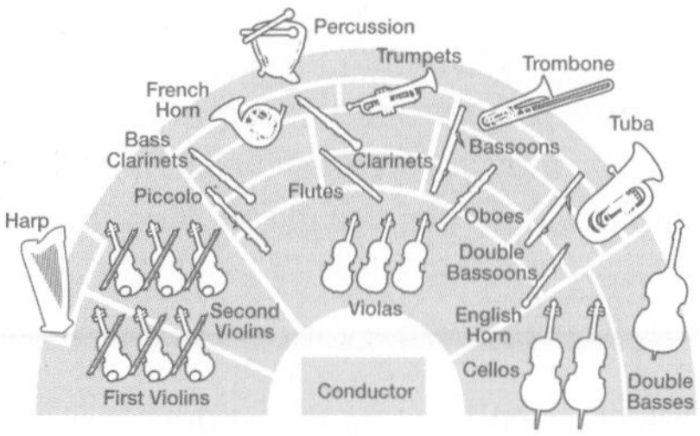

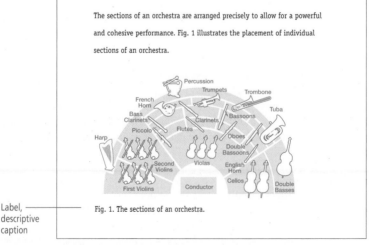

Label, descriptive caption

Fig. 1. The sections of an orchestra.

**FIGURE 28.6** Sample diagram from a student paper. © Cengage Learning.

## 4 Photographs

**Photographs** enable you to show exactly what something or someone looks like—an animal in its natural habitat, a painting, or an actor in costume, for example. Although it is easy to paste photographs directly into a text, you should do so only when they provide necessary explanation or support for your points. The photograph of a wooded trail in Figure 28.7 illustrates the student writer's description.

travelers are well advised to be prepared, to always carry water, and to dress for the conditions. Loose fitting, lightweight wicking material covering all exposed skin is necessary in summer, and layers of warm clothing are needed for cold-weather outings. Hats and sunscreen are always a good idea no matter what the temperature, although most of the trails are quite shady with huge oak trees. Fig. 1 shows a shady portion of the trail.

Photo sized and placed appropriately within text with consistent white space above and below

Reference to photo provides context

Fig. 1. Greenbelt Trail in springtime (author photo).

Label and descriptive caption

FIGURE 28.7 Sample photograph from a student paper. © Cengage Learning.

### Close-Up VISUALS AND COPYRIGHT

**Copyright** gives authors the legal right to control the copying of their work—visuals as well as text. The law makes a clear distinction between visuals used in documents prepared for school assignments and visuals used in documents that will be published. In general, you may use graphics from a source—print or electronic—in papers for your classes as long as you document the source, just as you would any other source.

If you use visuals in documents that will be published (on the Internet or in print), however, you must obtain permission in writing from the person or organization that holds the copyright. (Even images that are freely available on the Internet are copyrighted and usually require permission to use.) Sometimes the copyright holder will grant permission without charge, but often there will be a fee. Remember, it is your responsibility to determine whether or not permission is required.

### Using Visuals

When using visuals in your papers, follow these guidelines:

- ❑ Use a visual only when it contributes something important to the discussion, not for embellishment.
- ❑ Introduce each visual with a complete sentence.
- ❑ Follow each visual with a discussion of its significance.
- ❑ Leave wide margins around each visual.
- ❑ Place the visual as close as possible to the section of your paper in which it is discussed.
- ❑ Label each visual appropriately.
- ❑ Document each visual borrowed from a source.

### EXERCISE 3

Analyze the chart in Figure 28.8, noting the visual elements that are used to convey the billing costs of material, labor, and equipment on a construction project. Summarize the data in a brief paragraph. Then, list the advantages and disadvantages of presenting the data visually as opposed to verbally.

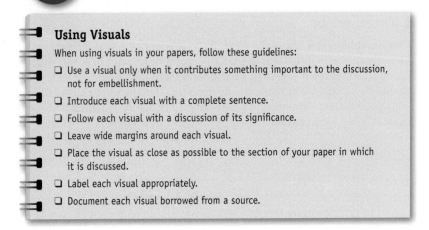

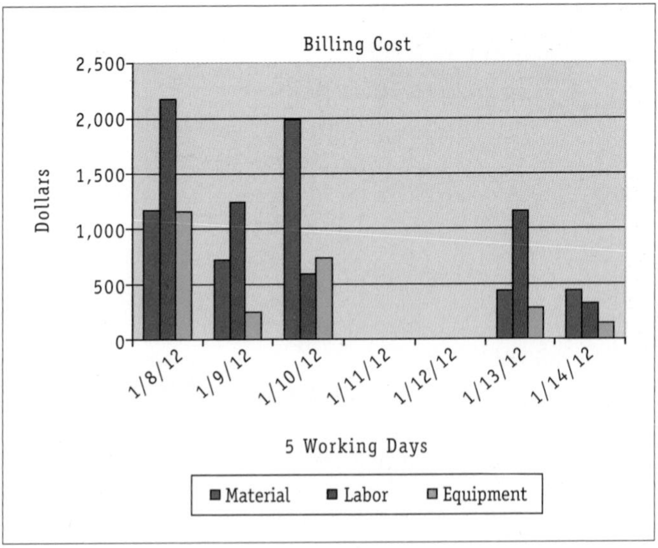


FIGURE 28.8 Billing cost chart. © Cengage Learning.

## 28e Using Desktop Publishing

During your college career, you may be required to use your computer for **desktop publishing**—using graphics as well as words to produce documents.

For example, you may produce a **brochure, flyer,** or newsletter for a student organization to which you belong or as a service-learning project for a course you are taking. (Figure 28.9 shows a page of a student brochure.) Brochures and flyers are frequently aimed at consumers of a product or service or at members of an organization. These documents may be informative, persuasive, or both.

See 32c–d

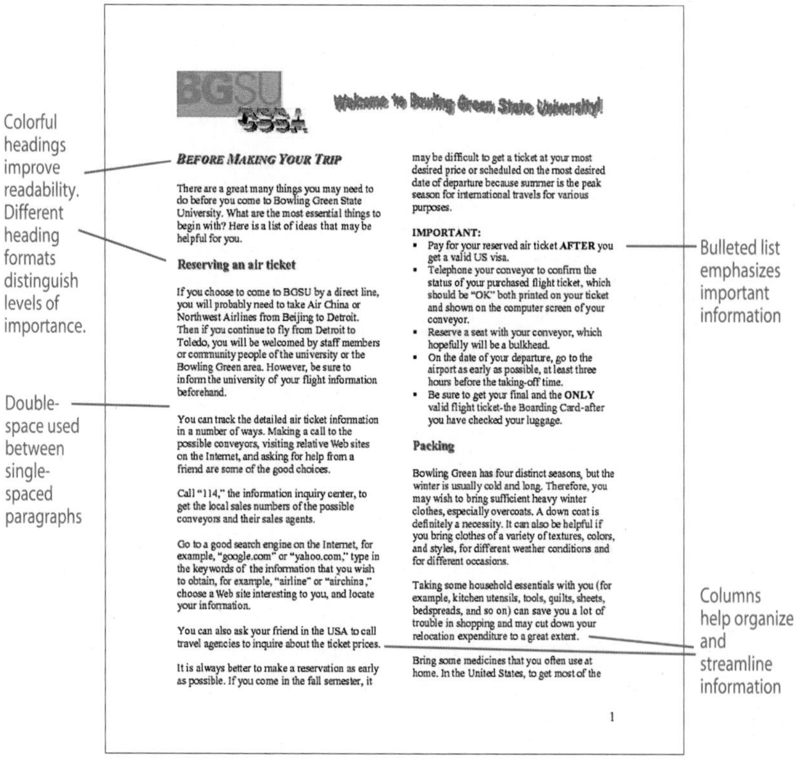
Colorful headings improve readability.
Different heading formats distinguish levels of importance.
Double-space used between single-spaced paragraphs
Bulleted list emphasizes important information
Columns help organize and streamline information

Welcome to Bowling Green State University!

*BEFORE MAKING YOUR TRIP*

There are a great many things you may need to do before you come to Bowling Green State University. What are the most essential things to begin with? Here is a list of ideas that may be helpful for you.

**Reserving an air ticket**

If you choose to come to BGSU by a direct line, you will probably need to take Air China or Northwest Airlines from Beijing to Detroit. Then if you continue to fly from Detroit to Toledo, you will be welcomed by staff members or community people of the university or the Bowling Green area. However, be sure to inform the university of your flight information beforehand.

You can track the detailed air ticket information in a number of ways. Making a call to the possible conveyors, visiting relative Web sites on the Internet, and asking for help from a friend are some of the good choices.

Call "114," the information inquiry center, to get the local sales numbers of the possible conveyors and their sales agents.

Go to a good search engine on the Internet, for example, "google.com" or "yahoo.com," type in the keywords of the information that you wish to obtain, for example, "airline" or "airchina," choose a Web site interesting to you, and locate your information.

You can also ask your friend in the USA to call travel agencies to inquire about the ticket prices.

It is always better to make a reservation as early as possible. If you come in the fall semester, it may be difficult to get a ticket at your most desired price or scheduled on the most desired date of departure because summer is the peak season for international travels for various purposes.

**IMPORTANT:**

- Pay for your reserved air ticket **AFTER** you get a valid US visa.
- Telephone your conveyor to confirm the status of your purchased flight ticket, which should be "OK" both printed on your ticket and shown on the computer screen of your conveyor.
- Reserve a seat with your conveyor, which hopefully will be a bulkhead.
- On the date of your departure, go to the airport as early as possible, at least three hours before the taking-off time.
- Be sure to get your final and the **ONLY** valid flight ticket-the Boarding Card-after you have checked your luggage.

**Packing**

Bowling Green has four distinct seasons, but the winter is usually cold and long. Therefore, you may wish to bring sufficient heavy winter clothes, especially overcoats. A down coat is definitely a necessity. It can also be helpful if you bring clothes of a variety of textures, colors, and styles, for different weather conditions and for different occasions.

Taking some household essentials with you (for example, kitchen utensils, tools, quilts, sheets, bedspreads, and so on) can save you a lot of trouble in shopping and may cut down your relocation expenditure to a great extent.

Bring some medicines that you often use at home. In the United States, to get most of the

1

FIGURE 28.9 First page of a student brochure. © Cengage Learning.

Most word-processing programs, such as *Microsoft Word*, contain templates (see Figure 28.10 on page 446) that can help you design your flyer, newsletter, or brochure. With these templates, you can select layout, color scheme, and typeface as well as document dimensions and paper size.

For more options, you can use one of the many desktop publishing software packages that are commercially available. *Microsoft Publisher,* like *Microsoft Word*, provides templates for a wide range of document types. More advanced desktop publishing programs include *The Print Shop Deluxe, PagePlus, QuarkXPress,* and *InDesign,* all of which are used extensively in business and industry.

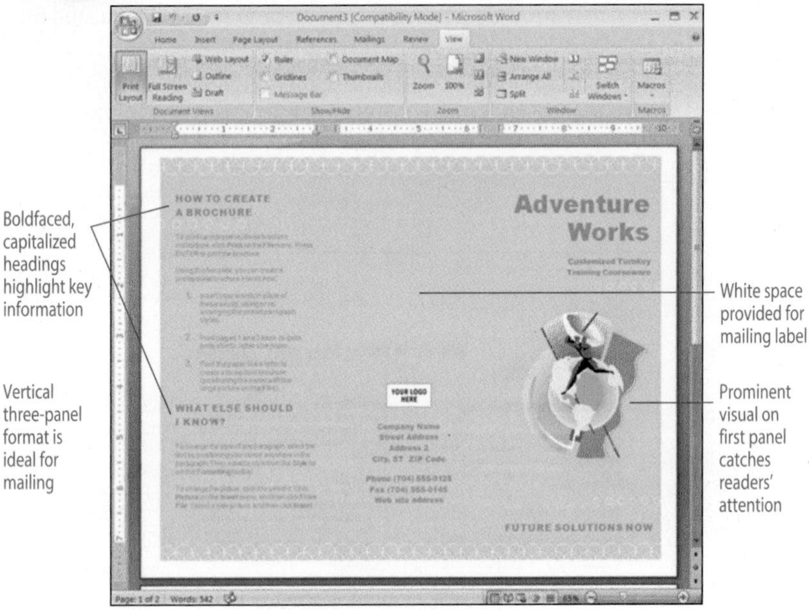
Boldfaced, capitalized headings highlight key information
Vertical three-panel format is ideal for mailing
White space provided for mailing label
Prominent visual on first panel catches readers' attention
HOW TO CREATE A BROCHURE
WHAT ELSE SHOULD I KNOW?
Adventure Works
FUTURE SOLUTIONS NOW

FIGURE 28.10 *Microsoft Word* brochure template. Copyright 2011, Microsoft Corporation. All Rights Reserved.

## EXERCISE 4

Create a promotional document for an organization on your campus. Before you begin the document design process, interview someone affiliated with the organization to determine the type of information you will need, the format in which the information should be delivered, and the image the organization wishes to project to the campus community.

CHAPTER 29

# Designing a Web Site

## Frequently Asked Questions



At some point in your college career—for example, as a course assignment or as a way of marketing your job skills—you may be asked to create a Web page or even a full Web site. Like other documents, Web pages follow the conventions of document design. Because so much of the content is meant to be read online, your choices of text, color, and navigation strategy are especially important.

See Ch. 28

### Close-Up COMPONENTS OF A WEB PAGE

A **personal home page** usually contains information about how to contact the author, along with a brief biography. A home page can also be the first page of a **Web site,** a group of related **Web pages** focusing on a personal, professional, or academic topic. In this case, the home page contains **links**—highlighted words, images, or URLs—that allow users to move from one page to another or to another Web site.

## 29a Planning a Web Site

When you plan your Web site, you should consider your purpose, audience, and tone, just as you would when planning a print document. You should also consider what content to include. Finally, just as an essay or research paper may have a set page limit, your Web site may have size and file-type limitations.

See 1a–c

CHECKLIST

**Planning a Web Site**

When you plan a Web site, consider the following questions:

- ❑ **What is your purpose?** Will your Web site be personal, educational, or job-related?
- ❑ **Who is the primary audience?** friends? students? potential employers? What type of information would be of interest to your audience? What would *not* be of interest?
- ❑ **What information will you include?** What information will appear on your home page? What information will appear on the other pages?
- ❑ **What mood do you want to convey?** What colors and type styles should you use to help you convey this mood?

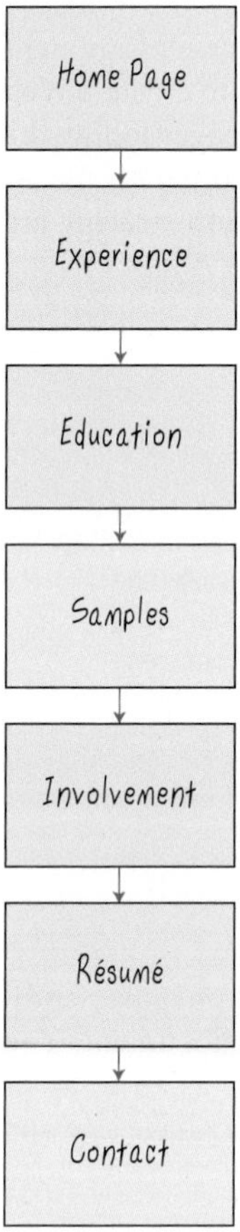

FIGURE 29.1 Linear storyboard.

Begin with a basic plan of your Web site's content (both text and visuals). Then, consider how your Web pages will be connected and what links you will provide to other Web sites. Because users will start with your home page and navigate from one part of your site to another, the home page should provide an overview of your site and give readers a clear sense of what material the site contains. As you lay out the pages of your Web site, place related items together, and use text and visuals sparingly. Keep in mind that too many graphics and elaborate type styles will distract or confuse users.

As you plan your Web site, consider how your pages will be organized. One way to map out your site's organization is to create a **storyboard**, using 3″ × 5″ index cards to represent the various elements of your Web site and moving these cards around until you arrive at an organization that makes sense. (You can also construct a storyboard by sketching a schematic—called a **wireframe**—of your Web site on a sheet of paper.)

If your Web site will be relatively simple, you can arrange pages in a **linear order** so that one page leads sequentially to the next. If your site will be relatively complicated, however, you will have to use a **hierarchical arrangement,** where pages are arranged in multiple ways—for example, in order of their relevance to a particular category or subject. Figures 29.1 and 29.2 show examples of linear and hierarchical arrangements. The home page of the student's Web site shown in Figure 29.3 indicates that information is grouped in linear order under the categories *Home, About Me, Résumé, My Photos,* and *Contact Me.*

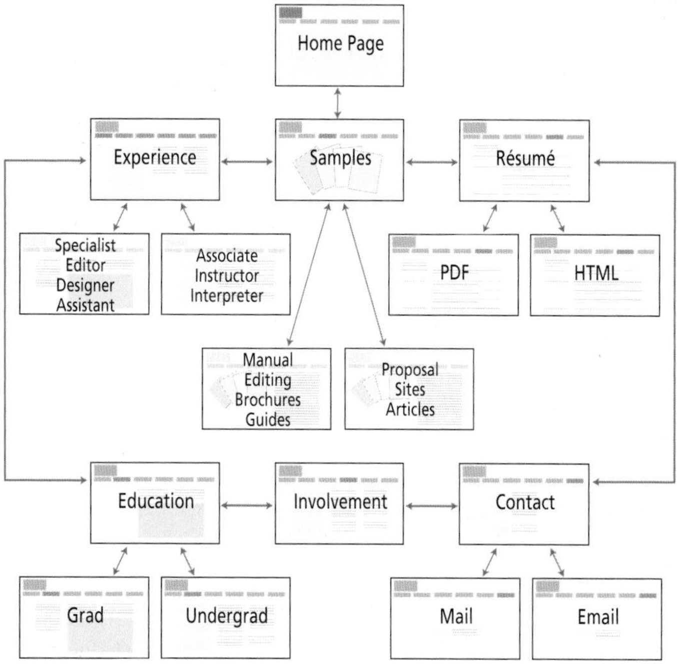


**FIGURE 29.2** Hierarchical storyboard. © Cengage Learning.

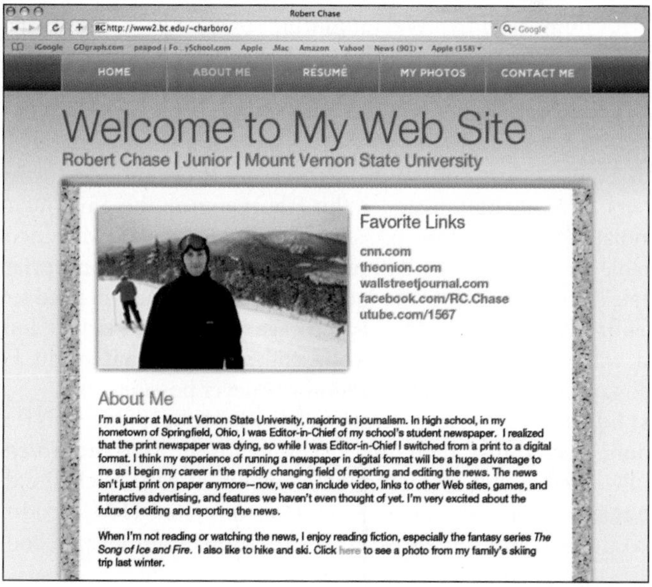


**FIGURE 29.3** The home page of a student's Web site. © Cengage Learning.

**EXERCISE 1**

Select three Web sites: one personal, one academic (such as your university's site), and one professional or organizational (such as that of the American Cancer Society). How do these sites differ in purpose, audience, and tone? How are these differences reflected in the design of each site?

## 29b Creating a Web Site

Once you have planned your Web site, you will need to select a method for creating the site. Essentially, there are three ways to do this: you can use Web-authoring software packages; you can use Web tools within your word-processing program; or you can create a page from scratch with a text editor that uses **HTML** (hypertext markup language) to convert standard documents into World Wide Web hypertext documents.

- **Web-Authoring Software** Many Web-authoring software packages—for example, *Adobe Dreamweaver* and *Microsoft Expression Web*—automatically translate your pages into HTML. The advantage of authoring software is that you do not need a working knowledge of HTML in order to develop your site. Some of this software even makes certain interactive functions—such as navigation bars, forms, or media effects—easier to design and implement.

  Note: A number of free Web-authoring software packages are available online. For example, *KompoZer* <kompozer.net>, *Amaya* <w3.org>, and *SeaMonkey* <seamonkey-project.org> are available for both Windows and Mac platforms.

- **Web Tools within Your Word-Processing Program** Most word processors have an option under the File menu or the Save menu that automatically saves word-processed documents as HTML documents suitable for Web delivery. Although this option may be appropriate for a simple document, it does not include the features you will need to create an entire Web site. In addition, the page you create will take longer to load, will be full of proprietary code, and will be difficult to edit. For this reason, you should avoid this option whenever possible.
- **Text Editors** If you have advanced knowledge of HTML, this is a good option. Text editors, including *TextMate* for the Mac and *Notepad* for the PC, enable you to control all elements of your Web site design. The major drawback of using a text editor is that HTML coding can be confusing, and some special effects require complicated codes.

EXERCISE 2

Find online reviews of the free Web-authoring software packages mentioned in the Note on page 450. What are the strengths of these packages? What are their weaknesses? Which do you think would be the best one for you? Why?

## 29c Selecting and Inserting Visuals

You can find visuals for your Web site by looking for sites on the Web that make visuals available for others to use. *Google*, for example, has an image directory that you can search. You can also find images explicitly licensed for noncommercial use at <search.creativecommons.org>. Finally, you can create and upload visuals yourself by using a digital camera or a scanner.

Once you have created a visual and saved it electronically, you can use a graphics package such as *Adobe Photoshop* to adjust the visual's size, contrast, or color scheme; to crop the image; or to add text. Other visual options include creating your own banners and backgrounds with special colors and textures. (In addition, you can use **multimedia**—movies and sound—as well as text.) Figure 29.4 shows a Web page that includes a visual.

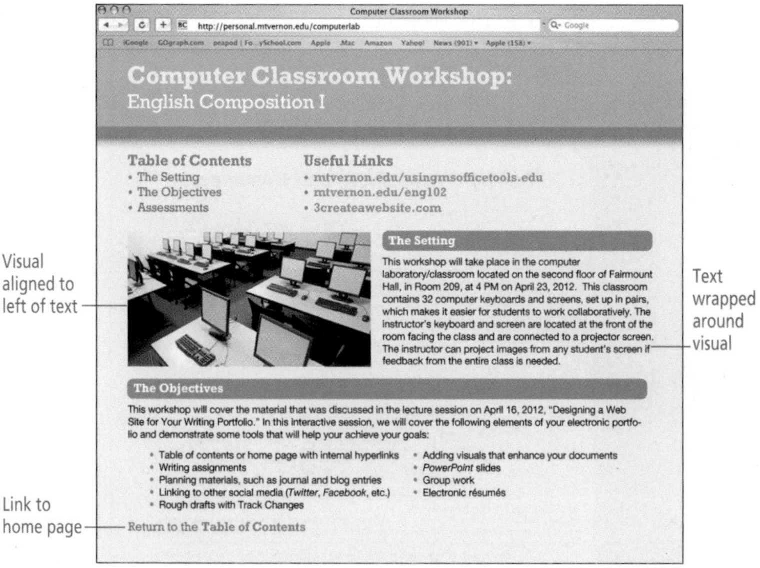


FIGURE 29.4 Web page that includes a visual. © Cengage Learning. Photo © Corbis Premium RF/Alamy.

**EXERCISE 3**

Select a visual you could include on a personal Web site. Download one of the free Web-authoring packages mentioned on page 450, and practice inserting and aligning the visual in an appropriate place and adjusting its height and width in relation to the text. How well does the visual thematically and visually support your written content and your overall design? What alterations can you make to the visual before you reinsert it? What changes in size and alignment should you make once the visual is reinserted on the page?

## 29d Planning Navigation

Web sites use a number of design features to make navigation easier. As you create the pages of your Web site, consider the following options for helping readers navigate your site:

- **Navigation Links, Buttons, and Bars** Navigation links, buttons, bars, and other graphic icons, such as arrows or pictures, enable readers to move from one page of a Web site to another (see Figure 29.5).
- **Anchors** Anchors (or **relative links**) enable readers to jump from one part of a Web page to another (see Figure 29.5).
- **Horizontal Rules** Horizontal rules divide sections and parts of a page (see Figure 29.5). You can use colored or patterned rules that coordinate with the color scheme of the Web site.

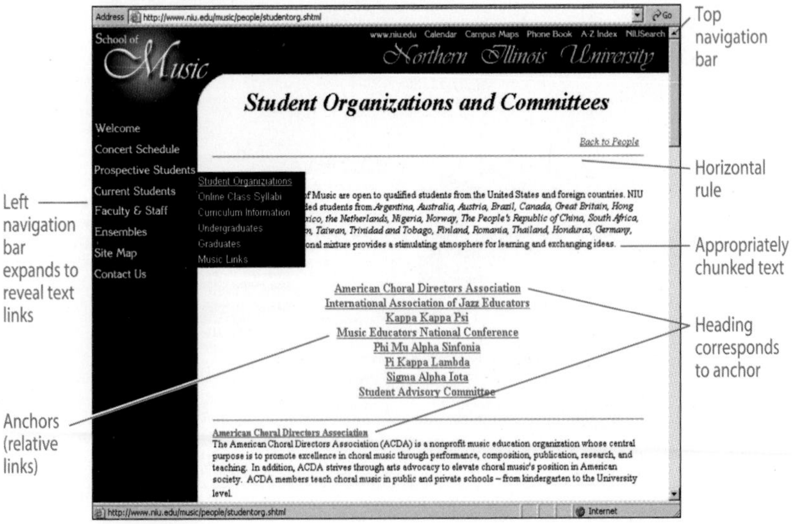


FIGURE 29.5 Web page with navigation links and anchors. © Cengage Learning.

- **Chunking or Clustering** Chunking or clustering means placing related items of text close to one another (see Figure 29.5). This technique cuts down on scrolling and helps users read content easily on the screen. By surrounding clusters of information with white space, you can create distinct areas of content.
- **Text Formatting Features** Like printed texts, Web texts follow the principles of **document design,** using design elements such as single-spaced text, headings, subheadings, and bulleted lists, as well as boldface and italics, to emphasize points. (Underlining is generally not used in Web texts because readers might mistake underlined text for a hyperlink.)

See Ch. 28

## Close-Up STYLE SHEETS

Web-authoring software packages contain style sheets that enable you to set in advance the standard features of your site—typefaces, type styles and sizes, and colors. This feature not only saves time but also helps you to create a consistent visual format.

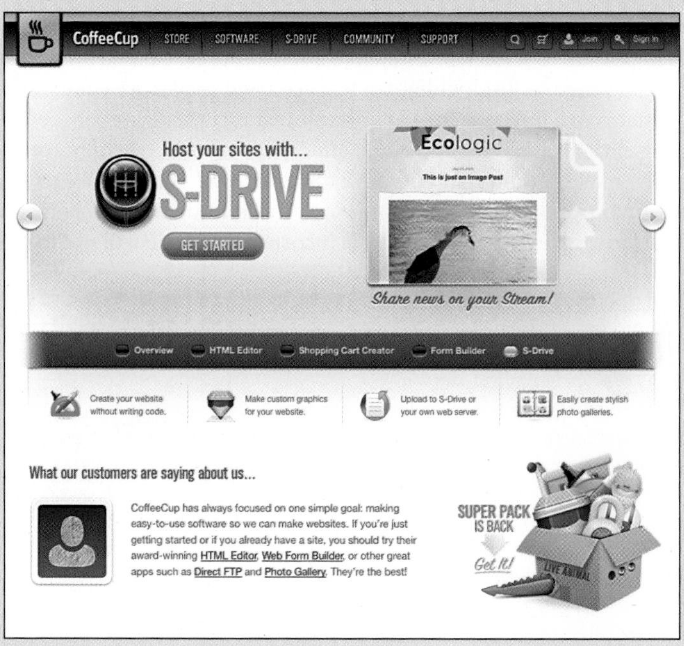


Courtesy of CoffeeCup

CHECKLIST

**Designing Effective Web Pages**

- ❑ Use the same type size and typeface for equivalent information. Keep headings consistent throughout your site.
- ❑ Use text, buttons, and bars to facilitate navigation.
- ❑ Use special multimedia effects in moderation.
- ❑ Avoid pages so full of text, graphics, and navigation aids that they make reading difficult and increase loading time.
- ❑ For best visibility, use text and background colors that contrast well.
- ❑ Preview your Web site on multiple machines and browsers as well as on both high-speed networks and slower-speed modems.
- ❑ Provide your email address so you can receive feedback from users.

## 29e Linking Content

**Links** (short for **hyperlinks**) are an important part of Web design. When you provide a link, you are directing people to a particular Web site. For this reason, you should make sure that the site you link to is up and running and that the information appearing there is both accurate and reliable.

It is important to select a prominent color for your text-based links to indicate that they are not just highlighted text. You will need three colors to indicate the status of a link: one for the link before it is clicked; one for the link as it is being clicked; and one for the link after it has been successfully accessed.

Finally, make certain that you have the exact URL for the sites to which you are linking. The Web relies on exact URLs to deliver information; if even one letter or punctuation mark is incorrect, the page will not load.

Close-Up WEB SITES AND COPYRIGHT

As a rule, assume that any material on a Web site is **copyrighted** unless the author makes an explicit statement to the contrary. This means you must obtain written permission if you are going to reproduce this material on your Web site. (You are, however, allowed to provide a link to a Web site without permission.) The only exception to this rule is the **fair use doctrine,** which allows the use of copyrighted material for the purpose of commentary, parody, or research and education.

How much of a work you use is a consideration when it comes to determining fair use. For example, you can quote a sentence of an article from the *New York Times* on your Web site for the purpose of commenting on it, but you must get permission if you want to reproduce a significant portion of the article. The purpose of your use—that is, whether you are using it commercially—is also a consideration. You can find more information about fair use at <fairuse.stanford.edu>.

*Note:* Material you quote in a research paper for one of your classes falls under the fair use doctrine and does not require permission.

## 29f Editing and Proofreading

Before you post your Web site, you should **edit and proofread** it just as you would any other document. (Even if you run a spell check and a grammar check, you must still proofread carefully.)

See 6d

CHECKLIST

### Style Conventions of Writing for the Web

- ❑ Avoid long, wordy sentences. Using active verbs will help keep your sentences short and concise.
- ❑ Avoid long paragraphs. Chunk content into small sections that are easy to read and access online.
- ❑ Speak directly to your audience, using the first person (*I*) and the second person (*you*) to establish a connection with readers.
- ❑ Avoid technical terminology that only a certain segment of your audience will understand.
- ❑ Choose your external links wisely. Do not provide so many that your audience is drawn away from your site.
- ❑ Use headings and bulleted lists to organize information visually and textually.
- ❑ Provide a title in the browser window for each page within your site to help users keep track of where they are.
- ❑ Proofread carefully offline before loading your content online.

## 29g Posting Your Web Site

Once you have designed a Web site, you will need to upload (**post**) it so you can view it on the Web. Most commonly, Web pages are posted with FTP (File Transfer Protocol) software.

To get your site up on the Web, you transfer your files to an **Internet server,** a computer that is connected at all times to the Internet. Your

Internet service provider will instruct you on how to use FTP to transfer your files. Once your site is up and running, any mistakes you have made will be apparent as soon as you view your pages on the Web.

### EXERCISE 4

Visit your university's Web site or Information Technology Center and obtain a Web server account. What are your file size limitations, and what content guidelines are provided? What online training or tutorials are available to help you develop and upload your site?

## 29h Creating Wiki Web Sites

Unlike a traditional Web site, a **wiki** Web site can be edited by anyone who has access to it. In other words, a wiki Web site is a collaborative effort of a community of users. Because wiki Web sites enable many people to create and edit content, they are used extensively by people working on group projects or by people who share common interests—for example, fantasy football fans or book lovers. Wikis are often used in the classroom, where a writing class can use a wiki site to edit a piece of writing or to create a brochure or a report.

*Wetpaint Central* <wetpaintcentral.com> and *Wikispaces* <wikispaces.com> are user-friendly wiki sites that enable anyone to design and launch a Web site. For example, with *Wetpaint Central*, you begin by selecting a site name, a URL, and a category for your site. Then, you indicate whether your site will be open to everyone or limited to just those you invite (see Figure 29.6).

Next, you choose a style for your Web site from a group of templates. Finally, you register the site and make a list of people you would like to invite to help construct it. Once you post your site, you (as well as others) can edit text, insert photos and videos—and even add new pages.

Wiki Web sites often grant different editing access to different pages. For example, the main page of the Web site might be blocked, while other pages might offer anything from limited to full editing access. The search engines *Wikia.com* <wikia.com>—founded by Jimmy Wales, one of the creators of *Wikipedia*—and *wiki.com* <wiki.com> give users access to thousands of wiki Web sites.

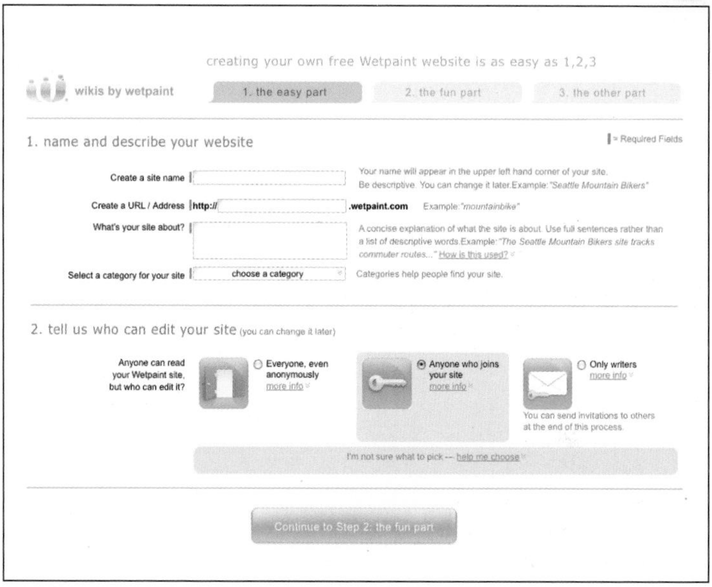


**FIGURE 29.6** *Wetpaint Central* wiki Web site creation page. Courtesy of wetpaint.com.

PART 8

# Developing Strategies for Academic and Professional Success

CHAPTER 30

# Creating a Writing Portfolio

## Frequently Asked Questions



A **writing portfolio,** a collection of coursework in print or electronic form, offers a unique opportunity for you to present your intellectual track record, showing where you've been and how you've developed as a writer. Increasingly, colleges have been using portfolios as a way to assess individual students' performance—and sometimes to see if the student body as a whole is meeting university standards.

The purpose of a writing portfolio is to demonstrate a writer's improvement and achievements. Portfolios allow writers to collect a body of writing in one place and to organize and present it in an effective, attractive format, giving the instructor a view of a student's writing that focuses more on the complete body of work than on individual assignments. While compiling individual items (sometimes called **artifacts**) to include in their portfolios, students reflect on their work and measure their progress; as they do so, they may improve their ability to evaluate their own work.

There are two kinds of portfolios:

1. **Growth** or **process portfolios** are designed to show a writer's improvement over time. They may include multiple essay drafts with instructor comments (and sometimes peer reviewers' comments as well) in addition to other work completed in and out of class for each assignment.
2. **Best-works** or **presentation portfolios** are designed to highlight a writer's notable achievements. They contain only finished products, such as the final drafts of essays or reports.

**Close-Up** PORTFOLIOS AND JOB APPLICATIONS

Just as your résumé provides a summary of your educational and professional responsibilities and accomplishments, best-works or presentation portfolios show prospective employers the range of writing-related skills that you have mastered and can use on the job.

Portfolios may be assembled in print or electronic form. A **print portfolio** collects and presents hard copy in a file folder. In contrast, an **electronic portfolio** compiles material in electronic files stored on a USB flash drive, a rewritable CD or DVD, or a Web site. Some portfolios combine print and electronic formats—for example, posting finished material on a Web site and collecting hard copies of early essay drafts with handwritten instructor comments in a folder.

### EXERCISE 1

List the items you might include in a portfolio for one of your classes, and think about how you could arrange this material. Then, write a paragraph outlining the specific content and format of your portfolio.

### EXERCISE 2

& Working in a group of three or four students, compare the paragraphs you wrote in response to Exercise 1. Discuss each student's proposed portfolio content and format. Then, consider whether you can incorporate any of your classmates' ideas into your own portfolio, and revise your paragraph accordingly.

## 30a Assembling a Print Portfolio

Before you begin assembling artifacts for a print portfolio, make sure you understand what items your instructor expects you to include.

CHECKLIST

### Content for Print Portfolios

The following material might be included in a print portfolio:

- ❑ **Table of contents** listing portfolio material
- ❑ Reflective statement in the form of a cover memo, letter, or essay. (Some portfolios also include brief reflections or descriptions of individual artifacts.) See 30c
- ❑ **Writing assignments** that provide a context for the artifacts in the portfolio
- ❑ **Planning material,** such as journal entries, freewriting exercises, brainstorming notes, and cluster diagrams
- ❑ **Shaping material,** such as thesis statements and informal and formal outlines
- ❑ **Rough drafts with comments** made by peer reviewers, instructors, and writing center tutors

*continued*

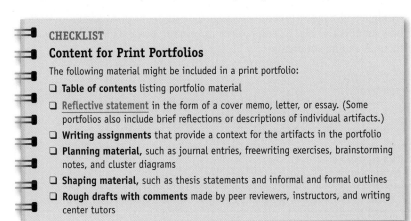

**Content for Print Portfolios *(continued)***

- ❑ **Rough drafts with revisions** made by hand or with Track Changes
- ❑ **Final drafts**
- ❑ **Photocopies and printouts** of source material
- ❑ **Visuals** that enhance your essays
- ❑ **Essay exam answers**
- ❑ **Transcripts of oral presentations** and supporting material
- ❑ **Group work** (collaborative work), with your own contributions clearly marked
- ❑ **Personal writing** that enhances the portfolio
- ❑ A **print résumé,** if the portfolio will be submitted to a prospective employer

Once you are sure you understand your instructor's requirements, you can begin to assemble your print portfolio, using the following checklist as a guide.

CHECKLIST

**Assembling a Print Portfolio**

As you assemble your print portfolio, keep the following guidelines in mind:

- ❑ **Select material** that follows your instructor's guidelines.
- ❑ **Revise individual artifacts as needed,** using comments made by peer reviewers and by your instructor.
- ❑ **Collect your material** in a file folder.
- ❑ **Format your material,** using the principles of effective document design to help you present your work.
- ❑ **Arrange your material** in the order specified by your instructor's guidelines, and include a table of contents.
- ❑ **Write a reflective statement** that demonstrates your thoughtful analysis of your portfolio and of the individual artifacts within it.

Figure 30.1 shows the contents page for a student's print portfolio. Notice how an effective design emphasizes important elements and distinguishes them from one another.

### EXERCISE 3

Using the checklist above as a guide, assemble your print portfolio. Then, reread your instructor's writing portfolio guidelines and add, remove, or rearrange material as necessary.

### EXERCISE 4

& Ask a classmate to evaluate the content and design of your print portfolio and the arrangement of the artifacts within it. Is material presented in a logical way? Is any content superfluous, or is any important content missing? After considering your classmate's suggestions, revise your portfolio if necessary.

Box highlights title, student's name, and skills demonstrated by portfolio

**English Composition I Portfolio**

**by**

**Samantha Mahoney**

Drafting and Revising | Thinking Critically | Identifying an Audience

Color-coded type can be used to emphasize elements and distinguish skill categories

**Contents**

Bulleted list identifies portfolio's contents

- Reflective Statement
- "Moments of Silence" (Relationship Essay)
- "Winter Meal" (Observational Descriptive Essay)
- "Pass the Brussels Sprouts" (Research Project)

Instructor — Professor Russell

Course — English 101, Section 046

Date submitted — 4 October 2012

**FIGURE 30.1** Table of contents for student's print portfolio. © Cengage Learning 2013.

## 30b Assembling an Electronic Portfolio

As with a print portfolio, the material you include in an electronic portfolio depends on individual course requirements. An electronic format allows for a wide range of possible content, including multimedia content—for example, video or audio clips, *PowerPoint* presentations, and Web pages.

Many academic disciplines are moving toward electronic portfolios because when posted on the Internet, they are immediately accessible to peers, instructors, and prospective employers. However, not all material lends itself to an electronic format. You may need to supplement your electronic portfolio with print documents if they cannot be easily scanned.

CHECKLIST

### Content for Electronic Portfolios

The following material might be included in an electronic portfolio:

- ❑ **Table of contents or home page with internal hyperlinks** to portfolio material
- ❑ **Reflective statement** in the form of a cover memo, letter, or essay, with internal hyperlinks to portfolio content See 30c
- ❑ **Writing assignments** that form the basis for portfolio content
- ❑ **Planning material,** such as electronic journal and blog entries
- ❑ **Shaping material,** such as thesis statements and informal and formal outlines
- ❑ **Rough drafts with revisions** made with Track Changes
- ❑ **Scanned rough drafts with comments** made by peer reviewers, instructors, and writing center tutors
- ❑ **Final drafts**
- ❑ **External hyperlinks** to online source material and other Web sites that support the portfolio
- ❑ **Visuals** that enhance your documents
- ❑ **Audio and video clips of oral presentations**
- ❑ ***PowerPoint* slides**
- ❑ **Group work** (collaborative work), with your own contributions clearly marked
- ❑ An **electronic résumé,** if the portfolio will be submitted to a prospective employer

Once you are sure you understand your instructor's requirements, you can assemble your electronic portfolio, using the following checklist as a guide.

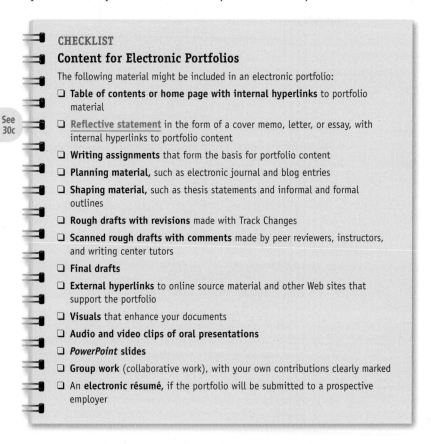

CHECKLIST

## Assembling an Electronic Portfolio

As you assemble your electronic portfolio, keep the following guidelines in mind:

- ❑ **Select material** that corresponds to your instructor's guidelines.
- ❑ **Revise your material,** using comments made by peer reviewers and by your instructor.
- ❑ **Compile your material** in electronic files and save your files on a storage device or post them to a Web site.
- ❑ **Format your material,** using principles of effective Web design to help you present your work.
- ❑ **Arrange your material** in the order specified by your instructor's guidelines, and include a home page.
- ❑ **Write a reflective statement** that demonstrates your thoughtful analysis of your portfolio and of the individual artifacts within it.
- ❑ **Collect additional materials** as hard copy in a folder (if necessary).

Close-Up **STORING FILES FOR ELECTRONIC PORTFOLIOS**

| Storage Device | Benefit | Limitation |
|---|---|---|
| USB flash drive/ external hard drive | Files can be resaved; compact and easy to transport | High storage capacity drives can be expensive; are easy to lose |
| Recordable CD (CD+/–R) | Relatively inexpensive | Files cannot be resaved |
| Recordable DVD (DVD+/–R) | Holds more content than CD+/–R | Files cannot be resaved; more expensive than CD+/–R |
| Rewritable CD (CD +/–RW) | Files can be resaved | Holds less content than DVD+/–RW; more expensive than CD+/–R |
| Rewritable DVD (DVD+/–RW) | Files can be resaved; holds more content than CD+/–RW | More expensive than CD+/–RW |
| Web site/cloud service | Files can be edited offline and uploaded | May require a subscription fee |

## Close-Up FREE VERSUS PROPRIETARY ELECTRONIC PORTFOLIO TOOLS

Electronic portfolio tools available through free or **open-source** software, such as *Drupal, Sakai,* and *uPortal,* allow users to edit the software's source code and customize their online portfolio experience. Because open-source software is free, users are granted unlimited access.

Proprietary or **closed-source** software, such as *Blackboard,* restricts users from editing its code but may still allow various customization options. Proprietary software requires a paid subscription that expires unless renewed. If you consider using an electronic portfolio tool, be sure to find out what its restrictions are before using it to assemble your portfolio.

Figure 30.2 shows the home page for a student's electronic writing portfolio. Notice how effective Web design elements highlight and distinguish key information on the page.

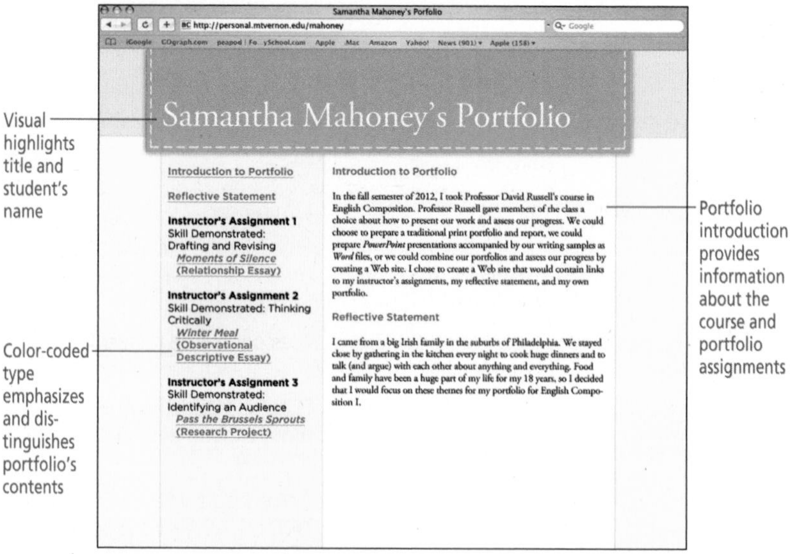


FIGURE 30.2 Home page for student's writing portfolio posted on the Internet.
© Cengage Learning.

### EXERCISE 5

Using the checklist on page 465 as a guide, assemble your electronic portfolio. Then, reread your instructor's guidelines and add, remove, or rearrange material as necessary.

**EXERCISE 6**

Ask a classmate to evaluate the content and design of your electronic portfolio and the arrangement of its content. Is material presented in an effective, attractive way? Is any content superfluous, or is any important content missing? If your portfolio is Web-based, is it easy to navigate from one item to another? After considering your classmate's suggestions, revise your portfolio if necessary.

## 30c Writing a Reflective Statement

Instructors usually require students to introduce their portfolios with a **reflective statement**—a memo, letter, or essay in which students honestly assess their writing improvement and achievements over a period of time. Reflective statements allow students to see themselves as writers and to discover both their strengths and the areas in which there is still room for improvement. Keep in mind that a reflective statement is not merely a summary of your completed work; it is an opportunity for you to look closely and analytically at your writing and thus to gain insights about your development as a writer.

CHECKLIST

### Writing a Reflective Statement

As you write your reflective statement, consider the following questions:

- ❑ What skills or knowledge does each item in your portfolio demonstrate? How do these skills and knowledge relate to your instructor's goals? How do they relate to your own academic or professional goals?
- ❑ How are the individual items in your portfolio related? What have you learned about each assignment in the context of your entire portfolio?
- ❑ How have comments made by peer reviewers and by your instructor helped you revise your work?
- ❑ How, specifically, has your writing changed throughout the course? What skills will you continue to work on?
- ❑ Which items in your portfolio best represent your development as a writer? Now that you have some distance from these pieces, do you have new insights about your writing that you didn't have before?

Following is an excerpt from the reflective statement for a student's print portfolio. Notice how both content and design highlight the achievements and improvement demonstrated by the student's writing portfolio.

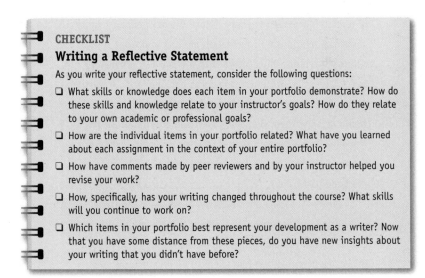

Mahoney 1

Opening component

**To:** Professor Russell

**From:** Samantha Mahoney

**Subject:** English Composition I Portfolio

**Date:** October 4, 2012

---

Purpose statement

This memo summarizes the knowledge and skills demostrated by my English Composition I Portfolio.

Color-coded headings can be used to emphasize and distinguish skill categories

**Drafting and Revising**

What scares me even more than staring at a blank computer screen is working hard on an essay only to have it returned covered in red ink. The relationship essay assignment made me confront my fear of revision and realize that revision is essential to my success as a writer—both in college and after I graduate.

Body of memo describes each assignment, how each essay responds to the assignment, and what the writer learned

This assignment asked us to explore the deep layers of a relationship. In my essay, "Moments of Silence," I wrote about the relationship I have with my hair and what it says about the relationships I have with my mother, my history, and my identity. While the topic was personal and interesting to me, I was unsure how to present it to my readers so that it would interest them. I ended up writing my first draft in a standard five-paragraph format, stating my main idea in a thesis statement and then discussing supporting points in the body paragraphs.

Explanation of how peer and instructor feedback helped student writer to revise

However, comments I received from peers and from you during our one-on-one conferences made me realize that my structure and general approach to my topic needed work. One peer reviewer told me that my essay's traditional organization made him feel distanced from a story that should have been both personal and unique. I worked through another draft before realizing that my essay needed

Mahoney 2

to show my readers why this particular relationship is so important to me. At that point, I changed the entire structure of the essay into a personal narrative to better convey the emotional impact of the relationship I was describing.

This assignment showed me that it is not enough to have a compelling topic; I also need to present that topic to readers in a compelling way. As I realized again and again throughout the semester, considering my audience and incorporating suggestions from my readers will help me to achieve my purpose for writing. This assignment made me see early in the semester how important revision is to my development as a college writer and (as I explain later) as an aspiring journalist.

Discussion of how revision relates to course goals as well as to student writer's academic and professional goals

**Thinking Critically**

The observational descriptive essay assignment asked us to describe a place twice using the same set of details: one description should emphasize the positive aspects of the place, while the other should emphasize the negative. I did not see the value of this assignment until I started working on it and realized it was harder than I had originally thought.

As I observed the restaurant I would write about in "Winter Meal," I began to see the complexities of the place and wonder how I could explain what I saw to others. I tried to view the restaurant from the perspective of a fictional character: a traveler taking refuge from a blizzard or a child who would rather be sledding than eating with his family. In this way, I could describe both the positive and negative qualities of the restaurant to an audience who had never been there. Writing this paper helped me to think critically about my subject and to see that any topic can be viewed from multiple angles.

Mahoney 3

This essay was the most creative and, in some ways, the most challenging of all my portfolio essays. I had to overcome my fear of "creative writing"—something I had never imagined myself doing. I learned that observing and describing a topic in detail meant analyzing it—turning it over again in my mind and on paper. I learned that creative writing and critical thinking are closely related, and that I could use the analytical skills I developed earlier in the semester (especially with my "Moments of Silence" paper) to write creatively. Now that the semester is over, I can see how much this assignment helped me in my final research project to persevere with my research and to think critically about each source I read.

Student writer makes connections among items in her portfolio and explains her insights as a developing writer

**Identifying an Audience**

Our end-of-the-semester research project asked us to explore the information available on a topic and argue our own position. In researching my topic on nutrition and writing my project, "Pass the Brussels Sprouts," I evaluated the credibility of my sources, examining their language for bias and deciding how they would fit into my paper. During one of our first conferences, you reminded me to keep my audience in mind as I wrote and revised this project. Because of the exploratory nature of the assignment, you suggested that I write for an audience much like myself: people who are not nutrition experts, but who are open to learning new information that challenges or even contradicts their ideas.

Explanation of how instructor feedback helped student writer to revise

EXERCISE 7

Using the checklist on page 467 as a guide, write a reflective statement for your portfolio. Ask a friend to read your statement and mark any sections that seem vague, unclear, or unfocused. Then, revise the statement to make it as readable and precise as possible.

## 30d Evaluating Writing Portfolios

Evaluation criteria for portfolios may differ from discipline to discipline, but all effective writing portfolios should be *comprehensive, well-organized, attractively presented,* and *consistent with your instructor's style and format guidelines.*

***Comprehensive*** A **comprehensive** portfolio includes a varied collection of coursework and demonstrates a writer's ability to respond to various writing situations. Be sure to include all the material requested by your instructor.

***Well-Organized*** A **well-organized** portfolio follows a consistent, logical organization that smoothly guides readers through a writer's work.

Portfolio content may be organized in various ways. For example, portfolios may be arranged chronologically, or they may be arranged by assignment, format, skill, level of improvement, or applicability to a student's major. Regardless of the method you use, be sure to label each item in your portfolio with a title, your name, your instructor's name, the course number, the date it was submitted, and any other information your instructor requires. To show the portfolio's content and organization at a glance, include a table of contents for print portfolios (refer back to Figure 30.1 on page 463) and a home page for electronic portfolios (refer back to Figure 30.2 on page 466).

***Attractively Presented*** An **attractively presented** portfolio shows a writer's work in the best possible light. You should use the principles of effective document design or Web design to enhance the readability and accessibility of your work. Remember, however, that design elements should never be superfluous or obtrusive; rather, they should always identify and emphasize important information on a page.

***Consistent with Your Instructor's Style and Format Guidelines*** A portfolio that is consistent with your instructor's style and format guidelines fulfills expectations established by the instructor and by his or her academic discipline. Carefully follow the documentation style and format guidelines your instructor requires for each assignment.

Note: Writing portfolios represent a writer's original work. To avoid committing unintentional plagiarism, be sure to distinguish your ideas from those of your sources.

**Close-Up** PORTFOLIOS IN OTHER DISCIPLINES

Portfolios are not limited to writing courses; in fact, instructors in disciplines other than writing often require portfolios that collect and assess students' work. For example, a math portfolio might indicate a student's progress during a particular unit of study or over an entire semester, and a Web design portfolio might demonstrate mastery of a particular set of skills.

### EXERCISE 8

& Using the checklists on pages 461–62 or 464–65 as a model, create a ten-item customized checklist that addresses the specific concerns you need to consider when assembling your writing portfolio. Compare your checklist with your classmates' and incorporate into your checklist any important steps you omitted. Then, use your checklist to help you assemble, revise, and fine-tune your portfolio.

CHAPTER 31

# Writing Essay Exams

## Frequently Asked Questions



See Ch. 16

Taking exams is a skill, one you have been developing throughout your life as a student. Although both short-answer and essay exams require you to study, to recall what you know, and to budget your time carefully as you write your answers, only essay questions ask you to synthesize information and to arrange ideas in a series of clear, logically connected sentences and paragraphs. To write an essay-length or even a paragraph-length answer, you must do more than memorize facts; you must see the relationships among them. In other words, you must think critically about your subject. See Ch. 8

## Close-Up WRITING IN-CLASS ESSAYS

Many of the strategies that can help you write strong responses to essay exams can also help you plan, write, and revise other kinds of in-class essays.

If you are asked to write an in-class essay, follow the steps outlined in this chapter, and be sure you understand exactly what you are being asked to do and how much time you have in which to do it. Keep in mind, however, that in-class essays, unlike essay exams, may be evaluated on their style and structure as well as on their content. This means, for example, that they should have fully developed introductory and concluding paragraphs.

Be sure you know beforehand the scope and format of the exam. How much of your text and class notes will be covered—the entire semester's work or only the material presented since the last exam? Will you have to answer every question, or will you be able to choose among alternatives? Will the exam be composed entirely of fill-in, multiple-choice, or true/false questions, or will it call for sentence-, paragraph-, or essay-length answers? Will the exam test your ability to recall specific facts, or will it require you to demonstrate your understanding of the course material by drawing conclusions?

### ESL TIP

Writing essay exam answers can be especially stressful because you have a short amount of time to write a thoughtful, accurate, and well-organized essay, using correct grammar and mechanics. One way to make this process easier is to have a clear plan before you begin writing. First decide what information you want to include in your answer and how you want to organize it, and then make an informal outline of your ideas to guide you as you write.

Different kinds of exams require different strategies. When you prepare for a short-answer exam, you may memorize facts without analyzing their relationship to one another or their relationship to a body of knowledge as a whole. When you prepare for an essay exam, however, you must do more than remember bits of information; you must also make connections among ideas.

When you are sure you know what to expect, see if you can anticipate the essay questions your instructor might ask. Try out likely questions on classmates in a **study group,** and see whether you can do some collaborative brainstorming to outline answers to possible questions. (If you have time, you might even practice answering one or two in writing.)

CHECKLIST

**Working in a Study Group**

Working collaboratively in a **study group** requires some degree of organization. To get the most out of your study group, you need to set some ground rules:

- ❑ Meet regularly.
- ❑ Decide in advance who will be responsible for each task.
- ❑ Set deadlines.
- ❑ Listen when someone else is speaking.
- ❑ Don't reject other people's ideas and suggestions without considering them very carefully.
- ❑ Take stock of the group's problems and progress at regular intervals.
- ❑ Be mindful of other students' learning styles and special needs.

## 31a Planning an Essay Exam Answer

Because you are under time pressure during an exam, you may be tempted to skip the planning and revision stages of the writing process. However, if you write in a frenzy and hand in your exam without a second glance, you are likely to produce a disorganized or even incoherent answer. With careful planning and editing, you can write an answer that demonstrates your understanding of the material.

### 1 Consider Your Audience and Purpose

See 1a–b

The audience for an exam is the instructor who prepared it. As you read the questions, think about what your instructor has emphasized in class. Keep in mind that your purpose is to demonstrate that you understand the material, not to make clever remarks or introduce irrelevant information. Also, make every effort to use the vocabulary of the particular academic discipline and to follow any discipline-specific stylistic conventions your instructor has discussed.

See Pt. 6

### 2 Read through the Entire Exam

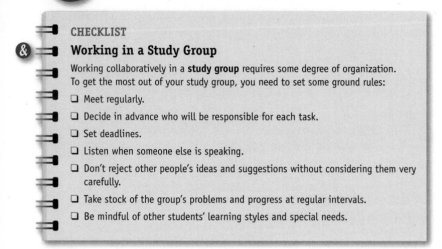

Before you begin to write, read the questions carefully to determine your priorities and your strategy. First, be sure that your copy of the test is complete and that you understand exactly what each question requires. If you need clarification, ask your instructor or proctor for help. Then, plan carefully, deciding how much time you should devote to answering each question. Often, the point value of each question or the number of questions on the exam indicates how much time you should spend on each answer. If an essay question is worth fifty out of one hundred points, for example, you should spend at least half (and perhaps more) of your time planning, writing, and proofreading your answer.

Next, decide where to start. Responding first to questions whose answers you are sure of is usually a good strategy. This tactic ensures that you will not become bogged down in a question that baffles you, left with too little time to write a strong answer to a question that you understand well. Moreover, starting with the questions that you are sure of can help build your confidence.

## 3 Read Each Question Carefully

To write an effective answer, you need to understand the question. As you read any essay question, you may find it helpful to underline key words and important terms.

> **Sociology:** Distinguish among Social Darwinism, instinct theory, and sociobiology, giving examples of each.
>
> **Music:** Explain how Milton Babbitt used the computer to expand Schoenberg's twelve-tone method.
>
> **Philosophy:** Define existentialism and identify three influential existentialist works, explaining why they are important.

Look carefully at the wording of each question. If the question calls for a comparison and contrast of two styles of management, an analysis of one style, no matter how comprehensive, will not be acceptable; if the question asks for causes and effects, a discussion of causes alone will not do.

**ESL TIP**

If you don't understand a word in an essay exam question, ask your instructor for clarification.

**Close-Up** KEY WORDS IN EXAM QUESTIONS

Pay careful attention to the words used in exam questions:

| | | |
|---|---|---|
| • explain | • clarify | • classify |
| • compare | • relate | • identify |
| • contrast | • justify | • illustrate |
| • trace | • analyze | • define |
| • evaluate | • interpret | • support |
| • discuss | • describe | • summarize |

The wording of the exam question suggests what you should emphasize. For instance, an American history instructor would expect very different responses to the following two questions:

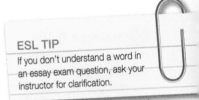

- Give a detailed explanation of the major causes of the Great Depression, noting briefly some of the effects of the economic collapse on the United States.
- Give a detailed summary of the effects of the Great Depression on the United States, briefly discussing the major causes of the economic collapse.

Although these two questions look alike, the first calls for an essay that stresses *causes,* whereas the second calls for one that stresses *effects.*

### 4 Brainstorm to Find Ideas

Once you think you understand the question, you need to find something to say. Begin by brainstorming, quickly listing all the relevant ideas you can remember. Then, identify the most important points on your list, and delete the others. A quick review of the exam question and your supporting ideas should lead you toward a workable thesis for your essay answer.

## 31b Shaping an Essay Exam Answer

See 5a

Like an essay, an effective exam answer has a thesis-and-support structure.

### 1 Stating a Thesis

Often, you can rephrase the exam question as a **thesis statement.** For example, the American history exam question "Give a detailed summary of the effects of the Great Depression on the United States, briefly discussing the major causes of the economic collapse" suggests the following thesis statement:

**Effective Thesis Statement:** The Great Depression, caused by the American government's economic policies, had major political, economic, and social effects on the United States.

This effective thesis statement addresses all aspects of the question but highlights only relevant concerns.

The following thesis statements are not effective:

**Vague Thesis Statement:** The Great Depression, caused largely by profligate spending patterns, had a number of very important results.

**Incomplete Thesis Statement:** The Great Depression caused major upheaval in the United States.

**Irrelevant Thesis Statement:** The Great Depression, caused largely by America's poor response to the 1929 stock market crash, had more important consequences than World War II did.

## 2 Constructing an Informal Outline

Because time is limited, you should plan your answer before you write it. Therefore, once you have decided on a suitable thesis, you should make an **informal outline** of your major points.

See 5d

On the inside cover of your exam book, or on its last sheet, list your supporting points in the order in which you plan to discuss them. Once you have completed your outline, check it against the exam question to make certain it covers everything the question calls for—and *only* what the question calls for.

An informal outline for an answer to the American history question introduced above ("Give a detailed summary of the effects of the Great Depression on the United States, briefly discussing the major causes of the economic collapse") might look like this:

**Thesis Statement:** The Great Depression, caused by the American government's economic policies, had major political, economic, and social effects on the United States.

**Supporting Points:**

Causes

American economic policies: income poorly distributed, factories expanded too much, more goods produced than could be purchased.

Effects

1. Economic situation worsened—farmers, businesses, workers, and stock market all affected.
2. Roosevelt elected—closed banks, worked with Congress to enact emergency measures.
3. Reform—TVA, AAA, NIRA, etc.
4. Social Security Act, WPA, PWA

# 31c Writing and Revising an Essay Exam Answer

Referring to your outline, you can now begin to draft your answer. Don't bother crafting an elaborate or unusual **introduction;** your time is precious, and so is your reader's. A simple statement of your thesis that summarizes your answer is your best introductory strategy: this approach is efficient, and it reminds you to address the question directly.

To develop the **body** of the essay, follow your outline point by point, using clear topic sentences and transitions to indicate your progression and to help your instructor see that you are answering the question in full. Such signals, along with **parallel** sentence structure and repeated key words, make your answer easy to follow.

See 43a

> **ESL TIP**
> Because of time pressure, it is difficult to write in-class essay exam answers that are as polished as your out-of-class writing. Even so, you should do your best to convey your ideas as clearly as you can, but keep in mind that instructors are usually more concerned with the accuracy of the content of your answers than with your writing style. Therefore, instead of wasting time searching for the "perfect" words or phrases, use words and grammatical constructions that are familiar to you. You can use any remaining time to check your grammar and mechanics. Finally, don't waste time recopying your work unless what you have written is illegible.

The most effective **conclusion** for an essay exam answer is a clear, simple restatement of the thesis or a summary of the essay's main points.

Although essay answers should be complete and detailed, they should not contain irrelevant material. Every unnecessary fact or opinion increases your chance of error, so don't repeat yourself or volunteer unrequested information, and don't express your own feelings or opinions unless you are asked to do so. In addition, be careful to support all your general statements with specific examples.

Be sure to leave enough time to revise what you have written. If you remember something you want to add, you can insert a few additional words with a caret (‸). Neatly insert a longer addition at the end of your answer, box it, and label it so your instructor will know where it belongs.

Finally, don't forget to leave a few minutes to proofread your essay to spot misspellings and mechanical errors.

The essay exam answer that appears below follows the outline on page 477. Notice how the student restates the question in her thesis statement and keeps the question in focus by repeating words that signal her focus on causes and effects (*cause, effect, result, response,* and *impact).*

### Effective Essay Exam Answer

**Question:** Give a detailed summary of the effects of the Great Depression on the United States, briefly discussing the major causes of the economic collapse.

Introduction—thesis statement rephrases question

The Great Depression, caused by the American government's economic policies, had major political, economic, and social effects on the United States.

Policies leading to Depression (¶2 summarizes causes)

The Depression was precipitated by the stock market crash of October 1929, but its actual causes were more subtle: they lay in the US government's economic policies. First, personal income was not well distributed. Although production rose during the 1920s, the farmers and other workers got too little of the profits; instead, a disproportionate amount of income went to the richest 5 percent of the population. The tax policies at this time made inequalities in income even worse. A good deal of income also went into development of new manufacturing plants. This expansion stimulated the economy but encouraged the production of more goods than consumers could purchase. Finally, during the economic boom of the 1920s, the government did not attempt to limit speculation or impose regulations on the securities market; it also did little to help build up farmers' buying power. Even after the crash began, the government made mistakes: instead of trying to address the country's deflationary economy, the government focused on keeping the budget balanced and making sure the United States adhered to the gold standard.

The Depression, devastating to millions of individuals, had a tremendous impact on the nation as a whole. Its political, economic, and social consequences were great.

Transition from causes to effects

Between October 1929 and Roosevelt's inauguration on March 4, 1932, the economic situation grew worse. Businesses were going bankrupt, banks were failing, and stock prices were falling. Farm prices fell drastically, and hungry farmers were forced to burn their corn to heat their homes. There was massive unemployment, with millions of workers jobless and humiliated, losing skills and self-respect. President Hoover's Reconstruction Finance Corporation made loans available to banks, railroads, and businesses, but Hoover thought state and local funds (not the federal government) should finance public works programs and relief. Confidence in the president declined as the country's economic situation worsened.

Early effects (¶s 4–8 summarize important results in chronological order)

One result of the Depression was the election of Franklin Delano Roosevelt. By the time of his inauguration, most American banks had closed, thirteen million workers were unemployed, and millions of farmers were threatened by foreclosure. Roosevelt's response was immediate: two days after he took office, he closed all the remaining banks and took steps to support the stronger ones with loans and to prevent the weaker ones from reopening. During the first hundred days of his administration, he kept Congress in special session. Under his leadership, Congress enacted emergency measures designed to provide "Relief, Recovery, and Reform."

Additional effects: Roosevelt's emergency measures

In response to the problems caused by the Depression, Roosevelt set up agencies to reform some of the conditions that had helped to cause the Depression in the first place. The Tennessee Valley Authority, created

Additional effects: Roosevelt's reform measures

in May 1933, was one of these. Its purposes were to control floods by building new dams and improving old ones, and to provide cheap, plentiful electricity. The TVA improved the standard of living of area farmers and drove down the price of power all over the country. The Agricultural Adjustment Administration, created the same month as the TVA, provided for taxes on basic commodities, with the tax revenues used to subsidize farmers to produce less. This reform measure caused prices to rise.

Additional effects: NIRA, other laws, and so on

Another response to the problems of the Depression was the National Industrial Recovery Act. This act established the National Recovery Administration, an agency that set minimum wages and maximum hours for workers and set limits on production and prices. Other laws passed by Congress between 1935 and 1940 strengthened federal regulation of power, interstate commerce, and air traffic. Roosevelt also changed the federal tax structure to redistribute American income.

Additional effects: Social Security, WPA, and so on

One of the most important results of the Depression was the Social Security Act of 1935, which established unemployment insurance and provided financial aid for the blind and disabled and for dependent children and their mothers. The Works Progress Administration (WPA) gave jobs to over two million workers, who built public buildings, roads, streets, bridges, and sewers. The WPA also employed artists, musicians, actors, and writers. The Public Works Administration (PWA) cleared slums and created public housing. In the National Labor Relations Act (1935), workers received a guarantee of government protection for their unions against unfair labor practices by management.

Conclusion—restatement of thesis

As a result of the economic collapse known as the Great Depression, Americans saw their government take responsibility for providing immediate relief, for helping the economy recover, and for taking steps to ensure that the situation would not be repeated. The economic, political, and social impact of the laws passed during the 1930s is still with us, helping to keep our government and our economy stable.

Notice that in her answer the student does not include any irrelevant material: she does not, for example, describe the conditions of people's lives in detail, blame anyone in particular, discuss the president's friends and enemies, or consider related events in other countries. She covers only what the question asks for. Notice, too, how topic sentences (**One result of the**

**Depression . . . ; In response to the problems caused by the Depression . . . ; One of the most important results of the Depression . . .**) keep the primary purpose of the discussion in focus and guide her instructor through the essay.

A well-planned essay like the preceding one is not easy to write. Consider the following ineffective answer to the same question.

### *Ineffective Essay Exam Answer*

The Great Depression is generally considered to have begun with the stock market crash of October 1929 and to have lasted until the defense buildup for World War II. It was a terrible time for millions of Americans, who were not used to being hungry or out of work. Perhaps the worst economic disaster in our history, the Depression left its scars on millions of once-proud workers and farmers who found themselves reduced to poverty. We all have heard stories of businessmen committing suicide when their investments failed, of people selling apples on the street, and of farmers and their families leaving the Dust Bowl in desperate search of work. My own great-grandfather, laid off from his job, had to support my great-grandmother and their four children on what he could make from odd carpentry jobs. This was the Depression at its worst.

No clear thesis; vague, subjective impressions of the Depression

What else did the Depression produce? One result of the Depression was the election of Franklin Delano Roosevelt. Roosevelt immediately closed all banks. Then, Congress set up the Federal Emergency Relief Administration, the Civilian Conservation Corps, the Farm Credit Administration, and the Home Owners' Loan Corporation. The Reconstruction Finance Corporation and the Civil Works Administration were two other agencies designed to provide "Relief, Recovery, and Reform." All these agencies helped Roosevelt in his efforts to lead the nation to recovery while providing relief and reform.

Gratuitous summary

Along with these emergency measures, Roosevelt set out to reform some of the conditions he felt were responsible for the economic collapse. Accordingly, he created the Tennessee Valley Authority (TVA) to control floods and provide electricity in the Tennessee Valley. The Agricultural Adjustment Agency levied taxes and got the farmers to grow less, causing prices to rise. Thus, these agencies, the TVA and the AAA, helped to ease things for the farmers.

Unsupported generalization

The National Industrial Recovery Act established the National Recovery Administration, which was designed to help workers. It established minimum wages and maximum hours, both of which made conditions better for workers. Other important agencies included the Federal Power Commission, the Interstate Commerce Commission, the Maritime Commission, and the Civil Aeronautics Authority. Changes in the tax structure at about this time made the tax system fairer and eliminated some inequities. Roosevelt, working smoothly with his cabinet and with Congress, took many important steps to ease the nation's economic burden.

Why were these agencies important? What did they do?

Despite the fact that he was handicapped by polio, Roosevelt was a dynamic president. His fireside chats, which millions of Americans heard on the radio every week, helped to reassure Americans that things would be fine. This increased his popularity. But he had problems, too. Not everyone agreed with him. Private electric companies opposed the TVA, big business disagreed with his support of labor unions, the rich did not like the way he restructured the tax system, and many people saw him as dangerously radical. Still, he was one of the most popular presidents ever.

Digression: discussion of Roosevelt is irrelevant

—Social Security Act: unemployment insurance, aid to blind and disabled and children

—WPA: built public projects

—PWA: public housing

—National Labor Relations Act: strengthened labor unions

Undeveloped information

This essay only indirectly answers the exam question. It devotes too much space to unnecessary elements: an emotional introduction, needlessly repeated words and phrases, gratuitous summaries, and unsupported generalizations. Without a thesis statement to guide her, the writer slips into a discussion of only the immediate impact of the Depression and never discusses its causes or its long-term effects. Although the body paragraphs do provide the names of many agencies created by the Roosevelt administration, they do not explain the purpose of most of them. Consequently, the student seems to consider the formation of the agencies, not their contributions, to be the Depression's most significant result.

Because the student took a time-consuming detour to discuss Roosevelt, she had to list some information at the end of the essay without discussing it fully; moreover, she was left with no time to sum up her main points, even in a one-sentence conclusion. Although it is better to include undeveloped information than to skip it altogether, many instructors will not give credit if you do not write your answer in full. More important, you cannot effectively show logical or causal relationships in a list.

## 31d Writing Paragraph-Length Essay Exam Answers

Some essay questions ask for a paragraph-length answer, not a full essay. A paragraph should be just that: not one or two sentences, not a list of points, not more than one paragraph.

A paragraph-length answer should be **unified** by a clear topic sentence. Just as an essay-length answer begins with a thesis statement, a paragraph-length answer opens with a topic sentence that summarizes what the paragraph will cover. You should phrase this sentence so that it echoes the wording of the exam question. The paragraph should also be **coherent**—that is, its statements should be linked by transitions that move the reader along. Finally, the paragraph should be **well developed**, with enough relevant detail to convince your reader that you know what you are talking about.

See 7a

See 7b–c

### *Effective Paragraph-Length Essay Exam Answer*

**Question:** In one paragraph, define the term *management by objectives*, give an example of how it works, and briefly discuss an advantage of this approach.

As defined by Horngren, *management by objectives* is an approach by which a manager and his or her superior together formulate goals, and plans by which they can achieve these goals, for a forthcoming period. For example, a manager and a superior can formulate a responsibility accounting budget, and the manager's performance can then be measured according to how well he or she meets the objectives defined by the budget. The advantage of this approach is that the goals set are attainable because they are not formulated in a vacuum. Rather, the objectives are based on what the entire team reasonably expects to accomplish. As a result, the burden of responsibility is shifted from the superior to the team: the goal itself defines all the steps needed for its completion.

Definition

Example

Advantage

In this answer, key phrases (**As defined by . . . ; For example . . . ; The advantage of this approach . . .**) clearly identify the various parts of the question being addressed. The writer includes just what the question asks for and no more. His use of the wording of the question helps make the paragraph orderly, coherent, and emphatic.

The student who wrote the following response may know what *management by objectives* is, but his paragraph sounds more like a casual explanation to a friend than an answer to an exam question.

### *Ineffective Paragraph-Length Essay Exam Answer*

Sketchy, casual definition; no example given

Management by objectives is when managers and their bosses get together to formulate their goals. This is a good system of management because it cuts down on hard feelings between managers and their superiors. Because they set the goals together, they can make sure they're attainable by considering all possible influences, constraints, and so on, that might occur. This way neither the manager nor the superior gets all the blame when things go wrong.

Vague

Remember, no response to an essay exam question will be effective unless you take the time to read the question carefully, plan your response, and outline your answer before you begin to write. It is always a good idea to use the wording of the question in your answer and to reread your answer to make sure it explicitly answers the question and contains no distracting grammatical or mechanical errors.

CHAPTER 32

# Writing for the Public and the Community

## Frequently Asked Questions



Some of the writing you do—such as diaries and journals—is strictly private, written just for yourself. Other writing—such as research papers and essay exams—is directed at an academic audience. At times, you may also be called upon to do **public writing,** producing documents directed to individuals and groups in the community outside your school.

In a composition course, a work-study job, a service-learning course, a co-op placement, or an internship (and, later, in the workplace), you may be required to write letters, proposals, flyers, brochures, media releases, and newsletters as well as Web pages, blog posts, and email messages directed at a community beyond the classroom.

See 32e

See 27b1–2

Many courses in various academic disciplines also include public-writing components. Depending on the discipline, you might be assigned to produce a variety of documents—for example, an op-ed piece for a criminal justice or political science course, a brochure for a public health course, book or film reviews for a literature class, or popular "translations" of scientific or technical material for a science or engineering course.

See Pt. 6

## Close-Up COLLABORATION AND PUBLIC WRITING

Many public writing projects in college classes are worked on collaboratively. Typically, an assignment will be given to a team of three to five students, who will then brainstorm collaboratively to come up with ideas. Different students will then take on different tasks—for example, contacting members of the community for feedback, making inquiries about possible funding sources to cover printing costs, or working with a graphic designer. Later on, students may write different sections of a document or revise and edit it at different stages before it is presented to the public.

Through public writing, you learn more about how to identify an audience and accommodate its needs as well as how to write for a variety of purposes. You also have an opportunity to practice the principles of good document design. And, of course, the skills you develop in public writing projects can help you succeed in the workplace. For example, you can develop rhetorical skills you might use in writing business reports, memos, and proposals or in developing a marketing campaign. More generally, working on public-writing projects can help you learn to write concise prose, to work as a member of a team, and to communicate with nonexpert audiences in business-to-business contexts.

See Ch. 28

The following sections discuss *media releases, proposals, brochures,* and *flyers*. These documents are typical of the kinds of writing students can create for the public.

## 32a Writing Media Releases

One common kind of public writing is the **media release,** a document designed to provide information about a project or event to media outlets (newspapers, magazines, online publications, and so on). This information can be used to help publications develop articles informing their readers about the subject of the media release.

The media release that follows was written by a student in an advanced composition course. It was sent to various local media outlets to advertise an upcoming conference on her university's campus. Note that the media release includes an attention-getting headline set in boldface and large type and a standard heading that provides contact information. (Sometimes a media release is accompanied by a cover letter. **See 33a** for information on business letter format.)

### *Sample Media Release*

For Immediate Release:

Contact:

Carol Hulse

Instructor of English at the University of West Florida

(850) 474-2933

chulse@uwf.edu

Linda Moore

Instructor of English at the University of West Florida

(850) 857-6074

lmoore@uwf.edu

**HIGH SCHOOL ARTICULATION CONFERENCE TO BE HELD AT UWF ON MARCH 8, 2011**

**UWF English Department Will Host Event for Escambia and Santa Rosa High Schools**

University of West Florida—On March 8, 2011, a high school articulation conference will be held for high school teachers in Escambia and Santa Rosa County from 8:00 a.m. to 3:00 p.m. The UWF English Department and students of composition are sponsoring this event, which will be held in Building 51. Students, teachers, and administrators are all invited to attend. The purpose of the conference is to establish better communication with local high schools in order to improve high school graduates' preparation for college-level coursework.

This year's keynote speaker will be Dr. David Jolliffe, the former Advanced Placement Exam Chief Reader and current Brown Chair in English Literacy at the University of Arkansas. Other speakers will include Dr. Peggy Jolly, Professor and Director of Freshman English and Developmental Studies at the University of Alabama at Birmingham; Bruce Swain, Chairperson of Communication Arts at UWF; and the winner of the "Call for Papers" abstract contest. The main topic of the conference will be "The Severity of Plagiarism."

A tour of the UWF Writing Lab will be available from 11:00 a.m. to 12:00 p.m., and lunch will be provided. Please contact Carol Hulse or Linda Moore for more information.

*The UWF English Department and students of composition are sponsoring this event in order to promote better college readiness and success.*

###

Sample Media Release: High School Articulation Conference to Be Held at UWF on March 8, 2011. Reprinted with permission.

### EXERCISE 1

Imagine that your school is sponsoring an open house for prospective students. Visit your school's Web site and survey the programs, services, and facilities highlighted there. Then, write a media release, directed at high school guidance counselors, announcing the open house. Your goal is to convince this audience to encourage students to attend the open house.

## 32b Writing Proposals

In public writing, **proposals** are often written to identify a specific problem in a community and propose a detailed, concrete plan for solving it.

After reading about the widespread problem of decreased literacy levels in the United States, students in an advanced composition course were asked to work in teams to design a new program, campaign, or service to improve literacy in their community. The following proposal outlines one team's idea, a campus book drive. The purpose of the proposal (directed at the university's student government association) was to appeal for funding to support the project. Note that the proposal includes internal headings to identify various sections and help readers locate information. (See p. 491 for the brochure the student team designed to promote the book drive.)

### *Sample Proposal*

To: April Jardine, University of West Florida Student Government Association President

From: Christian Cabral, Justin Ellis, Sara Holcomb, Sarah Neuland, Carl Shouppe (composition students)

Date: September 29, 2012

Subject: Proposal for Campus Book Drive

In our English Composition II class, we have been studying the problem of illiteracy in the United States. Our research has shown us that there is a great need to encourage reading, especially in young children. Many families would like to have books for their children but do not have the time or money to acquire reading materials. Because our campus is a part of a larger community, we believe that the University of West Florida has the responsibility to help such families. To do our part to increase literacy levels in the United States, we believe we must begin locally, increasing our community's literacy rates first. Therefore, we propose that a community book drive be held on campus during the month of November. We will need financial support as we plan, advertise, and implement this book drive, and we hope SGA will consider funding this important project.

**Background and Rationale**

Illiteracy is one of the great plagues of the twenty-first century. According to the article "Grim Illiteracy Statistics Indicate Americans Have a Reading Problem" published on the *Education Portal* Web site, 42 million American adults cannot read. In fact, as our society has become more and more technologically advanced, America's young people have been reading less. The online *Chronicle of Higher Education* article "Literary Reading Is Declining Faster than Before, Arts Endowment's New Report Says" describes "a steady drop, over two decades, in the percentage of Americans who read books of any sort. . . ." Many children do not own books, and many parents cannot afford to purchase books for their children. The book drive we propose can be a starting point for getting books into children's hands.

We are appealing to the SGA on behalf of our fellow students, requesting your financial assistance in support of our project. Our goal is to help children in our community whose families cannot afford to purchase books—particularly those children who live in foster homes and shelters.

**Plans**

To help spread awareness about our book drive, we plan to begin by creating a brochure for mass distribution. (We will also use other means to spread the word about the event, including posters, banners, flyers, and media releases to be sent to the *Pensacola News Journal,* the *Voyager,* and *Argus*.) The purpose of the brochure will be to publicize the book drive and explain its rationale to students, faculty, and staff on the University of West Florida campus. According to the *National Center for Family Literacy* Web site, "Children participating in family literacy programs demonstrated greater gains than children in child-focused programs." Our book drive can create an opportunity for families to read together, and the brochure—distributed on and around the University of West Florida campus—can spread awareness about the project and encourage members of the university community to donate books.

To publicize our project, we plan to appeal to the university community to design and produce flyers and posters, which we will distribute to local churches and shopping malls as well as throughout our campus. Distributing flyers and posters in high-volume areas will enable us to gather more books from wider sources—not only from college students but from members of the larger community as well.

Of course, advertising costs money. For example, we will need at least one thousand sheets of paper for flyers as well as poster board and paint. We would also like to set up drop boxes on campus—and, if possible, off campus as well—where people can donate books. In addition, we will need help recruiting volunteers to help design, produce, and distribute flyers, banners, and posters on campus and to assist in other areas if needed—for example, to sort the donated books by age and subject. Finally, we will need a room in which to meet as a group to set up, organize, collect, and sort the books we receive.

**Conclusion and Recommendations**

As the organization ProLiteracy Worldwide states in the report *The State of Adult Literacy 2006,* "there are 771 million illiterate adults in the world . . ." (3). Many of them are Americans. As ProLiteracy Worldwide points out, "If today's children are to become the adult readers of tomorrow, we must treat the acquisition of literacy skills as a neverending process" (13).

We know that the literacy problem cannot be solved overnight, but our group is committed to doing what it can. We ask that you, the president of SGA, approve our proposal and grant us the resources we need to support our book drive. A tentative budget and timetable are attached. Thank you for taking the time to consider our project.

### EXERCISE 2

Visit the Web sites of five area colleges and universities, and survey their academic programs and student services. Choose one program or service that is not available at the school you attend, and write a proposal explaining why it should be. Include background about the program at the other school, and explain how the program or service you recommend will serve your school's student population and improve the educational experience.

## 32c Designing Brochures

A **brochure** is a short pamphlet or booklet that provides information about a service, program, or event.

The student brochure on page 491, directed at the campus community (students, faculty, and staff) was designed to promote a book drive on a university campus in support of the school's efforts to fight illiteracy in the community.

### EXERCISE 3

& Working in a group of three students, design and write two brochures to be distributed at the open house described in Exercise 1. One brochure should be directed at prospective students, and the other should be directed at their parents. Your goal is to make your school as appealing as possible to each of these two very different audiences.

## Sample Brochure

**The following people are coordinating this project:**

Sara Holcomb
Christian Cabral
Justin Ellis
Carl Shouppe
Sarah Neuland

**For more information, please contact**

Student Government Association
University of West Florida
11000 University Parkway
Commons Bldg. 22, Room 227
Pensacola, FL 32514
Phone: (850) 474-2393
Fax: (850) 474-2390
www.uwf.edu/sga/

Campus Book Drive

**November 7-21**

Front and back cover of brochure. © Cengage Learning 2013.

**Why have a book drive?**

- To promote the importance of literacy throughout our community
- To provide books for people who cannot afford to buy them
- To supply books to residents of shelters for homeless families
- To encourage families to read together
- To improve literacy for future generations of children

**Why should you help to promote literacy?**

- 771 million people in the world are illiterate
- In the US alone, 42 million people cannot read
- Nonreaders lack the skills they need to succeed in the workplace

**How can you help make this book drive successful?**

- Look for bright green boxes around campus, and donate new or gently used books for children and adults
- Volunteer to help sort through and distribute the books that are collected
- SPREAD THE WORD!

Inside pages of brochure. © Cengage Learning 2013.

## 32d Designing Flyers

A **flyer** is a one-page document that uses text and graphics to advertise an upcoming event. (**See 28a** for information on creating an effective visual format.)

Students in a composition course created the flyer below to promote a benefit concert on their campus.

*Sample Flyer*

Mayland Community College
Benefit Concert
Featuring six local bands and appetizers donated by the State Street Grill
Art Building, Main Campus
March 21st – 7pm
$10
Proceeds from this event go to the Herter-O'Neal Scholarship fund sponsored by the Young Professionals student association.



**EXERCISE 4**

Assume that the new program or service you recommended in Exercise 2 has been implemented at your school. Design a flyer to announce this new program or service to students.

## 32e Writing for Service-Learning Courses

During your college career, you may take one or more service-learning courses. **Service-learning** courses are designed to help you learn course content by doing service in the community. By adding another dimension to your coursework, you can strengthen your critical thinking skills, sharpen your communications skills, and make more informed career decisions.

In service-learning components of college courses, students gain valuable experience while contributing to their communities:

- Students in an educational psychology course who are studying learning theory might observe a high school class in order to apply education theory to actual students; at the same time, the service-learning students can use what they have learned in their educational psychology course to help the high school students learn more effectively.
- In an advanced composition course studying the rhetoric of advertising campaigns, students might work in groups to design an ad campaign for a nonprofit agency. After interviewing workers and clients, the students could design effective print and visual documents to highlight the agency's services; at the end of the project, the agency would be given copies of the material the students designed.
- In a chemical engineering course, students might test water quality in area streams or creeks and share this information with their township or with a community environmental group. Using this baseline data, other students could later retest the water and report their conclusions to the same group.

Assignments in service-learning courses can range from proposals to oral histories to poetry. The most common assignment, however, is a **reflective journal,** a collection of informal responses that answer questions posed by the course instructor at various points during the semester. Before students begin the service-learning component of a course, the instructor might ask questions such as the following:

- Why did you decide to take this course?
- What do you hope to learn from your service-learning experience?

(In some cases, the instructor might ask a group of students to brainstorm collaboratively as they explore answers to these questions.) &

After the first week or two of the semester, the instructor's questions will typically become more specific. For example, in a math education class, the instructor might ask questions designed to help students focus on the issues that will be central to their experience:

- What did you expect the elementary math students to know?
- What difficulties did you expect them to have?
- Did you expect them to enjoy solving the math problems you prepared?
- How did you expect the school to be like or unlike the elementary school you attended?

For their service-learning experience, students in a biology class used material they had covered in lab to prepare basic science lessons for middle school students. Following is an excerpt from one student's reflective journal, written in response to her instructor's question, "What surprised you about your first meeting with your student?"

> The girl I was working with didn't seem to understand the material I'd prepared. The problem is that her reading level is somewhere around first grade. Her knowledge of words seemed to come only from memorization; she couldn't sound out words. She didn't seem to have any learning problems that would prevent her from reading. It just seemed as if she didn't know how. That concept is foreign to me. I'd heard of schools in this area passing kids even when they don't meet standards, but I never thought it was true. The interesting thing, though, was that reading seemed to get easier for her the longer we worked on the biology material. It began to seem as if maybe she did know how to read but her brain just needed to warm up. But why? Does it mean she doesn't read often enough, so she's just not used to it? Or could she for some reason be afraid to read? I thought I'd be teaching basic biology, but when the hour was up, we'd hardly started to talk about the material.

Students then write additional reflections after each visit to the service-learning site, with the instructor's questions—and their own responses—becoming more focused and analytical as the semester progresses. The goal is for the reflections to help students zero in on more than just what happened at the site; ideally, they should explore how their activities and observations relate to what they have learned in their own classes. At the end of the semester, students write a comprehensive reflective essay that sums up both what they learned and how their work benefited the community.

Another class's service-learning project was to introduce a genealogy curriculum to elementary school students in an inner-city school. An excerpt from a student's final reflection appears below.

> At the very beginning of the semester, I was kind of overwhelmed when I thought about the amount of work a service-learning class might require, but it didn't turn out to be any more work than my other courses, maybe because we did so much work in groups instead of on our own. Now that the semester is winding down, I'm glad I stuck with the class. Still, I would advise students not to take a class like this if they already have a very busy schedule because the collaborative work can sometimes be hard to schedule.
>
> I really didn't have any particular expectations when I started this class, so I was surprised by how much I enjoyed myself. Not only was the

course material interesting, but the bond our class developed was really strong. I think it would have been even better if we could have worked on at least one project all together; our class bond would have been even stronger if at the end of the semester we could have looked back and said we all did something as a group and made an impact as one.

At first, I was scared about all the writing, reading, and so on. Genealogy was new to me, and it took me a while to understand the concept well enough to explain it to kids who knew even less than I did. Still, after working on the project, I developed an interest in learning about my own family's past. So even if the curriculum we developed isn't put to use, at least I will have learned something about a topic I'd never thought much about before.

CHAPTER 33

# Writing for the Workplace

## Frequently Asked Questions



Employers value good writing skills. To make sure that job applicants can communicate effectively, some businesses include a writing assessment as part of the hiring process. They know that a good part of each workday is spent reading business communications. In addition, the higher people go in a company, the more they write, and poorly written memos, letters, and reports can cost businesses millions of dollars each year. For this reason, the writing skills you learn in college can give you a definite competitive advantage in the workplace.

## 33a Writing Business Letters

Business letters should be brief and to the point, with important information placed early in the letter. Be concise, avoid digressions, and try to sound as natural as possible.

The first paragraph of your letter should introduce your subject and mention any pertinent previous correspondence. The body of your letter should present the information readers need to understand your points. (If your ideas are complicated, present your points in a bulleted or numbered list.) Your conclusion should reinforce your message.

See 28c

Single-space within paragraphs, and double-space between paragraphs. Most often, business letters use **block format,** with all parts of the letter aligned with the left-hand margin. Proofread carefully to make sure there are no errors in spelling or punctuation.

## 33b Writing Letters of Application

A **letter of application** (also called a **cover letter**) summarizes your qualifications for a specific position. A letter of application (print or electronic) should be short and focused. Your primary objective in writing this letter is to obtain an interview.

Begin your letter of application by identifying the specific job you are applying for and stating where you heard about it—in a newspaper, in a professional journal, on a Web site, or from your school's job placement service, for example. Be sure to include the date of the advertisement and the exact title of the position. End your introduction with a statement that expresses your confidence in your ability to do the job.

In the body of your letter of application, provide the specific information that will convince readers of the strength of your qualifications—for example, relevant courses you have taken and pertinent job experience. Be sure to address any specific points mentioned in the advertisement. Above all, emphasize your strengths, and explain how they relate to the job for which you are applying. Remember, the prospective employer is primarily interested in what you can do for the company, so keep this in mind as you write.

Conclude by saying that you have enclosed your résumé and that you are available for an interview, noting any dates on which you will not be available. Be sure to include both your phone number and your email address in your letter.

### *Sample Letter of Application*

| | |
|---|---|
| Heading | 246 Hillside Drive<br>Urbana, IL 61801<br>Kr237@metropolis.105.com<br>(217) 283-3017<br><br>March 19, 2012 |
| Inside address | Mr. Maurice Snyder, Personnel Director<br>Guilford, Fox, and Morris<br>22 Hamilton Street<br>Urbana, IL 61822 |
| Salutation (followed by a colon) | Dear Mr. Snyder: |
| Body | My college advisor, Dr. Raymond Walsh, has told me that you are interested in hiring a summer accounting intern. I believe that my academic background and my work experience qualify me for this position.<br><br>I am presently a junior accounting major at the University of Illinois. During the past year, I have taken courses in taxation, trusts, and business law. I am also proficient in *PeachTree Complete* and *QuickBooks Pro*. Last spring, I gained practical accounting experience by working in our department's tax clinic. |
| Double-space → | |
| Single-space → | After I graduate, I hope to get a master's degree in taxation and then return to the Urbana area. I believe that my experience in taxation as well as my familiarity with the local business community would enable me to contribute to your firm.<br><br>I have enclosed a résumé for your examination. I will be available for an interview any time after midterm examinations, which end March 23. I look forward to hearing from you. |
| Complimentary close | Sincerely, |
| Written signature | *Sandra Kraft* |
| Typed signature | Sandra Kraft |
| Additional data | Enc: Résumé |

*Note:* Before you send your letter, proofread it very carefully. At this stage of the application process, even a single error in spelling or grammar could disqualify you.

## 33c Writing Follow-Up Emails

After you have been interviewed, send a **follow-up email** to the person (or persons) who interviewed you. First, thank your interviewer for taking the time to see you. Then, briefly summarize your qualifications and reinforce your interest in the position. Figure 33.1 shows a follow-up email. Because many applicants do not write follow-up emails, this kind of message can make a positive impression.

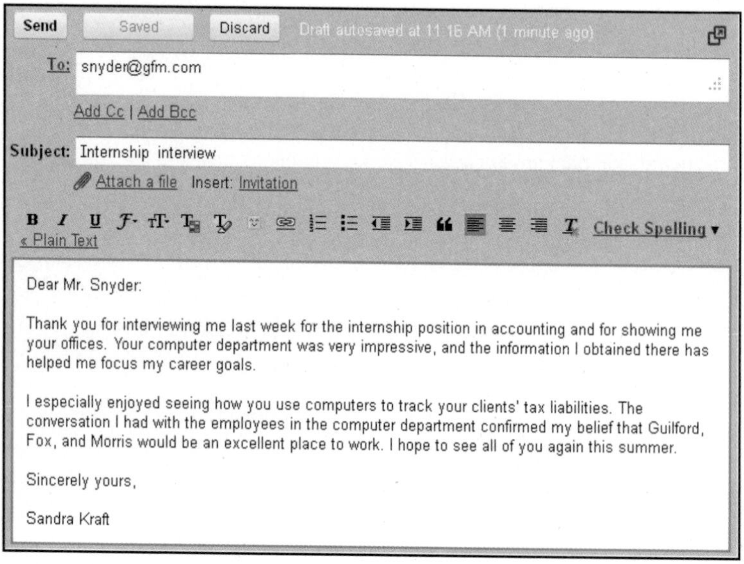


Dear Mr. Snyder:

Thank you for interviewing me last week for the internship position in accounting and for showing me your offices. Your computer department was very impressive, and the information I obtained there has helped me focus my career goals.

I especially enjoyed seeing how you use computers to track your clients' tax liabilities. The conversation I had with the employees in the computer department confirmed my belief that Guilford, Fox, and Morris would be an excellent place to work. I hope to see all of you again this summer.

Sincerely yours,

Sandra Kraft



FIGURE 33.1 Sample follow-up email.

*Note:* Before you begin your job search, make sure you delete any inappropriate material from your social networking sites. Many employers routinely search these sites during the hiring process.

### EXERCISE 1

Look through the employment advertisements in the files of your school's job placement service. Choose one job, and write a letter of application in which you summarize your achievements and discuss your qualifications for the position.

## 33d Designing Print Résumés

A **résumé** lists relevant information about your education, your job experience, your goals, and your personal interests.

There is no single correct format for a résumé. You will most likely arrange your résumé in **chronological order** (see p. 500), listing your education and work experience in sequence (beginning with the most recent). Whatever a résumé's arrangement, it should be brief—one page is usually sufficient for an undergraduate—easy to read, clear and emphatic, logically organized, and free of errors. If you include an employment objective, be sure you tailor it to the specific job you are applying for as well as to the employer your résumé is being sent to.

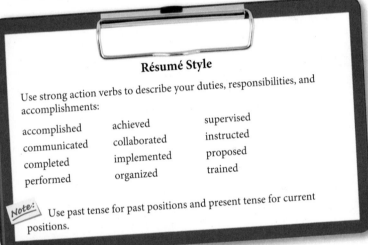

**Résumé Style**

Use strong action verbs to describe your duties, responsibilities, and accomplishments:

| | | |
|---|---|---|
| accomplished | achieved | supervised |
| communicated | collaborated | instructed |
| completed | implemented | proposed |
| performed | organized | trained |

*Note:* Use past tense for past positions and present tense for current positions.

### Close-Up RÉSUMÉ TEMPLATES

*Microsoft Word* contains **résumé templates,** preformatted documents that help you design a résumé. Keep in mind, however, that many employers and recruiters will dismiss résumés that strictly follow one of these standardized formats. In their view, if a candidate does not take the time to put together an original résumé, why should they take the time to read it?

These templates can give you ideas about what your résumé should look like, but you should not simply plug information into them. Take the time to create your own résumé, one that communicates your initiative and leads a prospective employer to conclude that you are a strong candidate for the job.

## Sample Résumé: Chronological Order

| KAREN L. OLSON | SCHOOL<br>3812 Hamilton St. Apt. 18<br>Philadelphia, PA 19104<br>215-382-0831<br>olsont@dunm.ocs.drexel.edu | HOME<br>110 Ascot Ct.<br>Harmony, PA 16037<br>412-452-2944 |
|---|---|---|

EDUCATION

DREXEL UNIVERSITY, Philadelphia, PA 19104
Bachelor of Science in Graphic Design
Anticipated Graduation: June 2013
Cumulative Grade Point Average: 3.2 on a 4.0 scale

COMPUTER SKILLS AND COURSEWORK

HARDWARE

Familiar with both Macintosh and PC systems

SOFTWARE

*Adobe Illustrator, Photoshop,* and *Type Align; QuarkXPress; CorelDRAW; Adobe InDesign*

COURSES

Corporate Identity, Environmental Graphics, Typography, Photography, Painting and Printmaking, Sculpture, Computer Imaging, Art History

EMPLOYMENT EXPERIENCE

*THE TRIANGLE,* Drexel University, Philadelphia, PA 19104
January 2010–present
Graphics Editor. Design all display advertisements submitted to Drexel's student newspaper.

UNISYS CORPORATION, Blue Bell, PA 19124
June–September 2010, Cooperative Education
Graphic Designer. Designed interior pages as well as covers for target marketing brochures. Created various logos and spot art designed for use on interoffice memos and departmental publications.

CHARMING SHOPPES, INC, Bensalem, PA 19020
June–December 2009, Cooperative Education
Graphic Designer/Fashion Illustrator. Created graphics for future placement on garments. Did some textile designing. Drew flat illustrations of garments to scale in computer. Prepared presentation boards.

DESIGN AND IMAGING STUDIO, Drexel University, Philadelphia, PA 19104
October 2008–June 2009
Monitor. Supervised computer activity in studio. Answered telephone. Assisted other graphic design students in using computer programs.

ACTIVITIES AND AWARDS

*The Triangle,* Graphics Editor: 2010–present
Kappa Omicron Nu Honor Society, vice president: 2010–present
Graphics Group, vice president: 2009–present
Dean's List: spring 2010, fall and winter 2011

REFERENCES AND PORTFOLIO

Available upon request.

## 33e Designing Electronic Résumés

The majority of résumés are still submitted on paper or as email attachments, but electronic résumés—both scannable and Web-based—are gaining in popularity.

> **ESL TIP**
>
> When describing honors that you received in another country and that may not be familiar to potential employers, it is wise to provide an explanation. For example, you might indicate what percentage of graduates receive this honor. You may also wish to indicate your visa status and your language skills on your résumé.
>
> *Note:* In some countries, job applicants list information about their age and marital status in their job application materials. However, in the United States, this is usually not done because employers are not legally allowed to discriminate on the basis of such factors.

### 1 Scannable Résumés

Many employers request scannable résumés that they can store in a database for future reference. If you prepare such a résumé, keep in mind that scanners will not pick up columns, bullets, or italics and that shaded or colored paper will make your résumé difficult to scan.

Whereas in a print résumé you use specific action verbs (**edited**) to describe your accomplishments, in a scannable résumé you also use key nouns (**editor**) that can be entered into a company database. These words will help employers find your résumé when they carry out a keyword search for applicants with certain skills. To facilitate a keyword search, applicants often include a Skills section on their résumé. For example, if you wanted to emphasize your computer skills, you would include keywords such as *WordPerfect, FileMaker Pro, PowerPoint*, and *C++*.

### *Sample Résumé: Scannable*

Deborah Keller
2000 Clover Lane
Fort Worth, TX 76107

Phone: (817) 735-9120
Email: kell5@aol.com

Employment Objective: Entry-level position in an organization that will enable me to use my academic knowledge and the skills that I learned in my work experience.

Education:

University of Texas at Arlington, Bachelor of Science in Civil Engineering, June 2012. Major: Structural Engineering. Graduated Magna Cum Laude. Overall GPA: 3.754 on a 4.0 base.

Scholastic Honors and Awards:

Member of Phi Eta Sigma First-Year Academic Honor Society, Chi Epsilon Civil Engineering Academic Society, Tau Beta Pi Engineering Academic Society, Golden Key National Honor Society.

Jack Woolf Memorial Scholarship for Outstanding Academic Performance.

Grant from the Society of Women Engineers.

Cooperative Employment Experience:

Johnson County Electric Cooperative, Clebume, TX, Jan. 2012 to June 2012. Junior Engineer in Plant Dept. of Maintenance and Construction Division. Inspected and supervised in-plant construction. Devised solutions to construction problems. Estimated costs of materials for small construction projects. Presented historical data relating to the function of the department.

Dallas-Fort Worth International Airport, Tarrant County, TX, Dec. 2010 to June 2011. Assistant Engineer. Supervised and inspected airfield paving, drainage, and utility projects as well as terminal building renovations. Performed on-site and laboratory soil tests. Prepared concrete samples for load testing.

Dallas-Fort Worth International Airport, Tarrant County, TX, Jan. 2010 to June 2010. Draftsperson in Design Office. Prepared contract drawings and updated base plans as well as designed and estimated costs for small construction projects.

Skills:

Organizational and leadership skills. Written and oral communication skills, C++, PC, Macintosh, DOS, Windows 7, Mac OSX Lion, Word, Excel, FileMakerPro, PowerPoint, WordPerfect, and Internet client software. Computer model development. Technical editor.

## 2 Web-Based Résumés

It is becoming common to have a version of your résumé posted on a Web site such as *Monster.com* (Figure 33.2) or *CareerBuilder.com*. Usually, a Web-based résumé is an alternative to a print résumé that you have mailed or a scannable version that you have submitted to a database or sent as an email attachment.

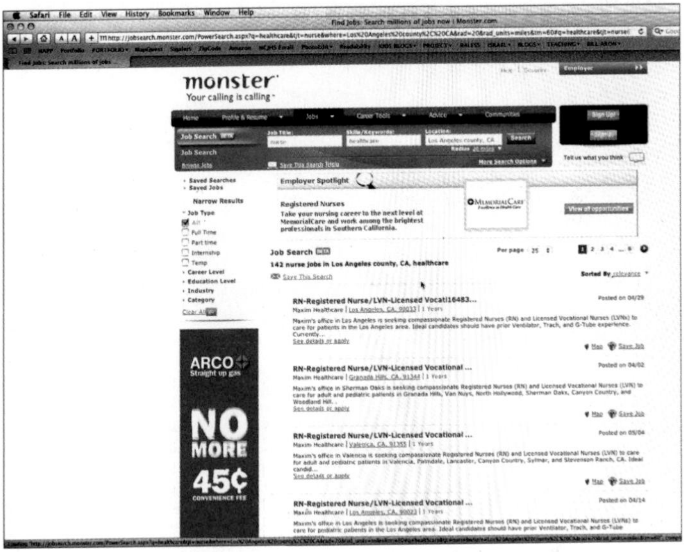


Bill Aron/PhotoEdit

FIGURE 33.2 *Monster.com*, a popular Web site for posting résumés.

### EXERCISE 2

Prepare two versions of your résumé—one print and the other scannable—that you could include with the letter of application you wrote for Exercise 1. How are these two résumés alike? How are they different?

### Close-Up ELECTRONIC PORTFOLIOS

Many disciplines are now recommending the use of **electronic portfolios,** Web-based collections of materials that represent a job applicant's skills and abilities. Prospective employers can select the items in the portfolio of most interest to them, perhaps following up on a reference in a cover letter or a link in an electronic résumé. Portfolios may also include personal statements, writing samples, and even video or audio clips.

*(continued)*

**ELECTRONIC PORTFOLIOS** *(continued)*

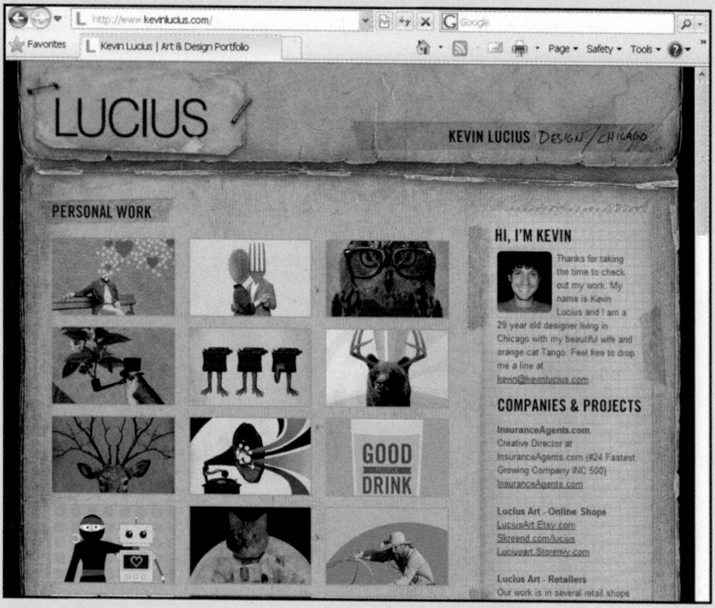


Courtesy of Kevin Lucius.

## 33f Writing Memos

Memos communicate information within an organization. A memo can be short or long, formal or informal, depending on its purpose. For example, some memos communicate trivial information (such as the time and location of a work-related social event) while others communicate important information in the form of reports or proposals. Given the increased use of electronic communication in organizations, most memos are either delivered as emails or as email attachments.

Begin your memo with a purpose statement that presents your reason for writing it. Follow this statement with a background section that gives readers the information they will need to understand the current situation. Then, in the body of your memo, present the detailed information that constitutes your support. If your document is short, use bulleted or numbered lists to emphasize information. If it is long—more than two or three paragraphs—use headings to designate the various sections of the memo (**Summary, Background, Benefits,** and so on). End your memo with a statement of your conclusions and recommendations.

***Sample Memo***

Opening component

TO: Ina Ellen, Senior Counselor
FROM: Kim Williams, Student Tutor Supervisor
SUBJECT: Construction of a Tutoring Center
DATE: November 9, 2012

Purpose statement

This memo proposes the establishment of a tutoring center in the Office of Student Affairs.

BACKGROUND

Under the present system, tutors must work with students at a number of facilities scattered across the university campus. As a result, tutors waste a lot of time running from one facility to another and are often late for appointments.

Body

NEW FACILITY

I propose that we establish a tutoring facility adjacent to the Office of Student Affairs. The two empty classrooms next to the office, presently used for storage of office furniture, would be ideal for this use. We could furnish these offices with the desks and file cabinets already stored in these rooms.

BENEFITS

The benefits of this facility would be the centralizing of the tutoring services and the proximity of the facility to the Office of Student Affairs. The tutoring facility could also use the secretarial services of the Office of Student Affairs.

RECOMMENDATIONS

Conclusion

To implement this project we would need to do the following:

1. Clean up and paint rooms 331 and 333
2. Use folding partitions to divide each room into five single-desk offices
3. Use stored office equipment to furnish the center

I am certain these changes would do much to improve the tutoring service. I look forward to discussing this matter with you in more detail.

### Close-Up COLLABORATIVE WRITING IN THE WORKPLACE

Writing in the workplace is frequently a collaborative effort. Often, a letter, memo, or report is the result of the combined efforts of many people who have different skills and access to different information. For example, one person might write the first draft of a memo and then pass it on to other people—coworkers and supervisors—for suggestions. Their suggestions can be written in the margins or inserted electronically using *Word*'s Comment feature or the highlighting feature of Track Changes. The final document, which incorporates these suggestions, will often be stronger than a document written by one person working alone.

## 33g Writing Emails and Using Voice Mail

### 1 Writing Emails

In many workplaces, virtually all internal (and much external) communications are transmitted as email. Although personal email tends to be quite informal, business email should observe the conventions of standard written letters. In addition, email should follow certain guidelines that can help you communicate more effectively in an electronic environment. (See **27b1** for a list of those guidelines.)

### 2 Using Voice Mail

Like email, voice mail can present challenges. The following tips can help you deliver a voice-mail message clearly and effectively.

CHECKLIST

**Using Voice Mail**

- ❑ **Organize your message before you deliver it.** Before you call, take the time to think about what you want to say. Long, meandering messages will frustrate listeners.
- ❑ **Begin your message by identifying yourself.** State your name and affiliation as well as the date and time of your call.
- ❑ **State the subject of your message first.** Then, fill in the details.
- ❑ **Speak slowly.** Many experts advise people to speak more slowly than they would in normal conversation.

- ❑ **Speak clearly.** Enunciate your words so that a listener will understand your message the first time.
- ❑ **Give your phone number twice.** No one wants to replay a long voice-mail message just to get a phone number.

### Close-Up WORKPLACE PRIVACY

In almost all cases, business emails are not considered private. Courts have held that an employer has the right to monitor all email sent over its system. (The same is true for voice mail as well as texts and instant messages.) For this reason, you should not assume that any message you send at work is private.

Some companies have policies that limit what an employee can post on social networking sites. Policies vary from company to company and are subject to state law, but derogatory comments about an employer or about the company (or any comments that could possibly damage the company) may be prohibited. You should check with your employer to find out if the company has a policy concerning social media.

CHAPTER 34

# Making Oral Presentations

## Frequently Asked Questions



At school and on the job, you may be called on to make **oral presentations.** Although many people are uncomfortable about giving oral presentations, the guidelines that follow can make the experience easier and less stressful.

## 34a Getting Started

Just as with writing an essay, the preparation stage of an oral presentation is as important as the speech itself. The time you spend on this stage of the process will make your task easier later on.

***Identify Your Topic*** The first thing you should do is identify the topic of your speech. Sometimes you are given a topic; at other times, you have the option of choosing your own. Once you have a topic, you will be able to decide how much information, as well as what kind of information, you will need.

***Consider Your Audience*** The easiest way to determine what kind of information you will need is to consider the nature of your audience. Is your audience made up of experts or of people who know little about your topic? How much background information will you have to provide? Can you use technical terms, or should you avoid them? Do you think your audience will be interested in your topic, or will you have to create interest? What opinions about your topic will the members of your audience bring with them?

> **ESL TIP**
>
> When making oral presentations, some ESL students choose topics related to their cultural background or home country. This is a good idea because you will often be able to provide information on these topics that is new to your instructor and your classmates. If you choose such a topic, determine beforehand how much background your audience has by speaking with your instructor and classmates.

***Consider Your Purpose*** Your speech should have a specific purpose that you can sum up concisely. To help you zero in on your purpose, ask yourself what you are trying to accomplish with your presentation. It is a good idea to write out this purpose and to keep it in front of you as you plan your speech.

**Purpose:** to convince an audience that college athletes should be paid a salary

***Consider Your Constraints*** How much time do you have for your presentation? (Obviously, a ten-minute presentation requires more information and preparation than a three-minute presentation.) Do you already know enough about your topic, or will you have to do research?

### & Close-Up GROUP PRESENTATIONS

Whether you are participating in a panel discussion or are part of a team making a long speech, you should be aware that group presentations require coordination. Before you begin to plan your speech, you should take these steps:

- Choose a leader who will coordinate the team's efforts.
- Determine who will be responsible for each part of the presentation.
- Determine who will prepare and display visuals.
- Agree on a schedule for both work and rehearsals.
- Agree on acceptable team behavior—for example, how to dress and how to behave during the presentation.

## 34b Planning Your Speech

In the planning phase, you develop a thesis; then, you decide what specific points you will discuss and divide your speech into a few manageable sections.

***Develop a Thesis Statement*** Before you actually plan your speech, you need to develop a thesis statement that clearly and concisely communicates your main idea to your audience. If you know a lot about your topic, you can develop a thesis on your own. If you do not know a lot, you will have to gather information before you can decide on a thesis.

See 5a–b

***Decide on Your Points*** Once you have decided on a thesis, you can decide what points you will discuss. Unlike readers, who can read and reread a passage until they understand it, listeners must understand information the first time they hear it. For this reason, effective speeches focus on points that are clear and easy to follow.

***Gather Support*** You cannot expect your listeners to automatically accept what you say. You must supply details, facts, and examples that will convince them that what you are saying is both accurate and reasonable. You can gather this supporting material in the library, on the Web, or from your own experience.

***Outline the Individual Parts of Your Speech*** Every speech has a beginning, a middle, and an end.

- The **introduction** should present your subject, engage your audience's interest, and state your thesis.
- The **body,** or middle section, of your speech should present the points that support your thesis. It should also include the facts, examples, and other information that will clarify your points and help convince listeners your thesis is reasonable.
- The **conclusion** should reinforce your thesis and bring your speech to a definite end.

*Note:* Be sure to plan your introduction and your conclusion carefully. Because these sections are what your audience hears first and last, they play a large part in determining the impression your speech makes. Don't make the mistake of thinking that you can make up an introduction or conclusion as you deliver your speech.

## 34c Preparing Your Presentation Notes

Most people use presentation notes of some kind when they give a speech. Each system of notes has advantages and disadvantages.

***Full Text*** Some people like to write out the full text of their speech and refer to it during their presentation. If the type is large enough, and if you triple-space, this strategy can be useful. The main disadvantage of using the full text of your speech is that it is easy to lose your place and become disoriented; another is that you may end up reading your speech.

***Note Cards*** Some people write important parts of their speech—for example, a list of key points or definitions—on note cards. Cards are portable, so they can be flipped through easily. They are also small, so they can be placed inconspicuously on a podium or a table. With some practice, you can learn to use note cards effectively. You have to be careful, however, not to become so dependent on the cards that you lose eye contact with your audience or begin fidgeting with the cards as you speak.

***Outlines*** Some people like to refer to an outline when they give a speech. As they speak, they can glance down at the outline to get their bearings or to remind themselves of a point they have to make. Because an outline does not contain the full text of a speech, the temptation to read is eliminated. However, if for some reason you draw a blank, an outline gives you very little to fall back on.

***iPads*** Some people use an iPad as a teleprompter. In order to do this, you need a stand for your iPad and an app, such as *Teleprompt+*, that turns an iPad into a teleprompter. *Teleprompt+* allows you to scroll your speech at various speeds, to pause it with a double-tap on the screen, and to time yourself as you speak. (*Teleprompt+* will even make video recordings of your presentation and of your practice sessions.) In addition, you can sync your iPad to your iPhone so that you can use your phone as a portable teleprompter as you walk around the room. Finally, *Teleprompt+* enables you to change the font and font size of your speech. With so many features, *Teleprompt+* takes time and practice to master—and, as with full-text presentation notes, you have to be careful not to simply read your speech.

## 34d Preparing Visual Aids

### 1 Using Visuals

**Visual aids,** such as overhead transparencies or posters, can reinforce important information and make your speech easier to understand. For a simple speech, a visual aid may be no more than a definition or a few key terms, names, or dates written on the board. A more complicated presentation might require charts, graphs, diagrams, or photographs—or even objects.

If you are using equipment such as a document camera, make sure you know how to operate it—and have a contingency plan in case the equipment does not work (for example, have handouts that you can distribute if the need arises). If possible, visit the room in which you will be giving your speech ahead of time, and see whether it has the equipment you need (and whether the equipment works). Finally, make sure that whatever visual aid you use is large enough for everyone in your audience to see. Print or type should be neat and free of errors, and graphics should be clearly labeled and easy to see.

## 2 Using Presentation Software

*Microsoft PowerPoint,* the most commonly used presentation software package, enables you to organize an oral presentation and prepare attractive professional slides. Effective slides are open and easy to read, and they reinforce important information (see Figure 34.1). Ineffective slides have the opposite effect and can undermine an otherwise effective presentation (see Figure 34.2 on page 512).

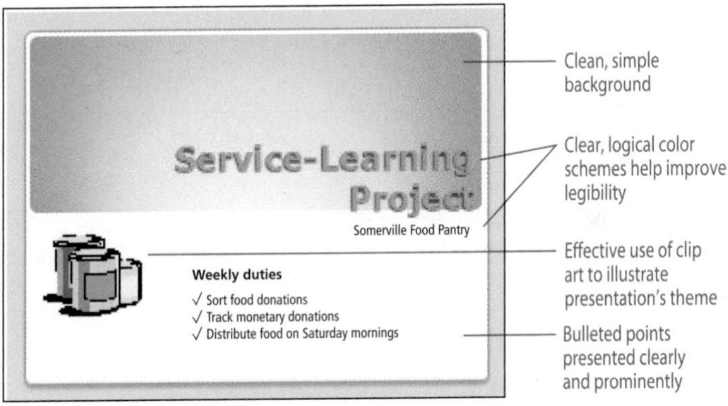


FIGURE 34.1 Effective *PowerPoint* slide. © Cengage Learning.

*PowerPoint*'s more advanced features enable you to create multimedia presentations that combine images, video, audio, and animation. You can also use the Insert menu to insert various items—for example, clip art, word art, and image files you have created with a digital camera or scanner—into your slide templates (see Figure 34.3 on page 512). You can even import charts and tables from *Microsoft Word* and *Excel* and download images from Internet sites directly into your slide templates.

**Note:** If possible, use the computer that you used to prepare your *PowerPoint* slides when you deliver your speech. That way, you can be sure that you will be able to open your files and that all the multimedia effects you included with your slides will work.

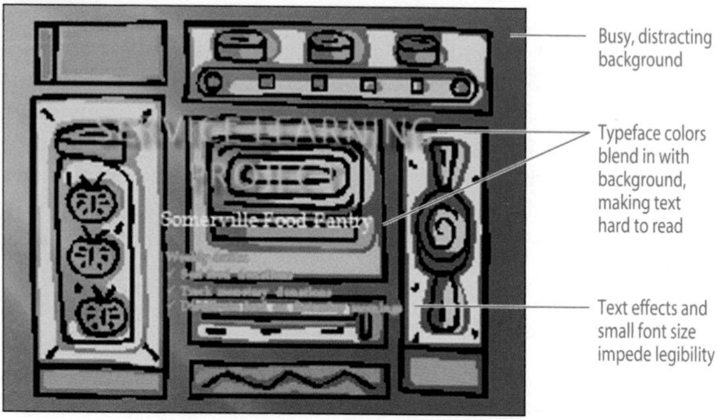


FIGURE 34.2 Ineffective *PowerPoint* slide. © Cengage Learning.

If you are using a MacBook, make sure that you have an Apple display adapter so that you can plug your computer into a data-projector. If you do not have an adapter, you will not be able to use your presentation software during your speech.

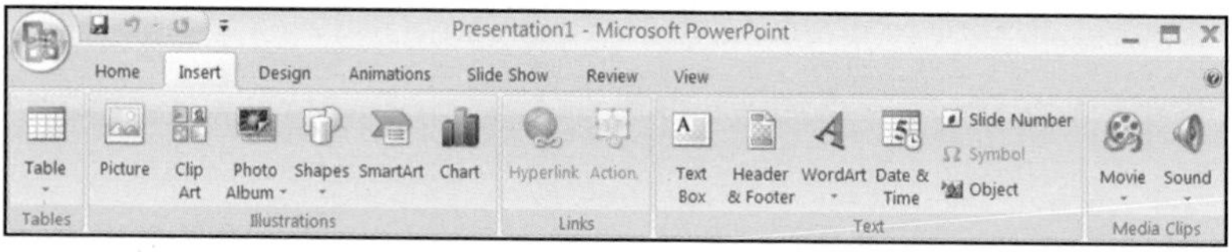


FIGURE 34.3 *Microsoft PowerPoint* Insert menu. © Microsoft Corporation.

**CHECKLIST**

**Creating *PowerPoint* Slides**

- ❑ Review your presentation notes, and decide where you need slides.
- ❑ Do not put more than three or four major points on a single slide.
- ❑ Use single words or short phrases, never complete sentences or paragraphs.
- ❑ Limit the number of slides. For a three- to five-minute presentation, five or six slides are usually enough. Too many slides will confuse listeners, especially if they are shown in quick succession.
- ❑ Use visuals to add interest to your presentation. Do not include distracting graphics or special effects just because your software allows you to do so.
- ❑ Use type and visuals that are large enough for your audience to see.

*Note:* Remember, your content, not your slides, should be the focus of your speech.

### Close-Up *PREZI*

An alternative to *PowerPoint* is *Prezi,* a cloud-based presentation tool that is available free on the Internet at <prezi.com>. It uses a single presentation screen or "stage" instead of individual slides. With *Prezi*, users can move around the stage (much the way a Skycam at a football game does) and zoom in and out, depending on what they want to emphasize. In addition, videos from *YouTube* (or other media) can easily be integrated into *Prezi*.

### Using Visual Aids in Your Presentation

| Visual Aid | Advantages | Disadvantages |
| --- | --- | --- |
| ***Computer presentations***<br><br>Bob Daemmrich/PhotoEdit | Clear<br>Easy to read<br>Professional<br>Graphics, video, sound, and animated effects<br>Portable (disk or CD-ROM) | Special equipment needed<br>Expertise needed<br>Special software needed<br>Software might not be compatible with all computer systems |
| ***Overhead projectors***<br><br>Lew Zimmerman/ istockphoto.com | Transparencies are inexpensive<br>Transparencies are easily prepared with computer or copier<br>Transparencies are portable<br>Transparencies can be written on during presentation<br>Projector is easy to operate | Transparencies can stick together<br>Transparencies can be accidentally placed upside down<br>Transparencies must be placed on projector by hand<br>Some projectors are noisy<br>Speaker must avoid tripping over power cord during presentation |

(*continued*)

### Using Visual Aids in Your Presentation (*continued*)

| Visual Aid | Advantages | Disadvantages |
|---|---|---|
| ***Document cameras (digital visualizers)***<br>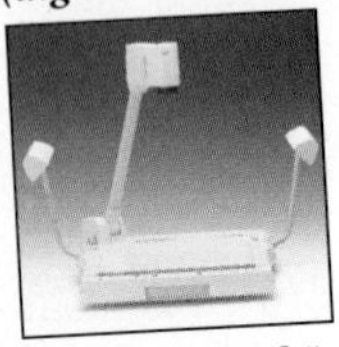<br>Business Wire/Handout/Getty Images Publicity/Getty Images | Captures visual images in real time<br>Projects images from a sheet of paper or projects 3D objects<br>Zooms in on small text, pictures, or objects<br>Interfaces with a white-board or a computer<br>Has a high-definition display | Much more expensive than an overhead projector<br>Must connect to another device to display an image<br>Not yet widely available |
| ***Slide projectors***<br><br>Andy Crawford/Dorling Kindersley/Getty Images | Slides are colorful<br>Slides look professional<br>Projector is easy to use<br>Order of slides can be rearranged during presentation<br>Portable (slide carousel) | Slides are expensive to produce<br>Special equipment needed for letter-ing and graphics<br>Dark room needed for presentation<br>Slides can jam in projector |
| ***Posters or flip charts***<br>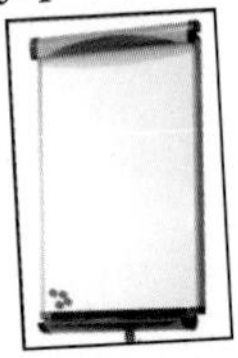<br>mbbirdy/istockphoto.com | Low-tech and personal<br>Good for small-group presentations<br>Portable | May not be large enough to be seen in some rooms<br>Artistic ability needed<br>May be expensive if prepared professionally<br>Must be secured to an easel |
| ***Chalkboards or whiteboard***<br><br>Jeffrey Coolidge/Stone/Getty Images | Available in most rooms<br>Easy to use<br>Easy to erase or change information during presentation | Difficult to draw complicated graphics<br>Handwriting must be legible<br>Must catch errors while writing<br>Cannot face audience when writing or drawing<br>Very informal |

## 3 Using *YouTube*

Because *YouTube* provides access to millions of videos, it is an excellent resource for oral presentations. You can find videos on almost any subject—for example, how to change the oil in a car, how to create a Web page, or even how to land a plane. You can also find videos showing current events, speeches, and television news shows. Figure 34.4 shows the *YouTube* home page.

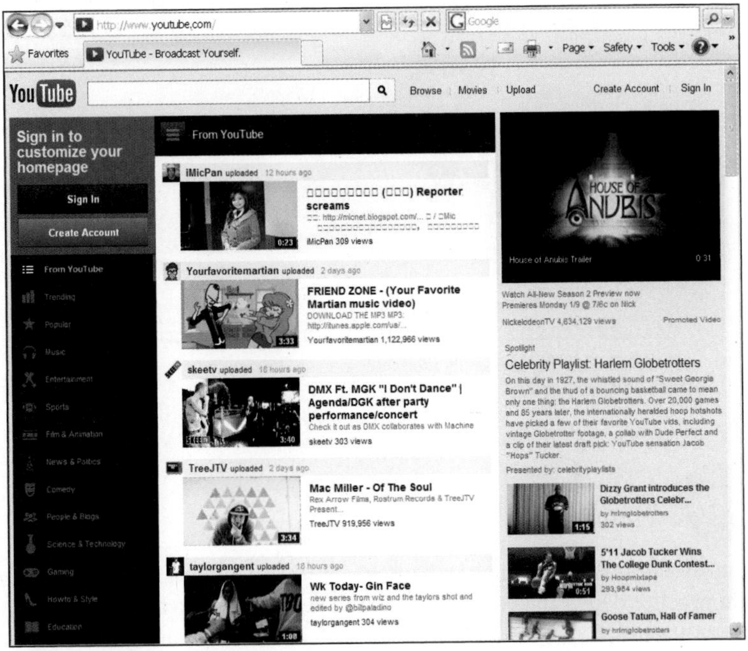


FIGURE 34.4 *YouTube* home page. © YouTube/Google, Inc.

*PowerPoint 2010* enables users to embed a *YouTube* video directly into a presentation (see Figure 34.5 on page 516). You can also download a *YouTube* link onto your computer and access it during your presentation.

During your speech, you should show only the part of the video that is necessary to illustrate your point. Long videos that contain irrelevant material will distract listeners and cause them to lose interest in your presentation. Also, before you play a video, make sure you introduce it, tell listeners why you are showing it to them, and identify the source.

Note: It is a good idea to have a backup plan in case a computer problem prevents you from using videos in your presentation.

FIGURE 34.5 *PowerPoint* screen that enables users to add *YouTube* video <addictivetips.com>.

## 34e Rehearsing Your Speech

You should practice your speech often—at least five times—and make sure you practice delivering your speech with your visuals. Do not try to memorize your entire speech, but be sure you know it well enough so you can move from point to point without constantly looking at your notes. Finally, time yourself. Make certain your three-minute speech actually takes three minutes to deliver.

## 34f Delivering Your Speech

The most important part of your speech is your delivery. Keep in mind that a certain amount of nervousness is normal, so try not to focus on it too much. Channel the nervous energy into your speech, and let it work for you. While you are waiting to begin, take some deep breaths. Once you get to the front of the room, don't start right away; wait until your audience settles down.

## Answering Audience Questions *(continued)*

- ❑ **Listen carefully.** Give your questioners your full attention, and don't interrupt them. Wait until they are finished asking their questions before you begin your answer.
- ❑ **Repeat questions.** By repeating questions, you make sure that everyone can hear them. You also give yourself time to put together an answer.
- ❑ **Answer questions concisely.** Keep your answers concise, direct, and focused. If a question is complicated and will require a long answer, summarize your response, and ask the questioner to see you after the presentation.
- ❑ **Be polite.** Don't indicate that you think a question is silly or misguided. Answer all questions respectfully.
- ❑ **Don't fake an answer.** If you don't know the answer to a question, say so. Then, tell the person that you will research the answer and email it to him or her.

CHECKLIST

**Delivering Your Speech**

As you deliver your speech, keep in mind the following tips on body language, eye contact, and pacing:

- ❑ Position yourself effectively.
- ❑ Stand up straight.
- ❑ Speak slowly and clearly.
- ❑ Maintain eye contact with the audience.
- ❑ Use natural gestures.
- ❑ Face the audience at all times.
- ❑ Do not just show or read visuals to your audience. Tell your audience more than they can see or read for themselves.
- ❑ Do not block your visuals.
- ❑ If you forget something, don't let your audience know. Work the informatio in later.
- ❑ Leave time for questions.
- ❑ Distribute any handouts before or after the speech, not during it.

## 34g Answering Audience Questions

Most speeches end with audience members askir question-and-answer session is as much a part of y prepared remarks are. Because the impression you part in how they judge your speech, you should ence questions.

As you review your presentation note questions listeners could ask—and th questions listeners could ask. Then, writ If necessary, prepare a note card wit facts—that you may need.

CHECKLIST

**Answering Audience**

Once the question-and-an following guidelines in

- ❑ **Control the situ** their hands. Don't

PART 9

# Sentence Style

CHAPTER 35

# Building Simple Sentences

## Frequently Asked Questions



A **sentence** is an independent grammatical unit that includes a subject and a predicate and expresses a complete thought.

The quick brown fox jumped over the lazy dog.

It came from outer space.

See 35b1

A **simple subject** is a noun or noun substitute (*fox, it*) that tells who or what the sentence is about. A **simple predicate** is a verb or verb phrase (*jumped, came*) that tells or asks something about the subject. The **complete subject** of a sentence includes the simple subject plus all its modifiers (*the quick brown fox*). The **complete predicate** includes the verb or verb phrase and all the words associated with it—such as modifiers, objects, and complements (*jumped over the lazy dog, came from outer space*).

**ESL TIP**

In some languages, such as Spanish and Italian, the subject of a sentence can sometimes be omitted (because the form of the sentence's verb clearly indicates who or what the subject of the sentence is). In English, however, every sentence must have a subject.

## 35a Constructing Simple Sentences

A **simple sentence** consists of at least one subject and one predicate. Simple sentences conform to one of five basic patterns.

### 1 Subject + Intransitive Verb (s + v)

See 47c1

The most basic simple sentence consists of just a subject and a verb or **verb phrase** (the main verb plus all its auxiliary verbs).

s v
The price of gold rose.

s v
Stock prices may fall.

Here the verbs *rose* and *may fall* are **intransitive**—that is, they do not need an object to complete their meaning.

## 2 Subject + Transitive Verb + Direct Object (s + v + do)

Another kind of simple sentence consists of the subject, a verb, and a direct object.

s v do
Van Gogh created *The Starry Night.*

s v do
Caroline saved *Jake.*

Here the verbs *created* and *saved* are **transitive**—each requires an object to complete its meaning in the sentence. In each sentence, the **direct object** indicates where the verb's action is directed and who or what is affected by it.

**ESL TIP**

To determine whether a verb is intransitive or transitive, consult a dictionary. Remember, though, that some verbs, such as *write,* can be intransitive or transitive.

She wrote all night. (intransitive)

She wrote an essay about her semester in Spain. (transitive)

## 3 Subject + Transitive Verb + Direct Object + Object Complement (s + v + do + oc)

Some simple sentences include an **object complement,** a word or phrase that renames or describes the direct object.

s v do oc
The class elected Bridget treasurer. (Object complement *treasurer* renames direct object *Bridget.*)

s v do oc
I found the exam easy. (Object complement *easy* describes direct object *exam.*)

## 4 Subject + Linking Verb + Subject Complement (s + v + sc)

Another kind of simple sentence consists of a subject, a **linking verb** (a verb that connects a subject to its complement), and the **subject complement** (the word or phrase that describes or renames the subject). See 47c1

s v sc
The injection was painless.

s v sc
Gordon Brown became prime minister.

Note that the linking verb is like an equal sign, equating the subject with its complement (*Gordon Brown = prime minister*).

### 5 Subject + Transitive Verb + Indirect Object + Direct Object (s + v + io + do)

Some simple sentences include an **indirect object,** which indicates to whom or for whom the verb's action was done.

s v io do
Cyrano wrote Roxanne a poem. (Cyrano wrote a poem for Roxanne.)

s v io do
The officer handed Frank a ticket. (The officer handed a ticket to Frank.)

**EXERCISE 1**

In each of the following sentences, underline the subject once and the predicate twice. Then, label direct objects, indirect objects, subject complements, and object complements.

sc
***Example:*** Isaac Asimov was a science fiction writer.

1. Isaac Asimov first saw science fiction stories in his parents' Brooklyn store.
2. He practiced writing by telling his schoolmates stories.
3. Asimov published his first story in *Astounding Science Fiction*.
4. The magazine's editor, John W. Campbell, encouraged Asimov to continue writing.
5. The young writer researched scientific principles to make his stories more accurate.
6. Asimov's "Foundation" series of novels is a "future history."
7. The World Science Fiction Convention gave the series a Hugo Award.
8. Sometimes Asimov used "Paul French" as a pseudonym.
9. *Biochemistry and Human Metabolism* was Asimov's first nonfiction book.
10. Asimov coined the term *robotics*.

## 35b Identifying Phrases and Clauses

### 1 Identifying Phrases

A **phrase** is a group of related words that lacks a subject or predicate or both and functions as a single part of speech. It cannot stand alone as a sentence.

- A **verb phrase** consists of a main verb and all its auxiliary verbs.

Time is flying.

- A **noun phrase** includes a noun or pronoun plus all related modifiers.

  I'll climb the highest mountain.

- A **prepositional phrase** consists of a preposition, its object, and any modifiers of that object.

  They discussed the ethical implications of the animal studies.

  He was last seen heading into the orange sunset.

- A **verbal phrase** consists of a **verbal** (participle, gerund, or infinitive) and its related objects, modifiers, or complements. A verbal phrase may be a **participial phrase,** a **gerund phrase,** or an **infinitive phrase.**

  Encouraged by the voter turnout, the candidate predicted a victory. (participial phrase)

  Taking it easy always makes sense. (gerund phrase)

  The jury recessed to evaluate the evidence. (infinitive phrase)

- An **absolute phrase** usually consists of a noun and a participle, accompanied by modifiers. It modifies an entire independent clause rather than a particular word or phrase.

  Their toes tapping, they watched the auditions.

## 2 Identifying Clauses

A **clause** is a group of related words that includes a subject and a predicate. An **independent** (main) clause can stand alone as a sentence, but a **dependent** (subordinate) **clause** cannot. It must always be combined with an independent clause to form a **complex sentence.**

See 36b

[Lucretia Mott was an abolitionist.] [She was also a pioneer for women's rights.] (two independent clauses)

[Lucretia Mott was an abolitionist] [who was also a pioneer for women's rights.] (independent clause, dependent clause)

[Although Lucretia Mott is widely known for her support of women's rights,] [she was also a prominent abolitionist.] (dependent clause, independent clause)

Dependent clauses may be *adjective, adverb,* or *noun* clauses.

- **Adjective clauses,** sometimes called **relative clauses,** modify nouns or pronouns and always follow the nouns or pronouns they modify. They are introduced by relative pronouns—*that, what, whatever, which, who, whose, whom, whoever,* or *whomever*—or by the adverbs *where* or *when.*

The television series *M*A*S*H,* which depicted life in an army hospital in Korea during the Korean War, ran for eleven years. (Adjective clause modifies the noun *M*A*S*H.*)

William Styron's novel *Sophie's Choice* is set in Brooklyn, where the narrator lives in a house painted pink. (Adjective clause modifies the noun *Brooklyn.*)

- **Adverb clauses** modify single words (verbs, adjectives, or adverbs), entire phrases, or independent clauses. They are always introduced by **subordinating conjunctions.** Adverb clauses provide information to answer the questions *how? where? when? why?* and *to what extent?*

  Exhausted after the match was over, Kim decided to take a long nap. (Adverb clause modifies *exhausted*, telling *when* Kim was exhausted.)

  Mark will go wherever there's a party. (Adverb clause modifies *will go*, telling *where* Mark will go.)

  Because 75 percent of its exports are fish products, Iceland's economy is heavily dependent on the fishing industry. (Adverb clause modifies independent clause, telling *why* the fishing industry is so important.)

- **Noun clauses** function as subjects, objects, or complements. A noun clause may be introduced by a relative pronoun or by *whether, when, where, why,* or *how.*

  What you see is what you get. (Noun clauses serve as subject and subject complement.)

  They finally decided which candidate was most qualified. (Noun clause serves as direct object of verb *decided.*)

*Note:* Some dependent clauses, called **elliptical clauses,** are grammatically incomplete but nevertheless can be easily understood from the context of the sentence. Typically, a part of the subject or predicate (or the entire subject or predicate) is missing: *Although [they were] full, they could not resist dessert.*

## EXERCISE 2

Which of the following groups of words are independent clauses? Which are dependent clauses? Which are phrases? Label each word group *IC, DC,* or *P.*

*Example:* Coming through the rye. (P)

1. Beauty is truth.
2. When knights were bold.
3. In a galaxy far away.
4. He saw stars.
5. I hear a symphony.
6. Whenever you're near.
7. The clock struck ten.
8. The red planet.
9. Slowly I turned.
10. For the longest time.

## 35c Expanding Simple Sentences

A **simple sentence** is a single independent clause. A simple sentence can consist of just a subject and a verb.

Jessica fell.

Or, a simple sentence can be expanded with modifying words and phrases.

Jessica and her younger sister Victoria almost immediately fell hopelessly in love with the very mysterious Henry Goodyear.

*Note:* Joined with other clauses, simple sentences can be expanded into **compound and complex sentences.**

See Ch. 36

### 1 Expanding Simple Sentences with Adjectives and Adverbs

**Adjectives and adverbs** can expand a simple sentence by modifying nouns, verbs, or other adjectives or adverbs. Read this sentence again:

See 51a

Jessica and her younger sister Victoria almost immediately fell hopelessly in love with the very mysterious Henry Goodyear.

In the sentence above, two adjectives describe nouns.

| **Adjective** | **Noun** |
|---|---|
| younger | sister |
| mysterious | Henry Goodyear |

Four adverbs describe the action of verbs or modify adjectives or other adverbs.

| **Adverb** | |
|---|---|
| almost | immediately (adverb) |
| immediately | fell (verb) |
| hopelessly | fell (verb) |
| very | mysterious (adjective) |

### EXERCISE 3

Label all the adjectives and adverbs in the following simple sentences.

adv adj adj

***Example:*** Marge listened secretly to the quiet conversation at the next table.

1. John swallowed the last of his cold coffee and gently set the thermos down. (Sherman Alexie, *Indian Killer*)
2. Each year I watched the field across from the Store turn caterpillar green, then gradually frosty white. (Maya Angelou, *I Know Why the Caged Bird Sings*)
3. He gingerly held the box and studied the old, familiar pictures. (Alan Lightman, *Good Benito*)
4. Stealthy and alert, he hunkers down like a predator and sneaks right up behind the seal, climbs decisively onto its back, and grips its cheeks in both hands. (Diane Ackerman, *The Rarest of the Rare*)
5. In late mammal times, the body evidently added a third brain. (Robert Bly, *The Sibling Society*)

### EXERCISE 4

Using the following sentences as models, write five original simple sentences. Use adverbs and adjectives where the model sentences use them, and then underline and label these modifiers.

adv adj

***Example:*** Manek gazed shyly at the beautiful girl.

adv adj

The cat ran wildly around the empty house.

1. Walkways from the Washington Monument to the Lincoln Memorial quickly filled.
2. People, shrugging off their winter coats, seemed to step more lightly around the mall.
3. Some sat on benches in carefully pressed white shirts, holding half-eaten sandwiches in pale hands.
4. Others, dressed in shiny spandex or torn T-shirts, spun wildly by on bikes or Rollerblades, sweatily celebrating the first days of spring.
5. Finally, the cherry blossoms were in flower.

## 2 Expanding Simple Sentences with Nouns and Verbals

Nouns and verbals that serve as modifiers can help you build richer simple sentences.

- **Nouns** can act as adjectives modifying other nouns.

He needed two cake pans for the layer cake.

- Some **verbals** (participles and infinitives) may also act as modifiers.

All the <u>living</u> former presidents attended the funeral. (Present participle acts as adjective.)

The Grand Canyon is the attraction <u>to visit</u>. (Infinitive acts as adjective.)

The puzzle was impossible <u>to solve</u>. (Infinitive acts as adverb.)

### Close-Up VERBALS USED AS NOUNS

A verbal may also act as a noun, serving as a subject, object, or complement in a sentence.

The <u>making</u> of a motion picture can be a complex and lengthy process. (Gerund acts as noun.)

<u>To err</u> is human. (Infinitive acts as noun.)

It took me the entire lab period to identify my <u>unknown</u>. (Past participle acts as noun.)

### EXERCISE 5

For additional practice in building simple sentences with individual words, combine each of the following groups of sentences into one simple sentence that contains several modifiers. You may have to add, delete, or reorder words.

***Example:*** The ~~night was~~ cold,/~~The night was~~ wet/~~The~~ night scared them/~~They were~~ terribly ~~scared.~~

1. The ship landed. The ship was from space. The ship was tremendous. It landed silently.
2. It landed in a field. The field was grassy. The field was deserted.
3. A dog appeared. The dog was tiny. The dog was abandoned. The dog was a stray.
4. The dog was brave. The dog was curious. He approached the spacecraft. The spacecraft was burning. He approached it carefully.
5. A creature emerged from the spaceship. The creature was smiling. He was purple. He emerged slowly.
6. The dog and the alien stared at each other. The dog was little. The alien was purple. They stared meaningfully.
7. The dog and the alien walked. They walked silently. They walked carefully. They walked toward each other.

8. The dog barked. He barked tentatively. He barked questioningly. The dog was uneasy.
9. The alien extended his hand. The alien was grinning. He extended it slowly. The hand was hairy.
10. In his hand was a bag. The bag was made of canvas. The bag was green. The bag was for laundry.

### 3 Expanding Simple Sentences with Prepositional Phrases

See 47f

ESL 64e

A preposition indicates the relationship between a noun or noun substitute and other words in a sentence. A **prepositional phrase** consists of the preposition, its object (the noun or noun substitute), and any modifiers of that object. Prepositional phrases can function in a sentence as adjectives or as adverbs.

prep obj
Carry Nation was a crusader for temperance. (Prepositional phrase functions as adjective modifying the noun *crusader*.)

prep mod obj
The Madeira River flows into the mighty Amazon. (Prepositional phrase functions as adverb modifying the verb *flows*.)

### EXERCISE 6

Read the following sentences. Underline each prepositional phrase, and then connect it with an arrow to the word it modifies. Label each prepositional phrase to indicate whether it functions as an adjective or an adverb.

adj adv
***Example:*** The porch of her grandmother's house wraps around all three sides.

1. Carol sat on the front porch and rocked in her grandmother's chair.
2. Age had surprised her in the middle of her life, crept up behind her in the mirror, and attacked her at the joints of her knees and hips.
3. Now she sat on the porch and felt that it too creaked in its joints.
4. Inside the house, her grandmother slept in a narrow bed under a worn chenille spread, the mattress sagging and spilling over the edges of the frame.
5. The slow rocking of the chair soothed the worries from Carol's mind.

### EXERCISE 7

For additional practice in using prepositional phrases, combine each of these sentence pairs to create one simple sentence that includes a prepositional phrase. You may add, delete, or reorder words. Some sentences may have more than one possible correct version.

***Example:*** America's drinking water is being contaminated by toxic ~~. Toxic~~ substances ~~are contaminating it.~~

1. Toxic waste disposal presents a serious problem. Americans have this problem.
2. Hazardous chemicals pose a threat. People are threatened.
3. Some towns, such as Times Beach, Missouri, were completely abandoned. Their residents abandoned them.
4. Dioxin is one chemical. It has serious toxic effects.
5. Dioxin is highly toxic. The toxicity affects animals and humans.
6. Toxic chemical wastes like dioxin may be found. Over fifty thousand dumps have them.
7. Industrial parks contain toxic wastes. Open pits, ponds, and lagoons are where the toxic substances are.
8. Toxic wastes pose dangers. The land, water, and air are endangered.
9. In addition, toxic substances are a threat. They threaten our public health and our economy.
10. Continuing toxic waste cleanup should be a high priority. Americans are the ones who will benefit.

## 4 Expanding Simple Sentences with Verbal Phrases

A **verbal phrase** consists of a **verbal** (participle, gerund, or infinitive) and its related objects, modifiers, or complements.

Some verbal phrases act as modifiers.

- **Participial phrases** always function as adjectives.

  Fascinated by Scheherazade's story, they waited anxiously for the next installment. (Participial phrase modifies the pronoun *they*.)

- **Infinitive phrases** may function as adjectives or as adverbs.

  It wasn't the ideal time to do homework. (Infinitive phrase modifies the noun *time*.)

  Henry M. Stanley went to Africa to find Dr. Livingstone. (Infinitive phrase modifies the verb *went*.)

### Close-Up USING MODIFIERS

When you use verbal phrases as modifiers, be especially careful not to create misplaced modifiers or dangling modifiers.

See Ch. 42

Other verbal phrases act as nouns.

- **Gerund phrases,** like gerunds themselves, are always used as nouns.

  Making a living is not always easy. (Gerund phrase serves as sentence's subject.)

  Wendy appreciated Tom's being honest. (Gerund phrase serves as object of the verb *appreciated.*)

  The entire town was shocked by their breaking up. (Gerund phrase is object of the preposition *by.*)

- **Infinitive phrases** may also be used as nouns.

  To know him is to love him. (Infinitive phrase *To know him* serves as sentence's subject; infinitive phrase *to love him* is subject complement.)

## EXERCISE 8

For practice in using verbal phrases, combine each of these sentence pairs to create one simple sentence that contains a participial phrase, a gerund phrase, or an infinitive phrase. Underline the verbal phrase in your sentence. You may have to add, delete, or reorder words, and you may find more than one way to combine each pair.

***Example:*** The American labor movement has helped millions of workers, ~~. It has won~~ *winning* them higher wages and better working conditions.

1. In 1912, the textile workers of Lawrence, Massachusetts, went on strike. They were demonstrating for "Bread and Roses, too."
2. The workers wanted higher wages and better working conditions. They felt trapped in their miserable jobs.
3. Mill workers toiled six days a week. They earned about $1.50 for this.
4. Most of the workers were women and children. They worked up to sixteen hours a day.
5. The mills were dangerous. They were filled with hazards.
6. Many mill workers joined unions. They did this to fight exploitation by their employers.
7. They wanted to improve their lives. This was their goal.
8. Finally, twenty-five thousand workers walked off their jobs. They knew they were risking everything.
9. The police and the state militia were called in. Attacking the strikers was their mission.
10. After sixty-three days, the American Woolen Company surrendered. This ended the strike with a victory for the workers.

(Adapted from William Cahn, *Lawrence 1912: The Bread and Roses Strike*)

## 5 Expanding Simple Sentences with Appositives

An **appositive** is a noun or a noun phrase that functions as an adjective, identifying or renaming an adjacent noun or pronoun.

> Farrington hated his boss, <u>a real tyrant</u>. (Appositive *a real tyrant* renames the noun *boss.*)
>
> <u>A barrier island off the coast of New Jersey</u>, Long Beach Island is a popular vacation spot. (Appositive *A barrier island off the coast of New Jersey* identifies the noun *Long Beach Island.*)

### Close-Up APPOSITIVES

An appositive is sometimes introduced by *such as, or, that is, for example, for instance, namely,* or *in other words*.

> A regional airline, <u>such as Southwest</u>, may account for more than half the departures at some second-tier airports.
>
> Rabies, or <u>hydrophobia</u>, was nearly always fatal until Pasteur's work.

*Note:* For information on punctuating sentences that include appositives, see **53d1.**

### EXERCISE 9

For practice in using appositives when you write, build five new simple sentences by combining each of the following pairs, turning one sentence in each pair into an appositive. (Note that each pair can be combined in a variety of ways and that the appositive can precede or follow the noun it modifies.) You may need to delete or reorder words in some cases.

***Example:*** ~~René Descartes was a~~ *A* noted French philosopher~~.~~ *, René* Descartes is best known for his famous declaration, "I think, therefore I am."

1. *I Know Why the Caged Bird Sings* is the first book in Maya Angelou's autobiography. It deals primarily with her life as a young girl in Stamps, Arkansas.
2. Catgut is a tough cord generally made from the intestines of sheep. Catgut is used for tennis rackets, for violin strings, and for surgical stitching.
3. Hermes was the messenger of the Greek gods. He is usually portrayed as an athletic youth wearing a cap and winged sandals.

4. Emiliano Zapata was a hero of the Mexican Revolution. He is credited with effecting land reform in his home state of Morelos.
5. Pulsars are celestial objects that emit regular pulses of radiation. Pulsars were discovered in 1967.

### 6 Expanding Simple Sentences with Compound Constructions

See 43a

A **compound construction** consists of two or more grammatically parallel items that are equivalent in importance. Within simple sentences, compound words or phrases—subjects, predicates, complements, or modifiers—may be joined in one of three ways:

- With commas:

  He took one long, loving look at his '57 Chevy.

See 36a1

- With coordinating conjunctions:

  They reeled, whirled, flounced, capered, gamboled, and spun. (Kurt Vonnegut Jr., "Harrison Bergeron")

- With **correlative conjunctions** (*both/and, either/or, neither/nor, not only/but also, whether/or*):

  Both milk and carrots contain Vitamin A.

  Neither the twentieth-century poet Sylvia Plath nor the nineteenth-century poet Emily Dickinson achieved recognition during her lifetime.

#### EXERCISE 10

A. Expand each of the following sentences by using compound subjects and/or predicates.

*Example:* Bill ^*and Juan* played guitar. ^*and sang.*

B. Then, expand your simple sentence with modifying words and phrases, using compound constructions whenever possible.

*Example:* ^*Despite butterflies in their stomachs and a restless audience,* Bill and Juan played guitar and sang.

1. Cortés explored the New World.
2. Virginia Woolf wrote novels.
3. Edison invented the phonograph.
4. PBS airs educational television programming.
5. Thomas Jefferson signed the Declaration of Independence.

#### EXERCISE 11

To practice building sentences with compound subjects, predicates, and modifiers, combine each of the following groups of sentences into one.

*Example:* Marion ~~studied~~/ ^and^ Frank studied/~~They studied~~ quietly/ ^and^ ~~They studied~~ diligently.

1. Robert Ludlum wrote best-selling spy thrillers. Tom Clancy writes best-selling spy thrillers. John le Carré writes best-selling spy thrillers.
2. Smoking can cause heart disease. A high-fat diet can cause heart disease. Stress can cause heart disease.
3. Walter Mosley and Sue Grafton write detective novels. They both write about "hard-boiled" detectives.
4. Successful rock bands give concerts. They record albums. They make videos. They license merchandise bearing their names and likenesses.
5. Sports superstars such as Tiger Woods and Michael Jordan earn additional income by making personal appearances. They earn money by endorsing products.

CHAPTER 36

# Building Compound and Complex Sentences

## Frequently Asked Questions



Writing that includes **varied sentences** is more interesting than writing that does not. One way to vary your sentences is to use compound and complex sentences along with simple sentences. See Ch. 37

## 36a Building Compound Sentences

A **compound sentence** is created when two or more independent clauses are joined with *coordinating conjunctions, transitional words or phrases, correlative conjunctions, semicolons,* or *colons.*

### 1 Using Coordinating Conjunctions

You can join two independent clauses with a **coordinating conjunction**—*and, or, nor, but, for, so,* or *yet.*

**ESL TIP**

Some languages, such as Arabic, tend to use coordination more than English does. If you think you are overusing compound sentences, try experimenting with complex sentences (see 37c).

She carried a thin, small cane made from an umbrella, and with this she kept tapping the frozen earth in front of her. (Eudora Welty, "A Worn Path")

In the fall the war was always there, but we did not go to it any more. (Ernest Hemingway, "In Another Country")

Note: Remember to use a comma before the coordinating conjunction that joins the two independent clauses.

### 2 Using Transitional Words or Phrases

You can join two independent clauses with a **transitional word or phrase.**

> Aerobic exercise can help lower blood pressure; however, people with high blood pressure should still limit salt intake.
>
> The saxophone does not belong to the brass family; in fact, it is a member of the woodwind family.

See 7b2

Commonly used transitional words and phrases include **conjunctive adverbs** like *however, therefore, nevertheless, consequently, finally, still,* and *thus* as well as expressions such as *for example, in fact, on the other hand,* and *for instance.*

Note: Remember to use a semicolon—not a comma—before the transitional word or phrase that joins the two independent clauses. Follow the transitional word or phrase with a comma.

### 3 Using Correlative Conjunctions

See 47g

You can use correlative conjunctions to join two independent clauses into a compound sentence.

> Diana not only passed the exam, but she also passed the course.
>
> Either he left his coat in his locker, or he left it on the bus.

## 4 Using Semicolons

You can use a **semicolon** to join two closely related independent clauses into a compound sentence.

See 54a

Alaska is the largest state; Rhode Island is the smallest.

Theodore Roosevelt was president after the Spanish-American War; Andrew Johnson was president after the Civil War.

## 5 Using Colons

You can use a **colon** to join two independent clauses into a compound sentence.

See 57a

He got his orders: he was to leave for Iraq on Sunday.

They thought they knew the outcome: Truman would lose to Dewey.

### Close-Up USING COMPOUND SENTENCES

When you join independent clauses to create compound sentences, you help readers to see the relationships between your ideas. Compound sentences can indicate the following relationships:

- Addition (*and, in addition, not only . . . but also*)
- Contrast (*but, however*)
- Causal relationships (*so, therefore, consequently*)
- Alternatives (*or, either . . . or*)

### EXERCISE 1

After reading the following paragraph, edit it to create as many compound sentences as you think your readers need to understand the relationships between ideas. When you have finished, bracket the independent clauses and underline the coordinating conjunctions, transitional words or phrases, correlative conjunctions, and punctuation marks that link clauses.

Paolo Soleri came to the United States from Italy. He came as an apprentice to Frank Lloyd Wright. Frank Lloyd Wright's designs celebrate the suburban lifestyle, with stand-alone homes meant for single families. Soleri's Utopian designs celebrate the city. Soleri believes that suburban lifestyles separate people from true nature. He also believes that our lifestyle separates us from the energy of the city. His first theoretical design was called Mesa

City. It proposed to house two million people. Soleri is currently building one of his dream cities, Arcosanti, in the desert outside of Scottsdale, Arizona. This project is funded privately by Soleri. He teaches design and building classes to students who help build the city. The students' tuition helps pay for construction. He also makes wind bells and chimes. He sells these all over the world. The profits further finance Arcosanti. The design for Arcosanti evokes images of colonies erected on space stations. It also resembles the hillside towns in Soleri's home country, Italy. The problems with our current city structures grow each year. People are looking for ways to revitalize the city. Some are looking at Soleri's Arcosanti as a model for sustainable urban development and renewal.

## EXERCISE 2

Add appropriate coordinating conjunctions, transitional words or phrases, or correlative conjunctions as indicated to combine each pair of sentences into one well-constructed compound sentence that retains the meaning of the original pair. Be sure to use correct punctuation.

***Example:*** The American population is aging. ~~People~~ *, so people* seem to be increasingly concerned about what they eat. (coordinating conjunction)

1. The average American consumes 128 pounds of sugar each year. Most of us eat much more sugar than any other food additive, including salt. (transitional word or phrase)
2. Many of us are determined to reduce our sugar intake. We have consciously eliminated sweets from our diets. (transitional word or phrase)
3. Unfortunately, sugar is not found only in sweets. It is also found in many processed foods. (correlative conjunction)
4. Processed foods like puddings and cake contain sugar. Foods like ketchup and spaghetti sauce do too. (coordinating conjunction)
5. We are trying to cut down on sugar. We find limiting sugar intake extremely difficult. (coordinating conjunction)
6. Processors may use sugar in foods for taste. They may also use it to help prevent foods from spoiling and to improve the texture and appearance of food. (correlative conjunction)
7. Sugar comes in many different forms. It is easy to overlook on a package label. (coordinating conjunction)
8. Sugar may be called sucrose or fructose. It may also be called corn syrup, corn sugar, brown sugar, honey, or molasses. (coordinating conjunction)
9. No sugar is more nourishing than the others. It really does not matter which is consumed. (transitional word or phrase)
10. Sugars contain empty calories. Whenever possible, they should be avoided. (transitional word or phrase)

(Adapted from *Jane Brody's Nutrition Book*)

## 36b Building Complex Sentences

A **complex sentence** consists of one **independent clause** and at least one **dependent clause**.

A dependent clause cannot stand alone; it must be combined with an independent clause to form a sentence. A **subordinating conjunction** or **relative pronoun** links the independent and dependent clauses and indicates the relationship between them.

dependent clause — independent clause
[After the town was evacuated,] [the hurricane began.]

independent clause — dependent clause
[Officials watched the storm,] [which threatened to destroy the town.]

*Note:* Sometimes a dependent clause may be embedded within an independent clause: *Town officials, [who were very concerned,] watched the storm.*

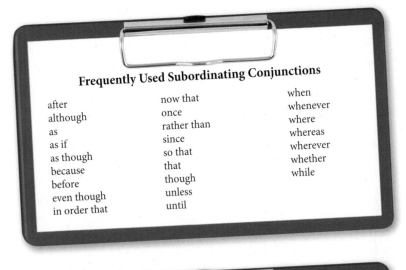

**Frequently Used Subordinating Conjunctions**

| | | |
|---|---|---|
| after | now that | when |
| although | once | whenever |
| as | rather than | where |
| as if | since | whereas |
| as though | so that | wherever |
| because | that | whether |
| before | though | while |
| even though | unless | |
| in order that | until | |

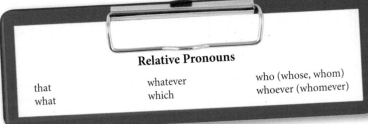

**Relative Pronouns**

| | | |
|---|---|---|
| that | whatever | who (whose, whom) |
| what | which | whoever (whomever) |

## Close-Up USING COMPLEX SENTENCES

When you join clauses to create complex sentences, you help readers to see the relationships between your ideas. Complex sentences can indicate the following relationships:

- Time relationships (*before, after, until, when, since*)
- Contrast (*however, although*)
- Causal relationships (*therefore, because, so that*)
- Conditional relationships (*if, unless*)
- Location (*where, wherever*)
- Identity (*who, which, that*)

## EXERCISE 3

Bracket the independent and dependent clauses in the following complex sentences. Then, using the five sentences as models, create two new complex sentences in imitation of each. For each pair of new sentences, use the same subordinating conjunction or relative pronoun that appears in the original sentence.

***Example:*** [Although life is sweet,] [it is sometimes hard.]
Although chemistry is difficult, it is often rewarding.
Although a computer may become obsolete, it can often be upgraded.

1. I said what I meant.
2. Savion Glover is the dancer who best exemplifies the phrase "poetry in motion."
3. Because she was considered a heretic, Joan of Arc was burned at the stake.
4. The oracle at Delphi predicted that Oedipus would murder his father and marry his mother.
5. The ghost vanished before Hamlet could question him further.

## EXERCISE 4

Use a subordinating conjunction or relative pronoun to combine each of the following pairs of sentences into one complex sentence. Be sure to choose a connecting word that indicates the relationship between the two sentences. You may have to change or reorder words.

***Example:*** ~~Some~~ [*Because some*] colleges are tightening admissions requirements. ~~Their~~ [*, their*] pool of students is growing smaller.

1. Many high school graduates are currently out of work. They need new skills for new careers.
2. Talented high school students are usually encouraged to go to college. A college education does not always guarantee them a job.
3. A college education can cost a student more than $100,000. Vocational education is becoming an increasingly attractive alternative.
4. Vocational students complete their work in less than four years. They can enter the job market more quickly.
5. Nurses' aides, paralegals, and computer technicians do not need college degrees. They can often find work.
6. Some four-year colleges are experiencing growth. Public community colleges and private trade schools are growing much more rapidly.
7. The best vocational schools try to meet the needs of local businesses. They train students for jobs that actually exist.
8. For instance, a school in Detroit might offer advanced automotive design. A school in New York City might focus on fashion design.
9. Other vocational schools offer courses in horticulture, respiratory therapy, and computer programming. They are able to place their graduates easily.
10. Laid-off workers, returning housewives, recent high school graduates, and even college graduates are reexamining vocational education. They all hope to find rewarding careers.

## Close-Up COMPOUND-COMPLEX SENTENCES

Another way to vary your sentences is to create an occasional compound-complex sentence. A **compound-complex sentence** consists of two or more independent clauses and at least one dependent clause.

dependent clause
[When small foreign imports began dominating the US automobile
independent clause — independent clause
industry,] [consumers were very responsive,] but [American auto workers were dismayed.]

CHAPTER 37

# Writing Varied Sentences

## Frequently Asked Questions



Using **varied sentences** can help make your writing livelier and more interesting, and it can also ensure that you emphasize the most important ideas in your sentences.

## 37a Varying Sentence Length

To add interest to your writing, try to mix sentences of different lengths.

### 1 Mixing Long and Short Sentences

A paragraph consisting entirely of short sentences (or entirely of long ones) can be dull.

> Drag racing began in California in the 1940s. It was an alternative to street racing. Street racing was illegal and dangerous. It flourished in the 1950s and 1960s. Eventually, it became almost a rite of passage. Then, during the 1970s, almost one-third of America's racetracks closed. Recently, however, drag racing has made a comeback.

Combining some of the paragraph's short sentences into longer ones creates a more interesting passage.

> Drag racing began in California in the 1940s as an alternative to street racing, which was illegal and dangerous. It flourished in the 1950s and 1960s, eventually becoming almost a rite of passage. Then, during the 1970s, almost one-third of America's racetracks closed. Recently, however, drag racing has made a comeback.

### 2 Following a Long Sentence with a Short One

Another way to add interest is to follow one or more long sentences with a short one. (This strategy also places emphasis on the short sentence.)

Over the years, vitamin boosters say, a misconception has grown that as long as there are no signs or symptoms of, say, scurvy, then we have all of the vitamin C we need. Although we know how much of a particular vitamin or mineral will prevent clinical disease, we have practically no information on how much is necessary for peak health. In short, we know how sick is sick, but we don't know how well is well. (*Philadelphia Magazine*)

### EXERCISE 1

Combine each of the following sentence groups into one long sentence. Then, compose a relatively short sentence to follow each long one. Finally, combine all the sentences into a paragraph, adding a topic sentence and any transitions necessary for coherence. Proofread your paragraph to be sure the sentences are varied in length.

1. Chocolate is composed of more than three hundred compounds. Phenylethylamine is one such compound. Its presence in the brain may be linked to the emotion of falling in love.
2. Americans now consume a good deal of chocolate. On average, they eat more than nine pounds of chocolate per person per year. The typical Belgian, however, consumes almost fifteen pounds per year.
3. In recent years, Americans have begun a serious love affair with chocolate. Elegant chocolate boutiques sell exquisite bonbons by the piece. At least one hotel offers a "chocolate binge" vacation. The bimonthly *Chocolate News* for connoisseurs is flourishing.

(Adapted from *Newsweek*)

## 37b Combining Choppy Simple Sentences

Strings of short simple sentences can be tedious—and sometimes hard to understand, as the following paragraph illustrates.

John Peter Zenger was a newspaper editor. He waged and won an important battle for freedom of the press in America. He criticized the policies of the British governor. He was charged with criminal libel as a result. Zenger's lawyers were disbarred. Andrew Hamilton defended him. Hamilton convinced the jury that Zenger's criticisms were true. Therefore, the statements were not libelous.

You can revise choppy sentences like the ones in the paragraph above by using *coordination*, *subordination*, or *embedding* to combine them with adjacent sentences.

### 1 Using Coordination

**Coordination** pairs similar elements—words, phrases, or clauses—giving equal weight to each.

Two choppy sentences linked with *and*, creating a compound sentence

John Peter Zenger was a newspaper editor. He waged and won an important battle for freedom of the press in America. He criticized the policies of the British governor, and he was charged with criminal libel as a result. Zenger's lawyers were disbarred by the governor. Andrew Hamilton defended him. Hamilton convinced the jury that Zenger's criticisms were true. Therefore, the statements were not libelous.

## 2 Using Subordination

**Subordination** places the more important idea in an independent clause and the less important idea in a dependent clause.

Complex sentence

John Peter Zenger was a newspaper editor who waged and won an important battle for freedom of the press in America. He criticized the policies of the British governor, and he was charged with criminal libel as a result. When Zenger's lawyers were disbarred by the governor, Andrew Hamilton defended him. Hamilton convinced the jury that Zenger's criticisms were true. Therefore, the statements were not libelous.

Complex sentence

## 3 Using Embedding

**Embedding** is the working of additional words and phrases into sentences.

The sentence *Hamilton convinced the jury . . .* becomes the phrase *convincing the jury*

John Peter Zenger was a newspaper editor who waged and won an important battle for freedom of the press in America. He criticized the policies of the British governor, and he was charged with criminal libel as a result. When Zenger's lawyers were disbarred by the governor, Andrew Hamilton defended him, convincing the jury that Zenger's criticisms were true. Therefore, the statements were not libelous.

This final revision of the original string of choppy sentences is interesting and readable because its sentences are varied and logically linked. (The short simple sentence at the end has been retained for emphasis.)

**ESL TIP**

Some ESL students rely on simple sentences and coordination in their writing because they are afraid of making sentence structure errors. The result is a monotonous style. To add variety, try using **subordination** and **embedding** in your sentences.

### EXERCISE 2

Using coordination, subordination, and embedding, revise this string of choppy simple sentences into a more varied and interesting paragraph.

The first modern miniature golf course was built in New York in 1925. It was an indoor course with 18 holes. Entrepreneurs Drake Delanoy and John Ledbetter built 150 more indoor and outdoor courses. Garnet Carter made miniature golf a worldwide fad. Carter built an elaborate miniature golf course.

He later joined with Delanoy and Ledbetter. Together they built more miniature golf courses. They abbreviated playing distances. They highlighted the game's hazards at the expense of skill. This made the game much more popular. By 1930, there were 25,000 miniature golf courses in the United States. Courses grew more elaborate. Hazards grew more bizarre. The craze spread to London and Hong Kong. The expansion of miniature golf grew out of control. Then, interest in the game declined. By 1931, most miniature golf courses were out of business. The game was revived in the early 1950s. Today, there are between eight and ten thousand miniature golf courses. The architecture of miniature golf remains an enduring form of American folk art. (Adapted from *Games*)

## 37c Breaking Up Strings of Compound Sentences

When you write, try to avoid creating an unbroken series of compound sentences. A string of compound sentences can be extremely monotonous; moreover, if you connect clauses only with coordinating conjunctions, you may find it difficult to indicate exactly how ideas are related and which is most important.

**All Compound Sentences:** A volcano that is erupting is considered *active*, but one that may erupt is designated *dormant,* and one that has not erupted for a long time is called *extinct*. Most active volcanoes are located in "The Ring of Fire," a belt that circles the Pacific Ocean, and they can be extremely destructive. Italy's Vesuvius erupted in AD 79, and it destroyed the town of Pompeii. In 1883, Krakatoa, located between the Indonesian islands of Java and Sumatra, erupted, and it caused a tidal wave, and more than 36,000 people were killed. Martinique's Mont Pelée erupted in 1902, and its hot gas and ash killed 30,000 people, and this completely wiped out the town of St. Pierre.

**Varied Sentences:** A volcano that is erupting is considered *active*. (simple sentence) One that may erupt is designated *dormant,* and one that has not erupted for a long time is called *extinct*. (compound sentence) Most active volcanoes are located in "The Ring of Fire," a belt that circles the Pacific Ocean. (simple sentence with modifier) Active volcanoes can be extremely destructive. (simple sentence) Erupting in AD 79, Italy's Vesuvius destroyed the town of Pompeii. (simple sentence with modifier) When Krakatoa, located between the Indonesian islands of Java and Sumatra, erupted in 1883, it caused a tidal wave that killed 36,000 people. (complex sentence with modifier) The eruption of Martinique's Mont Pelée in 1902 produced hot gas and ash that killed 30,000 people, completely wiping out the town of St. Pierre. (complex sentence with modifier)

**EXERCISE 3**

Revise the compound sentences in this passage so the sentence structure is varied. Be sure that the writer's emphasis and the relationships between ideas are clear.

Dr. Alice I. Baumgartner and her colleagues at the Institute for Equality in Education at the University of Colorado surveyed two thousand Colorado schoolchildren, and they found some startling results. They asked, "If you woke up tomorrow and discovered that you were a (boy) (girl), how would your life be different?" and the answers were sad and shocking. The researchers assumed they would find that boys and girls would see advantages in being either male or female, but instead they found that both boys and girls had a fundamental contempt for females. Many elementary school boys titled their answers "The Disaster" or "Doomsday," and they described the terrible lives they would lead as girls, but the girls seemed to feel they would be better off as boys, and they expressed feelings that they would be able to do more and have easier lives. (Adapted from *Redbook*)

## 37d Varying Sentence Types

Another way to achieve sentence variety is to mix **declarative sentences** (statements) with occasional **imperative sentences** (commands or requests), **exclamations,** and **rhetorical questions** (questions that readers are not expected to answer), as the following paragraph does.

Local television newscasts seem to be delivering less and less news. Although we stay awake for the late news, hoping to be updated on local, national, and world events, only about 30 percent of most newscasts is devoted to news. Up to 25 percent of the typical program—even more during "sweeps weeks"—can be devoted to feature stories, with another 25 percent reserved for advertising. The remaining time is spent on weather, sports, and casual conversation between anchors. Given this focus on "soft" material, what options do those of us wishing to find out what happened in the world have? (rhetorical question) Critics of local television have a few suggestions. First, write to your local station's management voicing your concern and threatening to boycott the news if changes are not made; then, try to get others who feel the way you do to sign a petition. (imperatives) If changes are not made, try turning off your television and reading the newspaper! (exclamation)

**EXERCISE 4**

The following paragraph is composed entirely of declarative sentences. To make it more varied, add three sentences—one exclamation, one rhetorical question, and one imperative—anywhere in the paragraph. Be sure the new sentences are consistent with the paragraph's purpose and tone.

When the Fourth of July comes around, the nation explodes with patriotism. Everywhere we look we see parades and picnics, firecrackers and fireworks. An outsider might wonder what all the fuss is about. We could explain that this is America's birthday party, and all the candles are being lit at once. There is no reason for us to hold back our enthusiasm—or to limit the noise that celebrates it. The Fourth of July is watermelon and corn on the cob, American flags and sparklers, brass bands and more. Everyone looks forward to this celebration, and everyone has a good time.

**Close-Up** VARYING SENTENCE TYPES

Other options for varying sentence types include mixing simple, compound, and complex sentences **(see Chs. 35–36** and **37b–c)**; mixing cumulative and periodic sentences **(see 38b)**; and using balanced sentences **(see 38c)**.

## 37e Varying Sentence Openings

Rather than beginning every sentence with the subject (*I* or *It*, for example), try beginning with a modifying *word, phrase,* or *clause.*

### *Beginning with Modifying Words*

Proud and relieved, they watched their daughter receive her diploma. (adjectives)

Hungrily, he devoured his lunch. (adverb)

### *Beginning with Modifying Phrases*

For better or worse, credit cards are now widely available to college students. (prepositional phrase)

Located on the west coast of Great Britain, Wales is part of the United Kingdom. (participial phrase)

His interests widening, Picasso designed ballet sets and illustrated books. (absolute phrase)

### *Beginning with Modifying Clauses*

After President Woodrow Wilson was incapacitated by a stroke, his wife unofficially performed many presidential duties. (adverb clause)

**GRAMMAR CHECKER Coordinating Conjunctions and Fragments**

If you begin a sentence with a coordinating conjunction, your grammar checker may identify the word group as a **fragment.** If so, you may need to revise your sentence, following the guidelines in **40b–d.**

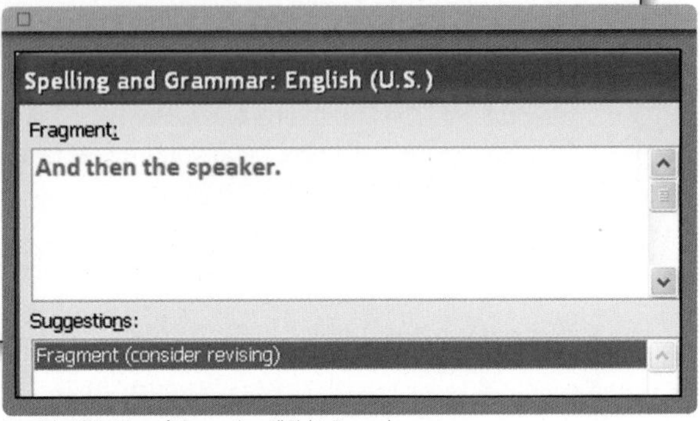




### EXERCISE 5

Each of these sentences begins with the subject. Revise each sentence so that it has a different opening; then, identify your opening strategy.

***Example:*** *In The Names,* N. Scott Momaday, the prominent Native American writer, tells the story of his first fourteen years ~~in *The Names*.~~ (prepositional phrase)

1. Momaday was taken as a very young child to Devil's Tower, the geological formation in Wyoming that is called Tsoai (Bear Tree) in Kiowa, and there he was given the name Tsoai-talee (Bear Tree Boy).
2. The Kiowa myth of the origin of Tsoai is about a boy who playfully chases his seven sisters up a tree, which rises into the air as the boy is transformed into a bear.
3. The boy-bear becomes increasingly ferocious and claws the bark of the tree, which becomes a great rock with a flat top and deeply scored sides.
4. The sisters climb higher and higher to escape their brother's wrath, and eventually they become the seven stars of the Big Dipper.
5. This story, from which Momaday received one of his names, appears in his works *The Way to Rainy Mountain, House Made of Dawn,* and *The Ancient Child.*

## 37f Varying Standard Word Order

ESL 64f

You can vary standard **word order** (subject-verb-object or subject-verb-complement) either by intentionally inverting this usual order or by inserting words between the subject and the verb.

### 1 Inverting Word Order

Sometimes you can place the complement or direct object *before* the verb instead of in its conventional position after the verb, or you can place the verb *before* the subject instead of after it. These strategies draw attention to the word or word group that appears in an unexpected place.

(object) (subject) (verb) (subject) (subject) (verb)

The north wall he painted red; the other walls he painted white.

(complement) (verb) (subject)

Crucial to the agreement is a clear understanding of the issues.

**Note:** Be careful to use inverted word order in moderation; when it is used in a series of sentences, inverted word order becomes distracting and hard to follow.

### 2 Separating Subject from Verb

You can also place words or phrases between subject and verb—but be sure that the word group does not obscure the connection between subject and verb or create an agreement error. See 50a

Many states require that infants and young children ride in government-approved child safety seats because they hope this regulation will reduce needless fatalities. (subject and verb together)

Many states, hoping to reduce needless fatalities, require that infants and young children ride in government-approved child safety seats. (subject and verb separated)

## EXERCISE 6

The following five sentences use conventional word order. To vary this standard word order, revise each sentence in one of two ways: either invert the sentence, or insert words between the subject and the verb. After you have completed your revisions, link all the sentences together to create a paragraph.

***Example:*** Dada, ~~was~~ an artistic and literary rebellion, ~~that~~ defied the conventional values of the early twentieth century. (words inserted between subject and verb)

1. The Dada movement first appeared in 1915 and effectively ended in 1925 with the rise of Surrealism.
2. The name *Dada*, French for "hobby horse," was selected at random from a dictionary.

3. The Dadaists ultimately rejected all traditional cultural values, and their goal became to destroy art as an aesthetic cult and replace it with "antiart" and "nonart."
4. The Dadaists rejected traditional art, and they substituted the nonsense poem, the ready-made object, and the collage.
5. The most notorious example of Dada art is the sculpture *Fountain* (1917), which was a urinal Marcel Duchamp found and signed *R. Mutt* and then entered into a gallery exhibit.

CHAPTER 38

# Writing Emphatic Sentences

## Frequently Asked Questions



In speaking, we emphasize certain ideas and deemphasize others with intonation and gesture; in writing, we convey **emphasis**—the relative importance of ideas—through the selection and arrangement of words.

## 38a Conveying Emphasis through Word Order

Because readers tend to focus on the beginning and end of a sentence, you should place the most important information there.

### 1 Beginning with Important Ideas

Placing key ideas at the beginning of a sentence stresses their importance. The unedited version of the following sentence places emphasis on the study, not on those who conducted it or on those who participated in it. Editing shifts this focus and puts the emphasis on the researcher, not on the study.

> ~~In a landmark study of alcoholism,~~/ Dr. George Vaillant of
> *, in a landmark study of alcoholism,*
> Harvard ^ followed two hundred Harvard graduates and four
> hundred inner-city, working-class men from the Boston area.

Straightforward assignments—laboratory reports, memos, technical papers, business correspondence, and the like—call for sentences that present vital information first and qualifiers later.

> Treating cancer with interferon has been the subject of a good deal of research. (emphasizes the treatment, not the research)
>
> Dividends will be paid if the stockholders agree. (emphasizes the dividends, not the stockholders)

### Close-Up USING *THERE IS* AND *THERE ARE*

Using an empty phrase like *there is* or *there are* at the beginning of a sentence generally weakens the sentence.

> *MIT places*
> ~~There is~~ heavy emphasis on the development of computational skills ~~at MIT~~.

## 2 Ending with Important Ideas

Placing key elements at the end of a sentence is another way to convey their importance.

***Using a Colon or a Dash*** A colon or a dash can add emphasis by isolating an important word or phrase at the end of a sentence.

> Beth had always dreamed of owning one special car: a 1953 Corvette.
>
> The elderly need a good deal of special attention—but they do not always get that attention.

### Close-Up PLACING TRANSITIONAL WORDS AND PHRASES

When they are placed at the end of a sentence, conjunctive adverbs or other transitional words lose their power to indicate the relationship between ideas. Placed earlier in the sentence, transitional words and phrases can link ideas and add emphasis.

See 7b2

> *however,*
> Smokers do have rights; they should not try to impose their habit on others. ~~however.~~

***Using Climactic Word Order*** **Climactic word order,** the arrangement of a series of items from the least to the most important, places emphasis on the last item in the series.

Binge drinking can lead to unwanted pregnancies, car accidents, and even death. (*Death* is the most serious consequence.)

## EXERCISE 1

Underline the most important idea in each sentence of the following paragraph. Then, identify the strategy that the writer uses to emphasize each idea. Is the key idea placed at the beginning or the end of a sentence? Does the writer use climactic order?

Listening to diatribes by angry callers or ranting about today's news, the talk radio host spreads ideas over the airwaves. Every day at the same time, the political talk show host discusses national events and policies, the failures of the opposing views, and the foibles of the individuals who espouse those opposing views. Listening for hours a day, some callers become recognizable contributors to many different talk radio programs. Other listeners are less devoted, tuning in only when they are in the car and never calling to voice their opinions. Political radio hosts usually structure their programs around a specific agenda, espousing the party line and ridiculing the opponent's position. With a style of presentation aimed both at entertainment and information, the host's ideas become caricatures of party positions. Sometimes, in order to keep the information lively and interesting, a host may either state the issues too simply or deliberately mislead the audience. A host can excuse these errors by insisting that the show is harmless: it's for entertainment, not information. Many are concerned about how the political process is affected by this misinformation.

### 3 Experimenting with Word Order

ESL 64f

In English sentences, the most common **word order** is subject-verb-object (or subject-verb-complement). By intentionally departing from this expected word order, you can place emphasis on the word, phrase, or clause that you have relocated.

> More modest and less inventive than Turner's paintings are John Constable's landscapes.

Here the writer calls attention to the modifying phrase *more modest and less inventive than Turner's paintings* by inverting word order, placing the complement and the verb before the subject.

**ESL TIP**

If English is not your first language, you may be reluctant to experiment with word order. However, to keep your sentences from becoming monotonous, you need to experiment occasionally. When you do, check with a native English speaker or with your instructor if you are uncertain about whether or not your sentences are grammatical.

## EXERCISE 2

Revise the following sentences to make them more emphatic. For each, decide which ideas should be highlighted, and place these key ideas at sentence beginnings or endings. Use climactic order or depart from conventional word order where appropriate.

1. Police want to upgrade their firepower because criminals are better armed than ever before.
2. A few years ago, felons used so-called Saturday night specials, small-caliber six-shot revolvers.
3. Now, semiautomatic pistols capable of firing fifteen to twenty rounds, along with paramilitary weapons like the AK-47, have replaced these weapons.
4. Police are adopting weapons such as new fast-firing shotguns and 9mm automatic pistols in order to gain an equal footing with their adversaries.
5. Faster reloading and a hair trigger are two of the numerous advantages that automatic pistols, the weapons of choice among law-enforcement officers, have over the traditional .38-caliber police revolver.

## 38b Conveying Emphasis through Sentence Structure

As you write, try to construct sentences that emphasize more important ideas and deemphasize less important ones.

### 1 Using Cumulative Sentences

A **cumulative sentence** begins with an independent clause, followed by additional words, phrases, or clauses that expand or develop it.

> She holds me in strong arms, arms that have chopped cotton, dismembered trees, scattered corn for chickens, cradled infants, shaken the daylights out of half-grown upstart teenagers. (Rebecca Hill, *Blue Rise*)

Because it presents its main idea first, a cumulative sentence tends to be clear and straightforward. (Most English sentences are cumulative.)

### 2 Using Periodic Sentences

A **periodic sentence** moves from supporting details, expressed in modifying phrases and dependent clauses, to the sentence's key idea, which is placed in the independent clause at the end of the sentence.

> Unlike World War II, which ended decisively with the unconditional surrender of Germany and Japan, the war in Vietnam did not have a clear-cut resolution.

Note: In some periodic sentences, the modifying phrase or dependent clause comes between subject and predicate: *Columbus, after several discouraging and unsuccessful voyages, finally reached America.*

### EXERCISE 3

A. Bracket the independent clause(s) in each sentence, and underline each modifying phrase and dependent clause. Label each sentence cumulative or periodic.
B. Relocate the supporting details to make cumulative sentences periodic and periodic sentences cumulative, adding words or rephrasing to make your meaning clear.
C. Be prepared to explain how your revision changes the emphasis of the original sentence.

***Example:*** Feeling isolated, sad, and frightened, [the small child sat alone in the bus terminal.] (periodic)

***Revised:*** The small child sat alone in the bus terminal, feeling isolated, sad, and frightened. (cumulative)

1. However different in their educational opportunities, both Jefferson and Lincoln as young men became known to their contemporaries as "hard students." (Douglas L. Wilson, "What Jefferson and Lincoln Read," *Atlantic Monthly*)
2. The road came into being slowly, league by league, river crossing by river crossing. (Stephen Harrigan, "Highway 1," *Texas Monthly*)
3. Without willing it, I had gone from being ignorant of being ignorant to being aware of being aware. (Maya Angelou, *I Know Why the Caged Bird Sings*)

### EXERCISE 4

Combine each of the following sentence groups into one cumulative sentence, subordinating supporting details to more important ideas. Then, combine each group into one periodic sentence. (Each group can be combined in a variety of ways, and you may have to add, delete, change, or reorder words.) How do the two versions of the sentence differ in emphasis?

***Example:*** More women than ever before are running for office. They are encouraged by the success of other female candidates.

***Cumulative:*** More women than ever before are running for office, encouraged by the success of other female candidates.

***Periodic:*** Encouraged by the success of other female candidates, more women than ever before are running for office.

1. Some politicians opposed the prescription drug program. They believed it was too expensive. They felt that a smaller, more limited program was preferable.
2. Smoking poses a real danger. It is associated with various cancers. It is linked to heart disease and stroke. It threatens even nonsmokers.

3. Infertile couples who want children sometimes go through a series of difficult processes. They may try adoption. They may also try artificial insemination or in vitro fertilization. They may even seek out surrogate mothers.
4. The Thames is a river that meanders through southern England. It has been the inspiration for such literary works as *Alice's Adventures in Wonderland* and *The Wind in the Willows.* It was also captured in paintings by Constable, Turner, and Whistler.
5. Black-footed ferrets are rare North American mammals. They prey on prairie dogs. They are primarily nocturnal. They have black feet and black-tipped tails. Their faces have raccoonlike masks.

## EXERCISE 5

Combine each of the following sentence groups into one sentence that subordinates supporting details to the main idea. In each case, create either a periodic or a cumulative sentence, depending on which structure you think will best convey the sentence's emphasis. Add, delete, change, or reorder words when necessary.

*, that there are too many graduates and too few jobs,*

***Example:*** The fears of today's college students^are based on reality. ~~They are afraid there are too many graduates and too few jobs.~~ (periodic)

1. Today's college students are under a good deal of stress. Job prospects in some fields are not very good. Financial aid is not as available as it was in the past.
2. Education has grown very expensive. The job market has become tighter. Pressure to get into graduate and professional schools has increased.
3. Family ties seem to be weakening. Students are not always able to count on family support.
4. College students have always had problems. Now, college counseling centers report more—and more serious—problems.
5. The term *student shock* was coined several years ago. This term describes a syndrome that may include depression, anxiety, headaches, and eating and sleeping disorders.
6. Many students are overwhelmed by the vast array of courses and majors offered at their colleges. They tend to be less decisive. They take longer to choose a major and to complete school.
7. Many drop out of school for brief (or extended) periods or switch majors several times. Many take five years or longer to complete their college education.
8. Some colleges are responding to the pressures that students feel. They hold stress-management workshops.They offer suicide-prevention seminars. They advertise the services of their counseling centers. They train students as peer counselors. They improve their vocational counseling services.

## 38c Conveying Emphasis through Parallelism and Balance

See 43a

By reinforcing the similarity between grammatical elements, parallelism can help you convey information clearly and emphatically.

We seek an individual who is a self-starter, who owns a late-model automobile, and who is willing to work evenings. (classified advertisement)

Do not pass Go; do not collect $200. (game instructions)

The Faust legend is central in Benét's *The Devil and Daniel Webster*, in Goethe's *Faust*, and in Marlowe's *Dr. Faustus*. (examination answer)

A **balanced sentence** is neatly divided between two parallel structures—for example, two independent clauses in a compound sentence. The symmetrical structure of a balanced sentence adds emphasis by highlighting similarities or differences between the ideas in the two clauses.

In the 1950s, the electronic miracle was the television; in the 1980s, the electronic miracle was the computer.

Alive, the elephant was worth at least a hundred pounds; dead, he would only be worth the value of his tusks, five pounds, possibly. (George Orwell, "Shooting an Elephant")

## 38d Conveying Emphasis through Repetition

See 39b

Unnecessary repetition makes sentences dull and monotonous as well as wordy.

He had a good arm and also could field well, and he was also a fast runner.

Effective repetition, however, can place emphasis on key words or ideas.

They decided to begin again: to begin hoping, to begin trying to change, to begin working toward a goal.

During those years when I was just learning to speak, my mother and father addressed me only in Spanish; in Spanish I learned to reply. (Richard Rodriguez, *Aria: Memoir of a Bilingual Childhood*)



### EXERCISE 6

Revise the sentences in this paragraph, using parallelism and balance to highlight corresponding elements, and using repetition of key words and phrases to add emphasis. You may combine sentences and add, delete, or reorder words.

Many readers distrust newspapers. They also distrust what they read in magazines. They do not trust what they hear on the radio and what television shows them, either. Of these media, newspapers have been the most responsive to audience criticism. Some newspapers even have ombudsmen.

They are supposed to listen to readers' complaints. They are also charged with acting on these grievances. One complaint that many people have is that newspapers are inaccurate. Newspapers' disregard for people's privacy is another of many readers' criticisms. Reporters are seen as arrogant, and readers feel that journalists can be unfair. They feel that reporters tend to glorify criminals, and they believe there is a tendency to place too much emphasis on bizarre or offbeat stories. Finally, readers complain about poor writing and editing. Polls show that despite its efforts to respond to reader criticism, the press continues to face hostility. (Adapted from *Newsweek*)

## 38e Conveying Emphasis through Active Voice

The active voice is generally more emphatic than the passive voice.

See 49d

ESL 64a6

**Passive:** The prediction that oil prices will rise is being made by economists.

**Active:** Economists are predicting that oil prices will rise.

Notice that the passive voice sentence above does not draw readers' attention to who is performing the action. In a passive voice sentence, the subject is the recipient of the action, so the actor fades into the background (*by economists*)—or may even be omitted entirely (*the prediction . . . is being made*). In contrast, active voice places the emphasis where it belongs: on the actor or actors (*Economists*).

Sometimes, of course, you *want* to stress the action rather than the actor; when this is the case, use the passive voice.

**Passive:** The West was explored by Lewis and Clark. (stresses the exploration of the West, not who explored it)

**Active:** Lewis and Clark explored the West. (stresses the contribution of the explorers)

### GRAMMAR CHECKER Avoiding Passive Voice

Your grammar checker will highlight passive voice constructions in your writing and offer revision suggestions.

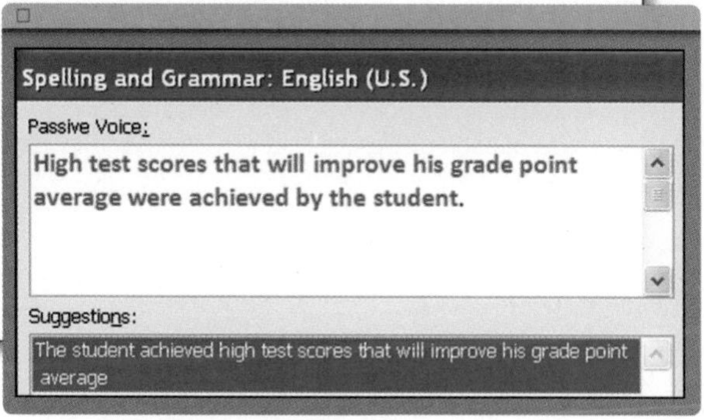
Spelling and Grammar: English (U.S.)
Passive Voice:
High test scores that will improve his grade point average were achieved by the student.
Suggestions:
The student achieved high test scores that will improve his grade point average

Note: Passive voice is also used when the identity of the person performing the action is irrelevant or unknown (*The course was canceled*). For this reason, the passive voice is frequently used in scientific and technical writing: *The beaker was filled with a saline solution.*

**GRAMMAR CHECKER Using Passive Voice**

Using passive voice is sometimes the clearest and most direct way to express your ideas. In the example sentence shown here, for instance, the use of passive voice is a good choice, and the grammar checker's suggestion is not only awkward but also incorrect.

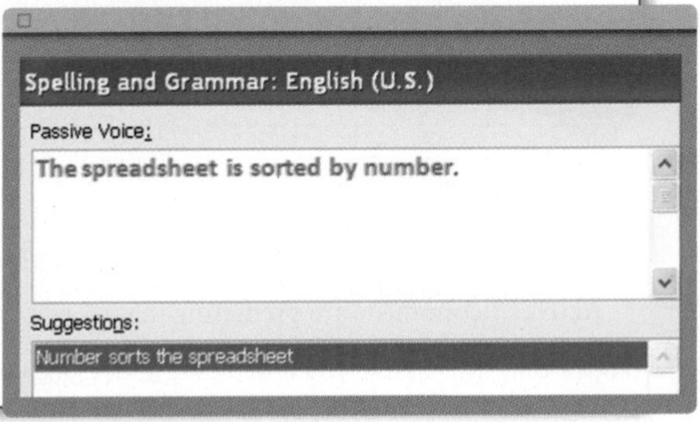
Spelling and Grammar: English (U.S.)
Passive Voice:
The spreadsheet is sorted by number.
Suggestions:
Number sorts the spreadsheet

## EXERCISE 7

Revise this paragraph to eliminate awkward or excessive use of passive constructions.

Jack Dempsey, the heavyweight champion between 1919 and 1926, had an interesting but uneven career. He was considered one of the greatest boxers of all time. Dempsey began fighting as "Kid Blackie," but his career did not take off until 1919, when Jack "Doc" Kearns became his manager. Dempsey won the championship when Jess Willard was defeated by him in Toledo, Ohio, in 1919. Dempsey immediately became a popular sports figure; President Franklin D. Roosevelt was one of his biggest fans. Influential friends were made by Jack Dempsey. Boxing lessons were given by him to the actor Rudolph Valentino. He made friends with Douglas Fairbanks Sr., Damon Runyon, and J. Paul Getty. Hollywood serials were made by Dempsey, but the title was lost by him to Gene Tunney, and Dempsey failed to regain it the following year. After his boxing career declined, a restaurant was opened by Dempsey, and many major sporting events were attended by him. This exposure kept him in the public eye until he lost his restaurant. Jack Dempsey died in 1983.

CHAPTER 39

# Writing Concise Sentences

## Frequently Asked Questions



A sentence is not concise simply because it is short; a **concise** sentence contains only the words necessary to make its point.

### Close-Up TEXT MESSAGES

If you send texts, which are limited to 140 characters, you already know how to be concise. In text messages, you omit articles and other nonessential words, and you use nonstandard spellings (*nite*) and shorthand (*ru home?*). This kind of language is not acceptable in college writing, where you need to use other strategies (such as those discussed in this chapter) to make your writing concise.

## 39a Eliminating Wordiness

A good way to find out which words are essential in a sentence is to underline the key words. Look carefully at the remaining words so you can determine which are unnecessary, and then eliminate wordiness by deleting them.

> It seems to me that it does not make sense to allow any bail to be granted to anyone who has ever been convicted of a violent crime.

The underlining shows you immediately that none of the words in the long introductory phrase are essential. The following revision includes just the words necessary to convey the key ideas.

> Bail should not be granted to anyone who has ever been convicted of a violent crime.

Whenever possible, delete nonessential words—*deadwood, utility words,* and *circumlocution*—from your writing.

## 1 Eliminating Deadwood

The term **deadwood** refers to unnecessary phrases that take up space and add nothing to meaning.

> ~~There were many~~ *Many* factors ~~that~~ influenced his decision to become a priest.
>
> The two plots are ~~both~~ similar in ~~the way~~ that they trace the characters' increasing rage.
>
> Shoppers ~~who are~~ looking for bargains often go to outlets.
>
> They played *an exhausting* ~~a~~ racquetball game ~~that was exhausting~~.
>
> ~~In this~~ *This* article ~~it~~ discusses lead poisoning.
>
> The most tragic character in Hamlet *is* ~~would have to be~~ Ophelia.

Deadwood also includes unnecessary statements of opinion, such as *I believe, I feel,* and *it seems to me.*

> ~~In my opinion, the~~ *The* characters seem undeveloped.
>
> ~~As far as I'm concerned, this~~ *This* course looks interesting.

## 2 Eliminating Utility Words

Utility words simply act as filler; they contribute nothing to the meaning of a sentence. **Utility words** include nouns with imprecise meanings (*factor, situation, type, aspect,* and so on); adjectives so general that they are almost meaningless (*good, bad, important*); and common adverbs denoting degree (*basically, actually, quite, very, definitely*). Often, you can just delete the utility word; if you cannot, replace it with a more precise word.

> ~~The registration situation~~ *Registration* was disorganized.
>
> The scholarship ~~basically~~ offered Fran *an* ~~a good~~ opportunity to study Spanish in Spain.
>
> It was ~~actually~~ a worthwhile book, but I did not ~~really~~ finish it.

### 3 Avoiding Circumlocution

**Circumlocution** is taking a roundabout way to say something (using ten words when five will do). Instead of complicated constructions, use concise, specific words and phrases that come right to the point.

> ~~It is not unlikely that the~~ *The* trend toward lower consumer spending will *probably* continue.
>
> The curriculum was ~~of a~~ unique ~~nature~~.
>
> Joe was in the army *while* ~~during the same time that~~ I was in college.

## Close-Up REVISING WORDY PHRASES

A wordy phrase can almost always be replaced by a more concise, more direct term.

| **Wordy** | **Concise** |
|---|---|
| at the present time | now |
| at this point in time | now |
| for the purpose of | for |
| due to the fact that | because |
| on account of | because |
| until such time as | until |
| in the event that | if |
| by means of | by |
| in the vicinity of | near |
| have the ability to | be able to |

### EXERCISE 1

Revise the following paragraph to eliminate deadwood, utility words, and circumlocution. Whenever possible, delete wordy phrases or replace them with more concise expressions.

For all intents and purposes, the shopping mall is no longer an important factor on the American cultural scene. In the '80s, malls became gathering places where teenagers met, walkers came to get in a few miles, and shoppers who were looking for a wide selection and were not concerned about value went to shop. There are several factors that have worked to undermine the mall's popularity. First, due to the fact that today's shoppers are more likely to be interested in value, many of them have headed to the discount stores. Today's shopper is now more likely to shop in discount stores or bulk-buying warehouse stores than in the small, expensive specialty shops in the large malls. Add to this a resurgence of the values of community, and we can see how mall shopping would have to be less attractive than shopping at local stores. Many malls actually have up to 20 percent empty storefronts, and some have had to close down altogether. Others have met the challenge by expanding their roles from shopping centers into community centers. They have added playgrounds for the children and more amusements and restaurants for the adults. They have also appealed to the growing sense of value shopping by giving gift certificates and discounts to shoppers who spend money in their stores. For a while, it seemed as if the huge shopping malls that had become familiar cultural icons were dying out, replaced by Internet shopping. Now, however, it looks as if some of those icons just might make it and survive by reinventing themselves as more than just places to shop.

## 39b Eliminating Unnecessary Repetition

See 38d

Repetition can make your sentences more **emphatic**, but unnecessary repetition and **redundant** word groups (repeated words or phrases that say the same thing, such as *free gift, halts to a stop,* and *unanticipated surprise*) can lessen the impact of your writing. You can correct unnecessary repetition by using one of the following strategies.

### 1 Deleting Redundancy

People's clothing ~~attire~~ can reveal a good deal about their personalities.

The twins kept having ~~recurring~~ cold symptoms.

The two candidates share several positions. ~~in common.~~

He always has his whole entire strategy planned out. ~~all the time.~~

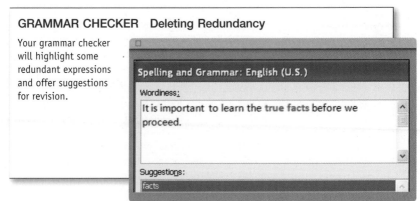

**GRAMMAR CHECKER Deleting Redundancy**

Your grammar checker will highlight some redundant expressions and offer suggestions for revision.

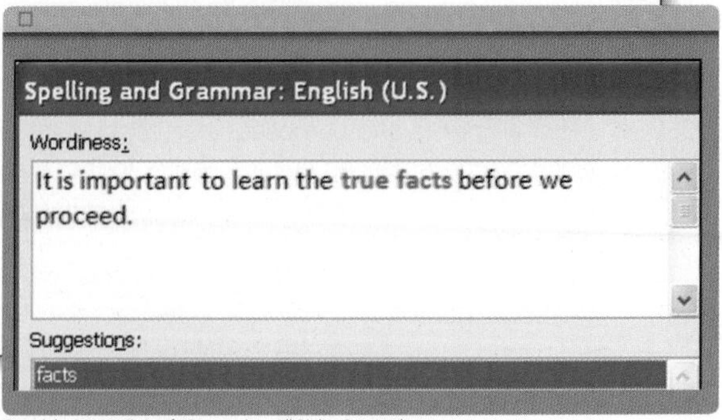
Spelling and Grammar: English (U.S.)
Wordiness:
It is important to learn the true facts before we proceed.
Suggestions:
facts

### 2 Substituting a Pronoun

The fictional detective Miss Marple solved many crimes. *The Murder at the Vicarage* was one of ~~Miss Marple's~~ *her* most challenging cases.

### 3 Creating an Appositive

Red Barber, ~~was~~ a sportscaster, ~~He~~ was known for his colorful expressions.

### 4 Creating a Compound

John F. Kennedy was the youngest man ever elected president/ *and* ~~He was~~ the first Catholic to hold this office.

### 5 Creating a Complex Sentence

Americans value freedom of speech/ *, which* ~~Freedom of speech~~ is guaranteed by the First Amendment.

**EXERCISE 2**

Eliminate any unnecessary repetition of words or ideas in this paragraph. Also, revise to eliminate deadwood, utility words, and circumlocution.

For a wide variety of different reasons, more and more people today are choosing a vegetarian diet. There are three kinds of vegetarians: strict vegetarians eat no animal foods at all; lactovegetarians eat dairy products, but they do not eat meat, fish, poultry, or eggs; and ovolactovegetarians eat eggs and dairy products, but they do not eat meat, fish, or poultry. Famous vegetarians include such well-known people as George Bernard Shaw, Leonardo da Vinci, Ralph Waldo Emerson, Henry David Thoreau, and Mahatma Gandhi. Like these well-known vegetarians, the vegetarians of today have good reasons for becoming vegetarians. For instance, some religions recommend a vegetarian diet. Some of these religions are Buddhism, Brahmanism, and Hinduism. Other people turn to vegetarianism for reasons of health or for reasons of hygiene. These people believe that meat is a source of potentially harmful chemicals, and they believe meat contains infectious organisms. Some people feel meat may cause digestive problems and may lead to other difficulties as well. Other vegetarians adhere to a vegetarian diet because they feel it is ecologically wasteful to kill animals after we feed plants to them. These vegetarians believe we should eat the plants. Finally, there are facts and evidence to suggest that a vegetarian diet may possibly help people live longer lives. A vegetarian diet may do this by reducing the incidence of heart disease and lessening the incidence of some cancers. (Adapted from *Jane Brody's Nutrition Book*)

## 39c Tightening Rambling Sentences

The combination of nonessential words, unnecessary repetition, and complicated syntax creates **rambling sentences.** Revising rambling sentences frequently requires extensive editing.

### 1 Eliminating Excessive Coordination

When you string a series of independent clauses together with coordinating conjunctions, you create a rambling, unfocused compound sentence that presents your ideas as if they all have equal weight. To revise such sentences, identify the main idea or ideas, and then subordinate supporting details to that main idea.

**Wordy:** Benjamin Franklin was the son of a candlemaker, but he later apprenticed as a printer, and this experience led to his buying the *Pennsylvania Gazette,* and he managed this periodical with great success.

**Concise:** Benjamin Franklin, the son of a candlemaker, later apprenticed as a printer, an experience that led to his buying the *Pennsylvania Gazette,* which he managed with great success. (Franklin's apprenticeship as a printer is the sentence's main idea.)

**Wordy:** Puerto Rico is a large island, and it is mountainous, and it has steep slopes, and they fall to gentle plains along the coast.

**Concise:** A large island, Puerto Rico is mountainous, with steep slopes falling to gentle plains along the coast. (Puerto Rico's mountainous terrain is the sentence's main idea.)

### 2 Eliminating Adjective Clauses

See 35b2

A series of adjective clauses is also likely to produce a rambling sentence. To revise, substitute more concise modifying words or phrases for the adjective clauses.

**Wordy:** *Moby-Dick*, which is a novel about a white whale, was written by Herman Melville, who was friendly with Nathaniel Hawthorne, who urged him to revise the first draft.

**Concise:** *Moby-Dick*, a novel about a white whale, was written by Herman Melville, who revised the first draft at the urging of his friend Nathaniel Hawthorne.

See 49d1

### 3 Eliminating Passive Constructions

ESL 64a6

Excessive use of the passive voice can create rambling sentences. Correct this problem when you revise by changing passive to active voice.

~~Water rights are being fought for in court by~~ Indian tribes, such as the Papago in Arizona and the Pyramid Lake Paiute in Nevada~~.~~ *, are fighting in court for water rights.*

## 4 Eliminating Wordy Prepositional Phrases

When you revise, substitute adjectives or adverbs for wordy **prepositional phrases**.

See 35c3

The trip was *dangerous* ~~one of danger~~ but also *exciting* ~~one of excitement~~.

He spoke *confidently* ~~in a confident manner~~ and *authoritatively* ~~with a lot of authority~~.

## 5 Eliminating Wordy Noun Constructions

Substitute strong verbs for wordy **noun phrases**.

See 35b1

We have *decided* ~~made the decision~~ to postpone the meeting until ~~the appearance of~~ all the board members *appear*.

Sometimes ~~there is an accumulation of~~ water *accumulates* on the roof.

### EXERCISE 3

Revise the rambling sentences in these paragraphs by eliminating excessive coordination; unnecessary use of the passive voice; and overuse of adjective clauses, prepositional phrases, and noun constructions. As you revise, make your sentences more concise by deleting nonessential words and unnecessary repetition.

Some colleges that have been in support of fraternities for a number of years are at this time in the process of conducting a reevaluation of the position of those fraternities on campus. In opposition to the fraternities are a fair number of students, faculty members, and administrators who claim fraternities are inherently sexist, which they say makes it impossible for the groups to exist in a coeducational institution, which is supposed to offer equal opportunities for members of both sexes. More and more members of the college community also see fraternities as elitist as well as sexist and favor their abolition. In addition, many point out that fraternities are associated with dangerous practices, such as hazing and alcohol abuse.

However, some students, faculty, and administrators remain wholeheartedly in support of traditional fraternities, which they believe are responsible for helping students make the acquaintance of people and learn the leadership skills that they believe will be of assistance to them in their future lives as adults. Supporters of fraternities believe that students should retain the right to make their own social decisions, and they think that joining a fraternity is one of those decisions, and they also believe fraternities are responsible for providing valuable services. Some of these are tutoring, raising money for charity, and running campus escort services. Therefore, these individuals are not of the opinion that the abolition of traditional fraternities makes sense.

PART 10

# Solving Common Sentence Problems

CHAPTER 40

# Revising Fragments

## Frequently Asked Questions



## 40a Recognizing Fragments

A **fragment** is an incomplete sentence—a phrase or clause that is punctuated as if it were a complete sentence. A sentence may be incomplete for any of the following reasons:

- **It lacks a subject.**

  Many astrophysicists now believe that galaxies are distributed in clusters. And even form supercluster complexes.

- **It lacks a verb.**

  Every generation has its defining moments. Usually the events with the most news coverage.

- **It lacks both a subject and a verb.**

  Researchers are engaged in a variety of studies. Suggesting a link between alcoholism and heredity. (*Suggesting* is a **verbal,** which cannot serve as a sentence's main verb.)

- **It is a dependent clause.**

  Bishop Desmond Tutu was awarded the 1984 Nobel Peace Prize. Because he fought to end apartheid.

  The pH meter and the spectrophotometer are two scientific instruments. That changed the chemistry laboratory dramatically.

Note: A sentence cannot consist of a single clause that begins with a subordinating conjunction (such as *because*) or a relative pronoun (such as *that*); moreover, unless it is a question or an exclamation, a sentence cannot consist of a single clause beginning with *when, where, who, which, what, why,* or *how.*

## Close-Up IDENTIFYING FRAGMENTS

A fragment is especially confusing when it comes between two independent clauses and readers cannot tell which of the two clauses completes the fragment's thought. For instance, it is impossible to tell to which independent clause the underlined fragment in each of the following sequences belongs.

> The course requirements were changed last year. Because a new professor was hired at the very end of the spring semester. I was unable to find out about this change until after preregistration.

> In *The Ox-Bow Incident*, the crowd is convinced that the men are guilty. Even though the men insist they are innocent and Davies pleads for their lives. They are hanged.

### GRAMMAR CHECKER Identifying Fragments

Your grammar checker will identify many (although not all) fragments. As you type, they will be highlighted in green, and you will be prompted to revise them. However, not every word group identified as a fragment will actually be a fragment. You, not your grammar checker, will have to make the final decision about whether or not a sentence is grammatically complete—and decide how to correct it.

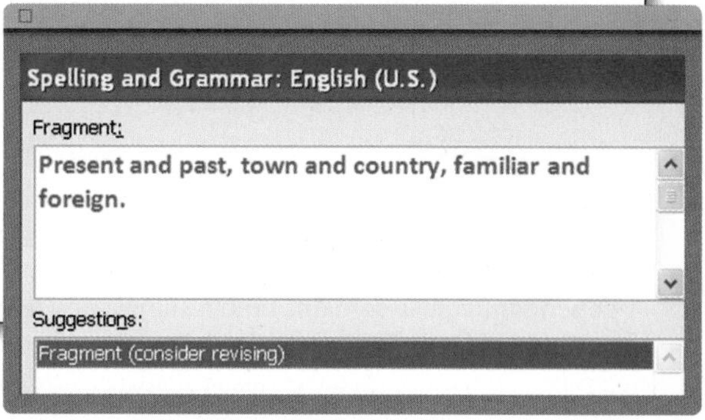
Spelling and Grammar: English (U.S.)
Fragment:
Present and past, town and country, familiar and foreign.
Suggestions:
Fragment (consider revising)

## EXERCISE 1

Identify each of the following word groups as either a fragment or a complete sentence. Be prepared to explain why each fragment is not a complete sentence. When you have finished, type each sentence into your word-processing program, and use the grammar checker to check your responses.

1. Consisting of shortness of breath, a high fever, and a racing pulse.
2. Held in contempt of court by the presiding judge.
3. Walking to the end of the road and back is good exercise.
4. On her own at last, after many years of struggle for independence.
5. Because he felt torn between two cultures.
6. With boundaries extending from the ocean to the bay.
7. Although language study can be challenging.

8. In addition, a new point guard will be a valuable addition to the team.
9. Defeated by his own greed but not in the least regretful.
10. Moreover, the continued presence of troops in Iraq.

## Close-Up REVISING FRAGMENTS

If you identify a fragment in your writing, use one of the following two strategies to revise it:

1. Attach the fragment to an adjacent independent clause.

   *and*
   According to German legend, Lohengrin is the son of Parzival/ ~~And~~ a knight of the Holy Grail.

   *because*
   Pioneers traveled west/ ~~Because~~ they hoped to find a better life.

2. Turn the fragment into a sentence.

   Lancaster County, Pennsylvania, is home to many Pennsylvania Dutch.
   *They are descended*
   ~~Descended~~ from German immigrants. (missing subject and verb added)

   *City*
   Property taxes rose sharply. ~~Although city~~ services declined. (subordinating conjunction *although* deleted)

## 40b Revising Dependent Clause Fragments

A **dependent clause** contains both a subject and a verb, but it cannot stand alone as a sentence. Because it needs an independent clause to complete its meaning, a dependent clause (also called a *subordinate clause*) must always be attached to at least one independent clause to form a complete sentence. You can recognize a dependent clause because it is always introduced by a subordinating conjunction (*although, because,* and so on) or a relative pronoun (*that, which, who,* and so on).

See 36b

In most cases, the best way to correct a dependent clause fragment is to join the dependent clause to an adjacent independent clause, creating a complex sentence.

*because*
The United States declared war/ ~~Because~~ the Japanese bombed Pearl Harbor. (Dependent clause has been attached to an independent clause, creating a complex sentence.)

*, which*
The battery is dead/ ~~Which~~ means the car won't start. (Dependent clause has been attached to an independent clause, creating a complex sentence.)

Another way to correct a dependent clause fragment is to delete the subordinating conjunction or relative pronoun, turning the fragment into a complete sentence.

> The United States declared war. ~~Because the~~ ^The Japanese bombed Pearl Harbor. (Subordinating conjunction *because* has been deleted; the result is a new sentence.)

> The battery is dead. ~~Which~~ ^This means the car won't start. (Relative pronoun *which* has been replaced by *this;* the result is a new sentence.)

*Note:* Simply deleting or replacing the subordinating conjunction or relative pronoun, as in the two examples above, is usually the least desirable way to revise a dependent clause fragment because it is likely to create two choppy sentences and because it does not clearly indicate the logical relationship between the two clauses.

### EXERCISE 2

Identify the fragments in the following paragraph. Then, correct each fragment either by attaching the fragment to an independent clause or by deleting or replacing the subordinating conjunction or relative pronoun to create a sentence that can stand alone. (In some cases, you will have to replace a relative pronoun with another word that can serve as the subject.)

> The drive-in movie came into being just after World War II. When both movies and cars were central to the lives of many Americans. Drive-ins were especially popular with teenagers and young families during the 1950s. When cars and gas were relatively inexpensive. Theaters charged by the carload. Which meant that a group of teenagers or a family with several children could spend an evening at the movies for a few dollars. In 1958, when the fad peaked, there were over four thousand drive-ins in the United States. While today there are fewer than three thousand. Many of these are in the Sunbelt, with most in California. Although many Sunbelt drive-ins continue to thrive because of the year-round warm weather. Many northern drive-ins are in financial trouble. Because land is so expensive. Some drive-in owners break even only by operating flea markets or swap meets in daylight hours. While others, unable to attract customers, are selling their theaters to land developers. Soon, drive-ins may be a part of our nostalgic past. Which will be a great loss for many who enjoy them.

## 40c Revising Phrase Fragments

A **phrase** provides information—description, examples, and so on—about other words or word groups in a sentence. However, because it lacks a subject, a verb, or both, a phrase cannot stand alone as a sentence.

See 7b2

## Close-Up FRAGMENTS INTRODUCED BY TRANSITIONS

Many phrase fragments are word groups that are introduced by transitional words and phrases, such as *also, finally, in addition,* and *now,* but are missing subjects and verbs. To correct such a fragment, you need to add the missing subject and verb.

*It was also*
~~Also~~ a step in the right direction.

*he found*
Finally, ^ a new home for the family.

*we need*
In addition, ^ three new keyboards for the computer lab.

### 1 Prepositional Phrase Fragments

See 35b1

ESL 64e1

A prepositional phrase consists of a preposition, its object, and any modifiers of the object.

To correct a prepositional phrase fragment, attach it to the independent clause that contains the word or word group modified by the prepositional phrase.

*for*
President Lyndon Johnson did not seek reelection~~.~~ ~~For~~ a number of reasons. (Prepositional phrase has been attached to an independent clause, creating a complete sentence.)

*in*
He ran sixty yards for a touchdown~~.~~ ~~In~~ the final minutes of the game. (Prepositional phrase has been attached to an independent clause, creating a complete sentence.)

## EXERCISE 3

Read the following passage and identify the fragments. Then, correct each one by attaching it to the independent clause that contains the word or word group it modifies.

Most college athletes are caught in a conflict. Between their athletic and academic careers. Sometimes college athletes' responsibilities on the playing field make it hard for them to be good students. Often, athletes must make a choice. Between sports and a degree. Some athletes would not be able to afford college. Without athletic scholarships. Ironically, however, their commitments (training, exercise, practice, and travel to out-of-town games, for example) deprive athletes. Of valuable classroom time. The role of college athletes is constantly being questioned. Critics suggest that athletes exist only to participate in and promote college athletics. Because of the importance of this role to academic institutions, scandals occasionally develop. With coaches and even faculty members arranging to inflate athletes' grades to help them remain eligible. For participation in sports. Some universities even lower admissions standards. To help remedy this and other inequities. The controversial Proposition 48, passed at the NCAA convention in 1982, established minimum College Board scores and grade standards for student athletes. But many people feel that the NCAA remains overly concerned. With profits rather than with education. As a result, college athletic competition is increasingly coming to resemble pro sports. From the coaches' pressure on the players to win to the network television exposure to the wagers on the games' outcomes.

## 2 Verbal Phrase Fragments

A verbal phrase consists of a **verbal**—a present participle (*walking*), past participle (*walked*), infinitive (*to walk*), or gerund (*walking*)—plus related objects and modifiers (*walking along the lonely beach*). Because a verbal cannot serve as a sentence's main verb, a verbal phrase is not a complete sentence and should not be punctuated as one.

To correct a verbal phrase fragment, you can attach the verbal phrase to an adjacent independent clause that contains the words (a subject or verb or both) that are needed to make the fragment a sentence.

> In 1948, India became an independent country/ ^*divided* ~~Divided~~ into the nations of India and Pakistan. (Verbal phrase has been attached to a related independent clause, creating a complete sentence.)

> A familiar trademark can increase a product's sales/ ^*, reminding* ~~Reminding~~ shoppers that the product has a long-standing reputation. (Verbal phrase has been attached to a related independent clause, creating a complete sentence.)

Or, you can change the verbal to a verb and add a subject.

> In 1948, India became an independent country. ^*It was divided* ~~Divided~~ into the nations of India and Pakistan. (Verb *was divided* has replaced verbal *divided*, and subject *it* has been added; the result is a complete sentence.)

> A familiar trademark can increase a product's sales. ^*It reminds* ~~Reminding~~ shoppers that the product has a long-standing reputation. (Verb *reminds* has replaced verbal *reminding*, and subject *it* has been added; the result is a complete sentence.)

### EXERCISE 4

Identify the fragments in the following paragraph and correct each one. Either attach the fragment to a related independent clause, or add a subject and a verb to create a complete sentence.

Many food products have well-known trademarks. Identified by familiar faces on product labels. Some of these symbols have remained the same, while others have changed considerably. Products like Sun-Maid Raisins, Betty Crocker potato mixes, Quaker Oats, and Uncle Ben's Rice use faces. To create a sense of quality and tradition and to encourage shopper recognition of the products. Many of the portraits have been updated several times. To reflect changes in society. Betty Crocker's portrait, for instance, has changed many times since its creation in 1936. Symbolizing women's changing roles. The original Chef Boy-ar-dee has also changed. Turning from the young Italian chef Hector Boiardi into a white-haired senior citizen. Miss Sunbeam, trademark of Sunbeam Bread, has had her hairdo modified several times since her first appearance in 1942; the Blue Bonnet girl, also created in 1942, now has a more modern look, and Aunt Jemima has also been changed. Slimmed down a bit in 1965. Similarly, the Campbell's Soup kids are less chubby now than in the 1920s when they first appeared. Still, manufacturers are very careful about selecting a trademark or modifying an existing one. Typically spending a good deal of time and money on research before a change is made.

### 3 Appositive Fragments

An **appositive**—a noun or noun phrase that identifies or renames an adjacent noun or pronoun—cannot stand alone as a sentence.

To correct an appositive fragment, attach the appositive to the independent clause that contains the word the appositive renames.

> Brian was the star forward of the Blue Devils~~.~~ *, the* ~~The~~ team with the best record. (Appositive has been attached to an independent clause, creating a complete sentence.)

> Piero della Francesca was a leader of the Umbrian school of painting~~.~~ *, a* ~~A~~ school that remained close to the traditions of Gothic art. (Appositive has been attached to an independent clause, creating a complete sentence.)

**Close-Up** LISTS

When an appositive fragment takes the form of a list, add a colon to connect the list to the independent clause that introduces it.

See 57a1

> Tourists often outnumber residents in four European cities~~.~~ *:* Venice, Florence, Canterbury, and Bath.

Sometimes an appositive consists of a word or phrase like *that is, for example, for instance, namely,* or *such as,* followed by an example.

To correct this kind of appositive fragment, attach the appositive to the preceding independent clause.

, such
Fairy tales are full of damsels in distress. ~~Such~~ as Cinderella and Rapunzel.

Note: Sometimes you can correct an appositive fragment by embedding the appositive within an independent clause.

—for example, Charles Dickens and Mark Twain—
Some popular novelists are highly respected in later generations. ~~For example, Charles Dickens and Mark Twain.~~

**EXERCISE 5**

Identify the fragments in this paragraph, and correct them by attaching each one to the independent clause containing the word the appositive identifies or renames.

Until the early 1900s, communities in West Virginia, Tennessee, and Kentucky were isolated by the mountains that surrounded them. The great chain of the Appalachian Mountains. Set apart from the emerging culture of a growing America and American language, these communities retained a language rich with the dialect of Elizabethan English and sprinkled with hints of a Scotch-Irish influence. In the 1910s and '20s, the communities in these mountains began to long for a better future for their children. The key to that future, as they saw it, was education. In some communities, that education took the form of Settlement Schools. Schools led by idealistic young graduates of eastern women's colleges. These teachers taught the basic academic subjects. Such as reading, writing, and mathematics. They also schooled their students in the culture of the mountains. For example, the crafts, music, and folklore of the Appalachians. In addition, they taught them skills that would help them survive when the coal market began to decline. The Settlement Schools attracted artisans from around the world. Quilters, weavers, basketmakers, and carpenters. The schools also opened the mountains to the world, leading to the decline of the Elizabethan dialect.

## 40d Revising Detached Compounds

The last part of a **compound predicate, compound object,** or **compound complement** cannot stand alone as a sentence.

To correct this type of fragment, connect the detached part of the compound to the sentence to which it belongs.

People with dyslexia have trouble reading~~. And~~ *and* may also find it difficult to write. (Detached part of the compound predicate has been connected to the sentence to which it belongs.)

They took only a compass and a canteen~~. And~~ *and* some trail mix. (Detached part of the compound object has been connected to the sentence to which it belongs.)

When their supplies ran out they were surprised~~. And~~ *and* hungry. (Detached part of the compound complement has been connected to the sentence to which it belongs.)

**EXERCISE 6**

Identify the fragments in this passage, and correct them by connecting each detached compound to the sentence to which it belongs.

As more and more Americans discover the pleasures of the wilderness, our national parks are feeling the stress. Wanting to get away for a weekend or a week, hikers and backpackers stream from the cities into nearby state and national parks. They bring with them a hunger for the wilderness. But very little knowledge about how to behave ethically in the wild. They also do not know how to keep themselves safe. Some of them think of the national parks as inexpensive amusement parks. Without proper camping supplies and lacking enough food and water for their trip, they are putting at risk their lives and the lives of those who will be called on to save them. One family went for a hike up a desert canyon with an eight-month-old infant. And their seventy-eight-year-old grandmother. Although the terrain was difficult, they were not wearing the proper shoes. Or good socks. They did not even carry a first aid kit. Or a map or compass. They were on an unmarked trail in a little-used section of Bureau of Land Management lands. And following vague directions from a friend. Soon, they were lost. They had not brought water or food. Or even rain gear or warm clothes. Luckily for them, they had brought a cell phone. By the time they called for help, however, it was getting dark and a storm was building. A rescue plane eventually located the family. And brought them to safety. Still, a little planning before they hiked in an inhospitable area, and a little awareness and preparedness for the terrain they were traveling in, would have saved this family much worry. And the taxpayers a lot of money.

## 40e Using Fragments Intentionally

Fragments are often used in speech and in personal email and other informal writing—as well as in journalism, political slogans, creative writing, bumper stickers, and advertising (see Figure 40.1).

In professional and academic writing, however, sentence fragments are generally not acceptable.

**CHECKLIST**

### Using Fragments Intentionally

In college writing, it is acceptable to use fragments in the following special situations:

- ❑ In lists
- ❑ In captions that accompany visuals
- ❑ In topic outlines
- ❑ In quoted dialogue
- ❑ In *PowerPoint* presentations
- ❑ In titles and subtitles of papers and reports

Image courtesy of The Advertising Archives

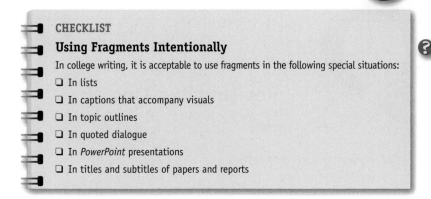

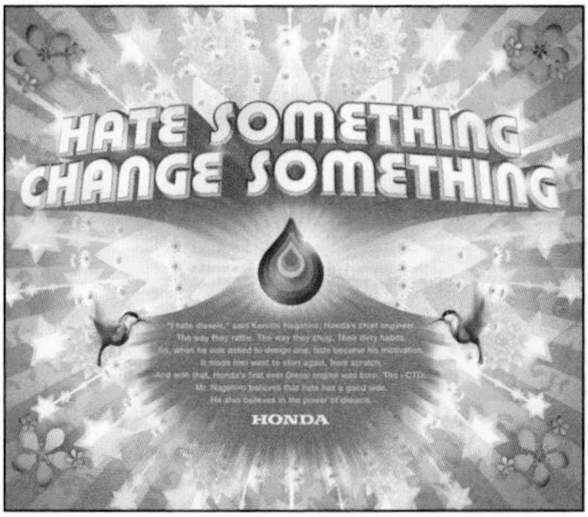


Image courtesy of The Advertising Archives

**FIGURE 40.1** Intentional fragments used in advertising.

## EXERCISE 7

Select several advertisements from magazines, newspapers, or the Internet. Identify word groups that you think are fragments. Then, type each into your word processor and run a grammar check. Keep in mind that some word groups may look like fragments but may in fact be imperative sentences (commands) that have an implied subject (*you*) and will therefore be recognized as grammatically correct sentences.

See 49c

Revise each fragment you identify so that it is a complete sentence. Then, decide which version—the fragment or your corrected sentence—is more effective for each advertisement's purpose and audience.

CHAPTER 41

# Revising Run-Ons

## Frequently Asked Questions



## 41a Recognizing Comma Splices and Fused Sentences

See 35b2

A **run-on** is an error that occurs when two independent clauses are joined incorrectly. There are two kinds of run-ons: *comma splices* and *fused sentences.*

A **comma splice** is a run-on that occurs when two independent clauses are joined by just a comma. A **fused sentence** is a run-on that occurs when two independent clauses are joined with no punctuation.

**Comma Splice:** Charles Dickens created the character of Mr. Micawber, he also created Uriah Heep.

**Fused Sentence:** Charles Dickens created the character of Mr. Micawber he also created Uriah Heep.

### GRAMMAR CHECKER Revising Comma Splices

Your grammar checker will highlight comma splices and prompt you to revise them.

Your grammar checker may also highlight fused sentences, but it may identify them simply as long sentences that need revision. Moreover, it will not offer suggestions for revising fused sentences.

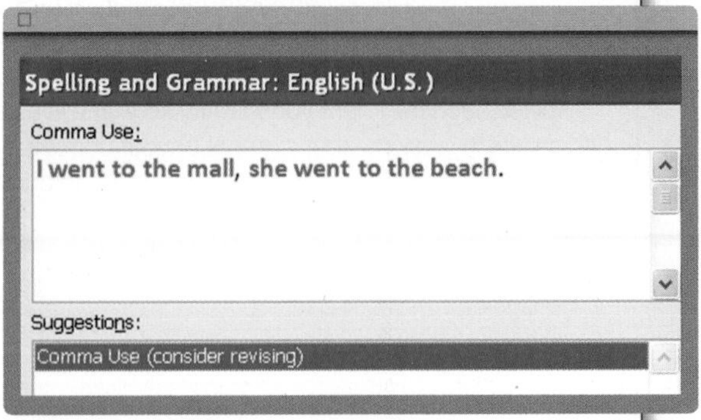

## 41b Correcting Comma Splices and Fused Sentences

To correct a comma splice or fused sentence, use one of the following four strategies:

1. Add a period between the clauses, creating two separate sentences.
2. Add a semicolon between the clauses, creating a compound sentence.
3. Add a coordinating conjunction between the clauses, creating a compound sentence.
4. Subordinate one clause to the other, creating a complex sentence.

### 1 Add a Period

You can correct a comma splice or fused sentence by adding a period between the independent clauses, creating two separate sentences. This is a good strategy to use when the clauses are long or when they are not closely related.

> In 1894, Frenchman Alfred Dreyfus was falsely convicted of
> *. His*
> treason~~,~~ ~~his~~ struggle for justice made his case famous.

**Close-Up** COMMA SPLICES AND FUSED SENTENCES

Using a comma to punctuate an interrupted quotation that consists of two complete sentences creates a comma splice. Instead, use a period.

> *. "In*
> "This is a good course," Eric said~~,~~ ~~"in~~ fact, I wish I'd taken it sooner."

### 2 Add a Semicolon

You can correct a comma splice or fused sentence by adding a semicolon between two closely related clauses that convey parallel or contrasting information. The result will be a **compound sentence.** See 54a

> In pre–World War II western Europe, only a small elite had access
> *;*
> to a university education~~,~~ however, this situation changed dramatically
> after the war.

*Note:* When you use a transitional word or phrase (such as *however, therefore,* or *for example*) to connect two independent clauses, the transitional element must be preceded by a semicolon and followed by a comma. If you link the two clauses with just a comma, you create a comma splice; if you omit punctuation entirely, you create a fused sentence. See 7b2

### 3 Add a Coordinating Conjunction

You can use a coordinating conjunction (*and, or, but, nor, for, so, yet*) to join two closely related clauses of equal importance into one **compound sentence.** The coordinating conjunction you choose indicates the relationship between the clauses: addition (*and*), contrast (*but, yet*), causality (*for, so*), or a choice of alternatives (*or, nor*). Be sure to include a comma before the coordinating conjunction.

> *and*
> Elias Howe invented the sewing machine,^ Julia Ward Howe was a poet and social reformer.

### 4 Create a Complex Sentence

When the ideas in two independent clauses are not of equal importance, you can use a subordinating conjunction or relative pronoun to join the clauses into one **complex sentence,** placing the less important idea in the dependent clause. The subordinating conjunction or relative pronoun you choose indicates how the clauses are related.

> *because*
> Stravinsky's ballet *The Rite of Spring* shocked Parisians in 1913~~,~~^ its rhythms seemed erotic.

> *, who*
> Lady Mary Wortley Montagu^ had suffered from smallpox herself, ~~she~~ helped spread the practice of inoculation.

**Close-Up** ACCEPTABLE COMMA SPLICES

In a few special cases, comma splices are acceptable. For instance, a comma is conventionally used in dialogue between a statement and a tag question, even though each is a separate independent clause.

> This is Ron's house, isn't it?
>
> I'm not late, am I?

In addition, commas may be used to connect two short, balanced independent clauses or two or more short parallel independent clauses, especially when one clause contradicts the other.

> Commencement isn't the end, it's the beginning.

#### EXERCISE 1

Identify the comma splices and fused sentences in the following paragraph. Correct each in two of the four possible ways discussed above. If a sentence is correct, leave it alone.

***Example:*** The fans rose in their seats, the game was almost over.
***Revised:*** The fans rose in their seats; the game was almost over.
The fans rose in their seats because the game was almost over.

Entrepreneurship is the study of small businesses, college students are embracing it enthusiastically. Many schools offer one or more courses in entrepreneurship these courses teach the theory and practice of starting a small business. Students are signing up for courses, moreover, they are starting their own businesses. One student started with a car-waxing business, now he sells condominiums. Other students are setting up catering services they supply everything from waiters to bartenders. One student has a thriving cake-decorating business, in fact, she employs fifteen students to deliver the cakes. All over the country, student businesses are selling everything from tennis balls to bagels, the student owners are making impressive profits. Formal courses at the graduate as well as undergraduate level are attracting more business students than ever, several schools (such as Baylor University, the University of Southern California, and Babson College) even offer degree programs in entrepreneurship. Many business school students are no longer planning to be corporate executives instead, they plan to become entrepreneurs.

## EXERCISE 2

Combine each of the following sentence pairs into one sentence without creating comma splices or fused sentences. In each case, subordinate one clause to the other to create a complex sentence. You may have to add, delete, reorder, or change words or punctuation.

***Example:*** ^*Because* I grew up at the New Jersey shore~~.~~^*, people* ~~People~~ think I'm lucky.

1. Other beach rats know better than to envy me. Inlanders romanticize life by the ocean.
2. The sound of the waves is comforting. The sand gets into everything.
3. In the summer, tourists clog the roads. In the winter, many of the locals are out of work.
4. Beach towns have a difficult time attracting industry. Taxes are often high.
5. After a while, going to the beach in the summer loses its charm. The beach in winter, empty of other people, is a beautiful sight.

## EXERCISE 3

Combine each of the following sentence pairs into one sentence without creating comma splices or fused sentences. In each case, either connect the clauses into a compound sentence (with a semicolon or with a comma and a coordinating conjunction) or subordinate one clause to the other to create a complex sentence. You may have to add, delete, reorder, or change words or punctuation.

1. Several recent studies indicate that many American high school students have little knowledge of history. This is affecting our future as a democratic nation and as individuals.
2. Surveys show that nearly one-third of American seventeen-year-olds cannot identify the countries the United States fought against in World War II. One-third think Columbus reached the New World after 1750.
3. Several reasons have been given for this decline in historical literacy. The main reason is the way history is taught.
4. This problem is bad news. The good news is that there is increasing agreement among educators about what is wrong with current methods of teaching history.
5. History can be exciting and engaging. Too often, it is presented in a boring manner.
6. Students are typically expected to memorize dates, facts, and names. History as adventure—as a "good story"—is frequently neglected.
7. One way to avoid this problem is to use good textbooks. Textbooks should be accurate, lively, and focused.
8. Another way to create student interest in historical events is to use primary sources instead of so-called comprehensive textbooks. Autobiographies, journals, and diaries can give students insight into larger issues.
9. Students can also be challenged to think about history by taking sides in a debate. They can learn more about connections among historical events by writing essays than by taking multiple-choice tests.
10. Finally, history teachers should be less concerned about specific historical details. They should be more concerned about conveying the wonder of history.

CHAPTER 42

# Revising Misplaced and Dangling Modifiers

## Frequently Asked Questions



A **modifier** is a word, phrase, or clause that describes, limits, or qualifies another word or word group in a sentence. A modifier should be placed close to the word it modifies.

> Wendy watched the storm, fierce and threatening. (*fierce and threatening* modifies *storm*)

**Faulty modification** is the awkward or confusing placement of modifiers or the modification of nonexistent words.

## 42a Revising Misplaced Modifiers

A **misplaced modifier** is a word or word group whose placement suggests that it modifies one word or word group when it is intended to modify another.

> *Wendy watched the storm, fierce*
> ~~Fierce~~ and threatening~~,~~ ~~Wendy watched the storm~~. (The storm, not Wendy, was fierce and threatening.)

> *The lawyer argued that the defendant, with*
> ~~With~~ an IQ of just 52, ~~the lawyer argued that the defendant~~ should not get the death penalty. (The defendant, not the lawyer, had an IQ of 52.)

### 1 Place Modifying Words Precisely

**Limiting modifiers**—such as *almost, only, even, hardly, merely, nearly, exactly, scarcely, simply,* and *just*—should always immediately precede the words they modify. A different placement will change the meaning of the sentence.

> Nick *just* set up camp at the edge of town. (He did it just now.)
>
> *Just* Nick set up camp at the edge of town. (He did it alone.)
>
> Nick set up camp *just* at the edge of town. (His camp was precisely at the edge.)

When a limiting modifier is placed so that it is not clear whether it modifies a word before it or one after it, it is called a **squinting modifier.**

The life that everyone thought would fulfill her totally bored her.

To correct a squinting modifier, place the modifier so that it is clear which word it modifies.

The life that everyone thought would totally fulfill her bored her. (Everyone expected her to be totally fulfilled.)

The life that everyone thought would fulfill her bored her totally. (She was totally bored.)

## EXERCISE 1

In the following sentence pairs, the modifier in each sentence points to a different word. Underline the modifier and draw an arrow to the word it modifies. Then, explain the meaning of each sentence.

***Example:*** She just came in wearing a hat. (She just now entered.)

She came in wearing just a hat. (She wore only a hat.)

1. He wore his almost new jeans.
   He almost wore his new jeans.
2. He had only three dollars in his pocket.
   Only he had three dollars in his pocket.
3. I don't even like freshwater fish.
   I don't like even freshwater fish.
4. I go only to the beach on Saturdays.
   I go to the beach only on Saturdays.
5. He simply hated driving.
   He hated simply driving.

## 2 Relocate Misplaced Phrases

Placing a modifying phrase incorrectly can change the meaning of a sentence or create an unclear or confusing (or even unintentionally humorous) construction.

To avoid ambiguity, place phrases as close as possible to the words they modify.

- Place **verbal phrase** modifiers directly before or immediately after the words or word groups they modify.

*Roller-skating along the shore,*
^Jane watched the boats.^ ~~roller skating along the shore.~~

- Place **prepositional phrase** modifiers immediately after the words they modify.

*with no arms*

*Venus de Milo* is a statue ^ created by a famous artist. ^ ~~with no arms.~~

EXERCISE 2

Underline the modifying verbal phrases or prepositional phrases in each sentence, and draw arrows to the words they modify.

***Example:*** Calvin is the Democrat running for town council.

1. The bridge across the river swayed in the wind.
2. The spectators on the shore were involved in the action.
3. Mesmerized by the spectacle, they watched the drama unfold.
4. The spectators were afraid of a disaster.
5. Within the hour, the state police arrived to save the day.
6. They closed off the area with roadblocks.
7. Drivers approaching the bridge were asked to stop.
8. Meanwhile, on the bridge, the scene was chaos.
9. Motorists in their cars were paralyzed with fear.
10. Struggling against the weather, the police managed to rescue everyone.

EXERCISE 3

Use the phrase that follows each sentence as a modifier in that sentence. Then, underline the modifier, and draw an arrow to indicate the word it modifies.

***Example:*** He approached the lion. (with fear in his heart)

With fear in his heart, he approached the lion.

1. The lion paced up and down in his cage, ignoring the crowd. (watching Jack)
2. Jack stared back at the lion. (in terror)
3. The crowd around them grew. (anxious to see what would happen)
4. Suddenly, Jack heard a terrifying growl. (from deep in the lion's throat)
5. Jack ran from the zoo, leaving the lion behind. (scared to death)

## 3 Relocate Misplaced Dependent Clauses

A dependent clause that serves as a modifier must be clearly related to the word it modifies.

- An **adjective clause** appears immediately *after* the word it modifies.

During the Civil War, Lincoln was the president who governed the United States.

- An **adverb clause** can appear in any of several positions, as long as its relationship to the word or word group it modifies is clear.

  When Lincoln was president, the Civil War raged.

  The Civil War raged when Lincoln was president.

### EXERCISE 4

Relocate the misplaced verbal phrases, prepositional phrases, or dependent clauses so that they clearly point to the words or word groups they modify.

***Example:*** *Silent Running* is a film ^with Bruce Dern^ about a scientist left alone in space. ~~with Bruce Dern.~~

1. She realized that she had married the wrong man after the wedding.
2. *The Prince and the Pauper* is a novel about an exchange of identities by Mark Twain.
3. The energy was used up in the ten-kilometer race that he was saving for the marathon.
4. He loaded the bottles and cans into his new car, which he planned to leave at the recycling center.
5. The manager explained the sales figures to the board members using a graph.

## 42b Revising Intrusive Modifiers

An **intrusive modifier** awkwardly interrupts a sentence, making it difficult to understand.

- Revise when a long modifying phrase comes between an auxiliary verb and a main verb.

  ^Without^ ~~She had, without~~ giving it a second thought or considering the consequences, ^she had^ planned to reenlist.

- Revise when an adverb phrase or clause comes between a subject and a verb (or between a verb and its object or complement).

  The election ^was contested^ because officials discovered that some people had voted more than once. ~~was contested.~~

- Revise when a modifier creates an awkward **split infinitive**—that is, when a modifier comes between the word *to* and the base form of the verb.

*defeat his opponent*
He hoped to ^ quickly and easily ^ ~~defeat his opponent.~~

*Note:* A split infinitive is acceptable when the intervening modifier is short, especially if the alternative would be awkward or ambiguous: *She expected to almost beat her previous record.*

**GRAMMAR CHECKER Revising Intrusive Modifiers**

Your grammar checker will identify some problems with intrusive modifiers, including certain awkward split infinitives. However, the grammar checker will not offer revision suggestions. You will have to revise these modification errors on your own, as illustrated in **42b.**

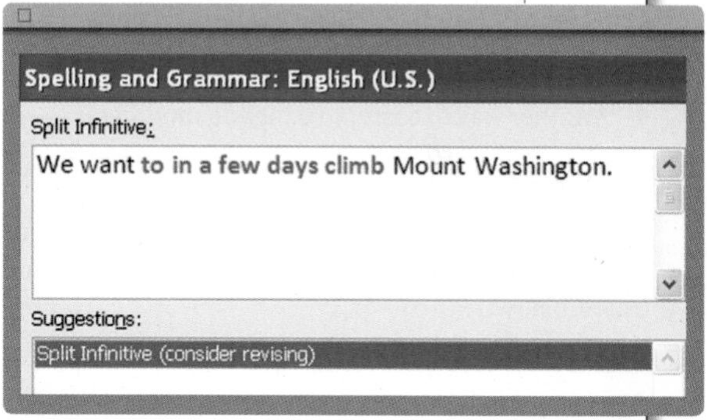
Spelling and Grammar: English (U.S.)
Split Infinitive:
We want to in a few days climb Mount Washington.
Suggestions:
Split Infinitive (consider revising)

## EXERCISE 5

Revise these sentences so that the modifying phrases or clauses do not interrupt an infinitive, separate an auxiliary verb from a main verb, or separate a subject from a verb or a verb from its object or complement.

*Despite the playwright's best efforts, a*
***Example:*** ^ ~~A~~ play can sometimes be ~~/despite the playwright's best efforts/~~ mystifying to the audience.

1. The people in the audience, when they saw the play was about to begin and realized the orchestra had finished tuning up and had begun the overture, finally quieted down.
2. They settled into their seats, expecting to very much enjoy the first act.
3. However, most people were, even after watching and listening for twenty minutes and paying close attention to the drama, completely baffled.
4. In fact, the play, because it had nameless characters, no scenery, and a rambling plot that did not seem to be heading anywhere, puzzled even the drama critics.
5. Finally, one of the three major characters explained, speaking directly to the audience, what the play was really about.

## 42c Revising Dangling Modifiers

A **dangling modifier** is a word or phrase that cannot logically modify any word in the sentence.

> **Dangling:** Using this drug, many undesirable side effects are experienced. (Who is using this drug?)

- One way to correct a dangling modifier is to **create a new subject** by adding a word or word group that *using this drug* can logically modify.

> **Revised:** Using this drug, patients experience many undesirable side effects.

- Another way to correct a dangling modifier is to **create a dependent clause.**

> **Revised:** Many undesirable side effects are experienced when this drug is used.

These two options for correcting dangling modifiers are further illustrated below.

### 1 Creating a New Subject

*the technician lifted*
Using a pair of forceps, ^ the skin of the rat's abdomen ~~was lifted~~. (Modifier cannot logically modify *skin.*)

*Meg found*
With fifty more pages to read, ^ *War and Peace* ~~was~~ absorbing. (Modifier cannot logically modify *War and Peace.*)

### 2 Creating a Dependent Clause

*Before* *was implemented,*
^ ~~To implement~~ a plus/minus grading system, ^ all students were polled. (Modifier cannot logically modify *students.*)

*Because the magazine had been on*
^ ~~On~~ the newsstands only an hour, its sales surprised everyone. (Modifier cannot logically modify *sales.*)

**Close-Up** REVISING DANGLING ELLIPTICAL CLAUSES

See 35b2

Elliptical clauses are incomplete constructions. Typically, the writer has intentionally omitted part of the subject or predicate (or the entire subject or predicate) from a dependent clause in order to create a more concise sentence. When such a clause cannot logically modify the subject of the sentence's main clause, it dangles. To revise a dangling elliptical clause, add a subject that the elliptical clause can logically modify.

> **Dangling:** While still in the Buchner funnel, you should press the crystals with a clear stopper to eliminate any residual solvent. (Elliptical clause cannot logically modify *you*.)
>
> **Revised:** While still in the Buchner funnel, the crystals should be pressed with a clear stopper to eliminate any residual solvent. (Subject of main clause has been changed from *you* to *crystals*, a word the elliptical clause can logically modify.)

### Close-Up DANGLING MODIFIERS AND THE PASSIVE VOICE

Most sentences that include dangling modifiers are in the passive voice. Changing the **passive voice** to **active voice** often corrects the dangling modifier.

See 49d

ESL 64a6

## EXERCISE 6

Eliminate the dangling modifier from each of the following sentences. Either supply a word or word group the dangling modifier can logically modify, or change the dangling modifier into a dependent clause.

***Example:*** Skiing down the mountain, my hat flew off. (dangling modifier)

***Revised:*** Skiing down the mountain, I lost my hat. (new subject added)
As I skied down the mountain, my hat flew off. (dependent clause)

1. Writing for eight hours every day, her lengthy books are published every year or so.
2. As an out-of-state student without a car, it was difficult to get to off-campus cultural events.
3. To build a campfire, kindling is necessary.
4. With every step upward, the trees became sparser.
5. Being an amateur tennis player, my backhand is weaker than my forehand.
6. When exiting the train, the station will be on your right.
7. Driving through the Mojave, the bleak landscape was oppressive.
8. By requiring auto manufacturers to further improve emission-control devices, the air quality will get better.
9. Using a piece of filter paper, the ball of sodium is dried as much as possible and placed in a test tube.
10. Surrounded by acres of farmland, my nearest neighbor was far away.

CHAPTER 43

# Revising Faulty Parallelism

## Frequently Asked Questions



**Parallelism**—the use of matching words, phrases, or clauses to express equivalent ideas—adds unity, balance, and force to your writing. Effective parallelism can help you write clearer sentences, but **faulty parallelism** can create awkward sentences that obscure your meaning and confuse readers.

See 43b

## 43a Using Parallelism Effectively

Parallelism highlights the correspondence between *items in a series, paired items,* and elements in *lists and outlines.*

### 1 With Items in a Series

Eat, drink, and be merry.

Baby food consumption, toy production, and school construction are likely to decline as the US population ages.

Three factors influenced his decision to seek new employment: his desire to relocate, his need for greater responsibility, and his dissatisfaction with his current job.

Note: For information on punctuating items in a series, **see 53b** and **54c.**

### 2 With Paired Items

The thank-you note was short but sweet.

Roosevelt represented the United States, and Churchill represented Great Britain.

Ask not what your country can do for you; ask what you can do for your country. (John F. Kennedy)

Paired elements linked by correlative conjunctions (such as *not only/ but also, both/and, either/or, neither/nor,* and *whether/or*) should always be parallel.

The design team paid close attention not only to color but also to texture.

Either repeat physics or take calculus.

Parallelism also highlights the contrast between paired elements linked by *than* or *as*.

Richard Wright and James Baldwin chose to live in Paris rather than to remain in the United States.

Success is as much a matter of hard work as a matter of luck.

### 3 In Lists and Outlines

Elements in a **list** should be parallel. See 28c

The Irish potato famine had four major causes:

1. The establishment of the landlord-tenant system
2. The failure of the potato crop
3. The reluctance of England to offer adequate financial assistance
4. The passage of the Corn Laws

Elements in an **outline** should also be parallel. See 6c4

## EXERCISE 1

Identify the parallel elements in these sentences by bracketing parallel phrases and clauses.

***Example:*** Manek spent six years in America [going to school] and [working for a computer company].

1. After he completed his engineering degree, Manek returned to India to visit his large extended family and to find a wife.
2. Unfamiliar with marriage practices in India and accustomed to the American notion of marriage for love, Manek's American friends disapproved of his plans.
3. Not only Manek but also his parents wanted an arranged marriage.
4. He didn't believe that either you married for love or you had a loveless marriage.
5. His parents' marriage, an arranged one, continues happily; his aunt's marriage, also arranged, has lasted thirty years.

## EXERCISE 2

Combine each of the following sentence pairs or sentence groups into one sentence that uses parallel structure. Be sure all paired items and items in a series (words, phrases, or clauses) are expressed in parallel terms.

1. Originally, there were five performing Marx Brothers. One was nicknamed Groucho. The others were called Chico, Harpo, Gummo, and Zeppo.

2. Groucho was very well known. So were Chico and Harpo. Gummo soon dropped out of the act. And later Zeppo did too.
3. They began in vaudeville. That was before World War I. Their first show was called *I'll Say She Is*. It opened in New York in 1924.
4. The Marx Brothers' first movie was *The Cocoanuts*. The next was *Animal Crackers*. And this was followed by *Monkey Business, Horse Feathers*, and *Duck Soup*. Then came *A Night at the Opera*.
5. In each of these movies, the Marx Brothers make people laugh. They also exhibit a unique, zany comic style.
6. In their movies, each brother has a set of familiar trademarks. Groucho has a mustache and a long coat. He wiggles his eyebrows and smokes a cigar. There is a funny hat that Chico always wears. And he affects a phony Italian accent. Harpo never speaks.
7. Groucho is always cast as a sly operator. He always tries to cheat people out of their money. He always tries to charm women.
8. In *The Cocoanuts*, Groucho plays Mr. Hammer, proprietor of the run-down Coconut Manor, a Florida hotel. In *Horse Feathers*, his character is named Professor Quincy Adams Wagstaff. Wagstaff is president of Huxley College. Huxley also has financial problems.
9. In *Duck Soup*, Groucho plays Rufus T. Firefly, president of the country of Fredonia. Fredonia was formerly ruled by the late husband of a Mrs. Teasdale. Fredonia is now at war with the country of Sylvania.
10. Margaret Dumont is often Groucho's leading lady. She plays Mrs. Teasdale in *Duck Soup*. In *A Night at the Opera*, she plays Mrs. Claypool. Her character in *The Cocoanuts* is named Mrs. Potter.

## 43b Revising Faulty Parallelism

**Faulty parallelism** occurs when elements that express equivalent ideas in a sentence are not presented in parallel terms.

> Many people in developing countries suffer because the countries lack sufficient housing, sufficient food, and ^*sufficient* ~~their~~ health-care facilities^. ~~are also insufficient.~~

To correct faulty parallelism, match nouns with nouns, verbs with verbs, and phrases or clauses with similarly constructed phrases or clauses.

> Popular exercises for men and women include yoga, weight ^*lifting* ~~lifters~~, Pilates, Zumba, and jogging.

> I look forward to hearing from you and to ^*having* ~~have~~ an opportunity to tell you more about myself.

## Close-Up REPEATING KEY WORDS

Although the use of similar grammatical structures may sometimes be enough to convey parallelism, sentences are often clearer if certain key words (for example, articles, prepositions, and the *to* in infinitives) are also repeated in each element of a pair or a series. In the following sentence, repeating the preposition *by* makes it clear that *not* applies only to the first phrase.

> Computerization has helped industry by not allowing labor costs to skyrocket, ^*by*^ increasing the speed of production, and ^*by*^ improving efficiency.

**GRAMMAR CHECKER Revising Faulty Parallelism**

Grammar checkers are not very useful for identifying faulty parallelism. Although your grammar checker may highlight some nonparallel constructions, it may miss others.

## EXERCISE 3

Identify and correct faulty parallelism in these sentences. Then, underline the parallel elements—words, phrases, and clauses—in your corrected sentences. If a sentence is already correct, mark it with a *C,* and underline the parallel elements.

***Example:*** Alfred Hitchcock's films include *North by Northwest*, *Vertigo*, *Psycho*, ~~and he also directed~~ *Notorious*^,^ and *Saboteur*.

1. The world is divided between those with galoshes on and those who discover continents.
2. World leaders, members of Congress, and religious groups are all concerned about global warming.
3. A national task force on education recommended improving public education by making the school day longer, higher teachers' salaries, and integrating more technology into the curriculum.
4. The fast food industry has expanded to include many kinds of restaurants: those that serve pizza, fried chicken chains, some offering Mexican-style menus, and hamburger franchises.
5. The consumption of Scotch in the United States is declining because of high prices, tastes are changing, and increased health awareness has led many whiskey drinkers to switch to wine or beer.

CHAPTER 44

# Revising Awkward or Confusing Sentences

## Frequently Asked Questions

- What is the difference between direct and indirect discourse? 593
- What's wrong with using *the reason is . . . because?* 596

The most common causes of awkward or confusing sentences are *unwarranted shifts, mixed constructions, faulty predication,* and *incomplete or illogical comparisons.*

**ESL TIP**

Some of the faulty example sentences in this chapter are similar to sentences that native English speakers sometimes use in conversation. Although such constructions may be acceptable in informal speech, they are not acceptable in your writing.

## 44a Revising Unwarranted Shifts

### 1 Shifts in Tense

Verb tense in a sentence (or in a group of related sentences) should not shift without good reason—to indicate changes of time, for example. Unwarranted shifts in tense can be confusing.

See 49b

ESL 64a2

I registered for the advanced philosophy seminar because I wanted a challenge. However, by the first week I ~~start~~ *started* having trouble understanding the reading. (unwarranted shift from past to present)

Jack Kerouac's novel *On the Road* follows a group of friends who ~~drove~~ *drive* across the United States in the 1950s. (unwarranted shift from present to past)

See 23b

*Note:* Discussions of literary works generally use the present tense.

See 49d

ESL 64a6

### 2 Shifts in Voice

Unwarranted shifts from active to passive voice (or from passive to active) can be confusing. In the following sentence, for instance, the shift from active (*wrote*) to passive (*was written*) makes it unclear who wrote *The Great Gatsby.*

he wrote
F. Scott Fitzgerald wrote *This Side of Paradise*, and later ^ *The Great Gatsby* ^ ~~was written~~.

Note: Sometimes a shift from active to passive voice within a sentence may be necessary to give the sentence proper emphasis: *Even though consumers protested, the sales tax was increased.* (To say *the legislature increased the sales tax* would draw the sentence's emphasis away from *consumers.*)

## 3 Shifts in Mood

Unwarranted shifts in mood can also create awkward sentences.

See 49c

be
Next, heat the mixture in a test tube, and ^ ~~you should make~~ sure it does not boil. (unwarranted shift from imperative to indicative)

## 4 Shifts in Person and Number

Person indicates who is speaking (first person—*I, we*), who is spoken to (second person—*you*), and who is spoken about (third person—*he, she, it, one,* or *they*). Most unwarranted shifts occur between the second and the third person.

ESL 64a1

you look
When ^ ~~one looks~~ for a car loan, you compare the interest rates of several banks. (unwarranted shift from third to second person)

Number indicates one (singular—*novel, it*) or more than one (plural—*novels, they, them*). Singular pronouns should refer to singular **antecedents** and plural pronouns to plural antecedents.

See 50b

ESL 64c1

he or she
If a person does not study regularly, ^ ~~they~~ will have a difficult time learning a foreign language. (unwarranted shift from singular to plural)

## 5 Shifts from Direct to Indirect Discourse

**Direct discourse** reports the exact words of a speaker or writer. It is always enclosed in quotation marks and is often accompanied by an **identifying tag** (*he says, she said*).

**Indirect discourse** summarizes the words of a speaker or writer. No quotation marks are used, and the reported words are often introduced with the word *that* or, in the case of questions, with *who, what, why, whether, how,* or *if*.

**Direct Discourse:** My instructor said, "I want your paper by this Friday."

**Indirect Discourse:** My instructor said that he wanted my paper by this Friday.

Unwarranted shifts between indirect and direct discourse can be confusing.

During the trial, John Brown repeatedly defended his actions and said that ~~I am~~ *he was* not guilty. (shift from indirect to direct discourse)

My mother asked, ~~was I~~ *"Are you* ever going to get a job~~.~~*?"* (neither indirect nor direct discourse)

## EXERCISE 1

Read the following sentences, and eliminate any shifts in tense, voice, mood, person, or number. Some sentences are correct, and some can be revised in more than one way.

***Example:*** When ~~one~~ *you* examine~~s~~ the history of the women's movement, you see that it had many different beginnings.

1. Some historians see World War II and women's work in the factories as the beginning of the push toward equal rights for women.
2. Women went to work in the textile mills of Lowell, Massachusetts, in the late 1800s, and her efforts at reforming the workplace are seen by many as the beginning of the equal rights movement.
3. Farm girls from New Hampshire, Vermont, and western Massachusetts came to Lowell to make money, and they wanted to experience life in the city.
4. The factories promised the girls decent wages, and parents were promised by them that their daughters would live in a safe, wholesome environment.
5. Dormitories were built by the factory owners; they are supposed to ensure a safe environment for the girls.
6. First, visit the loom rooms at the Boot Mills Factory, and then you should tour a replica of a dormitory.
7. When one visits the working loom room at the factory, you are overcome with a sense of the risks and dangers the girls faced in the mills.
8. For a mill girl, moving to the city meant freedom and an escape from the drudgery of farm life; it also meant they had to face many new social situations for which they were not always prepared.
9. Harriet Robinson wrote *Loom and Spindle,* the story of her life as a mill girl, and then a book of poems was published.
10. When you look at the lives of the loom girls, one can see that their work laid part of the foundation for women's later demands for equal rights.

## EXERCISE 2

Change the direct discourse in the following sentences to indirect discourse.

***Example:*** Anna Quindlen explained why she kept her maiden name when she married: "It was a political decision, a simple statement that I was somebody and not an adjunct of anybody, especially a husband."

Anna Quindlen explained that she kept her maiden name when she married as a political decision, a simple statement that she was somebody and not an adjunct of anybody, especially a husband.

1. Sally Thane Christensen, advocating the use of an endangered species of tree, the yew, as a treatment for cancer, asked, "Is a tree worth a life?"
2. Stephen Nathanson, considering the morality of the death penalty, asked, "What if the death penalty did save lives?"
3. Martin Luther King Jr. said, "I have a dream that one day this nation will rise up and live out the true meaning of its creed."
4. Benjamin Franklin once stated, "The older I grow, the more apt I am to doubt my own judgment of others."
5. Thoreau said, "The finest qualities of our nature, like the bloom on fruits, can be preserved only by the most delicate handling."

## 44b Revising Mixed Constructions

A **mixed construction** is an error created when an introductory dependent clause, prepositional phrase, or independent clause is incorrectly used as the subject of a sentence.

Because she studies every day^, ~~explains why~~ she gets good grades. (dependent clause used as subject)

*, you can*
By calling for information^ ~~is the way to~~ learn more about the benefits of ROTC. (prepositional phrase used as subject)

*Being*
^~~He was~~ late ~~was what~~ made him miss Act 1. (independent clause used as subject)

### EXERCISE 3

Revise the following mixed constructions so their parts fit together both grammatically and logically.

*Investing*
***Example:*** ^~~By investing~~ in commodities made her rich.

1. In implementing the "motor voter" bill has made it easier for people to register to vote.
2. She sank the basket was the reason they won the game.
3. Just because situations change, does not change the characters' hopes and dreams.
4. By dropping the course would be his only chance to avoid a low GPA.
5. Because she works for a tobacco company explains why she is against laws prohibiting smoking in restaurants.

## 44c Revising Faulty Predication

**Faulty predication** occurs when a sentence's subject and predicate do not logically go together.

### 1 Incorrect Use of *Be*

Faulty predication is especially common in sentences that contain a **linking verb**—a form of the verb *be,* for example—and a subject complement.

> Mounting costs and decreasing revenues *caused* ~~were~~ the downfall of the hospital.

This sentence incorrectly states that mounting costs and decreasing revenues *were* the downfall of the hospital when, in fact, they were the *reasons* for its downfall.

### 2 *Is When* or *Is Where*

Faulty predication occurs in one-sentence definitions that contain a construction like *is where* or *is when.* (In a definition, *is* must be preceded and followed by a noun or noun phrase.)

> Taxidermy is *the construction of* ~~where you construct~~ a lifelike representation of an animal from its preserved skin.

### 3 *The Reason . . . Is Because*

Faulty predication also occurs when the phrase *the reason is* precedes *because.* In this situation, *because* (which means "for the reason that") is redundant and should be deleted.

> The reason we drive is *that* ~~because~~ we are afraid to fly.

**GRAMMAR CHECKER Revising Faulty Predication**

Your grammar checker will highlight certain instances of faulty predication and offer suggestions for revision. However, the grammar checker will miss many unwarranted shifts, mixed constructions, and incomplete or illogical comparisons.

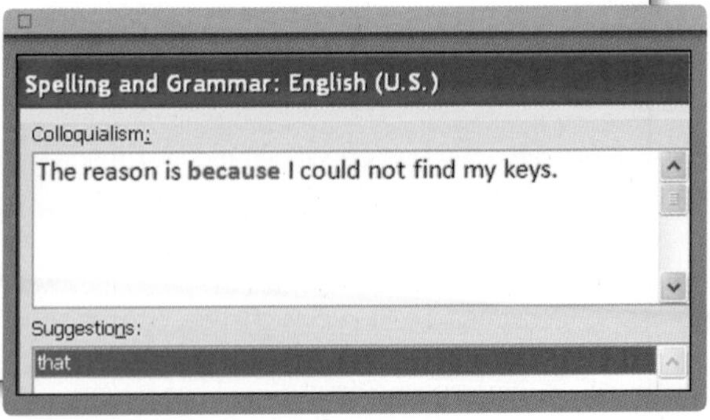
Spelling and Grammar: English (U.S.)
Colloquialism:
The reason is because I could not find my keys.
Suggestions:
that

### EXERCISE 4

Revise the following sentences to eliminate faulty predication. Keep in mind that each sentence may be revised in more than one way.

***Example:*** *Traffic* ~~The reason traffic~~ jams occur at 9 a.m. and 5 p.m. ~~is~~ because too many people work traditional rather than staggered hours.

1. Inflation is when the purchasing power of currency declines.
2. Hypertension is where blood pressure is elevated.
3. Television and the Internet were the decline in students' reading scores.
4. Some people say the reason for the increasing violence in American cities is because guns are too easily available.
5. The reason for all the congestion in American cities is because too many people live too close together.

## 44d Revising Incomplete or Illogical Comparisons

A comparison tells how two things are alike or unlike. When you make a comparison, be sure it is *complete* (that it identifies the two items that are being compared) and *logical* (that it equates two comparable items).

My chemistry course is harder/ *than Nina's.* (What two things are being compared?)

A pig's intelligence is greater than a ~~dog~~/ *dog's.* (illogically compares *a pig's intelligence* to *a dog*)

### EXERCISE 5

Revise the following sentences to correct any incomplete or illogical comparisons.

***Example:*** Technology-based industries are concerned about inflation as much as service industries/ *are.*

1. Opportunities in technical writing are more promising than business writing.
2. Technical writing is more challenging.
3. In some ways, technical writing requires more attention to detail and is, therefore, more difficult.
4. Business writers are concerned about clarity as much as technical writers.
5. Technology-based industries may one day create more writing opportunities than any other industry.

PART 11

# Using Words Effectively

CHAPTER 45

# Choosing Words

## Frequently Asked Questions



## 45a Choosing an Appropriate Level of Diction

**Diction,** which comes from the Latin word for *say,* refers to the choice and use of words. Different audiences and situations call for different levels of diction.

### 1 Formal Diction

**Formal diction** is grammatically correct and uses words that are familiar to an educated audience. A writer who uses formal diction often maintains emotional distance from the audience by using the impersonal *one* rather than the more personal *I* and *you.* In addition, the tone of the writing—as determined by word choice, sentence structure, and choice of subject—is dignified and objective.

> We learn to perceive in the sense that we learn to respond to things in particular ways because of the contingencies of which they are a part. We may perceive the sun, for example, simply because it is an extremely powerful stimulus, but it has been a permanent part of the environment of the species throughout its evolution, and more specific behavior with respect to it could have been selected by contingencies of survival (as it has been in many other species). (B. F. Skinner, *Beyond Freedom and Dignity*)

### 2 Informal Diction

**Informal diction** is the language that people use in conversation and in personal emails. You should use informal diction in your college writing only to reproduce speech or dialect or to give a paper a conversational tone.

***Colloquial Diction*** **Colloquial diction** is the language of everyday speech. Contractions—*isn't, I'm*—are typical colloquialisms, as are **clipped forms**—*phone* for *telephone, TV* for *television, dorm* for *dormitory.* Other colloquialisms include placeholders such as *kind of* and utility words such as *nice* for *acceptable, funny* for *odd,* and *great* for almost anything. Colloquial English also includes expressions such as *get across* for *communicate, come up with* for *find,* and *check out* for *investigate.*

***Slang*** **Slang,** language that calls attention to itself, is used to establish or reinforce identity within a group—urban teenagers, rock musicians, or computer users, for example. One characteristic of slang vocabulary is that it is usually relatively short-lived, coming into existence and fading out much more quickly than other words do. Because slang terms can emerge and disappear so quickly, no dictionary—not even a dictionary of slang—can list all or even most of the slang terms currently in use.

In personal email and instant messages, writers commonly use **emoticons**—typed characters, such as :-) or ;-), that indicate emotions or feelings—and **Internet slang,** (or **text shorthand**), such as BTW (by the way) or 2 Day. Although these typographical devices are common in informal electronic communication, they are always inappropriate in academic essays or emails to professors or supervisors.

***Regionalisms*** **Regionalisms** are words, expressions, and idiomatic forms that are used in particular geographical areas but may not be understood by a general audience. In eastern Tennessee, for example, a paper bag is a *poke,* and empty soda bottles are *dope bottles.* In Lancaster, Pennsylvania, which has a large Amish population, it is not unusual to hear an elderly person say *darest* for *dare not* or *daresome* for *adventurous.* And New Yorkers stand *on line* for a movie, whereas people in most other parts of the country stand *in line.*

***Nonstandard Diction*** **Nonstandard diction** refers to words and expressions not generally considered a part of standard English—words such as *ain't, nohow, anywheres, nowheres, hisself,* and *theirselves.*

No absolute rules distinguish standard from nonstandard usage. In fact, some linguists reject the idea of nonstandard usage altogether, arguing that this designation relegates both the language and those who use it to second-class status.

*Note:* Remember that colloquial expressions, slang, regionalisms, and nonstandard diction are almost always inappropriate in your college writing.

**ESL TIP**

Some of the expressions you learn from other students or from television are not appropriate for use in formal writing. When you hear new expressions, pay attention to the contexts in which they are used.

## 3 College Writing

The level of diction appropriate for college writing depends on your assignment and your audience. A personal-experience essay calls for a somewhat informal style, but a research paper, an exam, or a report requires a more formal level of diction. In general, most college writing falls somewhere between formal and informal English, using a conversational tone but maintaining grammatical correctness and using a specialized vocabulary when the situation requires it. (This is the level of diction that is used in this book.)

## Close-Up EMAILS TO INSTRUCTORS

Different instructors have different opinions about how students should address them. Unless you are told otherwise, however, think of emails to your instructors as business communications. Avoid highly informal salutations, such as "Hi prof"; instead, use a more formal salutation, such as "Dr. Sweeny."

### EXERCISE 1

The diction of this paragraph, from Toni Cade Bambara's short story "The Hammer Man," is informal. In order to represent the speech of a young girl, the writer intentionally uses slang expressions and nonstandard diction. Underline the words that identify the diction of this paragraph as informal. Then, rewrite the paragraph using standard diction.

> Manny was supposed to be crazy. That was his story. To say you were bad put some people off. But to say you were crazy, well, you were officially not to be messed with. So that was his story. On the other hand, after I called him what I called him and said a few choice things about his mother, his face did go through some piercing changes. And I did kind of wonder if maybe he sure was nuts. I didn't wait to find out. I got in the wind. And then he waited for me on my stoop all day and all night, not hardly speaking to the people going in and out. And he was there all day Saturday, with his sister bringing him peanut-butter sandwiches and cream sodas. He must've gone to the bathroom right there cause every time I looked out the kitchen window, there he was. And Sunday, too. I got to thinking the boy was mad.

### EXERCISE 2

After reading the following paragraph, underline the words and phrases that identify it as formal diction. Then, rewrite the paragraph, using the level of diction that you would use in your college writing. Consult a dictionary if necessary.

> In looking at many small points of difference between species, which, as far as our ignorance permits us to judge, seem quite unimportant, we must not forget that climate, food, etc., have no doubt produced some direct effect. It is also necessary to bear in mind that owing to the law of correlation, when one part varies and the variations are accumulated through natural selection, other modifications, often of the most unexpected nature, will ensue. (Charles Darwin, *The Origin of Species*)

## 45b Choosing the Right Word

Choosing the right word to use in a particular context is very important. If you use the wrong word—or even *almost* the right one—you run the risk of misrepresenting your ideas.

### 1 Denotation and Connotation

A word's **denotation** is its basic dictionary meaning, what it stands for without any emotional associations. A word's **connotations** are the emotional, social, and political associations it has in addition to its denotative meaning.

| Word | Denotation | Connotations |
|---|---|---|
| politician | someone who holds a political office | opportunist; wheeler-dealer |

Selecting a word with the appropriate connotation can be challenging. For example, the word *skinny* has negative connotations, whereas *thin* is neutral, and *slender* is positive. And words and expressions such as *mentally ill, insane, neurotic, crazy, psychopathic,* and *emotionally disturbed,* although similar in meaning, have different emotional, social, and political connotations that affect the way people respond. If you use terms without considering their connotations, you run the risk of undercutting your credibility, to say nothing of confusing and possibly angering your readers.

#### Close-Up USING A THESAURUS

Unlike a dictionary, which lists the definitions of words, a **thesaurus** lists **synonyms** (words that have the same meaning—for example, *well* and *healthy*) and **antonyms** (words that have opposite meanings—for example, *courage* and *cowardice*). Most online dictionaries, as well as *Microsoft Word*, enable you to access a thesaurus.

When you consult a thesaurus, remember that no two words have exactly the same meaning. Use synonyms carefully, checking your dictionary to make sure the connotation of the synonym is very close to that of the original word.

#### EXERCISE 3

The following words have negative connotations. For each, list one word with a similar meaning whose connotation is neutral and another whose connotation is positive.

*Example:* *Negative* skinny
*Neutral* thin
*Positive* slender

1. deceive
2. antiquated
3. pushy
4. pathetic
5. cheap
6. blunder
7. weird
8. politician
9. shack
10. stench

## 2 Euphemisms

A **euphemism** is a polite term used in place of a blunt or harsh term that describes something offensive, unpleasant, or embarrassing. College writing is no place for euphemisms. Say what you mean—*pregnant,* not *expecting; died,* not *passed away;* and *strike,* not *work stoppage.*

## 3 Specific and General Words

**Specific** words refer to particular persons, items, or events; **general** words denote entire classes or groups. *Queen Elizabeth II,* for example, is more specific than *monarch; jeans* is more specific than *clothing;* and *SUV* is more specific than *vehicle.* You can use general words to describe entire classes of items, but you should use specific words to clarify such generalizations.

### Close-Up USING SPECIFIC WORDS

Take particular care to avoid general words such as *nice, great,* and *terrific* that say nothing and could be used in almost any sentence. These utility words convey only enthusiasm, not precise meanings. Replace them with more specific words.

See 39a2

## 4 Abstract and Concrete Words

**Abstract** words—*beauty, truth, justice,* and so on—refer to ideas, qualities, or conditions that cannot be perceived by the senses. **Concrete** words name things that readers can see, hear, taste, smell, or touch. As with general and specific words, whether a word is abstract or concrete is relative. The more concrete your words and phrases, the more vivid the image you evoke in the reader's mind.

**EXERCISE 4**

Revise the following paragraph from a job application letter by substituting specific, concrete language for general or abstract words and phrases.

I have had several part-time jobs lately. Some of them would qualify me for the position you advertised. In my most recent job, I sold products in a store. My supervisor said I was a good worker who had a number of valuable qualities. I am used to dealing with different types of people in different settings. I feel that my qualifications would make me a good candidate for your job opening.

## 45c Using Figures of Speech

Writers often use **figures of speech** (such as *similes* and *metaphors*) to go beyond the literal meanings of words. By doing so, they make their writing more vivid or emphatic.

### Close-Up COMMONLY USED FIGURES OF SPEECH

- A **simile** is a comparison between two essentially unlike things on the basis of a shared quality. A simile is introduced by *like* or *as*.

  Like travelers with exotic destinations on their minds, the graduates were remarkably forgetful. (Maya Angelou, *I Know Why the Caged Bird Sings*)
- A **metaphor** also compares two essentially dissimilar things, but instead of saying that one thing is *like* another, it *equates* them.

  All the world's a stage,
  And all the men and women merely players; . . .
  (William Shakespeare, *As You Like It*)
- An **analogy** explains an unfamiliar item or concept by comparing it to a more familiar one.

  According to Robert Frost, writing free verse is similar to playing tennis without a net.
- **Personification** gives an idea or inanimate object human attributes, feelings, or powers.

  Truth strikes us from behind, and in the dark, as well as from before in broad daylight. (Henry David Thoreau, *Journals*)
- **Hyperbole** (or overstatement) is an intentional exaggeration for emphasis. For example, Jonathan Swift uses hyperbole in his essay "A Modest Proposal" when he suggests that eating Irish babies would help the English solve their food shortage.
- **Understatement** intentionally downplays the seriousness of a situation or sentiment by saying less than is really meant.

  According to Mao Tse-tung, a revolution is not a tea party.

## EXERCISE 5

Read the following paragraph from Mark Twain's *Life on the Mississippi*, and identify as many figures of speech as you can.

> Now when I had mastered the language of this water, and had come to know every trifling feature that bordered the great river as familiarly as I knew the letters of the alphabet, I had made a valuable acquisition. But I had lost something, too. I had lost something which could never be restored to me while I lived. All the grace, the beauty, the poetry, had gone out of the majestic river! I still keep in mind a certain wonderful sunset which I witnessed when steamboating was new to me. A broad expanse of the river was turned to blood; in the middle distance the red hue brightened into gold, through which a solitary log came floating black and conspicuous; in one place a long, slanting mark lay sparkling upon the water; in another the surface was broken by boiling, tumbling rings, that were as many-tinted as an opal; where the ruddy flush was faintest, was a smooth spot that was covered with graceful circles and radiating lines, ever so delicately traced; the shore on our left was densely wooded, and the somber shadow that fell from this forest was broken in one place by a long, ruffled trail that shone like silver; and high above the forest wall a clean-stemmed dead tree waved a single leafy bough that glowed like a flame in the unobstructed splendor that was flowing from the sun. There were graceful curves, reflected images, woody heights, soft distances; and over the whole scene, far and near, the dissolving lights drifted steadily, enriching it every passing moment with new marvels of coloring.

## EXERCISE 6

Rewrite the following sentences, adding a figure of speech to each sentence to make the ideas more vivid and exciting. Identify each figure of speech you use.

**Example:** The room was cool and still/ ^*like the inside of a cathedral.* (simile)

1. The last of the marathon runners limped toward the finish line.
2. The breeze gently stirred the wind chimes.
3. Jeremy has shoulder-length hair and a high forehead, and he wears small, red glasses.
4. The computer classroom was quiet.
5. The demolition crew worked slowly but efficiently.
6. Interstate highways often make for tedious driving.
7. Diego found calculus easy.
8. Music is essentially mathematical.
9. Katrina claims her dog is far more intelligent than her brother is.
10. Emotions are curious things.

## 45d Avoiding Inappropriate Language

### 1 Jargon

**Jargon**, the specialized or technical vocabulary of a trade, a profession, or an academic discipline, is useful for communicating in the field for which it was developed. Outside that field, however, it is often imprecise and confusing. For example, medical doctors may say that a procedure is *contraindicated* or that they are going to carry out a *differential diagnosis*. Business executives may want departments to *interface* effectively, and sociologists may identify the need for *perspectivistic thinking* to achieve organizational goals. If they are addressing other professionals in their respective fields, using these terms can facilitate communication. If, however, they are addressing a general audience, these terms will be confusing.

### 2 Neologisms

**Neologisms** are newly coined words that are not part of standard English. New situations call for new words, however, and frequently a neologism will become an accepted part of the language—*app, locavore, phishing, blog,* and *outsource,* for example. Other coined words are never fully accepted—for example, the neologisms created when the suffix *-wise* is added to existing words, creating nonstandard words like *weatherwise, sportswise, timewise,* and *productwise.*

### 3 Pretentious Diction

Good writing is clear and direct, not pompous or flowery. Revise to eliminate **pretentious diction,** inappropriately elevated and wordy language.

> As I fell ~~into slumber~~ ^asleep^, I ~~cogitated~~ ^thought^ about my day ~~ambling~~ ^hiking^ through ~~the splendor of~~ the Appalachian Mountains.

Frequently, pretentious diction is formal diction used in a relatively informal situation. In such a context, it is out of place. For every pretentious word, there is a clear and direct alternative.

| Pretentious | Clear | Pretentious | Clear |
|---|---|---|---|
| ascertain | discover | reside | live |
| commence | start | terminate | end |
| implement | carry out | utilize | use |
| minuscule | small | individual | person |

### 4 Clichés

**Clichés** are expressions that have been used so often that their power has been drained away. At one time, expressions such as "hit the nail on the head" or "pass the buck" might have called up vivid images in a reader's mind, but because of overuse, they have become clichés—pat, meaningless phrases.

back in the day
the bottom line
it is what it is
face the music
game plan
give 110 percent
smoking gun
a level playing field
a perfect storm
wake up and smell the coffee
old school
what goes around comes around

**ESL TIP**

Many ESL students have learned a long list of English idioms. Some of these, however, have become clichés. Although becoming familiar with these idioms can help you understand them when you encounter them, university instructors discourage students from using clichés in their writing, preferring language that is more original and more precise.

Writers sometimes resort to clichés when they run out of ideas. To capture your readers' attention, you should take the time to think of original expressions.

### 5 Mixed Metaphors

A **mixed metaphor** is created when a writer combines two or more incompatible images. The result can be illogical, humorous, or both. For this reason, you should revise mixed metaphors to make your imagery consistent.

**Mixed:** Management extended an olive branch in an attempt to break the ice between the company and the striking workers.

**Revised:** Management extended an olive branch with the hope that the striking workers would accept it.

### EXERCISE 7

Rewrite the following passage, eliminating jargon, neologisms, pretentious diction, and clichés. Feel free to add words and phrases and to reorganize sentences to make their meaning clear. If you are not certain about the meaning or status of a word, consult a dictionary.

At a given point in time, there coexisted a hare and a tortoise. The aforementioned rabbit was overheard by the tortoise to be blowing his horn about the degree of speed he could attain. The latter quadruped thereupon put forth a challenge to the former by advancing the suggestion that they interact in a running competition. The hare acquiesced, laughing to himself. The animals concurred in the decision to acquire the services of a certain fox to act in the capacity of judicial referee. This particular fox was in agreement, and, consequently, implementation of the plan was facilitated. In a relatively small amount of time, the hare had considerably outdistanced the tortoise and, after ascertaining that he himself was in a more optimized position distancewise than the tortoise, he arrived at the unilateral decision to avail himself of a respite. He made the implicit assumption in so doing that he would anticipate no difficulty in overtaking the tortoise when his suspension of activity ceased. An unfortunate development racewise occurred when the hare's somnolent state endured for a longer-than-anticipated time frame, facilitating the tortoise's victory in the contest and affirming the concept of unhurriedness and firmness triumphing in competitive situations. Thus, the hare was unable to snatch victory out of the jaws of defeat.

**EXERCISE 8**

Go through a newspaper or magazine, and list the examples of jargon, neologisms, pretentious diction, clichés, and mixed metaphors that you find. Then, substitute more appropriate words for the ones you identified. Be prepared to discuss your interpretation of each example and of the words you chose to put in its place.

## 45e Avoiding Offensive Language

The issue of when and how to avoid offensive language has generated much debate. On one side are those who say that groups of people who have traditionally been marginalized—women, minorities, gays, lesbians, transgendered individuals, people with special needs, and so on—deserve special treatment because the words that have been used to describe them have reinforced negative stereotypes and have put them at a great disadvantage. On the other side of the debate are those who say that this effort to change people's use of language is an extreme example of political correctness, where those with one view of society try to impose this view on others.

People on both sides of this debate make valid points. Clearly, offensive language has degraded members of certain groups on a daily basis and made it difficult—if not impossible—for them to fit into (or function in) society. But many people—even fairminded people—feel very strongly that they should be able to express themselves freely without worrying that their words might inadvertently further a stereotype.

As with most controversial issues, the truth is somewhat subtler than these two positions suggest. Most of us want to live in a society where everyone—regardless of background, gender, race, sexual orientation, age, or physical condition—is able to realize his or her full potential. Language that undercuts this goal has no place in civil discourse and should be avoided—in the workplace, in the classroom, and in our daily lives. Although people certainly have the right to express themselves, they should be aware of the potentially negative consequences—moral, ethical, and practical—of their words. Because the language we use not only expresses our ideas but also shapes our thinking, it is in everyone's best interest to make a reasonable effort to avoid using words that could insult, degrade, or otherwise harm others.

## 1 Stereotypes

***Race and Ethnicity*** When referring to any racial, ethnic, or religious group, use words with neutral connotations or words that the group uses in *formal* speech or writing to refer to itself—for example, *African American, latino* or *latina, Native American, Chinese American,* and so on.

*Note:* It is acceptable to use *black* in second references to *African Americans.*

***Age*** Avoid potentially offensive labels relating to age. Many older people prefer to call themselves *senior citizens* or *seniors,* and these terms are commonly used by the media and the government.

***Class*** Do not demean certain jobs because they are low paying or praise others because they have impressive titles. Similarly, do not use words—*hick, cracker, redneck,* and *trailer trash,* for example—that denigrate people based on their social or economic class.

***Sexual Orientation*** Always use neutral terms (such as *gay* and *lesbian*), but do not mention a person's sexual orientation unless it is relevant to your discussion.

***Physical Disability*** Use respectful language when referring to people with physical or mental disabilities. Mention a person's disability only when it is important to the discussion. Also, avoid outdated (and potentially hurtful) terms such as *retarded* and *crippled.* Instead, use terms such as *mentally challenged* and *physically disabled.* Keep in mind that the language used to describe people with disabilities changes over time.

## 2 Sexist Language

Avoid **sexist language**—language that reinforces and promotes gender stereotypes. Extending beyond the use of derogatory words, sexist language assumes that some professions are exclusive to one gender—for instance, that *nurse* denotes only women and that *doctor* denotes only men. The use of outdated job titles, such as *postman* for *letter carrier, fireman* for *firefighter,* and *stewardess* for *flight attendant,* is also considered sexist.

Sexist language also occurs when a writer fails to apply the same terminology to both men and women. For example, refer to two scientists with PhDs not as Dr. Sagan and Mrs. Yallow, but as Dr. Sagan and Dr. Yallow. Refer to two writers as James and Wharton, or Henry James and Edith Wharton, not James and Mrs. Wharton.

In your writing, always use *women*—not *girls, gals,* or *ladies*—when referring to adult females. Use *Ms.* as the form of address when a woman's marital status is unknown or irrelevant (for example, in business correspondence). Finally, avoid using the generic *he* or *him* when your subject could be either male or female. Use the third-person plural (*they*) or the phrase *he* or *she* (not *he/she*).

**Sexist:** Before boarding, each passenger should make certain that he has his ticket.

**Revised:** Before boarding, passengers should make certain that they have their tickets.

**Revised:** Before boarding, each passenger should make certain that he or she has a ticket.

*Note:* Remember not to use words to refer to a woman that you would not use to describe a man. For example, do not describe a woman as *pushy* if you would not use the same term to describe a man.

### Close-Up ELIMINATING SEXIST LANGUAGE

For every sexist usage, there is a nonsexist alternative.

| Sexist Usage | Possible Revisions |
|---|---|
| Mankind | People, human beings |
| Man's accomplishments | Human accomplishments |
| Man-made | Synthetic |
| Female engineer/lawyer/ accountant, and so on; male model | Engineer/lawyer/accountant, and so on; model |
| Policeman/woman | Police officer |
| Salesman/woman/girl | Salesperson, sales representative |
| Businessman/woman | Businessperson, executive |
| Everyone should complete his application by Tuesday. | Everyone should complete his or her application by Tuesday. |
| | All students should complete their applications by Tuesday. |

*Note:* When trying to avoid sexist use of *he* and *him* in your writing, be careful not to use the plural pronoun *they* or *their* to refer to a singular antecedent.

Drivers
~~Any driver~~ caught speeding should have their driving privileges suspended.

## EXERCISE 9

Suggest at least one alternative form for each of the following words or phrases. In each case, comment on the advantages and disadvantages of the alternative you recommend. If you feel that a particular term is not sexist, explain why.

forefathers
man-eating shark
manpower
the common man

point man
draftsman
workmen's compensation
men at work
waitress
first baseman
congressman
manhunt
longshoreman
committeeman
(to) man the battle stations
man overboard
fisherman
foreman
manned space program
gentleman's agreement
no man's land
spinster
old maid
old wives' tale

**EXERCISE 10**

Each of the following pairs of terms includes a feminine form that was at one time in wide use; most are still used to some extent. Which do you think are likely to remain in our language for some time, and which do you think will disappear? Explain your reasoning.

heir/heiress
benefactor/benefactress
murderer/murderess
actor/actress
hero/heroine
host/hostess
aviator/aviatrix
executor/executrix
author/authoress
poet/poetess
tailor/seamstress
comedian/comedienne
villain/villainess
prince/princess
widow/widower

CHAPTER 46

# Improving Spelling

## Frequently Asked Questions

- Why do I still need to proofread if I use a spell checker? 613
- Are there any spelling rules that I can memorize? 615
- What can I do to become a better speller? 619

Like most students, you probably use a spell checker when you write and revise your papers, but this does not eliminate your need to know how to spell. For one thing, a spell checker will only check words that are in its dictionary. In addition, a spell checker will not tell you if you have confused *principal* for *principle*, and it will not catch typos such as *form* for *from* or *its* for *it's*. What this means is that even if you use a spell checker, you still have to be a competent speller.

**Close-Up** RUNNING A SPELL CHECK

Even if you run a spell check, you still have to proofread your papers. Remember that a spell checker will not recognize the following kinds of errors:

- A word that is spelled correctly but used incorrectly—*accept* for *except* or *there* for *their*, for example.
- A typo that creates another word—*form* for *from* or *then* for *than*, for example.
- Many capitalization errors—*president Lincoln* instead of *President Lincoln*, for example.

## 46a Understanding Spelling and Pronunciation

Because pronunciation in English often provides few clues to spelling, you need to memorize the spellings of many words and use a dictionary or spell checker regularly.

### 1 Vowels in Unstressed Positions

Many unstressed vowels sound exactly alike. For instance, it is hard to tell from pronunciation alone that the *i* in *terrible* is not an *a*. In addition, the unstressed vowels *a*, *e*, and *i* are impossible to distinguish in the suffixes *-able* and *-ible*, *-ance* and *-ence*, and *-ant* and *-ent*.

| | | |
|---|---|---|
| comfortable | brilliance | servant |
| compatible | excellence | independent |

### 2 Silent Letters

Some English words contain silent letters, such as the *b* in *climb* and the *t* in *mortgage*.

| | | |
|---|---|---|
| aisle | depot | pneumonia |
| climb | knight | silhouette |
| condemn | mortgage | sovereign |

### 3 Words That Are Often Pronounced Carelessly

Most of us pronounce words rather carelessly in everyday speech. Consequently, when spelling, we may leave out, add, or transpose letters.

| | |
|---|---|
| candidate | perform |
| environment | quantity |
| February | recognize |
| government | specific |
| hundred | supposed to |
| library | surprise |
| lightning | used to |
| nuclear | |

### 4 American and British Spellings

Some words are spelled one way in the United States and another way in Great Britain and the Commonwealth nations.

| **American** | **British** |
|---|---|
| color | colour |
| defense | defence |
| honor | honour |
| judgment | judgement |
| theater | theatre |
| toward | towards |
| traveled | travelled |

### 5 Homophones

**Homophones** are words—such as *accept* and *except*—that are pronounced alike but spelled differently.

| | |
|---|---|
| accept | to receive |
| except | other than |
| affect | to have an influence on (*verb*) |
| effect | result (*noun*); to cause (*verb*) |
| its | possessive of *it* |
| it's | contraction of *it is* |
| principal | most important (*adjective*); head of a school (*noun*) |
| principle | a basic truth; rule of conduct |

For a full list of these and other homophones, along with their meanings and sentences illustrating their use, **see the Glossary of Usage.**

### Close-Up ONE WORD OR TWO?

Some words may be written as one word or two, depending on meaning.

*any way* vs. *anyway*
The early pioneers made the trip west any way they could.
It began to rain, but the game continued anyway.

*every day* vs. *everyday*
Every day brings new opportunities.
John thought of his birthday as an everyday event.

Other words are frequently misspelled because people are not sure whether they are one word or two.

| One Word | Two Words |
|---|---|
| already | a lot |
| cannot | all right |
| classroom | even though |
| overweight | no one |

## 46b Learning Spelling Rules

Most people can spell even difficult words "almost correctly"; usually only a letter or two are wrong. For this reason, memorizing a few rules and their exceptions and learning the correct spelling of the most commonly misspelled words can help you become a better speller.

### 1 The ie/ei Combinations

The old rule still stands: use *i* before *e* except after *c* (or when pronounced *ay*, as in *neighbor*).

| ***i* before *e*** | ***ei* after *c*** | ***ei* pronounced *ay*** |
|---|---|---|
| belief | ceiling | weigh |
| chief | deceit | freight |
| niece | receive | eight |

**Exceptions:** *either, neither, foreign, leisure, weird*, and *seize*. In addition, if the *ie* combination is not pronounced as a unit, the rule does not apply: *atheist, science.*

**EXERCISE 1**

Fill in the blanks with the proper *ie* or *ei* combination. After completing the exercise, use your dictionary or spell checker to check your answers.

***Example:*** conc_*ei*_ve

1. rec____pt
2. var____ty
3. caff____ne
4. ach____ve
5. kal____doscope
6. misch____f
7. effic____nt
8. v____n
9. spec____s
10. suffic____nt

## 2 Doubling Final Consonants

The only words that double their consonants before a suffix that begins with a vowel (*-ed, -ing*) are those that pass the following three tests:

1. They have one syllable or are stressed on the last syllable.
2. They contain only one vowel in the last syllable.
3. They end in a single consonant.

The word *tap* satisfies all three conditions: it has only one syllable, it contains only one vowel (*a*), and it ends in a single consonant (*p*). Therefore, its final consonant is doubled before a suffix beginning with a vowel (*tapped, tapping*).

The word *relent*, however, meets only two of the three conditions: it is stressed on the last syllable, and it has one vowel in the last syllable, but it does not end in a single consonant. Therefore, its final consonant is not doubled (*relented, relenting*).

## 3 Prefixes

The addition of a prefix never affects the spelling of the root (*mis* + *spell* = *misspell*). Some prefixes can cause spelling problems, however, because they are pronounced alike although they are not spelled alike: *ante-/anti-, en-/in-, per-/pre-*, and *de-/di-*.

| | |
|---|---|
| antebellum | antiaircraft |
| encircle | integrate |
| perceive | prescribe |
| deduct | direct |

### 4 Silent *e* before a Suffix

When a suffix that begins with a consonant is added to a word ending in silent *e*, the *e* is generally kept: *hope/hopeful; lame/lamely; bore/boredom.* **Exceptions:** *argument, truly, ninth, judgment,* and *acknowledgment.*

When a suffix that starts with a vowel is added to a word that ends in a silent *e*, the *e* is generally dropped: *hope/hoping; trace/traced; grieve/grievance; love/lovable.* **Exceptions:** *changeable, noticeable,* and *courageous.*

#### EXERCISE 2

Combine the following words with the suffixes in parentheses. Keep or drop the silent *e* as you see fit; be prepared to explain your choices.

***Example:*** fate (al)
fatal

1. surprise (ing)
2. sure (ly)
3. force (ible)
4. manage (able)
5. due (ly)
6. outrage (ous)
7. service (able)
8. awe (ful)
9. shame (ing)
10. shame (less)

### 5 *y* before a Suffix

When a word ends in a consonant plus *y*, the *y* generally changes to an *i* when a suffix is added (*beauty + ful = beautiful*). The *y* is kept, however, when the suffix *-ing* is added (*tally + ing = tallying*) and in some one-syllable words (*dry + ness = dryness*).

When a word ends in a vowel plus *y*, the *y* is retained (*joy + ful = joyful; employ + er = employer*). **Exception:** *day + ly = daily.*

#### EXERCISE 3

Add the endings in parentheses to the following words. Change or keep the final *y* as you see fit; be prepared to explain your choices.

***Example:*** party (ing)
partying

1. journey (ing)
2. study (ed)
3. carry (ing)
4. shy (ly)
5. study (ing)
6. sturdy (ness)
7. merry (ment)
8. likely (hood)
9. plenty (ful)
10. supply (er)

### 6 *seed* Endings

Endings with the sound *seed* are nearly always spelled *cede*, as in *precede, intercede, concede*, and so on. **Exceptions:** *supersede, exceed, proceed*, and *succeed.*

### 7 -able, -ible

If the root of a word is itself an independent word, the suffix *-able* is most often used. If the root of a word is not an independent word, the suffix *-ible* is most often used.

| | |
|---|---|
| *comfortable* | *compatible* |
| *agreeable* | *incredible* |
| *dryable* | *plausible* |

### 8 Plurals

Most nouns form plurals by adding *-s: savage/savages, tortilla/tortillas, boat/boats.* There are, however, a number of exceptions.

***Words Ending in -f or -fe*** Some words ending in *-f* or *-fe* form plurals by changing the *f* to *v* and adding *-es* or *-s: life/lives, self/selves.* Others add just *-s: belief/beliefs, safe/safes.* Words ending in *-ff* take *-s* to form plurals: *tariff/tariffs.*

***Words Ending in -y*** Most words that end in a consonant followed by *y* form plurals by changing the *y* to *i* and adding *-es: baby/babies.* **Exceptions:** proper nouns, such as the *Kennedys* (never the *Kennedies*).

Words that end in a vowel followed by a *y* form plurals by adding *-s: day/days, monkey/monkeys.*

***Words Ending in -o*** Words that end in a vowel followed by *o* form the plural by adding *-s: radio/radios, stereo/stereos, zoo/zoos.* Most words that end in a consonant followed by *o* add *-es* to form the plural: *tomato/tomatoes, hero/heroes.* **Exceptions:** *silo/silos, piano/pianos, memo/memos,* and *soprano/sopranos.*

***Words Ending in -s, -ss, -sh, -ch, -x, and -z*** These words form plurals by adding *-es: Jones/Joneses, mass/masses, rash/rashes, lunch/lunches, box/boxes, buzz/buzzes.* **Exceptions:** Some one-syllable words that end in *-s* or *-z* double their final consonants when forming plurals: *quiz/quizzes.*

***Compound Nouns*** **Compound nouns**—nouns formed from two or more words—usually form the plural with the last word in the compound construction: *welfare state/welfare states; snowball/snowballs.* However, where the first word of the compound noun is more important than the others, form the plural with the first word: *sister-in-law/sisters-in-law, attorney general/attorneys general, hole in one/holes in one.*

***Foreign Plurals*** Some words, especially those borrowed from Latin or Greek, keep their foreign plurals. Look up a foreign word's plural form in a dictionary if you do not know it.

| Singular | Plural |
|---|---|
| basis | bases |
| criterion | criteria |
| curriculum | curricula |
| datum | data |
| larva | larvae |
| medium | media |
| memorandum | memoranda |
| stimulus | stimuli |
| syllabus | syllabi |

## 46c Developing Spelling Skills

Besides studying the rules outlined in **46b,** you can take some additional steps to become a better speller.

### 1 Make Your Own Spelling List

Keep a list of your own problem words. When you read through a first draft, circle any words whose spellings you are unsure of. Then, look them up in your dictionary or spell checker, and add them to your list. When your instructor returns a paper, add to your list any words you have misspelled.

### 2 Uncover Patterns of Misspelling

Do you consistently have a problem with plurals or with *-ible*/*-able* endings? If so, review the spelling rules that apply to those particular problems. By using this strategy, you can eliminate the need to memorize single words.

### 3 Fix Each Word in Your Mind

Think of associations that will make the correct spellings stick in your mind. For example, you can remember the correct spelling of *definite* (often misspelled *definate*) by remembering that it contains the word *finite,* which suggests the concept of limit, as does *definite.*

### 4 Learn to Distinguish Commonly Confused Words

Learn to distinguish commonly confused **homophones** (words that sound exactly alike but have different spellings and meanings, such as *night* and *knight*) and near-homophones (words that sound similar, such as *accept* and *except*). For a list of homophones, **see the Glossary of Usage.**

See 46a5

PART 12

# Understanding Grammar

CHAPTER 47

# Using Parts of Speech

## Frequently Asked Questions



The eight basic **parts of speech**—the building blocks for all English sentences—are *nouns, pronouns, verbs, adjectives, adverbs, prepositions, conjunctions*, and *interjections*. How a word is classified depends on its function in a sentence.

## 47a Using Nouns

ESL 64b

Nouns name people, animals, places, things, ideas, actions, or qualities.

A **common noun** names any one of a class of people, places, or things: *artist, judge, building, event, city*.

A **proper noun,** always capitalized, designates a particular person, place, or thing: *Mary Cassatt, World Trade Center, Crimean War*.

A **count noun** names something that can be counted: five *dogs*, two dozen *grapes*.

A **noncount noun** names a quantity that is not countable: *time, dust, work, gold*. Noncount nouns generally have only a singular form.

See 50a5

A collective noun designates a group thought of as a unit: *committee, class, navy, band, family*. Collective nouns are generally singular unless the members of the group are referred to as individuals.

An **abstract noun** designates an intangible idea or quality: *love, hate, justice, anger, fear, prejudice*.

## 47b Using Pronouns

ESL 64c

Pronouns are words used in place of nouns or other pronouns. The word for which a pronoun stands is called its **antecedent.**

If you use a quotation in your paper, you must document it. (Pronoun *it* refers to antecedent *quotation*.)

A **personal pronoun** stands for a person or thing. Personal pronouns include *I, me, we, us, my, mine, our, ours, you, your, yours, he, she, it, its, him, his, her, hers, they, them, their,* and *theirs*.

The firm made Debbie an offer, and she couldn't refuse it.

An **indefinite pronoun** does not refer to any particular person or thing, so it does not require an antecedent. Indefinite pronouns include *another, any, each, few, many, some, nothing, one, anyone, everyone, everybody, everything, someone, something, either,* and *neither*.

See 50b3

Many are called, but few are chosen.

A **reflexive pronoun** ends with *-self* and refers to a recipient of the action that is the same as the actor. The reflexive pronouns are *myself, yourself, himself, herself, itself, oneself, themselves, ourselves,* and *yourselves*.

They found themselves in downtown Pittsburgh.

An **intensive pronoun** emphasizes a noun or pronoun that directly precedes it. (Intensive pronouns have the same form as reflexive pronouns.)

Darrow himself was sure his client was innocent.

A **relative pronoun** introduces an adjective clause or a noun clause in a sentence. Relative pronouns include *which, who, whom, that, what, whose, whatever, whoever, whomever,* and *whichever*.

Gandhi was the charismatic man who led India to independence. (introduces adjective clause)

Whatever happens will be a surprise. (introduces noun clause)

An **interrogative pronoun** introduces a question. Interrogative pronouns include *who, which, what, whom, whose, whoever, whatever,* and *whichever*.

Who is next?

A **demonstrative pronoun** points to a particular thing or group of things. *This, that, these,* and *those* are demonstrative pronouns.

This is one of Shakespeare's early plays.

A **reciprocal pronoun** denotes a mutual relationship. The reciprocal pronouns are *each other* and *one another*. *Each other* indicates a relationship between two individuals; *one another* denotes a relationship among more than two.

Romeo and Juliet declared their love for each other.

Concertgoers crowded one another in the ticket line.

## 47c Using Verbs

### 1 Recognizing Verbs

ESL 64a

A verb may express either *action* or a *state of being.*

He ran for the train. (physical action)

He worried about being late. (emotional action)

Elizabeth II became queen after the death of her father, George VI. (state of being)

Verbs can be classified into two groups: *main verbs* and *auxiliary verbs.*

***Main Verbs*** **Main verbs** carry most of the meaning in a sentence. Some main verbs are **action verbs.**

Emily Dickinson wrote poetry.

Other main verbs function as linking verbs. A **linking verb** does not show any physical or emotional action. Its function is to link the sentence's subject to a **subject complement,** a word or phrase that renames or describes the subject.

Carbon disulfide smells bad.

**Frequently Used Linking Verbs**

| | | | | |
|---|---|---|---|---|
| appear | believe | look | seem | taste |
| be | feel | prove | smell | turn |
| become | grow | remain | sound | |

***Auxiliary Verbs*** **Auxiliary verbs** (also called **helping verbs**), such as *be* and *have,* combine with main verbs to form **verb phrases.** Auxiliary verbs indicate tense, voice, or mood.

[auxiliary] [main verb] [auxiliary] [main verb]

The train has started. We are leaving soon.

[verb phrase] [verb phrase]

Certain auxiliary verbs, known as **modal auxiliaries,** indicate necessity, possibility, willingness, obligation, or ability.

In the future, farmers might cultivate seaweed as a food crop.

Coal mining would be safer if dust were controlled in the mines.

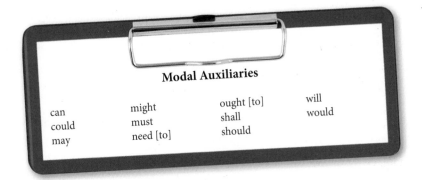

**Modal Auxiliaries**

| | | | |
|---|---|---|---|
| can | might | ought [to] | will |
| could | must | shall | would |
| may | need [to] | should | |

## 2 Recognizing Verbals

**Verbals,** such as *known* or *swimming* or *to go,* are verb forms that act as adjectives, adverbs, or nouns. A verbal can never serve as a sentence's main verb unless it is used with one or more auxiliary verbs (*has known, should be swimming*). Verbals include *participles*, *infinitives*, and *gerunds.*

***Participles*** Virtually every verb has a **present participle,** which ends in *-ing* (*loving, learning, going, writing*), and a **past participle,** which usually ends in *-d* or *-ed* (*agreed, learned*). Some verbs have **irregular** past participles (*gone, begun, written*). Participles may function in a sentence as adjectives or as nouns.

See 49a2

Twenty brands of running shoes were displayed at the exhibition. (Present participle *running* serves as adjective modifying noun *shoes.*)

The crowded bus went past those waiting at the corner. (Past participle *crowded* serves as adjective modifying noun *bus.*)

The wounded were given emergency first aid. (Past participle *wounded* serves as a noun, the sentence's subject.)

***Infinitives*** An **infinitive** is made up of *to* and the base form of the verb (*to defeat*). An infinitive may function as an adjective, an adverb, or a noun.

Ann Arbor was clearly the place to be. (Infinitive serves as adjective modifying noun *place.*)

They say that breaking up is hard to do. (Infinitive serves as adverb modifying adjective *hard.*)

Carla went outside to think. (Infinitive serves as adverb modifying verb *went.*)

To win was everything. (Infinitive serves as noun, the sentence's subject.)

***Gerunds*** **Gerunds** (which, like present participles, end in *-ing*) always function as nouns.

Seeing is believing. (Gerund *seeing* serves as sentence's subject; gerund *believing* serves as subject complement.)

He worried about interrupting. (Gerund *interrupting* is object of preposition *about*.)

Andrew loves skiing. (Gerund *skiing* is direct object of verb *loves*.)

*Note:* When the *-ing* form of a verb is used as a noun, it is a *gerund;* when it is used as an adjective, it is a *present participle.*

## 47d Using Adjectives

ESL 64d

Adjectives describe, limit, qualify, or in some other way modify nouns or pronouns.

### 1 Descriptive Adjectives

**Descriptive adjectives** name a quality of the noun or pronoun they modify.

After the game, they were exhausted.

They ordered a chocolate soda and a butterscotch sundae.

Some descriptive adjectives are formed from common nouns or from verbs (*friend/friendly, agree/agreeable*). Others, called **proper adjectives,** are formed from proper nouns.

A Shakespearean sonnet consists of an octave and a sestet.

See 60b1

*Note:* Two or more words may be joined (hyphenated before a noun, without a hyphen after a noun) to form a **compound adjective:** *His parents are very well-read people; most people are not so well read.*

### 2 Determiners

ESL 64b 2–3

When articles, pronouns, numbers, and the like function as adjectives, limiting or qualifying nouns or pronouns, they are referred to as **determiners.**

- **Articles** (*a, an, the*)

  The boy found a four-leaf clover.

- **Possessive nouns**

  Lesley's mother lives in New Jersey.

- **Possessive pronouns** (the personal pronouns *my, your, his, her, its, our, their*)

  Their lives depended on my skill.
- **Demonstrative pronouns** (*this, these, that, those*)

  This song reminds me of that song we heard yesterday.
- **Interrogative pronouns** (*what, which, whose*)

  Whose book is this?
- **Indefinite pronouns** (*another, each, both, many, any, some,* and so on)

  Both candidates agreed to return another day.
- **Relative pronouns** (*what, whatever, which, whichever, whose, whoever*)

  I forgot whatever reasons I had for leaving.
- **Numbers** (*one, two, first, second,* and so on)

  The first time I played baseball, I got only one hit.

## 47e Using Adverbs

ESL 64d

**Adverbs** describe the action of verbs or modify adjectives, other adverbs, or complete phrases, clauses, or sentences. They answer the questions "How?" "Why?" "Where?" "When?" "Under what conditions?" and "To what extent?"

He walked rather hesitantly toward the front of the room. (walked *how?*)

Let's meet tomorrow for coffee. (meet *when?*)

Adverbs that modify other adverbs or adjectives limit or qualify the words they modify.

He pitched an almost perfect game.

**Interrogative adverbs**—*how, when, why,* and *where*—introduce questions.

Why did the compound darken?

**Conjunctive adverbs** act as **transitional words,** joining and relating independent clauses. Conjunctive adverbs may appear in various positions in a sentence.

See 7b2

Jason forgot to register for chemistry. However, he managed to sign up during the drop/add period.

Jason forgot to register for chemistry; however, he managed to sign up during the drop/add period.

Jason forgot to register for chemistry. He managed, however, to sign up during the drop/add period.

Jason forgot to register for chemistry. He managed to sign up during the drop/add period, however.

**Frequently Used Conjunctive Adverbs**

| | | | |
|---|---|---|---|
| accordingly | furthermore | meanwhile | similarly |
| also | hence | moreover | still |
| anyway | however | nevertheless | then |
| besides | incidentally | next | thereafter |
| certainly | indeed | nonetheless | therefore |
| consequently | instead | now | thus |
| finally | likewise | otherwise | undoubtedly |

## 47f Using Prepositions

ESL 64e

A preposition introduces a noun or pronoun (or a phrase or clause functioning in the sentence as a noun), linking it to other words in the sentence. The word or word group the preposition introduces is called its **object.**

They received a postcard from (prep) Bobby (obj) telling about (prep) his trip (obj) to (prep) Canada (obj).

**Frequently Used Prepositions**

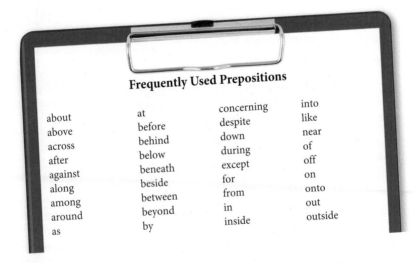

| | | | |
|---|---|---|---|
| about | at | concerning | into |
| above | before | despite | like |
| across | behind | down | near |
| after | below | during | of |
| against | beneath | except | off |
| along | beside | for | on |
| among | between | from | onto |
| around | beyond | in | out |
| as | by | inside | outside |

| | | | |
|---|---|---|---|
| over | through | under | upon |
| past | throughout | underneath | with |
| regarding | to | until | within |
| since | toward | up | without |

## 47g Using Conjunctions

**Conjunctions** connect words, phrases, clauses, or sentences.

- **Coordinating conjunctions** (*and, or, but, nor, for, so, yet*) connect words, phrases, or clauses of equal weight.

  The choice was simple: chicken or fish. (*Or* links two nouns.)

  The United States is a government "of the people, by the people, and for the people." (*And* links three prepositional phrases.)

  Thoreau wrote *Walden* in 1854, and he died in 1862. (*And* links two independent clauses.)

- **Correlative conjunctions,** always used in pairs, also link grammatically equivalent items.

  Both Hancock and Jefferson signed the Declaration of Independence. (Correlative conjunctions link two nouns.)

  Either I will renew my lease, or I will move. (Correlative conjunctions link two independent clauses.)

**Correlative Conjunctions**

| | |
|---|---|
| both . . . and | neither . . . nor |
| either . . . or | not only . . . but also |
| just as . . . so | whether . . . or |

- **Subordinating conjunctions** include *since, because, although, if, after, when, while, before,* and *unless*. A subordinating conjunction introduces

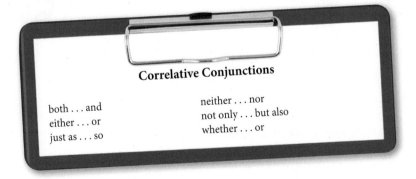

See 36b

a dependent (subordinate) clause, connecting it to the sentence's independent (main) clause to form a **complex sentence.**

Although drug use is a serious concern for parents, many parents are afraid to discuss it with their children.

It is best to diagram your garden before you start to plant it.

## 47h Using Interjections

**Interjections** are exclamations used to express emotion: *Oh! Ouch! Wow! Alas! Hey!* These words are grammatically independent; that is, they do not have a grammatical function in a sentence.

An interjection may be set off in a sentence by commas.

The message, alas, arrived too late.

For greater emphasis, an interjection can be punctuated as an independent unit, set off with an exclamation point.

Alas! The message arrived too late.

*Note:* Other kinds of words may also be used in isolation. They include *yes, no, hello, good-bye, please,* and *thank you.* All such words, including interjections, are collectively referred to as **isolates.**

CHAPTER 48

# Using Nouns and Pronouns

## Frequently Asked Questions

## 48a Understanding Case

**Case** is the form a noun or pronoun takes to indicate its function in a sentence. Nouns change form only in the possessive case: the *cat's* eyes, *Molly's* book. Pronouns, however, have three cases: *subjective, objective,* and *possessive.*

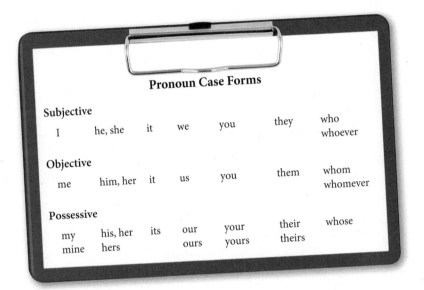

**Pronoun Case Forms**

| | | | | | | |
|---|---|---|---|---|---|---|
| **Subjective** | | | | | | |
| I | he, she | it | we | you | they | who<br>whoever |
| **Objective** | | | | | | |
| me | him, her | it | us | you | them | whom<br>whomever |
| **Possessive** | | | | | | |
| my<br>mine | his, her<br>hers | its | our<br>ours | your<br>yours | their<br>theirs | whose |

### 1 Subjective Case

A pronoun takes the **subjective case** in the following situations.

**Subject of a Verb:** I bought a new cell phone.

**Subject Complement:** It was he who volunteered at the shelter.

### 2 Objective Case

A pronoun takes the **objective case** in the following situations.

**Direct Object:** Our supervisor asked Adam and me to work on the project.

**Indirect Object:** The plumber's bill gave them quite a shock.

**Object of a Preposition:** Between us, we own ten shares of stock.

## Close-Up *I* AND *ME*

*I* is not always more appropriate than *me*. In compound constructions such as the following, *me* is correct.

> Just between you and me [not *I*], I think we're going to have a quiz. (*Me* is the object of the preposition *between*.)

### 3 Possessive Case

A pronoun takes the **possessive case** when it indicates ownership (*our* car, *your* book). The possessive case is also used before a **gerund.**

See 47c2

> Napoleon gave his approval to their ruling Naples. (*His* indicates ownership; *ruling* is a gerund.)

**EXERCISE 1**

Underline the correct form of the pronoun within the parentheses. Be prepared to explain why you chose each form.

***Example:*** Toni Morrison, Alice Walker, and (she, her) are perhaps the most widely recognized African-American women writing today.

1. Both Walt Whitman and (he, him) wrote a great deal of poetry about nature.
2. Our instructor gave Matthew and (me, I) an excellent idea for our project.
3. The sales clerk objected to (me, my) returning the sweater.
4. I understand (you, your) being unavailable to work tonight.
5. The waiter asked Michael and (me, I) to move to another table.

## 48b Determining Pronoun Case in Special Situations

### 1 Comparisons with *Than* or *As*

When a comparison ends with a pronoun, the pronoun's function in the sentence dictates your choice of pronoun case. If the pronoun functions as a subject, use the subjective case; if it functions as an object, use the objective case. You can determine the function of the pronoun by completing the comparison.

> Darcy likes John more than I. (*. . . more than I like John: I* is the subject.)
>
> Darcy likes John more than me. (*. . . more than she likes me: me* is the object.)

### 2 *Who* and *Whom*

The case of the pronouns *who* and *whom* depends on their function *within their own clause*. When a pronoun serves as the subject of its clause, use *who* or *whoever*; when it functions as an object, use *whom* or *whomever*.

The Salvation Army gives food and shelter to whoever is in need. (*Whoever* is the subject of the dependent clause *whoever is in need*.)

I wonder whom jazz musician Miles Davis influenced. (*Whom* is the object of *influenced* in the dependent clause *whom jazz musician Miles Davis influenced*.)

**Close-Up PRONOUN CASE IN QUESTIONS**

To determine whether to use subjective case (*who*) or objective case (*whom*) in a question, use a personal pronoun to answer the question. If the pronoun in your answer is the subject, use *who;* if the pronoun is the object, use *whom*.

Who wrote *The Age of Innocence*? She wrote it. (subject)

Whom do you support for mayor? I support her. (object)

### 3 Appositives

An **appositive** is a noun or noun phrase that identifies or renames an adjacent noun or pronoun. The case of a pronoun in an appositive depends on the function of the word the appositive identifies or renames. ESL 64c4

Two Motown recording artists, he and Smokey Robinson, had contracts with Motown Records. (*Artists* is the subject of the sentence, so the pronoun in the appositive *he and Smokey Robinson* takes the subjective case.)

We heard two Motown recording artists, Smokey Robinson and him. (*Artists* is the object of the verb *heard*, so the pronoun in the appositive *Smokey Robinson and him* takes the objective case.)

### 4 *We* and *Us* before a Noun

When a first-person plural pronoun directly precedes a noun, the case of the pronoun depends on how the noun functions in the sentence.

We women must stick together. (*Women* is the subject of the sentence, so the pronoun *we* must be in the subjective case.)

Teachers make learning easy for <u>us</u> students. (*Students* is the object of the preposition *for,* so the pronoun *us* must be in the objective case.)

**EXERCISE 2**

Using the word in parentheses, combine each pair of sentences into a single sentence. You may change word order and add or delete words.

***Example:*** After he left the band The Police, bass player Sting continued as a solo artist. He once taught middle-school English. (who)

***Revised:*** After he left the band The Police, bass player Sting, who once taught middle-school English, continued as a solo artist.

1. Herb Ritts has photographed world leaders, leading artistic figures in dance and drama, and a vanishing African tribe. He got his start by taking photographs of Hollywood stars. (who)
2. Tim Green has written several novels about a fictional football team. He played for the Atlanta Hawks and has a law degree. (who)
3. Some say Carl Sagan did more to further science education in America than any other person. He wrote many books on science and narrated many popular television shows. (who)
4. Jodie Foster has won two Academy Awards for her acting. She was a child star. (who)
5. Sylvia Plath met fellow poet Ted Hughes at Cambridge University in England. She later married him. (whom)

## 48c Revising Pronoun Reference Errors

ESL 64c1

An **antecedent** is the word or word group to which a pronoun refers. The connection between a pronoun and its antecedent should always be clear. If the <u>**pronoun reference**</u> is not clear, you will need to revise the sentence.

### 1 Ambiguous Antecedent

Sometimes it is not clear to which antecedent a pronoun—for example, *this, that, which,* or *it*—refers. In such cases, eliminate the ambiguity by substituting a noun for the pronoun.

The accountant took out his calculator and added up the list of numbers. Then, he put ~~it~~ *the calculator* into his briefcase. (The pronoun *it* can refer either to *calculator* or to *list of numbers.*)

When you make a promise to give someone a gift, you should keep ~~it.~~ *that promise.* (The pronoun *it* can refer either to *promise* or to *gift.*)

## 2 Remote Antecedent

If a pronoun is far from its antecedent, readers will have difficulty making a connection between them. To eliminate this problem, replace the pronoun with a noun.

During the mid-1800s, many Czechs began to immigrate to America.

By 1860, about 23,000 Czechs had left their country; by 1900, 13,000 Czech immigrants were coming to ~~its~~ *America's* shores each year.

## 3 Nonexistent Antecedent

Sometimes a pronoun—for example, *this*—refers to an antecedent that does not exist. In such cases, add the missing antecedent.

Some one-celled organisms contain chlorophyll yet are considered animals. This *paradox* illustrates the difficulty of classifying single-celled organisms. (Exactly what does *this* refer to?)

*Note:* Colloquial expressions such as "*It* says in the paper" and "*He* said on the news," which refer to unidentified antecedents, are not acceptable in college writing. Substitute the appropriate noun for the unclear pronoun: "*The article in the paper says . . .*"; "*In his commentary, Tom Brokaw observes. . . .*"

## 4 *Who, Which,* and *That*

*Who* is used to refer to people or to animals that have names. *Which* and *that* are used to refer to things or to unnamed animals. When referring to an antecedent, be sure to choose the appropriate pronoun (*who, which,* or *that*).

David Henry Hwang, who wrote the Tony Award-winning play *M. Butterfly*, also wrote *Yellow Face.*

The spotted owl, which lives in old growth forests, is in danger of extinction.

Houses that are built today are usually more energy efficient than those built twenty years ago.

Never use *that* to refer to a person.

The man ~~that~~ *who* holds the world record for eating hot dogs is my neighbor.

*Note:* Be sure to use *which* in **nonrestrictive clauses,** which are always set off with commas, and to use *that* in **restrictive clauses,** which are not set off with commas.

See 53d1

**EXERCISE 3**

Analyze the pronoun reference errors in each of the following sentences. After doing so, revise each sentence by substituting an appropriate noun or noun phrase for the underlined pronoun.

***Example:*** Jefferson asked Lewis to head the expedition, and Lewis selected ~~him~~ *Clark* as his associate. (*Him* refers to a nonexistent antecedent.)

1. The purpose of the expedition was to search out a land route to the Pacific and to gather information about the West. The Louisiana Purchase increased the need for it.
2. The expedition was going to be difficult. They trained the men in Illinois, the starting point.
3. Clark and most of the men who descended the Yellowstone River camped on the bank. It was beautiful and wild.
4. Both Jefferson and Lewis had faith that he would be successful in this transcontinental journey.
5. The expedition was efficient, and only one man was lost. This was extraordinary.

CHAPTER 49

# Using Verbs

## Frequently Asked Questions


- Which verbs are irregular? 637
- What is the difference between *lie* and *lay*? 640
- Is it always better to use the active voice? 647


## 49a Understanding Verb Forms

Every verb has four **principal parts:** a **base form** (the present tense form of the verb used with *I*), a **present participle** (the *-ing* form of the verb), a **past tense form,** and a **past participle.**

Note: The verb *be* is the one exception to this definition; its base form is *be*.

## 1 Regular Verbs

A **regular verb** forms both its past tense and its past participle by adding *-d* or *-ed* to the base form of the verb.

**Principal Parts of Regular Verbs**

| Base Form | Past Tense Form | Past Participle |
|---|---|---|
| smile | smiled | smiled |
| talk | talked | talked |
| jump | jumped | jumped |

## 2 Irregular Verbs

**Irregular verbs** do not follow the pattern discussed above. The chart that follows lists the principal parts of the most frequently used irregular verbs.

**Frequently Used Irregular Verbs**

| Base Form | Past Tense Form | Past Participle |
|---|---|---|
| arise | arose | arisen |
| awake | awoke, awaked | awoken, awaked |
| be | was/were | been |
| beat | beat | beaten |
| begin | began | begun |
| bend | bent | bent |
| bet | bet, betted | bet |
| bite | bit | bitten |
| blow | blew | blown |
| break | broke | broken |
| bring | brought | brought |
| build | built | built |

*(continued)*

**Frequently Used Irregular Verbs** ***(continued)***

| Base Form | Past Tense Form | Past Participle |
|---|---|---|
| burst | burst | burst |
| buy | bought | bought |
| catch | caught | caught |
| choose | chose | chosen |
| cling | clung | clung |
| come | came | come |
| cost | cost | cost |
| deal | dealt | dealt |
| dig | dug | dug |
| dive | dived, dove | dived |
| do | did | done |
| drag | dragged | dragged |
| draw | drew | drawn |
| drink | drank | drunk |
| drive | drove | driven |
| eat | ate | eaten |
| fall | fell | fallen |
| fight | fought | fought |
| find | found | found |
| fly | flew | flown |
| forget | forgot | forgotten, forgot |
| freeze | froze | frozen |
| get | got | gotten |
| give | gave | given |
| go | went | gone |
| grow | grew | grown |
| hang (execute) | hanged | hanged |
| hang (suspend) | hung | hung |
| have | had | had |
| hear | heard | heard |
| keep | kept | kept |
| know | knew | known |
| lay | laid | laid |
| lead | led | led |
| lend | lent | lent |
| let | let | let |
| lie (recline) | lay | lain |
| lie (tell an untruth) | lied | lied |
| make | made | made |
| prove | proved | proved, proven |
| read | read | read |
| ride | rode | ridden |
| ring | rang | rung |
| rise | rose | risen |

| Base Form | Past Tense Form | Past Participle |
|---|---|---|
| run | ran | run |
| say | said | said |
| see | saw | seen |
| set (place) | set | set |
| shake | shook | shaken |
| shrink | shrank, shrunk, | shrunk, shrunken |
| sing | sang | sung |
| sink | sank | sunk |
| sit | sat | sat |
| sneak | sneaked | sneaked |
| speak | spoke | spoken |
| speed | sped, speeded | sped, speeded |
| spin | spun | spun |
| spring | sprang | sprung |
| stand | stood | stood |
| steal | stole | stolen |
| strike | struck | struck, stricken |
| swear | swore | sworn |
| swim | swam | swum |
| swing | swung | swung |
| take | took | taken |
| teach | taught | taught |
| throw | threw | thrown |
| wake | woke, waked | waked, woken |
| wear | wore | worn |
| wring | wrung | wrung |
| write | wrote | written |

## GRAMMAR CHECKER Using Correct Verb Forms

Your grammar checker will highlight incorrect verb forms in your writing and offer revision suggestions.

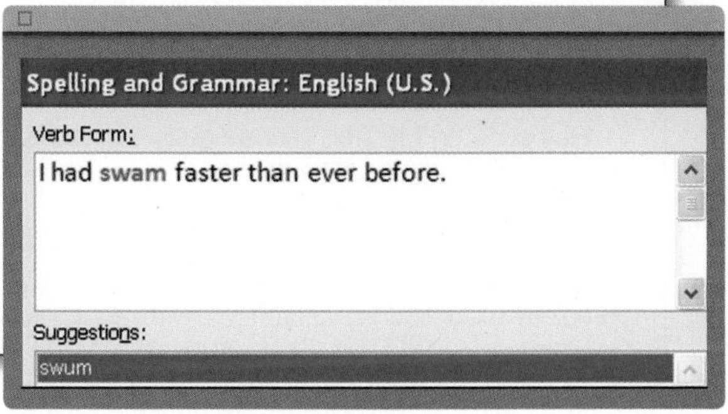
Spelling and Grammar: English (U.S.)
Verb Form:
I had swam faster than ever before.
Suggestions:
swum

## Close-Up *LIE/LAY* AND *SIT/SET*

*Lie* means "to recline" and does not take an object ("He likes to *lie* on the floor"); *lay* means "to place" or "to put" and does take an object ("He wants to *lay* a rug on the floor").

| Base Form | Past Tense Form | Past Participle |
|---|---|---|
| lie | lay | lain |
| lay | laid | laid |

*Sit* means "to assume a seated position" and does not take an object ("She wants to *sit* on the table"); *set* means "to place" or "to put" and usually takes an object ("She wants to *set* a vase on the table").

| Base Form | Past Tense Form | Past Participle |
|---|---|---|
| sit | sat | sat |
| set | set | set |

### EXERCISE 1

Complete each of the sentences in the following paragraph with an appropriate form of the verb in parentheses.

***Example:*** An air of mystery surrounds many of those who have ___*sung*___ (sing) and played the blues.

The legendary bluesman Robert Johnson supposedly ____________ (sell) his soul to the devil in order to become a guitar virtuoso. Myth has it that the young Johnson could barely play his instrument and annoyed other musicians by trying to sit in at clubs, where he ____________ (sneak) onto the bandstand to play every chance he got. He disappeared for a short time, the story goes, and when he returned he was a phenomenal guitarist, having ____________ (swear) a Faustian oath to Satan. Johnson's song "Crossroads Blues"—rearranged and recorded by the sixties band Cream as simply "Crossroads"—supposedly recounts this exchange, telling how Johnson ____________ (deal) with the devil. Some of his other songs, such as "Hellhound on My Trail," are allegedly about the torment he suffered as he ____________ (fight) for his soul.

### EXERCISE 2

Complete the following sentences with appropriate forms of the verbs in parentheses.

***Example:*** Mary Cassatt ___*laid*___ down her paintbrush. (lie, lay)

1. Impressionist artists of the nineteenth century preferred everyday subjects and used to ____________ fruit on a table to paint. (sit, set)
2. They were known for their technique of ____________ dabs of paint quickly on canvas, giving an "impression" of a scene rather than extensive detail. (lying, laying)
3. Claude Monet's *Women in the Garden* featured one woman in the foreground who ____________ on the grass in a garden. (sat, set)
4. In Pierre Auguste Renoir's *Nymphs,* two nude figures talk while ____________ on flowers in a garden. (lying, laying)
5. Paul Cézanne liked to ____________ in front of his subject as he painted and often painted out of doors rather than in a studio. (sit, set)

## 49b Understanding Tense

**Tense** is the form a verb takes to indicate when an action occurred or when a condition existed.

ESL 64a2

**English Verb Tenses**

**Simple Tenses**
Present (I *finish,* she or he *finishes*)
Past (I *finished*)
Future (I *will finish*)

**Perfect Tenses**
Present perfect (I *have finished,* she or he *has finished*)
Past perfect (I had *finished*)
Future perfect (I *will have finished*)

**Progressive Tenses**
Present progressive (I *am finishing,* she or he *is finishing*)
Past progressive (I *was finishing*)
Future progressive (I *will be finishing*)
Present perfect progressive (I *have been finishing*)
Past perfect progressive (I *had been finishing*)
Future perfect progressive (I *will have been finishing*)

## 1 Using the Simple Tenses

The **simple tenses** include *present, past,* and *future.*

- The **present tense** usually indicates an action that is taking place at the time it is expressed in speech or writing. It can also indicate an action that occurs regularly.

  I see your point. (an action taking place when it is expressed)

  We wear wool in the winter. (an action that occurs regularly)

> **Close-Up SPECIAL USES OF THE PRESENT TENSE**
>
> The present tense has four special uses.
>
> **To Indicate Future Time:** The grades arrive next Thursday.
>
> **To State a Generally Held Belief:** Studying pays off.
>
> **To State a Scientific Truth:** An object at rest tends to stay at rest.
>
> **To Discuss a Literary Work:** *Family Installments* tells the story of a Puerto Rican family.

- The **past tense** indicates that an action has already taken place.

  John Glenn orbited the earth three times on February 20, 1962. (an action completed in the past)

  As a young man, Mark Twain traveled through the Southwest. (an action that occurred once or many times in the past but did not extend into the present)

- The **future tense** indicates that an action will or is likely to take place.

  Halley's Comet will reappear in 2061. (a future action that will definitely occur)

  The growth of community colleges will probably continue. (a future action that is likely to occur)

## 2 Using the Perfect Tenses

ESL 64a2

The **perfect tenses** designate actions that were or will be completed before other actions or conditions. The perfect tenses are formed with the appropriate tense form of the auxiliary verb *have* plus the past participle.

- The **present perfect** tense can indicate two types of continuing action beginning in the past.

Dr. Kim has finished studying the effects of BHA on rats. (an action that began in the past and is finished at the present time)

My mother has invested her money wisely. (an action that began in the past and extends into the present)

- The **past perfect** tense indicates an action occurring before a certain time in the past.

  By 1946, engineers had built the first electronic digital computer.

- The **future perfect** tense indicates that an action will be finished by a certain future time.

  By Tuesday, the transit authority will have run out of money.

> **Close-Up** ***COULD HAVE, SHOULD HAVE,* AND *WOULD HAVE***
>
> Do not use the preposition *of* after *would, should, could,* and *might*. Use the auxiliary verb *have* after these words.
>
> I should ~~of~~ *have* left for class earlier.

### 3 Using the Progressive Tenses

ESL 64a2

The progressive tenses express continuing action. They are formed with the appropriate tense of the verb *be* plus the present participle.

- The **present progressive** tense indicates that something is happening at the time it is expressed in speech or writing.

  The volcano is erupting, and lava is flowing toward the town.

- The **past progressive** tense indicates two kinds of past action.

  Roderick Usher's actions were becoming increasingly bizarre. (a continuing action in the past)

  The French revolutionary Marat was stabbed to death while he was bathing. (an action occurring at the same time in the past as another action)

- The **future progressive** tense indicates a continuing action in the future.

  The treasury secretary will be carefully monitoring the money supply.

- The **present perfect progressive** tense indicates action continuing from the past into the present and possibly into the future.

  Rescuers have been working around the clock.

- The **past perfect progressive** tense indicates that a past action went on until another one occurred.

  Before President Kennedy was assassinated, he had been working on civil rights legislation.

- The **future perfect progressive** tense indicates that an action will continue until a certain future time.

  By eleven o'clock we will have been driving for seven hours.

## 4 Using Verb Tenses in a Sentence

Within a sentence, you use different tenses to indicate that actions are taking place at different times. By choosing tenses that accurately express these times, you enable readers to follow the sequence of actions.

- *When a **verb** appears in a dependent clause, its tense depends on the tense of the main verb in the independent clause.* When the main verb in the independent clause is in the past tense, the verb in the dependent clause is usually in the past or past perfect tense. When the main verb in the independent clause is in the past perfect tense, the verb in the dependent clause is usually in the past tense. (When the main verb in the independent clause is in any tense except the past or past perfect, the verb in the dependent clause may be in any tense needed for meaning.)

| **Main Verb** | **Verb in Dependent Clause** |
|---|---|
| George Hepplewhite was (past) an English cabinetmaker | who designed (past) distinctive chair backs. |
| The battle had ended (past perfect) | by the time reinforcements arrived. (past) |

- *When an **infinitive** appears in a verbal phrase, the tense it expresses depends on the tense of the sentence's main verb.* The *present infinitive* (the *to* form of the verb) indicates an action happening at the same time as or later than the main verb. The *perfect infinitive* (*to have* plus the past participle) indicates action happening earlier than the main verb.

| **Main Verb** | **Infinitive** |
|---|---|
| I went | to see the Phillies play last week. (The going and seeing occurred at the same time.) |
| I want | to see the Phillies play tomorrow. (Wanting occurs in the present, and seeing will occur in the future.) |
| I would like | to have seen the Phillies play. (Liking occurs in the present, and seeing would have occurred in the past.) |

- *When a* **participle** *appears in a verbal phrase, its tense depends on the tense of the sentence's main verb.* The *present participle* indicates action happening at the same time as the action of the main verb. The *past participle* or the *present perfect participle* indicates action occurring before the action of the main verb.

| **Participle** | **Main Verb** |
|---|---|
| Addressing the 1896 Democratic Convention, | William Jennings Bryan delivered his Cross of Gold speech. (The addressing and the delivery occurred at the same time.) |
| Having written her term paper, | Camille studied for her history final. (The writing occurred before the studying.) |

## EXERCISE 3

A verb is missing from each of the following sentences. Fill in the form of the verb indicated in parentheses.

***Example:*** The Outer Banks ___*stretch*___ (stretch: present) along the North Carolina coast for more than 175 miles.

1. Many portions of the Outer Banks of North Carolina __________ (give: present) the visitor a sense of history and timelessness.
2. Many students of history __________ (read: present perfect) about the Outer Banks and its mysteries.
3. It was on Roanoke Island in the 1580s that English colonists __________ (establish: past) the first settlement in the New World.
4. That colony vanished soon after it was settled, __________ (become: present participle) known as the famous "lost colony."
5. By 1718, the pirate Blackbeard __________ (made: past perfect) the Outer Banks a hiding place for his treasures.
6. It was at Ocracoke, in fact, that Blackbeard __________ (meet: past) his death.
7. Even today, people __________ (search: present progressive) the Outer Banks for Blackbeard's hidden treasures.
8. The Outer Banks are also famous for Kitty Hawk; even as technology has advanced into the space age, the number of tourists flocking to the site of the Wright brothers' epic flight __________. (grow: present perfect progressive)
9. Long before that famous flight occurred, however, the Outer Banks __________ (claim: past perfect) countless ships along its ever-shifting shores, resulting in its nickname—the "Graveyard of the Atlantic."
10. If the Outer Banks continue to be protected from the ravages of over-development and commercialization, visitors __________ (enjoy: future progressive) the mysteries of this tiny finger of land for years to come.

## 49c Understanding Mood

**Mood** is the form a verb takes to indicate whether a writer is making a statement or asking a question (*indicative mood*), giving a command (*imperative mood*), or expressing a wish or a contrary-to-fact statement (*subjunctive mood*).

- The **indicative** mood expresses an opinion, states a fact, or asks a question: *Jackie Robinson had a great impact on professional baseball.* (The indicative is the mood used in most English sentences.)
- The **imperative** mood is used in commands and direct requests. Usually, the imperative includes only the base form of the verb without a subject: *Use a dictionary.*
- The **subjunctive** mood was common in the past, but now it is used less and less often, and usually only in formal contexts.

### 1 Forming the Subjunctive Mood

The **present subjunctive** uses the base form of the verb, regardless of the subject. The **past subjunctive** has the same form as the past tense of the verb. (However, when *be* is used as an auxiliary verb, it takes the form *were* regardless of the number or person of the subject.)

Dr. Gorman suggested that I study the Cambrian Period. (present subjunctive)

The sign recommended that we be careful. (present subjunctive)

I wish I were going to Europe. (past subjunctive)

### 2 Using the Subjunctive Mood

The present subjunctive may be used in *that* clauses after words such as *ask, suggest, require, demand, recommend,* and *insist.*

The report recommended that juveniles be given mandatory counseling.

Captain Ahab insisted that his crew hunt the white whale.

The past subjunctive may be used in **conditional statements** (statements beginning with *if* that are contrary to fact, including statements that express a wish).

If John were here, he could see Marsha. (John is not here.)

The father acted as if he were having the baby. (The father couldn't be having the baby.)

I wish I were more organized. (expresses a wish)

**Note:** In many situations, the subjunctive mood can sound stiff or formal. To eliminate the need for a subjunctive construction, rephrase the sentence.

*to*

The group asked ~~that~~ the city council ^ ban smoking in public places.

## EXERCISE 4

Complete the sentences in the following paragraph by inserting the appropriate form (indicative, imperative, or subjunctive) of the verb in parentheses. Be prepared to explain your choices.

Harry Houdini was a famous escape artist. He __________ (perform) escapes from every type of bond imaginable: handcuffs, locks, straitjackets, ropes, sacks, and sealed chests underwater. In Germany, workers __________ (challenge) Houdini to escape from a packing box. If he __________ (be) to escape, they would admit that he __________ (be) the best escape artist in the world. Houdini accepted. Before getting into the box, he asked that the observers __________ (give) it a thorough examination. He then asked that a worker __________ (nail) him into the box. "__________ (place) a screen around the box," he ordered after he had been sealed inside. In a few minutes, Houdini __________ (step) from behind the screen. When the workers demanded that they __________ (see) the box, Houdini pulled down the screen. To their surprise, they saw the box with the lid still nailed tightly in place.

## 49d Understanding Voice

**Voice** is the form a verb takes to indicate whether its subject acts or is acted upon. When the subject of a verb does something—that is, acts—the verb is in the **active voice.** When the subject of a verb receives the action—that is, is acted upon—the verb is in the **passive voice.**

**Active Voice:** Hart Crane wrote *The Bridge.*

**Passive Voice:** *The Bridge* was written by Hart Crane.

### Close-Up ACTIVE VS. PASSIVE VOICE

Because the active voice emphasizes the person or thing performing an action, it is usually briefer, clearer, and more emphatic than the passive voice. For this reason, you should generally use the active voice in your college writing.

*(continued)*

**ACTIVE VS. PASSIVE VOICE** *(continued)*

Some situations, however, require use of the passive voice. For example, you should use passive constructions when the actor is unknown or unimportant or when the recipient of an action should logically receive the emphasis.

DDT was found in soil samples. (Passive voice emphasizes the discovery of DDT; who found it is not important.)

Grits are eaten throughout the South. (Passive voice emphasizes the fact that grits are eaten, not those who eat them.)

Note: Some scientific disciplines encourage writers to use the passive voice. The purpose is to convey objectivity—to shift the focus away from the scientists and to emphasize the experimental results.

## 1 Changing Verbs from Passive to Active Voice

You can change a verb from passive to active voice by making the subject of the passive verb the object of the active verb. The person or thing performing the action then becomes the subject of the new sentence.

**Passive:** The novel *Frankenstein* was written by Mary Shelley.

**Active:** Mary Shelley wrote the novel *Frankenstein*.

If a passive verb has no object, you must supply one that will become the subject of the active verb.

**Passive:** Baby elephants are taught to avoid humans. (By whom are baby elephants taught?)

**Active:** Adult elephants teach baby elephants to avoid humans.

## 2 Changing Verbs from Active to Passive Voice

You can change a verb from active to passive voice by making the object of the active verb the subject of the passive verb. The subject of the active verb then becomes the object of the passive verb.

**Active:** Sir James Murray compiled *The Oxford English Dictionary*.

**Passive:** *The Oxford English Dictionary* was compiled by Sir James Murray.

If an active verb does not have an object, it cannot be put into the passive voice. In such cases, you will need to supply an object that can become the subject of the passive sentence.

**Active:** Jacques Cousteau invented.
Cousteau invented ___?___.

**Passive:** ___?___ was invented by Jacques Cousteau.
The scuba was invented by Jacques Cousteau.

## EXERCISE 5

Determine which passive voice sentences in the following paragraph should be in the active voice, and rewrite those sentences.

Rockets were invented by the Chinese about AD 1000. Gunpowder was packed into bamboo tubes and ignited by means of a fuse. These rockets were fired by soldiers at enemy armies and usually caused panic. In thirteenth-century England, an improved form of gunpowder was introduced by Roger Bacon. As a result, rockets were used in battles and were a common—although unreliable—weapon. In the early eighteenth century, a twenty-pound rocket that traveled almost two miles was constructed by William Congreve, an English artillery expert. By the late nineteenth century, thought was given to supersonic speeds by the physicist Ernst Mach, and the sonic boom was predicted by him. The first liquid-fuel rocket was launched by the American Robert Goddard in 1926. A pamphlet written by him anticipated almost all future rocket developments. As a result of his pioneering work, he is known as the father of modern rocketry.

## EXERCISE 6

Determine which active voice sentences in the following paragraph should be in the passive voice, and rewrite those sentences.

The Regent Diamond is one of the world's most famous and coveted jewels. A slave discovered the 410-carat diamond in 1701 in an Indian mine. Over the years, people stole and sold the diamond several times. In 1717, the regent of France bought the diamond for an enormous sum, but during the French Revolution, it disappeared again. Someone later found it in a ditch in Paris. Eventually, Napoleon had the diamond set into his ceremonial sword. At last, when the French monarch fell, the government placed the Regent Diamond in the Louvre, where it remains today.

CHAPTER 50

# Revising Agreement Errors

## Frequently Asked Questions



ESL 64a1

**Agreement** is the correspondence between words in number, gender, and person. Subjects and verbs agree in **number** (singular or plural) and **person** (first, second, or third); pronouns and their antecedents agree in number, person, and **gender** (masculine, feminine, or neuter).

## 50a Making Subjects and Verbs Agree

Singular subjects take singular verbs, and plural subjects take plural verbs.

**Singular:** Hydrogen peroxide is an unstable compound.

**Plural:** Characters are not well developed in O. Henry's short stories.

ESL 64a2

ESL 64c3

Present tense verbs, except *be* and *have,* add *-s* or *-es* when the subject is third-person singular. Third-person singular subjects include nouns; the personal pronouns *he, she, it,* and *one;* and many **indefinite pronouns,** such as *everyone* and *anybody*.

The president has the power to veto congressional legislation.

She frequently cites statistics to support her assertions.

In every group, somebody emerges as a natural leader.

Present tense verbs do not add *-s* or *-es* when the subject is a plural noun, a first-person or second-person pronoun (*I, we, you*), or a third-person plural pronoun (*they*).

Experts recommend that dieters avoid salty processed meat.

In our Bill of Rights, we guarantee all defendants the right to a speedy trial.

At this stratum, you see rocks dating back fifteen million years.

They say that some wealthy people default on their student loans.

In the following special situations, subject-verb agreement can cause problems for writers.

## 1 When Words Come between Subject and Verb

If a modifying phrase comes between subject and verb, the verb should agree with the subject, not with the last word in the modifying phrase.

The sound of the drumbeats builds in intensity in Eugene O'Neill's play *The Emperor Jones.*

The games won by the intramural team are usually few and far between.

Note: This rule also applies to phrases introduced by *along with, as well as, in addition to, including,* and *together with*: *Heavy rain, together with high winds, causes hazardous driving conditions.*

## 2 When Compound Subjects Are Joined by *And*

Compound subjects joined by *and* usually take plural verbs.

Navigation systems and antilock brakes are standard on most new cars.

There are, however, two exceptions to this rule:

- Compound subjects joined by *and* that stand for a single idea or person are treated as a unit and take singular verbs.

  Rhythm and blues is a forerunner of rock and roll.

- When *each* or *every* precedes a compound subject joined by *and,* the subject takes a singular verb.

  Every desk and file cabinet was searched before the letter was found.

## 3 When Compound Subjects Are Joined by *Or*

Compound subjects joined by *or* (or by *either . . . or* or *neither . . . nor*) may take either a singular or a plural verb.

If both subjects are singular, use a singular verb; if both subjects are plural, use a plural verb. If one subject is singular and the other is plural, the verb agrees with the subject that is nearer to it.

Either radiation treatments or chemotherapy is combined with surgery for the most effective results. (Singular verb agrees with *chemotherapy*.)

Either chemotherapy or radiation treatments are combined with surgery for effective results. (Plural verb agrees with *treatments*.)

### 4 When Indefinite Pronouns Serve as Subjects

ESL 64c3

Most indefinite pronouns—*another, anyone, everyone, one, each, either, neither, anything, everything, something, nothing, nobody,* and *somebody*—are always singular and take singular verbs.

Anyone is welcome to apply for this grant.

Each of the chapters includes a review exercise.

Some indefinite pronouns—*both, many, few, several, others*—are always plural and take plural verbs.

Several of the articles are useful for my research.

A few indefinite pronouns—*some, all, any, more, most,* and *none*—can be singular or plural, depending on the noun they refer to.

Of course, some of this trouble is to be expected. (*Some* refers to *trouble*.)

Some of the spectators are getting restless. (*Some* refers to *spectators*.)

**GRAMMAR CHECKER Subject-Verb Agreement**

Your grammar checker will highlight and offer revision suggestions for many subject-verb agreement errors, including errors in sentences that have indefinite pronoun subjects.

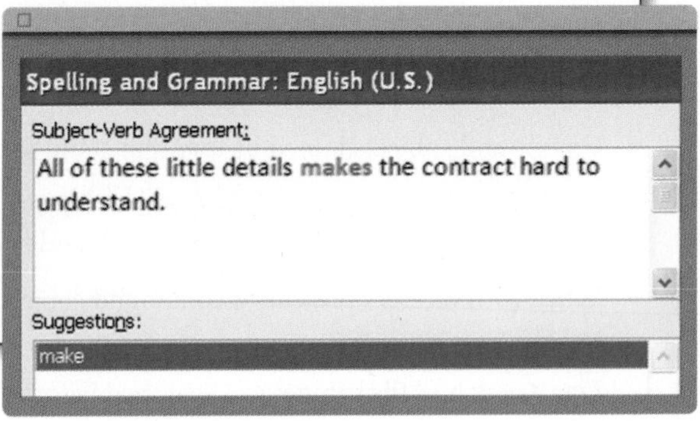
Spelling and Grammar: English (U.S.)
Subject-Verb Agreement:
All of these little details makes the contract hard to understand.
Suggestions:
make

**ESL TIP**

In British English, which you may have learned if you took ESL classes outside the United States, collective nouns tend to take plural verbs more often than they do in American English: *Management are considering giving workers a bonus.*

### 5 When Collective Nouns Serve as Subjects

A **collective noun** names a group of persons or things—for instance, *navy, union, association, band.* When it refers to a group as a unit (as it usually does), a collective noun takes a singular verb; when it refers to the individuals or items that make up the group, it takes a plural verb.

To many people, the royal family symbolizes Great Britain. (The family, as a unit, is the symbol.)

The family all eat at different times. (Each member eats separately.)

Note: If a plural verb sounds awkward with a collective noun, reword the sentence: *Family members all eat at different times.*

Phrases that name fixed amounts—*three-quarters, twenty dollars, the majority*—are treated like collective nouns. When the amount denotes a unit, it takes a singular verb; when it denotes part of the whole, it takes a plural verb.

Three-quarters of his usual salary is not enough to live on. (*Three-quarters* denotes a unit.)

Three-quarters of workshop participants improve dramatically. (*Three-quarters* denotes part of the group.)

Note: *The number* is always singular, and *a number* is always plural: *The number of voters has declined. A number of students have missed the opportunity to preregister.*

### 6 When Singular Subjects Have Plural Forms

A singular subject takes a singular verb, even if the form of the subject is plural.

Politics makes strange bedfellows.

Statistics deals with the collection, classification, analysis, and interpretation of data.

When such a word has a plural meaning, however, use a plural verb.

Her politics are too radical for her parents. (*Politics* refers not to the science of political government but, rather, to political principles or opinions.)

The statistics prove him wrong. (*Statistics* denotes not a body of knowledge but the numerical facts or data themselves.)

Note: Some words retain their Latin **plural** forms, which do not look like English plural forms. Be particularly careful to use the correct verbs with such words: *criterion is, criteria are; medium is, media are; bacterium is, bacteria are.* See 46b8

### 7 When Subject-Verb Order Is Inverted

Even when **word order** is inverted so that the verb comes before the subject (as it does in questions and in sentences beginning with *there is* or *there are*), the subject and verb must agree. ESL 64f

Is either answer correct?

There is a monument to Emiliano Zapata in Mexico City.

There are currently thirteen federal circuit courts of appeals.

### 8 With Linking Verbs

See 47c1

A **linking verb** should agree with its subject, not with the subject complement.

The problem was termites.

Here, the verb *was* correctly agrees with the subject *problem,* not with the subject complement *termites.* If *termites* were the subject, the verb would be plural.

Termites were the problem.

### 9 With Relative Pronouns

See 47b

When you use a **relative pronoun** (*who, which, that,* and so on) to introduce a dependent clause, the verb in that clause should agree in number with the pronoun's **antecedent** (the word to which the pronoun refers).

The farmer is among the ones who suffer during a grain embargo.
(Verb *suffer* agrees with plural antecedent *ones.*)

The farmer is the only one who suffers during a grain embargo.
(Verb *suffers* agrees with singular antecedent *one.*)

## EXERCISE 1

Each of these ten correct sentences illustrates one of the conventions just explained. Read each sentence carefully, and explain why each verb form is used.

***Example:*** Obedience in our schools is at an all-time low. (The verb is singular because *obedience,* not *schools,* is the subject.)

1. Jack Kerouac, along with Allen Ginsberg and William S. Burroughs, was a major figure in the "beat" movement.
2. Every American boy and girl needs to learn basic computational skills.
3. Aesthetics is not an exact science.
4. The audience was restless.
5. The Beatles' *Sergeant Pepper* album is one of those albums that remain popular long after they are issued.
6. All is quiet.
7. The subject was contagious diseases.
8. When he was young, Benjamin Franklin's primary concern was books.
9. Eighty dollars is too much to spend on one concert ticket.
10. "There are more things in heaven and earth, Horatio, than are dreamt of in your philosophy."

**EXERCISE 2**

Some of the following sentences are correct, but others contain common errors in subject-verb agreement. If a sentence is correct, mark it with a *C;* if it has an error, correct it.

1. *I Love Lucy* is one of those television shows that almost all Americans have seen at least once.
2. The committee presented their findings to the president.
3. Neither Western novels nor science fiction appeal to me.
4. Stage presence and musical ability makes a rock performer successful today.
5. *It's a Wonderful Life,* like many classic holiday movies, seems to be shown on television every year.
6. Hearts are my grandmother's favorite card game.
7. The best part of B. B. King's songs are the guitar solos.
8. Time and tide waits for no man.
9. Sports are my main pastime.
10. The lives of famous artists like Vincent Van Gogh interests many people.

## 50b Making Pronouns and Antecedents Agree

A pronoun must agree with its **antecedent**—the word or word group to which the pronoun refers. See 47b

Singular pronouns—such as *he, him, she, her, it, me, myself,* and *oneself*—should refer to singular antecedents. Plural pronouns—such as *we, us, they, them,* and *their*—should refer to plural antecedents. ESL 64c

In the following special situations, pronoun-antecedent agreement can present challenges for writers.

### 1 With Compound Antecedents

In most cases, use a plural pronoun to refer to a **compound antecedent** (two or more antecedents connected by *and* or *or*).

> Mormonism and Christian Science were influenced in their beginnings by Shaker doctrines.

However, this rule has several exceptions:

- If a compound antecedent denotes a single unit—one person, thing, or idea—use a singular pronoun to refer to the compound antecedent.

  > In 1904, the husband and father brought his family from Germany to the United States.

- Use a singular pronoun when a compound antecedent is preceded by *each* or *every.*

  > Every programming language and software application has its limitations.

- Use a singular pronoun to refer to two or more singular antecedents linked by *or* or *nor*.

  Neither Thoreau nor Whitman lived to see his work read widely.

- When one part of a compound antecedent is singular and one part is plural, the pronoun agrees in person and number with the antecedent that is nearer to it.

  Neither Dana nor her parents had their seatbelts fastened.

### 2 With Collective Noun Antecedents

If the meaning of the collective noun antecedent is singular (as it will be in most cases), use a singular pronoun. If the meaning is plural, use a plural pronoun.

The nurses' union announced its plan to strike. (All the members acted as one.)

The team ran onto the court and took their positions. (Each member acted individually.)

### 3 With Collective Noun Antecedents

See 50a4

Most **indefinite pronouns**—*each, either, neither, one, anyone,* and the like—are singular and require singular pronouns.

ESL 64c3

Neither of the men had his proposal ready by the deadline.

Each of these neighborhoods has its own traditions and values.

**Close-Up** PRONOUN-ANTECEDENT AGREEMENT

In speech and in informal writing, many people use the plural pronouns *they* or *their* with singular indefinite pronouns that refer to people, such as *someone, everyone,* and *nobody.*

**Informal:** Everyone can present their own viewpoint.

In college writing, however, you should avoid using a plural pronoun to refer to a singular subject. Instead, you can use both the masculine and the feminine pronoun.

**Correct:** Everyone can present his or her own viewpoint.

Or, you can make the sentence's subject plural.

**Correct:** All participants can present their own viewpoints.

The use of *his* alone to refer to a singular indefinite pronoun (*Everyone can present his own viewpoint)* is considered **sexist language**.

See 45e2

**GRAMMAR CHECKER Pronoun-Antecedent Agreement**

Your grammar checker will highlight and offer revision suggestions for many pronoun-antecedent agreement errors.

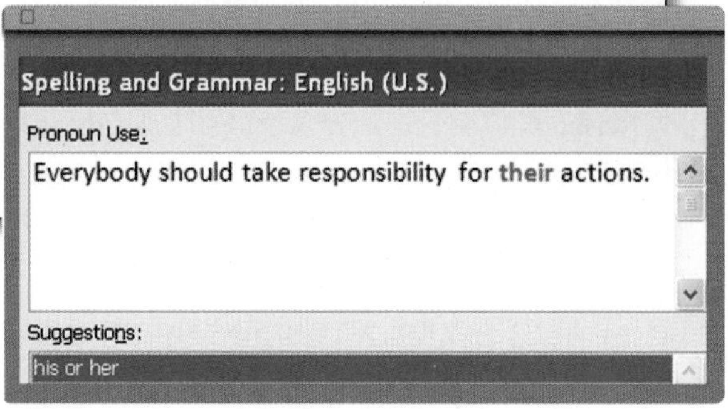
Spelling and Grammar: English (U.S.)
Pronoun Use:
Everybody should take responsibility for their actions.
Suggestions:
his or her

## EXERCISE 3

In the following sentences, find and correct any errors in subject-verb or pronoun-antecedent agreement.

1. The core of a computer is a collection of electronic circuits that are called the central processing unit (CPU).
2. Computers, because of advanced technology that allows the central processing unit to be placed on a chip, a thin square of semiconducting material about one-quarter of an inch on each side, has been greatly reduced in size.
3. Before broadband technologies, computers could "talk" to each other over phone lines through a modem, an acronym for *modulator-demodulator*.
4. Pressing keys on keyboards resembling typewriter keyboards generate electronic signals that are input for the computer.
5. Computers have built-in memory storage, and equipment such as discs or tapes provide external memory.
6. RAM (random-access memory), the erasable and reusable computer memory, hold the computer program, the computations executed by the program, and the results.
7. After computer programs are "read" from a disc or tape, the computer uses the instructions as needed to execute the program.
8. ROM (read-only memory), the permanent memory that is "read" by the computer but cannot be changed, are used to store programs that are needed frequently.
9. A number of video games with impressive graphics, sound, and color is available for home computers.
10. Although some computer users write their own programs, most buy ready-made software programs such as the ones that allows a computer to be used as a word processor.

## EXERCISE 4

The sentences below illustrate correct subject-verb and pronoun-antecedent agreement. Following the instructions in parentheses after each sentence, revise each so its verbs and pronouns agree with the newly created subject.

***Example:*** One child in ten suffers from a learning disability. (Change *One child in ten* to *Ten percent of all children*.)

***Revised:*** Ten percent of all children suffer from a learning disability.

1. The governess is seemingly pursued by evil as she tries to protect Miles and Flora from those she feels seek to possess the children's souls. (Change *The governess* to *The governess and the cook*.)
2. Insulin-dependent diabetics are now able to take advantage of new technology that can help alleviate their symptoms. (Change *diabetics* to *the diabetic.*)
3. All homeowners in coastal regions worry about the possible effects of a hurricane on their property. (Change *All homeowners* to *Every homeowner*.)
4. Federally funded job-training programs offer unskilled workers an opportunity to acquire skills they can use to secure employment. (Change *workers* to *the worker*.)
5. Foreign imports pose a major challenge to the American textile market. (Change *Foreign imports* to *The foreign import*.)
6. *Brideshead Revisited* tells how one family and its devotion to its Catholic faith influence Charles Ryder. (Delete *and its devotion to its Catholic faith.*)
7. *Writer's Digest* and *The Writer* are designed to aid writers as they seek markets for their work. (Change *writers* to *the writer.*)
8. Most American families have access to television; in fact, more have televisions than have indoor plumbing. (Change *Most American families* to *Almost every American family*.)
9. In Montana, it seems as though every town's elevation is higher than its population. (Change *every town's elevation* to *all the towns' elevations*.)
10. A woman without a man is like a fish without a bicycle. (Change *A woman/a man* to *Women/men*.)

CHAPTER 51

# Using Adjectives and Adverbs

## Frequently Asked Questions



## 51a Understanding Adjectives and Adverbs

**Adjectives** modify nouns and pronouns. **Adverbs** modify verbs, adjectives, or other adverbs—or entire phrases, clauses, or sentences. Both adjectives and adverbs describe, limit, or qualify other words, phrases, or clauses.

The function of a word in a sentence, not its form, determines whether it is an adjective or an adverb. Although many adverbs (such as *immediately* and *hopelessly*) end in *-ly*, others (such as *almost* and *very*) do not. Moreover, some words that end in *-ly* (such as *lively*) are adjectives.

**ESL TIP**

For information on correct placement of adjectives and adverbs in a sentence, **see 64d1.** For information on correct order of adjectives in a series, **see 64d2.**

## 51b Using Adjectives

Be sure to use an **adjective**—not an adverb—as a subject complement. A **subject complement** is a word that follows a linking verb and modifies the sentence's subject, not its verb. A **linking verb** does not show physical or emotional action. *Seem, appear, believe, become, grow, turn, remain, prove, look, sound, smell, taste, feel,* and the forms of the verb *be* are (or can be used as) linking verbs.

> Michelle seemed brave. (*Seemed* shows no action, so it is a linking verb. Because *brave* is a subject complement that modifies the subject *Michelle*, it takes the adjective form.)

Michelle smiled bravely. (*Smiled* shows action, so it is not a linking verb. *Bravely* modifies *smiled*, so it takes the adverb form.)

**Note:** Sometimes the same verb can function as either a linking verb or an action verb: *He remained stubborn.* (He was still stubborn.) *He remained stubbornly.* (He remained, in a stubborn manner.)

Use an adjective—not an adverb—as an **object complement,** a word that follows a sentence's direct object and modifies that object and not the verb. Objects are nouns or pronouns, so their modifiers must be adjectives.

Most people called him timid. (People consider him to be timid; here *timid* is an object complement that modifies *him*, the sentence's direct object, so the adjective form is correct.)

Most people called him timidly. (People were timid when they called him; here *timidly* modifies the verb *called*—not the object—so the adverb form is correct.)

## 51c Using Adverbs

Be sure to use an **adverb**—not an adjective—to modify verbs, adjectives, or other adverbs—or entire phrases, clauses, or sentences.

*very well*
Most students did ~~great~~ on the midterm.

*conservatively*
My friends dress a lot more ~~conservative~~ than I do.

### Close-Up USING ADJECTIVES AND ADVERBS

In informal speech, adjective forms such as *good, bad, sure, real, slow, quick,* and *loud* are often used to modify verbs, adjectives, and adverbs. Avoid these informal modifiers in college writing.

*really well*
The program ran ~~real good~~ the first time we tried it, but the new system
*badly*
performed ~~bad~~.

### EXERCISE 1

Revise each of the incorrect sentences in the following paragraph so that only adjectives modify nouns and pronouns and only adverbs modify verbs, adjectives, or other adverbs.

A popular self-help trend in the United States today is recorded motivational lectures. These recordings, with titles like *How to Attract Love, Freedom from Acne,* and *I Am a Genius,* are intended to address every problem known to modern society—and to solve these problems quick and easy. The lectures are said to work because they contain "hidden messages" that bypass conscious defense mechanisms. The listener hears only music or relaxing sounds, like waves rolling slow and steady. At decibel levels perceived only subconsciously, positive words and phrases are embedded, usually by someone who speaks deep and rhythmic. The top-selling lectures are those that help listeners lose weight or quit smoking. The popularity of such material is not hard to understand. They promise easy solutions to complex problems. But the main benefit of these lectures appears to be for the sellers, who are accumulating profits real fast.

### EXERCISE 2

Being careful to use adjectives—not adverbs—as subject complements and object complements, write five sentences in imitation of each of the following sentences. Consult the list of linking verbs in **47c1,** and use a different linking verb in each of your sentences.

1. Julie looked worried.
2. Dan considers his collection valuable.

## 51d Using Comparative and Superlative Forms

Most adjectives and adverbs have **comparative** and **superlative** forms.

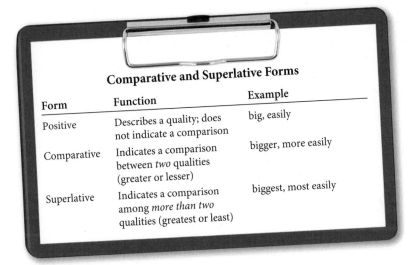

**Comparative and Superlative Forms**

| Form | Function | Example |
|---|---|---|
| Positive | Describes a quality; does not indicate a comparison | big, easily |
| Comparative | Indicates a comparison between *two* qualities (greater or lesser) | bigger, more easily |
| Superlative | Indicates a comparison among *more than two* qualities (greatest or least) | biggest, most easily |

### 1 Regular Comparative Forms

To form the comparative, all one-syllable adjectives and many two-syllable adjectives (particularly those that end in *-y, -ly, -le, -er,* and *-ow*) add *-er: slower, funnier*. (Note that a final *y* becomes *i* before *-er* is added.)

Other two-syllable adjectives and all long adjectives form the comparative with *more: more famous, more incredible.*

Adverbs ending in *-ly* also form the comparative with *more: more slowly.* Other adverbs use the *-er* ending to form the comparative: *sooner*.

All adjectives and adverbs indicate a lesser degree with *less: less lovely, less slowly*.

### 2 Regular Superlative Forms

Adjectives that form the comparative with *-er* add *-est* to form the superlative: *nicest, funniest*. Adjectives that indicate the comparative with *more* use *most* to indicate the superlative: *most famous, most challenging.*

The majority of adverbs use *most* to indicate the superlative: *most quickly*. Others use the *-est* ending: *soonest*.

All adjectives and adverbs use *least* to indicate the least degree: *least interesting, least willingly.*

**Close-Up** USING COMPARATIVES AND SUPERLATIVES

- Never use both *more* and *-er* to form the comparative or both *most* and *-est* to form the superlative.

  Nothing could have been ~~more~~ easier.

  Jack is the ~~most~~ meanest person in town.

- Never use the superlative when comparing only two things.

  Stacy is the *older* ~~oldest~~ of the two sisters.

- Never use the comparative when comparing more than two things.

  We chose the *earliest* ~~earlier~~ of the four appointments.

### 3 Irregular Comparatives and Superlatives

Some adjectives and adverbs have irregular comparative and superlative forms.

**Irregular Comparatives and Superlatives**

| | Positive | Comparative | Superlative |
|---|---|---|---|
| **Adjectives:** | good | better | best |
| | bad | worse | worst |
| | a little | less | least |
| | many, some, much | more | most |
| **Adverbs:** | well | better | best |
| | badly | worse | worst |

## 51e Avoiding Illogical Comparatives and Superlatives

Many adjectives—for example, *perfect, unique, excellent, impossible, parallel, empty,* and *dead*—are **absolutes** and therefore can have no comparative or superlative forms.

> "The Case of Amontillado" is a ~~more excellent~~ *better* story than "The Tell-Tale Heart."

> I saw ~~the most~~ *a* unique vase in the museum.

These words can, however, be modified by words that suggest approaching the absolute state—*nearly* or *almost,* for example.

> He revised until his draft was almost perfect.

*Note:* Some adverbs, particularly those indicating time, place, and degree (*almost, very, here, immediately*), do not have comparative or superlative forms.

### EXERCISE 3

Supply the correct comparative and superlative forms for each of the following adjectives or adverbs. Then, use each form in a sentence.

***Example:*** strange stranger strangest

The story had a *strange* ending.
The explanation sounded *stranger* each time I heard it.
This is the *strangest* gadget I have ever seen.

1. difficult
2. eccentric
3. confusing
4. bad
5. mysterious
6. softly
7. embarrassing
8. well
9. often
10. tiny

PART 13

# Understanding Punctuation and Mechanics

## OVERVIEW OF SENTENCE PUNCTUATION: COMMAS, SEMICOLONS, COLONS, DASHES, PARENTHESES

(Further explanations and examples are located in the sections listed in parentheses after each example.)

### SEPARATING INDEPENDENT CLAUSES

**With a Comma and a Coordinating Conjunction**

The House approved the bill, but the Senate rejected it. (**53a**)

**With a Semicolon**

Paul Revere's *The Boston Massacre* is traditional American protest art; Edward Hicks's paintings are socially conscious art with a religious strain. (**54a**)

**With a Semicolon and a Transitional Word or Phrase**

Thomas Jefferson brought two hundred vanilla beans and a recipe for vanilla ice cream back from France; thus, he gave America its all-time favorite ice-cream flavor. (**47a**)

**With a Colon**

A *U.S. News & World Report* survey has revealed a surprising fact: Americans spend more time at malls than anywhere else except at home and at work. (**57a2**)

### SEPARATING ITEMS IN A SERIES

**With Commas**

*Chipmunk*, *raccoon*, and *Mugwump* are Native American words. (**53b1**)

**With Semicolons**

Laramie, Wyoming; Wyoming, Delaware; and Delaware, Ohio were three of the places they visited. (**54c**)

### SETTING OFF EXAMPLES, EXPLANATIONS, OR SUMMARIES

**With a Colon**

She had one dream: to play professional basketball. (**57a2**)

**With a Dash**

"Study hard," "Respect your elders," "Don't talk with your mouth full"—Sharon had often heard her parents say these things. (**50b2**)

### SETTING OFF NONESSENTIAL MATERIAL

**With a Single Comma**

His fear increasing, he waited to enter the haunted house. (**53d4**)

**With a Pair of Commas**

Mark McGwire, not Sammy Sosa, was the first to break Roger Maris's home run record. (**53d3**)

**With Dashes**

Neither of the boys—both nine-year-olds—had any history of violence. (**57b1**)

**With Parentheses**

In some European countries (notably Sweden and France), high-quality day care is offered at little or no cost to parents. (**57c1**)

CHAPTER 52

# Using End Punctuation

## Frequently Asked Questions



## 52a Using Periods

### 1 Ending a Sentence

Use a period to signal the end of a statement, a mild command or polite request, or an indirect question.

Something is rotten in Denmark. (statement)

Be sure to have the oil checked before you start out. (mild command)

When the bell rings, please exit in an orderly fashion. (polite request)

They wondered whether the water was safe to drink. (indirect question)

### 2 Marking an Abbreviation

Use a period in most abbreviations.

| | | |
|---|---|---|
| Mr. Spock | 1600 Pennsylvania Ave. | 9 p.m. |
| Dr. Who | Aug. | etc. |

If an abbreviation ends the sentence, do not add another period.

He promised to be there at 6 a.m./

However, do add a question mark if the sentence is a question.

Did he arrive at 6 p.m.?

If the abbreviation falls *within* a sentence, use normal punctuation after the period.

He promised to be there at 6 p.m., but he forgot.

## Close-Up ABBREVIATIONS WITHOUT PERIODS

Abbreviations composed of all capital letters do not usually require periods unless they are the initials of people's names (E. B. White).

TMZ NYPD NFL PTSD ADHD

Familiar abbreviations of the names of corporations or government agencies and abbreviations of scientific and technical terms do not require periods.

EPA DNA FAA CD-ROM

**Acronyms**—new words formed from the initial letters or first few letters of a series of words—do not include periods.

| | | | |
|---|---|---|---|
| modem | op-ed | scuba | radar |
| OSHA | AIDS | NAFTA | CAT scan |

**Clipped forms** (commonly accepted shortened forms of words, such as *flu, dorm, math,* and *fax*) do not include periods.

**Postal abbreviations** do not include periods.

NY CA MS FL TX

### 3 Marking Divisions in Dramatic, Poetic, and Biblical References

Use periods to separate act, scene, and line numbers in plays; book and line numbers in long poems; and chapter and verse numbers in biblical references. (Do not space between the periods and the elements they separate.)

**Dramatic Reference:** *Hamlet* 2.2.1–5

**Poetic Reference:** *Paradise Lost* 7.163–67

**Biblical Reference:** Judges 4.14

*Note:* In MLA parenthetical references, titles of literary and biblical works are often abbreviated: (***Ham.* 2.2.1-5**); (**Judg. 4.14**).

See 18a1

### 4 Marking Divisions in Electronic Addresses

Periods, along with other punctuation marks (such as slashes and colons), are also used in electronic addresses (URLs).

http://cengage.com/english/kirsznermandell

*Note:* When you type a URL, do not follow it with a period or add spaces after periods within the address.

**EXERCISE 1**

Correct these sentences by adding missing periods and deleting unnecessary ones. If a sentence is correct, mark it with a *C*.

***Example:*** Their mission changed the war.

1. Julius Caesar was killed in 44 B.C.
2. Dr. McLaughlin worked hard to earn his Ph.D..
3. Carmen was supposed to be at A.F.L.-C.I.O. headquarters by 2 p.m.; however, she didn't get there until 10 p.m.
4. After she studied the fall lineup proposed by N.B.C., she decided to work for C.B.S.
5. Representatives from the U.M.W. began collective bargaining after an unsuccessful meeting with Mr. L Pritchard, the coal company's representative.

## 52b Using Question Marks

### 1 Marking the End of a Direct Question

Use a question mark to signal the end of a direct question.

Who was at the door?

### 2 Marking Questionable Dates and Numbers

Use a question mark in parentheses to indicate uncertainty about a date or number.

Aristophanes, the Greek playwright, was born in 448 (?) BC and died in 380 (?) BC.

### 3 Editing Misused Question Marks

Use a period, not a question mark, with an **indirect question** (a question that is not quoted directly).

The personnel officer asked whether he knew how to type~~?~~.

Do not use a question mark to convey sarcasm. Instead, suggest your attitude through your choice of words.

I refused his *not very* generous ~~(?)~~ offer.

*Note:* Never use more than one question mark to end a sentence.

**EXERCISE 2**

Correct the use of question marks and other punctuation in the following sentences.

***Example:*** She asked whether Freud's theories were accepted during his lifetime?.

1. He wondered whether he should take a nine o'clock class?
2. The instructor asked, "Was the Spanish-American War a victory for America."
3. Are they really going to China??!!
4. He took a modest (?) portion of dessert—half a pie.
5. "Is *data* the plural of *datum*?," he inquired.

## 52c Using Exclamation Points

Use an exclamation point to signal the end of an emotional or emphatic statement, an emphatic interjection, or a forceful command.

Remember the *Maine*!

"No! Don't leave!" he cried.

*Note:* Except for recording dialogue, exclamation points are almost never appropriate in college writing. Even in informal writing, use exclamation points sparingly—and never use two or more in a row.

**EXERCISE 3**

Add appropriate punctuation to this passage.

Dr Craig and his group of divers paused at the shore, staring respectfully at the enormous lake Who could imagine what terrors lay beneath its surface Which of them might not emerge alive from this adventure Would it be Col Cathcart Capt Wilks, the MD from the naval base Her husband, P L Fox Or would they all survive the task ahead Dr Craig decided some encouraging remarks were in order

"Attention divers," he said in a loud, forceful voice "May I please have your attention The project which we are about to undertake—"

"Oh, no" screamed Mr Fox suddenly "Look out It's the Loch Ness Monster"

"Quick" shouted Dr Craig "Move away from the shore" But his warning came too late

CHAPTER 53

# Using Commas

## Frequently Asked Questions



## 53a Setting Off Independent Clauses

See 47g

Use a comma when you form a compound sentence by linking two independent clauses with a coordinating conjunction or a pair of correlative conjunctions.

The House approved the bill, but the Senate rejected it.

Either the hard drive is full, or the modem is too slow.

**Note:** You may omit the comma if two clauses connected by a coordinating conjunction are very short: *Seek and ye shall find. Love it or leave it.*

### Close-Up SEPARATING INDEPENDENT CLAUSES

See 54b

Use a semicolon—not a comma—to separate two independent clauses linked by a coordinating conjunction when at least one of the clauses already contains a comma or when the clauses are especially complex.

The tourists visited Melbourne, the capital of Australia, for three days; and they toured Wellington, New Zealand, for two.

### EXERCISE 1

Combine each of the following sentence pairs into one compound sentence, adding commas where necessary.

***Example:*** Emergency medicine became an approved medical specialty in 1979/ ~~Now~~/ , and now pediatric emergency medicine is becoming increasingly important. (and)

1. The Pope did not hesitate to visit Cuba. He did not hesitate to meet with President Fidel Castro. (nor)
2. Agents place brand-name products in prominent positions in films. The products are seen and recognized by large audiences. (and)
3. Unisex insurance rates may have some drawbacks for women. These rates may be very beneficial. (or)
4. Cigarette advertising no longer appears on television. It does appear in print media. (but)
5. Dorothy Day founded the Catholic Worker movement in the 1930s. Her followers still dispense free food, medical care, and legal advice to the needy. (and)

## 53b Setting Off Items in a Series

### 1 Coordinate Elements

Use commas between items in a series of three or more **coordinate elements** (words, phrases, or clauses joined by a coordinating conjunction).

*Chipmunk*, *raccoon*, and *Mugwump* are Native American words.

You may pay by check, with a credit card, or in cash.

Brazilians speak Portuguese, Colombians speak Spanish, and Haitians speak French and Creole.

*Note:* To avoid ambiguity, always use a comma before the *and* (or other coordinating conjunction) that separates the last two items in a series: *He was inspired by his parents, the Dalai Lama, and Mother Teresa.*

*Note:* If phrases or clauses in a series already contain commas, use semicolons to separate the items.

See 54c

### 2 Coordinate Adjectives

Use a comma between items in a series of two or more **coordinate adjectives**—adjectives that modify the same word or word group—unless they are joined by a conjunction.

> **ESL TIP**
> If you have difficulty determining the correct order of adjectives in a series, **see 64d2.**

She brushed her long, shining hair.

The baby was tired and cranky and wet. (no commas required)

CHECKLIST

### Punctuating Adjectives in a Series

- ❑ If you can reverse the order of the adjectives or insert *and* between the adjectives without changing the meaning, the adjectives are coordinate, and you should use a comma.

  She brushed her long, shining hair.

  She brushed her shining, long hair.

  She brushed her long [and] shining hair.

- ❑ If you cannot reverse the order of the adjectives or insert *and,* the adjectives are not coordinate, and you should not use a comma.

  Ten red balloons fell from the ceiling.

  Red ten balloons fell from the ceiling.

  Ten [and] red balloons fell from the ceiling.

Note: Numbers—such as *ten*—are not coordinate with other adjectives.

## EXERCISE 2

Correct the use of commas in the following sentences, adding or deleting commas where necessary. If a sentence is punctuated correctly, mark it with a *C*.

***Example:*** Neither dogs, snakes, bees, nor dragons frighten her.

1. Seals, whales, dogs, lions, and horses, all are mammals.
2. Mammals are warm-blooded vertebrates that bear live young, nurse them, and usually have fur.
3. Seals are mammals, but lizards, and snakes, and iguanas are reptiles, and salamanders are amphibians.
4. Amphibians also include frogs, and toads and newts.
5. Eagles geese ostriches turkeys chickens and ducks are classified as birds.

## EXERCISE 3

Add two coordinate adjectives to modify each of the following phrases, inserting commas where required.

***Example:*** *strong, beautiful* ^classical music

1. distant thunder
2. silver spoon
3. New York Yankees
4. miniature golf
5. Rolling Stones
6. loving couple
7. computer science
8. wheat bread
9. art museum
10. new math

## 53c Setting Off Introductory Elements

In most cases, an introductory element is followed by a comma. If the sentence's meaning will be clear without it, the comma can be omitted. When in doubt, however, you should include the comma.

### 1 Dependent Clauses

A **dependent clause** that begins a sentence is generally set off from the rest of the sentence by a comma.

Although the CIA used to call undercover agents *penetration agents*, they now routinely refer to them as *moles*.

When war came to Baghdad, many victims were children.

If a dependent clause is short and designates time, you may omit the comma—provided the sentence will be clear without it.

When I exercise I drink plenty of water.

*Note:* Do not use a comma to set off a dependent clause at the *end* of a sentence: *I drink plenty of water/ when I exercise.*

See 53g8

### 2 Verbal and Prepositional Phrases

An introductory **verbal phrase** is usually set off by a comma.

Thinking that this might be his last chance, Peary struggled toward the North Pole. (participial phrase)

To write well, one must read a lot. (infinitive phrase)

**Close-Up USING COMMAS WITH VERBAL PHRASES**

A verbal phrase that serves as a subject is not set off by a comma.

See 35b1

Laughing out loud/ can release tension. (gerund phrase)

To know him/ is to love him. (infinitive phrase)

An introductory **prepositional phrase** is also usually set off by a comma.

During the Depression, movie attendance rose. (prepositional phrase)

However, if an introductory prepositional phrase is short and no ambiguity is possible, you may omit the comma.

After lunch I took a four-hour nap.

### 3 Transitional Words and Phrases

See 7b2

When a **transitional word or phrase** begins a sentence, it is usually set off from the rest of the sentence with a comma.

However, any plan that is enacted must be fair.

In other words, we cannot act hastily.

**EXERCISE 4**

Add commas in the following paragraph where necessary to set off an introductory element from the rest of a sentence.

While childhood is shrinking adolescence is expanding. Whatever the reason girls are maturing earlier. The average onset of puberty is now two years earlier than it was only forty years ago. What's more both boys and girls are staying in the nest longer. At present, it is not unusual for children to stay in their parents' home until they are twenty or twenty-one, delaying adulthood and extending adolescence. To some who study the culture this increase in adolescence portends dire consequences. With teenage hormones running amuck for longer the problems of teenage pregnancy and sexually transmitted diseases loom large. Young boys' spending long periods of their lives without responsibilities is also a recipe for disaster. However others see this "youthing" of American culture in a more positive light. Without a doubt adolescents are creative, lively, and more willing to take risks. If we channel their energies carefully they can contribute, even in their extended adolescence, to American culture and technology.

## 53d Setting Off Nonessential Material

Sometimes words, phrases, or clauses *contribute* to the meaning of a sentence but are not *essential* for conveying the sentence's main point. Use commas to set off such **nonessential material** whether it appears at the beginning, in the middle, or at the end of a sentence.

### 1 Nonrestrictive Modifiers

Use commas to set off **nonrestrictive modifiers,** which supply information that is not essential to the meaning of the word or word group they modify. (Do *not* use commas to set off **restrictive modifiers,** which supply information that is essential to the meaning of the word or word group they modify.)

**Nonrestrictive (commas required):** Actors, who have inflated egos, are often insecure. (*All* actors—not just those with inflated egos—are insecure.)

**Restrictive (no commas):** Actors who have inflated egos are often insecure. (Only those actors with inflated egos—not all actors—are insecure.)

In the following examples, commas set off only nonrestrictive modifiers—those that supply nonessential information. Commas do not set off restrictive modifiers, which supply essential information.

### *Adjective Clauses*

**Nonrestrictive:** He ran for the bus, which was late as usual.

**Restrictive:** Speaking in public is something that most people fear.

### *Prepositional Phrases*

**Nonrestrictive:** The clerk, with a nod, dismissed me.

**Restrictive:** The man with the gun demanded their money.

### *Verbal Phrases*

**Nonrestrictive:** The marathoner, running her fastest, beat her previous record.

**Restrictive:** The candidates running for mayor have agreed to a debate.

### *Appositives*

**Nonrestrictive:** *Citizen Kane*, Orson Welles's first film, made him famous.

**Restrictive:** The film *Citizen Kane* made Orson Welles famous.

**CHECKLIST**

**Restrictive and Nonrestrictive Modifiers**

To determine whether a modifier is restrictive or nonrestrictive, ask yourself these questions:

- ❑ Is the modifier essential to the meaning of the noun it modifies (*The man with the gun*, not just any man)? If so, it is restrictive and does not take commas.
- ❑ Is the modifier introduced by *that* (*something that most people fear*)? If so, it is restrictive. *That* cannot introduce a nonrestrictive clause.
- ❑ Can you delete the relative pronoun without causing ambiguity or confusion (*something [that] most people fear*)? If so, the clause is restrictive.
- ❑ Is the appositive more specific than the noun that precedes it (*the film* Citizen Kane)? If so, it is restrictive.

## Close-Up USING COMMAS WITH *THAT* AND *WHICH*

- *That* introduces only restrictive clauses, which are not set off by commas.

  I bought a used car that cost $2,000.

- *Which* generally introduces only nonrestrictive clauses, which are set off by commas.

  The used car I bought, which cost $2,000, broke down after a week.

### GRAMMAR CHECKER *That* or *Which*

Your grammar checker may label *which* as an error when it introduces a restrictive clause. It will prompt you to add commas (using *which* to introduce a nonrestrictive clause) or to change *which* to *that*. Carefully consider the meaning of your sentence, and revise accordingly.

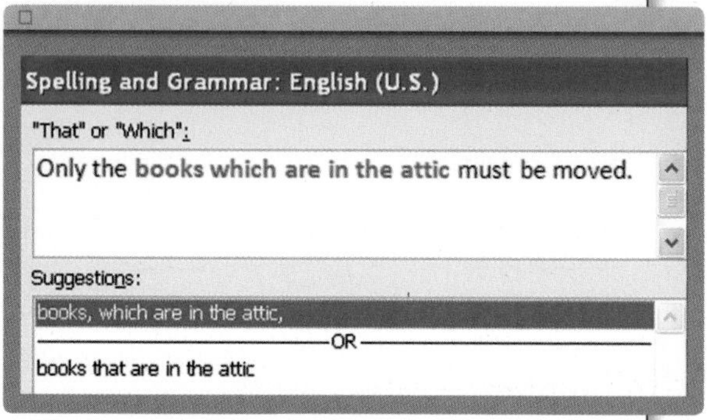
Spelling and Grammar: English (U.S.)
"That" or "Which":
Only the books which are in the attic must be moved.
Suggestions:
books, which are in the attic,
OR
books that are in the attic

### EXERCISE 5

Insert commas where necessary to set off nonrestrictive modifiers.

The Statue of Liberty which was dedicated in 1886 has undergone extensive renovation. Its supporting structure whose designer was the French engineer Alexandre Gustave Eiffel is made of iron. The Statue of Liberty created over a period of nine years by sculptor Frédéric-Auguste Bartholdi stands 151 feet tall. The people of France who were grateful for American help in the French Revolution raised the money to pay the sculptor who created the statue. The people of the United States contributing over $100,000 raised the money for the pedestal on which the statue stands.

## 2 Transitional Words and Phrases

See 7b2

Transitional words and phrases—which include conjunctive adverbs such as *however, therefore, thus,* and *nevertheless* as well as expressions such as *for example* and *on the other hand*—qualify, clarify, and make connections.

However, they are not essential to the sentence's meaning. For this reason, they are always set off by commas when they interrupt a clause or when they begin or end a sentence.

The Outward Bound program, for example, is considered safe.

In fact, Outward Bound has an excellent reputation.

Other programs are not so safe, however.

Note: When a transitional word or phrase joins two independent clauses, it must be preceded by a semicolon and followed by a comma: *Laughter is the best medicine; of course, penicillin also comes in handy sometimes.*

## 3 Contradictory Phrases

A phrase that expresses **contradiction** is usually set off by commas.

This medicine is taken after meals, never on an empty stomach.

Mark McGwire, not Sammy Sosa, was the first to break Roger Maris's home run record.

## 4 Absolute Phrases

An **absolute phrase,** which includes a noun or a pronoun and a participle and modifies an entire independent clause, is always set off by a comma from the independent clause it modifies.

His fear increasing, he waited to enter the haunted house.

Many soldiers were lost in Southeast Asia, their bodies never recovered.

## 5 Miscellaneous Nonessential Material

Other nonessential material usually set off by commas includes tag questions, names in direct address, mild interjections, and *yes* and *no*.

This is your first day on the job, isn't it?

I wonder, Mr. Honeywell, whether Mr. Albright deserves a raise.

Well, it's about time.

Yes, that's what I thought.

### EXERCISE 6

Set off the nonessential elements in these sentences with commas. If a sentence is correct, mark it with a *C*.

***Example:*** Piranhas, like sharks, will attack and eat almost anything if the opportunity arises.

1. Kermit the Frog is a Muppet a cross between a marionette and a puppet.
2. The common cold a virus is frequently spread by hand contact not by mouth.
3. The account in the Bible of Noah's Ark and the forty-day flood may be based on an actual deluge.
4. Many US welfare recipients, such as children, the aged, and the severely disabled, are unable to work.
5. The submarine *Nautilus* was the first to cross under the North Pole wasn't it?
6. The 1958 Ford Edsel was advertised with the slogan "Once you've seen it, you'll never forget it."
7. Superman was called Kal-El on the planet Krypton; on earth however he was known as Clark Kent not Kal-El.
8. Its sales topping any of his previous singles "Heartbreak Hotel" was Elvis Presley's first million-seller.
9. Two companies Nash and Hudson joined in 1954 to form American Motors.
10. A firefly is a beetle not a fly and a prairie dog is a rodent not a dog.

## 53e Using Commas in Other Conventional Contexts

### 1 With Direct Quotations

In most cases, use commas to set off a direct quotation from the **identifying tag**—the phrase that identifies the speaker (*he said, she answered,* and so on).

Emerson said to Whitman, "I greet you at the beginning of a great career."

"I greet you at the beginning of a great career," Emerson said to Whitman.

"I greet you," Emerson said to Whitman, "at the beginning of a great career."

When the identifying tag comes between two complete sentences, however, the tag is introduced by a comma but followed by a period.

"Winning isn't everything," Coach Vince Lombardi once said. "It's the only thing."

If the first sentence of an interrupted quotation ends with a question mark or exclamation point, do not use commas.

"Should we hold the front page?" she asked. "It's a slow news day."

"Hold the front page!" he cried. "There's breaking news!"

### 2 With Titles or Degrees Following a Name

Hamlet, prince of Denmark, is Shakespeare's most famous character.

Michael Crichton, MD, wrote *Jurassic Park*.

### 3 In Addresses and Dates

When a date or an address falls within a sentence, use a comma after the last element.

On January 28, 1986, the space shuttle *Challenger* exploded.

Do not use a comma to separate the street number from the street or the state name from the ZIP code.

Her address is 600 West End Avenue, New York, NY 10024.

*Note:* When only the month and year are given, do not use a comma to separate the month from the year: *August 1983*.

### 4 In Salutations and Closings

In informal correspondence, use commas following salutations and closings. Also use commas in both informal and business correspondence following the complimentary close.

| | |
|---|---|
| Dear John, | Love, |
| Dear Aunt Sophie, | Sincerely, |

*Note:* In business letters, always use a colon, not a comma, after the salutation. See 33a

### 5 In Long Numbers

For a number of four digits or more, place a comma before every third digit, counting from the right.

| | |
|---|---|
| 1,200 | 120,000 |
| 12,000 | 1,200,000 |

*Note:* Commas are not used in long page and line numbers, address numbers, telephone numbers, or ZIP codes (or in four-digit year numbers).

**ESL TIP**

In some countries, writers use commas for decimals where US writers use periods. When writing in English, remember to use periods in decimal numbers.

The total bill was $53/,75.

The number $1\frac{3}{4}$ can be represented as the decimal number 1/,75.

**EXERCISE 7**

Add commas where necessary to set off quotations, names, dates, addresses, and numbers.

1. India became independent on August 15 1947.
2. The UAW has more than 1500000 dues-paying members.
3. Nikita Khrushchev, former Soviet premier, once said "We will bury you!"
4. Mount St. Helens, northeast of Portland Oregon, began erupting on March 27 1980 and eventually killed at least thirty people.

5. Located at 1600 Pennsylvania Avenue Washington DC, the White House is a popular tourist attraction.
6. In 1956, playing before a crowd of 64519 fans in Yankee Stadium in New York New York, Don Larsen pitched the first perfect game in World Series history.
7. Lewis Thomas MD was born in Flushing New York and attended Harvard Medical School in Cambridge Massachusetts.
8. In 1967 2000000 people worldwide died of smallpox, but in 1977 only about twenty people died.
9. "The reports of my death" Mark Twain remarked "have been greatly exaggerated."
10. The French explorer Jean Nicolet landed at Green Bay Wisconsin in 1634, and in 1848 Wisconsin became the thirtieth state; it has 10355 lakes and a population of more than 4700000.

## 53f Using Commas to Prevent Misreading

In some cases, you need to use a comma to avoid ambiguity. For example, consider the following sentence.

Those who can, sprint the final lap.

Without the comma, *can* appears to be an auxiliary verb ("Those who can sprint . . ."), and the sentence seems incomplete. Because the comma tells readers to pause, it eliminates confusion.

Also use a comma to acknowledge the omission of a repeated word, usually a verb, and to separate words repeated consecutively.

Pam carried the box; Tim, the suitcase.

Everything bad that could have happened, happened.

### EXERCISE 8

Add commas where necessary to prevent misreading.

***Example:*** Whatever will be^, will be.

1. According to Bob Frank's computer is obsolete.
2. Da Gama explored Florida; Pizarro Peru.
3. By Monday evening students must begin preregistration for fall classes.
4. Whatever they built they built with care.
5. When batting practice carefully.
6. Brunch includes warm muffins topped with whipped butter and freshly brewed coffee.
7. Students go to school to learn not to play sports.
8. Technology has made what once seemed not possible possible.

**EXERCISE 9**

Add commas to the following sentences where needed, and be prepared to explain why each is necessary. If a sentence is correct, mark it with a *C*.

***Example:*** Once again, Congress is looking to make changes in immigration law.

1. According to some critics this test which new citizens must take before they are naturalized is simple and shallow.
2. Others claim that making the test more difficult would be unfair because many graduates of American high schools cannot answer the basic civics questions about the design of the American flag the structure of the US government and the events of American political history required by the test.
3. Some fear that too many new citizens from foreign countries will undermine core American values but others argue that those values came from earlier immigrants and that change is not necessarily bad.
4. Fear of immigrants while seemingly unfounded is not new.
5. In the 1940s the American government forced immigrants from Japan and their American-born children into internment camps after the Japanese bombed Pearl Harbor initiating America's involvement in World War II.

## 53g Editing Misused Commas

Do not use commas in the following situations.

### 1 To Join Two Independent Clauses

A comma alone cannot join two independent clauses; it must be followed by a coordinating conjunction. Using just a comma to connect two independent clauses creates a **comma splice**. See 41a

> The season was unusually cool, *but* the orange crop was not seriously harmed.

### 2 To Set Off Restrictive Modifiers

Commas are not used to set off **restrictive modifiers**. See 53d1

> Women/ who seek to be equal to men/ lack ambition.
>
> The film/ *Malcolm X*/ was directed by Spike Lee.

### 3 Before or After a Series

Do not use a comma to introduce or to close a series.

Three important criteria are~~,~~ fat content, salt content, and taste.

Quebec, Ontario, and Alberta~~,~~ are Canadian provinces.

### 4 Between Inseparable Grammatical Constructions

Do not place a comma between grammatical elements that cannot be logically separated: a subject and its predicate, a verb and its complement or direct object, a preposition and its object, or an adjective and the word or phrase it modifies.

A woman with dark red hair~~,~~ opened the door. (comma incorrectly placed between subject and predicate)

Louis Braille developed~~,~~ an alphabet of raised dots for the blind. (comma incorrectly placed between verb and object)

They relaxed somewhat during~~,~~ the last part of the obstacle course. (comma incorrectly placed between preposition and object)

Wind-dispersed weeds include the well-known and plentiful~~,~~ dandelions, milkweed, and thistle. (comma incorrectly placed between adjective and words it modifies)

### 5 Between a Verb and an Indirect Quotation or Indirect Question

Do not use a comma between a verb and an indirect quotation or between a verb and an indirect question.

General Douglas MacArthur vowed~~,~~ that he would return. (comma incorrectly placed between verb and indirect quotation)

The landlord asked~~,~~ if we would sign a two-year lease. (comma incorrectly placed between verb and indirect question)

### 6 Between Phrases Linked by Correlative Conjunctions

See 47g

Do not use a comma to separate two phrases linked by **correlative conjunctions.**

Forty years ago, most college students had access to neither photocopiers~~,~~ nor pocket calculators.

Both typewriters~~,~~ and tape recorders were generally available, however.

### 7 In Compounds That Are Not Composed of Independent Clauses

Do not use a comma before a coordinating conjunction (such as *and* or *but*) when it joins two elements of a compound subject, predicate, object, complement, or auxiliary verb.

Plagues,/ and pestilence were common during the Middle Ages. (compound subject)

Many women thirty-five and older are returning to college,/ and tend to be good students. (compound predicate)

Mattel has marketed a doctor's lab coat,/ and an astronaut suit for its Barbie doll. (compound object)

People buy bottled water because it is pure,/ and fashionable. (compound complement)

She can,/ and will be ready to run in the primary. (compound auxiliary verb)

## 8 Before a Dependent Clause at the End of a Sentence

Do not use a comma before a dependent clause that falls at the end of a sentence.

Jane Addams founded Hull House,/ because she wanted to help Chicago's poor.

### EXERCISE 10

Unnecessary commas have been intentionally added to some of the sentences that follow. Delete any unnecessary commas. If a sentence is correct, mark it with a *C*.

***Example:*** Spring fever,/ is a common ailment.

1. A book is like a garden, carried in the pocket. (Arab proverb)
2. Like the iodine content of kelp, air freight, is something most Americans have never pondered. (*Time*)
3. Charles Rolls, and Frederick Royce manufactured the first Rolls-Royce Silver Ghost, in 1907.
4. The hills ahead of him were rounded domes of grey granite, smooth as a bald man's pate, and completely free of vegetation. (Wilbur Smith, *Flight of the Falcon*)
5. Food here is scarce, and cafeteria food is vile, but the great advantage to Russian raw materials, when one can get hold of them, is that they are always fresh and untampered with. (Andrea Lee, *Russian Journal*)

CHAPTER 54

# Using Semicolons

## Frequently Asked Questions



A **semicolon** is used only between items of equal grammatical rank: two independent clauses, two phrases, and so on.

## 54a Separating Independent Clauses

Use a semicolon between closely related independent clauses that convey parallel or contrasting information but are not joined by a coordinating conjunction.

> Paul Revere's *The Boston Massacre* is traditional American protest art; Edward Hicks's paintings are socially conscious art with a religious strain.

See Ch. 41

*Note:* Using only a comma or no punctuation at all between independent clauses creates a **run-on.**

### EXERCISE 1

Add semicolons where necessary to separate independent clauses. Then, reread the paragraph to make certain no run-ons remain.

***Example:*** *Birth of a Nation* was one of the earliest epic movies; it was based on the book *The Klansman*.

During the 1950s movie attendance declined because of the increasing popularity of television. As a result, numerous gimmicks were introduced to draw audiences into theaters. One of the first of these was Cinerama, in this technique three pictures were shot side by side and projected onto a curved screen. Next came 3-D, complete with special glasses, *Bwana Devil* and *The Creature from the Black Lagoon* were two early 3-D ventures. *The Robe* was the first picture filmed in Cinemascope in this technique a shrunken image was projected on a screen twice as wide as it was tall. Smell-O-Vision (or Aroma-rama) enabled audiences to smell the scenes, it was impossible to get one odor out of the theater in time for the next smell to be introduced. William Castle's *Thirteen Ghosts* introduced special glasses for cowardly viewers, the red part of the glasses was the "ghost viewer," and the green part was the "ghost remover." Perhaps the ultimate in movie gimmicks accompanied the film *The Tingler* seats in the theater were wired to generate mild electric shocks. Unfortunately, the shocks set off a chain reaction that led to hysteria in the theater. During the 1960s, such gimmicks all but disappeared, viewers were able once again to simply sit back and enjoy a movie. In 1997, *Mr. Payback,* a short interactive film, introduced a new gimmick, it allowed viewers to vote on how they wanted the plot to unfold.

## EXERCISE 2

Combine each of the following sentence groups into one sentence that contains only two independent clauses. Use a semicolon to join the two clauses. You will need to add, delete, relocate, or change some words; keep experimenting until you find the arrangement that best conveys the sentence's meaning.

***Example:*** The Congo River Rapids was an early ride at Busch Gardens Africa
*; riders* *, gliding*
in Tampa, Florida. ~~Riders~~ rafted down the river. ~~They glided~~ alongside jungle plants and animals.

1. Theme parks today offer exciting rides. They are thrill packed. They flirt with danger.
2. The Great American Scream machine is located in Atlanta's Six Flags over Georgia. This ride is a wooden roller coaster. It has a top speed of 57 miles per hour.
3. In FireFall, riders go 60 feet up in the air and spin through fire and water effects. This ride is located in Great America. Great America is in Santa Clara, California.
4. The Storm can be found at the Wet 'n Wild park in Orlando, Florida. This ride features a long elevated chute. Riders spin into a giant bowl at the bottom.
5. Rolling Thunder is an exciting roller coaster ride. It is found at Six Flags Great Adventure in Jackson, New Jersey. This ride has an eighty-five-foot drop and ten hills.
6. The Beast is at Kings Island near Cincinnati, Ohio. The Beast is the longest wooden roller coaster in the world. It has a 7,400-foot track.
7. Son of Beast is also at Kings Island. It is the tallest and fastest wooden roller coaster in the world. It goes over 78 miles per hour.
8. Busch Gardens in Williamsburg, Virginia, features Escape from Pompeii. This is a thrilling and sometimes frightening water ride. It allows riders to explore ruins and see Mount Vesuvius erupt.
9. Wild Arctic is at Sea World in Orlando, Florida. This ride includes a simulated jet helicopter flight. The flight goes into an arctic storm. Riders confront polar bears, walruses, and beluga whales.
10. At Busch Gardens Africa, Egypt is a fascinating area of the park. It features Montu, an inverted steel roller coaster with cars hanging from the top. A replica of King Tut's tomb is also located there.

## 54b Separating Independent Clauses Introduced by Transitional Words and Phrases

See 7b2

Use a semicolon before a transitional word or phrase that joins two independent clauses. (The transitional element is followed by a comma.)

> Thomas Jefferson brought two hundred vanilla beans and a recipe for vanilla ice cream back from France; thus, he gave America its all-time favorite ice-cream flavor.

### EXERCISE 3

Combine each of the following sentence groups into one sentence that contains only two independent clauses. Use a semicolon and the transitional word or phrase in parentheses to join the two clauses, adding commas within clauses where necessary. You will need to add, delete, relocate, or change some words. There is no one correct version; keep experimenting until you find the arrangement you feel is most effective.

***Example:*** The Aleutian Islands, ~~are~~ located off the west coast of Alaska, ~~They~~ are an extremely remote chain of islands*; in fact, they* ~~They~~ are sometimes called America's Siberia. (in fact)

1. The Aleutians lie between the North Pacific Ocean and the Bering Sea. The weather there is harsh. Dense fog, 100-mph winds, and even tidal waves and earthquakes are not uncommon. (for example)
2. These islands constitute North America's largest network of active volcanoes. The Aleutians boast some beautiful scenery. The islands are relatively unexplored. (still)
3. The Aleutians are home to a wide variety of birds. Numerous animals, such as fur seals and whales, are found there. These islands may house the largest concentration of marine animals in the world. (in fact)
4. During World War II, thousands of American soldiers were stationed on Attu Island. They were stationed on Adak Island. The Japanese eventually occupied both islands. (however)
5. The islands' original population of native Aleuts was drastically reduced in the eighteenth century by Russian fur traders. Today, the total population is only about 8,500. US military employees comprise more than half of this. (consequently)

(Adapted from *National Geographic*)

## 54c Separating Items in a Series

Use semicolons between items in a series when one or more of the items include commas.

Three papers are posted on the bulletin board outside the building: a description of the exams; a list of appeal procedures for students who fail; and an employment ad from an automobile factory, addressed specifically to candidates whose appeals are turned down. (Andrea Lee, *Russian Journal*)

Laramie, Wyoming; Wyoming, Delaware; and Delaware, Ohio, were three of the places they visited.

## EXERCISE 4

Replace commas with semicolons where necessary to separate internally punctuated items in a series. (For information on the use of semicolons with quotation marks, **see 56e2.**)

***Example:*** Luxury automobiles have some strong selling points: they are status symbols,; some, such as the Corvette, appreciate in value,; and they are usually comfortable and well appointed.

1. The history of modern art seems at times to be a collection of "isms": Impressionism, a term that applies to painters who attempted to depict contemporary life by reproducing an "impression" of what the eye sees, Abstract Expressionism, which applies to artists who stress emotion and the unconscious in their nonrepresentational works, and, more recently, Minimalism, which applies to painters and sculptors whose work reasserts the physical reality of the object.
2. Although the term *Internet* is widely used to refer only to the World Wide Web and email, the Internet consists of a variety of discrete elements, including newsgroups, which allow users to post and receive messages on an unbelievably broad range of topics, interactive communication forums, such as blogs, discussion forums, and chat rooms, and FTP, which allows users to download material from remote computers.
3. Three of rock and roll's best-known guitar heroes played with the "British Invasion" group The Yardbirds: Eric Clapton, the group's first lead guitarist, went on to play with John Mayall's Bluesbreakers, Cream, and Blind Faith, and is now a popular solo act, Jeff Beck, the group's second guitarist, though not as visible as Clapton, made rock history with the Jeff Beck Group and inventive solo albums, and Jimmy Page, the group's third and final guitarist, transformed the remnants of the original group into the premier heavy metal band, Led Zeppelin.
4. Some of the most commonly confused words in English are *aggravate,* which means "to worsen," and *irritate,* which means "to annoy," *continual,* which means "recurring at intervals," and *continuous,* which means "an action occurring without interruption," *imply,* which means "to hint, suggest," and *infer,* which means "to conclude from," and *compliment,* which means "to praise," and *complement,* which means "to complete or add to."

5. Tennessee Williams wrote *The Glass Menagerie,* which is about Laura Wingfield, a disabled young woman, and her family, *A Streetcar Named Desire,* which starred Marlon Brando, and *Cat on a Hot Tin Roof,* which won a Pulitzer Prize.

### EXERCISE 5

Combine each of the following sentence groups into one sentence that includes a series of items separated by semicolons. You will need to add, delete, relocate, or change words. Try several versions of each sentence until you find the most effective arrangement.

***Example:*** Collecting baseball cards is a worthwhile hobby *because it* ~~It~~ helps children learn how to bargain and trade *; it* ~~It also~~ encourages them to compare data about ballplayers *; and, most* ~~Most~~ important, it introduces them to positive role models.

1. A good dictionary offers definitions of words, including some obsolete and nonstandard words. It provides information about synonyms, usage, and word origins. It also offers information on pronunciation and syllabication.
2. The flags of the Scandinavian countries all depict a cross on a solid background. Denmark's flag is red with a white cross. Norway's flag is also red, but its cross is blue, outlined in white. Sweden's flag is blue with a yellow cross.
3. Over one hundred international collectors' clubs are thriving today. One of these associations is the Cola Clan, whose members buy, sell, and trade Coca-Cola memorabilia. Another is the Citrus Label Society. There is also a Cookie Cutter Collectors' Club.
4. Listening to the radio special, we heard "Shuffle Off to Buffalo" and "Moon over Miami," both of which are about eastern cities. We heard "By the Time I Get to Phoenix" and "I Left My Heart in San Francisco," which mention western cities. Finally, we heard "The Star-Spangled Banner," which seemed to be an appropriate finale.
5. There are three principal types of contact lenses. Hard contact lenses, made of plexiglass or lucite, are seldom used today. Soft lenses, made of water-containing plastic, are more popular. Gas-permeable lenses, made of rigid, waterless plastic, are another option.

## 54d Editing Misused Semicolons

Do not use semicolons in the following situations.

### 1 Between a Dependent and an Independent Clause

Use a comma, not a semicolon, between a dependent and an independent clause.

Because new drugs can now suppress the body's immune reaction~~;~~, fewer organ transplants are rejected by the body.

**GRAMMAR CHECKER Editing Misused Semicolons**

Your grammar checker will highlight certain misused semicolons and frequently offer suggestions for revision.

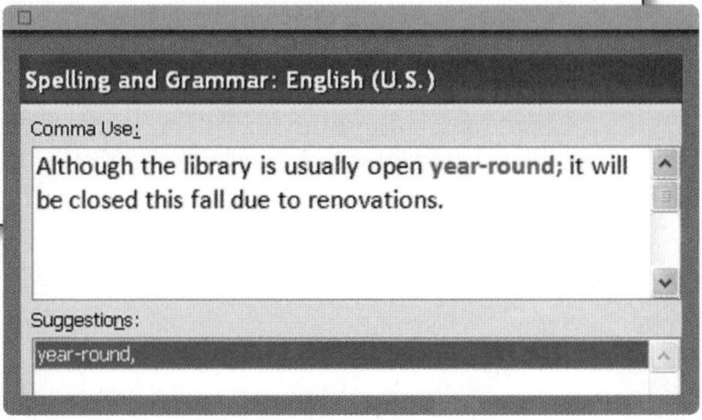
Spelling and Grammar: English (U.S.)
Comma Use:
Although the library is usually open year-round; it will be closed this fall due to renovations.
Suggestions:
year-round,

## 2 Between a Phrase and a Clause

Use a comma, not a semicolon, between a phrase and a clause.

Increasing rapidly~~;~~, computer crime poses a challenge for government, financial, and military agencies.

## 3 To Introduce a List

See 57a1

Use a colon, not a semicolon, to introduce a list.

Many people use all three of the most popular social networking sites~~;~~: *Facebook, Twitter,* and *LinkedIn.*

*Note:* Always introduce a list with a complete sentence followed by a colon.

## 4 To Introduce a Quotation

See 56a

Do not use a semicolon to introduce quoted speech or writing.

Marie Antoinette may not have said~~;~~, "Let them eat cake."

**EXERCISE 6**

Read the following paragraph carefully. Then, add semicolons where necessary, and delete incorrectly used ones, substituting other punctuation where necessary.

Barnstormers were aviators; who toured the country after World War I, giving people short airplane rides and exhibitions of stunt flying, in fact, the name *barnstormer* was derived from the use of barns as airplane hangars. Americans' interest in airplanes had all but disappeared after the war. The barnstormers helped popularize flying; especially in rural areas. Some were pilots who had flown in the war; others were just young men with a thirst for adventure. They gave people rides in airplanes; sometimes charging a dollar a minute. For most passengers, this was their first ride in an airplane, in fact, sometimes it was their first sight of one. After Lindbergh's 1927 flight across the Atlantic; Americans suddenly needed no encouragement to embrace aviation. The barnstormers had outlived their usefulness; and an era ended. (Adapted from William Goldman, *Adventures in the Screen Trade*).

CHAPTER 55

# Using Apostrophes

## Frequently Asked Questions



Use an apostrophe to form the possessive case, to indicate omissions in contractions, and to form certain plurals.

## 55a Forming the Possessive Case

The **possessive case** indicates ownership. In English, the possessive case of nouns and indefinite pronouns is indicated either with a phrase that includes the word *of* (the hands *of* the clock) or with an apostrophe and, in most cases, an *s* (the clock's hands).

### 1 Singular Nouns and Indefinite Pronouns

To form the possessive case of **singular nouns** and **indefinite pronouns,** add *-'s.*

"The Monk's Tale" is one of Chaucer's *Canterbury Tales.*

When we would arrive was anyone's guess.

### 2 Singular Nouns Ending in *-s*

To form the possessive case of **singular nouns that end in *-s*,** add *-'s* in most cases.

Reading Henry James's *The Ambassadors* was not Maris's idea of fun.

The class's time was changed to 8 a.m.

**Note:** With some singular nouns that end in *-s*, pronouncing the possessive ending as a separate syllable can sound awkward. In such cases, it is acceptable to use just an apostrophe: *Crispus Attucks' death, Aristophanes'* Lysistrata, *Achilles' left heel.*

An apostrophe is not used to form the possessive case of a title that already contains an *-'s* ending; use a phrase instead.

*The staging of*
^*A Midsummer Night's Dream*~~'s staging~~ presents a challenge.

### 3 Regular Plural Nouns

To form the possessive case of **regular plural nouns** (those that end in *-s* or *-es*), add only an apostrophe.

*The Readers' Guide to Periodical Literature* is available online.

Laid-off employees received two weeks' severance pay and three months' medical benefits.

The Lopezes' three children are triplets.

### 4 Irregular Plural Nouns

To form the possessive case of **nouns that have irregular plurals,** add *-'s.*

Long after they were gone, the geese's honking could still be heard.

*The Children's Hour* is a play by Lillian Hellman; *The Women's Room* is a novel by Marilyn French.

The two oxen's yokes were securely attached to the cart.

### 5 Compound Nouns or Groups of Words

To form the possessive case of **compound nouns** (nouns formed from two or more words) or of word groups, add *-'s* to the last word.

The editor-in-chief's position is open.

He accepted the Secretary of State's resignation under protest.

This is someone else's responsibility.

### 6 Two or More Items

To indicate **individual ownership** of two or more items, add *-'s* to each item.

> Ernest Hemingway's and Gertrude Stein's writing styles have some similarities. (Hemingway and Stein have two separate writing styles.)

To indicate **joint ownership,** add *-'s* only to the last item.

> Gilbert and Sullivan's operettas include *The Pirates of Penzance* and *The Mikado.* (Gilbert and Sullivan collaborated on both operettas.)

## EXERCISE 1

Change the modifying phrases that follow the nouns to possessive forms that precede the nouns.

***Example:*** the pen belonging to my aunt
my aunt's pen

1. the songs recorded by Ray Charles
2. the red glare of the rockets
3. the idea that Warren had
4. the housekeeper Rick and Leslie hired
5. the first choice of everyone
6. the dinner given by Harris
7. furniture designed by William Morris
8. the climate of the Virgin Islands
9. the sport the Russells play
10. the role created by the French actress

## EXERCISE 2

Change each word or phrase in parentheses to its possessive form. In some cases, you may have to use a phrase to indicate the possessive.

***Example:*** The (children) toys were scattered all over their (parents) bedroom.

The children's toys were scattered all over their parents' bedroom.

1. Jane (Addams) settlement house was called Hull House.
2. (*A Room of One's Own*) popularity increased with the rise of feminism.
3. The (chief petty officer) responsibilities are varied.
4. Vietnamese (restaurants) numbers have grown dramatically in ten (years) time.
5. (Charles Dickens) and (Mark Twain) works have sold millions of copies.

## **55b**  Indicating Omissions in Contractions

### **1** Omitted Letters

Apostrophes replace omitted letters in contractions that combine a pronoun and a verb (*he + will = he'll*) or the elements of a verb phrase (*do + not = don't*).

### Frequently Used Contractions

it's (it is, it has)
he's (he is, he has)
she's (she is, she has)
who's (who is, who has)
isn't (is not)
wouldn't (would not)
couldn't (could not)
don't (do not)
won't (will not)

let's (let us)
we've (we have)
they're (they are)
we'll (we will)
I'm (I am)
we're (we are)
you'd (you would)
we'd (we would)
they'd (they had)

*Note:* Contractions are very informal. Do not use contractions in college writing unless you are quoting a source that uses them.

**GRAMMAR CHECKER**   Revising Contractions

Your grammar checker will highlight contractions and offer suggestions for revision.

Spelling and Grammar: English (U.S.)

Contraction Use:

You'll want to be sure to bring your laptop.

Suggestions:

You will

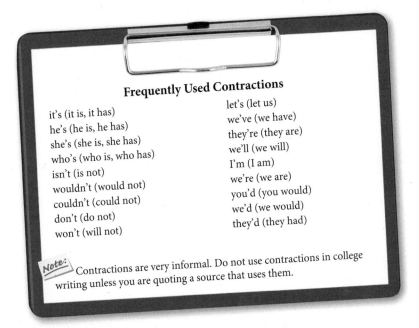

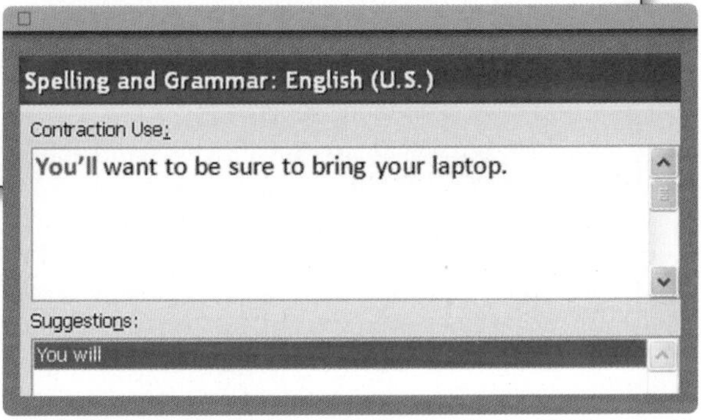

## Close-Up USING APOSTROPHES

Be careful not to confuse contractions (which always include apostrophes) with the possessive forms of personal pronouns (which never include apostrophes).

| **Contractions** | **Possessive Forms** |
|---|---|
| Who's on first? | Whose book is this? |
| They're playing our song. | Their team is winning. |
| It's raining. | Its paws were muddy. |
| You're a real pal. | Your résumé is very impressive. |

### 2 Omitted Numbers

In informal writing, an apostrophe may be used to represent the century in a year.

Crash of '29     class of '10     '57 Chevy

In college writing, however, write out the year in full: *the Crash of 1929, the class of 2010, a 1957 Chevrolet.*

### EXERCISE 3

In the following sentences, correct any errors in the use of apostrophes. (Remember, apostrophes are used in contractions but not in possessive pronouns.) If a sentence is correct, mark it with a *C*.

***Example:*** ~~Who's~~ *Whose* troops were sent to Afghanistan?

1. Its never easy to choose a major; whatever you decide, your bound to have second thoughts.
2. Olive Oyl asked, "Whose that knocking at my door?"
3. Their watching too much television; in fact, they're eyes are glazed.
4. Whose coming along on the backpacking trip?
5. The horse had been badly treated; it's spirit was broken.
6. Your correct in assuming its a challenging course.
7. Sometimes even you're best friends won't tell you your boring.
8. They're training had not prepared them for the hardships they faced.
9. It's too early to make a positive diagnosis.
10. Robert Frost wrote the poem that begins, "Who's woods these are I think I know."

## 55c Forming Plurals

In a few special situations, add -*'s* to form plurals.

- **Plurals of Letters**

  The Italian language has no *j* 's, *k* 's, or *w* 's.

- **Plurals of Words Referred to as Words**

  The supervisor would accept no *if* 's, *and* 's, or *but* 's.

Note: **Elements spoken of as themselves** (letters, numerals, or words) are set in italic type; the plural ending, however, is not. See 59c

Apostrophes are not used in plurals of abbreviations (including acronyms) or numbers.

DVDs    PACs    1960s

### EXERCISE 4

In the following sentences, form correct plurals for the letters and words in parentheses. Underline to indicate italics where necessary.

***Example:*** The word *bubbles* contains three (b).
The word *bubbles* contains three *b*'s.

1. She closed her letter with a row of (x) and (o) to indicate kisses and hugs.
2. The three (R) are reading, writing, and 'rithmetic.
3. The report included far too many (maybe) and too few (definitely).
4. The word bookkeeper contains two (o), two (k), and three (e).
5. His letter included many (please) and (thank you).

## 55d Editing Misused Apostrophes

Do not use apostrophes with plural nouns that are not possessive.

The Thompson's are not at home.

Down vest's are very warm.

The Philadelphia 76er's have had good years and bad.

Do not use apostrophes to form the possessive case of personal pronouns.

This ticket must be your's or her's.

The next turn is their's.

Her doll had lost it's right eye.

The next great moment in history is our's.

*Note:* Be especially careful not to confuse the possessive forms of personal pronouns with contractions.

See 55b1

### GRAMMAR CHECKER Editing Misused Apostrophes

Your grammar checker will highlight misused apostrophes in your writing and offer revision suggestions.

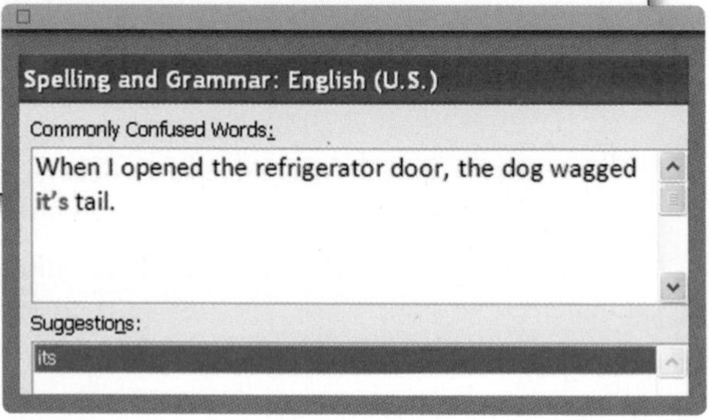
Spelling and Grammar: English (U.S.)
Commonly Confused Words:
When I opened the refrigerator door, the dog wagged it's tail.
Suggestions:
its

### EXERCISE 5

In the following sentences, correct all errors in the use of apostrophes to form noun plurals or the possessive case of personal pronouns.

***Example:*** Dr. Sampson's lecture's were more interesting than her's.

1. The Schaefer's seats are right next to our's.
2. Most of the college's in the area offer computer courses open to outsider's as well as to their own students.
3. The network completely revamped it's daytime programming.
4. Is the responsibility for the hot dog concession Cynthia's or your's?
5. Romantic poets are his favorite's.
6. Debbie returned the books to the library, forgetting they were her's.
7. Cultural revolution's do not occur very often, but when they do they bring sweeping change's.
8. Roll-top desk's are eagerly sought by antique dealer's.
9. A flexible schedule is one of their priorities, but it isn't one of our's.
10. Is your's the red house or the brown one?

CHAPTER 56

# Using Quotation Marks

## Frequently Asked Questions



Use quotation marks to set off brief passages of quoted speech or writing, to set off certain titles, and to set off words used in special ways. Do not use quotation marks when quoting long passages of prose or poetry.

## 56a Setting Off Quoted Speech or Writing

When you quote a word, phrase, or brief passage of someone else's speech or writing, enclose the quoted material in a pair of quotation marks.

> Gloria Steinem observed, "We are becoming the men we once hoped to marry."

> Galsworthy writes that Aunt Juley is "prostrated by the blow" (329). (Note that in this example from a student paper, the end punctuation follows the parenthetical documentation.)

### Close-Up USING QUOTATION MARKS WITH DIALOGUE

When you record **dialogue** (conversation between two or more people), enclose the quoted words in quotation marks. Begin a new paragraph each time a new speaker is introduced.

When you are quoting several paragraphs of dialogue by one speaker, begin each new paragraph with quotation marks. However, use closing quotation marks only at the end of the *entire quoted passage,* not at the end of each paragraph.

Special rules govern the punctuation of a quotation when it is used with an **identifying tag,** a phrase (such as *he said*) that identifies the speaker or writer. Punctuation guidelines for various situations involving identifying tags are outlined below.

## 1 Identifying Tag in the Middle of a Quoted Passage

Use a pair of commas to set off an identifying tag that interrupts a quoted passage.

"In the future," pop artist Andy Warhol once said, "everyone will be world famous for fifteen minutes."

If the identifying tag follows a completed sentence but the quoted passage continues, use a period after the tag. Begin the new sentence with a capital letter, and enclose it in quotation marks.

"Be careful," Erin warned. "Reptiles can be tricky."

## 2 Identifying Tag at the Beginning of a Quoted Passage

Use a comma after an identifying tag that introduces quoted speech or writing.

The Raven repeated, "Nevermore."

See 57a3

Use a colon instead of a comma before a quotation if the identifying tag is a complete sentence.

She gave her final answer: "No."

**GRAMMAR CHECKER Checking Punctuation with Quotation Marks**

Your grammar checker will often highlight missing punctuation in sentences containing quotation marks and offer suggestions for revision.

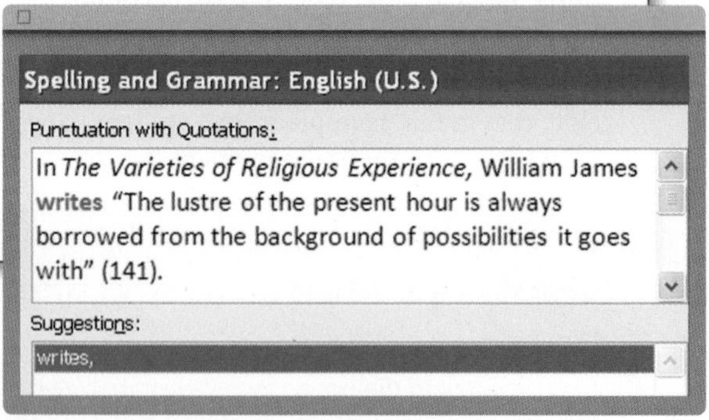
Spelling and Grammar: English (U.S.)
Punctuation with Quotations:
In The Varieties of Religious Experience, William James writes "The lustre of the present hour is always borrowed from the background of possibilities it goes with" (141).
Suggestions:
writes,

## 3 Identifying Tag at the End of a Quoted Passage

Use a comma to set off a quotation from an identifying tag that follows it.

"Be careful out there," the sergeant warned.

If the quotation ends with a question mark or an exclamation point, use that punctuation mark instead of the comma. In this situation, the tag begins with a lowercase letter even though it follows end punctuation.

"Is Ankara the capital of Turkey?" she asked.

"Oh boy!" he cried.

*Note:* A comma or period at the end of a quotation is always placed *before* the closing quotation marks. For information on placement of other punctuation marks with quotation marks, **see 56e.**

### EXERCISE 1

Add quotation marks to these sentences where necessary to set off quotations from identifying tags.

***Example:*** Wordsworth's phrase "splendour in the grass" was used as the title of a movie about young lovers.

1. Few people can explain what Descartes's words I think, therefore I am actually mean.
2. Gertrude Stein said, You are all a lost generation.
3. Freedom of speech does not guarantee anyone the right to yell fire in a crowded theater, she explained.
4. There's no place like home, Dorothy insisted.
5. If everyone will sit down the teacher announced the exam will begin.

## 56b Setting Off Long Prose Passages and Poetry

### 1 Long Prose Passages

Do not enclose a **long prose passage** (a passage of more than four lines) in quotation marks. Instead, set it off by indenting the entire passage one inch from the left-hand margin. Treat the quoted passage like regular text: double-space above and below it, and double-space between lines within it. Introduce the passage with a colon, and place parenthetical documentation one space *after* the end punctuation.

The following portrait of Aunt Juley illustrates several of the devices Galsworthy uses throughout *The Forsyte Saga,* such as a journalistic detachment that is almost cruel in its scrutiny, a subtle sense of the grotesque, and an ironic stance:

> Aunt Juley stayed in her room, prostrated by the blow. Her face, discoloured by tears, was divided into compartments by the little

ridges of pouting flesh which had swollen with emotion. . . . At fixed intervals she went to her drawer, and took from beneath the lavender bags a fresh pocket-handkerchief. Her warm heart could not bear the thought that Ann was lying there so cold. (329)

Many similar portraits of characters appear throughout the novel.

**Close-Up QUOTING LONG PROSE PASSAGES**

When you quote a long prose passage that is a single paragraph, do not indent the first line. When quoting two or more paragraphs, however, indent the first line of each paragraph (including the first) an additional one-quarter inch. If the first sentence of the quoted passage does not begin a paragraph in the source, do not indent—but do indent the first line of each subsequent paragraph. If the passage you are quoting includes material set in quotation marks, keep the quotation marks.

See 19b

*Note:* APA guidelines differ from those summarized here, which follow MLA style.

### 2 Poetry

Treat one line of poetry like a short prose passage: enclose it in quotation marks, and run it into the text.

One of John Donne's best-known poems begins with the line, "Go and catch a falling star."

See 57e2

If you quote two or three lines of poetry, separate the lines with slashes (/), and run the quotation into the text. (Leave one space before and one space after the slash.)

Alexander Pope writes, "True Ease in Writing comes from Art, not Chance, / As those move easiest who have learned to dance."

See 56b2

If you quote more than three lines of poetry, set them off like a long prose passage. (For special emphasis, you may set off fewer lines in this manner.) Do not use quotation marks, and be sure to reproduce punctuation, spelling, capitalization, and indentation *exactly* as they appear in the poem.

Wilfred Owen, a poet who was killed in action in World War I, expressed the horrors of war with vivid imagery:

> Bent double, like old beggars under sacks.
> Knock-kneed, coughing like hags, we cursed through sludge.
> Till on the haunting flares we turned our backs
> And towards our distant rest began to trudge. (lines 1-4)

## 56c Setting Off Titles

Titles of short works and titles of parts of long works are enclosed in quotation marks. Other titles are **italicized**.

See 59a

### Titles Requiring Quotation Marks

**Articles in Magazines, Newspapers, and Professional Journals**

"Why Johnny Can't Write"

**Essays, Short Stories, Short Poems, and Songs**

"Fenimore Cooper's Literary Offenses"
"Flying Home"
"The Road Not Taken"
"The Star-Spangled Banner"

**Chapters or Sections of Books**

"Miss Sharp Begins to Make Friends" (Chapter 10 of *Vanity Fair*)

**Episodes of Radio or Television Series**

"Lucy Goes to the Hospital" (*I Love Lucy*)

**See 59a** for a list of titles that require italics.

### EXERCISE 2

Add quotation marks to the following sentences where necessary to set off titles. If italics are incorrectly used, substitute quotation marks. Place commas and periods inside quotation marks.

***Example:*** Margaret Atwood has written stories, such as *"Happy Endings,"* ~~Happy Endings~~/ and poems, such as "You Fit Into Me."

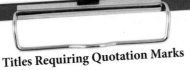

1. One of the essays from her new book *Good Bones and Simple Murder* was originally published in *Harper's* magazine.
2. Her collection of poems, *Morning in the Burned House,* contains the moving poem *In the Secular Night.*
3. You may have seen the movie *The Handmaid's Tale,* starring Robert Duvall, based on her best-selling novel.
4. *Surfacing* was the first book of hers I read, but my favorite work of hers is the short story Hair Ball.
5. I wasn't surprised to find her poems The Animals in the Country and This Is a Photograph of Me in our English textbook last year.

## 56d Setting Off Words Used in Special Ways

Enclose a word used in a special or unusual way in quotation marks. (If you use *so-called* before an unusual usage, do not use quotation marks as well.)

> It was clear that adults approved of children who were "readers," but it was not at all clear why this was so. (Annie Dillard)

Also enclose a **coinage**—an invented word—in quotation marks.

> After the twins were born, the minivan became a "babymobile."

## 56e Using Quotation Marks with Other Punctuation

At the end of a quotation, punctuation is sometimes placed before the closing quotation marks and sometimes placed after them.

### 1 With Final Commas or Periods

At the end of a quotation, place a comma or period *before* the quotation marks.

> Many, like the poet Robert Frost, think about "the road not taken," but not many have taken "the one less traveled by."

### 2 With Final Semicolons or Colons

At the end of a quotation, place a semicolon or colon *after* the quotation marks.

> Students who do not pass the test receive "certificates of completion"; those who pass are awarded diplomas.

> Taxpayers were pleased with the first of the candidate's promised "sweeping new reforms": a balanced budget.

### 3 With Question Marks, Exclamation Points, and Dashes

If a question mark, exclamation point, or dash is part of the quotation, place the punctuation mark *before* the quotation marks.

> “Who’s there?” she demanded.
>
> “Stop!” he cried.
>
> “Should we leave now, or—” Vicki paused, unable to continue.

If a question mark, exclamation point, or dash is *not* part of the quotation, place the punctuation mark *after* the quotation marks.

> Did you finish reading “The Black Cat”?
>
> Whatever you do, don’t yell “Uncle”!
>
> The first story—Updike’s “A&P”—provoked discussion.

If both the quotation and the sentence are questions or exclamations, place the punctuation mark *after* the quotation marks.

> Who asked, “Is Paris burning”?

**Close-Up** QUOTATIONS WITHIN QUOTATIONS

Use *single* quotation marks to enclose a quotation within a quotation.

> Claire noted, “Liberace always said, ‘I cried all the way to the bank.’ ”

Also use single quotation marks within a quotation to indicate a title that would normally be enclosed in double quotation marks.

> I think what she said was, “Play it, Sam. Play ‘As Time Goes By.’ ”

Use *double* quotation marks around quotations or titles within a long prose passage.

See 56b1

## 56f Editing Misused Quotation Marks

Do not use quotation marks in the following situations.

### 1 To Convey Emphasis

Do not use quotation marks to convey emphasis.

> William Randolph Hearst’s “fabulous” home is a castle called San Simeon.

## 2 To Set Off Slang or Technical Terms

Do not use quotation marks to set off slang or technical terms. (Note that slang is almost always inappropriate in college writing.)

> Dawn is ~~“into”~~ very involved in running.
>
> ~~“~~Biofeedback~~”~~ is sometimes used to treat migraine headaches.

## 3 To Enclose Titles of Long Works

See 59a

Titles of long works are italicized, not set in quotation marks.

> The classic novel ~~“~~*War and Peace*~~”~~ is even longer than the epic poem ~~“~~*Paradise Lost.*~~”~~

**Note:** Do not use quotation marks (or italics) to set off titles of your own papers.

## 4 To Set Off Terms Being Defined

Terms being defined are italicized.

> The word ~~“~~*tintinnabulation,*~~”~~ meaning the ringing sound of bells, is used by Poe in his poem “The Bells.”

## 5 To Set Off Indirect Quotations

Quotation marks should not be used to set off **indirect quotations** (someone else’s written or spoken words that are not quoted exactly).

> Freud wondered ~~“~~what a woman wanted.~~”~~

### EXERCISE 3

In the following paragraph, correct the use of single and double quotation marks to set off direct quotations, titles, and words used in special ways. Supply quotation marks where they are required, and delete those that are not required, substituting italics where necessary.

In her essay ‘The Obligation to Endure’ from the book “Silent Spring,” Rachel Carson writes: As Albert Schweitzer has said, ‘Man can hardly even recognize the devils of his own creation.’ Carson goes on to point out that many chemicals have been used to kill insects and other organisms which, she writes, are “described in the modern vernacular as pests.” Carson believes such “advanced” chemicals, by contaminating our environment, do more harm than good. In addition to “Silent Spring,” Carson is also the author of the book “The Sea Around Us.” This work, divided into three sections (Mother Sea, The Restless Sea, and Man and the Sea About Him), was published in 1951.

## EXERCISE 4

Correct the use of quotation marks in the following sentences. If a sentence is correct, mark it with a *C*.

***Example:*** The “Watergate” incident brought many new expressions into the English language.

1. Kilroy was here and Women and children first are two expressions Bartlett’s Familiar Quotations attributes to “Anon.”
2. Neil Armstrong said he was making a small step for man but a giant leap for mankind.
3. “The answer, my friend”, Bob Dylan sang, “is blowin’ in the wind”.
4. The novel was a real “thriller,” complete with spies and counterspies, mysterious women, and exotic international chases.
5. The sign said, Road liable to subsidence; it meant that we should look out for potholes.
6. One of William Blake’s best-known lines—To see a world in a grain of sand—opens his poem Auguries of Innocence.
7. In James Thurber’s short story The Catbird Seat, Mrs. Barrows annoys Mr. Martin by asking him silly questions like Are you tearing up the pea patch? Are you scraping around the bottom of the pickle barrel? and Are you lifting the oxcart out of the ditch?
8. I’ll make him an offer he can’t refuse, promised “the godfather” in Mario Puzo’s novel.
9. What did Timothy Leary mean by “Turn on, tune in, drop out?”
10. George, the protagonist of Bernard Malamud’s short story, A Summer’s Reading, is something of an “underachiever.”

CHAPTER 57

# Using Other Punctuation Marks

## Frequently Asked Questions

## 57a Using Colons

The **colon** is a strong punctuation mark that points readers ahead to the material that follows it. When a colon introduces a list or series, explanatory material, or a quotation, *it must be preceded by a complete sentence.*

### 1 Introducing Lists or Series

Use a colon to set off a list or a series, including one introduced by a phrase such as *the following* or *as follows.*

Waiting tables requires three skills: memory, speed, and balance.

### 2 Introducing Explanatory Material

Use a colon to introduce material that explains, exemplifies, or summarizes. Frequently, this material is presented in the form of an **appositive,** a word group that identifies or renames an adjacent noun or pronoun.

Diego Rivera is well known for a controversial mural: the one commissioned for Rockefeller Center in the 1930s.

She had one dream: to play professional basketball.

Sometimes a colon separates two independent clauses, the second illustrating or explaining the first.

*A U.S. News & World Report* survey revealed a surprising fact: Americans spend more time at malls than anywhere else except at home and at work.

**Close-Up** USING COLONS

When a complete sentence follows a colon, it may begin with either a capital or a lowercase letter. However, if the sentence is a quotation, the first word is always capitalized (unless it was not capitalized in the source).

### 3 Introducing Quotations

See 56b

When you quote a **long prose passage,** always introduce it with a colon. Also use a colon before a short quotation when it is introduced by a complete sentence.

With dignity, Bartleby repeated the familiar words: "I prefer not to."

### Other Conventional Uses of Colons

**To Separate a Title from a Subtitle**

*Family Installments*: *Memories of Growing Up Hispanic*

**To Separate Minutes from Hours**

6:15 a.m.

**After the Salutation in a Business Letter** See 33a

Dear Dr. Evans:

**To Separate Place of Publication from Name of Publisher in a Works-Cited List** See 18a2

Boston: Wadsworth, 2013

## 4 Editing Misused Colons

Do not use colons in the following situations.

***After Expressions Like* For Example** Do not use colons after *for example, such as, namely,* and *that is.* Remember that when a colon introduces a list or series, a complete sentence must precede the colon.

> The Eye Institute treats patients with a wide variety of conditions, such as~~:~~ myopia, glaucoma, and cataracts.

***In Verb and Prepositional Constructions*** Do not place colons between verbs and their objects or complements or between prepositions and their objects.

> James A. Michener wrote~~:~~ *Hawaii, Centennial, Space,* and *Poland.*
>
> Hitler's armies marched through~~:~~ the Netherlands, Belgium, and France.

### EXERCISE 1

Add colons where appropriate in the following sentences, and delete any misused colons.

***Example:*** There was one thing he really hated: getting up at 7:00 every morning.

1. Books about the late John F. Kennedy include the following *A Hero for Our Time; Johnny, We Hardly Knew Ye; One Brief Shining Moment;* and *JFK: Reckless Youth.*

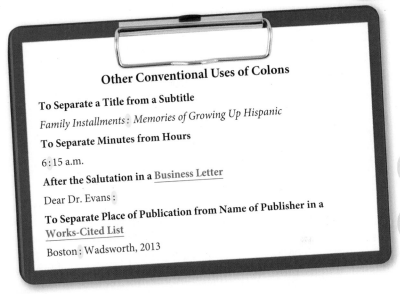

2. Only one task remained to tell his boss he was quitting.
3. The story closed with a familiar phrase "And they all lived happily ever after."
4. The sergeant requested: reinforcements, medical supplies, and more ammunition.
5. She kept only four souvenirs a photograph, a matchbook, a theater program, and a daisy pressed between the pages of *William Shakespeare The Complete Works*.

## 57b Using Dashes

### 1 Setting Off Nonessential Material

See 53d

Like commas, **dashes** can set off nonessential material, but unlike commas, dashes call attention to the material they set off. Indicate a dash with two unspaced hyphens (which your word-processing program will automatically convert to a dash).

For emphasis, you may use dashes to set off explanations, qualifications, examples, definitions, and appositives.

> Neither of the boys—both nine-year-olds—had any history of violence.

> Too many parents learn the dangers of swimming pools the hard way—after their toddler has drowned.

### 2 Introducing a Summary

Use a dash to introduce a statement that summarizes a list or series before it.

> "Study hard," "Respect your elders," "Don't talk with your mouth full"—Sharon had often heard her parents say these things.

### 3 Indicating an Interruption

In dialogue, a dash can mark a hesitation or an unfinished thought.

> "I think—no, I know—this is the worst day of my life," Julie sighed.

### 4 Editing Overused Dashes

Too many dashes can make your writing seem disorganized and out of control, so you should be careful not to overuse them.

> Registration was a nightmare~~—~~. ~~most~~ Most of the courses I wanted to take—geology and conversational Spanish, for instance—met at inconvenient times~~—~~or were closed by the time I tried to sign up for them~~—~~. ~~it~~ It was really depressing~~—~~, even for registration.

**EXERCISE 2**

Add dashes where needed in the following sentences. If a sentence is correct, mark it with a *C*.

***Example:*** World War I—called "the war to end all wars"—was, unfortunately, no such thing.

1. Tulips, daffodils, hyacinths, lilies all these flowers grow from bulbs.
2. St. Kitts and Nevis two tiny island nations are now independent after 360 years of British rule.
3. "But it's not" She paused and thought about her next words.
4. He considered several different majors history, English, political science, and business before deciding on journalism.
5. The two words added to the Pledge of Allegiance in the 1950s "under God" remain part of the Pledge today.

## 57c Using Parentheses

### 1 Setting Off Nonessential Material

Use **parentheses** to enclose material that expands, clarifies, illustrates, or supplements.

> In some European countries (notably Sweden and France), high-quality day care is offered at little or no cost to parents.

When a complete sentence set off by parentheses falls within another sentence, it should not begin with a capital letter or end with a period.

> The region is so cold (temperatures average in the low twenties) that it is virtually uninhabitable.

If the parenthetical sentence does *not* fall within another sentence, however, it must begin with a capital letter and end with appropriate punctuation.

> The region is very cold. (Temperatures average in the low twenties.)

**Close-Up USING PARENTHESES WITH OTHER PUNCTUATION**

When parentheses fall within a sentence, punctuation never immediately precedes the opening parenthesis. Punctuation may follow the closing parenthesis, however.

> George Orwell's *1984*/ (1949), which focuses on the dangers of a totalitarian society, is required reading.

### 2 Using Parentheses in Other Situations

Use parentheses around letters and numbers that identify points on a list, dates, cross-references, and documentation.

> All reports must include the following components: (1) an opening summary, (2) a background statement, and (3) a list of conclusions.
>
> Russia defeated Sweden in the Great Northern War (1700–1721).
>
> Other scholars also make this point (see p. 54).
>
> One critic has called the novel "puerile" (Arvin 72).

**EXERCISE 3**

Add parentheses where appropriate in the following sentences. If a sentence is correct, mark it with a *C*.

***Example:*** The greatest battle of the War of 1812 (the Battle of New Orleans) was fought after the war was declared over.

1. During the Great War 1914–1918, Britain censored letters written from the front lines.
2. Those who lived in towns on the southern coast such as Dover could often hear the mortar shells across the channel in France.
3. Wilfred Owen wrote his most famous poem "Dulce et Decorum Est" in the trenches in France.
4. The British uniforms with bright red tabs right at the neck were responsible for many British deaths.
5. It was difficult for the War Poets as they are now called to return to writing about subjects other than the horrors of war.

## 57d Using Brackets

Use brackets in the following situations.

### 1 Setting Off Comments within Quotations

**Brackets** within quotations tell readers that the enclosed words are yours and not those of your source. You can bracket an explanation, a clarification, a correction, or an opinion.

> "Even at Princeton he [F. Scott Fitzgerald] felt like an outsider."

If a quotation contains an error, indicate that the error is not yours by following the error with the Latin word *sic* ("thus") in brackets.

> As the Web site notes,"The octopuss [sic] is a cephalopod mollusk with eight arms."

See 15d1

Note: Use brackets to indicate changes that you make in order to fit a quotation smoothly into your sentence.

## 2 Replacing Parentheses within Parentheses

When one set of parentheses falls within another, use brackets in place of the inner set.

> In her study of American education between 1945 and 1960 (*The Trouble Crusade* [New York: Basic, 1963]), Diane Ravitch addresses issues such as progressive education, race, educational reforms, and campus unrest.

# 57e Using Slashes

Use slashes in the following situations.

## 1 Separating One Option from Another

When separating one option from another with a **slash,** do not leave a space before or after the slash.

> The either/or fallacy is a common error in logic.
>
> Writer/director Spike Lee will speak at the film festival.

## 2 Separating Lines of Poetry Run into the Text

When separating lines of poetry run into the text, leave one space before and one space after the slash.

> The poet James Schevill writes, "I study my defects / And learn how to perfect them."

# 57f Using Ellipses

Use ellipses in the following situations.

## 1 Indicating an Omission in Quoted Prose

Use an **ellipsis**—three *spaced* periods—to indicate that you have omitted words from a prose quotation. (Note that an ellipsis in the middle of a quoted passage can indicate the omission of a word, a sentence or two, or even a whole paragraph or more.) When deleting material from a quotation, be very careful not to change the meaning of the original passage.

> **Original:** "When I was a young man, being anxious to distinguish myself, I was perpetually starting new propositions." (Samuel Johnson)

**With Omission:** "When I was a young man, . . . I was perpetually starting new propositions."

Note that when you delete words immediately after an internal punctuation mark (such as the comma in the example above), you retain the punctuation before the ellipsis.

When you delete material at the end of a sentence, place the ellipsis after the sentence's period or other end punctuation.

According to humorist Dave Barry, "from outer space Europe appears to be shaped like a large ketchup stain. . . . " (period followed by ellipsis)

*Note:* Never begin a quoted passage with an ellipsis.

When you delete material between sentences, place the ellipsis after any punctuation that appears in the original passage.

**Deletion from Middle of One Sentence to End of Another:** According to Donald Hall, "Everywhere one meets the idea that reading is an activity desirable in itself. . . . People surround the idea of reading with piety and do not take into account the purpose of reading." (period followed by ellipsis)

**Deletion from Middle of One Sentence to Middle of Another:** "When I was a young man, . . . I found that generally what was new was false." (Samuel Johnson) (comma followed by ellipsis)

*Note:* If a quoted passage already contains an ellipsis, MLA recommends that you enclose any ellipses of your own in brackets to distinguish them from those that appear in the original quotation.

### Close-Up USING ELLIPSES

If a quotation ending with an ellipsis is followed by parenthetical documentation, the final punctuation comes *after* the documentation.

As Jarman argues, "Compromise was impossible . . ." (161).

## 2 Indicating an Omission in Quoted Poetry

Use an ellipsis when you omit a word or phrase from a line of poetry. When you omit one or more lines of poetry, use a line of spaced periods. (The length may be equal either to the line above it or to the missing line—but it should not be longer than the longest line of the poem.)

**Original:**

Stitch! Stitch! Stitch!
In poverty, hunger, and dirt,
And still with a voice of dolorous pitch,
Would that its tone could reach the Rich,
She sang this "Song of the Shirt!"

(Thomas Hood)

**With Omission:**

Stitch! Stitch! Stitch!
In poverty, hunger, and dirt,
. . . . . . . . . . . . . . . . . . . . . . . . .
She sang this "Song of the Shirt!"

## EXERCISE 4

Read the following paragraph, and follow the instructions after it, taking care in each case not to delete essential information.

The most important thing about research is to know when to stop. How does one recognize the moment? When I was eighteen or thereabouts, my mother told me that when out with a young man I should always leave a half-hour before I wanted to. Although I was not sure how this might be accomplished, I recognized the advice as sound, and exactly the same rule applies to research. One must stop *before* one has finished; otherwise, one will never stop and never finish. (Barbara Tuchman, *Practicing History*)

1. Delete words from the middle of one sentence to the end of another, marking the omission with an ellipsis.
2. Delete words from the middle of one sentence to the middle of another, marking the omission with an ellipsis.
3. Delete words at the end of any sentence, marking the omission with an ellipsis.
4. Delete one complete sentence from the middle of the passage, marking the omission with an ellipsis.

## EXERCISE 5

Add appropriate punctuation—colons, dashes, parentheses, brackets, or slashes—to the following sentences. If a sentence is correct, mark it with a *C*.

***Example:*** There was one thing she was sure of: if she did well at the interview, the job would be hers.

1. Mark Twain Samuel L. Clemens made the following statement "I can live for two months on a good compliment."
2. Liza Minnelli, the actress singer who starred in several films, is the daughter of legendary singer Judy Garland.

3. Saudi Arabia, Oman, Yemen, Qatar, and the United Arab Emirates all these are located on the Arabian Peninsula.
4. John Adams 1735–1826 was the second president of the United States; John Quincy Adams 1767–1848 was the sixth.
5. The sign said, "No tresspassing sic."
6. *Checkmate* a term derived from the Persian phrase meaning "the king is dead" announces victory in chess.
7. The following people were present at the meeting the president of the board of trustees, three trustees, and twenty reporters.
8. Before the introduction of the potato in Europe, the parsnip was a major source of carbohydrates in fact, it was a dietary staple.
9. In the well-researched book *Crime Movies* (New York Norton, 1980), Carlos Clarens studies the gangster genre in film.
10. I remember reading though I can't remember where that Upton Sinclair sold plots to Jack London.

CHAPTER 58

# Knowing When to Capitalize

## Frequently Asked Questions



### Close-Up REVISING CAPITALIZATION ERRORS

In *Microsoft Word,* the AutoCorrect tool will automatically capitalize certain words—such as the first word of a sentence or the days of the week. You can also designate additional words to be automatically capitalized for you as you type. To do this, select the AutoCorrect option, and type in the words you want to capitalize. Be sure to proofread your documents after using the AutoCorrect tool, though, since it may introduce capitalization errors into your writing.

## 58a Capitalizing the First Word of a Sentence

Capitalize the first word of a sentence, including a sentence of quoted speech or writing.

As Shakespeare wrote, "Who steals my purse steals trash."

Do not capitalize a sentence set off within another sentence by dashes or parentheses.

Finding the store closed—it was a holiday—they went home.

The candidates are Frank Lester and Jane Lester (they are not related).

**Close-Up** USING CAPITAL LETTERS IN POETRY

The first word of a line of poetry is generally capitalized. If the poet uses a lowercase letter to begin a line, however, you should follow that style when you quote the line.

## 58b Capitalizing Proper Nouns

**Proper nouns**—the names of specific persons, places, or things—are capitalized, and so are adjectives formed from proper nouns.

**ESL TIP**

If you are not sure whether a noun should be capitalized, look it up in a dictionary. Do not capitalize a word simply because you want to emphasize its importance.

### 1 Specific People's Names

Always capitalize people's names: Olympia Snowe, Barack Obama.

Capitalize a title when it precedes a person's name (Senator Olympia Snowe) or is used instead of the name (Dad). Do not capitalize titles that *follow* names (Olympia Snowe, the senator from Maine) or those that refer to the general position, not the particular person who holds it (a stay-at-home dad).

You may, however, capitalize titles that indicate very high-ranking positions even when they are used alone or when they follow a name: the Pope; Barack Obama, President of the United States. Never capitalize a title denoting a family relationship when it follows an article or a possessive pronoun (an uncle, his mom).

Capitalize titles that represent academic degrees or abbreviations of those degrees even when they follow a name: Dr. Sanjay Gupta; Sanjay Gupta, MD.

### 2 Names of Particular Structures, Special Events, Monuments, and So On

| | |
|---|---|
| the Brooklyn Bridge | the Taj Mahal |
| the Eiffel Tower | Mount Rushmore |
| the World Series | the *Titanic* |

**Note:** Capitalize a common noun, such as *bridge, river, county,* or *lake,* when it is part of a proper noun (Lake Erie, Kings County).

### 3 Places and Geographical Regions

| | |
|---|---|
| Saturn | the Straits of Magellan |
| Budapest | the Fiji Islands |
| Walden Pond | the Western Hemisphere |

Capitalize *north, south, east,* and *west* when they denote particular geographical regions but not when they designate directions.

There are more tornadoes in Kansas than in the East. (*East* refers to a specific region.)

Turn west at Broad Street and continue north to Market. (*West* and *north* refer to directions, not specific regions.)

### 4 Days of the Week, Months, and Holidays

| | |
|---|---|
| Saturday | Cinco de Mayo |
| January | Diwali |

### 5 Historical Periods, Events, Documents, and Names of Legal Cases

| | |
|---|---|
| the Industrial Revolution | the Treaty of Versailles |
| the Reformation | the Voting Rights Act |
| the Battle of Gettysburg | *Brown v. Board of Education* |

**Note:** Names of court cases are italicized in the text of your papers, but not in works-cited entries.

### 6 Philosophic, Literary, and Artistic Movements

| | |
|---|---|
| Naturalism | Dadaism |
| Neoclassicism | Expressionism |

### 7 Races, Ethnic Groups, Nationalities, and Languages

| | |
|---|---|
| African American | Korean |
| Latino/Latina | Farsi |

*Note:* When the words *black* and *white* denote races, they have traditionally not been capitalized. Current usage is divided on whether or not to capitalize *black*.

### 8 Religions and Their Followers; Sacred Books and Figures

| | | |
|---|---|---|
| Islam | the Qur'an | Buddha |
| the Talmud | Jews | God |

*Note:* It is not necessary to capitalize pronouns that refer to God (although some people do so).

### 9 Specific Groups and Organizations

the Democratic Party
the International Brotherhood of Electrical Workers
the New York Yankees
the American Civil Liberties Union
the National Council of Teachers of English
the Rolling Stones

*Note:* When the name of a group or organization is abbreviated, the **abbreviation** uses capital letters in place of the capitalized words. See 61b

| | | |
|---|---|---|
| IBEW | ACLU | NCTE |

### 10 Businesses, Government Agencies, and Other Institutions

| | |
|---|---|
| General Electric | the Environmental Protection Agency |
| Lincoln High School | the University of Maryland |

### 11 Brand Names and Words Formed from Them

| | | | | |
|---|---|---|---|---|
| Velcro | Coke | Post-it | Rollerblades | Astroturf |

*Note:* Brand names that over long use have become synonymous with the product—for example, *nylon* and *aspirin*—are no longer capitalized. (Consult a dictionary to determine whether or not to capitalize a familiar brand name.)

## Close-Up USING BRAND NAMES

In general, use generic references, not brand names, in college writing—*photocopy,* not *Xerox,* for example. These generic names are not capitalized.

### 12 Specific Academic Courses

Sociology 201 English 101

**Note:** Do not capitalize a general subject area (sociology, zoology) unless it is the name of a language (English, Spanish).

### 13 Adjectives Formed from Proper Nouns

| | |
|---|---|
| Freudian slip | Elizabethan era |
| Platonic ideal | Shakespearean sonnet |
| Aristotelian logic | Marxist ideology |

When words derived from proper nouns have lost their original associations, do not capitalize them: *china bowl, french fries.*

## GRAMMAR CHECKER Recognizing Proper Nouns

Your spell checker may not recognize the proper nouns you use in your documents, particularly those that have irregular capitalization, such as *Leonardo da Vinci,* and therefore will identify these nouns as spelling errors. It may also fail to recognize certain discipline-specific proper nouns.

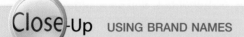

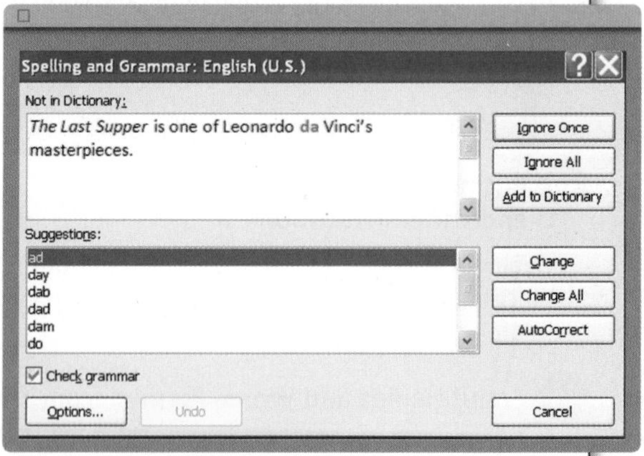



To solve this problem, click Ignore Once to instruct the spell checker to ignore the word one time and Ignore All to instruct the spell checker to ignore all uses of the word in your document.

## 58c Capitalizing Important Words in Titles

In general, capitalize all words in titles with the exception of articles (*a*, *an*, and *the*), prepositions, coordinating conjunctions, and the *to* in infinitives (unless they are the first or last word in the title or subtitle).

"Dover Beach"
The Declaration of Independence
*Across the River and into the Trees*
*On the Waterfront*
*Madame Curie: A Biography*
"What Friends Are For"

## 58d Capitalizing the Pronoun *I*, the Interjection *O*, and Other Single Letters in Special Constructions

Always capitalize the pronoun *I* even if it is part of a contraction (*I'm*, *I'll*, *I've*).

Sam and I finally went to Mexico, and I'm glad we did.

Always capitalize the interjection *O*.

Give us peace in our time, O Lord.

However, capitalize the interjection *oh* only when it begins a sentence.

Note: Many other single letters are capitalized in certain usages: *an A in history*, *vitamin B*, *C major*. Check your dictionary to determine whether or not to use a capital letter.

## 58e Capitalizing Salutations and Closings of Letters

Always capitalize the first word of the salutation of a personal or business letter.

See 33a

Dear Fred,          Dear Mr. Reynolds:

Always capitalize the first word of the complimentary close.

Sincerely,          Very truly yours,

## 58f Editing Misused Capitals

Do not capitalize words for emphasis or as an attention-getting strategy. If you are uncertain about whether or not a word should be capitalized, consult a dictionary.

### 1 Seasons

Do not capitalize the names of the seasons—summer, fall, winter, spring—unless they are personified, as in *Old Man Winter.*

### 2 Centuries and Loosely Defined Historical Periods

Do not capitalize the names of centuries or general historical periods.

seventeenth-century poetry
the automobile age

Do, however, capitalize names of specific historical, anthropological, and geological periods: *Iron Age; Renaissance; Paleozoic Era.*

### 3 Diseases and Other Medical Terms

Do not capitalize names of diseases or medical tests or conditions unless a proper noun is part of the name or unless the name of the disease is an **acronym**.

See 52a2

| | | |
|---|---|---|
| smallpox | Apgar test | AIDS |
| Lyme disease | mumps | SIDS |

## EXERCISE 1

Capitalize words where necessary in these sentences.

***Example:*** John F. Kennedy won the P~~p~~ulitzer P~~p~~rize for his book *P~~p~~rofiles* in *C~~c~~ourage.*

1. Two of the brontë sisters wrote *jane eyre* and *wuthering heights,* nineteenth-century novels that are required reading in many english classes that focus on victorian literature.
2. It was a beautiful day in the spring—it was april 15, to be exact—but all Ted could think about was the check he had to write to the internal revenue service and the bills he had to pay by friday.
3. Traveling north, they hiked through british columbia, planning a leisurely return on the cruise ship *canadian princess*.
4. Alice liked her mom's apple pie better than aunt nellie's rhubarb pie, but she liked grandpa's punch best of all.
5. A new elective, political science 30, covers the vietnam war from the gulf of tonkin to the fall of saigon, including the roles of ho chi minh, the viet cong, and the buddhist monks; the positions of presidents johnson and nixon; and the influence of groups like the student mobilization committee and vietnam veterans against the war.

6. When the central high school drama club put on a production of shaw's *pygmalion,* the director xeroxed extra copies of the parts for eliza doolittle and professor henry higgins so he could give them to the understudies.
7. Shaking all over, Bill admitted, "driving on the los angeles freeway is a frightening experience for a kid from brooklyn, even in a bmw."
8. The new united federation of teachers contract guarantees teachers many paid holidays, including columbus day, veterans day, and washington's birthday; a week each at christmas and easter; and two full months (july and august) in the summer.
9. The sociology syllabus included the books *beyond the best interests of the child, regulating the poor: the functions of public welfare,* and *a welfare mother;* in anthropology, we were to begin by studying the stone age; and in geology, we were to focus on the Mesozoic era.
10. Winners of the nobel peace prize include lech walesa, former leader of the polish trade union solidarity; the reverend dr. martin luther king jr., founder of the southern christian leadership conference; and archbishop desmond tutu of south africa.

CHAPTER 59

# Using Italics

## Frequently Asked Questions



## 59a Setting Off Titles and Names

Use italics for the titles and names listed in the following box. Most other titles are set off with quotation marks.

See 56a

**Titles and Names Set in Italics**

**Books:** *The Kite Runner, Beloved*
**Newspapers:** the *Washington Post*, the *Philadelphia Inquirer* (According to MLA style, the word *the* is not italicized in titles of newspapers.)
**Magazines and Journals:** *Rolling Stone, Scientific American*
**Online Magazines and Journals:** *salon.com, theonion.com*
**Web Sites or Home Pages:** *urbanlegends.com, movie-mistakes.com*
**Pamphlets:** *Common Sense*
**Films:** *The Matrix, Citizen Kane*
**Television Programs:** *60 Minutes, The Apprentice, Fear Factor*
**Radio Programs:** *All Things Considered, A Prairie Home Companion*
**Long Poems:** *John Brown's Body, The Faerie Queen*
**Plays:** *Macbeth, A Raisin in the Sun*
**Long Musical Works:** *Rigoletto, Eroica*
**Software Programs:** *Microsoft Word, PowerPoint*
**Search Engines and Web Browsers:** *Google, Internet Explorer, Safari*
**Databases:** *Academic Search Premier, Expanded Academic ASAP Plus*
**Paintings and Sculpture:** *Guernica, Pietà*
**Video Games:** *Halo: Combat Evolved, Grand Theft Auto V*
**Ships:** *Lusitania*, U.S.S. *Saratoga* (S.S. and U.S.S. are not italicized.)
**Trains:** *City of New Orleans, The Orient Express*
**Aircraft:** *The Hindenburg, Enola Gay* (Only particular aircraft, not makes or types such as Piper Cub or Airbus, are italicized.)
**Spacecraft:** *Challenger, Enterprise*

*Note:* Names of sacred books, such as the Bible and the Qur'an, and well-known documents, such as the Constitution and the Declaration of Independence, are neither italicized nor placed within quotation marks.

## 59b Setting Off Foreign Words and Phrases

Italics are often used to set off foreign words and phrases that have not become part of the English language.

"*C'est la vie,*" Madeline said when she saw the long line for the concert.

*Spirochaeta plicatilis* is a corkscrewlike bacterium.

If you are not sure whether a foreign word has been assimilated into English, consult a dictionary.

## 59c Setting Off Elements Spoken of as Themselves and Terms Being Defined

Use italics to set off letters, numerals, and words that refer to the letters, numerals, and words themselves.

Is that a *p* or a *g*?

I forget the exact address, but I know it has a *3* in it.

Does *through* rhyme with *cough*?

Welsh Scrabble sets have seven *Y*s, one *LL* and two *FF*s. (Note that only the letter referred to, not the plural *s*, is italicized.)

Also use italics to set off words and phrases that you go on to define.

A *closet drama* is a play meant to be read, not performed.

Note: When you quote a dictionary definition, put the word you are defining in italics and the definition itself in quotation marks.

To *infer* means "to draw a conclusion"; to *imply* means "to suggest."

## 59d Using Italics for Emphasis

Italics can occasionally be used for emphasis.

Initially, poetry might be defined as a kind of language that says *more* and says it *more intensely* than does ordinary language. (Lawrence Perrine, *Sound and Sense*)

However, overuse of italics is distracting. Instead of italicizing, try to indicate emphasis with word choice and sentence structure.

### EXERCISE 1

Underline to indicate italics where necessary, and delete any italics that are incorrectly used. If a sentence is correct, mark it with a *C*.

***Example:*** <u>However</u> is a conjunctive adverb, not a coordinating conjunction.

1. I said Carol, not Darryl.
2. A *deus ex machina,* an improbable device used to resolve the plot of a fictional work, is used in Charles Dickens's novel Oliver Twist.

3. He dotted every i and crossed every t.
4. The Metropolitan Opera's production of Carmen was a tour de force for the principal performers.
5. *Laissez-faire* is a doctrine holding that government should not interfere with trade.
6. Antidote and anecdote are often confused because their pronunciations are similar.
7. Hawthorne's novels include Fanshawe, The House of the Seven Gables, The Blithedale Romance, and The Scarlet Letter.
8. Words such as mailman, policeman, and fireman have been replaced by nonsexist terms such as letter carrier, police officer, and firefighter.
9. A classic black tuxedo was considered de rigueur at the charity ball, but Jason preferred to wear his *dashiki*.
10. Thomas Mann's novel Buddenbrooks is a bildungsroman.

CHAPTER 60

# Using Hyphens

## Frequently Asked Questions



**Hyphens** have two conventional uses: to break a word at the end of a line and to link words in certain compounds.

## 60a Breaking a Word at the End of a Line

A computer never breaks a word at the end of a line; if the full word will not fit, it is brought down to the next line. Sometimes, however, you will want to break a word with a hyphen—for example, to fill in space at the end of a line when you want to increase a document's visual appeal.

When you break a word at the end of a line, divide it only between syllables, consulting a dictionary if necessary. Never divide a word at the end of a page, and never hyphenate a one-syllable word. In addition, never leave a single letter at the end of a line or carry only one or two letters to the next line.

If you divide a compound word at the end of a line, put the hyphen between the elements of the compound (*snow-mobile,* not *snowmo-bile*).

See 60b

**Close-Up DIVIDING ELECTRONIC ADDRESSES (URLs)**

Never insert a hyphen to divide an electronic address (URL) at the end of a line. (Readers might think the hyphen is part of the address.) MLA style recommends that you break the URL after a slash. If this is not possible, break it in a logical place—after a period, for example—or avoid the problem altogether by moving the entire URL to the next line.

## 60b Dividing Compound Words

A **compound word** consists of two or more words. Some familiar compound words are always hyphenated: *no-hitter, helter-skelter.* Other compounds are always written as one word: *fireplace, peacetime.* Finally, some compounds are always written as two separate words: *labor relations, bunk bed.* A dictionary can tell you whether a particular compound requires a hyphen.

**GRAMMAR CHECKER Hyphenating Compound Words**

Your grammar checker will highlight certain compound words with incorrect or missing hyphenation and offer suggestions for revision.

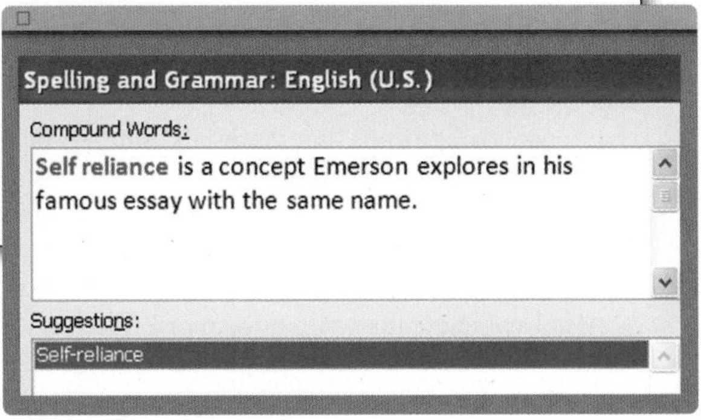
Spelling and Grammar: English (U.S.)
Compound Words:
Self reliance is a concept Emerson explores in his famous essay with the same name.
Suggestions:
Self-reliance

### 1 Hyphenating with Compound Adjectives

A **compound adjective** is a series of two or more words that function together as an adjective. When a compound adjective *precedes* the noun it modifies, use hyphens to join its elements.

> The research team tried to use nineteenth-century technology to design a space-age project.

When a compound adjective *follows* the noun it modifies, do not use hyphens to join its elements.

The three government-operated programs were run smoothly, but the one that was not government operated was short of funds.

Note: A compound adjective formed with an adverb ending in *-ly* is not hyphenated, even when it precedes the noun: *Many upwardly mobile families are on tight budgets.*

Use **suspended hyphens**—hyphens followed by a space or by appropriate punctuation and a space—in a series of compounds that modify the same word.

Graduates of two- and four-year colleges were eligible for the grants.

The exam called for sentence-, paragraph-, and essay-length answers.

## 2 Hyphenating with Certain Prefixes and Suffixes

Use a hyphen between a prefix and a proper noun or proper adjective.

mid-July pre-Columbian

Use a hyphen to connect the prefixes *all-*, *ex-*, *half-*, *quarter-*, *quasi-*, and *self-* and the suffix *-elect* to a noun.

ex-senator self-centered president-elect

Note: The words *selfhood, selfish,* and *selfless* do not include hyphens. In these words, *self* is the root, not a prefix.

## 3 Hyphenating in Compound Numerals and Fractions

Hyphenate compounds that represent numbers below one hundred (even if they are part of a larger number).

the twenty-first century
three hundred sixty-five days

Also hyphenate the written form of a fraction when it modifies a noun.

a two-thirds share of the business

## 4 Hyphenating for Clarity

Hyphenate to prevent readers from misreading one word for another.

Before we can reform criminals, we must re-form our ideas about prisons.

Hyphenate to avoid certain hard-to-read combinations, such as two *i*'s (*semi-illiterate*) or more than two of the same consonant (*shell-less*).

In most cases, hyphenate between a capital initial and a word when the two combine to form a compound: *A-frame, T-shirt, D-day.*

## 5 Hyphenating in Coined Compounds

A **coined compound,** one that uses a new combination of words as a unit, requires hyphens.

He looked up with a who-do-you-think-you-are expression.

### EXERCISE 1

Form compound adjectives from the following word groups, inserting hyphens where necessary.

***Example:*** a *three-year* contract ~~for three years~~

1. a relative who has long been lost
2. someone who is addicted to video games
3. a salesperson who goes from door to door
4. a display calculated to catch the eye
5. friends who are dearly beloved
6. a household that is centered on a child
7. a line of reasoning that is hard to follow
8. the border between New York and New Jersey
9. a candidate who is thirty-two years old
10. a computer that is friendly to its users

### EXERCISE 2

Add hyphens to the compounds in these sentences wherever they are required. Consult a dictionary if necessary.

***Example:*** Alaska was the forty-ninth state to join the United States.

1. One of the restaurant's blue plate specials is chicken fried steak.
2. Virginia and Texas are both right to work states.
3. He stood on tiptoe to see the near perfect statue, which was well hidden by the security fence.
4. The five and ten cent store had a self service makeup counter and stocked many up to the minute gadgets.
5. The so called Saturday night special is opposed by pro gun control groups.
6. He ordered two all beef patties with special sauce, lettuce, cheese, pickles, and onions on a sesame seed bun.
7. The material was extremely thought provoking, but it hardly presented any earth shattering conclusions.
8. The Dodgers Phillies game was rained out, so the long suffering fans left for home.
9. Bone marrow transplants carry the risk of what is known as a graft versus host reaction.
10. The state funded child care program was considered a highly desirable alternative to family day care.

CHAPTER 61

# Using Abbreviations

## Frequently Asked Questions



Generally speaking, **abbreviations** are not appropriate in college writing except in tables, charts, and works-cited lists. Some abbreviations are acceptable only in scientific, technical, or business writing, or only in a particular academic **discipline**. If you have any questions about the appropriateness of a particular abbreviation, check a style manual in your field.

See Pt. 6

**Close-Up** ABBREVIATIONS IN ELECTRONIC COMMUNICATIONS

Like emoticons and acronyms, which are popular in email and instant messages, shorthand abbreviations and symbols—such as *GR8* (great) and *2NITE* (tonight)—are common in text messages. Although they are acceptable in informal electronic communications, such abbreviations are not appropriate in college writing or in business communications.

## 61a Abbreviating Titles

Titles before and after proper names are usually abbreviated.

| | |
|---|---|
| Mr. Homer Simpson | Rep. Nydia Velázquez |
| Henry Kissinger, PhD | Prof. Elie Weisel |

Do not, however, use an abbreviated title without a name.

*doctor*
The ~~Dr.~~ diagnosed tuberculosis.

## 61b Abbreviating Organization Names and Technical Terms

Well-known businesses and government, social, and civic organizations are frequently referred to by capitalized initials. These abbreviations fall into two categories: those in which the initials are pronounced as separate units (MTV) and acronyms, in which the initials are pronounced as a word (FEMA).

To save space, you may also use accepted abbreviations for complex technical terms that are not well known, but be sure to spell out the full term the first time you mention it, followed by the abbreviation in parentheses.

> Citrus farmers have been using ethylene dibromide (EDB), a chemical pesticide, for more than twenty years. Now, however, EDB has contaminated water supplies.

**Close-Up** ABBREVIATIONS IN MLA DOCUMENTATION

See 18a

MLA documentation style requires abbreviations of publishers' company names—for example, **Columbia UP** for *Columbia University Press*—in the works-cited list. Do not, however, use such abbreviations in the body of your paper.

MLA style also permits the use of abbreviations that designate parts of written works (**ch. 3, sec. 7**)—but only in the works-cited list and parenthetical documentation.

Finally, MLA recommends abbreviating classic literary works and books of the Bible in parenthetical citations: ***Oth.*** (*Othello*), ***Exod.*** (Exodus). These words should not be abbreviated in the text of your paper or in the works-cited list.

## 61c Abbreviating Dates, Times of Day, and Temperatures

Dates, times of day, and temperatures are often abbreviated.

| | |
|---|---|
| 50 BC (*BC* follows the date) | AD 432 (*AD* precedes the date) |
| 6 a.m. | 3:03 p.m. |
| 20°C (Centigrade or Celsius) | 180°F (Fahrenheit) |

Always capitalize *BC* and *AD*. (The alternatives *BCE,* for "before the common era," and *CE,* for "common era," are also capitalized.) Use lowercase letters for *a.m.* and *p.m.*, but use these abbreviations only when they are accompanied by numbers.

> We will see you in the ~~a.m.~~ *morning.*

*Note:* Avoid the abbreviation *no.* (written either *no.* or *No.*), except in technical writing, and then use it only before a specific number: *The unidentified substance was labeled no. 52.*

## 61d Editing Misused Abbreviations

In college writing, abbreviations are not used in the following cases.

### 1 Names of Days, Months, or Holidays

Do not abbreviate days of the week, months, or holidays.

> *Saturday, December* *Christmas*
> On^ ~~Sat., Dec.~~ 23, I started my^ ~~Xmas~~ shopping.

### 2 Names of Streets and Places

In general, do not abbreviate names of streets and places.

> *Drive* *New York City.*
> He lives on Riverside^ ~~Dr.~~ in^ ~~NYC.~~

**Exceptions:** The abbreviation *US* is often acceptable (*US Coast Guard*), as is *DC* in *Washington, DC.* Also permissible are *Mt.* before the name of a mountain (*Mt. Etna*) and *St.* in a place name (*St. Albans*).

### 3 Names of Academic Subjects

Do not abbreviate names of academic subjects.

> *Psychology* *literature*
> ^ ~~Psych.~~ and English^ ~~lit.~~ are required courses.

### 4 Names of Businesses

Write company names exactly as the firms themselves write them, including the distinction between the **ampersand** (&) and the word *and: AT&T, Charles Schwab & Co., Inc.* Abbreviations for *company, corporation,* and the like are used only along with a company name.

> *corporation* *company*
> The^ ~~corp.~~ merged with a^ ~~co.~~ in Ohio.

### 5 Latin Expressions

Abbreviations of the common Latin phrases *i.e.* ("that is"), *e.g.* ("for example"), and *etc.* ("and so forth") are generally not appropriate in college writing except in notes and bibliographic citations.

> *for example,*
> Other musicians (^ ~~e.g.,~~ Bruce Springsteen) have also been influenced by Bob Dylan.

Poe wrote "The Raven," "Annabel Lee," ~~etc.~~ *and other poems.*

## 6 Units of Measurement

In technical writing, some units of measurement are abbreviated when they are preceded by a numeral.

The hurricane had winds of 35 mph.

One new hybrid gets over 50 mpg.

However, MLA style requires that you write out units of measurement and spell out words such as *inches, feet, years, miles, pints, quarts,* and *gallons.*

## 7 Symbols

The symbols =, +, and # are acceptable in technical and scientific writing but not in nontechnical college writing. The symbols % and $ are acceptable only when used with **numerals** (15%, $15,000), not with spelled-out numbers.

See 62b4,7

### EXERCISE 1

Correct any incorrectly used abbreviations in the following sentences, assuming that all are intended for a college audience. If a sentence is correct, mark it with a *C*.

***Example:*** *Romeo* ~~&~~ *and* *Juliet* is a play by Shakespeare.

1. The committee meeting, attended by representatives from Action for Children's Television (ACT) and NOW, Sen. Putnam, & the pres. of ABC, convened at 8 A.M. on Mon. Feb. 24 at the YWCA on Germantown Ave.
2. An econ. prof. was suspended after he encouraged his students to speculate on securities issued by a corp. under investigation by the SEC.
3. Benjamin Spock, who wrote *Baby and Child Care,* was a respected dr. known throughout the USA.
4. The FDA banned the use of Red Dye no. 2 in food in 1976, but other food additives are still in use.
5. The Rev. Dr. Martin Luther King Jr., leader of the SCLC, led the famous Selma, Ala., march.
6. Wm. Golding, a novelist from the U.K., won the Nobel Prize in lit.
7. The adult education center, financed by a major computer corp., offers courses in basic subjects such as introductory bio. and tech. writing as well as teaching HTML and XML.

8. All the fraternity brothers agreed to write to Pres. Dexter appealing their disciplinary probation under Ch. 4, Sec. 3, of the IFC constitution.
9. A 4 qt. (i.e., 1 gal.) container is needed to hold the salt solution.
10. According to Prof. Morrison, all those taking the exam should bring two sharpened no. 2 pencils to the St. Joseph's University auditorium on Sat.

CHAPTER 62

# Using Numbers

## Frequently Asked Questions



Convention determines when to use a **numeral** (22) and when to spell out a number (twenty-two). Numerals are commonly used in scientific and technical writing and in journalism, but they are used less often in the humanities.

Note: The guidelines in this chapter are based on the *MLA Handbook for Writers of Research Papers,* 7th ed. (2009). APA style, however, requires that all numbers below ten be spelled out if they do not represent specific measurements and that numbers ten and above be expressed in numerals.

## 62a Spelled-Out Numbers versus Numerals

Unless a number falls into one of the categories listed in **62b,** spell it out if you can do so *in one or two words.*

The Hawaiian alphabet has only twelve letters.

Class size stabilized at twenty-eight students.

The subsidies are expected to total about two million dollars.

Numbers *more than two words* long are expressed in figures.

The dietitian prepared 125 sample menus.

The developer of the community purchased 300,000 doorknobs and 153,000 faucets.

Never begin a sentence with a numeral. If necessary, reword the sentence.

**Faulty:** 250 students are currently enrolled in World History 106.

**Revised:** Current enrollment in World History 106 is 250 students.

*Note:* When one number immediately precedes another in a sentence, spell out the first, and use a numeral for the second: *five 3-quart containers.*

**GRAMMAR CHECKER Spelled-Out Numbers versus Numerals**

Your grammar checker will often highlight numerals in your writing and suggest that you spell them out. Before clicking Change, be sure that the number does not fall into one of the categories listed in **62b**.

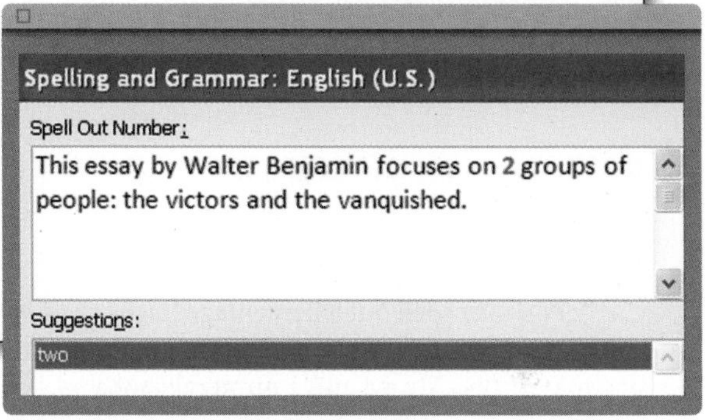
Spelling and Grammar: English (U.S.)
Spell Out Number:
This essay by Walter Benjamin focuses on 2 groups of people: the victors and the vanquished.
Suggestions:
two

## 62b Conventional Uses of Numerals

### 1 Addresses

1920 Walnut Street, Philadelphia, PA 19103

### 2 Dates

January 15, 1929    1914–1919

### 3 Exact Times

9:16    10 a.m. (or 10:00 a.m.)

**Exceptions:** Spell out times of day when they are used with *o'clock: eleven o'clock,* not *11 o'clock.* Also spell out times expressed as round numbers: *They were in bed by ten.*

### 4 Exact Sums of Money

$25.11 $6,752.00

Note: Always use a numeral (not a spelled-out number) with a $ symbol. You may spell out a round sum of money if you use sums infrequently in your paper, provided you can do so in two or three words: *five dollars; two thousand dollars.*

### 5 Divisions of Written Works

Use arabic (not roman) numerals for chapter and volume numbers; acts, scenes, and lines of plays; chapters and verses of the Bible; and line numbers of long poems.

### 6 Measurements before an Abbreviation or Symbol

12″ 55 mph
32° 15 cc

### 7 Percentages and Decimals

80% 3.14

Note: You may spell out a percentage (*eighty percent*) if you use percentages infrequently in your paper, provided the percentage can be expressed in two or three words. Always use a numeral (not a spelled-out number) with a % symbol.

### 8 Ratios, Scores, and Statistics

See Ch. 19, Ch. 21

In a paper that follows APA or CSE style, use numerals for numbers presented as a comparison.

Children preferred Fun Flakes over Graino by a ratio of 20 to 1.

The Orioles defeated the Phillies 6–0.

The median age of the patients was 42; the mean age was 40.

### 9 Identification Numbers

Route 66 Track 8 Channel 12

Note: When writing out large numbers, insert a comma every three digits from the right, beginning after the third digit.

3,000 25,000 6,751,098

Do not, however, use commas in four-digit page and line numbers, addresses, or year numbers.

page 1202 3741 Laurel Ave. 1968

## EXERCISE 1

Following MLA guidelines, revise the use of numbers in these sentences, making sure usage is correct and consistent. If a sentence uses numbers correctly, mark it with a *C*.

***Example:*** The Empire State Building is ~~one hundred and two~~ *102* stories high.

1. *1984,* a novel by George Orwell, is set in a totalitarian society.
2. The English placement examination included a 30-minute personal-experience essay, a 45-minute expository essay, and a 150-item objective test of grammar and usage.
3. In a control group of two hundred forty-seven patients, almost three out of four suffered serious adverse reactions to the new drug.
4. Before the Thirteenth Amendment to the Constitution, slaves were counted as 3/5 of a person.
5. The intensive membership drive netted 2,608 new members and additional dues of over 5 thousand dollars.
6. They had only 2 choices: either they could take the yacht at Pier Fourteen, or they could return home to the penthouse at Twenty-seven Harbor View Drive.
7. The atomic number of lithium is three.
8. Approximately 3 hundred thousand schoolchildren in District 6 were given hearing and vision examinations between May third and June 26.
9. The United States was drawn into the war by the Japanese attack on Pearl Harbor on December seventh, 1941.
10. An upper-middle-class family can spend more than 250,000 dollars to raise each child up to age 18.

## REVIEW EXERCISE: PUNCTUATION AND MECHANICS

Read the essay below, and then answer the questions on page 744.

**Is This the Future of Punctuation!?**

*By Henry Hitchings*

Punctuation arouses strong feelings. You have probably come across the pen-wielding vigilantes who skulk around defacing movie posters and amending handwritten signs that advertise "Rest Room's" or "Puppy's For Sale."

People fuss about punctuation not only because it clarifies meaning but also because its neglect appears to reflect wider social decline. And while the big social battles seem intractable, smaller battles over the use of the apostrophe feel like they can be won.

Yet the status of this and other cherished marks has long been precarious. The story of punctuation is one of comings and goings.

Early manuscripts had no punctuation at all, and those from the medieval period suggest haphazard innovation, with more than 30 different marks. The modern repertoire of punctuation emerged as printers in the 15th and 16th centuries strove to limit this miscellany.

Many punctuation marks are less venerable than we might imagine. Parentheses were first used around 1500, having been observed by English writers and printers in Italian books. Commas were not employed until the 16th century; in early printed books in English one sees a virgule (a slash like this /), which the comma replaced around 1520.

Other marks enjoyed briefer success. There used to be a clunky paragraph sign known as a pilcrow; initially it was a C with a slash drawn through it. Similar in its effect was one of the oldest punctuation symbols, a horizontal ivy leaf called a hedera. It appears in 8th-century manuscripts, separating text from commentary, and after a period out of fashion it made an unexpected return in early printed books. Then it faded from view.

Another mark, now obscure, is the *point d'ironie,* sometimes known as a "snark." A back-to-front question mark, it was deployed by the 16th-century printer Henry Denham to signal rhetorical questions, and in 1899 the French poet Alcanter de Brahm suggested reviving it. More recently, the difficulty of detecting irony and sarcasm in electronic communication has prompted fresh calls for a revival of the point d'ironie. But the chances are slim that it will make a comeback.

In fact, Internet culture generally favors a lighter, more informal style of punctuation. True, emoticons have sprung up to convey nuances of mood and tone. Moreover, typing makes it easy to amplify punctuation: splattering 20 exclamation marks on a page, or using multiple question marks to signify theatrical incredulity. But, overall, punctuation is being renounced.

How might punctuation now evolve? The dystopian view is that it will vanish. I find this conceivable, though not likely. But we can see harbingers of such change: editorial austerity with commas, the newsroom preference for the period over all other marks, and the taste for visual crispness.

Though it is not unusual to hear calls for new punctuation, the marks proposed tend to cannibalize existing ones. In this vein, you may have encountered the interrobang, which signals excited disbelief.

Such marks are symptoms of an increasing tendency to punctuate for rhetorical rather than grammatical effect. Instead of presenting syntactical and logical relationships, punctuation reproduces the patterns of speech.

One manifestation of this is the advance of the dash. It imitates the jagged urgency of conversation, in which we change direction sharply and with punch. Dashes became common only in the 18th century. Their appeal is visual, their shape dramatic. That's what a modern, talky style of writing seems to demand.

By contrast, use of the semicolon is dwindling. Although colons were common as early as the 14th century, the semicolon was rare in English books before the 17th century. It has always been regarded as a useful hybrid—a separator that's also a connector—but it's a trinket beloved of people who want to show that they went to the right school.

More surprising is the eclipse of the hyphen. Traditionally, it has been used to link two halves of a compound noun and has suggested that a new coinage is on probation. But now the noun is split (fig leaf, hobby horse) or rendered without a hyphen (crybaby, bumblebee). It may be that the hyphen's last outpost will be in emoticons, where it plays a leading role.

Graphic designers, who favor an uncluttered aesthetic, dislike hyphens. They are also partly responsible for the disappearance of the apostrophe. This little squiggle first appeared in an English text in 1559. Its use has never been completely stable, and today confusion leads to the overcompensation that we see in those handwritten signs. The alternative is not to use apostrophes at all—an act of pragmatism easily mistaken for ignorance.

Defenders of the apostrophe insist that it minimizes ambiguity, but there are few situations in which its omission can lead to real misunderstanding.

The apostrophe is mainly a device for the eye, not the ear. And while I plan to keep handling apostrophes in accordance with the principles I was shown as a child, I am confident that they will either disappear or be reduced to little baubles of orthographic bling.



*(continued)*

### QUESTIONS

1. Review the guidelines discussed in **Chapters 52–57** and **Chapter 60,** and then review Hitchings's use of punctuation marks in his essay. Would you add or delete any punctuation? Would you substitute different punctuation marks anywhere?
2. Hitchings notes that semicolons and hyphens are falling out of favor. Do you see this trend as positive? Why or why not?
3. According to Hitchings, the dash is more popular than ever. Do your observations support his conclusion? Do you think greater use of the dash is a good thing?
4. Do you think apostrophes are necessary to avoid confusion, or do you think the English language would be just fine without them? Explain your reasoning.
5. What is your favorite punctuation mark? Why?
6. Suggest a new punctuation mark that should be added to the language. What function would this punctuation mark serve?

PART 14

# Bilingual and ESL Writers

CHAPTER 63

# Adjusting to the US Classroom

## Frequently Asked Questions



If you went to school outside of the United States, you may not be familiar with the way writing is taught in US composition classes.

### Close-Up CHARACTERISTICS OF US CLASSROOMS

Here are some aspects of US classrooms that may be unfamiliar to you:

- **Punctuality** Students are expected to be in their seats and ready to begin class at the scheduled time. If you are late repeatedly, your grade may be lowered.
- **Student–Instructor Relationships** The relationship between students and instructors may be more casual and friendly than what you are used to. However, instructors still expect students to abide by the rules they set.
- **Class Discussion** Instructors typically expect students to volunteer ideas in class and may even enjoy it when students challenge their opinions (as long as the students can make good arguments for their positions). Rather than being seen as a sign of disrespect, this is usually considered to be evidence of interest and involvement in the topic under discussion.

## 63a Understanding the Writing Process

See Chs. 4–6

Typically, US composition instructors teach writing as a process. This process usually includes the following components:

See 4e3–5

- **Planning and shaping your writing** Your instructor will probably help you get ideas for your writing by assigning relevant readings, conducting class discussions, and asking you to keep a journal or engage in freewriting, brainstorming, or clustering.

- **Writing multiple drafts** After you write your paper, you will probably get feedback from your instructor or your classmates so that you can **revise** (improve) your paper before receiving a grade on it. Instructors expect students to use the suggestions they receive to make significant improvements to their papers. (For more information on the drafting process, **see 6a–b.**)
- **Looking at sample papers** Your instructor may provide the class with sample student papers of the type that he or she has assigned. Such samples can help you understand how to complete the assigned paper. Sometimes the samples are strong papers that can serve as good examples of what to do. However, most samples will have both strengths and weaknesses, so be sure you understand your instructor's opinion of the samples he or she provides.
- **Engaging in** peer review (sometimes called peer editing) Your instructor may ask the class to work in small groups or individually to exchange ideas about an assigned paper. You will be expected to provide other students with feedback on the strengths and weaknesses of their papers. Afterward, you should think carefully about your classmates' comments and make changes to improve your paper. See 6c2
- **Attending conferences** Your instructor may schedule one or more appointments with you to discuss your writing and may ask you to bring a draft of the paper you are working on. Your instructor may also be available to help you with your paper without an appointment during his or her office hours. In addition, many educational institutions have **writing centers,** where tutors help students get started on their papers or improve their drafts. When you meet with your instructor or writing center tutor, bring your paper and a list of specific questions, and be sure to make careful notes about what you discuss. You can refer to these notes when you revise your paper.

### Close-Up USING YOUR NATIVE LANGUAGE

Depending on your language background and skills, you may find it helpful to use your native language in some stages of your writing.

When you are making notes about the content of your paper, you may be able to generate more ideas and record them more quickly if you do some of the work in your native language. In addition, when you are drafting your paper and cannot think of a particular word in English, it may be better simply to write the word in your native language (and come back to it later) so you do not lose your train of thought.

However, if you use another language a great deal as you draft your writing and then try to translate your work into English, the English may sound awkward or be hard to understand. The best strategy when you draft your papers is to write in English as much as you can, using the vocabulary and structures that you already know.

## 63b Understanding English Language Basics

Getting used to writing and editing your work in English will be easier if you understand a few basic principles:

ESL 64a

- **In English, words may change their form according to their function.** For example, verbs change form to communicate whether an action is taking place in the past, present, or future.
- **In English, context is extremely important to understanding function.** In the following sentences, for instance, the word *walk* performs different functions according to its relationships to other words.

  Juan and I are taking a walk. (*Walk* is a noun, a direct object of the verb *taking,* with an article, *a,* attached to it.)

  If you walk instead of driving, you will help conserve the Earth's resources. (*Walk* is a verb, the predicate of the subject *you.*)

See Ch. 46

- **Spelling in English is not always phonetic and sometimes may seem illogical.** Spelling in English may be related more to the history of the word and to its origins in other languages than to the way the word is pronounced. Therefore, learning to spell correctly is often a matter of memorization, not of sounding out the word phonetically. For example, "ough" is pronounced differently in *tough, though,* and *thought.*

ESL 64f

- **Word order is extremely important in English sentences.** In English sentences, word order may indicate which word is the subject of the sentence and which is the object, whether the sentence is a question or a statement, and so on.

## 63c Learning to Edit Your Work

See 6d

Editing your paper involves focusing on grammar, spelling, punctuation, and mechanics. The approach you take to editing for grammar errors should depend on your strengths and weaknesses in English.

**CHECKLIST**

### Editing Strategies

- ❑ **If you learned English mostly by speaking it, if you have strong oral skills, and if you usually make correct judgments about English by instinct,** the best approach for you may be reading your paper aloud and listening for mistakes, correcting them by deciding what sounds right. You may even find that as you read aloud, you automatically correct your written mistakes as you speak. (Be sure to transfer those corrections to your paper.) In addition to proofreading your paper from beginning to end, you might find it helpful to start from the end of the paper, reading and proofreading sentence by sentence. This strategy can keep you from being distracted by your ideas, allowing you to focus on grammar alone.

- ❑ **If you learned English mostly by reading, studying grammar rules, and/or translating between your native language and English,** you may not feel that you have good instincts about what sounds right in English. If this is the case, you should take a different approach to editing your papers. First, identify the errors you make most frequently by looking at earlier papers your instructor has marked or by asking your instructor for help. Once you have identified your most common errors, read through your paper, checking each sentence for these errors. Try to apply the grammar and mechanics rules you already know, or check the relevant grammar explanations in **Chapter 64** for help.

After you check your paper for grammar errors, you should check it again to make sure that you have used proper punctuation, capitalization, and spelling. If you have difficulty with spelling, you can use a spell checker to help you, but remember that spell checkers cannot catch every error. After you have made grammar and mechanics corrections on your own, you can seek outside help in identifying errors you might have missed. You should also keep a notebook with a list of your most frequent grammatical errors and review these errors regularly.

CHECKLIST

### Getting Outside Help with Editing

- ❑ **Ask a tutor or a friend for help.** After you have done your best to edit your own paper, you may want to ask for help from a writing center tutor, from your instructor, or from a friend whose English skills you trust. Ask your helper to point out any errors. Then, try to correct these errors.
- ❑ **Use a grammar checker.** Your computer's grammar checker may give you some help with editing, but you may not find it very helpful because such grammar checkers are usually not designed to catch the types of errors typically made by ESL students.
- ❑ **Use a dictionary.** The dictionary can also be a good source of grammar help, especially if you use a dictionary designed for nonnative English speakers.

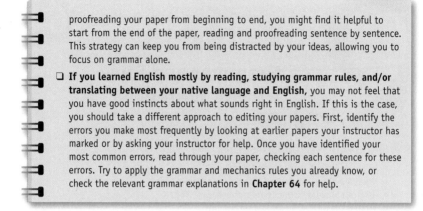

CHAPTER 64

# Grammar and Style for ESL Writers

## Frequently Asked Questions



For ESL writers (as for many native English writers), grammar can be a persistent problem. Grammatical knowledge in a second language usually develops slowly, with time and practice, and much about English is idiomatic (not subject to easy-to-learn rules). This chapter is designed to provide you with the tools you will need to address some of the most common grammatical problems ESL writers face.

## 64a Using Verbs

### 1 Subject-Verb Agreement

See Ch. 49

English verbs change their form according to person, number, and tense. The verb in a sentence must **agree** with the subject in both person and number. Person refers to *who* or *what* is performing the action of the verb (for example, **I, you,** or someone else), and number refers to *how many* people or things are performing the action (one or more than one).

See 50a

In English, the rules for **subject-verb agreement** are very important. Unless you use the correct person and number in the verbs in your sentences, you will confuse your English-speaking audience by communicating meanings you do not intend.

## Close-Up SUBJECT-VERB AGREEMENT

Follow these basic guidelines when selecting verbs for your sentences:

- If the subject consists of only one noun or pronoun, use a singular verb.

  He is at the park.

- If the subject consists of two or more nouns or pronouns connected with the word *and,* use a plural verb.

  Bob and Carol are at the park.

- If the subject contains both a singular and a plural noun or pronoun connected with the word *or,* the verb should agree with the noun that is nearer to it.

  Bob or the boys are at the park.

  The boys or Bob is at the park.

Note: Don't be confused by phrases that come between the subject and the verb. The verb should agree with the subject of the sentence, not with a noun that appears within an intervening phrase.

The woman with all of the children is at the park.

The coach, as well as the players, is nervous.

For information on subject-verb agreement with **indefinite pronouns,** such as *each, everyone,* and *nobody,* see **50a4.**

### 2 Verb Tense

**Tense** refers to *when* the action of the verb takes place. One problem that many nonnative speakers of English have with English verb tenses results from the large number of **irregular verbs** in English. For example, the first-person singular present tense of *be* is not "I be" but "I am," and the past tense is not "I beed" but "I was."

See 49b

See 49a2

Note: ESL writers whose first language is Chinese, Japanese, Korean, Russian, Thai, or Vietnamese are especially likely to have difficulty with verb tenses.

**Close-Up CHOOSING THE SIMPLEST VERB FORMS**

Some nonnative English speakers use verb forms that are more complicated than they need to be. They may do this because their native language uses more complicated verb forms than English does or because they "overcorrect" their verbs into complicated forms. Specifically, nonnative speakers tend to use progressive and perfect verb forms instead of simple verb forms. To communicate your ideas clearly to an English-speaking audience, choose the simplest possible verb form.

### 3 Auxiliary Verbs

The **auxiliary verbs** (also known as **helping verbs**) *be, have,* and *do* are used to create some present, past, and future forms of verbs in English: "Julio is taking a vacation"; "I have been tired lately"; "He does not need a license." The auxiliary verbs *be, have,* and *do* change form to reflect the time frame of the action or situation and to agree with the subject.

Note: ESL writers whose first language is Arabic, Chinese, Creole, Haitian, or Russian may have difficulty with auxiliary verbs because their first language sometimes omits the *be* verb.

**Close-Up AUXILIARY VERBS**

Only auxiliary verbs, not the verbs they "help," change form to indicate person, number, and tense.

**Present:** We have to eat.

**Past:** We had to eat. (*not* "We had to ate.")

See 47c1

Modal auxiliaries (such as *can* and *should*) do not change form to indicate tense, person, or number.

**EXERCISE 1**

A student wrote the following two paragraphs as part of a paper for his ESL composition class. He was asked to write about several interviews he conducted with people in his future profession, hotel management. The paragraphs contain errors in subject-verb agreement and verb tense, which the student's instructor underlined. Correct the underlined verbs by changing their form: begin by considering when the action took place, and then choose the simplest appropriate verb form to express that time. (Be sure to pay attention to the meaning and context of the sentences to determine which verb form is appropriate.)

In the past, when someone (1) <u>ask</u> me why I was interested in the hotel business, I always (2) <u>have</u> a hard time answering that question. I do not know exactly when and why I (3) <u>decide</u> to be a hotel manager. The only reason I can think of is my father. In his current job, he (4) <u>travel</u> a lot, and I have had a few chances to follow him and see other cities. Every time I went with him on a business trip, we (5) <u>spended</u> the night in a hotel, and I was surprised at how much hotels (6) <u>does</u> to satisfy their customers. All the employees are always friendly and polite. This gave me a positive image of hotels that made me (7) <u>decided</u> that the hotel business would be right for me.

For this paper, I (8) <u>spended</u> almost two weeks interviewing department heads at a local Hilton Hotel. Mr. Andrew Plain, the person who (9) <u>spend</u> the most time with me, (10) <u>share</u> an experience related to when he first got into the business. One of his first jobs was to plan a wedding, and he (11) <u>feel</u> a lot of responsibility because he (12) <u>believe</u> that a wedding is a one-time life experience for most people. So he wanted to take care of everything and make sure that everything was on track. To prepare for the wedding, he (13) <u>need</u> to work almost every Sunday, and one night he even (14) <u>have</u> to sleep in his office to attend the early wedding ceremony the next morning. From my experience with this interview, I realized that the people who are interested in the hotel business (15) <u>needs</u> great dedication to their career.

## 4 Negative Verbs

The meaning of a verb may be made negative in English in a variety of ways, chiefly by adding the words *not* or *does not* to the verb (is, is *not;* can ski, *can't* ski; drives a car, *does not* drive a car).

**GETTING HELP FROM A DICTIONARY**

You may have trouble with items 5, 8, and 9 of Exercise 1 if you do not know the correct past tense forms of the verb *spend,* which is irregular. For help, look up the word *spend* in a dictionary. The first word after the word *spend* is the simple past form of *spend.*

### Close-Up CORRECTING DOUBLE NEGATIVES

A **double negative** occurs when the meaning of a verb is made negative not just once but twice in a single sentence.

> Henry doesn't have ~~no~~ *any* friends. (*or* Henry ~~doesn't have~~ *has* no friends.)
>
> I looked for articles in the library, but there were~~n't~~ none. (*or* I looked for articles in the library, but there weren't ~~none~~ *any*.)

*Note:* Some ESL writers whose first language is Spanish tend to use double negatives.

## 5 Phrasal Verbs

Many verbs in English are composed of two or more words that are combined to create a new idiomatic expression—for example, *check up on, run for, turn into,* and *wait on.* These verbs are called **phrasal verbs.** It is important to become familiar with phrasal verbs and their definitions so you will recognize these verbs as phrasal verbs (instead of as verbs that are followed by prepositions).

***Separable Phrasal Verbs*** Often, the words that make up a phrasal verb can be separated from each other by a direct object. In these **separable phrasal** verbs, the object can come either before or after the preposition. For example, "Ellen turned down the job offer" and "Ellen turned the job offer down" are both correct. However, when the object is a pronoun, the pronoun must come before the preposition. Therefore, "Ellen turned *it* down" is correct, but "Ellen turned down *it*" is incorrect.

### Close-Up SEPARABLE PHRASAL VERBS

| Verb | Definition |
| --- | --- |
| call off | cancel |
| carry on | continue |
| cheer up | make happy |
| clean out | clean the inside of |
| cut down | reduce |
| figure out | solve |

| Verb | Definition |
|---|---|
| fill in | substitute |
| find out | discover |
| give back | return something |
| give up | stop doing something or stop trying |
| leave out | omit |
| pass on | transmit |
| put away | place something in its proper place |
| put back | place something in its original place |
| put off | postpone |
| start over | start again |
| talk over | discuss |
| throw away/out | discard |
| touch up | repair |

***Inseparable Phrasal Verbs*** Some phrasal verbs—such as *look into, make up for,* and *break into*—consist of words that can never be separated. With these **inseparable phrasal verbs,** you do not have a choice about where to place the object; the object must always directly follow the preposition. For example, "Anna cared for her niece" is correct, but "Anna cared her niece for" is incorrect.

### Close-Up INSEPARABLE PHRASAL VERBS

| Verb | Definition |
|---|---|
| come down with | develop an illness |
| come up with | produce |
| do away with | abolish |
| fall behind in | lag |
| get along with | be congenial with |
| get away with | avoid punishment |
| keep up with | maintain the same achievement or speed |
| look up to | admire |
| make up for | compensate |
| put up with | tolerate |
| run into | meet by chance |
| see to | arrange |
| show up | arrive |
| stand by | wait or remain loyal to |
| stand up for | support |
| watch out for | beware of or protect |

### 6 Voice

See 49d

Verbs may be in either active or passive voice. When the subject of a sentence performs the action of the verb, the verb is in **active voice.** When the action of the verb is performed on the subject, the verb is in **passive voice.**

Karla and Miguel purchased the tickets. (active voice)

The tickets were purchased by Karla and Miguel. (passive voice)

The tickets were purchased. (passive voice)

Because your writing will usually be clearer and more concise if you use the active voice, you should use the passive voice only when you have a good reason to do so.

When deciding whether to use the passive or active voice, you need to consider what you want to focus on. In the first example above, the focus is on Karla and Miguel. However, the second and third examples above, which use the passive voice, put the focus on the fact that the tickets were *purchased* rather than on *who* purchased them.

Note: ESL writers whose first language is Creole, Japanese, Korean, Russian, Thai, or Vietnamese may encounter unique challenges with voice when writing in English.

### 7 Transitive and Intransitive Verbs

Many nonnative English speakers find it difficult to decide whether or not a verb needs an object and in what order direct and indirect objects should appear in a sentence. Learning the difference between transitive verbs and intransitive verbs can help you with such problems.

A **transitive verb** is a verb that has a direct object: "My father asked a question" (subject + verb + direct object). In this example, *asked* is a transitive verb; it needs an object to complete its meaning.

An **intransitive verb** is a verb that does not take an object: "The doctor smiled" (subject + verb). In this example, *smiled* is an intransitive verb; it does not need an object to complete its meaning.

A transitive verb may be followed by a direct object or by both an indirect object and a direct object. (An indirect object answers the question "To whom?" or "For whom?") The indirect object may come before or after the direct object. If the indirect object follows the direct object, the preposition *to* or *for* must precede the indirect object.

s v do
Keith wrote a letter. (subject + verb + direct object)

s v io do
Keith wrote his friend a letter. (subject + verb + indirect object + direct object)

s v do io
Keith wrote a letter to his friend. (subject + verb + direct object + *to*/*for* + indirect object)

Some verbs in English look similar and have similar meanings, except that one is transitive and the other is intransitive. For example, *lie* is intransitive, *lay* is transitive; *sit* is intransitive, *set* is transitive; *rise* is intransitive, *raise* is transitive. Knowing whether a verb is transitive or intransitive will help you with troublesome verb pairs like these and will help you place words in the correct order. (See the **Glossary of Usage** for more on these verb pairs.)

Note: It is also important to know whether a verb is transitive or intransitive because only transitive verbs can be used in the **passive voice.** To determine whether a verb is transitive or intransitive—that is, to determine whether or not it needs an object—consult the example phrases in a dictionary. See 49d

## 8 Infinitives and Gerunds

In English, two verb forms may be used as nouns: **infinitives,** which always begin with *to* (as in *to work, to sleep, to eat*), and **gerunds,** which always end in *-ing,* (as in *working, sleeping, eating*).

To bite into this steak requires better teeth than mine. (infinitive used as a noun)

Cooking is one of my favorite hobbies. (gerund used as a noun)

Sometimes the gerund and the infinitive form of the same verb can be used interchangeably. For example, "He continued *to sleep*" and "He continued *sleeping*" convey the same meaning. However, this is not always the case. Saying, "Marco and Lisa stopped *to eat* at Julio's Café" is not the same as saying, "Marco and Lisa stopped *eating* at Julio's Café." In this example, the meaning of the sentence changes depending on whether a gerund or infinitive is used.

Note: ESL writers whose first language is Arabic, Chinese, Farsi, French, Greek, Korean, Portuguese, Spanish, or Vietnamese may have difficulty with gerunds.

## 9 Participles

In English, verb forms called **present participles** and **past participles** are frequently used as adjectives. Present participles usually end in *-ing,* as in *working, sleeping,* and *eating,* and past participles usually end in *-ed, -t,* or *-en,* as in *worked, slept,* and *eaten.*

According to the Bible, God spoke to Moses from a burning bush. (present participle used as an adjective)

Some people think raw fish is healthier than cooked fish. (past participle used as an adjective)

A **participial phrase** is a group of words consisting of the participle plus the noun phrase that functions as the object or complement of the action being expressed by the participle. To avoid confusion, the participial phrase must be placed as close as possible to the noun it modifies.

Having visited San Francisco last week, Jim and Lynn showed us pictures from their vacation. (The participial phrase is used as an adjective that modifies *Jim and Lynn.*)

See 53d

*Note:* When a participial phrase falls at the beginning of a sentence, a comma is used to set it off. When a participial phrase is used in the middle of a sentence, commas should be used only if the phrase is not essential to the meaning of the sentence. No commas should be used if the participial phrase is essential to the meaning of the sentence.

### 10 Verbs Formed from Nouns

In English, nouns can sometimes be used as verbs, with no change in form (other than the addition of an *-s* for agreement with third-person singular subjects or the addition of past tense endings). For example, the nouns *chair, book, frame,* and *father* can all be used as verbs.

She chairs a committee on neighborhood safety.

We booked a flight to New York for next week.

I will frame my daughter's diploma after she graduates.

He fathered several children out of wedlock.

## 64b Using Nouns

See 47a

Nouns name things: people, animals, objects, places, feelings, ideas. If a noun names one thing, it is singular; if a noun names more than one thing, it is plural.

### 1 Recognizing Noncount Nouns

Some English nouns do not have a plural form. They are called **noncount nouns** because what they name cannot be counted.

Note: ESL writers whose first language is Chinese or Japanese may have trouble with noncount nouns.

Close-Up NONCOUNT NOUNS

The following commonly used nouns are noncount nouns. These words have no plural forms. Therefore, you should never add *-s* to them.

| | | |
|---|---|---|
| advice | evidence | knowledge |
| clothing | furniture | luggage |
| education | homework | merchandise |
| equipment | information | revenge |

**EXERCISE 2**

An ESL student wrote the following paragraph as part of a composition paper about her experiences learning English. Read the paragraph, and decide which of the underlined words need to be made plural and which should remain unchanged. If a word should be made plural, make the necessary correction. If a word is correct as is, mark it with a *C*.

Visiting Ireland for three (1) month expanded my (2) knowledge of English. I took a part-time English (3) course, which was the key to improving my writing. The (4) course helped me understand the essential (5) rule of English, and I learned a lot of new (6) vocabulary and expressions. In the first three (7) lecture, the teacher, Mr. Nelson, explained the fundamentals of writing in English. My (8) enthusiasm for the English language increased because I realized the importance of this (9) language for my (10) future. Mr. Nelson recommended that I read more English (11) book. I took his advice, and my English got better.

## 2 Using Articles with Nouns

English has two kinds of **articles,** indefinite and definite.

Use an **indefinite article** (*a* or *an*) with a noun when readers are not familiar with the noun you are naming—for example, when you are introducing a noun for the first time. To say, "Jim entered *a* building," signals to the audience that you are introducing the idea of the building for the first time. The building is indefinite, or not specific, until it has been identified.

**GETTING HELP FROM A DICTIONARY**

Some of the nouns in Exercise 2 are noncount nouns, which cannot be made plural. If you are not sure whether a noun is countable or not, look it up in a dictionary.

The indefinite article *a* is used when the word following it (which may be a noun or an adjective) begins with a consonant or with a consonant sound: *a tree, a onetime offer.* The indefinite article *an* is used if the word following it begins with a vowel (*a, e, i, o,* or *u*) or with a vowel sound: *an apple, an honor.*

Use the **definite article** (*the*) when the noun you are naming has already been introduced, when the noun is already familiar to readers, or when the noun to which you refer is specific. To say, "Jim entered *the* building," signals to readers that you are referring to the same building you mentioned earlier. The building has now become specific and may be referred to by the definite article.

*Note:* ESL writers whose first language is Chinese, Farsi, Russian, or Swahili are likely to have difficulty with articles.

## Close-Up USING ARTICLES WITH NOUNS

There are three main exceptions to the rules governing the use of articles with nouns:

1. **Plural nouns** do not require indefinite articles: "I love horses," not "I love *a* horses." (However, plural nouns do require definite articles if you have already introduced the noun to your readers or if you are referring to a specific plural noun: "I love *the* horses in the national park near my house.")

2. **Noncount nouns** may or may not require articles.

   "Love conquers all," not "*A* love conquers all" or "*The* love conquers all."

   "*A* good education is important," not "Good education is important."

   "*The* homework is difficult" or "Homework is difficult," not "*A* homework is difficult."

   To help determine whether or not a noncount noun requires an article, look up that noun in a dictionary and consult the sample sentences provided.

3. **A proper noun,** which names a particular person, place, or thing, sometimes takes an article and sometimes does not. When you use an article with a proper noun, do not capitalize the article unless the article is the first word of the sentence.

   "*The* Mississippi River is one of the longest rivers in the world," not "Mississippi River is one of the longest rivers in the world."

   "Teresa was born in *the* United States," not "Teresa was born in United States."

   "China is the most populous nation on earth," not "*The* China is the most populous nation on earth."

To find out whether or not a proper noun requires an article, look up that noun in a dictionary, and consult the sample sentences provided.

## EXERCISE 3

The following introductory paragraph of a paper about renewable energy power sources was written for an ESL composition course. Read the paragraph, and decide whether or not each of the underlined noun phrases requires an article. If a noun phrase is correct as is, mark it with a *C*. If a noun phrase needs an article, indicate whether that article should be *a, an,* or *the*.

(1) Use of electrical power has increased dramatically over (2) last thirty years and continues to rise. (3) Most ordinary sources of (4) electricity require (5) oil, (6) gas, or (7) uranium, which are not (8) renewable resources. Living without (9) electrical power is not feasible as long as everything in our lives depends on (10) electricity, but (11) entire world will be in (12) big crisis if (13) ignorance regarding renewable energy continues. (14) Renewable energy, including (15) solar energy, (16) wind energy, (17) hydro energy, and (18) biomass energy, need (19) more attention from (20) scientists.

### 3 Using Other Determiners with Nouns

**Determiners** are words that function as **adjectives** to limit or qualify the meaning of nouns. In addition to articles, **demonstrative pronouns, possessive nouns and pronouns, numbers** (both **cardinal** and **ordinal**), and other words indicating number and order can function in this way.

**GETTING HELP FROM A DICTIONARY**

If you are uncertain whether or not to use an article with a certain noun, look up that noun in a dictionary, and use the sample sentences provided as a guide. When dealing with a noun phrase, be sure to look up the main noun. For example, in Exercise 3 item 1, look up *use*, and in item 2, look up *year*.

See 47d2

**Close-Up** USING OTHER DETERMINERS WITH NOUNS

- **Demonstrative pronouns** (*this, that, these, those*) communicate the following:
  1. the relative nearness or farness of the noun from the speaker's position (*this* and *these* for things that are *near*, *that* and *those* for

*(continued)*

**USING OTHER DETERMINERS WITH NOUNS** *(continued)*

things that are *far*): *this* book on my desk, *that* book on your desk; *these* shoes on my feet, *those* shoes in my closet.

2. the number of things indicated (*this* and *that* for *singular* nouns, *these* and *those* for *plural* nouns): *this* (or *that*) flower in the vase, *these* (or *those*) flowers in the garden.

- **Possessive nouns** and **possessive pronouns** (*Ashraf's, his, their*) show who or what the noun belongs to: *Maria's* courage, *everybody's* fears, the *country's* natural resources, *my* personality, *our* groceries.
- **Cardinal numbers** (*three, fifty, a thousand*) indicate how many of the noun you mean: *seven* continents. **Ordinal** numbers (*first, tenth, thirtieth*) indicate in what order the noun appears among other items: *third* planet.
- Words other than numbers may indicate **amount** (*many, few*) and **order** (*next, last*) and function in the same ways as cardinal and ordinal numbers: *few* opportunities, *last* chance.

## 64c Using Pronouns

See 47b, Ch. 48

Any English noun may be replaced by a **pronoun**. Pronouns enable you to avoid repeating a noun over and over. For example, *doctor* may be replaced by *he* or *she, books* by *them,* and *computer* by *it.*

### 1 Pronoun Reference

See 48c

**Pronoun reference** is very important in English sentences, where the noun the pronoun replaces (the **antecedent**) must be easily identified. In general, you should place the pronoun as close as possible to the noun it replaces so the noun to which the pronoun refers is clear. If this is impossible, use the noun itself instead of replacing it with a pronoun.

**Unclear:** When Tara met Emily, she was nervous. (Does *she* refer to Tara or to Emily?)

**Clear:** When Tara met Emily, Tara was nervous.

**Unclear:** Stefano and Victor love his DVD collection. (Whose DVD collection—Stefano's, Victor's, or someone else's?)

**Clear:** Stefano and Victor love Emilio's DVD collection.

*Note:* ESL writers whose first language is Spanish or Thai may have difficulty with pronoun reference.

## 2 Pronoun Placement

Never use a pronoun immediately after the noun it replaces. For example, do not say, "Most of my classmates they are smart"; instead, say, "Most of my classmates are smart."

The only exception to this rule occurs with an **intensive pronoun,** which ends in *-self* and emphasizes the preceding noun or pronoun: *Marta herself was eager to hear the results.*

## 3 Indefinite Pronouns

Unlike **personal pronouns** (*I, you, he, she, it, we, they, me, him, her, us, them,* and so on), **indefinite pronouns** do not refer to a particular person, place, or thing. Therefore, an indefinite pronoun does not require an antecedent. **Indefinite pronoun subjects** (*anybody, nobody, each, either, someone, something, all, some*), like personal pronouns, must agree in number with the sentence's verb.

See 50a4

Nobody ~~have~~ has failed the exam. (*Nobody* is a singular subject and requires a singular verb.)

## 4 Appositives

**Appositives** are nouns or noun phrases that identify or rename an adjacent noun or pronoun. An appositive usually follows the noun it explains or modifies but can sometimes precede it.

My parents, Mary and John, live in Louisiana. (*Mary and John* identifies *parents.*)

*Note:* The case of a pronoun in an appositive depends on the case of the word it identifies.

See 48b3

If an appositive is *not* essential to the meaning of the sentence, use commas to set off the appositive from the rest of the sentence. If an appositive *is* essential to the meaning of the sentence, do not use commas.

His aunt Trang is in the hospital. (*Trang* is necessary to the meaning of the sentence because it identifies which aunt is in the hospital.)

Akta's car, a 1997 Jeep, broke down last night, so she had to walk home. (*a 1997 Jeep* is not essential to the meaning of the sentence.)

## 5 Pronouns and Gender

A pronoun must agree in **gender** with the noun to which it refers.

My sister sold her old car.

Your uncle is walking his dog.

Keep in mind that in English, most nonhuman nouns are referred to as *it* because they do not have grammatical gender. However, exceptions are sometimes made for pets, ships, and countries. Pets are often referred to as *he* or *she,* depending on their sex, and ships and countries are sometimes referred to as *she.*

Note: ESL writers whose first language is Bengali, Farsi, Gujarati, or Thai may have problems with pronouns and gender.

**EXERCISE 4**

There are no pronouns in the following passage. The repetition of the nouns again and again would seem strange to a native English speaker. Rewrite the passage, replacing as many of the nouns as possible with appropriate pronouns. Be sure that the connection between the pronouns and the nouns they replace is clear.

The young couple seated across from Daniel at dinner the night before were newlyweds from Tokyo. The young couple and Daniel ate together with other guests of the inn at long, low tables in a large dining room with straw mat flooring. The man introduced himself immediately in English, shook Daniel's hand firmly, and, after learning that Daniel was not a tourist but a resident working in Osaka, gave Daniel a business card. The man had just finished college and was working at the man's first real job, clerking in a bank. Even in a sweatsuit, the man looked ready for the office: chin closely shaven, bristly hair neatly clipped, nails clean and buffed. After a while the man and Daniel exhausted the man's store of English and drifted into Japanese.

The man's wife, shy up until then, took over as the man fell silent. The woman and Daniel talked about the new popularity of hot springs spas in the countryside around the inn, the difficulty of finding good schools for the children the woman hoped to have soon, the differences between food in Tokyo and Osaka. The woman's husband ate busily. From time to time the woman refilled the man's beer glass or served the man radish pickles from a china bowl in the middle of the table, and then returned to the conversation.

## 64d Using Adjectives and Adverbs

See Ch. 51

Adjectives and adverbs are words that **modify** (describe, limit, or qualify) other words.

### 1 Position of Adjectives and Adverbs

**Adjectives** in English usually appear before the nouns they modify. A native speaker of English would not say, "*Cars red and black* are involved in more accidents than *cars blue or green*" but would say instead, "*Red and black cars* are involved in more accidents than *blue or green cars.*"

However, adjectives may appear *after* linking verbs ("The name seemed *familiar.*"), *after* direct objects ("The coach found them *tired* but *happy.*"), and *after* indefinite pronouns ("Anything *sad* makes me cry.").

**Adverbs** may appear before or after the verbs they describe, but they should be placed as close to the verb as possible: not "I *told* John that I couldn't meet him for lunch *politely*," but "I *politely told* John that I couldn't meet him for lunch" or "I *told* John *politely* that I couldn't meet him for lunch." When an adverb describes an adjective or another adverb, it usually comes *before* that adjective or adverb: "The essay has *basically sound* logic"; "You must express yourself *absolutely clearly.*"

Never place an adverb between the verb and the direct object.

**Incorrect:** Rolf *drank quickly* the water.

**Correct:** Rolf *drank* the water *quickly* (or, Rolf *quickly drank* the water).

**Incorrect:** Suong *took quietly* the test.

**Correct:** Suong *quietly took* the test (or, Suong *took* the test *quietly*).

Note: ESL writers whose first language is Creole or Haitian may have problems with adverbs.

## 2 Order of Adjectives

A single noun may be modified by more than one adjective, perhaps even by a whole list of adjectives. Given a list of three or four adjectives, most native speakers would arrange them in a sentence in the same order. If, for example, shoes are to be described as *green* and *big,* numbering *two,* and of the type worn for playing *tennis,* a native speaker would say "two big green tennis shoes." Generally, the adjectives that are most important in completing the meaning of the noun are placed closest to the noun.

### Close-Up ORDER OF ADJECTIVES

1. Articles (*a, the*), demonstratives (*this, those*), and possessives (*his, our, Maria's, everybody's*)
2. Amounts (*one, five, many, few*), order (*first, next, last*)
3. Personal opinions (*nice, ugly, crowded, pitiful*)
4. Sizes and shapes (*small, tall, straight, crooked*)
5. Age (*young, old, modern, ancient*)
6. Colors (*black, white, red, blue, dark, light*)
7. Nouns functioning as adjectives to form a unit with the noun (*soccer ball, cardboard box, history class*)

**EXERCISE 5**

Write five original sentences in which two or three adjectives describe a noun. Be sure that the adjectives are in the correct order.

## 64e Using Prepositions

See 47f

In English, prepositions (such as *to, from, at, with, among, between*) give meaning to nouns by linking them with other words and other parts of the sentence. Prepositions convey several kinds of information:

- Relations to **time** (*at* nine o'clock, *in* five minutes, *for* a month)
- Relations of **place** (*in* the classroom, *at* the library, *beside* the chair) and **direction** (*to* the market, *onto* the stage, *toward* the freeway)
- Relations of **association** (go *with* someone, the tip *of* the iceberg)
- Relations of **purpose** (working *for* money, dieting *to* lose weight)

### 1 Commonly Used Prepositional Phrases

In English, the use of prepositions is often idiomatic rather than governed by grammatical rules. In many cases, therefore, learners of English as a second language need to memorize which prepositions are used in which phrases.

In English, some prepositions that relate to time have specific uses with certain nouns, such as days, months, and seasons:

- *On* is used with days and specific dates: *on* Monday, *on* September 13, 1977.
- *In* is used with months, seasons, and years: *in* November, *in* the spring, *in* 1999.
- *In* is also used when referring to some parts of the day: *in* the morning, *in* the afternoon, *in* the evening.
- *At* is used to refer to other parts of the day: *at* noon, *at* night, *at* seven o'clock.

**Close-Up DIFFICULT PREPOSITIONAL PHRASES**

The following phrases (accompanied by their correct prepositions) sometimes cause difficulties for ESL writers:

| | | |
|---|---|---|
| according *to* | *at* least | relevant *to* |
| apologize *to* | *at* most | similar *to* |
| appeal *to* | refer *to* | subscribe *to* |
| different *from* | | |

## 2 Commonly Confused Prepositions

The prepositions *to, in, on, into,* and *onto* are very similar to one another and are therefore easily confused.

### Close-Up USING COMMON PREPOSITIONS

- *To* is the basic preposition of direction. It indicates movement toward a physical place: "She went *to* the restaurant"; "He went *to* the meeting." (*To* is also used to form the infinitive of a verb: "He wanted *to deposit* his paycheck before noon"; "Irene offered *to drive* Maria to the baseball game.")
- *In* indicates that something is within the boundaries of a particular space or period of time: "My son is *in* the garden"; "I like to ski *in* the winter"; "The map is *in* the car."
- *On* indicates position above or the state of being supported by something: "The toys are *on* the porch"; "The baby sat *on* my lap"; "The book is *on* top of the magazine."
- *Into* indicates movement to the inside or interior of something: "She walked *into* the room"; "I threw the stone *into* the lake"; "He put the photos *into* the box." Although *into* and *in* are sometimes interchangeable, note that usage depends on whether the subject is stationary or moving. *Into* usually indicates movement, as in "I jumped *into* the water." *In* usually indicates a stationary position relative to the object of the preposition, as in "Mary is swimming *in* the water."
- *Onto* indicates movement to a position on top of something: "The cat jumped *onto* the chair"; "Crumbs are falling *onto* the floor." Both *on* and *onto* can be used to indicate a position on top of something (and therefore they can sometimes be used interchangeably), but *onto* specifies that the subject is moving to a place from a different place or from an outside position.

### Close-Up PREPOSITIONS IN IDIOMATIC EXPRESSIONS

Many nonnative speakers use incorrect prepositions in idiomatic expressions. Compare the incorrect expressions in the left-hand column below with the correct expressions in the right-hand column.

| **Incorrect** | **Correct** |
| --- | --- |
| according *with* | according *to* |
| apologize *at* | apologize *to* |

*(continued)*

**PREPOSITIONS IN IDIOMATIC EXPRESSIONS** *(continued)*

| Incorrect | Correct |
|---|---|
| appeal *at* | appeal *to* |
| believe *at* | believe *in* |
| different *to* | different *from* |
| *for* least, *for* most | *at* least, *at* most |
| refer *at* | refer *to* |
| relevant *with* | relevant *to* |
| similar *with* | similar *to* |
| subscribe *with* | subscribe *to* |

## EXERCISE 6

An ESL student in a composition class wrote the following paragraphs as part of a paper about her experiences learning to write in English. In several cases, she chose the wrong prepositions. The student's instructor has underlined the misused prepositions. Your task is to replace each underlined preposition with a correct preposition. (In some cases, there may be more than one possible correct answer.) If you have trouble, see the "Getting Help from a Dictionary" box, which follows the exercise.

My first experience writing (1) of English took place (2) at my early youth. I don't remember what the experience was like, but I do know that I have improved my writing skills since then. The improvement stems from various reasons. One major impact (3) to my writing was the fact that I attended an American school (4) of my country. This helped a lot because the first language (5) to the school was English. Being surrounded (6) in English helped me improve both my verbal skills and my writing skills. Another major factor that helped me develop my English writing skills, especially my grammar and vocabulary, was reading novels.

(7) At the future, I plan to improve my writing skills in English by participating (8) to several activities. I plan to read more novels so I can further develop the grammar and vocabulary skills that will help me earn my degree. I also plan to communicate verbally with native speakers and to listen (9) at public speeches (such as the president's state of the union address), which usually contain rich vocabulary. But my main plan is to keep writing more papers and discussing my writing (10) to my instructor. The more I write, the more confident I will become and the more my writing will improve. And there is always room for improvement.

## 64f Understanding Word Order

In English, word order is extremely important, contributing a good deal to the meaning of a sentence.

> **GETTING HELP FROM A DICTIONARY**
>
> In some cases, you can determine which preposition to use by consulting a dictionary. For example, you can find the answers to items 3, 6, 7, 8, 9, and 10 in Exercise 6 by consulting a dictionary. Look up a noun or verb that is part of the phrase in question, and within the dictionary entry for each of these words, you will find example phrases containing the correct preposition. *Hint:* For item 3, look up the word *impact,* and for item 6, look up *surround*.

### 1 Standard Word Order

Like Chinese, English is an SVO language, or one in which the most typical sentence pattern is "subject-verb-object." (Arabic, by contrast, is an example of a VSO language.)

### 2 Word Order in Questions

Word order in questions can be particularly troublesome for speakers of languages other than English, partly because there are so many different ways to form questions in English.

#### Close-Up WORD ORDER IN QUESTIONS

1. To create a **yes/no question** from a statement whose verb is a form of *be* (*am, is, are, was, were*), move the verb so it precedes the subject.

   Rasheem is in his laboratory.

   Is Rasheem in his laboratory?

   When the statement is *not* a form of *be,* change the verb to include a form of *do* as a helping verb, and then move that helping verb so it precedes the subject.

   Rasheem researched the depletion of the ozone level.

   Did Rasheem research the depletion of the ozone level?

2. To create a **yes/no question** from a statement that includes one or more helping verbs, move the first helping verb so it precedes the subject.

   Rasheem is researching the depletion of the ozone layer.

   Is Rasheem researching the depletion of the ozone layer?

*(continued)*

**WORD ORDER IN QUESTIONS** *(continued)*

3. To create a **question asking for information,** replace the information being asked for with an **interrogative** word (*who, what, where, why, when, how*) at the beginning of the question, and invert the order of the subject and verb as with a yes/no question.

   Rasheem is in his laboratory.

   Where is Rasheem?

   Rasheem is researching the depletion of the ozone layer.

   What is Rasheem researching?

   Rasheem researched the depletion of the ozone level.

   What did Rasheem research?

   If the interrogative word is the subject of the question, however, do *not* invert the subject and verb.

   Who is researching the depletion of the ozone level?

4. You can also form a question by adding a **tag question** (such as *won't he?* or *didn't I?*) to the end of a statement. If the verb of the main statement is *positive,* then the verb of the tag question is *negative;* if the verb of the main statement is *negative,* then the verb of the tag question is *positive*.

   Rasheem is researching the depletion of the ozone layer, isn't he?

   Rasheem doesn't intend to write his dissertation about the depletion of the ozone layer, does he?

## 3 Word Order in Imperative Sentences

**Imperative** sentences state commands. It is common for the subject of an imperative sentence to be left out because the word *you* is understood to be the subject: "Go to school"; "Eat your dinner." Therefore, the word order pattern in an imperative sentence is usually "verb-object," or VO.

# Glossary of Usage

This glossary of usage lists words and phrases that writers often find troublesome and explains how they are used.

a, an   Use *a* before words that begin with consonants and words with initial vowels that sound like consonants: *a* person, *a* historical document, *a* one-horse carriage, *a* uniform. Use *an* before words that begin with vowels and words that begin with a silent *h: an* artist, *an* honest person.

accept, except   *Accept* is a verb that means "to receive"; *except* as a preposition or conjunction means "other than" and as a verb means "to leave out": The auditors will *accept* all your claims *except* the last two. Some businesses are *excepted* from the regulation.

advice, advise   *Advice* is a noun meaning "opinion or information offered"; *advise* is a verb that means "to offer advice to": The broker *advised* her client to take his attorney's *advice.*

affect, effect   *Affect* is a verb meaning "to influence"; *effect* can be a verb or a noun—as a verb it means "to bring about," and as a noun it means "result": We know how the drug *affects* patients immediately, but little is known of its long-term *effects.* The arbitrator tried to *effect* a settlement between the parties.

all ready, already   *All ready* means "completely prepared"; *already* means "by or before this or that time": I was *all ready* to help, but it was *already* too late.

all right, alright   Although the use of *alright* is increasing, current usage calls for *all right.*

allusion, illusion   An *allusion* is a reference or hint; an *illusion* is something that is not what it seems: The poem makes an *allusion* to the Pandora myth. The shadow created an optical *illusion.*

a lot   *A lot* is always two words.

among, between   *Among* refers to groups of more than two things; *between* refers to just two things: The three parties agreed *among* themselves to settle the case. There will be a brief intermission *between* the two acts. (Note that *amongst* is British, not American, usage.)

amount, number   *Amount* refers to a quantity that cannot be counted; *number* refers to things that can be counted: Even a small *amount* of caffeine can be harmful. Seeing their commander fall, a large *number* of troops ran to his aid.

an, a   See **a, an.**

and/or In business or technical writing, use *and/or* when either or both of the items it connects can apply. In college writing, however, avoid the use of *and/or.*

as . . . as . . . In such constructions, *as* signals a comparison; therefore, you must always use the second *as*: John Steinbeck's *East of Eden* is *as* long *as* his *The Grapes of Wrath.*

as, like *As* can be used as a conjunction (to introduce a complete clause) or as a preposition; *like* should be used as a preposition only: In *The Scarlet Letter,* Hawthorne uses imagery *as* (not *like*) he does in his other works. After classes, Fred works *as* a manager of a fast food restaurant. Writers *like* Carl Sandburg appear once in a generation.

at, to Many people use the prepositions *at* and *to* after *where* in conversation: *Where* are you working *at*? Where are you going *to*? This usage is redundant and should not appear in college writing.

awhile, a while *Awhile* is an adverb; *a while,* which consists of an article and a noun, is used as the object of a preposition: Before we continue, we will rest *awhile* (modifies the verb *rest*). Before we continue, we will rest for *a while* (object of the preposition *for*).

bad, badly *Bad* is an adjective, and *badly* is an adverb: The school board decided that *Adventures of Huckleberry Finn* was a *bad* book. American automobile makers did not do *badly* this year. After verbs that refer to any of the senses or after any other linking verb, use the adjective form: He looked *bad.* He felt *bad.* It seemed *bad.*

being as, being that These awkward phrases add unnecessary words, thereby weakening your writing. Use *because* instead.

beside, besides *Beside* is a preposition meaning "next to"; *besides* can be either a preposition meaning "except" or "other than" or an adverb meaning "as well": *Beside* the tower was a wall that ran the length of the city. *Besides* its industrial uses, laser technology has many other applications. Edison invented not only the lightbulb but the phonograph *besides.*

between, among See **among, between.**

bring, take *Bring* means "to transport from a farther place to a nearer place"; *take* means "to carry or convey from a nearer place to a farther place": *Bring* me a souvenir from your trip. *Take* this message to the general, and wait for a reply.

can, may *Can* denotes ability; *may* indicates permission: If you *can* play, you *may* use my piano.

cite, site *Cite* is a verb meaning "to quote as an authority or example"; *site* is a noun meaning "a place or setting"; it is also a shortened form of *Web site:* Jeff *cited* five sources in his research paper. The builder cleared the *site* for the new bank. Marisa uploaded her *site* to the Web.

climactic, climatic *Climactic* means "of or related to a climax"; *climatic* means "of or related to climate": The *climactic* moment of the movie occurred unexpectedly. If scientists are correct, the *climatic* conditions of Earth are changing.

complement, compliment *Complement* means "to complete or add to"; *compliment* means "to give praise": A double-blind study would *complement* their preliminary research. My instructor *complimented* me on my improvement.

conscious, conscience *Conscious* is an adjective meaning "having one's mental faculties awake"; *conscience* is a noun that means the moral sense of right and wrong: The patient will remain *conscious* during the procedure. His *conscience* would not allow him to lie.

continual, continuous *Continual* means "recurring at intervals"; *continuous* refers to an action that occurs without interruption: A pulsar is a star that emits a *continual* stream of electromagnetic radiation. (It emits radiation at regular intervals.) A small battery allows the watch to run *continuously* for five years. (It runs without stopping.)

could of, should of, would of The contractions *could've, should've,* and *would've* are often misspelled as the nonstandard constructions *could of, should of,* and *would of.* Use *could have, should have,* and *would have* in college writing.

couple, couple of *Couple* means "a pair," but *couple of* is often used colloquially to mean "several" or "a few." In your college writing, specify "four points" or "two examples" rather than using "a couple of."

criterion, criteria *Criteria,* from the Greek, is the plural of *criterion,* meaning "standard for judgment": Of all the *criteria* for hiring graduating seniors, class rank is the most important *criterion.*

data *Data* is the plural of the Latin *datum,* meaning "fact." In colloquial speech and writing, *data* is often used as the singular as well as the plural form. In college writing, use *data* only for the plural: The *data* discussed in this section *are* summarized in Appendix A.

different from, different than *Different than* is widely used in American speech. In college writing, use *different from.*

disinterested, uninterested *Disinterested* means "objective" or "capable of making an impartial judgment"; *uninterested* means "indifferent or unconcerned": The American judicial system depends on *disinterested* jurors. Finding no treasure, Hernando de Soto was *uninterested* in going farther.

don't, doesn't *Don't* is the contraction of *do not; doesn't* is the contraction of *does not.* Do not confuse the two: My dog *doesn't* (not *don't*) like to walk in the rain. (Note that contractions are generally not acceptable in college writing.)

economic, economical *Economic* refers to the economy—to the production, distribution, and consumption of goods. *Economical* means "avoiding waste" or "careful use of resources": There was strong *economic* growth this quarter. It is *economical* to have roommates in this city.

effect, affect See **affect, effect.**

e.g. *E.g.* is an abbreviation for the Latin *exempli gratia,* meaning "for example" or "for instance." In college writing, do not use *e.g.* Instead, use for *example* or *for instance.*

emigrate from, immigrate to To *emigrate* is "to leave one's country and settle in another"; to *immigrate* is "to come to another country and reside there." The noun forms of these words are *emigrant* and *immigrant:* My great-grandfather *emigrated from* Warsaw along with many other *emigrants* from Poland. Many people *immigrate to* the United States for economic reasons, but *immigrants* still face great challenges.

eminent, imminent *Eminent* is an adjective meaning "standing above others" or "prominent"; *imminent* means "about to occur": Oliver Wendell Holmes Jr. was an *eminent* jurist. In ancient times, a comet signaled *imminent* disaster.

enthused *Enthused,* a colloquial form of *enthusiastic,* should not be used in college writing.

etc. *Etc.,* the abbreviation of *et cetera,* means "and the rest." Do not use it in your college writing. Instead, use *and so on*—or, better yet, specify what *etc.* stands for.

everyday, every day *Everyday* is an adjective that means "ordinary" or "commonplace"; *every day* means "occurring daily": In the Gettysburg Address, Lincoln used *everyday* language. She exercises almost *every day.*

everyone, every one *Everyone* is an indefinite pronoun meaning "every person"; *every one* means "every individual or thing in a particular group": *Everyone* seems happier in the spring. *Every one* of the packages had been opened.

except, accept See **accept, except.**

explicit, implicit *Explicit* means "expressed or stated directly"; *implicit* means "implied" or "expressed or stated indirectly": The director *explicitly* warned the actors to be on time for rehearsals. Her *implicit* message was that lateness would not be tolerated.

farther, further *Farther* designates distance; *further* designates degree: I have traveled *farther* from home than any of my relatives. Critics charge that welfare subsidies encourage *further* dependence.

fewer, less Use *fewer* with nouns that can be counted: *fewer* books, *fewer* people, *fewer* dollars. Use *less* with quantities that cannot be counted: *less* pain, *less* power, *less* enthusiasm.

firstly (secondly, thirdly, . . .) Archaic forms meaning "in the first . . . second . . . third place." Use *first, second, third* instead.

further, farther See **farther, further.**

good, well *Good* is an adjective, never an adverb: She is a *good* swimmer. *Well* can function as an adverb or as an adjective. As an adverb, it means "in a good manner": She swam *well* (not *good*) in the meet. *Well* is used as an adjective meaning "in good health" with verbs that denote a state of being or feeling: I feel *well.*

got to *Got to* is not acceptable in college writing. To indicate obligation, use *have to, has to,* or *must.*

hanged, hung Both *hanged* and *hung* are past participles of *hang. Hanged* is used to refer to executions; *hung* is used to mean "suspended": Billy Budd was *hanged* for killing the master-at-arms. The stockings were *hung* by the chimney with care.

he, she Traditionally, *he* has been used in the generic sense to refer to both males and females. To acknowledge the equality of the sexes, however, avoid the generic *he*. Use plural pronouns whenever possible. **See 45f2.**

historic, historical *Historic* means "important" or "momentous"; *historical* means "relating to the past" or "based on or inspired by history": The end of World War II was a *historic* occasion. *Historical* records show that Quakers played an important part in the abolition of slavery.

hopefully The adverb *hopefully,* meaning "in a hopeful manner," should modify a verb, an adjective, or another adverb. Do not use *hopefully* as a sentence modifier meaning "it is hoped." Rather than "*Hopefully,* scientists will soon discover a cure for AIDS," write "*People hope* scientists will soon discover a cure for AIDS."

i.e. *I.e.* is an abbreviation for the Latin *id est,* meaning "that is." In college writing, do not use *i.e.* Instead, use its English equivalent.

if, whether When asking indirect questions or expressing doubt, use *whether:* He asked *whether* (not *if*) the flight would be delayed. The flight attendant was not sure *whether* (not *if*) it would be delayed.

illusion, allusion See **allusion, illusion.**

immigrate to, emigrate from See **emigrate from, immigrate to.**

implicit, explicit See **explicit, implicit.**

imply, infer *Imply* means "to hint" or "to suggest"; *infer* means "to conclude from": Mark Antony *implied* that the conspirators had murdered Caesar. The crowd *inferred* his meaning and called for justice.

infer, imply See **imply, infer.**

inside of, outside of *Of* is unnecessary when *inside* and *outside* are used as prepositions. *Inside of* is colloquial in references to time: He waited *inside* (not *inside of*) the coffee shop. He could run a mile in *under* (not *inside of*) eight minutes.

irregardless, regardless *Irregardless* is a nonstandard version of *regardless.* Use *regardless* or *irrespective* instead.

is when, is where These constructions are faulty when they appear in definitions: A playoff is (not *is when* or *is where*) an additional game played to establish the winner of a tie.

its, it's *Its* is a possessive pronoun; *it's* is a contraction of *it is: It's* no secret that the bank is out to protect *its* assets.

kind of, sort of The use of *kind of* and *sort of* to mean "rather" or "somewhat" is colloquial and should not appear in college writing: It is well known that Napoleon was rather (not *kind of*) short.

lay, lie See **lie, lay.**

leave, let *Leave* means "to go away from" or "to let remain"; *let* means "to allow" or "to permit": *Let* (not *leave*) me give you a hand.

less, fewer See **fewer, less.**

let, leave See **leave, let.**

lie, lay *Lie* is an intransitive verb (one that does not take an object) meaning "to recline." Its principal forms are *lie, lay, lain, lying:* Each afternoon she would *lie* in the sun and listen to the surf. *As I Lay Dying* is a novel by William Faulkner. By 1871, Troy had *lain* undisturbed for two thousand years. The painting shows a nude *lying* on a couch.

*Lay* is a transitive verb (one that takes an object) meaning "to put" or "to place." Its principal forms are *lay, laid, laid, laying:* The Federalist Papers *lay* the foundation for American conservatism. In October 1781, the British *laid* down their arms and surrendered. He had *laid* his money on the counter before leaving. We watched the stonemasons *laying* a wall.

life, lifestyle *Life* is the time that a living thing exists; *lifestyle* is a way of living that reflects a person's values or attitudes: Before he was hanged, Nathan Hale said, "I only regret that I have but one *life* to lose for my country." The writer Virginia Woolf was known for her unconventional *lifestyle.*

like, as See **as, like.**

loose, lose *Loose* is an adjective meaning "not rigidly fastened or securely attached"; *lose* is a verb meaning "to misplace": The marble facing of the building became *loose* and fell to the sidewalk. After only two drinks, most people *lose* their ability to judge distance.

lots, lots of, a lot of These words are colloquial substitutes for *many, much,* or *a great deal of.* Avoid their use in college writing: The students had *many* (not *lots of* or a *lot of*) options for essay topics.

man Like the generic pronoun *he, man* has been used in English to denote members of both sexes. This usage is being replaced by *human beings, people,* or similar terms that do not specify gender. **See 45e2.**

may, can See **can, may.**

may be, maybe *May be* is a verb phrase: *maybe* is an adverb meaning "perhaps": She *may be* the smartest student in the class. *Maybe* her experience has given her an advantage.

media, medium *Medium,* meaning "a means of conveying or broadcasting something," is singular; *media* is the plural form and requires a plural verb: The *media have* distorted the issue.

might have, might of *Might of* is a nonstandard spelling of the contraction of *might have* (*might've*). Use *might have* in college writing.

number, amount See **amount, number.**

OK, O.K., okay All three spellings are acceptable, but this term should be avoided in college writing. Replace it with a more specific word or words: The lecture was *adequate* (not *okay*), if uninspiring.

outside of, inside of See **inside of, outside of.**

passed, past *Passed* is the past tense of the verb *pass; past* means "belonging to a former time" or "no longer current": The car must have been going eighty miles per hour when it *passed* us. In the envelope was a bill marked *past* due.

percent, percentage *Percent* indicates a part of a hundred when a specific number is referred to: "*10 percent* of his salary." *Percentage* is used when no specific number is referred to: "a *percentage* of next year's receipts." In technical and business writing, it is permissible to use the % sign after percentages you are comparing. Write out the word *percent* in college writing.

phenomenon, phenomena A *phenomenon* is a single observable fact or event. It can also refer to a rare or significant occurrence. *Phenomena* is the plural form and requires a plural verb: Many supposedly paranormal *phenomena are* easily explained.

plus As a preposition, *plus* means "in addition to." Avoid using *plus* as a substitute for *and:* Include the principal, *plus* the interest, in your calculations. Your quote was too high; *moreover* (not *plus*), it was inaccurate.

precede, proceed *Precede* means "to go or come before"; *proceed* means "to go forward in an orderly way": Robert Frost's *North of Boston* was *preceded* by an earlier volume. In 1532, Francisco Pizarro landed at Tumbes and *proceeded* south.

principal, principle As a noun, *principal* means "a sum of money (minus interest) invested or lent" or "a person in the leading position"; as an adjective, it means "most important"; a *principle* is a noun meaning a rule of conduct or a basic truth: He wanted to reduce the *principal* of the loan. The *principal* of the high school is a talented administrator. Women are the *principal* wage earners in many American households. The Constitution embodies certain fundamental *principles.*

quote, quotation *Quote* is a verb. *Quotation* is a noun. In college writing, do not use *quote* as a shortened form of *quotation:* Scholars attribute these *quotations* (not *quotes*) to Shakespeare.

raise, rise *Raise* is a transitive verb, and *rise* is an intransitive verb—that is, *raise* takes an object, and *rise* does not: My grandparents *raised* a large family. The sun will *rise* at 6:12 tomorrow morning.

real, really *Real* means "genuine" or "authentic"; *really* means "actually." In college writing, do not use *real* as an adjective meaning "very."

reason is that, reason is because *Reason* should be used with *that* and not with *because,* which is redundant: The *reason* he left is *that* (not *because*) you insulted him.

regardless, irregardless See **irregardless, regardless.**

respectably, respectfully, respectively *Respectably* means "worthy of respect"; *respectfully* means "giving honor or deference"; *respectively* means "in the order given": He skated quite *respectably* at his first Olympics. The seminar taught us to treat others *respectfully*. The first- and second-place winners were Tai and Kim, *respectively.*

rise, raise See **raise, rise.**

set, sit *Set* means "to put down" or "to lay." Its principal forms are *set* and *setting:* After rocking the baby to sleep, he *set* her down carefully in her crib. After *setting* her down, he took a nap.

*Sit* means "to assume a sitting position." Its principal forms are *sit, sat,* and *sitting:* Many children *sit* in front of the television five to six hours a day. The dog *sat* by the fire. We were *sitting* in the airport when the flight was canceled.

shall, will *Will* has all but replaced *shall* to express all future action.

should of See **could of, should of, would of.**

simple, simplistic *Simple* means "plain, ordinary, or uncomplicated"; *simplistic* means "overly or misleadingly simplified": Because she had studied, Tanya thought the test was *simple.* His explanation of how the Internet works is *simplistic.*

since Do not use *since* for *because* if there is any chance of confusion. In the sentence "*Since* President Nixon traveled to China, trade between China and the United States has increased," *since* could mean either "from the time that" or "because." To be clear, use *because.*

sit, set See **set, sit.**

so Avoid using *so* as a vague intensifier meaning "very" or "extremely." Follow *so* with *that* and a clause that describes the result: She was *so* pleased with their work *that* she took them out to lunch.

sometime, sometimes, some time *Sometime* means "at some time in the future"; *sometimes* means "now and then"; *some time* means "a period of time": The president will address Congress *sometime* next week. All automobiles, no matter how reliable, *sometimes* need repairs. It has been *some time* since I read that book.

sort of, kind of See **kind of, sort of.**

supposed to, used to *Supposed to* and *used to* are often misspelled. Both verbs require the final *d* to indicate past tense.

take, bring See **bring, take.**

than, then *Than* is a conjunction used to indicate a comparison; *then* is an adverb indicating time: The new shopping center is bigger *than* the old one. He did his research; *then,* he wrote a report.

that, which, who Use *that* or *which* when referring to a thing; use *who* when referring to a person: It was a speech *that* inspired many. The movie, *which* was a huge success, failed to impress her. Anyone *who* (not *that*) takes the course will benefit.

their, there, they're *Their* is a possessive pronoun; *there* indicates place and is also used in the expressions *there is* and *there are; they're* is a contraction of *they are:* Watson and Crick did *their* DNA work at Cambridge University. I love Los Angeles, but I wouldn't want to live *there. There* is nothing we can do to resurrect an extinct species. When *they're* well treated, rabbits make excellent pets.

themselves, theirselves, theirself *Theirselves* and *theirself* are nonstandard variants of *themselves.*

then, than See **than, then.**

till, until, 'til *Till* and *until* have the same meaning, and both are acceptable. *Until* is preferred in college writing. *'Til,* a contraction of *until,* should be avoided.

to, at See **at, to.**

to, too, two *To* is a preposition that indicates direction; *too* is an adverb that means "also" or "more than is needed"; *two* expresses the number 2: Last year we flew from New York *to* California. "Tippecanoe and Tyler, *too*" was William Henry Harrison's campaign slogan. The plot was *too* complicated for the average reader. Just north of *Two* Rivers, Wisconsin, is a petrified forest.

try to, try and *Try and* is the colloquial equivalent of the more formal *try to:* He decided to *try to* (not *try and*) do better. In college writing, use *try to.*

-type Deleting this empty suffix eliminates clutter and clarifies meaning: Found in the wreckage was an incendiary (not *incendiary-type*) device.

uninterested, disinterested See **disinterested, uninterested.**

unique Because *unique* means "the only one," not "remarkable" or "unusual," never use constructions like *the most unique* or *very unique.*

until See *till, until, 'til.*

used to See *supposed to, used to.*

utilize In most cases, replace *utilize* with *use* (*utilize* often sounds pretentious).

wait for, wait on To *wait for* means "to defer action until something occurs." To *wait on* means "to act as a waiter": I am *waiting for* (not *on*) dinner.

weather, whether *Weather* is a noun meaning "the state of the atmosphere"; *whether* is a conjunction used to introduce an alternative: The *weather* will improve this weekend. It is doubtful *whether* we will be able to ski tomorrow.

well, good See *good, well.*

were, we're *Were* is a verb; *we're* is the contraction of *we are:* The Trojans *were* asleep when the Greeks attacked. We must act now if *we're* going to succeed.

whether, if See **if, whether.**

which, who, that See **that, which, who.**

who, whom When a pronoun serves as the subject of its clause, use *who* or *whoever;* when it functions in a clause as an object, use *whom* or *whomever:* Sarah, *who* is studying ancient civilizations, would like to visit Greece. Sarah, *whom* I met in France, wants me to travel to Greece with her. **See 48b2.**

who's, whose *Who's* means "who is" or "who has"; *whose* indicates possession: *Who's* going to take calculus? *Who's* already left for the concert? The writer *whose* book was in the window was autographing copies.

will, shall See **shall, will.**

would of See **could of, should of, would of.**

your, you're *Your* indicates possession; *you're* is the contraction of *you are:* You can improve *your* stamina by jogging two miles a day. *You're* certain to be the winner.

# Glossary of Grammatical and Rhetorical Terms

absolute phrase See **phrase.**

abstract noun See **noun.**

acronym A word formed from the first letters or initial sounds of a group of words: *NATO* = North Atlantic Treaty Organization.

active voice See **voice.**

adjective A word that describes, limits, qualifies, or in any other way modifies a noun or pronoun. A **descriptive adjective** names a quality of the noun or pronoun it modifies: *junior* year. A **proper adjective** is formed from a proper noun: *Hegelian philosophy.* **47d, 51b**

adjective clause See **clause.**

adverb A word that describes the action of verbs or modifies adjectives, other adverbs, or complete phrases, clauses, or sentences. Adverbs answer the questions "How?" "Why?" "Where?" "When?" and "To what extent?" Adverbs are formed from adjectives, many by adding *-ly* to the adjective form (*dark/darkly, solemn/solemnly*), and may also be derived from prepositions (*Joe carried on*). Other adverbs that indicate time, place, condition, cause, or degree are not derived from other parts of speech: *then, never, very,* and *often,* for example. The words *how, why, where,* and *when* are classified as **interrogative adverbs** when they ask questions (*How did we get into this mess?*). See also **conjunctive adverb. 47e, 51c**

adverb clause See **clause.**

adverbial conjunction See **conjunctive adverb.**

agreement The correspondence among words in number, person, and gender. Subjects and verbs must agree in number (singular or plural) and person (first, second, or third): *Soccer is a popular European sport; I play* soccer too. **50a** Pronouns and their antecedents must agree in number, person, and gender (masculine, feminine, neuter): *Lucy loaned Charlie her car.* **50b**

allusion A reference to a well-known historical, literary, or biblical person or event that readers are expected to recognize.

analogy A kind of comparison in which the writer explains an unfamiliar idea or object by comparing it to a more familiar one: *Sensory pathways of the central nervous system are bundles of nerves rather like telephone cables that feed information about the outside world into the brain for processing.*

antecedent The word or word group to which a pronoun refers: *Brian finally bought the car he had always wanted.* (*Brian* is the antecedent of the pronoun *he.*)

appositive A noun or noun phrase that identifies or renames an adjacent noun or pronoun: *Columbus, the capital of Ohio, is in the central part of the state.* Appositives may be used without special introductory phrases, as in the preceding example, or they may be introduced by *such as, or, that is, for example,* or *in other words: Japanese cars, such as Hondas, now have a large share of the US automobile market.* **35c5** In a **restrictive appositive,** the appositive precedes the noun or pronoun it modifies: *Singing cowboy Gene Autry was once the owner of the California Angels.* **53d1**

article The word *a, an,* or *the.* Articles signal that a noun follows and are classified as **determiners. 64b2–3**

auxiliary verb See **verb.**

balanced sentence A sentence neatly divided between two parallel structures. Balanced sentences are typically **compound sentences** made up of two parallel clauses (*The telephone rang, and I answered*), but the parallel clauses of a **complex sentence** can also be balanced. **38c**

base form See **principal parts.**

cardinal number A number that expresses quantity—*seven, thirty, one hundred.* (Contrast **ordinal number.**)

case The form a noun or pronoun takes to indicate how it functions in a sentence. English has three cases. A pronoun takes the **subjective** (or **nominative**) **case** when it acts as the subject of a sentence or a clause: *I am an American.* **48a1** A pronoun takes the **objective case** when it acts as the object of a verb or of a preposition: *Fran gave me her dog.* **48a2** Both nouns and pronouns take the **possessive case** when they indicate ownership: *My house is brick, Brandon's T-shirt is red.* This is the only case in which nouns change form. **48a3**

clause A group of related words that includes a subject and a predicate. An **independent (main) clause** may stand alone as a sentence (*Yellowstone is a national park in the West*), but a **dependent (subordinate) clause** must always be accompanied by an independent clause (*Yellowstone is a national park in the West that is known for its geysers*). Dependent clauses are classified according to their function in a sentence. An **adjective clause** (sometimes called a **relative clause**) modifies a noun or pronoun: *The ficus, which grew to be twelve feet tall, finally died* (the clause modifies *ficus*). An **adverb clause** modifies a single word (verb, adjective, or adverb) or an entire phrase or clause: *The film was exposed when Bill opened the camera* (the clause modifies *exposed*). A **noun clause** acts as a noun (as subject, direct object, indirect object, or complement) in a sentence: *Whoever arrives first wins the prize* (the clause is the subject of the sentence). An **elliptical clause** is grammatically incomplete—that is, part or all of the subject or predicate is missing. If the missing part can be inferred from the context of the sentence, such a construction is acceptable: *When (they are) pressed, the committee members will act.* **35b2** climactic word order The writing strategy of moving from the least important to the most important point in a sentence and ending with the key idea. **38a2**

collective noun See **noun.**

comma splice A type of **run-on** created when two independent clauses are incorrectly joined by just a comma. Correct comma splices by separating the independent clauses with a period, a semicolon, or a comma and a coordinating conjunction, or by using subordination. **Ch. 41**

**Comma Splice:** The Mississippi River flows south, the Nile River flows north.

**Revised:** The Mississippi River flows south. The Nile River flows north.

**Revised:** The Mississippi River flows south; the Nile River flows north.

**Revised:** The Mississippi River flows south, and the Nile River flows north.

**Revised:** Although the Mississippi River flows south, the Nile River flows north.

common noun See **noun.**

comparative degree See **degree.**

complement A word or word group that describes or renames a subject, an object, or a verb. A **subject complement** is a word or phrase that follows a linking verb and renames the subject. It can be an adjective (called a **predicate adjective**) or a noun (called a **predicate nominative**): *Clark Gable was a movie star.* An **object complement** is a word or phrase that describes or renames a direct object. Object complements can be either adjectives or nouns: *We call the treehouse our hideout.*

complete predicate See **predicate.**

complete subject See **subject.**

complex sentence See **sentence.**

compound Two or more words that function as a unit, such as **compound nouns:** *attorney-at-law, boardwalk;* **compound adjectives:** *hardhitting editorial;* **compound prepositions:** *by way of, in addition to;* **compound subjects:** *April and May are spring months;* and **compound predicates:** *Many try and fail to climb Mount Everest.*

compound adjective See **compound.**

compound noun See **compound.**

compound predicate See **compound.**

compound preposition See **compound.**

compound sentence See **sentence.**

compound subject See **compound.**

compound-complex sentence See **sentence.**

conjunction A word or words used to connect single words, phrases, clauses, and sentences. **Coordinating conjunctions** (*and, or, but, nor, for, so, yet*) connect words, phrases, or clauses of equal weight: *crime and punishment* (coordinating conjunction *and* connects two words). **Correlative conjunctions** (*both . . . and, either . . . or, neither . . . nor,* and so on), always used in pairs, also link items of equal weight: *Neither Texas nor Florida crosses the Tropic of Cancer.* **Subordinating conjunctions** (*since, because, although, if, after,* and so on) introduce adverb clauses: *You will have to pay for the tickets now because I will not be here later.* **47g**

conjunctive adverb An adverb that joins and relates independent clauses in a sentence (*also, anyway, besides, hence, however, nevertheless, still,* and so on): *Howard tried out for the Yankees; however, he didn't make the team.* **47e**

connotation The emotional associations that surround a word. (Contrast **denotation.**) **45b1**

contraction The combination of two words with an apostrophe replacing the missing letters: *We + will = we'll; was + not = wasn't.*

coordinate adjective One of a series of adjectives that modify the same word or word group: *The park was quiet, shady, and cool.* **53b2**

coordinating conjunction See **conjunction.**

coordination The pairing of similar elements (words, phrases, or clauses) to give equal weight to each. Coordination is used in simple sentences to link similar elements into compound subjects, predicates, complements, or modifiers. It can also link two independent clauses to form a compound sentence: *The sky was cloudy, and it looked like rain.* **37b1**

correlative conjunction See **conjunction.**

count noun See **noun.**

cumulative sentence A sentence that begins with a main clause followed by additional words, phrases, or clauses that expand or develop it: *On the hill stood a schoolhouse, paint peeling, windows boarded, playground overgrown with weeds.* **38b1**

dangling modifier A word or phrase that cannot logically modify any word in the sentence. To correct dangling modifiers, either create a new subject that the dangling modifier can logically modify, or change the dangling modifier into a dependent clause.

*they continued the trip.*

Thinking about their destination, ~~the trip continued.~~ **42c**

deductive argument An argument that begins with a general statement or proposition and establishes a chain of reasoning that leads to a conclusion. **9b**

degree Most adjectives and adverbs change form to indicate degree. The **positive degree** describes a quality without indicating a comparison (*Frank is tall*). The **comparative degree** indicates a comparison between two persons or things (*Frank is taller than John*). The **superlative degree** indicates a comparison between one person or thing and two or more others (*Frank is the tallest boy in his scout troop*). **51d**

demonstrative pronoun See **pronoun;** see also **determiner.**

denotation The dictionary meaning of a word. (Contrast **connotation.**) **45b1** dependent clause See **clause.**

descriptive adjective See **adjective.**

determiner Determiners are words that function as adjectives to limit or qualify nouns. Determiners include **articles** (*a, an, the*): *the book, a peanut;* **possessive nouns** (*Janet's*): *Janet's dog;* **possessive pronouns** (*my, your, his,* and so on): *their apartment, my house;* **demonstrative pronouns** (*this, these, that, those*): *that table, these chairs;* **interrogative pronouns** (*what, which, whose,* and so on): *Which car is yours?;* **indefinite pronouns** (*another, each, both, many,* and so on): *any minute, some day;* **relative pronouns** (*what, whatever, which, whichever, whose, whosoever*): *Bed rest was what the doctor ordered;* and **ordinal** and **cardinal numbers** (*one, two, first, second,* and so on): *Claire saw two robins.* **47d2; 51a; 64b2–3**

direct object See **object.**

direct quotation See **quotation.**

documentation The formal acknowledgment of the sources used in a piece of writing. **Pts. 4–5**

documentation style A format for providing information about the sources used in a piece of writing. Documentation formats vary from discipline to discipline. **Pts. 4–5**

double negative A nonstandard combination of two negative words:

**Double Negative:** She didn't have no time.

**Revised:** She had no time. *or* She didn't have any time. **64a4**

ellipsis Three spaced periods used to indicate the omission of a word or words from a quotation: "*The time has come . . . and we must part.*" **57f**

elliptical clause See **clause.**

embedding A strategy for varying sentence structure that involves changing some sentences into modifying phrases and working them into other sentences. **37b3**

enthymeme A syllogism in which one of the premises—usually the major premise—is implied rather than stated. **9b3**

faulty parallelism See **parallelism.**

figurative language Language that departs from the literal meaning or order of words to create striking effects or new meanings. Types of figurative language (called **figures of speech**) include **simile, metaphor,** and **personification. 45c**

figure of speech See **figurative language.**

finite verb A verb that can serve as the main verb of a sentence. Unlike **participles, gerunds,** and **infinitives** (see also **verbal**), finite verbs do not require an auxiliary in order to function as the main verb: *The rooster crowed.*

fragment See **sentence fragment.**

function word An article, a preposition, a conjunction, or an auxiliary verb that indicates the function of and the grammatical relationships among nouns, verbs, and modifiers in a sentence.

fused sentence A type of **run-on** created when two independent clauses are joined without punctuation. Correct fused sentences by separating the independent clauses with a period, a semicolon, or a comma and a coordinating conjunction, or by using **subordination. Ch. 41**

**Fused Sentence:** Protein is needed for good nutrition lipids and carbohydrates are too.

**Revised:** Protein is needed for good nutrition. Lipids and carbohydrates are too.

**Revised:** Protein is needed for good nutrition; lipids and carbohydrates are too.

**Revised:** Protein is needed for good nutrition, but lipids and carbohydrates are too.

gender The classification of nouns and pronouns as masculine (*father, boy, he*), feminine (*mother, girl, she*), or neuter (*radio, kitten, them*).

gerund A special verb form ending in *-ing* that is always used as a noun: *Fishing is relaxing* (gerund *fishing* serves as subject; gerund *relaxing* serves as subject complement).

Note: When the *-ing* form of a verb is used as a modifier, it is considered a **present participle.** See also **verbal.**

gerund phrase See **phrase.**

helping verb See **verb.**

idiom An expression that is characteristic of a particular language and whose meaning cannot be predicted from the meaning of its individual words: *lend a hand.*

imperative mood See **mood.**

indefinite pronoun See **pronoun;** see also **determiner.**

independent clause See **clause.**

indicative mood See **mood.**

indirect object See **object.**

indirect question A question that tells what has been asked but, because it does not report the speaker's exact words, does not take quotation marks or end with a question mark: *He asked whether he could use the family car.*

indirect quotation See **quotation.**

inductive argument An argument that begins with observations or experiences and moves toward a conclusion. **9a**

infinitive The base form of the verb preceded by *to.* An infinitive can serve as an adjective (*He is the man to watch*), an adverb (*Chris hoped to break the record*), or a noun (*To err is human*). See also **verbal.**

infinitive phrase See **phrase.**

intensifier A word that adds emphasis but not additional meaning to words it modifies. *Much, really, too, very,* and *so* are typical intensifiers.

intensive pronoun See **pronoun.**

interjection A grammatically independent word, expressing emotion, that is used as an exclamation. An interjection can be set off by a comma, or, for greater emphasis, it can be punctuated as an independent unit, set off by an exclamation point: *Ouch! That hurt.* **47h**

interrogative adverb See **adverb.**

interrogative pronoun See **pronoun;** see also **determiner.**

intransitive verb See **verb.**

irregular verb A verb that does not form both its past tense and past participle by adding *-d* or *-ed* to the base form of the verb. **49a2**

isolate Any word, including an **interjection,** that can be used in isolation: *Yes. No. Hello. Good-bye. Please. Thanks.*

linking verb A verb that connects a subject to its complement: *The crowd became quiet.* Words that can be used as linking verbs include *seem, appear, believe, become, grow, turn, remain, prove, look, sound, smell, taste, feel,* and forms of the verb *be.*

main clause See **clause.**

main verb See **verb.**

metaphor A **figure of speech** in which the writer makes an implied comparison between two unlike items, equating them in an unexpected way: *The subway coursed through the arteries of the city.* (Contrast **simile.**) **45c**

misplaced modifier A modifier whose placement suggests that it modifies one word or word group when it is intended to modify another. **42a**

*Dan smiled at his baby son, finally*
~~Finally~~ asleep in his crib~~.~~. ~~Dan smiled at his baby son.~~

mixed construction A sentence made up of two or more parts that do not fit together grammatically. **44b**

**Mixed:** The Great Chicago Fire caused terrible destruction was what prompted changes in the fire code. (independent clause used as a subject)

**Revised:** The terrible destruction of the Great Chicago Fire prompted changes in the fire code.

**Revised:** Because of the terrible destruction of the Great Chicago Fire, the fire code was changed.

mixed metaphor The combination of two or more incompatible images in a single figure of speech: *During the race, John kept a stiff upper lip as he ran like the wind.* **45d5**

modal auxiliary See **verb.**

modifier A word, phrase, or clause that acts as an adjective or an adverb, describing, limiting, or qualifying another word or word group in the sentence.

mood The verb form that indicates the writer's basic attitude. There are three moods in English. The **indicative mood** is used for statements and questions: *Nebraska became a state in 1867.* The **imperative mood** specifies commands or requests and is often used without a subject: (*You*) *Pay the rent.* The **subjunctive mood** expresses wishes or hypothetical conditions: *I wish the sun were shining.* **49c**

nominal A word, phrase, or clause that functions as a noun.

nominative case See **case.**

noncount noun See **noun.**

nonfinite verb See **verbal.**

nonrestrictive modifier A modifying phrase or clause that does not limit or particularize the words it modifies, but rather supplies additional information about them. Nonrestrictive modifiers are set off by commas: *Oregano, also known as marjoram or suganda, is a member of the mint family.* (Contrast **restrictive modifier.**) **53d1**

noun A word that names people, places, things, ideas, actions, or qualities. A **common noun** names any of a class of people, places, or things: *lawyer, town, bicycle.* A **proper noun,** always capitalized, refers to a particular person, place, or thing: *Mother Teresa, Chicago, Schwinn.* A **count noun** names something that can be counted: *a dozen eggs, two cats in the yard.* A **noncount noun** names a quantity that is not countable: *sand, time, work.* An **abstract noun** refers to an intangible idea or quality: *bravery, equality, hunger.* A **collective noun** designates a group of people, places, or things thought of as a unit: *Congress, police, family.* **47a**

noun clause See **clause.**

noun phrase See **phrase.**

number The form taken by a noun, pronoun, or verb to indicate one (**singular**): *car, he, this, boast;* or many (**plural**): *cars, they, those, boasts.* **44a4**

object A noun, pronoun, or other noun substitute that receives the action of a **transitive verb, verbal,** or **preposition.** A **direct object** indicates where the verb's action is directed and who or what is affected by it: *John caught a butterfly.* An **indirect object** tells to or for whom the verb's action was done: *John gave Nancy the butterfly.* An **object of a preposition** is a word or word group introduced by a preposition: *John gave Nancy the butterfly for an hour.*

object complement See **complement.**

object of a preposition See **object.**

objective case See **case.**

ordinal number A number that indicates position in a series: *seventh, thirtieth, one-hundredth.* (Contrast **cardinal number.**)

parallelism The use of similar grammatical elements in sentences or parts of sentences: *We serve beer, wine, and soft drinks.* Words, phrases, clauses, or complete sentences may be parallel, and parallel items may be paired or presented in a series. When elements that have the same function in a sentence are not presented in the same terms, the sentence is flawed by **faulty parallelism. 38c; Ch. 43**

participial phrase See **phrase.**

participle A verb form that generally functions in a sentence as an adjective. Virtually every verb has a **present participle,** which ends in *-ing* (*breaking, leaking, taking*), and a **past participle,** which usually ends in *-d* or *-ed* (*agreed, walked, taken*). (See also **verbal.**) *The heaving seas swamped the dinghy* (present participle *heaving* modifies noun *seas*); *Aged people deserve respect* (past participle *aged* modifies noun *people*).

parts of speech The eight basic building blocks for all English sentences: *nouns, pronouns, verbs, adjectives, adverbs, prepositions, conjunctions,* and *interjections.*

passive voice See **voice.**

past participle See **participle.**

periodic sentence A sentence that moves from a number of specific examples to a conclusion, gradually building in intensity until a climax is reached in the main clause: *Sickly and pale and looking ready to crumble, the marathoner headed into the last mile of the race.* **38b2**

person The form a pronoun or verb takes to indicate the speaker (**first person**): *I am/we are;* those spoken to (**second person**): *you are;* and those spoken about (**third person**): *he/she/it is; they are.* **44a4**

personal pronoun See **pronoun.**

personification A form of **figurative language** in which the writer describes an idea or inanimate object in human terms: *The big feather bed beckoned to my tired body.* **45c**

phrase A grammatically ordered group of related words that lacks a subject or a predicate or both and functions as a single part of speech. A **verb phrase** consists of an auxiliary (helping) verb and a main verb: *The wind was blowing hard.* A **noun phrase** includes a noun or pronoun plus all related modifiers: *She broke the track record.* A **prepositional phrase** consists of a preposition, its object, and any modifiers of that object: *The ball sailed over the fence.* A **verbal phrase** consists of a verbal and its related objects, modifiers, or complements. A verbal phrase may be a **participial phrase** (*Undaunted by the sheer cliff, the climber scaled the rock*), a **gerund phrase** (*Swinging from trees is a monkey's favorite way to travel*), or an **infinitive phrase** (*Wednesday is Bill's night to cook spaghetti*). An **absolute phrase** includes a noun and a participle, accompanied by modifiers: *His heart racing, he dialed her number.* It modifies an entire independent clause. **35b1**

plural See **number.**

positive degree See **degree.**

possessive case See **case.**

possessive noun See **determiner.**

possessive pronoun See **determiner.**

predicate A verb or verb phrase that tells or asks something about the subject of a sentence is called a **simple predicate:** *Well-tended lawns grow green and thick.* (*Grow* is the simple predicate.) A **complete predicate** includes all the words associated with the predicate: *Well-tended lawns grow green and thick.* (*Grow green and thick* is the complete predicate.)

predicate adjective See **complement.**

predicate nominative See **complement.**

prefix A letter or group of letters put before a root or a word that adds to, changes, or modifies it.

preposition A part of speech that introduces a noun or pronoun (or a phrase or clause functioning in the sentence as a noun), linking it to other words in the sentence: *Jeremy crawled under the bed.* **47f**

prepositional phrase See **phrase.**

present participle See **participle.**

principal parts The forms of a verb from which all other forms can be derived. The principal parts are the **base form** (*give*), the **present participle** (*giving*), the **past tense** (*gave*), and the **past participle** (*given*).

pronoun A word that may be used in place of a noun in a sentence. The noun for which a pronoun stands is called its **antecedent.** There are eight types of pronouns. Some have the same form but are distinguished by their function in the sentence. A **personal pronoun** stands for a person or thing: *I, me, we, us, my,* and so on (*They broke the window*). A **reflexive pronoun** ends in *-self* or *-selves* and refers to the subject of the sentence or clause: *myself, yourself, himself,* and so on (*They painted the house themselves*). An **intensive pronoun** ends in *-self* or *-selves* and emphasizes a preceding noun or pronoun (*Custer himself died in the battle*). A **relative pronoun** introduces an adjective or noun clause in a sentence: *which, who, whom,* and so on (*Sitting Bull was the Sioux chief who defeated Custer*). An **interrogative pronoun** introduces a question: *who, which, what, whom,* and so on (*Who won the lottery?*). A **demonstrative pronoun** points to a particular thing or group of things: *this, that, these, those* (*Who was that on the phone?*). A **reciprocal pronoun** denotes a mutual relationship: *each other, one another* (*We still have each other*). An **indefinite pronoun** refers to persons or things in general, not to specific individuals. Most indefinite pronouns are singular—*anyone, everyone, one, each*—but some are always plural—*both, many, several* (*Many are called, but few are chosen*). **47b**

proper adjective See **adjective.**

proper noun See **noun.**

quotation The use of the written or spoken words of others. A **direct quotation** is a passage borrowed word for word from another source. Quotation marks (" ") establish the boundaries of a direct quotation: "*Those tortillas taste like cardboard,*" *complained Beth.* **56a** An **indirect quotation** reports someone else's written or spoken words without quoting that person directly. Quotation marks are not used: *Beth complained that the tortillas tasted like cardboard.*

reciprocal pronoun See **pronoun.**

reflexive pronoun See **pronoun.**

regular verb A verb that forms both its past tense and its past participle by the addition of *-d* or *-ed* to the base form of the verb. **49a1**

relative clause See **clause.**

relative pronoun See **pronoun.**

restrictive appositive See **appositive.**

restrictive modifier A modifying phrase or clause that limits the meaning of the word or word group it modifies. Restrictive modifiers are not set off by commas: *The Ferrari that ran over the fireplug was red.* (Contrast **nonrestrictive modifier.**) **53d1**

root A word from which other words are formed. An understanding of a root word increases a reader's ability to understand unfamiliar words that incorporate the root.

run-on An incorrect construction that results when the proper connective or punctuation does not appear between independent clauses. A run-on occurs either as a **comma splice** or as a **fused sentence. Ch. 41**

sentence An independent grammatical unit that contains a *subject* and a *predicate* and expresses a complete thought: *Carolyn sold her car.* A **simple sentence** consists of one subject and one predicate: *The season ended.* **35a;** a **compound sentence** is formed when two or more simple sentences are connected with coordinating conjunctions, conjunctive adverbs, semicolons, or colons: *The rain stopped, and the sun began to shine.* **36a;** a **complex sentence** consists of one simple sentence, which functions as an independent clause in the complex sentence, and at least one dependent clause, which is introduced by a subordinating conjunction or a relative pronoun: *When he had sold three boxes* [dependent clause], *he was halfway to his goal.* [independent clause] **36b;** and a **compound-complex sentence** consists of two or more independent clauses and at least one dependent clause: *After he prepared a shopping list* [dependent clause], *he went to the store* [independent clause], *but it was closed.* [independent clause]. **36b**

sentence fragment An incomplete sentence; a phrase or clause that is punctuated as if it were a complete sentence. **Ch. 40**

shift A change of *tense, voice, mood, person, number,* or *type of discourse* within or between sentences. Some shifts are necessary, but problems occur with unnecessary or illogical shifts. **44a**

simile A **figure of speech** in which the writer makes a comparison, introduced by *like* or *as,* between two unlike items on the basis of a shared quality: *Like sands through the hourglass, so are the days of our lives. The wind was as savage as his neighbor's Doberman.* (Contrast **metaphor.**) **45c**

simple predicate See **predicate.**

simple sentence See **sentence.**

simple subject See **subject.**

singular See **number.**

split infinitive An infinitive whose parts are separated by a modifier.

She expected ~~to~~ one day soon [to] swim the channel. **42b**

squinting modifier A modifier that seems to modify either a word before it or one after it and that conveys a different meaning in each case. **42a1**

subject A noun or noun substitute that tells who or what a sentence is about is called a **simple subject:** *Healthy thoroughbred horses run like the wind.* (*Horses* is the simple subject.) The **complete subject** of a sentence includes all the words associated with the subject: *Healthy thoroughbred horses run like the wind.* (*Healthy thoroughbred horses* is the complete subject.) **35a**

subject complement See **complement.**

subjective case See **case.**

subjunctive mood See **mood.**

subordinate clause See **clause.**

subordinating conjunction See **conjunction.**

subordination Making one or more clauses of a sentence grammatically dependent on another element in a sentence: *Preston was only eighteen when he joined the firm.* **37b2**

suffix A syllable added at the end of a word or root that changes its part of speech.

superlative degree See **degree.**

suspended hyphen A hyphen that is followed by a space or by the appropriate punctuation and a space: *The wagon was pulled by a two-, four-, or six-horse team.*

syllogism A three-part set of statements or propositions, devised by Aristotle, that contains a major premise, a minor premise, and a conclusion. **9b2**

tag question A question, consisting of an auxiliary verb plus a pronoun, that is added to a statement and set off by a comma: *You know it's going to rain, don't you?*

tense The form of a verb that indicates when an action occurred or when a condition existed. **49b**

transitive verb See **verb.**

verb A word or phrase that expresses action (He painted the fence) or a state of being (*Henry believes in equality*). A **main verb** carries most of the meaning in the sentence or clause in which it appears: *Winston Churchill smoked long, thick cigars.* A main verb is a **linking verb** when it is followed by a **subject complement:** *Dogs are good pets.* An **auxiliary verb** (sometimes called a **helping verb**) combines with the main verb to form a **verb phrase:** *Graduation day has arrived.* The auxiliaries *be* and *have* are used to indicate the tense and voice of the main verb. The auxiliary *do* is used for asking questions and forming negative statements. Other auxiliary verbs, known as

**modal auxiliaries** (*must, will, can, could, may, might, ought* [*to*], *should,* and *would*), indicate necessity, possibility, willingness, obligation, and ability: *It might rain next Tuesday.* A **transitive verb** requires an **object** to complete its meaning in the sentence: *Pete drank all the wine* (*wine* is the direct object). An **intransitive verb** has no direct object: *The candle flame glowed.* **47c1; Ch. 49**

verb phrase See **phrase.**

verbal (nonfinite verb) Verb forms—**participles, infinitives,** and **gerunds**—that are used as nouns, adjectives, or adverbs. Verbals do not behave like verbs. Only when used with an auxiliary can such a verb form serve as the main verb of a sentence. *The wall painted* is not a sentence; *The wall was painted* is. **47c2**

verbal phrase See **phrase.**

voice The form that determines whether the subject of a verb is acting or is acted upon. When the subject of a verb performs the action, the verb is in the **active voice:** *Tiger Woods sank a thirty-foot putt.* When the subject of a verb receives the action—that is, is acted upon—the verb is in the **passive voice:** *A thirty-foot putt was sunk by Tiger Woods.* **38e; 44a2; 49d, 64a6**

# Index

*Note:* Page numbers in blue indicate definitions.

## B

## G

## H

## P

## S